E. B. Segel

The Semblance of Peace

The Semblance of Peace

THE POLITICAL SETTLEMENT
AFTER
THE SECOND WORLD WAR

by

Sir John Wheeler-Bennett

K.C.V.O., C.M.G., O.B.E., F.R.S.L., Hon. D.C.L.(Oxon.)

and

Anthony Nicholls

The Norton Library
W·W·NORTON & COMPANY·INC·
NEW YORK

First published in the Norton Library 1974
by arrangement with St. Martin's Press, Inc.

Books That Live
The Norton imprint on a book means that in the publisher's
estimation it is a book not for a single season but for the years.
W. W. Norton & Company, Inc.

*Note: The St. Martin's Press edition of this book contains a section
of documents which does not appear in the Norton Library edition.*

Library of Congress Cataloging in Publication Data
Wheeler-Bennett, Sir John Wheeler, 1902–
    The semblance of peace.
    (The Norton library)
    Reprint of the ed. published by St. Martin's
Press, New York.
    Bibliography: p.
    1. World War, 1939–1945—Diplomatic history.
2. World War, 1939–1945—Peace. I. Nicholls,
Anthony James 1934–   joint author. II. Title.
[D748.W47   1974]   940.53'14   73-18247
ISBN 0-393-00709-X

Printed in the United States of America
1 2 3 4 5 6 7 8 9 0

Contents

List of Plates

List of Maps

Cartoons

Preface

IN writing this book, which has occupied the better part of five years, our research has necessarily ranged over a wide field. We have consulted with due care the books and documents listed in the Bibliography and believe that our conclusions from this research are accurate and justified.

We could not, however, have arrived at these deductions merely from research alone. In the course of our work we have been aided in many ways by the kindness of friends who have placed themselves and their memories at our disposal or have guided us to sources of information of which we might otherwise not have been aware, or have materially aided us by their criticism and counsel. In this respect we are especially and sincerely grateful to Dr Alan Bullock, the Master of St Catherine's College, Oxford, for having read part of our typescript and for the wise and excellent comments which he has made. We are also greatly indebted to Mr Richard Storry of St Antony's College, Oxford, for his invaluable advice in connection with our Oriental chapters, and our deepest thanks are due to Mr Rex Allen and Mr Alan Hunt of The Macmillan Press and Mr Thomas J. McCormack and Mr Frank Upjohn of St Martin's Press, New York, for their unfailing and indefatigable aid in many aspects of the production of this book.

In addition, there are many who, either by personal conversation or by the written word, have helped us to arrive at our conclusions. Among them are the following: the late Hon. Dean Acheson, Mr Herbert Agar, Mr Hamilton Fish Armstrong, the late Baroness Asquith of Yarnbury, the late Earl Attlee and the Earl of Avon; Mr George Backer of New York, Sir John Balfour and the late Hon. Francis Biddle; Lord Caccia, the late Sir Alexander Cadogan, Lord Conesford and Mr John Counsell; Sir Patrick Dean, Mr Piers Dixon, M.P., the Hon. Lewis Douglas and the late Hon. Allen Dulles; Miss Eileen Gaylord and Lord Gladwyn; the Hon. Averell Harriman; Sir Charles Johnston; the Hon. Philip Kaiser, the Hon. George Kennan and the Hon. W. John Kenney; Mr Lansing Lamont and Mr Walter Lippman; the late Mr René

MacColl, Sir Andrew McFadyean, the Rt Hon. Harold Macmillan, Mr Leonard Miall, General Sir William Morgan and Mr Malcolm Muggeridge; the late Lord Normanbrook; Count Edward Raczyński, the Hon. Samuel Reber and Mr Franklin D. Roosevelt, Jr; Lord Shawcross, Lord Strang and Major-General Sir Kenneth Strong; Mr A. J. P. Taylor and Mr George Malcolm Thomson; and the management of the Hotel Waldorf-Astoria, New York, for valuable information.

For the varied help which all of the above have given us we offer our sincere gratitude. It is understood, however, that the opinions expressed in this book are our responsibility alone.

The staffs of the Embassies in London of the United States of America, the Union of Soviet Socialist Republics and of Japan have been uniformly helpful and we gratefully acknowledge this assistance. Our very sincere thanks are also due to the staff of the Library of the Royal Institute of International Affairs for their cheerful and unwearying willingness to help us in every possible way and for the outstanding efficiency of their efforts. We are similarly obligated to the staffs of the London Library and the Library of St Antony's College, and of the Photographic Division of the Imperial War Museum. To all we offer our warmest thanks.

Finally, a special word of warm thanks and appreciation is due to Miss Frances Coulson who, once again, has coped successfully and uncomplainingly with the execrable handwriting of Sir John Wheeler-Bennett and with our passion for redrafting; her checking of facts and dates has also proved of the greatest assistance.

J.W.-B.
A.J.N.

Garsington – New York – Charlottesville, Virginia – Oxford, 1965–November 1970

PART ONE

WAR AND PEACE

Civilization is hooped together, brought
Under a rule, under the semblance of peace
By manifold illusion.
　　　　　W. B. YEATS, 'Meru', from *Supernatural Songs*

1 | Introduction: Some Thoughts on Peace-making

MANY books have already been written on the Peace Conference of Paris and the settlement which concluded the First World War – and 'the end is not yet'. Historians will be disputing the failings and virtues of these remarkable achievements for decades to come, and the same will probably be true of the Second World War, its termination and its repercussions.

Here we cannot speak of a settlement, for in the case of Germany no treaty of peace has yet been signed and indeed there is no longer a united Germany with which it could be signed. In the following pages an attempt has been made to show how these strange circumstances came about and how the post-war aims of the Allies, beginning with the hypothesis of a united Germany and finishing with a divided one, gradually developed and evolved, changing in definition and emphasis as the exigencies of the times demanded, as the kaleidoscope of Fate dictated and as the course of the war required. We have also attempted to tell the story of what happened to the other senior Axis partners, Italy and Japan, and to their satellite 'hangers-on'.

The gentle art of peace-making has greatly changed since the days of grace and elegance at Vienna. Even the Peace Conference of Paris subscribed to the conventional standards of diplomacy – despite what followed. At least for a while we enjoyed the Semblance of Peace and indeed became all too wedded to it for our own good – hence the diplomatic defeat of the West at Munich in 1938 and the collapse of France two years later. But since the termination of hostilities with Germany and Japan in 1945 the world has enjoyed only the very flimsiest illusion of peace. Indeed the Cold War began at Potsdam – or even before. Then, however, there followed major crises – the Berlin airlift, the Berlin Wall, Cuba – when the peace of the world has seemed to quiver in the balance; and any one of them could all too easily have developed into a conventional war had it not been for the nuclear deterrent. But even in the quiescent periods we have been sternly aware of tension, of provocation and of danger. It may well be that we shall never again enjoy the full blessings of peace as we once knew them and shall have to console ourselves, like Mr Chadband, with 'What is peace? Is it war? No.' Perhaps it is only the Semblance of Peace that matters.

II

We have it on the authority of Pericles that men rarely adhere to the same views during the course of a war which they held upon entering it, and are likely to change their beliefs as to causes when they look back from the consequences of their actions.[1] Centuries later, the egregious Prince von Bülow wrote that 'One knows where a war begins but one never knows where it ends'.[2]

There is profound truth in both these statements, but both need a certain elaboration. Indeed one knows where a war begins in the sense that the rupture of diplomatic relations or an exchange of missiles constitutes the end of peace and the commencement of hostilities. But who can say why or where? It may well be that the First World War began at Sedan or at the Algeciras Conference or at Sarajevo. It may well be that the Second World War began as the ink dried on the parchment of the Treaty of Versailles and to some keen listener there came the sound of a child weeping.* Historians will be debating these points for many years to come in answer to the question 'When?'

And the question 'Why?' is also elusive of solution. For example, Britain ostensibly went to war in 1914 in opposition to the violation by Germany of Belgian neutrality, and in 1939 by virtue of her treaty of alliance with Poland. But there were more reasons to it than this in either case, and the truth was more clearly declared by Duff Cooper in his great speech of resignation in protest against the Munich Agreement:

> It was not for Serbia that we fought in 1914. It was not even for Belgium, although it originally suited some people to say so. We were fighting then, as we should have been fighting last week, in order that one Great Power should not be allowed, in disregard of treaty obligations, of the laws of nations and the decrees of morality, to dominate by brutal force the continent of Europe. . . .[4]

This was as true in 1939 as in 1914.

* A famous cartoon of 1919, which has remained vividly in the memories of many, depicted a statesman of the Versailles Treaty saying at the conclusion to his colleagues: 'Curious! I seem to hear a child weeping!' A baby labelled '1940 Class' was in the background weeping bitterly. This memorable picture was recalled by the then Mr Attlee at the Peace Conference of Paris on 30 July 1946, with the words: 'The foreboding was justified. The child cried in the Second World War. Let it not cry again.'[3] (See below, pp. 432 ff.)

The Tiger: "Curious! I seem to hear a child weeping!"

Cartoon by Will Dyson for the *Daily Herald*, 1919. It shows the principals at the Versailles Peace Conference – Lloyd George, Orlando, Clemenceau and Wilson.

Nor was Pericles wide of the mark. There were few in August 1914 who envisaged as an outcome of the war the disappearance of the Hohenzollern, Romanov, Habsburg and Ottoman dynasties, or the dismemberment or disintegration of the German, Russian, Austro-Hungarian and Turkish Empires, the introduction of the principle of self-determination or the establishment of a League of Nations.

Similarly, in 1939 the original attitude of the Western Allies towards Germany was defined by Neville Chamberlain in his broadcast on 4 September. 'In this war', he had said, 'we are not fighting against you, the German people, for whom we have no bitter feelings, but against a tyrannous and forsworn régime.'[5] In the course of the next six years it was clearly apparent that, whatever their inner reservations may have been, the German people were either unable or unwilling to free themselves from the Nazi régime, with the inevitable result that they became identified in the minds of those arrayed against them with an upsurging of bitterness – a bitterness which found its ultra-logical apogee in the Morgenthau Plan. This plan, formally considered and initialled at the second Quebec Conference of September 1944, provided that a defeated Germany would be forcibly transformed from an industrial into an agricultural state.* Though this idea of 'pastoralizing' Germany did not survive, the very fact that it was officially advanced marks a notable change from the sentiments expressed by Mr Chamberlain. The formula of Unconditional Surrender, promulgated at Casablanca in 1943, set the pattern for the ultimate conclusion of the war – a pattern which was finally fulfilled in the schoolhouse of Rheims on 7 May 1945, but which had its own startling sequels in the establishment of two German republics and the reappearance of a rearmed and resurgent Federal Republic as an equal partner in the North Atlantic Treaty Organization.

Furthermore, the fact that Britain's *casus belli* in September 1939 had been in defence of the independence and integrity of Poland became somewhat obscured by the subsequent events of the ensuing six years. The emergence of the Soviet Union as a leading partner in the Grand Alliance had a further – and again, perhaps, an inevitable – sequel in the virtual abandonment of Poland by the Western Powers at Yalta. For though Poland emerged from the conflict possessed of large tracts of German territory, she had also ceded considerable areas to the Soviet Union and had become politically a satellite of Moscow.†

Moreover, though it had been accepted during the war that Germany should be compelled to disgorge the ill-gotten gains which she had

---

* See below, pp. 174–87.

† By the various agreements which constituted the modern Polish state, Poland received 40,157 sq. miles of German territory and ceded 70,049 sq. miles to Russia.

annexed from Czechoslovakia, Poland and France and to restore the independence of Austria, the complete disappearance of the German Reich had been as little foreseen as the subsequent disintegration of the overseas empires of France, the Netherlands and Belgium in a welter of nationalism and bloodshed – a fate which the British Empire largely escaped by reason of its genius for improvisation and adaptability, as, for example, in the achievement of the interpretative formula of April 1949, whereby it was found possible to include sovereign independent republics within the basically monarchic framework of the Commonwealth.*

Above all, it can have occurred to very few in September 1939 that before the end of hostilities the world would have crossed the threshold of the Nuclear Age.

A comparison of the evolution and definition of Allied war aims during the two world wars reveals some striking divergences and similarities. The First World War saw early diplomatic interchanges which, *inter alia*, promised Constantinople to Russia, the Rhine frontier to France and substantial territorial cessions from Austria–Hungary to Italy. It closed with the formidable Treaty of Versailles and its ancillary treaties of St Germain, Trianon, Neuilly and Sèvres (or rather Lausanne) which, together with the creation of the League of Nations, had changed both the face of Europe and the form and tempo of international diplomacy. The Second World War opened with promises of a peace of understanding to a non-Nazi Germany and offered 'a shadow of good things to come' in the Atlantic Charter. It closed untidily with a European continent acutely divided by the Iron Curtain and in such a condition that, whereas it was possible to negotiate treaties of peace in 1946 with Germany's allies, no such agreement could be reached with a Germany divided. No treaty of peace has so far been signed with Germany, and the Contractual Agreement of 1954 merely restored sovereignty to the Federal German Republic and ended the state of war which had existed since 1939 and the state of occupation which had obtained since 1945. On the other hand, the Treaty of San Francisco in 1951 concluded the war with Japan along conventional lines. Unlike the Covenant of the League of Nations, which formed an integral part of all the treaties of the Paris Peace Conference,† the Charter of the United Nations was hammered out and accepted in 1945 as a separate instrument of inter-

---

* This formula was achieved at the Meeting of Commonwealth Prime Ministers of 1949, and bears the date of 27 April. It ranks in importance in the development and evolution of the British Commonwealth with the Balfour Formula of 1926 and the Statute of Westminster of 1931.[6]

† In respect of Turkey, this was only true of the Treaty of Sèvres. When the Treaty of Lausanne came to be signed in July 1923, the Covenant had already become sufficiently controversial as to be dropped from the text.

national policy, having no connection with any other treaty or agreement. Moreover, it had the profound advantage that the United States was not only a prime mover in the drafting of the Charter and one of its founding signatories (this indeed she had been in 1919!), but that the Senate saw fit to ratify her membership.

The Allied discussions preceding the settlements after both world wars were carried on in each case under the impulse of an ailing American President. It is now widely believed that, according to all evidence available after the fact, Woodrow Wilson's illness in April 1919 in the midst of the Peace Conference – an illness which was currently diagnosed as influenza[7] – was in fact a thrombosis of the brain,[8] and the President's decisions and actions taken subsequent to this affliction must be considered accordingly. Correspondingly, despite the vehement contrary statements of his medical adviser,[9] it must be accepted that Franklin Roosevelt was not himself, either physically or mentally, at the Yalta Conference of February 1945. His appearance – a ghastly pallor accentuating the almost skeletal thinness of his face – shocked those of his British colleagues who had known him closely during the war, and his conduct of affairs convinced them that he was already failing in strength and grasp.[10]

Each of these American Presidents was imbued with an immutable desire to dominate the peace settlement following his respective war and to impose upon friend and foe alike a formula designed by him personally as a panacea for the world's ills. President Wilson visualized a *Pax Americana* based on the Fourteen Points, functioning with and through the Covenant of the League of Nations. Of this he was balked, first by the contrary views of David Lloyd George and Georges Clemenceau, then at the hands of the United States Senate, and finally because his own intransigent obstinacy would not permit him to sanction a qualified American ratification – 'with reservations' – of the Treaty of Versailles.

President Roosevelt's ambition was to establish the United Nations but to superimpose upon it an American–Soviet alliance, which should dominate world affairs to the detriment of Britain and France, and to this end he made copious concessions to Marshal Stalin. He was not spared the frustration and disappointment of disillusionment, for between Yalta and Potsdam the predatory designs of Moscow had become all too evident. His successor, President Truman, after a hesitant beginning, was quick to take the full measure of the Soviet threat.

The conclusion of both world wars was overshadowed by this threat – but with a difference. In 1919 Russia had reached the nadir of political and military disintegration and perhaps the apogee of pure revolutionary fervour. The impact upon the world of Bolshevism as a new ideology was greater even than that of Wilsonism, and even more dangerous to the survival of the old order. Dependent almost entirely for its success on the external effect of its propaganda – for it was not until considerably later that the Red Army was reorganized as an effective fighting force – Bolshevism seemed to constitute a threat to the countries of Eastern and Central Europe, but the authority of established Governments was sufficiently strong to combat it successfully. It also provided a bogey to the more firmly founded Western European nations who feared a possible spread of the revolutionary views from the East. This spectre was in the thoughts of the statesmen at the Peace Conference of Paris and influenced their decisions not a little. 'We are running a race with Bolshevism and the world is on fire,' President Wilson said on one occasion.[11]

A quarter of a century later, however, the position had greatly changed. By 1945 the inspirational genius of Lenin and the revolutionary fanaticism of Trotsky had both disappeared and in their place was the crude materialism, the stark *Realpolitik*, of Stalin. As a result of the Second World War the Soviet Union became second only to the United States as a military world power. By 1950 she was able to exercise a rigid and ruthless control over all Eastern, Central and South-eastern Europe, with the exception of Finland, Austria, Yugoslavia and Greece, and exhibited a very patent intention of extending permanently her ideological and political hegemony over all those territories. Thirty years after the Revolution of 1917 Russia had regained nearly all that she had lost by the diplomatic débâcle of Brest-Litovsk and the decisions of the Paris Peace Conference, and had achieved the realization of the most wildly imaginative ambitions of the Romanovs – all, indeed, except the possession of Constantinople and the Straits which had in the course of time greatly diminished in political and strategic significance.

In one sense a parallel – albeit a scarcely comforting one – can be drawn between the conclusion and outcome of the two world conflicts. Whereas both wars were fought with the greatest endurance and courage, the most appalling expenditure of lives and fortunes and resources, to the end that German militarism should be destroyed, the undeniable fact remains that after both Germany has emerged from a state of complete and utter defeat as a rearmed military power. To be sure, the conditions were different in each case. In the twenties the rearmament of the *Reichswehr* and the plans for its development and expansion were carried on clandestinely by General von Seeckt under the noses of the Allied Control Commission, with the knowledge of the German Government, the connivance of German big business and heavy industry, and the active collaboration of Soviet Russia.[12]

Things were very different in 1945. Germany, in accordance with the agreement between the four Allied Powers on 20 September, and by subsequent rulings of the Allied Control Council, was prohibited from military organization in any form, and when the West German Federal Republic was established in 1949 particular care was taken to safeguard the permanency of these provisions. A large and vocal section of West German public opinion was just as hostile to any form of rearmament as were Germany's neighbours. Whatever effects the Second World War was to have on Europe, the permanent extinction of German military power seemed bound to be one of them.

Yet in the 1950s there occurred a complete transmogrification of the German scene. In a far shorter period than after the First World War Germany emerged rearmed, not in contravention of treaty provisions, but with the open – and indeed avid – encouragement of her occupiers. The cause of this extraordinary shift in policy was the progressive collapse of the war-time alliance which had united the Western Powers against Hitler. From being regarded by the British and Americans as respected comrades in arms, the Russians began to be suspected of being potential aggressors and saboteurs of peace. So complete was this transformation that the Western Continental Powers, backed by the United States, Great Britain and Canada, were constrained to take extraordinary precautions to protect their security and independence. This unavoidably involved a reversal of the policy universally accepted for Germany at the close of the war. It entailed the creation of the North Atlantic Treaty Organization, into which a new German Army, the *Bundeswehr*, became integrated. Europe – and indeed the world – was divided into armed camps after a fashion more suited to a state of war than a time of peace.

Let it be said at once that the policy pursued by the Western Governments was essentially the only one to follow under the exigencies of the circumstances. The courageous doctrine preached long ago by Sir Winston Churchill, the doctrine of opposing aggression and tyranny, from whatever quarter they may come, with steadfastness and courage – the doctrine also of taking first things first – made it imperative that the dream of post-war co-operation between East and West had to be subordinated to the requirements of a new danger. The rearmament of Germany was only one unsought consequence of this danger; high levels of military expenditure, the sacrifice of schemes for social betterment and the dashing of hopes for international amity were others. After a catastrophic conflict which had lasted nearly six years, neither Europe nor the rest of the world could claim to have created peace. Instead there reigned an armed truce.

As this book is being printed attempts are being made to create a 'détente' between East and West based on the newly flexible *Ostpolitik* of the West German Government. The painful slowness of this laudable policy illustrates how deep the gulf which separates East from West in Europe still is. Even if this 'détente' is achieved it will only succeed in giving formal recognition to a situation which has existed since 1945 – a situation in which not only Germany but the whole of Europe has been effectively divided. All this is doubtless inevitable. But in accepting it, yet remembering the promises and sacrifices of two world wars, may we not say with Othello, 'Oh the pity of it, Iago, the pity of it'?

In the pages which follow the authors of this volume have not attempted to present the reader with a chronological diplomatic history. It has been our aim to illuminate the origins and significance of the uneasy and interrupted peace which followed the defeat of the Axis Powers; to do this it has sometimes been necessary to anticipate events in one theatre of war or diplomacy before describing contemporary occurrences elsewhere. We trust that this arrangement will meet with our readers' approval and forbearance.

2 | From the Phoney War to the Atlantic Charter

BRITAIN placed herself in a state of war with Germany on 3 September 1939, but almost immediately the situation became confused by the official pronouncement of the Prime Minister on 4 September that she had no quarrel with the German people but only with the German Government.

The reasons for this remarkable statement lie farther back in the penumbra of the inter-war years. From 1920 onwards there had existed a school of thought in Britain which believed that Germany had suffered certain grievous wrongs and unjustified humiliations at the hands of the Allies under the Treaty of Versailles. The adherents of this school campaigned consistently during the ensuing years for a revision of the Treaty – more especially in relation to disarmament and reparations – warning that if such rectification were not made Germany would one day be strong enough to take unilateral action in this respect, and that when this day came the former Allied Powers would find themselves in the embarrassing position of either having to 'put up or shut up' – in Theodore Roosevelt's immortal phrase. However wrong this school of thought may have been in its initial premise, it was proved woefully but indubitably correct in its subsequent deduction. One of the salient elements which swept Adolf Hitler into power in 1933 was his promise to free Germany from 'the shackles of Versailles', and this he proceeded consistently to fulfil.

The Revisionist School in Britain was now in its element. Every step taken by Nazi Germany in violation of her treaty obligations was hailed as inevitable and indeed justified, an argument which reached its apogee of unreality and stupidity when Hitler's occupation and remilitarization of the Rhineland was characterized as 'merely going into his own back yard'. Thereafter, however, there occurred a split in the ranks of the Revisionists. As Hitler's villainy became revealed and his predatory intentions upon his neighbours were gradually disclosed, the 'die-hards' among the Revisionists continued to condone, if not to applaud, whereas a dissenting group, appalled at the visage which the new Germany presented, however mistreated she may originally have been, stood in mesmerized horror as act after act of aggression was committed unchallenged.

Neither group, however, abandoned its basic Germanophilism. The Nazis and Hitler they were prepared to deprecate or condemn, according to their respective progressive lights, but they clung obstinately to their belief in the essential and fundamental decency of the German people. Both groups, therefore, were receptive to the line of argument purveyed by many of those Germans who had fled their Fatherland as victims of Nazi persecution. Manifestly these refugees were as genuinely anti-Nazi as could possibly be required, but most of them were also sincere German patriots, consumed with a desire to protect Germany – *their* Germany – from the consequences of Hitler's crimes. It was these men and women who conscientiously preached the doctrine that, while National Socialism and all its manifestations was a thing accursed, the innate good qualities of the German people as a whole were 'not dead but sleeping', not suffocated beneath the brown cloak of Nazi terror but lying dormant in temporary thrall, ready to remanifest themselves as soon as liberty and freedom should be restored to Germany.

In addition to this German line of argument persistently purveyed outside Germany, there were certain evidences produced from within the Reich which indicated opposition and dissent. During the summer of 1938 secret German envoys had besought Britain to remain firm in opposing Nazi aggression against Czechoslovakia, suggesting that if this were done a military *coup* would overthrow Hitler and destroy the Nazi régime. Once the Munich Agreement was a *fait accompli*, these same elements in Germany at once declared that only Mr Chamberlain's journey to Berchtesgaden had prevented this military *coup* from operation and success.[1] During the summer months preceding the outbreak of war in 1939 there had been a repetition of these proceedings. As late as June – and therefore well after Germany's designs upon Poland had been made plain and the British guarantees given in consequence – these secret envoys of the Opposition were in London again dangling the prospect of a military overthrow of Hitler yet seeking assurances that a non-Nazi Germany would retain all that the Führer's policies had gained for her and even hinting that, should the overthrow of Hitler be delayed until after the conquest of Poland, Britain and France might condone a certain German aggrandizement at Polish expense.[2]

Although these German efforts bore no fruit in influencing immediate policy, they did, nevertheless, have some effect on the thinking of the professional Germanophils and of those responsible for the presentation of the Allied case to the German people after the outbreak of hostilities. There was, it was argued, the possibility that a plot against Hitler *might* indeed exist and that it *might* indeed succeed. Again, it was possible that once a new Government had seized power in Berlin the German people as a whole *might* rise in their strength, throw off the shackles of Nazi oppression and demonstrate their innate decency by revenging themselves upon their recent oppressors before re-establishing a *Rechtsstaat*.

This belief, which was held more fervently by some than others, had an inherent weakness. It entirely overlooked the age-long and mutual hatred between Germany and Poland. An 'isolated war' against Poland was something of which the German General Staff had dreamed and planned for nearly a generation, and the overthrow of Hitler could not have been further from their minds until the 'small conflict' had been conducted to a successful conclusion. Then, perhaps (for they abhorred the idea of a general war), the Generals might contemplate a *coup de main*, but not until spoils of war in the East had been safely garnered; and in this they were not without a generous measure of support from the German people as a whole.

The Revisionist School in Britain was either ignorant or unheeding of this essential factor. They believed in the possibility of driving a wedge between the Nazi régime and the German people, and it was to this end that Mr Chamberlain made his now historic broadcast on 4 September – a primitive, clumsy and amateurish essay in the field of political warfare. After recounting the crimes of the Führer and his Government, he declared:

> In this war we are not fighting against the German people, for whom we have no bitter feelings, but against a tyrannous and forsworn régime which has betrayed not only its own people but the whole of Western civilization and all that you and we hold dear.

By implication it was conveyed to the German people that, once Hitler and the Nazi régime had been disposed of, Germany might expect a generous peace, and the measure of the generosity may be gauged by the fact that as late as 1940 and 1941 there were still those in England who considered that the Sudetenland and even Austria should form a part of post-war Germany, and that it was not until 1942 that the Munich Agreement was formally abrogated and the restoration of Austrian independence declared to be a part of the official policy of the British Government.[3]*

---

* See below, App. A, 'Note on the Present Position of the Munich Agreement'.

II

The British people went to war in 1939 in a very different frame of mind from that of 1914. There was neither the inspiration nor the genius of a Rupert Brooke to thank God 'Who has matched us with His hour', nor to rejoice with Laurence Binyon in that 'We step from days of sour division into the grandeur of our fate'. The prevailing feeling was in a sense one of relief that the decision to 'stop Hitler', long pending, had at last been taken. But there was little passion or enthusiasm about it, only a grim determination to see it through at all costs and to a finish – a finish which should liberate Europe from fear and aggression. What had happened was that the nation had passed in a twelvemonth from the ignoble relief consequent upon Mr Chamberlain's diplomatic defeat at Munich to an awakening to the starkness of reality; from the mood of flat rejection of war into acceptance of its virtual inevitability.

Similarly there was little or none of the fierce anti-German feeling of 1914 when hostile demonstrations against all Germans in the country, or against persons or shops with German names, and an epidemic of spy-mania forced the Government to arrest and intern many Germans and Austrians – most of them entirely innocent – for their own protection. In 1939 these conditions did not obtain. The persecution by the Nazi régime since 1933 of numerous classes of German citizens on political and religious grounds had resulted in a great influx into the United Kingdom of refugees from oppression who were in many cases willing or anxious to work, and even to fight, for the defeat of National Socialism, and it was believed by many that these people were representative of many others in Germany who had not been fortunate enough to escape but who longed for the day of liberation.

Then there was a definite – if impracticable – distinction in the British mind between the Nazi régime and the German people, and in this respect Mr Chamberlain's broadcast of 4 September was a not inaccurate reflection of the prevailing spirit. Indeed Charles Hamilton Sorley's lines 'To Germany' written in April 1915, were more indicative of thought at the beginning of the Second World War than of the First:

> You are blind like us. Your hurt no man designed,
> And no man claimed the conquest of your land.
> But gropers both through fields of thought confined
> We stumble and we do not understand.
> You only saw your future bigly planned,
> And we, the tapering paths of our own mind,
> And in each other's dearest ways we stand,
> And hiss and hate. And the blind fight the blind.

When it is peace, then we may view again
With new-won eyes each other's truer form
And wonder. Grown more loving-kind and warm
We'll grasp firm hands and laugh at the old pain,
When it is peace. But until peace, the storm,
The darkness and the thunder and the rain.[4]

It was not until 1940, when the glorious reverse of Dunkirk and the consequent threat of invasion brought with them the menace of the Fifth Column, that public outcry – often ill-directed – arose against the danger of those German refugees who were still at large.[5] It was the Battle of Britain, when all Britain was suddenly in the fighting line, which clarified the public mind as to the strategic value of any distinction which existed between 'good' and 'bad' Germans.

But in the meantime this dichotomy of thought prevailed and created in the British mind – both official and public – a kind of counterpart to the 'Maginot mentality' in France, which paralysed and mesmerized the military and political thinking of that country. Having remained virtually quiescent during the slaughter of Poland, the Western Allies settled down behind the Maginot Line, awaiting Hitler's next move and at the same time expectant of insurrection from the Opposition within the Reich.*

Strangely enough, tentative proposals for peace were forthcoming through no less than four channels. The first was Hitler. Returned in triumph from his victory in the East, the Führer at once began his planning for prosecuting the war against Britain and France. Before launching this, however, he determined upon a peace offer to the West which might conceivably save him the trouble of mounting an offensive. On 6 October, in his speech to the Reichstag, he made a definite offer of peace on the basis of the recognition by the Western Powers of his Polish conquests; satisfaction to be given to German colonial aims by Britain, but no further demands to be made upon France. 'I have refused', he said, 'even to mention the problem of Alsace-Lorraine.'

Édouard Daladier replied on 10 October. France, he said, would never lay down her arms until guarantees for a real peace and general security had been obtained. But it was not M. Daladier's reactions which primarily interested the Führer. He knew that once again – as at Munich in 1938 and as in September 1939 – the key to any decision lay, in the

---

* A positive aversion to the idea of a more active prosecution of the war existed in Government circles in London. When Leopold Amery proposed to the Air Minister that, in view of Germany's shortage of timber, some attempt should be made to set fire to the Black Forest, Sir Kingsley Wood replied that there was no question of the R.A.F. bombing even the munition works at Essen 'which were private property'.[6]

last instance, in the hands of Britain. It was for Mr Chamberlain's reply that he seemed to be waiting, and he took the opportunity of a second speech in the Sportpalast on 10 October to re-emphasize his readiness for peace: 'Germany has no cause for war against the Western Powers.'

Mr Chamberlain's reply was delivered in the House of Commons on 12 October, and once again the technique of attempting to drive a wedge between the Führer and the German people was employed.[7] The Führer's proposals he dismissed as 'vague and uncertain', offering no suggestion for righting the wrongs done to Czechoslovakia and to Poland. The Prime Minister then proceeded to elaborate the formula of his broadcast of 4 September:

> It is no part of our policy to exclude from her rightful place in Europe a Germany which will live in amity and confidence with other nations. On the contrary, we believe that no effective remedy can be found for the world's ills that does not take account of the just claims and needs of all countries, and whenever the time may come to draw the lines of a new peace settlement, His Majesty's Government would feel that the future would hold little hope unless such a settlement could be reached through the method of negotiation and agreement.
>
> It was not, therefore, with any vindictive purpose that we embarked on war, but simply in defence of freedom. . . .
>
> We seek no material advantage for ourselves; we desire nothing from the German people which should offend their self-respect. We are not aiming only at victory but rather look beyond it to the laying of a foundation of a better international system which will mean that war is not to be the inevitable lot of every succeeding generation.
>
> I am certain that all the peoples of Europe, including the people of Germany, long for peace, a peace which will enable them to live their lives without fear, and to devote their energies and their gifts to the development of their culture, the pursuit of their ideals and the improvement of their material prosperity.

Finding that his gambit of a 'peace offer' had failed, Hitler summoned his generals on 27 October and informed them that they must make final preparations for a Western Offensive. X-day was to be 12 November and the objectives were to include the occupation of Belgium and the Netherlands, with both of which states Germany had treaties of non-aggression.

Paris and London were, of course, ignorant of these developments at the Führer's headquarters; indeed it was widely believed in those capitals that Hitler, rather than risk a frontal attack upon the legendary Maginot Line, was prepared to accept the strategy of a war of attrition, and this was welcomed by the West, since it was believed that Britain was well equipped to win such a war because of her superiority at sea. Hopes were raised for a struggle of endurance which might prove of comparatively little cost in loss of life. It was in this belief that the *Sitzkrieg* was conducted, and it came therefore as somewhat of a surprise when on 7 November an appeal for peace to all belligerents was received from the sovereigns of Belgium and the Netherlands, who offered their good offices as intermediaries.

What had happened was that King Leopold III had on 6 November received tidings from his Legation in Berlin, where secret contacts had been maintained with anti-Nazi elements, warning him of the imminence of the Western Offensive and of the fact that the Low Countries were among its targets. This news was enough to send the King racing through the night from Brussels to The Hague by car to confer with Queen Wilhelmina on their common approaching danger. He found that the Queen had also received similar information, and the two agreed upon concerted action to forestall their peril.[8]

King George VI and President Lebrun did not make known their respective replies to this appeal until 12 November – the original X-day of the German offensive – and these contained a courteous refusal of the offer. After recapitulating the reasons why Britain was at war and the reasons why she must continue to be so, the King wrote to his fellow sovereigns: 'Should Your Majesty be able to communicate to me any proposals from Germany of such a character as to afford real prospect of achieving the purpose I have described above, I can say at once that my Government would give them their most earnest consideration.'[9]

The immediate danger passed, but only the inclemency of the weather had prevented the offensive from taking place and it had been but temporarily postponed.* The forced landing near Malines in Belgium on 10 January 1940 of a *Luftwaffe* plane carrying two staff officers with important 'top secret' papers concerning the forthcoming attack, which they were unable to destroy and which were communicated by the Belgian authorities to the British, French and Netherlands Governments, gave further evidence that the strange condition of 'All Quiet on the Western Front' was but a lull before the storm.[10]

In the meantime, however, the latter part of Mr Chamberlain's reply of 12 October to the Führer's 'peace offer' had caused a flutter among the Opposition in Germany. Though his remarks had been originally addressed, *inter alia*, by the Prime Minister to the House of Commons, his statement had been reported over the German Service of the B.B.C. and had therefore been heard by many Germans who, regardless of pains and penalties, listened regularly to these broadcasts. At once the

---

* The original order for attack on 12 November had been cancelled on 7 November. Between then and the final order of 9 May 1940 there were fourteen postponements of the offensive for meteorogical reasons. The German Army leaders were relieved by these postponements since they regarded Hitler's precipitate haste as recklessly dangerous.

question arose, what exactly did Mr Chamberlain mean? What terms had he in mind for a Germany which had proved her good faith by disposing of Hitler and overthrowing the Nazi régime? In short, the very natural question: 'What is there in it for us?'

The leaders of the Opposition had long been anxious to elucidate this query and to this end they had utilized a number of channels. Theodor Kordt, a former member of the German Embassy staff in London, had been appointed to the Legation in Berne where he was visited periodically by his British friend, Philip Conwell-Evans, a dedicated follower of the Revisionist School. An eminent Munich lawyer, Dr Josef Müller, had been dispatched to Rome to keep in touch with certain Vatican circles; while the former German Ambassador to Italy, Ulrich von Hassell, made contact with the British Foreign Office through another Englishman, J. Lonsdale Bryans, who was described as 'an English associate of Lord Halifax'.

It was Philip Conwell-Evans who now intervened with a message that Mr Chamberlain's House of Commons statement of 12 October constituted 'a solemn obligation' which would be 'unconditionally observed'.[11] As such it was hoped by the leaders of the Opposition to provide a powerful trump card in 'gingering up' the German generals to make their *coup* against Hitler before the launching of the Western Offensive.

But what did Mr Chamberlain's statement really mean? To this end von Hassell and Josef Müller bent their renewed energies. To Lord Halifax in February 1940 von Hassell sent a memorandum, by the hand of Lonsdale Bryans, declaring it to be the aim of the German Opposition to lay the foundation for the 'permanent pacification and re-establishment of Europe as a solid basis and a security against a renewal of warlike tendencies'. To achieve this end von Hassell laid it down as a necessity that Germany should retain both Austria and the Sudetenland and that the German–Polish border should be 'more or less identical with the German frontier of 1914'. Apart from these amputations, Poland and Czechoslovakia should be restored to independence and there should be no discussion of Germany's western frontiers. There followed certain general aphorisms on human rights, Christian ethics and social welfare as the *Leitmotiv* of the new Europe.[12]

Mr Bryans duly showed this paper to Lord Halifax and to Sir Alexander Cadogan, the Permanent Under-Secretary, at the Foreign Office and it was his impression that its contents received general agreement and sympathy.* But he was given nothing in writing and it

---

* This is not entirely beyond the bounds of possibility in view of the feelings about Austria and Czechoslovakia which prevailed in London until as late as 1942 (see above, pp. 11–14).

was nearly two months before he was again able to meet von Hassell in Switzerland, by which time the course of events had rendered all discussion of peace terms academic.

Josef Müller in Rome, on the other hand, had been more successful. Through the good offices of Pope Pius XII's Private Secretary, Father Robert Leiber, and the former Chairman of the German Centre Party, Monsignor Ludwig Kaas, he had succeeded in establishing indirect contact with the British Minister to the Holy See, D'Arcy Osborne (later Duke of Leeds), and his first tentative feelers were apparently sufficiently encouraging as to establish the fact that all doors to a negotiated peace with a Germany which had eliminated Hitler and the Nazi régime were not irrevocably barred and that there were still those in London with whom it was possible to talk. By the end of October these Papal soundings had disclosed a very evident willingness in London to make a 'soft peace' with a non-Nazi Germany. According to what Müller reported back to Germany, the Pope was prepared to go to surprising lengths in his understanding of German interests, whereas Lord Halifax, while accepting the general principles of the German formula, had cagily touched upon such points as the 'decentralization' of Germany and the possibility of a 'referendum in Austria'. The Holy Father himself was stated to be ready to act as an intermediary and as a guarantor for an understanding with Britain on the following terms:

1. The removal of the Nazi régime.
2. The formation of a new German Government and the restoration of the *Rechtsstaat* in Germany.
3. No attack in the West by either side.
4. The settlement of the Eastern question in favour of Germany.

Müller also conveyed the impression that the British Government were actually prepared for an understanding on these conditions.[13]

The generals, however, did not rise to this fly. They were beginning to stand in increasingly unholy awe of their Führer and, in addition, many of the fears and objections which had beset them at the prospect of mounting an offensive in mid-winter had greatly diminished when it become more and more clear that the attack would now be launched in the spring or early summer. The generals, therefore, rejected the advances of the Opposition and it was many months before they found themselves again in a receptive mood – and then it was too late.

For the war was rapidly passing from that passive phase in which one could discuss the possibility of a negotiated peace. First the Scandinavian campaign in April and then the attack in the West a month later suddenly broadened the field of operations past all previous belief, with the inevitable results that the German generals, once again triumphant in battle and recipient of the honours and laurels of war, banished all thought of overthrowing the Führer from their minds; while the British, in the throes of their struggle for survival, were equally unwilling to discuss the possibility of peace. There was no revival of this pacific interest while Britain 'stood alone', though it recurred thereafter in a more practical form than heretofore.

There was, however, one final pendant to the Phoney War period, a strange and anomalous echo which found no respondent chord.

It was early in August 1940. The Battles of the Low Countries and of France had been fought and lost and the preliminary phase of the Battle of Britain had begun, though the main battle had not yet been joined. At this moment of comparative quiet, the moment before the storm of fire and blast was to break over Britain, that Nestor of European sovereigns, King Gustav V of Sweden, made a last attempt to effect a negotiated peace before the coming bitter conflict rendered this impossible. In secret letters to King George VI and to Hitler he offered his services as an intermediary 'to enable contact to be made between the two groups of belligerents in order to examine the possibilities of peace'.

The nature of Hitler's reply, if any were made, is unknown, but on 12 August the King handed to the Swedish Minister in London his own courteous but unequivocal rejection of King Gustav's offer. In view of the criminal record of the enemy, wrote the King, he saw not the slightest cause to recede from the principles and resolves which he and his Ministers had already set forth:

> . . . On the contrary the intention of my peoples to prosecute the war until their purposes have been achieved has been strengthened. They will not falter in their duty and they firmly believe that with the help of God they will not lack the means to discharge their task.

King George spoke not only for himself and his Ministers in the United Kingdom but on behalf of the Governments of the British Dominions Beyond the Seas, for all had been consulted. His own personal reaction, which typified that of the great majority of his subjects, was recorded in his diary on 5 August (three days after he had received King Gustav's letter):

> How can we talk of peace with Germany now after they have overrun & demoralized the peoples of so many countries in Europe? Until Germany is prepared to live peaceably with her neighbours in Europe, she will always be a menace. We have got to get rid of her aggressive spirit, her engines of war & the people who have been taught to use them.[14]

III

To the westward, the United States was an anxious observer of the events in Europe. Geographically more detached than was Britain from the imminence of danger from a Nazi-dominated Europe, the United States was directly and vitally concerned with the course of the Battle of the Atlantic, a phase of the war which continued unrelentingly, despite the quiescence of events on the Continent. President Franklin Roosevelt appreciated better than most of his countrymen the vital importance for America of Britain's winning this battle, for the British Navy provided a sure shield for the North American continent against possible Nazi aggression. The President was also keenly aware of the fact that the apparent stalemate in Europe was most unlikely to continue after spring had brought open campaigning weather, and he knew, moreover, that once a general conflict had been joined the prospects of restoring peace would be extremely tenuous.

President Roosevelt was confronted by more than one profound difficulty. The majority of Americans, though in general sympathizing with Britain and France, rejected the idea of America's becoming involved in 'a shooting war' with every fibre of their being. They looked with some confidence to the President and that veteran statesman Cordell Hull, who was his Secretary of State, to keep them out of war, and this he sincerely hoped he would be able to do, provided there were some hopes of peace before the summer. Once the war had become general, Roosevelt was personally convinced that America would sooner or later be drawn in, but he could not mention this belief even to his closest colleagues, so great was the national feeling against involvement.*

Other difficulties which perplexed the President were that he was preparing to introduce a Selective Service Act for the first time in American history in time of peace and, furthermore, was considering the far graver decision of shattering political precedent and seeking nomination in the Democratic Party Convention of July 1940 for a third presidential term. Peace, or the enhanced chances of peace, was a very necessary element for the success of both projects, and President Roosevelt was greatly involved in plans towards this end.

From the very morrow of the conquest of Poland the United States

* 'I do not know anyone in official Washington who, as you say, "feels it inevitable that this country should be drawn into the European conflict"', wrote the President in reply to a violent protest from that arch-isolationist General Robert E. Wood (future leader of the 'America First' Committee) in October 1939. 'You make all kinds of wild and wholly incorrect statements. "The whole Department of State" is *not* permeated with this feeling, nor are "some of the Ambassadors", neither is "notably the Ambassador to France" [William C. Bullitt]. Neither do I share this feeling. Neither does Mrs Roosevelt share this feeling.'[15]

Government had been in receipt of persistent hints and suggestions from a variety of sources that the President should take the initiative in mediation. In the early days of October 1939 Dr Otto Dietrich, the Nazi Chief Press Officer, had urged the President to take action in order to prevent 'the most gruesome blood-bath in history', and there were further indications that Hitler was ready to make peace if only Mr Roosevelt would take the initiative. The existence of the 'peace feelers' became public, and on 7 and 10 October the President authorized positive denials that he was in any way impressed by these Nazi overtures.[16]

Some six weeks later a further German approach was made to the White House, this time on the part of *émigrés* who had been stimulated by the visit of an active and impeccable member of the Opposition, Adam von Trott zu Solz. Utilizing his ability to visit America as a neutral country, Adam von Trott had attended a conference of the Institute of Pacific Relations at Virginia Beach during the third week of November where he had met a number of distinguished representatives of the academic and business worlds of Britain, Canada and the United States – and also one of the writers of this book. In the plenary sessions and committees of the conference he had observed a very 'correct' attitude, confining himself to the recapitulation of the German 'case' without openly defending Nazi principles. In conversations held in private rooms, however, and in long horseback rides with John Wheeler-Bennett along the broad grey sands of the Virginia shore, von Trott frankly declared himself to be an anti-Nazi and made us acquainted with the thinking and planning of the German Opposition. He stressed the readiness of nearly all Germans, Nazis and anti-Nazis alike, for a 'quick peace' based on the *status quo* before her conquest of Poland, and urged the Western Allies to reiterate and redefine their peace terms along the lines of Mr Chamberlain's statements of 4 September and 12 October, both of which were fresh in our memories. If this were done, he declared – and done in time – the Army would effect a *coup* and over-throw the Nazi régime.

Von Trott's proposals reached the British Embassy in Washington (and were subsequently reported to London), the United States Department of State and the Canadian Department of External Affairs; in all these quarters they were viewed with the greatest suspicion. Von Trott himself was further successful in persuading virtually all the leading non-Socialist German *émigrés* in the country – with the exception of Dr Heinrich Brüning, the former Reich Chancellor – to subscribe to a memorandum which reached the White House urging upon the President the importance and desirability of making public a statement on war aims and peace terms and emphasizing the significant effect which such publication would have upon 'the internal situation in Germany'.[17]

Nor were these the only indications of pressure brought to bear on the Administration in the interests of peace. Throughout the winter the President and the State Department were besieged by persons pleading for American mediatory intervention before the war entered upon a more violent phase. Businessmen with foreign connections, like Thomas Watson of I.B.M. and James Mooney of the General Motors Export Corporation, were productive of schemes for peace of which a salient feature was that they should be conducted by businessmen appointed as secret envoys. American liberals, such as Oswald Garrison Villard, returned from Europe urging that intervention might still get results. Appeasement-minded foreign visitors, like Axel Wennergren, the Swedish capitalist, who offered his own services as a go-between, energetically argued that it was not too late to intervene.[18]

In the face of this 'peace barrage' the President sought to winnow the sense from the nonsense, the genuine from the self-interest, the practical from the idealism. He pondered deeply. Experience as a junior member of President Wilson's Administration had bred in him a fine distaste for the employment of secret emissaries of the type of Colonel House, and in any case this was not that type of war. Roosevelt discussed the matter in broad outline with Secretary Hull and with Bernard Baruch, his unofficial elder-statesman adviser, and with others of the higher echelons of the State Department such as Norman Davis, himself a veteran negotiator. From these discussions it became very clear that Mr Hull was opposed to any peace initiative on the part of the United States on the grounds that, with all the military successes so far on the German side, it could scarcely be expected that Hitler would consider for a moment the surrender of Austria, Czechoslovakia and Poland and that a peace leaving these gains in German hands was not one which the Allies ought to accept or the United States to encourage.[19] Another school of thought, less forthright than the Secretary of State, urged that premature appearance as a mediator would detract from the subsequent effectiveness of the United States as a peace-maker, and yet another faction argued that to talk repeatedly of peace until peace did indeed arrive would give America the useful character of the voice of common sense.[20]

Partly as a result of these consultations and partly of his own deep inner communion, President Roosevelt had by the end of the year reached a decision to act. On 24 December, in a Christmas letter to Pope Pius XII, he announced that he was appointing Myron C. Taylor, an eminent Quaker and former League of Nations High Commissioner for Refugees, with the personal rank of Ambassador, to be his representative at the Vatican. Mr Taylor's primary and ostensible duties would be in connection with co-operation in meeting the increasingly pressing problem of refugees from Germany and Nazi-occupied countries, but it was also President Roosevelt's hope that, by friendly collaboration with the Vatican, his envoy might be of service in preventing the spread of the war – especially Italian participation – and in promoting a just peace.

A second decision taken by the President early in the New Year was to send a fact-finding mission to Europe for the purpose of establishing whether there were any prospects of peace. This task he confided to his old school-friend the Under-Secretary of State, Sumner Welles.

Both the origins and the ultimate objectives of the Welles Mission are somewhat obscure. At least two members of the President's Cabinet, the Secretary of the Interior – Harold Ickes – and the Secretary of State, believed that the idea had originated with Welles himself;[21] but Harold Ickes was ever a mordant chronicler, and between Cordell Hull and his Under-Secretary of State there was little love lost, Hull suspecting that Welles discussed and conducted policy with the President behind his back – a suspicion in which there was more than a substratum of truth.* There is little doubt that Sumner Welles was indeed anxious to 'get into the act' in some form or other, but there is good reason to believe that President Roosevelt had had the idea of a mission to Europe well in mind for some time before, and that he had even considered naming as his emissary the President of Johns Hopkins University, Dr Isaiah Bowman, that great geographer who had been one of Woodrow Wilson's advisers at the Peace Conference at Paris.[23] He had discussed the matter tentatively with Cordell Hull late in January. Sumner Welles returned to Washington from sick-leave at the beginning of February, and the idea of sending his old friend on this mission very soon thereafter crystallized in the President's mind. He had complete trust in Welles's ability as an observer and was not unaware of his fondness for formal negotiations. He therefore sought the general approval of Secretary Hull early in February, and having announced it to his Cabinet on 7 February, made the matter public two days later.

As to the ultimate objectives of the Welles Mission, there is also some

---

* Hull himself was a believer in the delegation of work and did so on all possible occasions. 'This practice worked very well', he wrote in his memoirs, 'in most instances. Later on, however, instances occurred where an assistant badly abused his trust by going over my head to see the President without instructions from me and undertaking in one way or another virtually to act as Secretary of State. Sumner Welles was the principal offender.'[22]

uncertainty. According to what the President told the Cabinet, Welles was instructed to visit the Foreign Ministries in Rome, Berlin, Paris and London in order to receive and co-ordinate information on the ground with a view to transmitting it later to the President and the Secretary of State. The President made it clear that his envoy went without any specific instructions or any power to make or act on proposals; his information would not even be passed on to the other members of the Cabinet,[24] and this was certainly in accordance with Mr Hull's views. There is, however, evidence from one of the President's biographers, Rexford Tugwell, who was at this time one of his close familiars, that Roosevelt had a broader aim for the Welles Mission than the mere getting of information. The accumulation of reports presaging a German offensive in the late spring or early summer had inspired the President with a desire to make one last effort to effect mediation before the European structure disappeared in a final holocaust. Did he give Welles certain secret instructions which justified the envoy in describing his mission as a 'forlorn hope'?[25] It is Tugwell's contention that, if the Under-Secretary had brought back any substantial degree of encouragement for an agreement on peace terms, the President would have proposed to Hitler, Mussolini, Chamberlain and Reynaud that they should meet with him on neutral soil or possibly at sea, when 'the famous charm, backed by the mightily increasing power of the United States, would have its chances'.[26]

Whatever the President may have had in mind as an ultimate objective, he had first to deal with the immediate repercussions of his announcement both at home and abroad. The idea of the Welles Mission caused alarm in isolationist circles and consternation among the pro-Allied supporters. It at once gave rise to a crop of rumours of dissension between the President and his Secretary of State and between Hull and Welles.* It was given a mixed reception by the American Embassies in the capitals concerned, for whereas in Rome and Berlin the Ambassador and *Chargé d' Affaires*, respectively, had but formal touch with the Italian and German Governments and therefore welcomed a new point of contact, William Bullitt in Paris and Joseph Kennedy in London considered themselves on such intimate relations with the Governments to which they were accredited that they deemed Mr Welles's visitation superfluous. The Governments whom Mr Welles was to visit gave, with the exception of the German, a most cordial response to the suggestion of his coming, but it was evident that in both

---

* So irresponsible did these rumours become that Hull on 14 February issued an official statement emphasizing his almost uniform agreement with the President on foreign affairs and paying a graceful compliment to Sumner Welles.[27]

London and Paris there was considerable apprehension of his approach.[28]

Despite these difficulties Sumner Welles eventually sailed from New York on his tour of exploration in the *Rex*, accompanied by Jay Pierpoint Moffat, Chief of the Division of Western European Affairs in the State Department, and arrived with personal holograph letters from the President to Mr Chamberlain, Paul Reynaud and Mussolini (but not to Hitler), introducing Welles as 'my old boyhood friend'.[29] To the American diplomats it was almost as if they were entering a different world. Europe, poised on the razor edge of a general war, was still very much in a reminiscent mood. Hitler could not forgive the fact that Britain had given a 'blank cheque' to Poland 'and had therefore made war inevitable'; Mussolini could not forgive the sanctions episode of 1935; Neville Chamberlain could not forgive Hitler for the violation of the Munich Agreement in March 1939; France had many memories which she found it difficult to forget or forgive. All the belligerents were deeply concerned for their own security. Germany alone envisaged an expansion of the field of operations; Britain and France would not shrink from this but equally would not consider a peace with Nazi Germany. Italy had no desire to enter the war, but if Germany in her coming offensive – of which all talked openly – overran Holland and Belgium and inflicted some rapid and crushing defeats on France Welles considered that Mussolini would not resist the temptation of bringing Italy into the war on the side of the Axis. On the other hand, Welles believed that, such was the obsession with the problem of security, if the President of the United States, with the support of a united Western Hemisphere, should propound a practical plan for security and disarmament even the Nazis might consider it a basis for negotiation.

Such was the burden of the report which Sumner Welles made to the President on his return to America on 28 March.[30] It was a brilliant piece of reportage, but if Roosevelt had really expected any practical outcome of this mission he must have been bitterly disappointed. Though no one could have gleaned more than Welles from the leaders of Europe, the fact remained that neither Hitler, nor Mussolini, nor Neville Chamberlain, nor Paul Reynaud, nor Pope Pius, nor their respective Foreign Ministers, had offered any real hope of peace; and, though Mr Hull might describe Welles's report as 'superb', he was also compelled to add that 'nothing he learned gave us any basis for action'.[31] The President, nevertheless, issued an official statement on the Welles Mission on 29 March, concluding with the words: 'Even though there may be scant immediate prospect for the establishment of any just, stable and lasting peace in Europe, the information made available to this Government as a result of Mr Welles' mission will undoubtedly be of the greatest value when the time comes for the establishment of such a peace.'[32]

The passage of events – eleven days after this statement Hitler invaded Denmark and Norway and within two months had defeated France and driven the British Army out of Europe – postponed the making of peace for another five years, and when hostilities closed Reynaud was in political obscurity, Hitler, Mussolini and Chamberlain were dead – and so was Franklin Delano Roosevelt.

IV

It is an undeniable fact that, of all the states concerned, Russia was most immediately conscious of the danger to herself and to Europe presented by the National Socialist Revolution in Germany. The advent of Hitler to power meant, in a sense, far more to the Soviet Union than to any other Power in Europe, and the dislocation of her foreign policy was also greater. To Britain and to France the rupture of the Locarno Pact and of the foreign policy of Stresemann and Brüning was a source of disillusionment and shock, but for the Soviet Union the termination of the Rapallo policy of Brockdorff-Rantzow, Maltzan and Seeckt entailed a complete reorientation of all aspects of foreign policy.

It was, perhaps, because of the extreme Russian sensibility to the problem of security, or, perhaps, because of the acute ideological antithesis which existed between National Socialism and Marxism, that the Government of the Soviet Union was more vividly aware of the menace of the Third Reich than were the majority of the Western Powers. But, whatever the cause, Soviet leadership and Soviet diplomacy were quick to recognize both the dangers and the advantages which might accrue from this new manifestation. Russia was concerned for her own safety from the militant Moloch which was gradually emerging in Central Europe, but she was also alive to the fact that the effect of this apparition might redound to her own benefit, since it would inevitably compel the Western Powers to woo Russia from the isolationist policy which she had pursued for twelve years or more and to facilitate her return to active membership in the family of Europe. The calculations of Moscow proved exactly right.

By a curious amalgam of the Leninist and Wilsonian interpretations of the principle of self-determination, Russia, at the close of the First World War, had been separated from a large amount of territory over which she had formerly exercised sovereignty. The Grand Duchy of Finland and the provinces of Lithuania, Estonia and Latvia declared their independence; what had been Russian Poland was incorporated in the new Polish state; Bessarabia was ceded to Rumania and the vilayets of Kars, Ardahan and Batum to Turkey. Finally, as a result of the Russo-Polish war, the Treaty of Riga awarded to Poland a considerable portion of the western Ukraine and White Russia. As the years passed and the basis of Soviet foreign policy developed and clarified, it was found to have three basic long-term principles which continued adamant despite all mutations and tergiversations of current diplomacy. These were: first, to hold firmly to what remained of the old Russian Empire; secondly, to regain the territories lost by the Treaty of Brest-Litovsk, at the Paris Peace Conference and by the Treaty of Riga; thirdly, to regain for the Soviet Union the territorial strength and political influence which Tsarist Russia had exercised in the past and, if possible, to exceed it. In all these ambitions, with the exception of the re-annexation of Finland, the Soviet Union was successful at the close of the Second World War.

The first step was the famous Russian 'return to Europe' in 1934, the fruit of the statesmanship of those veteran diplomatists, Louis Barthou and Maxim Litvinov, and of President Beneš of Czechoslovakia. It took the form of the entry of the Soviet Union into the League of Nations, preceded by the conclusion of treaties of neutrality and non-aggression between Russia and France, Finland, Poland, Estonia and Latvia, and followed by pacts of mutual assistance between Russia and France and Czechoslovakia. This was satisfactory as far as it went, but where Soviet diplomacy failed, and failed signally, was to arrive at any agreement for a collective security pact directed against the onmarch of Nazi aggression. There was nothing altruistic in this policy. Stalin had realized that only at the expense of Russia could Germany's ambitions for *Lebensraum* be achieved in their ultimate entirety, and that Austria, Czechoslovakia, Memel and Poland were but stepping-stones to the Ukraine, the Urals, and eventually to world dominion.

This Soviet effort failed for a variety of reasons. In Eastern Europe two important factors, Poland and Rumania, feared the threat of Soviet aid almost as acutely as the menace of Nazi aggression; while in the West the distrust of Bolshevism in France and Britain distorted their perspective in regard to German policy. The school of thought in Paris which murmured 'Better Hitler than Blum' and, later on, 'Better Hitler than Stalin', was already vocal, and there was a profound dislike in London and in Paris for any idea of an active alliance with a régime which liquidated its political opponents and decimated its General Staff and High Command. Fear of Russia and of Bolshevism on the part of the Appeasers in Britain and France divided their peoples and weakened their own attitudes towards Hitler. Nor was the Führer slow to take advantage. By identifying himself with the struggle against Bolshevism he successfully wooed and won the support of many who also entertained a lively aversion to the brutality and gangsterism of his domestic and foreign policies.

It was this road which led directly to the humiliation of the Western Powers at Munich in September 1938 when Russia, although a vitally interested party, was ignored. For among the benefits accruing to the Führer from his triumph, other than the fulfilment of his immediate demands upon Czechoslovakia, were the isolation of Poland and exclusion of the Soviet Union from the new Concert of Europe. When the West reawakened to a sense of reality after the Rape of Czechoslovakia in March 1939 and began its limping and half-hearted attempts to forge an alliance with Moscow, it was too late to realize the aims for which Maxim Litvinov had striven for the previous five years. By this time it was widely believed in Moscow that the governing aim of British and French policy was to do a deal with Hitler and turn Nazi Germany against Bolshevik Russia, hoping thereby to effect their mutual exhaustion.*

In the interests of his three basic principles of policy Stalin took allies where he could find them. He was as ever brutally realistic in his diplomacy, but now he placed a number of his cards face upwards on the table. The Soviet Union was ready to align itself with any political combination which favoured Soviet policy and, while the British and French Governments hesitated and swithered, Hitler made haste to clinch a bargain. The result was the Nazi–Soviet Pact of 23 August 1939.

This agreement not only provided a basis of non-aggression between the two countries – the aspect in which Hitler was most interested; it opened for Stalin the way to the realization of the first and second of his basic principles of policy and even to the beginning of the third. By supplementary protocols and subsequent agreements Russia achieved the annexation of the Baltic Republics; the recognition of the fact that Finland was within her sphere of influence; a substantial share in the partition of Poland, wiping out the losses sustained by the Treaty of Riga; the retrocession by Rumania of the province of Bessarabia; and the cession by the same country of the province of Bukovina, which had

---

* As Edward Crankshaw has so wisely written, 'Looking backward now it is easy to see that the only practical way of stopping Hitler without war was in fact to come to terms with Russia and to rearm. But those who were ready to treat with Russia, who saw Hitler as the immediate danger, were reluctant to rearm; and those who were ready to rearm were those who were inclined to think that Bolshevism was more dangerous than Fascism.'[33] The outstanding exception to this dictum in Britain is that of Sir Winston Churchill, whose wisdom in regard to the necessity of taking first things first never faltered.

never been a part of Tsarist Russia but was now claimed as being an integral part of the western Ukraine.[34]

Virtually all Russia's territorial losses at the conclusion of the First World War were made good between September 1939 and June 1940. The outstanding exception was Finland, and an early attempt to correct this omission was made by the use of the mailed fist. On 28 November 1939 Stalin denounced the Soviet Union's treaty of non-aggression with Finland and within forty-eight hours launched an all-out offensive across the Finnish frontier. There followed a war in which the victim of unprovoked aggression defended itself with utmost gallantry against the aggressor, the while appealing to the rest of the civilized world for assistance. None was forthcoming, though public opinion in Britain and France, in the United States and among Finland's Scandinavian neighbours was outraged. At length she could fight no more and, her resistance at an end, she sought terms of peace. Her defeat, however, was not total. By the Treaty of Moscow (12 March 1940) Finland retained her independence but suffered severe losses in territory, population and economic concessions to Russia.[35]*

Having thus achieved much of what she desired as an intermediate stage in the fulfilment of her basic principles of policy, Russia pursued towards Germany a policy of appeasement beside which the record of Britain and France is pallid by comparison. But all to no purpose. Hitler, as early as July 1940, had determined on an assault upon his Eastern partner and had set his planners to work forthwith. The result was that 'Operation Barbarossa' was launched at dawn on 22 June 1941 and achieved much of the element of surprise. It achieved still more, for not only was the Soviet Union thus bulldozed into the Allied camp, but she also became a vital factor, as a major partner in war, in the making of peace.

V

The events which occurred between the summer solstices of 1940 and 1941 changed not only the whole aspect of the Second World War but also the course of history. Germany was established in military dominance along the west coast of Europe, and Axis might controlled the European continent from the North Cape to Cape Matapan. France had disappeared as an ally, but the flame of continued resistance was kept alive by the kindling indomitability of General de Gaulle. Britain, the Britain of Mr Churchill, a very different Britain from that of Mr Chamberlain, had fought and won her gigantic struggle in the Battle of Britain, and was enduring with courage and fortitude the ghastly and

* See below, p. 461.

continuous aerial assault of the Blitz; she had, moreover, defeated the Italians in the Western Desert* but was hard pressed in a struggle for survival in the Battle of the Atlantic. The United States of America, with the 'bases for destroyers' deal and the passage of the Lend-Lease Act,† had passed from neutrality to non-belligerency, and there was little doubt, as the Irishman said, whom she was 'non-belligerent against'. Russia remained an enigma.

It was now apparent that Hitler's tide of victory had been halted and held on the shores of the Channel and that he could no longer 'win at a canter'. The Battle of Britain had resulted in a major defeat for the *Luftwaffe*, and the unconquerable spirit, which Mr Churchill had stimulated and sustained, was geared to a long war of attrition. With the resources of the Commonwealth now mobilized in her support and with America functioning as the 'Arsenal of Democracy', Britain could keep up the struggle indefinitely, *provided* – and this was the crucial condition – *provided* she could win the Battle of the Atlantic and assure the continued flow of supplies into the beleaguered island fortress.

There was little talk of peace at this time and much of an enduring struggle. A vitally important decision was reached on 27 May 1941 when President Roosevelt, as a result of the sinking by U-boat attack of the merchantman *Robin Moor*, flying the American flag in Brazilian waters, declared a state of emergency and claimed the right of American warships to protect American shipping. In a 'fireside chat' on the same day he stated with emphasis that the United States could never tolerate an Axis victory.[36]‡ A few weeks later, on 12 June, the representatives of thirteen Allied Governments and of General de Gaulle, 'leader of Free Frenchmen', met at St James's Palace for the solemn purpose of proclaiming their resolution:§

1. That they will continue the struggle against German or Italian oppression until victory is won, and will mutually assist each other in this struggle to the utmost of their respective capacities;

* Italy had entered the war on the side of Germany on 10 June 1940, thereby fulfilling Sumner Welles's prophecy of a few weeks before (see above, p. 27). President Roosevelt, in a speech at the University of Virginia, Charlottesville, on the same day, branded this action as 'the hand that held the dagger has stuck it into the back of its neighbour'.

† The 'bases for destroyers' agreement was signed on 2 September 1940; the Lend-Lease Act became law on 11 March 1941.

‡ On 11 June 1941, Henry Stimson, Secretary of War, told the Cadets of the U.S. Military Academy at West Point that 'there is no possibility for America to live safely in a world dominated by the methods and practices of the Nazi leaders. The issue raised by the Axis Powers not only demonstrates that any compromise between their system and ours is impossible, but that their system is doomed to eventual and total failure.'[37]

§ The Governments concerned were those of the United Kingdom, Canada, Australia, New Zealand, South Africa, Belgium, Czechoslovakia, Greece, Luxembourg, the Netherlands, Norway, Poland and Yugoslavia.

2. That there can be no settled peace and prosperity so long as free peoples are coerced by violence into submission to domination by Germany or her associates, or live under the threat of such coercion;

3. That the only true basis of enduring peace is the willing co-operation of free peoples in a world in which, relieved of the menace of aggression, all may enjoy economic and social security; and that it is their intention to work together, and with other free peoples, both in war and peace, to this end.[38]

It was into this climate of grim determination that there was interjected the new and sudden development of the Nazi invasion of Russia. To the British people as a whole it came as a welcome surprise. A new ally of great potential strength was in the field, albeit very reluctantly. The advent of the Soviet Union in this new guise was further embellished by a marked decrease of aerial assault upon Britain and a diminution of any threat of invasion. Such was the popular reaction. But there were many who thought deeper into the past and saw further into the future, and they did not like what they thought and saw. Although Russia had admittedly shown to advantage in her struggle for collective security in the late thirties, her international record since the beginning of her dalliance with Nazi Germany after Munich had offset in the minds of many the previous good impression.* To some of these persons Mr Churchill's dictum that 'The Nazi régime is indistinguishable from the worst features of Communism' epitomized the situation and their thinking stopped there.

Mr Churchill, however, had a broader vision and a greater understanding. His broadcast on the night of 22 June 1941 was a masterpiece of integrity and statesmanship. He took back nothing that he had said in the past about Soviet Russia – and he had said plenty!; he was unchanged in his views on Communism, but here was a new victim of Nazi aggression and as such he welcomed Russia as an ally, to whom aid would be given unstintingly in the struggle against the Nazi régime and for the destruction of Hitler. 'The Russian danger is therefore our danger, and the danger of the United States, just as the cause of any Russian fighting for his hearth and home is the cause of free men and free principles in every quarter of the globe.'

Nevertheless, as Mr Churchill has also pointed out, the Soviet Union was far from being an unalloyed asset. It was true that Britain was afforded important relief at home and in the Mediterranean by the diversion of Nazi activities, but, in order to keep Russia 'in the ring', heavy diversions had also to be made by the Allies. The 'Arsenal of Democracy' was not inexhaustible, nor was the necessary supply of

* See above, pp. 30–1.

shipping necessitated by the demands made upon it. Raw materials and weapons originally destined for Britain had now to find their perilous way to Murmansk and Archangel, and upon Britain fell the burden of organizing and carrying out the convoys which brought them there. Thus, though the effect on morale in Britain, and conversely in Germany, of Russia's entry into the war was great, it was true that for more than a year Russia presented herself as a burden rather than a help. 'None the less we rejoiced to have this mighty nation in the battle with us.'[39]

If, moreover, Russia was to some extent an embarrassment as a military ally, she was infinitely more so as a political partner. This became fully apparent almost at once in regard to Poland. These two states, now involuntary allies, were technically in a state of war. The burden of effecting something which might pass for a reconciliation fell upon the British Government and specifically on Anthony Eden. Thorny though the subject was, it could not have been consigned to hands more efficient or more adroit. In modern British diplomacy there has rarely been a more effective, indefatigably patient or brilliant negotiator than Mr Eden.

The conversations began in London on 5 July 1941, between the Polish Premier, General Wladyslaw Sikorski, and the Soviet Ambassador, Ivan Maisky, and each party arrived with an irreconcilable premise. The aims of the Poles were twofold: a declaration by the Soviet Government that the partition of Poland of 28 September 1939 between Germany and Russia was null and void, and the effective liberation of all Polish prisoners of war and civilians deported from Poland to the Soviet Union. On the first of these points the Soviet Government was adamant. Under no circumstances would any such declaration be made; the question of Russia's western frontier was not open to discussion. On the second point, they were prepared to give a guarded agreement.

The position of the British Government as an 'honest broker' was difficult in the extreme; even Mr Eden's capacities were taxed to the utmost. Britain had gone to war in 1939 as a direct result of her guarantee to Poland and was therefore under a strong moral obligation to her. It was felt strongly that Britain could in no wise accept the situation created by the Nazi–Soviet Agreement of September 1939. On the other hand, it was equally urgent not to discourage the Soviet Union in these first few weeks of its struggle for survival, when the tide of war was running strongly against her and there was little immediate help on the horizon. 'We could not force our new and sorely threatened ally', wrote Mr Churchill, 'to abandon, even on paper, regions on her frontier which she had regarded for generations as vital to her security.'[40]

The deadlock was complete. Only a compromise could solve the dilemma. In return for an undertaking by Russia to permit the formation of a Polish army from the prisoners of war held in the Soviet Union, the Poles agreed, under British pressure, to rely upon Soviet good faith in the future settlement of Soviet–Polish relations and to forgo at the moment any written guarantees for the future. This line of argument was accepted by the Polish Government-in-exile on condition that the British Government gave a written statement describing as null and void all agreements concluded after 1 September 1939 in regard to Polish territory and subsequent acts relating to it. This suggestion, the idea of the singularly able Ambassador and subsequent Minister of Foreign Affairs, Count Edward Raczyński,[41] was accepted by Mr Eden, who formally notified the House of Commons on 30 July – in informing them of the Soviet–Polish Agreement signed on that day – that an exchange of Notes to this effect had been made with the Polish Government. He added, in reply to a parliamentary question: 'The exchange of Notes which I have just read to the House does not involve any guarantee of frontiers by His Majesty's Government.'[42]

This first contact with Soviet diplomacy as an ally was certainly an unpleasant one for the British Government and should have proved salutary. Unfortunately the episode contained the germ of that element which bedevilled the relations of Britain and America with the Soviet Union from then onwards to the close of the war: namely, an obsession with the suspicious fear that Russia would make a separate peace with Germany, even though she had adhered to the Allied Declaration of St James's Palace of 12 June 1941.* Mr Eden was more far-sighted in this matter than Mr Churchill. He did not believe in the probability of such an event, but as will be seen the bogey manifested itself in various forms during the next four years.

Though it is all too easy for the historian to be wise after the event and to profit from hindsight, it must be recorded as an opinion that at no time between 1941 and 1945 was this a real danger. When the tide of war was running against her, Russia dared not make peace with Germany because she had too much to lose; when later the tide turned in her favour, she was equally disinclined because as a member of the victorious Allies she had too much to gain. From first to last Stalin was motivated by the three guiding principles of Soviet foreign policy,† and none of these could be served by the making of a separate peace.

The circumstances of the negotiation of the Russo-Polish Agreement of 30 July 1941 did, however, have one vitally important and constructive effect upon Anglo-American relations in that they played an undoubted part in one of the most dramatic episodes of the war – the Atlantic Charter.

---

* See above, p. 32.   † See above, p. 29.

VI

If credit may be given to any one person for the inspiration of the rendezvous in Placentia Bay on 9 August 1941, it must go to Harry Hopkins. Ever since his first historic visit to England in January of that year, this most intimate of all Franklin Roosevelt's personal advisers had striven to arrange a meeting between the two great leaders of the Anglo-Saxon world, who were on such intimate terms of correspondence and telephone conversation and were yet unknown to one another in the flesh. Nor was there any reluctance on the part of either the President or the Prime Minister. Both were eager for an encounter and it was only circumstances which prevented them time and again.

At last, however, the circumstances proved to be confederate to Harry Hopkins's efforts. The new situation created by the events of 22 June 1941 rendered a meeting between President Roosevelt and Mr Churchill not only desirable and expedient but imperative. When, therefore, on his second visit to England in July, Hopkins brought to Churchill the President's invitation to some northern bay early in August, the Prime Minister, after consultation with King George VI, accepted with alacrity and satisfaction.[43] Thus it was that on the morning of Saturday, 9 August, the newest British battleship, *Prince of Wales*, sailed into Placentia Bay, Newfoundland, there to make rendezvous with the U.S.S. *Augusta*, and two 'former naval persons' held their first historic meeting.*

Of the various subjects discussed between the two statesmen at this time, the only one that affects us here is that of the Atlantic Charter, over the origins of which a curious degree of divergence has arisen among the authorities.[45] Sir Winston Churchill writes that the initiative came from President Roosevelt,[46] whereas Sumner Welles asserts that 'There had been no prior exchange of views between the President and Mr Churchill about issuing a declaration such as the Atlantic Charter. The initiative was taken by Mr Churchill after his arrival at Argentia on the evening of 9 August.'[47]

Now the full weight of all the evidence indicates that Sir Winston is correct in his record and Mr Welles is wrong. Certainly there had been no 'prior exchange of views' between the President and the Prime Minister, but neither had there been any discussion in Whitehall prior

---

* In strict accuracy it must be recorded that these two great men *had* already met in July 1918. Young Mr Roosevelt, then Assistant Secretary of the Navy, had come to London and at a banquet had been introduced to Mr Churchill, then a member of the British Cabinet. Though the meeting had made a vivid impression on Mr Roosevelt, Mr Churchill had apparently completely forgotten it, a matter which became a mildly sore point with the President.[44]

to Mr Churchill's departure. Neither in his discussions with Mr Eden, his Foreign Secretary, nor in the deliberations in Cabinet was there any suggestion of a proposal for a joint declaration, nor did the matter arise during his talks with Sir Alexander Cadogan as *Prince of Wales* ploughed her majestic way across the Atlantic.

Indeed the whole idea of any discussion of war aims was inimical to Mr Churchill. He was engaged first and last in winning the war and was content to leave the definition of Allied objectives to a moment when victory should be nearer than it seemed in August 1941. He certainly had no such object in view when he left England, and it is safe to say that the idea never entered his head until his dinner party with the President in *Augusta* on the evening of 9 August. It was at this point that the President expressed the thought 'that it would be well if we could draw up a joint declaration laying down certain basic principles which should guide our policies along the same road'.

Just when President Roosevelt had conceived this idea it is difficult to say. The evidence is lacking and, as Harry Hopkins kept no record of his *tête-à-tête* talks with Mr Churchill prior to their departure in *Prince of Wales*, it is impossible to say definitely whether the thought was conveyed indirectly by the Presidential envoy to the Prime Minister; the strong supposition is, however, that it was not, and that the initiative was a fortuitous and spontaneous inspiration of the President's. It was a golden opportunity to get at least part of the principles of his Four Freedoms publicly endorsed by the chief Allied belligerent and also to extract from the British a declaration against territorial or economic imperialism. He desired above all things that his fundamental principle of peace and international co-operation should not be undermined – as it was strongly believed that the effect of President Wilson's Fourteen Points had been undermined – by Allied intrigues behind the President's back, and this thought had certainly been transmitted by Harry Hopkins to Mr Churchill.[48]

Mr Churchill took back with him to *Prince of Wales* for further cogitation the various points which had been canvassed at the dinner table and afterwards. The chief attraction of a joint declaration must have been that the mere issuing of such a statement would intensify and dramatize the working unity of the two Atlantic Powers. By breakfast time next morning, therefore, he was disturbing Sir Alexander Cadogan's matutinal bacon and eggs with a demand for the text for a joint declaration, the broad outline of which he sketched in vigorous language. Sir Alexander caught the spirit of his thought in a first draft which he submitted to the Prime Minister, who expressed general but not very enthusiastic approval but made only a few small verbal

changes.* This British draft was then handed by Cadogan to Sumner
Welles after the famous church parade service on the quarter-deck of
Prince of Wales on Sunday, 10 August.† The text was as follows:

> The President of the United States of America and the Prime
> Minister, Mr Churchill, representing His Majesty's Government in
> the United Kingdom, being met together‡ to resolve and concert the
> means of providing for the safety of their respective countries in face
> of Nazi and German aggression and of the dangers to all peoples
> arising therefrom, deem it right to make known certain principles
> which they both accept for guidance in the framing of their policy and
> on which they base their hopes for a better future for the world.
>
> First, their countries seek no aggrandizement, territorial or other;
>
> Second, they desire to see no territorial changes that do not accord
> with the freely expressed wishes of the peoples concerned;
>
> Third, they respect the right of all peoples to choose the form of
> government under which they will live; they are only concerned to
> defend the rights of freedom of speech and thought without which
> such choice must be illusory;
>
> Fourth, they will strive to bring about a fair and equitable distri-
> bution of essential produce not only within their territorial boundaries
> but between the nations of the world;
>
> Fifth, they seek a peace which will not only cast down forever the
> Nazi tyranny but by effective international organization will afford to
> all States and peoples the means of dwelling in security within their
> own bounds and of traversing the seas and oceans without fear of
> lawless assault or the need of maintaining burdensome armaments.

The first three of Mr Churchill's points commended themselves to
Welles as being 'both essential in their import and admirable in their
clarity'. The fourth and fifth, however, he considered 'either question-
able in meaning, or far too limited in their scope'. He was particularly
anxious that any declaration made should include provision for the

* Sir Winston Churchill later revised his opinion of the original British draft, for in
his memoirs he writes: 'Considering all the tales of my reactionary Old World outlook,
and the pain this is said to have caused the President, I am glad it should be on record
that the substance and spirit of what came to be known as the "Atlantic Charter" was in
its first draft a British production cast in my own words.'[49]

† It is perhaps curious that neither of the principals at the Atlantic Meeting was
accompanied by his chief foreign adviser. The President came supported by Welles,
Hopkins, Averell Harriman and his military advisers; the Prime Minister by Sir
Alexander Cadogan, the Chiefs of Staff, Lord Beaverbrook and Lord Cherwell ('The
Prof.'). Moreover, whereas the British Cabinet was kept fully informed of what was in
progress both before and during the meeting, the preparations on the American side
had been, in so far as foreign affairs were concerned, entirely in the hands of Sumner
Welles; Secretary Hull, who had been recuperating from an illness, was only informed
of the forthcoming conference on 28 July.

‡ The three words 'being met together' were Sir Alexander Cadogan's own contribution and were in the original British draft. They were not inserted by Mr Churchill,
as is alleged by H. V. Morton in his book, *Atlantic Meeting*, p. 129.

post-war elimination of all such impediments to world trade as American high protectionist tariffs and the British Commonwealth Ottawa Agreements.

Welles therefore prepared an alternative draft which he submitted to President Roosevelt early on the morning of 11 August:

> The President of the United States of America and the Prime Minister, Mr Churchill, representing His Majesty's Government in the United Kingdom, being met together, to consider and to resolve the steps which their Governments should take in order to provide for the safety of the respective countries in face of the policies of world-wide domination and of military conquest upon which the Hitlerite Government of Germany and the other dictatorships associated therewith have embarked, and in face of the dangers to all peoples arising therefrom, deem it right and proper to make known certain principles which they both accept for guidance in the framing of their respective policies and on which they base their hopes for a better future for the world.
>
> First, their countries seek no aggrandizement, territorial or other;
>
> Second, they desire to see no territorial changes that do not accord with the freely expressed wishes of the peoples concerned;
>
> Third, they respect the right of all peoples to choose the form of government under which they will live;
>
> Fourth, they will strive to promote mutually advantageous economic relations between them through the elimination of any discrimination in either the United States of America or in the United Kingdom against the importation of any product originating in the other country; and they will endeavour to further the enjoyment by all peoples of access on equal terms to the markets and to the raw materials which are needed for their economic prosperity;
>
> Fifth, they hope to see established a peace, after the final destruction of Nazi tyranny, which by effective international organization, will afford to all states and peoples the means of dwelling in security within their own boundaries, and the means of assurance that human beings may live out their lives in freedom from fear. They likewise hope to see established by such a peace safety for all peoples on the high seas and oceans, and the adoption of such measures as will prevent the continuation of expenditures for armaments other than those which are purely defensive.

President Roosevelt considered both drafts with great care and made his own alterations and amendments. In particular he struck out the greater part of the proposed preamble and also all reference to 'international organization' which had been in both the British and the American draft proposals. Welles was then sent away to prepare a third draft which was discussed formally by the President and the Prime Minister and their advisers later in the morning. This draft was as follows:

The President of the United States of America and the Prime
Minister, Mr Churchill, representing His Majesty's Government in
the United Kingdom, being met together, deem it right to make
known certain common principles in the national policies of their
respective countries on which they base their hopes for a better future
for the world.

First, their countries seek no aggrandizement, territorial or other;

Second, they desire to see no territorial changes that do not accord
with the freely expressed wishes of the people concerned;

Third, they respect the right of all peoples to choose the form of
government under which they will live; and they wish to see self-
government restored to those from whom it has been forcibly
removed;

Fourth, they will endeavour to further the enjoyment by all peoples
of access, without discrimination and on equal terms, to the markets
and to the raw materials of the world which are needed for their
economic prosperity;

Fifth, they hope to see established a peace, after the final destruction
of the Nazi tyranny, which will afford to all nations the means of
dwelling in security within their own boundaries, and which will
afford assurance to all peoples that they may live out their lives in
freedom from fear and want;

Sixth, they desire such a peace to establish for all safety on the high
seas and oceans;

Seventh, they believe that all of the nations of the world, for
realistic as well as spiritual reasons, must come to the abandonment of
the use of force. Because no future peace can be maintained if land,
sea or air armaments continue to be employed by nations which
threaten, or may threaten, aggression outside of their frontiers, they
believe that the disarmament of such nations is essential. They will
likewise further all other practicable measures which will lighten for
peace-loving peoples the crushing burden of armaments.

It was during the discussion of the second Welles draft that Mr
Churchill pleaded that the provision for 'effective international
organization' be restored. The President, however, was adamant.
Twenty-one years before, as a young man of thirty-eight, he had
campaigned as Democratic Vice-Presidential candidate as a supporter
of the League of Nations and had seen that cause go down to hopeless
defeat at the hands of the American electorate. Subsequent observation
and experience had not enhanced his opinion of the League as an
organization nor of its chances of achieving success; to him it appeared
to have become the tool of British and French diplomacy. Moreover, he
was haunted by the ghost of Woodrow Wilson and his failure. Any
suggestion of a repetition of the Fourteen Points, with their memories
of an American Expeditionary Force and a false 'peace', would arouse
the intransigence of the extreme isolationists and the unrealism of the

extreme internationalists. He dared not risk this at that moment,* and it was for this reason that he was unyielding on the subject. In reply to Mr Churchill's arguments, the President is recorded by Sumner Welles as saying that he did not feel he could agree

> because of the suspicions and opposition that such a statement on his part would create in the United States. He said that he himself would not be in favour of the creation of a new Assembly of the League of Nations, at least until after a period of time had passed and during which an international police force composed of the United States and Great Britain had had an opportunity of functioning.[51]

It was more than two years before the President felt himself strong enough to endorse boldly the proposal for a post-war international organization, and by that time he had reached the conclusion that the two pillars of such an organization must be the United States and the U.S.S.R.†

As a result of the discussions on board *Augusta* on the morning of 11 August, sufficient agreement was reached for the Prime Minister to submit by telegram to his colleagues in London the full text of the draft of the joint declaration. The telegram reached London at midnight (G.M.T.) and Mr Attlee at once convened an emergency Cabinet meeting which met at 1.45 a.m. on the morning of 12 August. The upshot of a careful discussion was the suggestion of one small amendment and the recommendation that a new paragraph be added dealing with social security. A telegram was immediately sent to *Prince of Wales* and thus, within twelve hours of the dispatch of his original telegram from Placentia Bay, Mr Churchill had received the advice of his colleagues in London. They could hardly have done better had they been next door rather than thousands of miles apart.[52]

The British amendments were incorporated in a fourth draft prepared by Welles and Cadogan, which became the final version adopted by President Roosevelt and Mr Churchill at their final meeting on 12 August and has survived in history as the Atlantic Charter:

> The President of the United States of America and the Prime Minister, Mr Churchill, representing His Majesty's Government in the United Kingdom, being met together, deem it right to make known certain common principles in the national policies of their

---

* How correctly President Roosevelt gauged the spirit of the times may be judged from the fact that at the very moment that he was in conference with Mr Churchill in Placentia Bay the House of Representatives in Washington passed the bill to extend the Selective Service Act by the perilous margin of one vote, on 12 August. 'The news of it dropped like enemy bombs on the decks of the *Augusta* and the *Prince of Wales*.'[50]

† See below, p. 540.

respective countries on which they base their hopes for a better future for the world.

First, their countries seek no aggrandizement, territorial or other.

Second, they desire to see no territorial changes that do not accord with the freely expressed wishes of the peoples concerned.

Third, they respect the right of all peoples to choose the form of government under which they will live; and they wish to see sovereign rights and self-government restored to those who have been forcibly deprived of them.

Fourth, they will endeavour, with due respect to their existing obligations, to further the enjoyment of all States, great or small, victor or vanquished, of access, on equal terms, to the trade and to the raw materials of the world which are needed for their economic prosperity.

Fifth, they desire to bring about the fullest collaboration between all nations in the economic field, with the object of securing for all improved labour standards, economic advancement, and social security.

Sixth, after the final destruction of the Nazi tyranny they hope to see established a peace which will afford to all nations the means of dwelling in safety within their own boundaries, and which will afford assurance that all the men in all the lands may live out their lives in freedom from fear and want.

Seventh, such a peace should enable all men to traverse the high seas and oceans without hindrances.

Eighth, they believe that all the nations of the world, for realistic as well as spiritual reasons, must come to the abandonment of the use of force. Since no future peace can be maintained if land, sea, or air armaments continue to be employed by nations which threaten, or may threaten, aggression outside of their frontiers, they believe, pending the establishment of a wider and more permanent system of general security, that the disarmament of such nations is essential. They will likewise aid and encourage all other practicable measures which will lighten for peace-loving peoples the crushing burden of armaments.[53]

As far as is known, the problem of Soviet Russia was only discussed at Placentia Bay in terms of the support which could be given her in terms of arms and supplies – what America could give; what Britain could spare. It was still a matter of conjecture whether the Red Army could stand up to the hammer-blows of the *Wehrmacht* – whether indeed they would be compelled by force of circumstances to retreat behind the Urals and abandon Russia in Europe to the Nazis while depending upon a war of attrition. This event was more than suspected by the most competent military authorities in Britain and America, and the participation of the Soviet Union as a 'planner for peace' seemed curiously academic. Yet there must have been a certain degree of satisfaction for those who entertained optimistic views on the intentions of the Moscow Government when on 24 September the Soviet Union joined with nine other Allies, gathered once again at St James's Palace,* in making known that, having taken note of the principles of the Joint Declaration, they adhered 'to the common principles of policy set forth in that Declaration and their intention to co-operate to the best of their ability in giving effect to them'.[54]

* The nine other signatories were Belgium, Czechoslovakia, Greece, Luxembourg, the Netherlands, Norway, Poland, the United Kingdom and the representative of General de Gaulle.

3 | The Anglo–Russian Treaty

IT was not long before the principles of the Atlantic Charter underwent their first acid test of exposure to traditional diplomacy in Moscow and in London.

The United States Government took their stand on the Charter as a reason for postponing all discussion of post-war territorial settlement until the war had been won and a peace conference convened, their hope being that the settlement of frontiers could thereby be made to subscribe to the terms of the Charter.

The Soviet attitude was one of profound suspicion, and though Marshal Stalin had generally acceded to the principles of the Charter he still resented the fact that he had not been consulted beforehand. He scented a private agreement between President Roosevelt and Mr Churchill to exclude Russia from the peace settlement; he feared that the specific denial contained in the Charter of aggrandizement, 'territorial or other', and of territorial changes not in accordance with 'the freely expressed wishes of the peoples concerned', was directed against the Soviet Union; he sensed that, once the strain of war was over, Britain and the United States might not be prepared to take what he, the Marshal, considered sufficiently harsh measures to render Germany harmless.[1]

The British Government was placed in the difficult position of being an active belligerent ally of Russia and a non-belligerent partner of the United States. Throughout the autumn of 1941 Stalin had been increasingly acerbic in his communications with the Prime Minister, demanding that Britain declare war on Finland, Rumania and Hungary, requiring of Britain a greater contribution of aid to Russia and requesting a clarification of British views on war aims. Herein was the rub. It could not be ignored that the views of Moscow and Washington in respect of post-war policies were mutually incompatible. Moscow desired definite decisions as between allies; Washington insisted upon procrastination.

In an attempt to keep troth with both sides, Mr Churchill informed Stalin on 21 November that Mr Eden would come to Moscow shortly, accompanied by high military and other experts, and would be empowered to discuss every question concerning the conduct and prosecution of the war. In so far as post-war matters were concerned, the Foreign Secretary would be able 'to discuss the whole of this field with you', wrote the Prime Minister to the Marshal. But he also intimated that such discussion would be general rather than specific in nature:

> Our intention is to fight the war in alliance with you and in constant consultation with you to the utmost of our strength, and however long it lasts, and when the war is won, as I am sure it will be, we expect that Soviet Russia, Great Britain and the United States will meet at the council table of the victors as the three principal partners and agencies by which Nazism will have to be destroyed. Naturally, the first object will be to prevent Germany, and particularly Prussia, from breaking out upon us for the third time.[2]

To this proposal Marshal Stalin agreed, and the plans for Mr Eden's visit went forward. His intention to go to Moscow was communicated to Washington, with immediate repercussions. Though the United States and Britain were not yet full allies, they were co-partners in the Atlantic Charter; the State Department at once voiced its fears and warnings. On 4 December two messages reached Mr Eden from Washington, one from Sumner Welles urging that no concurrence be given to the annexation of the Baltic States by the Soviet Union, and a second from Cordell Hull going much further. The Secretary of State went far beyond a mere note of caution. He strongly emphasized that, as all three of the Great Powers had committed themselves to the principles of the Atlantic Charter, no specific terms of post-war settlement should be agreed upon before the final peace conference. Above all, warned the Secretary – 'no secret agreements'.[3]

Mr Eden's visit to Moscow could scarcely have been undertaken in circumstances less propitious for British and American prestige. As he arrived at Scapa on 7 December, preparatory to sailing, he was given the news of the Japanese attack on Pearl Harbor and the elimination of the U.S. Pacific Fleet. These tidings of disaster were scarcely calculated to stimulate the morale of the Foreign Secretary, who was already suffering from acute gastro-influenza. Nor was he further cheered on his arrival at Murmansk on the twelfth to receive word of the loss off Malaya of *Prince of Wales* and *Repulse*.[4] Mr Eden therefore entered upon his conversation with the Marshal at a disadvantage. He was irritated, in addition, by the very necessary precautions which he was compelled to take against his quarters being microphoned by the N.K.V.D., remarking to Sir Alexander Cadogan that the Embassy car was probably the only place where they could speak freely – a degree of optimism certainly dangerous to entertain.

There was nothing enigmatic, ambiguous or evasive about the Marshal's approach. He had it all cut and dried. His cards were spread openly on the table – and all Mr Hull's worst fears and prognostications were realized.

Two draft treaties were presented to Mr Eden at the outset: one for a military alliance for the duration of hostilities, the second for an agreement on common post-war action between Britain and the Soviet Union, both in respect of territorial adjustment and of the prevention of further German aggression, including partition of the Reich. These two instruments were to be published, but the latter contained a secret protocol dealing in some detail with European frontiers.

In their subsequent discussions the Marshal spelled out just what he wished to see happen in Europe after the war was ended. Austria, he proposed, should be restored as an independent sovereign state; the Rhineland detached from Prussia and given independence; Bavaria too was to be separated from the Reich; East Prussia should be ceded to Poland and the Sudetenland restored to Czechoslovakia. Looking beyond Germany, the Marshal envisaged the reconstitution of Yugoslavia, with augmentations at the expense of Italy; Albania should once again become independent, and certain of the Italian island possessions in the Aegean should go to Greece. Turkey should receive the major part of the Dodecanese as well as territorial accretions from Bulgaria and in northern Syria. The Soviet Union would welcome the establishment of British bases in France, Belgium, the Netherlands, Norway and Denmark; while for her part the Soviet Union demanded the restoration of the *status quo ante* to the German invasion of June 1941, namely the Baltic States, certain parts of Finland, Bukovina and Bessarabia, with the 'Curzon Line'* forming the basis for the future Russo-Polish frontier.

Russia, in short, was to retain all the fruits of her partnership with Nazi Germany, while offering a handsome concession to Britain in the shape of military bases on the continent of Europe as a *quid pro quo* – or, more brutally, a bribe. Moreover, the Marshal made any consideration of an Anglo-Russian agreement dependent upon the immediate recognition by Britain of the future frontiers of the U.S.S.R. and more

---

* This was the line proposed by Lord Curzon, the British Foreign Secretary, as a basis for an armistice agreement in July 1920, when the Poles were being severely mauled in a war with Soviet Russia. It was never accepted by the Poles, who were able to obtain a much more favourable frontier when the tide of battle changed in their favour.

specifically of the incorporation therein of the Baltic States and the restoration of the Soviet–Finnish frontier of 1940.

Faced with the fact that Stalin thought in terms of the Old Diplomacy of Machiavelli, Metternich and Talleyrand, whereas he himself was pledged to uphold the principles of the New Diplomacy as evidenced in the Atlantic Charter, Mr Eden wisely temporized. He would, he said, consult his Prime Minister (then in Washington) and his War Cabinet colleagues in London. While he personally agreed with much of what the Marshal had said about the post-war treatment of Germany, it must be understood that at the present juncture Britain, because of her understanding with the United States precluding secret treaties and agreements on territorial adjustments concluded prior to the end of hostilities, could not enter into such treaties as the Marshal had proposed, without consulting not only the United States Government but also the Governments of the British Dominions. This he undertook to do. His argument, however, was one which the Marshal did not hesitate to treat with contempt as an equivocation.

The Foreign Secretary telegraphed at length both to Washington and to London, making his own views clear and emphasizing the necessity of not being drawn into a final commitment at this time. From Mr Churchill and from the War Cabinet came support and confirmation of his attitude, and although Mr Eden reported that they 'took leave of one another [on 20 December] in a very friendly atmosphere',* the fact remained that the *impasse* regarding a post-war settlement remained unresolved and Stalin had firmly refused to consider, on account of Russian military weakness, a declaration of war upon Japan. To this Mr Eden retorted that, for similar reasons, Britain could not in the near future envisage the opening of a second front in Europe or the sending of troops to the Eastern Front.

The Moscow meeting had proved a failure in so far as concrete results were concerned. It had, however, provided a not unsalutary illustration of what the Russians intended to do after the war had ended and how little they considered themselves to be inhibited in so doing by the terms and principles of the Atlantic Charter.

Thus far the policy of the British Government had been entirely consistent with that of President Roosevelt and Mr Hull. London and

---

* It was at their final dinner together that the Marshal told Mr Eden, with great gusto, the story of Molotov's visit to Berlin in November 1940 when, in the course of a dinner party, a raid by the R.A.F. compelled them to take shelter in Ribbentrop's official dug-out. The German Foreign Minister waxed eloquent on the theme that the British Empire was finished and her resistance at an end, to which Molotov acidly replied: 'If the war is over, why are we in this dug-out and whose bombs have put us here?'[5]

Washington thought as one and spoke as one. But with the coming of the New Year a certain deviationist tendency, a note of dissonance began to manifest itself in Whitehall. An agreement with Russia, it was said, was essential both for the prosecution of the war and for the provision of a makeweight against Germany after the war's conclusion. Moreover, when the consultations between London and Washington became protracted and dilatory, Stalin, while pressing for the speedy conclusion of an agreement, also brought into play that weapon of political warfare and blackmail, the threat of a separate peace with Germany. Though it is to be doubted whether at any time the Russians ever seriously contemplated taking this step, their intention to do so was bruited on more than one occasion and did not fail to cause apprehension and division in the councils of the Western Allies. At this juncture the reaction of Sir Stafford Cripps was significant. Speaking at Bristol on 8 February 1942, with all the authority of a former Ambassador to Moscow, who was shortly to become a member of the War Cabinet, he adjured the United States as follows:

> We want our American friends to realize that, if they are going to partake with us in the reconstruction of Europe, it is vital that these decisions should not be too long delayed. Delay will add to the suspicions between this country and the Soviet Union – suspicions which have not, because of their historical foundations, completely disappeared.[6]

Mr Eden and the Foreign Office were of the opinion that, though, if the final crunch came, Britain must unquestionably cast her lot with America rather than with Russia, it was her duty to attempt a conciliation of the discordant concepts of Washington and Moscow. The first step towards such a harmonization would be to persuade the President to agree to some recognition of Soviet claims for a guarantee of the return of the Russian territory lost as a result of the German invasion. If President Roosevelt would not consent to this, Britain should propose, as an alternative, that she and the United States should agree to support Russian post-war claims for bases in territories contiguous to the Soviet Union and for Soviet control of the defence and foreign policies of the Baltic States.[7]

The Foreign Secretary was successful in getting his colleagues in the War Cabinet to accept his policy. Mr Churchill by now no longer entertained the repugnance for Stalin's claims which he had evinced at the time of Mr Eden's conference in Moscow. He was just as anxious as Stalin to see an agreement signed and, with his authority, Mr Eden proceeded to convince the American Ambassador, John Winant, then about to depart for Washington, of the British point of view. Winant in his turn successfully converted Harry Hopkins, and on 7 March Mr Churchill weighed in with a personal appeal to the President:

> The increasing gravity of the war has led me to feel that the principles of the Atlantic Charter ought not to be construed so as to deny Russia the frontiers she occupied when Germany attacked her [cabled the Prime Minister]. This was the basis on which Russia acceded to the Charter. . . . I hope therefore that you will give us a free hand to sign the treaty which Stalin desires as soon as possible.[8]

'Now there was war in Heaven.' In reply to the British frontal assault on American policy, supported by the Winant–Hopkins flank attack, the State Department mounted a massive counter-offensive. Every battalion, every battery, was called into play, and Cordell Hull, Sumner Welles and William C. Bullitt, a former Ambassador to Moscow, were found in fantastic and infelicitous alignment. The President was bombarded with memoranda urging him to stand firm on the principles of the Charter and reject 'appeasement' of the British and Soviets. Roosevelt himself was inclined to a direct approach to Stalin through the Soviet Ambassador in Washington, Maxim Litvinov, and the newly appointed American Ambassador in Moscow, Admiral William H. Standley. When Mr Eden indicated a preference for a tripartite discussion of the matter, this was refused; the President informed the Marshal that, while the United States was in favour of promoting the post-war security of the Soviet Union, they would have nothing to do with any treaty on frontiers during the course of hostilities, and he gave a specific assurance to this effect to the Polish Prime Minister, General Sikorski, during the latter's visit to Washington in April.[9]

Despite this barrage of objections from the Americans, the British Government decided to go ahead and negotiate with the Russians on the basis of recognition of the 1941 frontiers in respect of the Baltic States and Rumania, but specifically excluding the Russo-Polish border. Mr Eden now displayed a further example of diplomatic brilliance. Caught between the cross-fire of American disapproval and Russian importunity, he acquitted himself with outstanding ability. The negotiations which began in London with M. Maisky, the Soviet Ambassador, early in April were protracted and complex. It was found at the outset that the Russians had intensified their demands. Not only were they claiming British assent to the Curzon Line but also to a secret protocol according agreement to Russo-Finnish and Russo-Rumanian pacts of mutual assistance after the war. With infinite patience Mr Eden reasserted the British objections to such terms, which ran counter not only to American sensibilities and the principles of the Atlantic Charter, but also to the spirit of the Anglo-Polish Treaty of Alliance concluded in April 1939.

As a counter-proposal he offered a twenty-year post-war alliance with Russia which would guarantee to her British support in the event of renewed German aggression. There would be no mention of frontiers in this agreement.

M. Molotov arrived in London on 20 May and the Anglo-Russian negotiations entered upon a more delicate but penultimate phase. Molotov was at first disposed to reject the British counter-proposals and to stand pat on the original Soviet demands. However, the firmness of the views expressed by Mr Churchill and Mr Eden as to the un-acceptability of these terms by Britain, and the further advice tendered by Mr Winant on the damage which would be occasioned to the Russian image in the United States by a treaty concluded on these lines, ultimately convinced him that, if a treaty were to be signed at all, it must be on the lines of the British proposals. After consultation with Moscow, therefore, he agreed to accept them and the Anglo-Russian Treaty was signed at the Foreign Office on 26 May 1942.[10]

The final and favourable conclusion of the negotiations was a personal triumph for Mr Eden, who had achieved the apparent marvel of reconciling Russian acquisitiveness with American susceptibilities, while maintaining the amiability of both parties. Even that veteran of American professional diplomacy, Sumner Welles, declared it to be 'a miracle', and the Foreign Secretary received the warm congratulations of the Prime Minister and his Cabinet colleagues. It was indeed a major diplomatic achievement. Unfortunately it had not achieved what was hoped of it. The Russians, *reculant pour mieux sauter*, bided their time for a more favourable occasion to attain their territorial ambitions, and in the end they were to receive the whole-hearted approval of the United States and the tacit consent of the United Kingdom.

4 | Casablanca and Unconditional Surrender

I

LORD ISMAY described 1943 as 'Conference Year'.[1] It was a year in which the two Western Allies achieved a degree of military and political co-operation quite unprecedented in the history of war. It also saw the first meeting between the leaders of the three Great Powers engaged in the struggle against Hitler.

The summer of 1942 had brought the Allies safely past the lowest point in their fortunes. The trail of disaster which had led from Pearl Harbor to Singapore and Tobruk was at last brought to an end. By the following December Axis offensives had not merely been blunted; they were being thrown back. In North Africa the Battle of El Alamein was the first conclusive land victory achieved by an Allied army against Hitler. To the west, the 'Torch' operation – the Allied landings in Morocco and Algeria – had been a brilliant success. On the Russian front General Friedrich Paulus's Sixth Army was already in a death-grip near Stalingrad.

Victory, as King George VI remarked, was good for the nerves.[2] But it would be of little permanent value unless it were followed up with the utmost vigour. In the words of Sir John Slessor, 'The time was ripe for the emergence of the master plan, the blue-print for how to set about winning the war'.[3] The forces of the United Nations must grasp the initiative and impose it upon their enemies.* Their manner of so doing would not only decide the outcome of the war. It would shape the forth-coming peace. Strategic decisions would have diplomatic implications and, as experience in the First World War had shown, diplomatic engagements lightly entered upon in time of conflict might be regretted when the moment came to forge a peace settlement.

The first necessity was for agreement between the United States and Britain about the way in which their great successes in North Africa should be exploited. In December 1942 it seemed clear that the expulsion of Rommel's forces from the southern shores of the Mediter-

* The term 'United Nations', signifying 'the Allies', had been in use since the Declaration of Washington of 1 January 1942.

ranean was only a matter of time, and although the strategic ideas of Adolf Hitler actually prolonged the conflict there for several months the final outcome was even more beneficial to the Allied cause than the Western leaders had dared to hope.

At the same time the Battle of the Atlantic had yet to be won, and the problem of co-operation with the Russian war effort had not been satisfactorily settled. In Britain the Prime Minister was determined that the Western Powers should strike decisive blows against the Axis in 1943. He was very concerned lest what he regarded as the springboard of North Africa should turn out to be a sofa upon which large and well-equipped forces of Allied troops would rest without causing Hitler any real inconvenience.[4] Mr Churchill felt himself obliged to do all he could to help the Russians by creating a second front in Europe. He also feared that the demands of the American Navy in the Far East might cause a dangerous hiatus in the European theatre, a hiatus which could enable Hitler to regain the initiative. On 24 November 1942, for example, information had reached London which seemed to suggest that the United States might be restricting its efforts in Europe.[5] To Mr Churchill's anxious queries President Roosevelt returned a soothing but not altogether conclusive reply in which he remarked that American forces were more heavily engaged in the South-west Pacific than he had at first anticipated.[6]

The Prime Minister was adamant in opposing any weakening of the Allied assaults against Hitler. He urged his planners to provide him with offensive schemes to extend the struggle with the Axis. At first he wished to press on with the idea of a cross-Channel operation as soon as possible, but his military advisers gradually persuaded him that this was not practicable.[7] Nevertheless, Mr Churchill would not accept any scheme which condemned the Allies to a passive role in 1943. He wanted priority to be given to more ambitious operations in the Mediterranean, operations which might knock Italy out of the war, set the Balkans aflame and perhaps so weaken German forces elsewhere that a major front could be opened in Western Europe.[8]

In addition to these military problems, political matters arising from the success of Allied arms were also demanding attention. The most immediate difficulty was the question of French civilian and military administration in North Africa. When General Eisenhower's forces had landed in Morocco and Algeria on 8 November they had been faced with a very dangerous and difficult situation, since the local French commanders and officials were largely loyal to Vichy. There was a distinct possibility that the Anglo-American expeditionary force would be bogged down by the need to pacify a large area of difficult terrain.

The diplomatic preparations for the American landing had not been at all satisfactory, and the American candidate for the French leadership, General Henri Giraud, proved incapable of asserting his authority.

The situation had been saved by the fortunate presence in Algiers of Admiral Darlan. François Darlan was a notorious collaborator who was violently anti-British. But he was able to persuade most French military officials to cease resistance to General Eisenhower's forces and turn their guns against the Germans. When Hitler invaded Vichy France it became more obvious that the duty of all patriotic Frenchmen in North Africa was to support the Allies. Both Eisenhower and his subordinate field commander, General Mark Clark, had behaved with skilful prudence in their handling of Darlan. But the arrangement with him had provoked strong reaction in both the United States and Britain.* It was felt that, since the West was waging a struggle against Fascism, there could be no place for pacts with anti-democratic enemies of the United Nations. If Darlan was to be treated with such favour, might not the same sort of bargain be made with more pliable Fascist elements in Italy, or even men like Goering in Berlin?

For the British Government the affair was particularly embarrassing because it led to further deterioration in the Government's relations with the Free French. General de Gaulle had not been told of the plan to attack North Africa, largely because the Americans insisted that the Gaullists be completely excluded from the entire venture. One of Mr Churchill's most irritating diplomatic headaches was the need to avoid an open clash between General de Gaulle and the American Government. It had always been erroneously believed in Washington that special American relations with Vichy would bring great rewards, and that the Gaullist faction in London was simply upsetting the Allied apple-cart.

The Darlan episode – culminating in his assassination on 24 December – was also important because it had raised the whole issue of Allied attitudes towards liberated territory and the settlement of Europe once the Axis had been destroyed. These questions could not be ignored, but false or over-hasty answers might endanger the stability of a future plan for world peace. Inter-Allied consultations were obviously needed.

* Eisenhower was shocked and indignant at suggestions that he was insufficiently involved with anti-Fascist idealism. 'I can't understand', he burst out to Harold Macmillan, 'why these long-haired, starry-eyed guys keep gunning for me. I'm no reactionary. Christ on the Mountain! I'm as idealistic as Hell.' No such complaints about his lack of idealism come from Moscow. Marshal Stalin – being better acquainted with the techniques required by a struggle for power than some of his anti-Fascist brethren in the West – fully approved of Eisenhower's action. As he wrote to Mr Churchill on 27 November 1942, 'Military diplomacy should know how to use for the war aims not only the Darlans, but even the devil and his grandmother'.[9]

When, on 26 November 1942, Mr Churchill received a suggestion from the President that American, British and Soviet military staffs should meet at the earliest opportunity to co-ordinate plans, he was quick to insist that there should be consultation between Heads of Governments rather than just a gathering of military leaders.[10] The reason that he put to the President was certainly unanswerable. Generals – and in particular Soviet generals – would have no authority to take major decisions, and there would be a tiresome waste of energy – as well as a danger to security – involved in the exchange of cipher telegrams between three capitals and the scene of the meeting. The Prime Minister undoubtedly had other considerations in his mind as well – considerations which he could less easily make known to the President. If there were to be a tripartite meeting of staffs, the British delegation would be unlikely to obtain agreement to the broad lines of its strategy. The American Naval Chief of Staff, Admiral Ernest King – a man so tough the President used to claim he shaved with a blow-torch – would weaken the Western case from the outset by pressing for more effort in the Pacific. General George Marshall would support operations in Europe, but was quite out of sympathy with the British conception of those operations. For him the only way to beat Germany was to launch a cross-Channel assault into France. Efforts elsewhere were dangerous and time-consuming irrelevances. From the British viewpoint this American obsession with the Western Front was particularly dangerous because it would naturally coincide with Soviet inclinations. The belief that the way to victory was to 'keep plugging away at the point where the enemy was strongest'[11] died hard, especially among soldiers who had not been involved in the first three years of the previous Great War. In Britain both the military staffs and their political superiors were aware how serious an obstacle the Channel was and how demoralizing would be the effect of failure on a Western offensive. As Mr Churchill later remarked to General Eisenhower, 'We must take care that the tides do not run with the blood of American and British youth, or the beaches be choked with their bodies'.[12]

President Roosevelt finally accepted the force of Churchill's argument that the meeting should be between Heads of Governments rather than military experts, but he still seemed more willing to emphasize the strategic rather than the political aspects of the proposed conference. He pointedly refused to enlarge the scope of the meeting by the inclusion of representatives of the American State Department. Mr Churchill had wished to bring Anthony Eden, the Foreign Secretary, with him to any summit meeting, but this suggestion was politely vetoed by the President. When the conference, which was to meet in North

Africa, finally assembled, Roosevelt was accompanied by Harry Hopkins and Averell Harriman. Cordell Hull was left behind.

This was clearly a deliberate decision by the President and leaves room for speculation about his motives. He may have been personally disinclined to encumber his delegation with a Secretary of State who was not always likely to accept the Presidential line of thought. He may have felt that the attitude of the State Department was so hostile to the Gaullists that Hull would simply be an embarrassment in North Africa. There is reason to suppose that he regarded the French problem as being his own most important responsibility at the conference. When it took place he told General Eisenhower's naval aide, Captain Harry C. Butcher, that he saw himself as 'something of a father confessor to all the boys and hoped to help Ike with some of his political troubles while here by having Giraud and, if possible, de Gaulle, in for a unity talk'.[13] Harry Hopkins felt that the President was personally inclined to get out of Washington, where his arduous political labours were becoming a burden to him.[14]

But it seems very probable that President Roosevelt did not feel that the moment had yet come for far-reaching commitments on political questions. In particular, he did not wish to appear to be making arrangements for the settlement of the post-war world before establishing a relationship of trust between Washington and Moscow. His conception of post-war peace-keeping was based on his belief in the need for a 'special relationship' between the United States and Russia. This was indeed a pathetic fallacy, though not an ignoble one.*

What was needed in 1943 was a formula which would enable the President to temporize when the question of war aims was raised publicly in the United States. It was an unavoidable feature of the American political system that the President would be pressed to specify the terms upon which his Government would be prepared to make peace. President Wilson had been eager to publicize his thoughts on this question, and his attempts at a rational formulation of democratic war aims had led him into the diplomatic catastrophe of the Fourteen Points. In the First World War, United States diplomacy had been characterized by a good deal of thinking aloud and a serious lack of consultation with the Allied Powers. President Roosevelt intended to avoid both these pitfalls. At the same time it would be unwise to imitate the French and the British Governments in the earlier war by giving

---

* On 18 March 1942 President Roosevelt had written to Mr Churchill: 'I hope you will not mind my being brutally frank when I tell you that I can personally handle Stalin better than either your Foreign Office or my State Department. Stalin hates the guts of your top people. He thinks he likes me better and I hope he will continue to do so.'[15]

secret undertakings to other friendly countries which might prove
embarrassing before the struggle was over.

The solution considered by the President was one which committed
him to no precise line of action, satisfied the inclinations of public
opinion in Britain and America and was designed to reassure his ally in
the East. This was the concept of Unconditional Surrender by the Axis.

As early as April 1942 a subcommittee in the American State
Department, headed by Norman Davis, had been set up to advise on
problems of security. This subcommittee had reached the conclusion
that war had come a second time to the United States only because
Germany had not been compelled to admit her absolute defeat in 1918.
The German people had been allowed to believe that their country had
somehow been tricked into accepting an unworthy peace even though
she had never been beaten on the battlefield. To prevent a repetition of
this disastrous misconception the sub-committee recommended, on
21 May 1942, that 'On the assumption that the victory of the United
Nations will be conclusive, unconditional surrender rather than an
armistice should be sought from the principal enemy states, except
perhaps Italy'.

Before the President left for Casablanca he told his Joint Chiefs of
Staff that he intended to support the concept of Unconditional Surrender
as being the ultimate military objective of the Allies. His intention was
not opposed by the Chiefs of Staff. Indeed, it seems to have been accepted
as such a self-evident representation of Allied policy that no attempt was
made to study its military implications.[16]

II

The decision was finally taken to hold the Allied Conference in
Casablanca during the third week of January 1943. The plan for a
tripartite meeting had been jettisoned owing to Stalin's unwillingness to
leave the Soviet Union at a time when his country was involved in one
of the most crucial battles of the entire war. Soviet requirements were,
in any case, perfectly clear. Stalin wanted to hold the Western leaders to
their promises for a second front in 1943. He was not interested in
substitutes. Proposals for air forces to be sent to his own southern
theatre of war – Operation 'Velvet' – had seemed attractive when the
Germans were on the point of breaking through near Stalingrad. Now
that the Russians themselves were on the offensive, Stalin had no desire
for Western visitors to be present on his front.

On 14 January the British Chiefs of Staff and Mr Churchill arrived
at Casablanca. The Prime Minister was fortunate enough to have a

specially equipped Liberator placed at his disposal by the Americans and made the flight in reasonable comfort. His senior staff had to sample the less obvious pleasures of a bitterly cold bomb-bay in rarefied atmosphere. Consequently they did not appear to be as spruce as their American colleagues, who turned up some hours later in well-appointed Sky-masters.[17] But this advantage was short-lived. For the British delegation had at its disposal an excellently organized staff team which had been sent ahead in the converted liner *Bulolo* and which was now established in the harbour at Casablanca. Expert advice buttressed the arguments of the British staff throughout the discussions of the next few days. Mr Churchill had even been able to take his Map Room with him. He established it in his villa where it was kept up to date by the omniscient Captain Richard Pim. It was useful to be able to point out to American guests just how many U-boats there were in the Atlantic, in case any of them were inclined to overlook the problems posed by the naval war.[18]

The British staffs were headed by General Sir Alan Brooke – a man of great intellectual capacity, whose thoughts ran so fast that neither his tongue nor his listeners could easily keep up with them.[19] Brooke represented the voice of caution at the military councils of the conference. He regarded Churchill's own designs for 1943 as over-sanguine, and was rather contemptuous of American plans.[20] Fortunately his sharpness of tongue was counterbalanced by the diplomatic skill of the British liaison officer in Washington, Field-Marshal Sir John Dill, whose value to the Allies as a cohesive force was demonstrated beyond question at the conference. The other leading figures in the British delegation were the brilliant air strategist, Air Chief Marshal Sir Charles Portal, and Admiral of the Fleet Sir Dudley Pound. Admiral Pound was a taciturn but immensely knowledgeable First Sea Lord, whose habit of appearing to be asleep at the conference table disconcerted his colleagues without impairing his own efficiency.

It was these three men, along with Mr Churchill's own Chief of Staff, Lieutenant-General Sir Hastings Ismay, who had to bear the burden of putting Britain's case for vigorous but intelligently planned action against Hitler in 1943. The Prime Minister himself gave them the keynote to successful negotiations with their American allies – they must be patient and reasonable but utterly persistent, 'like water dripping on a stone'.[21] It was good advice, and it worked.

There were, as has already been indicated, a number of factors favouring the British at Casablanca. The first was their larger staff organization which could provide them with fuller information to support their views. The second was the lack of co-ordination between the three American services, none of which was enthusiastic about

Mediterranean operations but which had no coherent plan to suggest in the place of the British one. Admiral King confused the issue by demanding that 30 per cent of Allied efforts should be devoted to the Pacific – a demand which, as General Brooke was quick to point out, could hardly be justified in any military sense.[22] Marshall fought a determined battle to wind up Mediterranean operations as quickly as possible and turn Allied attention to the Western Front, but he was faced with detailed arguments about the transport difficulties involved in assembling a credible force during 1943. In this respect the Americans had suffered a fortuitous set-back as their delegation from Washington was travelling to the conference. At Trinidad the President's own Chief of Staff, Admiral William Leahy, had succumbed to a bout of bronchitis and had had to be left behind. Leahy was a man for whom the Mediterranean theatre of operations had had no attraction whatever. In the words of one English writer, he regarded it 'as a kind of dark hole into which one entered at one's peril. If large forces were committed . . . the door would suddenly and firmly be shut behind one.'[23] From the British point of view the Admiral's illness may have been a blessing in disguise.*

The crisis in the military talks at Casablanca came on 18 January, after a morning of vigorous argument. General Brooke was in despair about the chances for making a good Allied plan, but the more flexible Field-Marshal Dill persuaded him to put forward a conciliatory paper stressing those areas of policy about which agreement had been reached. That afternoon a statement drafted by Air Marshal Sir John Slessor was presented to the Americans who accepted it without difficulty. The military staffs were able to report on their success to the President and the Prime Minister the same evening.[25]

The Casablanca Conference was thus at least a limited success for the British strategists. Germany was to be considered the main Axis enemy in 1943. First priority was to be given to the defeat of the U-boat, air attacks on Germany were to be stepped up, the clearance of North Africa was to proceed as rapidly as possible and Allied offensives were to extend from there into Sicily. Churchill's hope that Italy might be knocked out of the war and that Turkish participation might then open up the whole of the Balkans to Allied penetration had been materially enhanced by the events of the conference.

On the political side the results were less striking. While the military men were locked in combat, Mr Churchill and the President had been consulting about diplomatic issues. The difficulties over General

---

* Indeed, the Admiral found little to enthuse over when the conference was finished. He was disappointed over the lack of precision about operations on the Western Front and gloomy about North Africa.[24]

de Gaulle and the administration of French North Africa were exacerbated by the General's own reluctance to come to the conference himself. Only very great pressure from Mr Churchill and Mr Eden at the Foreign Office prevailed upon him to do so. There followed a frigid meeting between de Gaulle and General Giraud which was of value to the President and the Prime Minister politically, but which marked no very great improvement in the relations between the Gaullists and their North African colleagues. Admiral Leahy, who had himself been an American Ambassador in Vichy France, revealed his view of the arrangements made between Giraud and de Gaulle in his memoirs when he wrote:

> Some small approach was made towards getting a political agreement between Giraud, who was fighting in North Africa, and de Gaulle, who was talking in England. I was unable to see any military advantage that would be gained by the type of agreement that was proposed.[26]

If the problem of the French had been evaded rather than solved, larger questions of world organization did not come up in any very specific form and could hardly be dealt with in the absence of Soviet representatives. But President Roosevelt still felt the need for some kind of political declaration which would emphasize Allied determination to go on waging war until the Axis Powers had been rendered impotent. The more ambivalent the Allied position in North Africa was made to seem by the difficulties with de Gaulle, the more necessary it was to expunge the memory of Darlan by making a firm statement about the purposes of the war against Fascism.

The President was also motivated by a desire to ensure that America's war against Japan would not be neglected by her allies after the Germans and the Italians had been beaten. Mr Churchill had reassured him on this point so far as Britain was concerned, but he hoped if possible to be able to gain a firm commitment from the Russians to join the struggle in the Pacific once Germany was out of the war.[27]

The President was therefore of the opinion that a public statement should be made in which the two Western Allies pledged themselves to wage war against the Axis Powers until they should be willing to offer their Unconditional Surrender. He broached the subject to Mr Churchill at lunch one afternoon in the presence of Elliott Roosevelt, who afterwards noted that the Prime Minister pronounced the phrase 'perfect' and remarked that he could just see how 'Goebbels and the rest of 'em'll squeal'.[28] However accurate this recollection was – and Mr Churchill himself could not recall the occasion – there is no doubt that the President and the Prime Minister had discussed the idea of such a declaration. On 20 January the War Cabinet in London had received a progress report from the conference in which Mr Churchill had remarked on the President's desire to employ the Unconditional Surrender formula.[29] In Mr Churchill's report Italy was to be excluded from the scope of such an announcement. He hoped that the Italians might be encouraged to seek a separate peace if hopes of a more lenient settlement could be held out to the reluctant warriors in Rome.

The War Cabinet met that afternoon to consider the Prime Minister's communication, of which the section dealing with Unconditional Surrender was but a small part. The phrase itself aroused no opposition, but the Cabinet felt that it should be strengthened by adding Italy to the enemies affected by the formula. Mr Attlee and his colleagues in London were of the opinion that the exclusion of Italy would have a disheartening effect on potential allies in the Balkans and would not necessarily hasten the withdrawal of Italy from the war. On the contrary, 'knowledge of all rough stuff coming to them' would be more likely to have the desired effect on the Italians' morale.[30]

The matter was then dropped until 24 January – the day on which Mr Churchill and the President finally obtained a token reconciliation between Giraud and de Gaulle. After these two stiff and unbending figures had been hustled into demonstrating an attitude of reluctant amity for the benefit of photographers, the surprised and delighted Press correspondents in Casablanca were addressed by the President and the Prime Minister. Roosevelt spoke first. His statement was to make history, and he himself fully realized the importance of what he was saying. He spoke from notes and his intentions had been discussed and considered beforehand. The impact of his remarks was a factor which he was less easily able to judge.

The notes which the President held in his hand as he faced the Press reporters that day contained the following paragraph:*

The President and the Prime Minister, after a complete survey of the world war situation, are more than ever determined that peace can come to the world only by a total elimination of German and Japanese war power. This involves the simple formula of placing the objective of this war in terms of unconditional surrender by Germany, Italy and Japan. Unconditional surrender by them means a reasonable assurance of world peace for generations. Unconditional surrender means not the destruction of the German populace, nor of the Italian or Japanese populace, but does mean the destruction of a philosophy in Germany, Italy and Japan which is based on the conquest and subjugation of other peoples.[31]

* It should be remembered that this was a Press conference statement, not the official conference communiqué. No mention of Unconditional Surrender was contained in the latter.

There was nothing very new in the thoughts which underlay this paragraph. It still implied a distinction between the German, Italian and Japanese peoples and their rulers. Indeed, Unconditional Surrender was itself a logical extension of the principles governing the Allied attitude towards the Axis since the beginning of the war. Mr Chamberlain had drawn a contrast between the Germans and Hitler.* The latter must be removed; the former could be expected to find a place in the community of civilized nations. Now the Allies had ceased to hope that their enemies could rid themselves of wicked leaders. The only solution was complete defeat and a new start. Had the war simply been regarded as a struggle for power between rival nation-states there would have been no need for the Unconditional Surrender formula. The Allies could then have regarded any Axis Government as acceptable which offered them generous enough concessions to make peace. This approach was not considered by any of the Allied statesmen. It would have been swiftly rejected by their peoples had they done so.

Mr Churchill seems to have been surprised by the President's statement, since the issue had not been discussed after the British had insisted on including Italy in the Unconditional Surrender Formula. Nevertheless, there had been a clear understanding that the aim of the Allies to fight the Axis to a finish should be stated at the Conference. The Prime Minister therefore staunchly backed the President up in his declaration of Allied policy."† Since his own Cabinet had been in favour of accepting the President's statement in the sense in which it was finally made, there was no need to fear repercussions in London. It was only Mr Churchill's tactical plan for dealing with Italy which had suffered a set-back.

In other respects the declaration seemed a heart-warming statement of Allied resolution in the face of an enemy which had enslaved nearly all of Europe and much of Asia. It did not give cause for alarm in any of the other Allied capitals. Had not Anthony Eden declared on 12 July 1941 that Britain was 'not prepared to negotiate with Hitler on any subject'?‡ There was little doubt anywhere in the Allied camp at this

* See above, p. 14.

† President Roosevelt claimed after the conference that he had not planned his statement very clearly in advance, but that in the confusion after the withdrawal of the two recalcitrant French generals the thought of making it had 'popped into his mind'. The difficulty with which the Frenchmen had been brought together had reminded him of the efforts needed to get Grant and Lee to meet at Appomattox. Notions like this might have flashed through the President's mind at that moment. But we cannot be expected to believe that he could have been influenced in making a statement of great political importance by the recollection of a Republican President who had not even been a very good general. The President himself was an expert at managing Press conferences. His notes made it quite clear that he was not speaking off the cuff.

‡ On the occasion of the signing of the first accord with the Soviet Union.[33]

time that the Axis must be not only defeated but be seen to be defeated. This was especially true of the Germans. No more Wilsonian illusions could be allowed to blossom among the enemy if they found the fortunes of war turning against them. It was important – and indeed in President Roosevelt's view essential – that the Allied view on this should be put on record at a time when the Axis still believed itself strong enough to win the war. The Axis Powers, as the President pointed out when he returned to America, were hoping that even if the Allies did start winning they would quickly fall out among themselves.[34] This belief was supported by the heterogeneous political composition of the anti-Fascist coalition and the example of the conflicts which had attended peace-making at the end of the First World War. If such Axis hopes could be quashed, the morale of its members would suffer accordingly.

Since the end of the war the President's statement has come in for intense criticism. Even men who had themselves shouldered responsibility for the policy of Unconditional Surrender tried later on to dissociate themselves from it. The most famous instance of this type of amnesia was perhaps the occasion upon which Ernest Bevin claimed that Unconditional Surrender had been foisted upon the British War Cabinet without its consent, and that it had been the cause of reconstruction problems in Germany after the war. This policy, claimed Bevin,

> left us with a Germany without Law, without a Constitution, without a single person with whom we could deal, without a single institution to grapple with the situation, and we have had to build right from the bottom with nothing at all.[35]

Mr Bevin meant these remarks as a condemnation of Unconditional Surrender. At the time he made them to the House of Commons, Germany's plight was a serious one. But when one examines his statement more carefully it appears that he was inadvertently justifying the policy he had chosen to attack. Germany had to be rebuilt right from the bottom. During the war there were few in the West who did not believe this. After victory was won it was easy to forget it. One might ask, as Wilson Harris did in the same parliamentary debate:

> What kind of a constitution could we have inherited in 1945? Hitler had smashed every scrap of democracy in Germany. Despotic autocrats at the top and a subservient *Reichstag* and *Gauleiters* all over the country. Was that the kind of constitution that would have recommended itself to the Hon. members opposite?[36]

Sometimes this question is countered by suggesting that without Unconditional Surrender there would have been a revolution within Germany – the sort of thing for which Mr Chamberlain had hoped so pathetically in the autumn and winter of 1939. Yet it was precisely this kind of development which might have caused most embarrassment to the United Nations. President Roosevelt did not wish for the destruction of the German people. That was made clear in his public statements time and again after the Casablanca Conference. But nor could he wish to see a German Darlan. No Government which could conceivably have taken power in Germany during the war would have been acceptable to the Allies as being free from the taint of German militarism.

III

In any case there is no evidence that the Unconditional Surrender formula caused the Germans to delay revolution and peace-making for fear of Allied harshness. The Italians were not deterred by it and did indeed manage 'to work their passage home'. The fact was that the anti-Nazi forces in Germany were too weak in numbers and determination to overthrow Hitler. The Führer was, in Churchill's words, 'a maniac with supreme power to play out his hand to the end, which he did; and so did we'.[37]

One might also ask, what were the alternatives to Unconditional Surrender? Precise terms upon which a peace might have been based? As Mr Churchill has again pointed out, these would have been far less palatable to the Germans than the realities of Unconditional Surrender actually turned out to be. Even if we lay aside the extremes of the Morgenthau Plan,* there was general agreement among the Allies in 1943 that Germany should be dismembered. Soviet claims for reparations alone were likely to be colossal.

Nor would it have been possible for the Allied Governments to go through the war without giving their long-suffering peoples some idea of how they proposed to end it. Pressure for some sort of statement of war aims was bound to build up in the democracies when victory began to seem likely. Only shortly after the President returned from Casablanca to Washington he found that the United States Senate was bestirring itself to inquire what stake America would have in the post-war world.† The formula of Unconditional Surrender was the most satisfactory solution which could be found for a problem which threatened to jeopardize a future peace.‡

* See below, pp. 174–87.
† In particular, the Republican Party, which had entered the war in a spirit of sulky mistrustfulness, was casting about for a platform which would enable it to seem more patriotic than the Administration whilst accepting the facts of international life. This was to appear in September 1943 as the 'Mackinac Resolution'.[38] (See below, pp. 540–1.)
‡ Care should be taken not to exaggerate the effect of Unconditional Surrender on German public opinion. Contrary to popular belief, Dr Goebbels did not greet the

Lastly, it should perhaps be emphasized again that neither the President nor the Prime Minister ever committed himself to a policy of blind destruction against enemy peoples. The keynote of the Unconditional Surrender policy was that it gave the vanquished no rights against the victors. It did not absolve the Allies from their duties as civilized nations. President Roosevelt explicitly underlined this point on 14 February 1943 when he said that the Allies meant no harm to the common people of the Axis, although they would 'impose punishment and retribution in full upon their guilty and barbaric leaders'.[40] This policy was not modified as the war progressed. On 18 January 1945 Mr Churchill told the House of Commons that nothing would induce Britain and America to abandon the principle of Unconditional Surrender. But he went on to point out:

> ... the President of the United States and I, in your name, have repeatedly declared that the enforcement of unconditional surrender upon the enemy in no way relieves the victorious powers of their obligations to humanity or their duties as civilized and Christian nations. . . .[41]

The Prime Minister then drew on his knowledge of classical Greece, and reminded the House that the Athenians, having on one occasion conquered a hostile tribe and herded them on the beach naked for the slaughter, set them free, saying:

> This is not done because they were men.
> It was done because of the nature of man.

Seen in this light, 'Unconditional Surrender' ceases to be an instrument of blind hatred and can be judged as what it was – the only civilized formula which could satisfy free peoples waging a life-and-death struggle against Fascism.[42]

Casablanca formula as a heaven-sent gift to his propaganda organization. After the conference, directives to the Berlin Press put no stress on Unconditional Surrender, and in his famous 'total war' speech at the Berlin Sportpalast on 18 February 1943 Goebbels made no reference to the Allied statement. His 'total war' campaign was a reaction to the defeat at Stalingrad. Unconditional Surrender was scarcely discussed at all in the Nazi Press in the early months of 1943. The fact was that the declaration gave Goebbels little that was of propaganda value. More detailed statements about Germany's future would have been much more damaging to the Allied cause. When, on a later occasion, the Morgenthau Plan was published in the American Press, it was seized upon at once by the German propaganda machine.[39]

5 | The Unconditional Surrender of Italy

I

DISCUSSION of the armistice terms to be imposed on beaten foes had more than academic significance in 1943. Neither of the Allies' major enemies was even approaching collapse, but martial feeling in Rome was very much more tremulous than in Tokyo or Berlin. The Italians had been led into the war on the mistaken impulse of their erratic dictator. Many of the more intelligent Fascist leaders had regarded this rash action with alarm, for they knew that Italy was not equipped for such a struggle. By the end of 1942 their worst fears had been realized. The American and British armies in North Africa were threatening to link arms. Mussolini had to face the prospect of invasion. He could have little confidence in his ability to repel it. Morale in Italy was sagging. Constant military reverses, the absence of some of their best soldiers on the Russian front, the ill-concealed contempt of the Germans and the new terror of Allied air-raids made it unlikely that there would be any very heroic resistance to a determined Anglo-American assault.

The Casablanca Conference was important for Allied policy towards Italy for two reasons. It enabled Mr Churchill to ensure that at least the first steps would be taken in his proposed Mediterranean offensive. This encouraged him in the hope that Italy would be knocked out of the war in 1943, and could be used as a base for operations against Southern Europe. But, on the other hand, the Unconditional Surrender declaration – applying as it did to all the Axis Powers – might tend to make dissatisfied Italians less likely to attempt to break away from Germany. For this reason the Prime Minister had attempted to avoid applying the declaration to Italy, feeling that her exclusion would increase the distrust between Berlin and Rome.[1]

There was, indeed, a good deal of ambivalence in the attitude of both the Western Powers towards Italy. Public statements by leaders in Britain and America had made a very much more emphatic distinction between the Italians and their Fascist rulers than between the Germans and Hitler. Speaking to the British nation on 29 November 1942, the

Prime Minister said of the Italians:

> One man and the régime he has created have brought these measureless calamities upon the hard-working, gifted and once happy Italian people, with whom, until the days of Mussolini, the English-speaking world had so many sympathies and never a quarrel. How long must this endure?[2]

This was an open invitation to the Italian people to throw off their Government and come over to the Allies. A similar implication was to be found in the speech delivered two weeks earlier to the Mazzini Society in New York by the Assistant Secretary of State, Adolf A. Berle, who told his Italian–American audience that 'Freedom is not a gift; it is an achievement. You must attain it yourselves. But when that freedom is won, certain pledges have been made to you and to the world.'[3]

This remark had a very Wilsonian ring. Although Mr Berle made it plain that he was referring to the Atlantic Charter when he spoke of 'pledges', the implied promise was clear.

At the same time public opinion in neither Britain nor the United States was prepared to tolerate any sort of truck with Italian Fascism – if for reasons which were not identical. The British had no particular cause to exempt Italy from any retribution coming to the Axis Powers. From the political viewpoint the bacillus of Fascism had been bred in Rome. Mussolini had been a constant source of trouble for the League of Nations. His role in the Spanish Civil War had aroused deep resentment. The British had been forced to stand helplessly by whilst Italy stabbed their French ally in the back and made her 'brief promenade by German permission along the Riviera',[4] as Mr Churchill contemptuously described it. There had followed a bitter war against Mussolini's armies in North Africa.

The strong reaction which the Darlan episode aroused in London was likely to be far exceeded if any tenderness was shown towards Fascism in Italy. Concern about this was not confined to the Left wing of British political opinion. The British Foreign Office was led by a brilliant young Minister who had good reason to despise the Italians for the humiliations they had inflicted on Britain and the League of Nations before the war. At a still higher level King George VI again mirrored the thoughts of his people when he wrote in his diary on 16 February 1943:

> I feel that we must have a cut and dried joint plan for this [the Italian problem] and that we must be firm and not deal with any of the Fascist régime or Mussolini's people, or any kind of Quisling.[5]

Nevertheless, there were cross-currents in British policy towards Italy. Mussolini, though he was now despised, had never been hated with the same venom as had been directed at Hitler. Had the Duce not been at one time the confidant of British Prime Ministers and the darling of the Conservative Press? Did he not deserve some recognition as the saviour of Italy from Bolshevism, the man who had brought order from chaos in Rome?[6]

From the Prime Minister's viewpoint there could, indeed, be no question of an arrangement with Mussolini, but Italian defeat was a means to an end rather than an end in itself. He wished to utilize the Italian peninsula for his strategic plans in Europe. So long as an Italian Government could be found which would provide him with the military facilities he required, he was not inclined to be too finicky about the technicalities of surrender. Italy was a nation which would find it difficult to threaten the peace after the war, whatever real or imagined grievances she might have about the ending of hostilities.

On the American side the situation was perhaps even more complex. American public opinion drew a very sharp distinction between Fascism and the Italian nation. There were many Americans of Italian origin who hoped that the war might bring democratic and, if possible, republican government to Italy. On the other hand, Italy was not regarded as a major enemy in the United States as was Germany or Japan. American forces had scarcely come into contact with Italians since they entered the war.

America's military chiefs – particularly General Marshall and Secretary of War Henry Stimson – were preoccupied with their desire to avoid committing large numbers of American troops to operations in Italy. Political advantages to be gained by the rapid exploitation of Italian political problems were unlikely to be regarded by them as sufficiently attractive to offset any possible weakening of their proposed offensive in the West. On the diplomatic side the State Department and the President's advisers – notably Harry Hopkins – were opposed to an arrangement with compromised elements in Rome. The shade of Admiral Darlan brooded over Washington.[7]

On 10 July the invasion of Sicily began. Although the Americans and the British were still not clear what form the exploitation of their Mediterranean offensive should take, the Sicilian invasion was a direct menace to Mussolini's régime. Preparations were made in London and Washington for eventual peace moves by the Italians, and Allied propaganda aimed at the Italian population was intensified. President Roosevelt had drawn up a declaration to the Italian people which he submitted to Mr Churchill for amendment. It was dropped over Italian cities on 17 July in the form of a statement signed by both statesmen.[8] The message pointed to the overwhelming power of British

and American forces concentrated in the Mediterranean, forces which
were at that moment 'carrying the war deep into the territory of your
country'. The Italians were told that their brave soldiers had been sent
to fight for the Germans, who had not hesitated to desert them on every
battlefield from El Alamein to Cape Bon. The blame for this situation
was placed squarely on Mussolini. Italy's sole hope for survival lay in
honourable capitulation to the forces of the United Nations. 'The time
has come', the Italians were told, 'for you to decide whether Italians
shall die for Mussolini and Hitler – or live for Italy, and for civilization.'

This statement underlined the Allied principle that distinctions were
to be made between conquered peoples and their Governments. It
encouraged the Italians to revolt, but gave no opportunity for a Fascist
régime to make peace by negotiation. In fact there was never very much
suggestion that Mussolini would be able to nerve himself to approach
the Allies. The Chief of the Italian General Staff, General Vittorio
Ambrosio, was urging Mussolini to end the war as soon as possible, and
the Duce is said to have promised King Victor Emmanuel III that he
would disengage Italy from the conflict by 15 September,[9] but nothing
came of these aspirations. Mussolini knew only too well that he could not
trifle with his German ally.

It may also be noticed that the Allied declaration made no promises
to the Italians which were inconsistent with the principle of Unconditional Surrender. No bargain was offered to the people of Italy. They
were simply given the prospect of restoring 'national dignity, security
and peace'. These benefits were eventually bestowed on Italy, although
many bitter months of turmoil and bloodshed lay in front of her.

II

When Mussolini was overthrown a week later, after what can only be
described as a palace revolution,* Mr Churchill's reaction was to
consult with President Roosevelt on measures to be taken to exploit
the new situation. The President had been taken by surprise in his
country residence and only heard the news as the result of a public
wireless broadcast.[10] There was, in any case, little that the Allies could
do immediately except to ensure that their objectives in Italy were not
at cross-purposes. Roosevelt urged that the whole of Italy and her

---

* Mussolini and the Fascist régime in Italy were overthrown on 25 July 1943. The
King of Italy entrusted the Government to Marshal Pietro Badoglio and placed
Mussolini under arrest. After several moves he was housed in the mountain resort of
Gran Sasso. Thence he was 'kidnapped to freedom' on 12 September, in a daring
commando operation under the direction of *Luftwaffe* General Kurt Student and S.S.
Captain Otto Skorzeny.

communications system must be made available to the Allies for use against the Germans in the north and the Balkans. If the new Italian Government wished to make peace, 'we should come as close as possible to unconditional surrender, followed by good treatment of the Italian populace. But I think also that the Head Devil should be surrendered, together with his chief partners in crime. . . .'[11] The Prime Minister sent back a memorandum on the fall of Mussolini in which he said that he did not feel that the Allies should be too particular in dealing with any non-Fascist Government, 'even if it is not all we should like', so long as it could deliver the goods.[12] The goods were to be the use of Italy and her dominions by Allied forces, the surrender of the Italian fleet, the withdrawal of Italian garrisons from France, Corsica and the Balkan Peninsula, the release of Allied prisoners held in Italy and an attempt by the Italians to intern German troops on their soil.

Both statesmen were agreed that no precipitate action should be taken which might encourage the Italians to think that the Allies would offer generous terms. Their plan was to play a waiting game whilst discreetly establishing contact with King Victor Emmanuel.* Mr Churchill described their policy most effectively when addressing the House of Commons on 27 July 1943:

> We should let the Italians, to use a homely phrase, stew in their own juice for a bit and hot up the fire to the utmost in order to accelerate the process, until we obtain from their Government – or whoever possesses the necessary authority – all the indispensable requirements we demand for carrying on the war against our prime and capital foe, which is not Italy but Germany. . . .[14]

In this statement the Prime Minister made it clear that the Allies would go on waging war on Italy without mercy so long as she remained in the ranks of their enemies. But he added that

> it would be a grave mistake when Italian affairs are in this fluid, formative condition for the rescuing powers, Britain and the U.S.A., so to act as to break down the whole structure and expression of the Italian State. We certainly do not seek to reduce Italian life to a condition of chaos and anarchy and to find ourselves without any authorities with whom to deal.[15]

The line adopted by Washington and London was cautious and consistent with military realities. The Allies were not in a position to intervene at that moment on the mainland of Italy. They had every reason to play a waiting game which would encourage Italian submission but avoid embarrassing commitments.

* Unfortunately the Germans were aware of these Allied tactics. They intercepted a transatlantic telephone conversation between the President and Mr Churchill on 29 July in which their intentions were made clear.[13]

But in the theatre of war itself the situation looked rather different. General Eisenhower was only too eager to bring the Italians over into the Allied camp and thus facilitate the dangerous and difficult operations of his troops. As soon as Eisenhower heard of Mussolini's fall he wanted to exploit the situation by issuing a radio message to Rome explaining that Unconditional Surrender would not mean dishonourable terms. He hoped that King Victor Emmanuel would be encouraged to co-operate with the Allies. Only the persuasion of his two political advisers prevented him from making this broadcast.[16]

The chief American political representative in North Africa was Robert Murphy, an experienced member of the American diplomatic service who had been representing the United States in Algiers before the Allied landings. He had been at least partly responsible for the misplaced American confidence in General Giraud as a North African leader, and his task became no easier after the assassination of Darlan. At that time the British Government had felt it necessary to send its own representative to North Africa to prevent political difficulties from jeopardizing the magnificent work of Eisenhower's military command.

The man chosen was Harold Macmillan. He faced a tricky assignment which promised to provide many headaches and few opportunities for distinction. The British Government did not want to make it appear that they were interfering with Eisenhower's control of what was primarily an American military operation. In fact, Eisenhower worked well with both Murphy and Macmillan, though he seems to have had some initial suspicions over the latter's appointment. He felt that these civilian experts could lighten the burden of political decisions on his shoulders. Robert Murphy was later to testify to Mr Macmillan's personal influence in the Mediterranean theatre.*

Although Murphy, at least, was not scheduled by his superiors to play any part in political developments concerning Italy, he and Macmillan were asked by Eisenhower's staff to help straighten out the awkward diplomatic problems which lay ahead in connection with the Italian campaign.[18]

Such help was very welcome in the summer of 1943. Not for the last time in his career as a soldier General Eisenhower found himself facing a military–political dilemma of peculiar complexity. If he encouraged the Italians to change sides in the war he might seem to cast doubts on the Unconditional Surrender formula which had only recently won

---

* According to Murphy, Macmillan told his British staff that 'these Americans represent the new Roman Empire, and we Britons, like the Greeks of old, must teach them how to make it go'.[17]

public acclaim in the West. On the other hand, a rigid insistence on total surrender might cause the Italians to regret their decision to overthrow Mussolini; it would certainly delay their military capitulation. Not unnaturally, General Eisenhower wanted to accomplish this capitulation as quickly as possible. He favoured offering the Italians a military armistice of a short and uncomplicated character. President Roosevelt – and Mr Macmillan – sympathized with this, but the British Government feared any arrangement which might offer the Italians an excuse for claiming the right to lenient terms at a peace settlement. Mr Churchill, being more easily swayed by strategic considerations, was willing to be persuaded by the Americans, but his Foreign Secretary and the War Cabinet demanded that Marshal Badoglio's régime should subscribe to detailed terms of surrender which spelled out the political as well as the military consequences of total capitulation. Mr Macmillan found this policy difficult to comprehend. He wrote of his colleagues in London: 'I wish some of them would come and try landing on a defended and mined beach out of a barge, in which one has been three or four days at sea (and sick half that time) in the middle of the night!'[19]

He therefore favoured Eisenhower's plan of facing the Italians with only brief armistice agreement and, despite pressure from London, he was able to watch this scheme come to fruition. Nevertheless, the danger of subsequent misunderstanding if only the 'short' and not the 'long' terms were imposed on the Italians was not imaginary. The events of November 1918 had shown how important the nature of any armistice agreement might become in post-war politics.

Meanwhile the new Italian Government was desperately trying to face both ways at once and avoid the destruction which threatened it from two sides. While Hitler was being assured of Italy's loyalty to the Axis, peace feelers were being extended to the Western Allies.* On 3 August Marshal Badoglio authorized a representative in Lisbon to make contact with the British Embassy there. Six days later further overtures were made in Tangier.[21] Then, on 15 August, a properly accredited representative of the Italian Government arrived in Madrid and made contact with the British Ambassador, Sir Samuel Hoare. This

---

* The Italians had good reason to desert Hitler. Apart from their lamentable military situation, there were signs that the Germans were planning to overthrow Badoglio's Government. Hitler actually ordered General Student to kidnap the Italian King, his cabinet and members of the royal family. They were to be transported to Germany and a 'loyal' Fascist régime set up. This scheme, planned in early August 1943, was never implemented, partly owing to Italian precautions and partly owing to the reluctance of German commanders in Italy to involve themselves in such an act of treachery.[20]

envoy was General Giuseppe Castellano, a high-ranking professional soldier who had served with distinction in the First World War.[22]

The proposal he made to Hoare was of a far-reaching character and was relayed to Quebec, where Mr Churchill and President Roosevelt were conferring with their service chiefs. The Allied leaders ordered General Eisenhower to send two staff officers to open negotiations with Castellano. The men they designated for this assignment were General Walter Bedell Smith, Eisenhower's Chief of Staff, and Brigadier K. W. D. Strong, the British Chief of Intelligence at Eisenhower's headquarters. These officers were to give General Castellano the terms of Italian surrender to be exacted by the Allies. They were only to cover the military aspects of surrender and were not to be regarded as covering political questions.[23] At 10 p.m. on 19 August the two Allied generals, having flown to Portugal on forged British passports and in civilian clothes, met Castellano at the British Ambassador's residence in Lisbon. Also present at the meeting were the British Ambassador, Sir Ronald Campbell, and an Italian diplomat, Franco Montanari. The latter acted as interpreter, but General Castellano was the real spokesman on the Italian side.[24]

The meeting was made more difficult than it otherwise would have been by the fact that the two parties concerned were talking at cross-purposes. The Italian envoy had come to arrange for Italy to join the United Nations in opposition to Germany. General Bedell Smith had to state at the outset that he was prepared only to discuss the terms on which the Allied forces would be prepared to cease hostilities against the Italians. The question of Italian participation in the war against Germany was one of high policy and would have to be decided by the Governments concerned. However, he did promise that Allied forces would assist any Italians who fought against or obstructed the Germans. He then read out the armistice conditions.[25] Attached to these conditions was a pro-memoria which emphasized that the terms did not visualize the active assistance of Italy in fighting the Germans, and that the extent to which the terms could be modified would depend on how far the Italian Government and people aided the United Nations during the war. But the Allies would give all support to Italians fighting Germans and would direct their bombing attacks against German targets in Italy so long as information about them was supplied by the Italians.[26] Meanwhile the Italians were urged to adopt at once an attitude of passive resistance to the Germans. They were to sabotage communications, safeguard Allied prisoners of war and if necessary release them, prevent Italian ships from falling into German hands and ensure that the Germans did not take over Italian coastal defence systems.

General Bedell Smith and Brigadier Strong found that Castellano was not able to accept the armistice conditions without reference to his Government, although he reacted to them fairly calmly and simply asked for clarification on some details. He was more concerned to know what help the Allies could give to the Italians against their erstwhile German friends. He asked with especial interest when the Allies were going to attack the Italian mainland and where the landing would be made. He pointed out that German S.S. units were poised to occupy Rome, which was itself denuded of Italian troops. Bedell Smith refused to answer this question on the very proper military grounds that the detailed plans of the Allied Commander would have to be kept secret until very shortly before the actual landings took place. Castellano was unhappy about this because it would leave the Italians little time to prepare their own moves vis-à-vis the Germans.[27]

Castellano returned to consult with Badoglio, taking with him a wireless set and codes with which to keep in contact with the Allies. On 26 August another envoy, General Giacomo Zanussi, appeared in Lisbon, accompanied by a British prisoner of war, General Adrian Carton de Wiart. This visit was not altogether felicitous from the Italian point of view. It seems to have increased the suspicion harboured by Bedell Smith that the Italian negotiations might be a ruse to obtain information about the timing and location of Allied operations.* In any case the Allied military authorities had no intention of giving away any confidential information to the Italians. Zanussi himself went to Algiers, where he attempted to persuade the Allied Commander to make a landing of airborne troops in the vicinity of Rome. This landing was to coincide with the main attack on the Italian coast and would be designed to protect the Italian Government against German forces which lay near the city. According to Zanussi, the Italians had six well-equipped divisions available to help fight Nazi units in the area,[29] a statement which did not entirely square with the information given earlier by Castellano. Both Murphy and Macmillan were enthusiastic about Zanussi's suggestion, and military advisers at Eisenhower's headquarters believed that the daring scheme might work.† Castellano was called to meet the Allied representatives again, this time in Sicily.

The next meetings were to take place at Cassibile, the headquarters of General Sir Harold Alexander, the British Commander-in-Chief in Sicily. Bedell Smith, Robert Murphy and Harold Macmillan were

---

* In a letter written by General Bedell Smith to General Castellano on 5 December 1943, the suspicion aroused by Zanussi's visit is mentioned, together with the Allied determination not to reveal confidential information to the Italians.[28]

† Macmillan and Murphy even volunteered to be flown with the airborne force to deal with the political aspect of the operation.

present there, as was General Zanussi. The atmosphere at Alexander's headquarters was very favourable to a rapid agreement with the Italians. The British Commander was being urged by Mr Churchill to make greater efforts in the expansion of Allied strength in Italy so that a major operation could be launched.[30] He was only too well aware of the weakness of Allied forces vis-à-vis those of the Axis. To him an armistice with the Italians seemed an urgent military necessity. He confided to Murphy and Macmillan that he would be prepared to resign from the Army if the British Government did not approve of his insistence on immediate Italian surrender, in return for which the Allies should accept Italian co-operation.* Since Eisenhower was also eager for a settlement with Italy, there can be no doubt that the leading figures on the Allied side in the Mediterranean were pressing hard for an armistice.

General Castellano arrived in Sicily on the morning of 31 August. He was taken to Cassibile, which lay in olive groves not far from Syracuse. With him he carried instructions from Marshal Badoglio to the effect that Italy would accept the peace terms offered only if the Allies pledged themselves to land in sufficient force to protect the Italian Government from the Germans. Otherwise, as the Italian Cabinet's memorandum put it, Italy would become a second Poland.[32] This Italian enthusiasm for a massive invasion of their own homeland was curiously embarrassing for the Allied representatives, who knew very well that they lacked the force to meet Italian demands. The bizarre truth – which neither side wished to state openly – was that the Anglo-American conquerors could not advance fast enough to satisfy their defeated Italian foes. The dilemma was naturally more cruel for the Italians than for the Western leaders. As Murphy wrote to President Roosevelt, 'It is a nice balance in their minds whether we or the Germans will work the most damage in Italy. They are between the hammer and the anvil.'[33]

Nevertheless, the situation had its poignancy for the Allies too. Every day that was wasted saw Rommel move more German soldiers into Italy. Although the Anglo-American force could do nothing to prevent this, might not energetic action by the Italian Army succeed in disrupting the German lines of communication, freeing Allied prisoners and seizing bases for the Allied air forces? It was an attractive prospect, but an

---

* Alexander explained these anxieties to Bedell Smith, Murphy and Macmillan after they had arrived in Cassibile from North Africa. He pointed out that in the initial landings on the Italian coast the Allies would have only from three to five Anglo-American divisions to pit against the nineteen German divisions already deployed in Italy and the sixteen Italian divisions whose loyalty was still uncertain. Murphy claimed that both General Alexander and Mr Macmillan were very disturbed at the effect a repulse in Italy would have on British morale.[31]

illusory one. The Italian Army would only strike at the Nazis if enough American and British troops were available to ensure victory anyway. Since the Allies wanted to use Italian soldiers instead of their own, no real community of interest existed. The fact was that Italy's Army and her Government were too demoralized to offer effective resistance to the Germans.

One possible method of overcoming Italian nervousness seemed to be offered in the proposal made by General Zanussi that an airborne force should be landed near Rome. Bedell Smith mentioned this to Castellano's delegation at Cassibile, and it was received by them with enthusiasm. General Castellano – apparently forgetting the gloomier statement he had made in Lisbon* – told Bedell Smith that the airfields in the neighbourhood of the capital could be defended by the Italian Army.[34] The meeting was then broken off to enable Castellano to consult once again with his masters. This time he was left in no doubt that the moment for procrastination had passed. Macmillan and Murphy pointed out to him that, should the surrender terms not be accepted, King Victor Emmanuel would lose all claim to be considered Head of the Italian State. The Allies would have to stir up revolution against him throughout the peninsula and bombard Italian cities from the air. Castellano flew back to Rome at 5 p.m. that afternoon with the unpleasant knowledge that if he did not return by midnight on the next day with the armistice signed Rome would be subjected to air attack.[35]

On 1 September Eisenhower authorized the plan to drop Allied airborne troops into the Rome area on the night of 8 September. News was then received from the Italians that they would return to Sicily on 2 September. The Allied representatives there expected them to bring the signed armistice with them, but they did nothing of the kind. Instead they declared that the King and Badoglio were only prepared to accept the armistice terms after Allied troops had been landed in force on the Italian pensinsula. To General Alexander and his political advisers this was dangerous prevarication and had to be squashed without delay. The British Commander-in-Chief treated his guests to an outburst of well-judged but by no means simulated fury, having donned his full-dress uniform for the purpose. Castellano and his party were not allowed to leave the camp.[36] Permission to sign the peace terms was finally sent to the Italian negotiators from Rome on 3 September. General Eisenhower flew from North Africa to add his signature for the Allied Powers.

The terms which General Eisenhower and Castellano signed were

* See above, p. 73.

concerned entirely with the war situation and took the form of a military capitulation. Eisenhower had been instructed to obtain the signature for these and then to present the Italians with a longer document itemizing political, economic and financial conditions. They were of necessity much more unpalatable than the purely military terms.* When poor Castellano saw the longer surrender document he was understandably shocked, and decided to withold its contents from his superiors until after the armistice had been publicly announced. This event was due to take place a few hours before the main Allied landings.[41]

When the Italian delegation flew back to Rome after the signature of the surrender they bore with them the impression that a large Allied force was soon to be landed by air in the neighbourhood of Rome. General Eisenhower and General Bedell Smith has indeed done their best to implement this decision, to the vocal indignation of General Mark Clark, who regarded the 82nd Airborne Division as vital to the success of his Salerno operation.[42] Nor were the commanders of the division itself at all attracted by their new mission, which they saw as a hazardous military gamble forced on them for political reasons.[43] The deputy commander of the airborne troops, General Maxwell Taylor, was sent to Ascona in an Italian frigate to spy out the land in Rome. He was not reassured by the situation he found there. General Castellano likened him to the hapless Colonel Hentsch at the battle of the Marne,[44] but there seems no reason to doubt that Allied reservations about the Rome landings were fully justified. On 8 September the Allies received a wireless message from Badoglio, admitting that he could no longer protect his airfields against the Germans. 'Operation Giant II' (the code-name of the airborne attack) would have to be cancelled. In

---

* General Eisenhower was unhappy about this procedure, describing it as a 'crooked deal'.[37] It should be remembered that Eisenhower was always inclined to treat the Italians leniently, hoping thereby to facilitate his own operations. On the British side, Anthony Eden felt that the Italian Government should be forced to accept the full terms of the surrender as soon as possible, so that they should have no opportunity to evade their responsibilities. When General Zanussi was in Lisbon in late August the British Foreign Office had demanded that he be sent back to Rome with the full text of the surrender terms. General Eisenhower, however, had not wished to face Badoglio with the longer and more draconian instrument of surrender at that stage.[38] The responsibility for the 'crooked deal' – in so far as there was one – lay therefore with the military authorities and not with the diplomats.

The British Prime Minister and the American President took the view that military considerations must predominate over political ones at that critical moment in the Italian negotiations. Mr Churchill wrote to his Foreign Secretary that 'If we get emergency terms it means that the Italians will have given themselves up to us lock, stock and barrel. There would be nothing improper in our requiring them to hand over the pull-through and other cleaning materials afterwards.'[39]

After the military surrender, pressure from the British Government – reinforced by the support of Marshal Stalin – eventually led to the full instrument of surrender being signed in Malta on 29 September.[40]

consequence of this Badoglio said that he could no longer accept an immediate armistice, since it would result in a German occupation of Rome.[45]

General Eisenhower reacted vigorously, telling the wretched Marshal that news of Italy's armistice would be broadcast at 6.30 p.m. on 8 September, and that unless Badoglio co-operated the full records of the whole affair would be published. Badoglio was to take all steps to defend Rome and to inform Eisenhower when the postponed air operation could take place. Any failure of the Italian Government to carry out the obligations which it had taken upon itself would lead to a breakdown of Allied confidence in it. The message ended with the ominous statement that '. . . consequently the dissolution of your Government and nation would ensue'.[46]

At 6.30 p.m. Algiers Radio broadcast the Italian surrender. Two hours later Allied forces started their assault of Salerno. The Italians in Rome hesitated, but then reluctantly announced their acceptance of the armistice. Italy had left the Axis. The first of the Allies' enemies had surrendered unconditionally.

III

The military gains resulting from this diplomatic victory were not very remarkable. The Germans were now firmly established on the mainland of Italy. General Eisenhower's appeal to Marshal Badoglio to defend Rome was not heeded. The Italian King and his Prime Minister bundled themselves into motor-cars and escaped to Pescara, where they embarked on an Italian cruiser and sailed for Brindisi. The news of the armistice had given the German forces the excuse they needed to take over Italy's coastal defences, and the landing at Salerno was fiercely resisted. Most Italian soldiers were cut off and disarmed by the Germans. The Italian Government delayed declaring war on Germany until 13 October – largely owing to the Fabian tactics of King Victor Emmanuel.[47] The only real gain for the Allies was at sea, for the Italian fleet did manage to make its way to Malta in the face of severe German air attacks. This marked an important improvement in the Allied naval position.

Unconditional Surrender had really been of little consequence to the course of events in Italy. The crucial factors were military ones. The Allies found themselves in the curious position of liberating a hostile nation which was more eager to welcome their invasion than they were to embark upon it. The slowness of the Allied advance into Italy was not caused by delays over the armistice negotiations. It was the result of a strategic decision to hold back Allied forces for the attack on northern France. There is no evidence that a more rapid acceptance of Badoglio's terms would have prevented German consolidation in central Italy. Badoglio did not, in fact, propose any terms. He wanted Allied intervention to protect him from Hitler. Had the Allies not insisted on Unconditional Surrender from Badoglio they would have gained nothing in the military sense and might have been seriously embarrassed once the war was won. In particular, it might have been difficult to reject Italy's colonial claims if she had not formally surrendered.

The delays in obtaining Italian surrender did not alter the Allied military timetable. Their only practical effect was to rob General Mark Clark of the 82nd Airborne Division during his initial operations at Salerno. When one remembers how that division had later to be landed behind the American lines when the whole beach-head was threatened with destruction, there seems good reason to be thankful that 'Operation Giant II' was never put to the test.* In 1943 the Italian Army was a spent force. Only as the war in Italy unfolded did the Italian people – fighting as partisans – throw off the lethargy and demoralization which Fascism had induced in them and begin to 'work their passage home'. The result was an Italy which retained its national frontiers and re-established itself with great rapidity as a respected member of the free European community. The principles which underlay Allied foreign policy were demonstrated to be neither irrational nor unjust.

* In his letter to General Castellano of 5 December 1943, General Bedell Smith said that he believed the airborne operation could have succeeded 'had there been in command of the Italian Divisions around Rome an officer of courage, firmness and determination who was convinced that success was possible'.[48] The qualifying sentence is a vital one.

6 | 'Trident', 'Quadrant' and the Moscow Conference of Foreign Ministers

I

BY midsummer 1943 the fortunes of the Grand Alliance had experienced a remarkable transformation. Germany was being defeated on all major fronts, on land, on sea, and in the air. One of the Axis partners had been overthrown. The speed at which events were moving rendered consultation among the Allies more necessary than it had been during the period when Hitler had held the initiative, for now the direction of Allied military offensives would have very important political implications.

The first major Allied controversy to be thrashed out in the summer of 1943 was the military argument which had been raging for almost two years between the Americans and the British over the question of the second front. As has already been shown,* at Casablanca the British had been able to persuade President Roosevelt and General Marshall that operations in the Mediterranean should be carried on until all Germans had been cleared from North Africa and Sicily could be threatened. This was still regarded as the preliminary to a smashing blow in the West. Marshall, Leahy and Stimson were quite determined not to be led away from their major objective by further British temptations in Italy or the Balkans. Yet, as the year went on, operations in North Africa were so successful, and the prospects in Italy seemed so full of promise, that the old proverb about 'a bird in the hand' began to recommend itself ever more forcefully to the British Government. Mr Churchill and General Brooke had never been very enthusiastic about the prospects for a cross-Channel assault unless the Germans were seriously weakened by diversionary actions elsewhere. The British Chief of Staff, in particular, had a strategic conception embracing all theatres of war in which the Germans were fighting, and did not regard different geographical areas as fronts of greater or lesser value according to their position on a map. The Germans should be fought

* See above ,p. 58.

where they could be beaten. They could be beaten most easily where their lines of communication were inadequate. In 1943 this meant Southern Europe. Only when sufficient Axis strength had been drawn off into that theatre could the Germans be defeated in the West.[1] On the political plane, Mr Churchill was aware of fear and distress among Germany's satellites in the Balkans and the Danube Basin. He remembered how the sudden collapse of Bulgaria had signalled the end of the First World War. He felt that Hitler was more vulnerable in Central Europe than on his Western Wall.

In May 1943 Mr Churchill and his military advisers went to Washington to participate in a conference to which was given the code-name 'Trident'. Since this took place on the American Chiefs of Staffs' home ground, they were rather better equipped to withstand British pressure than at Casablanca, even though the usual thoroughness had gone into British staff preparations. Admiral Leahy, himself a firm opponent of Mediterranean entanglements, took the chair at staff meetings, and arguments over the exploitation of Allied victories in North Africa could not be resolved to the satisfaction of the British. It was agreed that the Allied Commander in North Africa should be instructed to 'plan such operations in the exploitation of "Husky" [the capture of Sicily] as are best calculated to eliminate Italy from the war, and to contain the maximum number of German forces'.[2] Mr Churchill's vivid persuasiveness could not compel the Americans to accept more definite commitments in Italy, nor would they consider any extensions into Yugoslavia and Greece.[3]

The British, on the other hand, were forced to accept a definite commitment to launch a cross-Channel assault in the spring of 1944. The President was quite adamant in advocating this; Admiral Leahy and General Marshall warmly supported him. If plans to build up forces in Britain for an attack on the coast of France were to be pushed ahead without reference to major successes in other theatres, the resources available for operations in the Mediterranean would be bound to suffer limitation. All in all, the conference was not a marked success for the British, although it did leave the question of operations against Italy an open one. As has been seen, they were to be pressed home with no little effect.* On the other hand operational discussions about the Far East has proved very embarrassing for the British, since Field-Marshal Sir Archibald Wavell's Command could hold out no prospect of effective action against the Japanese in Burma.[4] This British weakness irked Mr Churchill and he determined to have a better story to tell at the next inter-Allied conference.

* See above, pp. 67 ff.

President Roosevelt and his advisers were better pleased with 'Trident' than they had been with Casablanca.[5] Although the cross-Channel assault lay far in the future, it had been definitely accepted as a top-priority operation once Sicily had been captured. Strategically the argument seemed to be tilting America's way, and the fact that the United States would soon be contributing more in manpower to European operations that the British themselves seemed likely to increase the weight of American views.* The President was, meanwhile, eager to balance his military effort with progress in the diplomatic field. The Grand Alliance was a triple coalition. Until then, the only close co-operation had been between Britain and America. Mr Churchill was the only Allied leader who had met both his counterparts face to face. Roosevelt wished to create the same bond of personal trust between himself and Marshal Stalin that had helped to sustain relations between the White House and No. 10 Downing Street. He believed that he was much more likely to charm Stalin than was Mr Churchill, whose fierce hostility to Bolshevism was thought to be an ideological hindrance in his relations with the Russians.

This view had the support of Averell Harriman, a close personal adviser and friend, who had accompanied Mr Churchill on his visit to Moscow in August 1942. Harriman was convinced that Stalin wanted a firm understanding with Roosevelt more than anything else apart from the destruction of Hitler. The Russian leader saw his country's post-war reconstruction more soundly based on this than on any other alternative.[6]

The President had on several previous occasions expressed his desire for a personal meeting with Stalin.[7] He now felt that this confrontation was a matter of urgency. On 5 May he wrote a remarkable letter to Marshal Stalin and sent it to Moscow in the care of a personal envoy, Joseph E. Davies, who had himself been Ambassador there until 1939. The fact that Admiral Standley, the official Ambassador to the Soviet Union, was on very bad terms with his host Government undoubtedly encouraged Roosevelt to use his personal form of contact, and it may have been a factor in encouraging him to get on friendlier relations with Stalin himself.[8]

In his letter to Stalin, Roosevelt made it quite clear that he wanted a *tête-à-deux* with the Russian leader. Mr Churchill was not to be present. The President urged that the meeting should be informal and free from 'the difficulties of large staff conferences or the red tape of diplomatic

* It should not be thought that British efforts to exploit opportunities in the Mediterranean theatre meant that they wanted to concentrate on it to the exclusion of a Western offensive. For an authoritative discussion of this problem see Michael Howard, *The Mediterranean Strategy in the Second World War* (London, 1968).

conversations'. It was to be 'a meeting of minds' with no need for official agreements or declarations.[9] Davies was cordially received in Moscow, and on 27 May he could report that Stalin agreed in principle to the President's request. It was hoped that the meeting could be arranged in July or August. Stalin does not seem to have reacted with enormous enthusiasm to the suggestion of a purely bilateral meeting,[10] although President Roosevelt felt obliged to tell Mr Churchill that the initiative for such an exclusive arrangement had come from the Russians.[11] The British Prime Minister, for his part, became involved in a decidedly acrimonious exchange of communications with Stalin over the question of the second front. It was here that the President found his private relations with London and Moscow becoming tangled. For, at the moment when he was trying – unbeknown to his British friends – to establish a personal *rapport* with Stalin, the decisions taken at the 'Trident' conference were about to precipitate a crisis of confidence between the Eastern and the Western elements in the forces fighting Hitler.

At the end of the 'Trident' discussions Mr Churchill had invited General Marshall to fly with him to North Africa to see for himself the beneficial results of the 'Torch' operation. The Prime Minister hoped to be able to persuade Eisenhower to press home his attack on Italy with the utmost vigour, and it was felt that it would be unsuitable for him to confer with the American General if Marshall was not present.[12] Marshall proved useful in another and unexpected way. Before the Prime Minister's aircraft left for Gibraltar he and the President had been working on a draft communiqué about the conference to be sent to Stalin. Since this proved a tricky task, they agreed that the Prime Minister should take the draft away with him and work on it in the aeroplane. When the journey had begun Churchill gave 'a bundle of drafts' with emendations in their various 'scrawls' to Marshall, and asked him to make something of them. In two hours he returned with a fair copy which delighted both Mr Churchill and the President.[13] It did not please Marshal Stalin.

For the Soviet Government the vital news in the communiqué from Washington was that the second front in France would not be opened until the spring of 1944. On 11 June 1943 Stalin sent a message to both his allies in which he upbraided them for going back on earlier promises to attack across the Channel in August or September of that year. The Soviet Government, he added ominously, 'cannot align itself with this decision, which, moreover, was adopted without its participation and without any attempt at a joint discussion of this highly important matter and which may gravely affect the subsequent course of the war'.[14]

Mr Churchill replied by emphasizing the difficulties involved in the second-front operation, and by stressing the tremendous efforts already being made against Germany by the Western Powers. He answered Stalin's complaints about consultation by assuring the Russians that he would 'go at any risk to any place that you and the President may agree upon'.[15] This could not have been altogether welcome to President Roosevelt, to whom Mr Churchill sent a copy of his telegram. Nevertheless, he had little option but to support the Prime Minister in a message of his own to Moscow.[16] This drew forth a yet more offensive communication in which the Russian leader rebutted Mr Churchill's explanations by citing passages from British statements made earlier in the war. He was also very skilful in making use of information which the Prime Minister had given him about Anglo-American military achievements to belittle the difficulties facing an assault in the West. Had not the Allied position improved since the previous February? Had not the Germans suffered defeats in Russia and North Africa? Had not the Western Allies begun to vanquish the submarine? Were they not wresting air superiority from the *Luftwaffe*? Conditions for launching a second front must therefore have improved rather than deteriorated. Perhaps the most sinister aspect of Stalin's last message had been its final paragraph, which ran thus:

> You say that you 'quite understand' my disappointment. I must tell you that the point here is not just the disappointment of the Soviet Government, but the preservation of its confidence in its allies, a confidence which is being subjected to severe stress. One should not forget that it is a question of saving millions of lives in the occupied areas of Western Europe and Russia and of reducing the enormous sacrifices of the Soviet armies, compared with which the sacrifices of the Anglo-American armies are insignificant.[17]

Mr Churchill was not prepared to sit tongue-tied under these provocations and he sent off a strongly worded reply. There followed an almost total breach in communications between the Kremlin and the West. Stalin withdrew his Ambassadors from London and Washington. For what was certainly the last time in the war it seemed remotely possible that the Russians might be reconsidering their alignment with the rest of the United Nations. Certainly tentative Soviet peace feelers were put out in Stockholm during the summer of 1943.* Hitler, however,

---

* According to Peter Kleist, a member of the Nazi diplomatic service and a specialist in Eastern European affairs, a number of attempts were made by the Russians to start negotiations for a compromise peace. Their go-between was a businessman in Stockholm called Edgar Clauss who approached Kleist on three occasions – in December 1942, in June 1943 and in September 1943. Kleist also claimed that he received information about the Moscow and Tehran Conferences from Clauss. It has been

showed no interest in negotiating with the Russians. He was arrogantly convinced that the shame of Stalingrad could be wiped out by another vigorous offensive. On 5 July 1943 the Nazis launched a large-scale attack on the central part of the Russian front. But then came a surprise. The Soviet forces held back this onslaught, and after about a week they were able to reply with a successful counter-offensive. It soon became clear that the Red Army could sustain itself against the *Wehrmacht* even without the assistance of the Russian winter. The dubious advantages to be gained by negotiation were completely overshadowed by the glorious prospect of total victory.

All these developments had seriously damaged President Roosevelt's efforts to establish personal intimacy with Stalin. No more was heard of Davies's proposal in Moscow until early in August, by which time the whole diplomatic situation had changed.

While the negotiations had been going on between Davies and the Russians, Roosevelt had thought it more discreet to avoid mentioning his Soviet scheme to his British friends. Mr Churchill had, of course, been in Washington for much of that period, and the President had doubtless felt it an awkward subject to broach with the Prime Minister face to face, especially when it was not clear that anything would come of his initiatives in Moscow. But after it had begun to appear that Stalin would accept his proposal, the President sent Mr Harriman to London to explain matters. It was a mission which caused Harriman some embarrassment.

He arrived in London on 23 June. At midnight, after a bad-tempered dinner party, at which Lord Beaverbrook had succeeded in upsetting the Prime Minister, Harriman had had to break the news of Roosevelt's scheme for a bilateral meeting with the Russians. Fortunately Harriman himself was on good personal terms with Churchill, and the Prime Minister accepted the sincerity of the American's arguments, even though he did not agree with them. Harriman stressed the value of an intimate understanding between Roosevelt and Stalin, an understanding impossible if the meeting had to be between three persons. He also put forward the view that public opinion in America would react more favourably to a confrontation between Stalin and Roosevelt than to a meeting of the three statesmen at which Churchill would appear to be the broker.[19]

The Prime Minister rapidly sent a message to Roosevelt pointing out

---

impossible to verify this story because Clauss died in April 1946. However, even if it were true, there is no real evidence that the Soviet feelers were meant as the prelude to a genuine offer of peace to Germany. Kleist's German superiors were, by his own account, very suspicious of Soviet motives.[18]

the use which Axis propaganda would make of a meeting from which Mr Churchill was excluded.[20] The Prime Minister also dispatched his firm reply to Stalin's second salvo about the Western Front without referring it first to President Roosevelt, as was his normal habit. The Americans were upset about this, since they would have preferred to tone down the Prime Minister's message in order to smooth Stalin's ruffled temper.[21]

Although the whole Russo-American project was to prove abortive, it did have a very important result so far as relations between London and Washington were concerned. In order to mollify Churchill, Roosevelt suggested that, immediately after his meeting with Stalin, there should be another conference between the British and the Americans at the Citadel in Quebec. All these various confabulations should then be regarded as preliminary to a full-dress meeting of the three statesmen which would take place in the autumn.[22] Mr Churchill was by now so anxious about Stalin's 'bearish' attitude that he dropped his objections to the idea of an exclusive meeting between his two partners, but by that time the fate of President Roosevelt's *tête-à-tête* with the Soviet leader had been sealed.[23]

II

The meeting to be held at Quebec, however, was not cancelled. On the contrary, the news from the Mediterranean and Russia made it all the more important that the Americans and British should confer together once again. For their part Mr Churchill and his advisers were eager to exploit the fall of Mussolini and the shivers of apprehension which this event had caused in Central Europe.* In the spring of 1943 it had come to be noticed in Ankara that the Bulgarians and the Hungarians were trying to make contact with the Allies. At the same time the Rumanian Foreign Minister, Mihai Antonescu, was apparently inspiring similar contacts in both Switzerland and Turkey.[24] The British Foreign Office had some hopes of the democratic opposition in Hungary, for example, which was supposedly based on the trade unions, the peasants' political organizations and the Socialist Party.[25] When Mussolini fell from power at the end of July, the situation in Hungary became yet more promising. Even the Press and radio in Budapest began to carry reports of anti-Nazi activity.[26] In August both the Bulgarians and the Magyars established serious contacts with the Allies. They wished to negotiate their withdrawal from the Axis on the understanding that action should only be taken when Anglo-American forces reached their borders.[27]

* See above, p. 68.

Coupled with the prospect of seizing most of the Italian peninsula and reinforcing partisan resistance in the Balkans, these favourable conditions on Hitler's southern and eastern flanks left no doubt in Mr Churchill's mind that operations in the Mediterranean should be pursued with the utmost vigour. But to the Americans such views were very disturbing, since they seemed once again to suggest that the British were half-hearted about the priority to be given to a cross-Channel attack.

These feelings of distrust were voiced when Mr Stimson, the American Secretary of War, came to Britain in July 1943. He was subjected to great pressure by Mr Churchill and Mr Eden for a more flexible policy towards the Mediterranean and Southern Europe. He got the impression that both military and political authorities in Britain were inclined against the attack on the French coast. The British general in charge of the planning for this operation – 'Overlord' – Lieutenant-General Frederick Morgan,* expressed the fear to Stimson that diversions in the Mediterranean might cause dangerous delays in the Western operation. Stimson himself engaged in verbal struggles with Mr Churchill on this issue, and the Prime Minister admitted to him that, had he been in supreme command, the assault on France would not have been part of his operational plan, although he emphasized his complete loyalty to it now that it had been accepted as part of Allied strategy.[28] The Prime Minister may well have been carried away by his own enthusiasm and the excellent news from the Sicilian theatre.[29] He may also have been influenced by advice from his old friend Field-Marshal Smuts.

Stimson, who followed his visit to London with a tour of inspection in North Africa, was determined that the British view of strategy should not once again be imposed upon the Americans. On 10 August he was back in Washington writing a most remarkable letter to Roosevelt, a letter which he handed to the President in person later that day. In it he advised that British lack of confidence in the cross-Channel operation was so serious as not to warrant the appointment of a British Commander-in-Chief. 'The shadows of Passchendaele and Dunkirk', he wrote, 'still hang too heavily over the imagination of these leaders.' He went on to speak of the 'vital difference of faith' between the Americans, who thought that Germany could only be really defeated by massing forces under an air umbrella in France, and the British, who believed it possible 'to gain victory by a series of attritions in Northern Italy, in the Eastern Mediterranean, in Greece, in the Balkans, in Rumania and other satellite countries . . .'.[30] Stimson found this latter view quite unaccept-

* General Morgan's official designation was COSSAC (Chief of Staff to the Supreme Allied Commander).

able. As he put it, the United States was pledged to a second front, and 'None of these methods of pin-prick warfare can be counted on by us to fool Stalin into the belief that we have kept that pledge'.

Stimson found the President in whole-hearted agreement. In fact, Roosevelt himself had been turning over large strategic problems in his mind in the weeks which had followed the 'Trident' conference, and he had rejected extended operations in Italy or the Balkans. Two points of entry into *Festung Europa* recommended themselves to the President. The first and most obvious was the Channel coast. The second lay through Rumania and the Danube Plains. For this the co-operation of Turkey and Russia would be required.[31] In either case it was unlikely that the British would be satisfied.

At a meeting of the American Chiefs of Staff which followed his interview with Stimson, Roosevelt pleased his military advisers by showing a resolution unusual for him in strategic matters.[32] The Americans went to Quebec confident that this time they could hold their own in any duel between the staffs.

If the Western Allies were experiencing friction in the planning of their military operations, the arrangements to be made for the establishment of a future peace were also the cause of disagreement and frustration. Once again, large questions of principle were at issue, and the answers to these questions would often be complementary to the military decisions taken by Allied leaders.

Although the end of the war was still far off, the Allies felt confident that they would eventually gain an absolute victory. Whereas in 1941 this had been a matter of faith, it was now reinforced by the tide of events and the numerical inequality of the conflicting forces. Winning the war could only be a prelude to the infinitely more complicated task of securing the peace. And it was to this problem that the Allies had now begun to turn their attention.

Many acute minds had already applied themselves to a consideration of the failures of the peace-makers at the end of the First World War. It was in 1943 that Harold Nicolson published a second edition of his own personal record of the Paris Peace Conference. He included in it some thoughts on the peace negotiations which, he assumed, would follow the conclusion of the Second World War. The authors of Versailles, he wrote, had not realized that

> the turbulent waters of any post-war world can be contained only by the concrete of rigid principle and the dykes of a firmly enforced programme. They relied on the wattle of improvisation and a few hastily gathered sods of compromise; these were quickly overrun by the flood.[33]

The Foreign Offices of the Western Powers also knew how important it was not to be taken unawares by the sudden outbreak of peace. Having seen the fruits of one victory thrown away by inept and slothful diplomacy, they did not want to be accused of inadequate foresight a second time. Although military matters still dominated Allied counsels during the early part of 1943, attention was being paid to the question of post-war settlements and the maintenance of peace.

In both Britain and America groups of experts were formed to plan ahead for the coming victory. In the United States a committee for post-war planning had been established, and in the British Foreign Office Mr Eden and his senior officials – foremost among them Sir Alexander Cadogan and Gladwyn Jebb* – had, since the autumn of 1942, been giving serious consideration to the problems of peace and security.

For the United States, the Secretary of State, Cordell Hull, was a veteran diplomatist who liked to think of himself as a statesman rather than a politician. His was a prickly and rather dry personality, the narrowness and self-righteousness of which was offset by a sincere dedication to high principles. He was a man for whom Mr Gladstone would have felt considerable admiration. Hull himself had good reasons for striving to avoid the errors made by the Western Powers in the closing stages of the First World War. As a young Congressman he had been a warm admirer of President Wilson, and had seen that statesman's dream of international co-operation brought to ruin partly as a result of America's own opposition to overseas entanglements. Like President Roosevelt, Hull was determined to succeed where Wilson had failed, but his over-all objectives were somewhat different from those of the President. Hull wanted agreement on a world-wide system of peace-keeping, a system based on the armed strength of the four great Allies – Britain, China, Russia and the United States.

This policy would involve a complete change of attitude on the part of the American public towards the acceptance of overseas obligations during peace-time. Hull realized that, if his plan were to succeed, it would have to be presented to the American people as an imaginative and yet practicable scheme which would ensure a real break with the grasping selfishness of power politics in the pre-war era. Hence he was resolved not to commit America to any action which would seem to pledge United States support to the narrow interests of individual allies – especially if those allies were in Europe. He could rightly point to the disastrous effect of similar promises made during the First World War.

'There is little doubt', he had written to Roosevelt on 4 February 1942,

* Later Lord Gladwyn.

that if the principle is once admitted that agreements relating to frontiers may be entered into prior to the peace conference, the association of nations opposed to the Axis, which thus far has been based upon the common aim of defeating the enemy, may be weakened by the introduction among its members of mutual suspicion and by efforts of various members to intrigue in order to obtain commitments with regard to territory at the expense of other members.[34]

This was sound enough if it was assumed – acting on the precedents set by the earlier war – that the embattled nations would make claims far in excess of what they themselves were able to gain by force of arms. That had certainly been the case with Tsarist Russia and pre-Fascist Italy. Unfortunately Hull seems to have forgotten that it is as dangerous to renegotiate obsolete peace settlements as it is to refight dead campaigns. By trying to postpone the territorial arrangement of Europe until a larger Four-Power scheme for world organization had been created, Hull made it easier for Europe to be divided along lines which very nearly corresponded to the positions of the Allied armies when the war came to an end.

On the British side Mr Eden's view was rather less Olympian, and infinitely more practical. He and his advisers felt that Britain could only continue to function in the role of a Great Power if she was able to act in co-operation with her war-time allies, and in particular with the United States. This would inevitably mean that post-war diplomacy would be dominated by a mighty constellation of victor Powers. It was a prospect not entirely pleasing to Britain, and likely to be far less attractive to other, smaller nations. Nevertheless, there was no foreseeable alternative which did not leave Britain vulnerable to Russia or a revived Germany.[35]

The British were therefore eager to support Mr Hull in his grand design for world security, if only because it would bind the United States to participate in world affairs as she had omitted to do in the years between the wars. However, Mr Eden and his colleagues were not disposed to content themselves with grandiose schemes which might prove wanting when tested by unwelcome and unexpected crises in the future. Just as France had wished for concrete guarantees of security at the Peace Conference in 1919, so now the British were determined to establish a European settlement which would prevent them having to face hostile neighbours in impotent isolation.

Furthermore, the British felt that no scheme for international peace could survive if it were not based on a foundation of European security, coupled with safeguards against further outbreaks of aggression in the Far East. On 13 April 1943 Sir Alexander Cadogan, the Under-

Secretary of State for Foreign Affairs, minuted that, so long as the Great Powers remained ready to hold back German and Japanese aggression, it should not be difficult to construct what he called 'ancillary organs which may have their uses'. Therefore it was necessary to reach an agreement with the United States and Russia about the arrangements for an armistice, the occupation of enemy countries, the maintenance of disarmament, economic control and other practical details. Once these matters had been decided upon, it might be possible to organize the policing of Europe. Britain should concentrate on obtaining such an agreement before trying to design 'all the outbuildings of the future Palace of Peace'.[36]

It was therefore upon the details of the European settlement that Mr Eden wished to concentrate. In this he was supported by Mr Churchill, who felt that security for the world could best be established on a regional basis. Mr Churchill had publicly proposed that there should be a Council of Europe and a Council of Asia as part of a world security system. The former would be established after the defeat of the European Axis, that is, while the war against Japan was still in progress.[37] The Americans were upset by this public announcement and, when Mr Eden went to the United States in March 1943, he was pressed for an assurance that Churchill had not intended to exclude the United States from European affairs.[38]

One of the British Foreign Secretary's most emphatic aims was the re-establishment of a strong French nation, liberated from Vichy as well as from occupation by the Germans. France, it was hoped, would provide Britain with a reliable Continental ally. Hence the British Foreign Office was eager to raise the status of the French within the Alliance. Mr Eden, in particular, was sympathetic to General de Gaulle, and, when the Free French Committee of National Liberation was formed at the beginning of June 1943, he was in favour of giving it official recognition.

This was a source of friction within the Alliance. The Americans were very suspicious of General de Gaulle. They were contemptuous of his Free French supporters, whom they regarded as indifferent fighters and masters of intrigue.[39] Furthermore, they had no particular desire to see a powerful France re-emerging after the war because this would make the business of Four-Power peace-keeping more difficult. President Roosevelt was of the opinion that France and Poland, for example, should be kept in a state of disarmament after the war. His view was that if Germany were properly disarmed the French would not need a big military establishment.[40] After the Free French Committee had been established, President Roosevelt had exerted strong pressure on

Mr Churchill to break with de Gaulle, pressure which had already been brought to bear several times during the preceding months.[41] Although the Prime Minister had himself often been vexed by the General's autocratic and uncompromising attitude, he refused to jettison the Free French leader, and in this he had the firm support of his colleagues in the War Cabinet. Mr Eden, in particular, realized that to snub de Gaulle would create a serious rift in the French community outside France, as well as giving heart to the Vichyites.[42]

The fact was that the Americans were not so interested in the revival of a strong France as were the British. The Americans did not trust the French, nor did they feel them to be necessary for their future system of international security. Indeed, the French might well increase the complexity of the Alliance and the strains within it. On 12 July Mr Eden wrote to Mr Churchill that the Americans disliked the growth of an independent French spirit and wished the French authorities to comply without question with their demands. For Britain this would be a mistaken policy. Her major problem after the war would be the containment of Germany. The treaty with the Soviet Union would have to be balanced by an understanding with a powerful France in the West. He went on to say:

> Our whole policy towards France and Frenchmen should therefore be governed by this consideration ... in dealing with European problems of the future we are likely to have to work more closely with France even than with the United States, and while we should naturally concert our French policy so far as we can with Washington, there are limits beyond which we ought not to allow our policy to be governed by theirs. . . .
>
> Europe expects us to have a European policy of our own and to state it. . . .[43]

One feature of this European policy was Mr Eden's effort to establish a regional security organization for Europe based on a Continental settlement which would ensure an effective balance of power. The chief object of the balance would be the containment of Germany, but independence from undue Soviet influence was an unspoken objective of great importance in British circles. This did not mean that the British Government expected the Soviet Union to be a hostile element once the war was over. Like the Americans, they were eager to see the Grand Alliance carried over from war to peace. But they were also aware of their own comparative weakness in the league of the Great Powers. A European continent consisting only of weak or hostile states from the Channel to the Russian frontier would be an uncomfortable neighbour for Great Britain. As Mr Churchill put it, 'the prospect of having no strong country between England and Russian was not attractive'.[44]

The chief difficulty, from the British point of view, lay in Eastern Europe. It was, after all, the area which posed most problems when planning a stable post-war settlement. The independent states established between Germany and Russia after the First World War had been the object of predatory ambitions from East and West, ambitions which had revealed themselves most clearly in the Nazi–Soviet Pact of 1939. It was for Poland that Britain and France had entered the war. The Czechs had lost their independence as a result of the notorious Munich Agreement, which had already been declared null and void by the Free French and the British in 1942.[45]* The exiled Governments of Poland and Czechoslovakia were active and vocal in London, whilst the gallantry of their expatriate soldiers and airmen had intensified public sympathy for their cause. Yet Eastern Europe was almost inaccessible to the Western Powers. Only if there was a dramatic collapse of German influence in the Danube Basin could the British and the Americans hope to create a physical presence in this region. After Stalingrad the chances were that Soviet, rather than Western, troops would liberate Poland and Czechoslovakia and press into the Danube Basin.

From the point of view of the Western Allies it was therefore essential that agreement be reached about the independence and territorial integrity of Eastern European states. The Poles, especially, were in a very awkward situation. For them the Soviet Union had been nearly as much to blame in encompassing their doom as the Germans. It would need skilful diplomacy to create a Polish–Soviet settlement favourable to Poland. Unhappily the Poles were better at fighting than at diplomacy. Their physical courage was only too well matched by their inflated political appetites. It was a very uncomfortable fact, for example, that the Poles had played the part of jackals – if not accomplices – when Hitler had dismembered Czechoslovakia in 1938. Far from trying to protect Czechoslovakia, they had seized the economically valuable area of Teschen from their helpless Czech neighbours. This had not been a good beginning for a state whose security might depend on the moral support of other nations.[46] As for Russia's annexations in 1939, it was unfortunate for the Poles that most of this territory lay to the east of a frontier line accepted by Allied statesmen in 1920. The boundary had roughly corresponded to the eastern limits of 'Congress Poland' as recognized by the European Powers at Vienna in 1815.† The area seized by the Russians was regarded by the Poles as historically Polish because much of it had only gone to Russia under the terms of the third

* See below, App. A, 'Note on the Present Position of the Munich Agreement'.
† This later became known as the 'Curzon Line' (see above, p. 46 n.).

Polish partition in 1795. But it was of mixed nationality, and historical claims of this nature could scarcely be expected to carry much weight under the desperate circumstances of the Second World War.

The leaders of Poland's Government-in-exile believed that the way to safeguard their country's interests was to insist on the maximum territorial claims they could possibly advance in all areas. They refused to consider any modification of their pre-war frontier with the Soviet Union. They notified their allies that they intended to retain their claim to Teschen, despite the odious circumstances under which it had been obtained.[47] In addition to this, they made it clear that East Prussia ought to go to Poland after the war as a safeguard against renewed German aggression.[48] These were certainly breathtaking aspirations for a nation, every inch of whose territory was occupied by enemy forces. They aroused a good deal of irritation among Poland's allies in the West, for whom good relations with Russia seemed more important than the territorial claims of an exiled Polish Government. Both the British and the Americans were willing to see East Prussia go to Poland, and it was known that Stalin also favoured this change.[49] On the other hand it was realized that it would be much more difficult to guarantee the Poles their eastern territories. Stalin had made Russian views on this subject quite clear in December 1941.[50] The British Foreign Office and the American State Department were in a dilemma over the Polish frontier question. It had been accepted as a principle of Allied diplomacy that no territorial arrangements should be made until they could be properly discussed at a peace conference. For this reason the Western Powers had not accepted the demands put by Stalin to Mr Eden in Moscow.[51] Concessions to Russia in the case of Poland would also involve acceptance of Soviet claims to the Baltic States and to parts of Finland and Rumania. On the other hand, if the Polish question was left until the end of the war, the Poles might be left in a perilous situation.

Had the Poles themselves pressed for a territorial settlement with the Soviet Union they might have persuaded their Western Allies to accept it. Certainly, by the summer of 1943, the British and the Americans were coming round to the view that such an agreement was necessary, although they failed to align their policies in an effective way.* But the Poles themselves were quite inflexibly determined that no inch of their territory should be surrendered to Stalin.

In December 1941, for example, Stalin suggested to General Sikorski, the leader of the exiled Polish Government, that it might be possible to agree on a territorial settlement based on Poland's pre-war frontiers, with certain minor 'rectifications' in Russia's favour.[52] It was not clear how

* See below, pp. 109 and 116.

large these changes were going to be, but Stalin insisted that they were very small.* Sikorski refused even to listen to the Soviet proposals. He claimed that he was not empowered by his Government to entertain the possibility of a reduction in Polish territory. It was a refusal which illustrated the limitations in Sikorski's character, limitations which were tragically characteristic of Poland's exiled leaders.

By 1943 the situation had changed in a way unfavourable to the Poles. The Soviet Government had gained in self-confidence as a result of its victories against the Germans. It began to feel that it could settle Russo-Polish frontier questions without much reference either to the Western Allies or to the Polish Government in London. The Poles, for their part, became even more suspicious of the Russians, and directed their efforts towards arousing Anglo-American resistance to Soviet demands in Eastern Europe. The Poles were certainly right to distrust the Soviet Union. Unfortunately their tactics were very inept. Propaganda emphasizing Polish territorial claims was ill-received in the West. The British and the Americans began to find their gallant Polish allies a source of irritation.† It was damaging for Poland that her Government was regarded in London and Washington as basically undemocratic, expressing the wishes of the feckless, if delightful, Polish ruling class. In 1939 this had been an advantage. Nobody could accuse the Warsaw régime of being inclined towards Bolshevism, as had been the case with the Czech Government in Prague.‡ But after Russia's entry into the war the political climate in London had changed. Now 'Fascism' was the great enemy, and it could plausibly be argued that the Poles were not free of an anti-democratic taint. This criticism of the Polish Government, together with a human if not altogether heroic desire to avoid difficulties with Russia, contributed to a Press campaign in London against the Poles. The intransigent behaviour of some exiled Polish leaders did not improve matters.[54]

The Russians well knew how to exploit this situation. When, in 1943, the Nazis made known the horrifying details of the Katyn massacres,§

---

* He described them as merely being a '*chut-chut*', or barely perceptible, change. This was certainly disingenuous.

† When Mr Eden visited Washington in March 1943 he complained to the President and Harry Hopkins about the difficulties being made by the Poles. For example, he described how Sikorski insisted that a cruiser offered to the Polish navy by the British Government should be called the *Lwow*. This was a city in the area disputed between Russia and Poland. It had no naval significance, since it was not a seaport. This was clearly designed to score off the Russians. When the British refused to cede the cruiser if it were given such a provocative name, Sikorski rejected it altogether.[53]

‡ There was, of course, no truth in this allegation against the Czech Government.

§ On 5 April 1943 the Germans announced that they had found the bodies of over 10,000 Polish officers who had been taken prisoner by the Russians in 1939 and cold-bloodedly murdered. The bodies had been discovered buried in a wood at Katyn, not

Polish demands for an independent inquiry were used by the Soviet authorities as a pretext to withdraw recognition from the Polish Government in London.* This led to intensified Allied pressure on the Poles to be conciliatory towards the Russians, because it was feared that Stalin might otherwise establish his own pro-Communist Polish Government and make arrangements with that. It was thus at a desperate moment in Poland's fortunes that, on 4 July 1943, General Sikorski was killed in an air crash at Gibraltar.† For the Poles fighting under Allied leadership in the Middle East, the Soviet Union and elsewhere, the chances of their homeland regaining its integrity began to look very slender.

In the case of Czechoslovakia the situation was apparently more promising. Soviet relations with the Czechs had always been more cordial than with almost any other Eastern European country. A close feeling of affinity existed between the Czechs and their Slav brothers in Russia. More important than this was the advantage the Czechs possessed in their exiled President, Dr Eduard Beneš. A statesman of the highest quality, his masterly diplomacy had been unable to save his small country from Nazi occupation, but it had unmasked Hitler's aggressive nature before the eyes of the world. Having taken refuge in London, Beneš applied himself to the creation of a stable balance of power in Europe once the war had been brought to a successful conclusion. He believed that, if peace was to be lasting in Eastern Europe, smaller states like his own would have to establish genuine friendly relations with their most powerful neighbours and co-operate with them in a system of collective security. He was therefore eager to come to an agreement with the Soviet Union, a policy which recommended itself to his Western allies.

---

far from Smolensk. Since the Poles themselves had long been trying to trace several thousand of their officers who had disappeared in Russia in the spring of 1940, the German claim that the massacre had been committed by the Russians seemed plausible. The Poles demanded an independent Red Cross inquiry. The Soviet Government alleged that the massacre had been carried out by the Germans. There seems little doubt that the murders were, in fact, the work of the Russian security forces. When, in 1945, Goering and other war criminals were indicted at Nuremberg as being responsible for the Katyn murders, they were acquitted of these particular charges, and the accusation was quietly dropped.[55]

* The Polish Government, for its part, suspended diplomatic relations with the Soviet Union and delegated the supervision of its interests to the Australian Government.

† The ludicrous charge was subsequently made by the German writer Rolf Hochhuth, in his play *The Soldiers*, that General Sikorski's plane had been sabotaged with the connivance of Mr Churchill, in order to remove a source of Anglo-Russian friction and to prevent Stalin from making a separate peace with Germany. A spirited riposte, based on copious research and travel, was later written by Carlos Thompson.[56]

Czechoslovakia did, indeed, enjoy a number of advantages vis-à-vis Poland when trying to obtain Allied support for her policy. The Czechs, unlike the Poles, made no ambitious demands for territory from their neighbours, and since they had no common frontier with the Soviet Union it seemed unlikely that they would be under pressure to cede parts of their country to Russia. The chief aim of Beneš's Government was to restore the *status quo* as it had existed before the Munich Agreement in 1938, with the proviso that the Czechs should be allowed to expel German minorities from Czechoslovak territory. The Allies were only too willing to accept this moderate programme. In May and June 1943 Beneš made a very successful visit to Washington, where he obtained President Roosevelt's agreement to a transfer of the Sudeten German population from Czechoslovakia to Germany.[57] He was encouraged in his desire to go to Moscow to arrange an understanding with the Soviet Government, and arrangements were made for him to visit Russia towards the end of 1943.

The British Government opposed a Czech–Soviet pact on the grounds that Russia and Britain had agreed not to make separate agreements with smaller states while the war was in progress. But at the Conference of Foreign Ministers in Moscow in October 1943, Mr Eden dropped his objections to Beneš's scheme.[58]

Beneš may have been mistaken in believing that co-operation with the Soviet Union was possible after the war. But he was surely right in thinking that arrangements made before Russian troops arrived in Eastern Europe were better than no arrangements at all.

Whatever the Soviet attitude to exiled Governments in London, it was obvious that the pre-war settlement of Eastern Europe could not be restored with any hope of permanence. Mr Eden and his colleagues in the British Foreign Office were stimulated to produce more ambitious plans for the development and security of Germany's eastern neighbours. The British Foreign Office projected a scheme for a Federation of Eastern and Central European States which would be capable of resisting further German aggression. This would participate in a wider scheme of European security. There should also be a Scandinavian Federation to protect Northern Europe from a repetition of the Hitlerite aggressions in 1940. It was at first hoped that the Eastern Federation could include Poland, Rumania and Bulgaria as well as Czechoslovakia, Hungary, Austria and Yugoslavia.* The Soviet Government showed

---

* The Poles had been eager supporters of an Eastern European Federation. In October 1939 August Zaleski, the Foreign Minister in the new Polish Government under Sikorski, proposed in London that there should be a federation of Poland with the Danubian countries, perhaps in the form of a monarchy under the Archduke Otto von Habsburg.[59] This proposal was unlikely to find much favour with the old members

no enthusiasm for any such far-reaching proposal. However, in conversation with Mr Eden in London, M. Maisky, the Soviet Ambassador, said that his Government would probably not object to a Balkan Federation, provided it excluded Rumania, or to a Scandinavian Federation, provided that it excluded Finland. Nor did he reject the idea of a Polish–Czechoslovak Federation so long as Poland possessed a Government friendly to the Soviet Union.[61] The British, therefore, entertained hopes of achieving some form of Danubian Federation to be incorporated in a Council of Europe.

Unfortunately, the American Government was not at all enthusiastic about this conception. To Mr Hull, for example, it smacked of power politics and spheres of interest. The President, for his part, was eager to see world peace-keeping managed by four Great Powers, with the old states of Europe kept firmly under control by the mighty forces to the West and the East. He hoped to be able to extend the principle of United Nations trusteeship – in which he placed great faith – into Europe. This would eliminate the need for creating new power structures there. For example, the President was quite convinced that Serbs and Croats should no longer be forced to live in unwelcome proximity, and suggested that Croatia be placed under United Nations supervision.[62]

The differences between London and Washington were not confined to problems of international security. There were other matters about which entirely opposing views were held, and foremost among these was the question of colonies. President Roosevelt's belief in the trusteeship system extended far beyond the boundaries of Europe. He was very eager that it should be used to help liberate dependent territories from their former rulers. In particular, he wished to set up trusteeships in the Far East when those areas overrun by the Japanese should be freed by the Allies. The Americans wished to see France relinquish her hold on Indo-China and Britain give up Hong Kong. In both these cases China was to be the beneficiary.[63] These proposals were not calculated to cheer the British Prime Minister or his Foreign Secretary. Mr Churchill remarked that he had not become Prime Minister in order to preside over the dissolution of the British Empire, an observation prompted by an obvious American interest in the granting of independence to

of the East European 'Little Entente', and particularly with the Czechs. The Poles later urged the Czechs to join with them at least in a bilateral federation, but the Czechs rightly suspected that Poland hoped to be the leading partner in such a union, and that Polish leaders were more favourably inclined towards Hungary than towards Czechoslovakia.[60] In any case, the Federation scheme was connected more with the anti-Russian Poles than with the more pro-Soviet Czechs, and this itself was enough to weaken the proposal's chances in both Moscow and Washington.

India.* As for Mr Eden, he had already made his views on Asia clear when he visited Washington in March 1943. When President Roosevelt stressed his desire to build China up as a Great Power, Mr Eden prophetically commented that the Chinese might well experience a revolution after the war, and he 'did not much like the idea of the Chinese running up and down the Pacific'.[65] In response to suggestions that Britain might surrender Hong Kong as a gesture of goodwill, the British Foreign Secretary remarked that the Americans had not proposed any similar gestures on their part.[66] Mr Eden also noted the apparent disregard for French interests shown by the President. On 27 March Roosevelt suggested that Britain and the United States might act as 'policemen' at Dakar and Bizerta after the war. He was not pleased when Sumner Welles reminded him that America had promised France the restoration of all her overseas possessions.[67]

Mr Eden, although just as determined not to surrender on the colonial issue as was his chief, had not wished to appear intransigent or unreasonable. In deference to American wishes a British declaration of intent about colonial territories was drafted and submitted for approval by the War Cabinet on 9 December 1942.[68] This had been sent to Washington for consideration, but had proved insufficiently radical to satisfy the American Government. At the end of March 1943 Hull had presented Eden with some counter-proposals of a most far-reaching kind. These placed all dependent territories under United Nations trusteeship and pledged the colonial Powers responsible for them to promise independence within a stated period. Although a British *aide-mémoire* had been passed to the American Ambassador, John Winant, in London outlining British objections to this plan, Mr Hull had either not been shown these British comments or had chosen to ignore them.[69] In either case he was not likely to drop the question, which was, as he later remarked, 'a subject very close to my heart'.[70]

Thus it was that the conference at Quebec in August 1943 – originally conceived by President Roosevelt as a sequel to his own *tête-à-tête* with Stalin – became a wide-ranging discussion of strategic and diplomatic objectives, a discussion held against a comforting background of military victory, but disturbed by many serious differences of principle and approach.

* During his visit to Washington in September 1943 Mr Churchill was introduced by President Roosevelt to Mrs Helen Ogden Mills Reid, a Vice-President of the *New York Herald Tribune* and a severe critic of British policy in India. After lunch at the White House the conversation turned to this subject. The Prime Minister at once said: 'Before we proceed further let us get one thing clear. Are we talking about the brown Indians of India, who have multiplied alarmingly under the benevolent British rule? Or are we speaking of the red Indians of America who, I understand, are almost extinct?' The President laughed heartily and Mrs Reid did not pursue the argument.[64]

III

On 5 August Mr Churchill and a delegation of over two hundred persons, including Orde Wingate* and Wing-Commander Guy Gibson,† set sail in the *Queen Mary* for Halifax, Nova Scotia. On the voyage – which was, as usual, a hard-working affair – the question of the Western landings was taken in hand. General Morgan and Vice-Admiral Lord Louis Mountbatten explained to the Prime Minister their plans for overcoming the natural obstacles to a Channel crossing.[71] Yet, despite this diligence, the Quebec Conference – code-named 'Quadrant' – was not destined to be as successful for the British strategists as Casablanca or even 'Trident'. President Roosevelt and his advisers were absolutely determined that this time they should not be deflected from their grand design in the West, no matter how enticing the prospects might be elsewhere. The staffs in the Pentagon had 'analysed at length the technique of previous conferences, the debating techniques of the British and even the precise number of planners required to cope on equal terms with the British staffs. . . . They went to Quebec determined to make their ideas prevail by all means at their disposal.'[72] General Marshall told his colleagues that 'we must go into this argument in the spirit of winning'. He and Admiral King were agreed on a conception of global strategy in which expanded Mediterranean activities had no part. For one thing, there would be no landing craft available, since King was taking the lion's share for his assaults on the Gilbert Islands.

The British delegation, on the other hand, was not quite so united in its policies as had been the case at Casablanca. On the one hand both Mr Churchill and his military advisers wished to exploit the Mediterranean situation to the utmost. On the other, they were eager to gain general agreement for the plans for a cross-Channel operation which had been drawn up in London. Even General Brooke – normally a severe critic – was prompted to express cautious praise when considering

---

* Major-General Orde Charles Wingate, D.S.O., R.A. (1903–44). An original leader of guerrilla forces, Wingate had seen service before the war in the Sudan, Transjordan and Palestine, where he won the first of two D.S.O.s. In 1942, having directed irregular forces with great success in Ethiopia, he was given command of a mixed brigade of British, Gurkha and Burmese troops in Burma. Supplied from the air, these 'Chindits', as they came to be called, were able to penetrate into the jungle far behind the Japanese lines. In 1944 Wingate was appointed to lead an airborne force to invade central Burma, but in March of that year he was killed in an air crash.

† Wing-Commander Guy Penrose Gibson, V.C., D.S.O., D.F.C., R.A.F. (1918–44). The Commander of 617 Squadron, a specialist bomber force entrusted with particularly hazardous operations. Its most famous exploit was the bombing of the Möhne and the Eder dams on 16 May 1943. Experience gained by this squadron was important in the development of precision techniques used by Bomber Command at a later stage in the war. Gibson himself was killed in action on 19 September 1944.

General Morgan's proposals. It was, said the C.I.G.S., 'a good plan, but too optimistic as to the rate of advance to be expected'.[73] From the British point of view the attack on the French coast could only succeed if diversions in the Mediterranean weakened the German opposition in the West. Yet the Americans were in a strong position to argue that, since the number of troops and vessels which could be supplied to Europe was limited, they should be concentrated on the Western offensive and not dissipated elsewhere.

The British were also on difficult ground when it came to discussing the Far East. British operations in Burma had not been proceeding with any success, and Mr Churchill was eager to settle on some stroke in the South-east Asian theatre that would restore British prestige. He had an exaggerated respect for the Japanese as jungle fighters, claiming that to wage war against them in this element was like 'going into the water to fight a shark'.[74] He hit on a scheme for seizing the north-western tip of Sumatra in an amphibious operation. This plan – which he had also espoused during his earlier visit to Washington and now championed with redoubled vigour – was to be an Oriental 'Torch' which would utilize Allied sea power and might prove an effective substitute for jungle warfare.

Hence the Quebec Conference opened with the British delegation being unaware that the American staffs did not share their basic premises. They assumed that the Pacific would be firmly relegated to the background, though they were ready to discuss proposals for improving their own operations against the Japanese. The Americans, on the other hand, wished to close down any further aggressive operations in the Mediterranean and were not willing to bring the number of troops to Britain which the British staffs felt to be essential for the Western assault. Brooke insisted on 25 per cent more landing craft for 'Overlord' than the plans recommended, and urged on the most rapid build-up of American troops.[75] When the Americans refused to accept his requirements he and his colleagues emphasized that, without satisfaction on this point, the Allies would have to reduce German strength in France and the Low Countries by diversionary operations elsewhere. It was over this point that the British ran into rock-like opposition from Admiral King. No landing craft could be diverted from his theatre.[76] On 15 August Marshall actually threatened that the war would be reoriented towards Japan.[77] This was probably an exaggerated threat, but it exemplified American determination to reject British proposals for a modification of their own European plans.

The confused reports coming in from Italy meant that a great deal of time had to be spent considering the exploitation of Italian surrender, and the fact that Mr Churchill had offered the Supreme Command of the cross-Channel operation to the Americans meant that General Brooke tended to have a weak position in the strategic argument vis-à-vis General Marshall. Mr Churchill had done his best to support his military chiefs, but his interventions in matters of Far Eastern strategy had not always been very helpful. He had, it is true, advanced his usual and always powerful warnings of the appalling casualties that might be suffered in the Western operation – warnings which apparently served only to reinforce American fears that the cross-Channel venture was in danger of being shelved.

After much fierce argument agreement was finally reached, but the result was by no means entirely encouraging for the British. The Chief of the Imperial General Staff wrote: 'I am not really satisfied with the results. We have not really arrived at the best strategy, but I suppose when working with allies, compromises, with all their evils, become inevitable.'[78]

The Allied deliberations established as objectives a second front in France in May 1944, a stabilization of the Italian offensive north of Rome, an increased air assault on Germany and combined operations of an extensive character against the Japanese. It was not a result which entirely suited Mr Churchill, but he put a brave face upon it when reporting back to the War Cabinet in London. 'Everything here', he cabled, 'has gone off well. We have secured a settlement of a number of hitherto intractable questions – e.g. the South-East Asia Command,* "Tube Alloys",† and French Committee‡ recognition. On this last we had an awful time with Hull, who has at last gone off in a pretty sulky mood, especially with the Foreign Secretary, who bore the brunt. . . .'[79]

Mr Eden had, indeed, been experiencing a rough passage with Cordell Hull. When the two Foreign Secretaries met in the Citadel at Quebec on 20 August, the French Committee of Liberation was the first issue to demand their attention. Mr Eden put the case for recognizing de Gaulle's Committee very strongly. He pointed out to Hull that the British had to live twenty miles from France and wanted to rebuild her as far as they could.[80] Hull was firmly against any concession to the Gaullists. He sought to exploit the differences which were thought to exist on this issue between Mr Eden and the Prime Minister by remarking that Mr Churchill's telegrams to the President had at no time expressed disagreement with American policy.[81] He also accused the

* Admiral Mountbatten had been appointed to the Supreme Command in that theatre in an effort to inject new vigour into the British effort there.
† The code-name for atom-bomb research.
‡ The French Committee of Liberation – the Gaullist Free French organization in London. It demanded recognition as the true government of France.

British of financing de Gaulle, implying that this money was being used to attack American policy.[82] Mr Eden sturdily defended the Free French leader, saying that in 1940 he had been Britain's only friend – a statement which did not altogether please his American colleague.[83] The discussion became really very acrimonious, although both men were much too experienced in the business of diplomacy to lose their tempers entirely. But the French question proved intractable, despite Mr Churchill's cheerful claim to his Government colleagues. After at least two days of argument the British and the Americans resigned themselves to issuing different statements about their policies towards the Free French Committee.[84]

Nor was this the only matter on which the two Foreign Secretaries found themselves at cross-purposes. Mr Hull began to press Eden persistently on the colonial question. He referred to the American proposals guaranteeing independence to colonial territories within a measurable period. When he brought this matter up for the third time, the British Foreign Secretary had to tell him frankly that he disliked the American proposals. He pointed out that the word 'independence' would create great difficulties within the British Empire, in which there were varying degrees of autonomy and subjugation. Some colonies had complete self-government, whilst others were so backward that it was thought unlikely they would ever be ready for independence.[85] There was also the question of Dominion susceptibilities. Australia and New Zealand, for example, had colonies which they would be loath to surrender.

Mr Hull's anti-imperialism was not dimmed by this rebuff. In his own words he believed that the subject was 'too important for the long-range advancement of the world to let it drop'.[86] He dug in his toes for a lengthy struggle.

In face of these set-backs there were some positive achievements, although they marked no very great development in the thinking of either Government. Mr Hull put the American plan for a Four-Power Declaration on peace-keeping after the war to Mr Eden and, as was to be expected, the Foreign Secretary expressed satisfaction with it. This was of great significance from the American viewpoint. Yet it did not mark any very large step forward in the settlement of post-war problems. It was a declaration of intent which involved no detailed commitments and which had yet to be accepted by the Soviet Union.

Both men also agreed that the Western Powers should co-ordinate their policy on the question of Russia's western frontiers. If they had to make concessions to Russia they should be ready to table their needs in return.[87] Mr Eden was particularly eager to get some agreement about this before the Russians actually entered Polish territory, since then the Polish–Soviet problem would be much more difficult to solve.[88] He gave Mr Hull a note outlining the demands which Russia would probably make on her western neighbours. A somewhat stormy meeting thus ended on a note of co-operation, if not of triumph.

The next stage in any discussion of Allied war aims would clearly have to involve the Russians themselves. Since Stalin's renewed friendliness, or at least willingness to communicate, had coincided with Mr Churchill's departure for the United States, the Prime Minister had taken the opportunity to renew suggestions for a tripartite meeting. Stalin this time expressed his willingness to meet his co-belligerents. However, it proved impossible to agree on a meeting-place, since Stalin claimed that his presence was needed at home to direct military operations, and President Roosevelt was not inclined to go to Russia. Stalin suggested that, in the meantime, a preparatory meeting of 'responsible representatives of our states' should be held. It was agreed that this should take the form of a conference of Foreign Ministers who could exchange views and prepare the ground for a summit conference. Mr Churchill suggested that London would be a good place to hold the meeting, but Stalin plumped firmly for Moscow. He promised to meet Churchill and Roosevelt himself in November or December, and proposed that their meeting could be held in Persia.[89] In this, as in most of his other demands, Stalin was to be satisfied.

IV

The Moscow Conference, which began on 19 October 1943, was really the first genuine step taken towards a tripartite conduct of Allied policy since the Allies had begun to seize the initiative in military operations. It came after the crisis had been successfully passed, but in a situation still capable of catastrophic developments. It had to overcome many years of accumulated – and usually well-merited – hostility and suspicion. The negotiators bore with them all the time the knowledge that the special conditions which forged a mighty alliance might disappear when peace came. In any case, the Allied Powers had serious divergences of interest in many parts of the world.

For the Soviet Union the first priority at the meeting was to pin the British and the Americans down on the question of a second front. They cleverly made this their only requirement when the agenda of the meeting was being arranged in September 1943.[90] Since the Russians were advancing towards Eastern Europe there was no need for them to concern themselves unduly about the regulation of frontiers there. This would be especially true if the Western Powers were persuaded to throw their major effort against Hitler's Western Wall.

Otherwise the Soviet Government intended to maintain its freedom of action in Eastern Europe and to obtain the greatest possible influence over other territories which might be liberated by its allies. The Russians wanted no agreement to any form of political settlement in Central and Eastern Europe which would prevent them establishing their influence there. Hence they wished to avoid committing themselves to definite principles of conduct governing the administration of liberated territories, and they had no desire to consider schemes for possible federation among the old successor states of the Austro-Hungarian Empire. Above all they did not want to reopen relations with the Polish Government in London or come to any agreement about the manner of Poland's liberation. There was a large underground army inside Poland supported by the four major Polish parties – none of which was Communist.[91] The Russians wanted no Western collaboration with this Polish patriotic movement. Nor did they wish to be embarrassed by the political demands of the Polish Government in London. They were equally unwilling to discuss the future of Yugoslavia. In the case of Czechoslovakia the Soviet Government was eager to see the British and the Americans accept Beneš's proposed Czech–Soviet pact.* This would simply emphasize Soviet influence in Eastern Europe without tying Russia's hands politically.

If Britain and America were to keep their noses out of Eastern Europe, Stalin saw no reason why the Soviet Union should exercise any such restraint further west. The Soviet authorities wished to be associated with the Allied administration in Italy and to have a say in the political future of France. On the one hand, they might thereby assist the progress of Communism in those two countries, and on the other they could use claims for a part in the administration of these areas as a bargaining counter against possible Western demands to supervise developments in Eastern Europe.

Generally speaking, the Russians were cautious about the future of Germany, and preferred to let their allies commit themselves to proposals which might later prove embarrassing.[92] On questions of international security and economic aid the Soviet Government was quite willing to accept American proposals so long as they did not limit Soviet action in its chosen spheres, and so long as the Soviet Union was not restricted in her claim for reparations from Germany.

The British had more complex aims, although they, like the Americans, were motivated by a genuine desire to come to a good understanding

* See above, pp. 95–6.

with Russia. Mr Churchill was well aware how bitter the disappointment over the 'Trident' decisions had been in Moscow, and he particularly wanted to avoid making promises of a grandiose character which might be impossible to fulfil.[93] At the same time he was worried about the situation in the Mediterranean, regarding the Anglo-American plans for deployment there as inadequate for either the capture of Rome or the exploitation of possible opportunities in the Balkans. He felt that to sacrifice all the possible gains in the Mediterranean simply because of a 'lawyer's agreement' about the timetable for 'Overlord' would be an act of military folly. He feared that by hurrying 'Overlord' on too fast the Western Powers might incur defeats on two fronts instead of winning two decisive victories.

On 11 October 1943 the Prime Minister drew up a set of instructions for Mr Eden's guidance at the Moscow meetings. These stressed that Britain sought no territory or special advantage for herself as the outcome of the war, but that she strongly supported a League of Nations which would include a Council of Europe, with an International Court and an armed force capable of implementing its decisions. The armistice period at the end of the war might be prolonged, and during that period the three Great Powers, together with the Chinese, should remain united and well armed. Countries occupied by the Axis should have their sovereign rights restored. It was made fairly clear that Britain would accept an alteration of Poland's pre-war frontiers in favour of Russia in the east. This should be balanced by Polish acquisitions of German territory to the west. Nazi and Fascist Governments were to be extirpated from hostile countries, but this was not to exclude the possibility of negotiation with interim Governments if such negotiations would save Allied lives. This stipulation once again illustrated that Unconditional Surrender was a formula which did not impose insufferably rigid restrictions on the Allies or their diplomacy. As for Germany, her future was to be decided by the victor Powers. She was to be disarmed and prevented from rearming. In any event, Mr Churchill clearly envisaged special treatment for Prussia, a state towards which he had retained the hostility generally felt during the First World War.[94]

The British Foreign Office had also begun to make preparations for the discussions in Moscow. The most pressing problems were those in which diplomatic difficulties seemed likely to hamper military operations. Thus Mr Eden was determined to ensure that Italy should be administered in a manner which, whilst recognizing inter-Allied responsibility, left control firmly in the hands of the theatre commander. He also wished to see some movement towards recognition of the Free French

National Committee. Above all, he wanted to establish machinery for the investigation of problems connected with the termination of hostilities in Europe.

Originally he had proposed a politico-military commission in Algiers to deal with the political side of the Italian settlement. The rapid march of events in Italy had made it necessary to have a separate administrative organization there. The Foreign Secretary then proposed a body with much wider terms of reference. Although concerning itself mainly with questions related to armistice terms, it would serve two wider purposes. It would prevent the confusion which had characterized Allied negotiations at the end of the First World War, and it would clarify conflicts about the future of Europe which might exist within the Alliance.[95]

Such a clarification could only be of benefit to the Western Powers. Mr Eden was well aware of the dangers which faced Europe as the result of Soviet military successes. He knew that 'liberation' was a word likely to find a different interpretation in Moscow from that accepted in Washington or London. He felt that definite commitments should be made about the policy to be pursued in areas occupied by United Nations forces. The political future of Eastern and Central Europe should be planned in such a way that the smaller nations there should be assured of genuine independence. All the Allies should renounce any desire to establish spheres of influence there. More specifically, Mr Eden wanted the Polish question raised, although he had scant hopes of Russian concessions on territorial matters. Yugoslavia was another area which required attention if Russo-British friction was to be avoided. The two Allies were in danger of supporting hostile groups among the Yugoslav partisans.

In the Middle East there were doubts about Russian policy towards Persia. This was a very important matter for any future peace settlement. Persia was the only part of the world occupied by Russian and British troops. It had been a traditional area of dispute between the two countries since long before the Bolshevik Revolution. After the war was over it would be certain to excite international ambitions because of its geographical location and its oil deposits. The British and the Americans hoped for a tripartite declaration on Persia which would eliminate fears of possible disharmony.[96]

On the American side, the Foreign Ministers' conference presented President Roosevelt with an awkward personal problem. He wanted to send the Under-Secretary of State, Sumner Welles, whose colourful personality and lively imagination were more attractive to him than the ponderous autocracy of Cordell Hull. Unfortunately, relations between Hull and Welles had become very strained in the summer of 1943. While

Mr Eden was at Quebec, Harry Hopkins told him that if Welles was sent to Moscow Hull would do his best to torpedo the meeting.[97] When Roosevelt then suggested that Welles might go to Moscow as a special emissary in order to save Mr Hull from such an arduous journey at his advanced age, the Secretary of State took prompt and effective action to squash any such possibility.[98]* Despite his own wish to send a man with whom he had established a close personal *rapport*, Roosevelt could not easily risk an open breach with Hull. The Secretary had enormous prestige in the American Congress, and the President knew that he had to carry the Legislature with him in foreign policy if he was to avoid the fate which had overtaken Wilson after the Paris Peace Conference.

From the British point of view this was an unfortunate development because Mr Eden was more likely to find willing co-operation from Welles than from Hull. Nevertheless, the main lines of American policy were probably not affected by the Secretary's determination to go to Moscow. He and the President shared common views on the need for a second front, and in any case Hull was far too cautious to commit himself on military matters. Mr Hull, like President Roosevelt, was eager to draw the Russians into a scheme of international collaboration and peace-keeping after the war was over. He therefore made up his mind to obtain Russian agreement to the Four-Power Declaration which he had shown the British at Quebec. Mr Hull had sent the draft of the Declaration to Moscow after it had been approved by Mr Churchill and his Foreign Secretary, but M. Molotov refused to accept it on the grounds that China had no interest in European matters. Mr Hull was alarmed and upset, if not entirely surprised. The aim of the Americans had been to gain from Russia recognition that the Chinese were of equal standing with the other Allies. For one thing Russia was not at war with Japan, and Mr Hull himself had grave doubts about their intention to embark upon hostilities in the Far East before the Japanese had been virtually defeated by the Western Powers.[99] Then he feared that Russia might intervene to occupy Manchuria and other frontier areas.

The American Government had every reason to concern itself about Russia's future policy towards China, since, if the Soviet Union recognized the Chinese as full partners in the Alliance, it could scarcely appropriate Chinese territory. There was also the problem of the Chinese Communist movement. The Americans wanted order and stability to return to China after the war. They thought that China would then be a co-operative ally.[100] The Communists were a divisive element and it was hoped that Russia might exercise a 'moral influence'

* Shortly after this Welles's position became so difficult that, on 25 September 1943, he resigned his post.

over them.[101] In this respect the dissolution of the Comintern in May 1943 had seemed a hopeful development.

The Americans gave priority to this question, and it was made the first item on their proposed agenda for the meeting. Mr Hull and President Roosevelt agreed that the former should come away from Moscow without having reached any agreement on a joint declaration if the Four-Power principle was not accepted.[102] Indeed, they expected trouble not only from the Russians, but also from the British. It was felt that Mr Churchill did not like China, and he may have had good reason for such an opinion in view of the American belief that China should be supported because of 'her influence over British India'.[103]

This question was discussed at a meeting in the White House on 5 October 1943. President Roosevelt ran over a number of general problems with Mr Hull and some other senior advisers, among them the new Under-Secretary of State, Edward Stettinius. After the Four-Power Declaration had been dealt with, the President turned to Germany. He had very strong views about this, claiming that his own experiences as a student in Germany had given him an insight into that country which his colleagues lacked. He advocated partition of the Reich into three or more states, although he thought there should be some common economic institutions such as a customs union and rail and postal services. Germany should be disarmed, Prussia detached from it and all dangerous elements of the population forcibly removed. The men from the State Department did not accept these views without reservation. Partition, it was argued, would have undesirable results, and the customs union would either fail to work or would become an instrument in a drive for reunification.[104] Indeed, the President does not seem to have had any very clear-cut ideas about Germany, despite his claim to expert knowledge. His suggested solution to the German problem was a contradictory rectification of both the territorial and the economic failings of the Versailles Treaty. He was forced to admit that his experience of Germany was rather far in the past, and the transitional period in that country would have to be one of trial and error. Reparations, he felt – and in this the Allies were all agreed – would have to be in manpower and equipment rather than money.[105] This, at least, was one lesson which had been learned from Versailles.

The conversation then turned to the matter of European frontiers outside Germany. Roosevelt spoke of making an appeal to Stalin on grounds of 'high morality' so that plebiscites should be held in the Baltic States and eastern Poland. This seems to have been largely designed to quell the rumblings of Western consciences. It was evident that the President – like Mr Churchill – expected the Russians to retain both the Baltic States and eastern Poland, and that neither of the Western Powers would be prepared to do anything to push Stalin out.[106]* On the question of the Low Countries the President had idiosyncratic views. He regarded Belgium as an artificial, bilingual state and referred to a German study drawn up in 1940 which had proposed a federal union of Alsace, Lorraine, Luxembourg and the two parts of Belgium. This was not a suggestion likely to find much favour anywhere in liberated Europe.† Fortunately the Americans did not persevere with it.

Lastly, the American desire for a new trusteeship system was stressed, and some idea was given of specific areas in which it might be applied. The Baltic passages and the Persian Gulf were mentioned, as well as Hong Kong and Indo-China. Other key points to be under international control included Dakar, Ascension Island and parts of the Dutch East Indies. By applying a form of trusteeship to colonial areas the inspection and publicity involved would encourage the imperial Powers to grant rapid independence. Once again, this was not a scheme which could be expected to find an easy passage at the conference table.[108] Great Britain, in particular, would oppose it at many points.

For the time being the Americans were not so much concerned about the reaction of their British colleagues. They were determined to fulfil their original intention of establishing their own special relationship with the Russians. At the very least they wished to eradicate any impression in Russian minds that the United States and Britain were bound together by particular ties of interest which excluded the Soviet Union. Above all, the Americans fostered the hope of encouraging Russia to commit herself to fight the Japanese.

On the British side, the situation was very different. Mr Churchill had always been inclined to arrange meetings with his American colleagues before going to see Stalin. Britain needed American support for her European security schemes, and if this was not forthcoming her hopes of achieving them would be very slender. Hence the British were eager for an opportunity to co-ordinate their preparations for the conference with those of the American delegation.

At the beginning of October Mr Eden suggested that he should meet the American Secretary of State in Cairo for a preliminary discussion before they went on to the Soviet Union. Hull firmly refused.[109] During the air flight to Moscow the American delegation did have a stop-over in Tehran and Mr Eden took this opportunity to visit Hull. The American

* Roosevelt wanted the boundary 'somewhat east of the Curzon Line'.

† It is fair to say that Stalin also showed up badly when discussing this particular region. In February 1948 he flatly told a delegation of Bulgarian and Yugoslav leaders that Holland was not a member of the Benelux customs union.[107]

restricted himself to 'a few greetings and casual observations', and although Mr Eden was not much perturbed by this taciturnity[110] Hull's attitude illustrated the line he was to follow once they were in Russia.

V

The lack of close Anglo-American collaboration at the conference was to prove of some importance in the course of the negotiations, especially during their early stages. Despite Mr Hull's refusal to meet his British colleague in Cairo, Mr Eden was not to be put off by American aloofness. On the day after their arrival in Moscow he visited the Secretary of State accompanied by the British Ambassador, Sir Archibald Clark Kerr. The American was living in Spaso House, the ex-home of a Tsarist sugar-king which had subsequently become the American Embassy. Eden arrived at noon on 18 October, the day before the conference held its first formal meeting. After discussing certain aspects of the publicity for the conference, Hull impressed upon his British visitors that the Soviet Government should be given every indication possible that both the United States and the British delegations were ready to discuss any matters separately with the Russians. Everything should be done to avoid a 'feeling of suspicion' on the part of the Soviet authorities that the British and American groups, living together as they were in the National Hotel, 'were conferring without giving the Soviet Government the benefit of their discussions'. It might have been retorted that the Russians had made the arrangements about the conference, and that, if there were difficulties of communication between them and the Western delegates, these came from the Soviet rather than the Western side.

In the face of this bleak introduction, the British Foreign Secretary did manage to raise a few concrete points. In particular, he pressed for the expansion of the Mediterranean Commission and its removal from Algiers to London, where it was to be the basis of the commission to study problems of European administration after liberation from the Axis. He also urged the American delegation to support him in pressing the Russians to reopen diplomatic relations with the exiled Polish Government. Hull did not commit himself very far and it was not a satisfactory meeting from a British viewpoint.[111]

As the conference progressed the two Western Foreign Secretaries seemed to be constantly falling foul of one another. The British had been prepared for trouble from Molotov; instead they were surprised by his affability.[112] On the other hand, Anglo-American co-operation was felt to be the natural order of things, and so when even minor differences cropped up they caused perhaps excessive irritation. Added to this was the fact that Mr Eden was possibly less pro-American and more 'European' in his outlook than other members of the War Cabinet, and that no close personal understanding existed between him and Mr Hull to compare with that between Mr Churchill and the American President.

All kinds of frictions contributed to Anglo-American difficulties. Even the temperature of the conference room was a matter about which the aged Mr Hull and his youthful British colleague had diametrically opposing views. On the first day of the proceedings Mr Hull was so cold that he sent for his overcoat. Apparently he liked to work in a temperature of about 90 degrees Fahrenheit. The Russians duly stoked up their boilers and the unfortunate Mr Eden thought he was going to faint. A compromise was eventually reached which was acceptable to both sides.[113]

Another cause of distrust was Mr Eden's *entrée* with Stalin. On breaking his journey at Tehran, Eden had not been overjoyed to find a telegram from the Prime Minister telling him of an offensive message sent by Stalin with reference to Arctic convoys. Mr Churchill had returned this with a diplomatic flourish to the new Russian Ambassador, Fedor Gusev.* It was now up to the Foreign Secretary to see Stalin and smooth matters over. Shortly after his arrival he asked Molotov to arrange a meeting with Stalin, and this duly took place on 21 October. The problem of the convoys was satisfactorily explained.[114] Mr Hull seems to have imagined that this conversation with Stalin had been prearranged by the British Government, and that it was part of an attempt to short-circuit the conference by going over the head of M. Molotov.[115] He virtuously resolved to arrange matters through the Russian Foreign Minister, and duly had an interview with Stalin himself.†

At the conference table itself the Western delegations did not at first fare much better. When the proceedings began in the Spiridonovka Palace on 19 October, there was a slight difference of opinion between Mr Eden and Mr Hull over the vexed question of Press releases, a point on which the American delegation was always politically sensitive. M. Molotov's smooth interjection to the effect that he did not see any real differences between the views of the two Western Foreign Secretaries was hardly calculated to increase the feelings of amity among his guests.[117]

---

* Mr Churchill used the phrase *'nul et non avenu'* when returning the Note to M. Gusev. It is unlikely that this meant very much to the Russian, whose French and English were limited.

† There was, of course, no foundation in Hull's suspicion since Eden had arranged his interview through Molotov.[116]

The next meeting saw a long and important explanation of Western strategy delivered to the Russians by Generals Ismay and John R. Deane. Although highly successful as a justification of the decisions taken at Quebec, some aspects of the meeting irritated the British diplomats present. The American General Deane seemed to them to be over-stressing his country's contribution to the war effort. In particular, the American day bomber offensive was put on an apparently equal footing with the R.A.F.'s night-time assaults on Germany, even though the latter were much more highly developed. General Deane made only passing references to the R.A.F. when discussing Allied bombing, and all his concrete examples were drawn from American operations.[118] He also urged co-operation between the Russian and United States Air Forces without mentioning the R.A.F. Mr Eden was provoked to intervene himself at the end of the military exposition, in order to give facts and figures about the size of Britain's contribution to Allied air power.[119]

This American tendency to play down British air strength evidently rankled with Mr Eden. After his conversation with Stalin on 21 October he wrote that, whereas Stalin fully understood the contribution Britain was making to the war, 'It is a danger to the future that his people don't [understand this] and now the Americans are making claims to a share in the bomber offensive which is by no means justified, but further dims our glory'.[120]

Then there was the question of Turkey and Sweden. The Russians raised this after the plans for a Western offensive had been explained to them. M. Molotov said that Russia wished to see both Sweden and Turkey enter the war. Cordell Hull primly declined to comment on military matters of that kind. He referred them to his Government. But Mr Eden was much more willing to discuss Molotov's proposals. The reason was not far to seek. For the Americans, the Soviet suggestions must have seemed an uncomfortable echo of Churchillian plans for military 'adventures' in the Mediterranean and Scandinavia. They might divert forces from the major theatre in France. But the British were exasperated at their failure to put more bite into operations in the Eastern Mediterranean, and Mr Churchill had been urging that Turkey be pressed into the war ever since the 'Torch' landings in North Africa.[121] It cannot have been very reassuring for the Americans to hear Mr Eden say that the British would be open to persuasion from the Russians on this issue, especially after he had pointed out the difficulty of involving Turkey in the war whilst Allied troops were having to be drawn away from the Eastern Mediterranean to bolster up other theatres.[122] Although Hull courteously stated that he thought his Government would share Eden's views on this subject, he was very much more reluctant to discuss it than was the British Foreign Secretary. When he did receive his instructions from Washington they were firmly negative ones.[123]*

On 23 October the conference turned its attention to the Balkans. Mr Eden urged that action should be taken to create a common policy towards the partisans in Yugoslavia. This – it was hoped – would eliminate the feuding between the two rival Yugoslav groups and intensify guerrilla activity against the Germans. It was clear that Molotov had no great interest in pursuing this question, and Hull flatly stated that he had nothing to add to Eden's remarks. The only further American contribution was an offer by General Deane to send O.S.S. units into the Balkans to carry out sabotage operations. Their purpose would, he assured M. Molotov, be 'purely military'. Neither the substance nor the form of this offer was likely to please the British Foreign Secretary.[125]

The conference had earlier begun to discuss the British proposal for an advisory commission to consider non-military problems arising from the war. Originally a draft had been produced for a body which would direct and co-ordinate the activities of armistice commissions set up to regulate the surrender of Axis Powers. It would be responsible for the maintenance of order in the countries concerned. In this respect it could be seen simply as a tool of diplomacy, an attempt to prevent Allied soldiers finding themselves in the same difficulties as General Eisenhower in Algiers some nine months earlier. But by October the situation had changed. Italian surrender, a problem which had loomed large in July and which had then seemed likely to be a major matter for such a commission to tackle, was now in the past. The proposal for a commission could, Mr Eden felt, be usefully turned to wider purposes. As he saw it at the conference it should be a 'form of clearing-house . . . with broad consultative powers to deal with general questions arising out of the war'.[126]

M. Molotov was not enthusiastic. He preferred the narrower definition in the earlier draft. This was not surprising, for, apart from an inevitable suspicion of new plans thrust on them from London, the Russians had no particular desire to see effective machinery established to iron out European problems. They preferred to let these problems ripen and solve themselves. Nevertheless, the prospects for the commission began to brighten as the conference progressed. A number of difficult matters – the occupation of Germany, the declaration on the treatment of liberated

---

* Churchill was eager to 'give Russia the right hand' by getting ships, supplies and other forces through the Black Sea. He cabled this view to Roosevelt on 23 October. There is no record of Roosevelt's reply.[124]

areas and the question of the civil administration of France – were referred to it.[127] The Russians did persuade Mr Eden to limit the terms of reference of the commission more specifically to matters connected with ending the war,[128] but it was still possible for it to be regarded as an institution which might play an important part in shaping a forthcoming peace settlement. This would largely depend on the use to which it was put by the three Allied Governments.

In fact Mr Eden did not press very strongly for the wider interpretation of the commission's powers, and he himself may not have been quite clear what its optimum role should be. He was preoccupied with the need to prevent Russian interest in Italy from hampering the effectiveness of the Allied Commander there. M. Molotov made great play with Soviet proposals for the extirpation of Fascism in Italy and went on to complicate the issue by demanding immediate delivery of some Italian warships and cargo vessels to the Soviet Union.[129]

Mr Eden had more success over Austria, and this was indeed the one territorial problem that was definitely settled at the conference. A British proposal was accepted according to which the *Anschluss* of March 1938 was declared null and void. After the war Austria should be separated from Germany.[130]* No conclusion was reached, however, about the treatment of Germany itself. Nor was M. Molotov much embarrassed by a British suggestion that there should be agreement about the right of liberated European nations to decide their own future. This involved the opportunity to form associations with other states so long as they did not endanger third parties. The Allied Powers should also renounce any thought of creating spheres of influence in Europe. The Russians scarcely needed to trouble themselves about this proposal because Mr Hull expressed his decided opposition to it. He urged that particular areas or special questions ought not to be considered before general principles were agreed on and said that

> he personally felt very strongly that the only orderly and reasonable approach to the entire question of international collaboration and the creation of a stable and lasting basis for world peace was to take the general questions first.[131]

Nevertheless, British interest in Eastern Europe, and in particular the suggestion that federations might be formed there, aroused M. Molotov to display his powerful negative qualities. He read a statement affirming Soviet eagerness to liberate small states but claiming that

> the premature and possibly artificial attachment of these countries to theoretically planned groupings would be full of danger, both for the

* See below, pp. 467–8.

1 Churchill on board the
Prince of Wales, looking
towards the *Augusta*, at
Placentia Bay, August 1941

2 President Roosevelt leaves
Union Station, Washington,
D.C., with Secretary of
State Cordell Hull after
returning from the Atlantic
Conference, 17 August 1941

3   Tehran: Mr Churchill entertains President Roosevelt and Marshal Stalin on 30 November 1943 – the Prime Minister's birthday

4   Tehran: Stalin – with Marshal Voroshilov on his left – talking to Harry Hopkins (fourth from left), 2 December 1943. Mr Eden is behind Stalin's right shoulder

small countries themselves as well as for the peaceful development of Europe. Such an important step as federation with other states and the possible renunciation of part of their sovereignty is admissible only as a result of a free, peaceful and well-considered expression of the will of the people.[132]

He doubted the ability of what he called *émigré* Governments, or even of Governments set up immediately after the war, to express the real will of the people.

It is astonishing that neither Mr Eden nor Mr Hull objected to the wording of this document, casting doubt as it did on the authority of numerous Allied Governments-in-exile, and making it clear that the Russians would put their own interpretation on the means by which the 'real will and permanent aspirations'[132] of European populations were to be ascertained. The British may have been thrown on to the defensive by a clever Soviet reference to a '*cordon sanitaire*' directed against Russia.[133] As for Mr Hull, Russian objections to the consideration of federations were in line with his desire to avoid specific commitments before general principles had been established. It was also fortunate for the Russians that American distaste for the Free French National Committee made it difficult for them to express blanket approval for all exiled Governments.*

There was, indeed, every reason for M. Molotov to feel satisfied with the conference's treatment of Continental Europe. Vagueness was the keynote of all declarations on this subject, and the farther east the problem was the vaguer and more negative the outcome. For example, on 27 October Mr Eden suggested that his proposal for a declaration on the treatment of liberated areas be referred to the London Commission,† a body which did not yet exist and whose terms of reference were to be severely limited by the conference itself.[135]

Perhaps the most pressing issue of all and the one on which the British felt that decisions ought to be taken was that of Poland. The Western Powers were really resigned to Poland losing territory to Russia after the war, but Eden felt that some efforts had to be made on behalf of the Polish Government in London before Poland's future was allowed to fall completely into the hands of the Soviet Union.[136] Expatriate Polish morale had to be taken into consideration, especially in view of the promises given to the Poles in London in July 1941.‡

The Foreign Secretary tried to press Hull into taking action about

* On the following day – 27 October – Mr Hull remarked that 'you might have governments in exile several of which would be entirely acceptable to our three governments and others concerning which there might be some doubt'.[134]

† The name given at the conference to the European Advisory Commission.

‡ See above, p. 35.

Poland, but, once again, the American was not willing to co-operate. He argued that he had no instructions on this point. It was hardly a convincing argument, since Mr Eden was not even suggesting that they raise the ticklish question of frontiers, but was simply urging a demonstration of 'keen concern for Poland's future'. Once again, Hull seems to have been motivated by a desire to avoid offending the Russians and his belief that territorial bargains should not be struck between the Great Powers in secret conclave. He was certainly well informed on the Polish side of the problem, and could not plead ignorance as an excuse for inaction.*

When Eden raised this issue at the conference on 29 October, Hull showed no conspicuous desire to back him up. He remarked that 'when two neighbours fell out the other neighbours, without going into the causes or merits of the dispute, were entitled to express the hope that these differences could be patched up'.[138] This was – as Mr Eden later remarked – 'a detached view of neighbourliness'. It is perhaps only fair to remark that the British do not themselves seem to have expected too much from these exchanges – Mr Eden closed his remarks by saying that 'he had spoken his piece on Poland and merely desired to reiterate that his Government was prepared to make any contribution which would be found possible looking toward the re-establishment of friendly relations between the Soviet Union and Poland'. Nevertheless, Mr Hull's apparently lukewarm attitude was not something which M. Molotov would be likely to overlook.

This tendency for the British and American delegations to work, if not at cross-purposes, at least in comparative isolation, was paralleled by private conversations between both groups and M. Molotov. Generally speaking, Eden seems to have informed Hull about his intention to sound Molotov out on specific topics like Poland and Yugoslavia. Hull, on the other hand, was eager to establish a personal relationship with Molotov. He hoped that mutual confidence between the Russian and American delegations could bring lasting rewards. Two hours after Eden had visited him on the first day after their arrival, Hull received Molotov. The Secretary of State stressed the need for co-operation between America and Russia after the war. Misunderstandings and suspicions between their peoples should be broken down. He therefore urged that subordinate members of the American delegation should meet their opposite numbers in the Soviet Government so that they could get to know one another and discuss common problems. He assured Molotov that he wanted co-operation between the three

---

* Before he left for Moscow Hull had received the Polish Ambassador, who explained Polish wishes at length.[137]

countries on an equal footing and that there should be no secrets between the three of them. Naturally enough, the Russian Foreign Minister expressed hearty approval.

At first, indeed, Molotov seemed to be responding to Mr Hull's treatment. When the American Secretary brought forward his proposals for a Four-Power Declaration on 21 October, Molotov was inclined to object to the inclusion of China in the statement. During an intermission for tea Hull pressed the Russian privately to give way on this issue. He made clear America's concern about the repercussions which could follow if China were to be treated with contempt by Russia, Great Britain and the United States. Hull took the opportunity of this private conversation to re-emphasize the practicability of developing closer relations between their two countries. There were, he claimed, no material or international interests which were not common to both countries. In matters of trade and economic affairs they were supplementary. He offered to discuss methods of establishing closer relations and better understanding between the two nations. The Russian Foreign Minister made suitably appreciative noises. What may have impressed him more than these offers of co-operation was the Secretary's remark that failure to obtain the Four-Power agreement might necessitate readjustments in United States policy designed to stabilize the situation in the Far East.[139] At any rate, he agreed to leave the question of Chinese participation open for the time being.[140]

Despite his persistent efforts to create closer understanding, Mr Hull became dissatisfied with the lack of positive action on matters which the Americans were eager to settle. The Four-Power Declaration, the meeting of the three Allied leaders and economic co-operation were apparently as far from being settled as ever. At another quiet talk during a tea-time recess Hull found himself being pressed by Molotov on the Turkish question, and, when he tried to discuss peace-time projects for economic collaboration, Molotov rather caustically asked if it was not true that isolationism had nearly been the ruin of the United States. Hull had to reply in the affirmitive, but pointed out that the same was true of the Soviet Union.[141]

The American Secretary of State felt that the conference was grinding on without achieving much result. His attempts at wooing the Russians, though successful socially, seemed to be falling flat so far as concrete achievements were concerned. This was especially true in relation to the fixing of the personal meeting between Roosevelt, Stalin and Churchill. Hull was coming under strong pressure from Washington on this point. Roosevelt was willing to travel far to meet Stalin, but he felt that some concessions to his own position should also be made by the Russians.

The furthest Stalin was prepared to travel was Tehran. He argued that he could not keep in close contact with his battle fronts from any greater distance. Roosevelt, on the other hand, had been told that air communications between Tehran and Cairo were very bad. He thought it would be impossible for documents which, under the American Constitution, needed his signature, to be flown out to him. He therefore refused to go to Tehran. For his part, Stalin was equally unyielding. Probably his major consideration was the control of the communications between the meeting-place and the home countries concerned. In Tehran the Russians would have complete security in this respect, and would even be in a position to eavesdrop on their allies. But had the meeting taken place in Basra, for example, telephone links would have been passed through British territory. Hull, acting on instructions from the President, had a meeting with Stalin on 25 October and put the American case very strongly. Stalin was gracious, but did not budge.[142]

When the tea interval arrived on the next day Hull called Eden across to his table. The conference, he said, was getting nowhere. The Western delegates were being 'strung along'. What could they do about it? Eden suggested he might see Stalin again, and Hull agreed.[143] It seemed that his confidence in the Russians was waning.

Yet when the proceedings were renewed after tea, Molotov presented the Americans with their first major achievement. He agreed to accept their views on the association of China with the three other Allies in the Four-Power Declaration. By the end of the session this item on the agenda had been successfully settled.[144] Molotov's behaviour on the following day was even more gracious, and when Hull pointed out that he wanted to leave Moscow by 31 October the Russian Foreign Minister assured him that the business of the conference could be worked out accordingly.[145]

The Russian was as good as his word, although Mr Hull did have to delay his departure by two days. By the beginning of November decisions had been taken on many major issues. Hull had achieved agreement to the Four-Power Declaration, Mr Eden had persuaded the conference to establish consultative machinery in London for the investigation of European problems, an agreement had been made over the administration of Italy, and the Russians had been reassured about Western strategy. Even on the Turkish question, the British and the Soviet delegations had signed an undertaking to ask for air bases from Turkey and bring her into the war as soon as possible. This was adhered to by President Roosevelt subject to the firm proviso that no troops needed for 'Overlord' or Italy should be sacrificed as a result.[146]

Trickier problems had been shelved without much difficulty. Mr Hull's references to the colonial question had been greeted with polite interest by the Russians and a definite negative by Mr Eden. Nothing more had been done about it.[147] Mr Eden had not had very much luck over Yugoslavia or Poland, and the Russians were not successful in pressing Sweden into the war.

The three Allied representatives were able to record whole-hearted agreement on the matter of punishment to be meted out to German war criminals. As the Germans fell back across Eastern and Southern Europe it was becoming clear that the scale of their atrocities exceeded anything which could have been expected from nominally civilized belligerents. The British Government feared that as the Nazis' position grew more perilous the number of their crimes would multiply. Mr Churchill drew up a declaration warning the Germans against further such atrocities. After the war the perpetrators would be taken back to the scene of their crimes for trial. This declaration was submitted to the Moscow Conference. With some minor modifications, it was duly inserted in the protocols over the names of Churchill, Roosevelt and Stalin. There could, however, have been little doubt who had drafted it. Nobody, friend or foe, could mistake the Churchillian menace in the words:

> Let those who have hitherto not imbrued their hands with innocent blood beware lest they join the ranks of the guilty, for most assuredly the three allied powers will pursue them to the uttermost ends of the earth and will deliver them to their accusers in order that justice may be done.[148]*

A principle had been enunciated which was to redress the moral balance tipped so sharply on the side of injustice and wickedness by two world wars and an uneasy peace. The Second World War was the first great international conflict in modern times after which those responsible for atrocities were called to account individually for their crimes.†

VI

When the results of the conference are examined it becomes clear that M. Molotov and his delegation had won a discreet but decisive success. They had been reassured over Western plans for a second front and had not been forced to make uncomfortable commitments about inter-Allied

---

* See below, pp. 391 ff.

† The Entente Powers had made noises about the trial of war criminals in 1918, but little had been done except in purely military cases. The Kaiser and Ludendorff escaped scot-free. It should be pointed out that the Moscow Declaration was largely concerned with individual atrocities committed outside Germany. It specifically reserved the trial and punishment of major war criminals to the Allied Governments.[149] Negotiations to establish a United Nations Commission for War Crimes were already far advanced by the time the Moscow meeting occurred.[150]

co-operation in Yugoslavia or Poland. Pressure was to be put on Turkey to enter the war. Mr Hull had been given his Four-Power Declaration, a brave statement of intent which bound the Soviet Government to no practical line of conduct. The Soviet statement opposing plans for federation in Central and Eastern Europe[151] was included in the protocol of the conference. It was listed as referring to 'the future of Poland and Danubian and Balkan countries' so that the Allies seemed to be accepting Russia's interpretation of the political situation in that region. On the other hand, the Soviet Government had obtained the right to be represented in an Allied Commission to control the civilian administration of Italy.* The conditions under which Allied government in France should be established were stated in great detail.[152] The contrast between the silence on the fate of territories due to be liberated by the Red Army and the attentive interest shown towards areas already occupied or about to be liberated by the Western Allies was very remarkable. It cannot but have encouraged the Soviet Government in its belief that it was about to receive *carte blanche* in Eastern Europe. The Soviet leaders were quite willing to demonstrate their satisfaction to their Western colleagues. Stalin entertained them with every mark of favour in the last days of their stay.[153] Molotov was clearly pleased and eager to be friendly. Both Mr Hull and Mr Eden were gratified by such unusual cordiality. The British Foreign Secretary wrote to the Prime Minister:

> When I came here I had no conception of how much they wanted this Conference to succeed. There were of course checks and setbacks, but general progress was cumulative and we ended at the top. Our exchanges since the Conference have been on a still more intimate footing.[154]

Most enthusiastic of all were the Americans. Cordell Hull constantly noted the benevolent attitude of Stalin.[155] So far as the results of the conference were concerned, Mr Hull had his eyes fixed on wider and more general issues than those which exercised the British and Soviet Governments. He had, after all, not only achieved the Four-Power Declaration which would establish the foundation for an international peace-keeping organization, but he had obtained agreement to statements of policy on international trade in the post-war era. These would he hoped, prevent the reappearance of national barriers to world trade, restrict cartels, regulate production in competitive markets and create stable foreign-exchange rates. Other proposals had been made on inter-

---

* The conference approved a scheme for an Advisory Council for Italy and a Declaration promising to restore democracy and political and religious freedom there.

national shipping, air traffic, communications, nutritional standards and labour conditions.[156]

This section of the conference's work was indeed a triumph for Mr Hull and, even if the era of co-operation which it foreshadowed was not always to include the Soviet Union, it did at least help to lay the foundation of an international attitude towards economic matters far in advance of that which had existed before the Second World War.

Even more encouraging from the American viewpoint was the apparently unsolicited promise made by Stalin to Mr Hull at a banquet to the effect that Russia would enter the war against Japan once Germany was beaten. This was heartening news indeed.*

Unfortunately for the Americans their delight at the achievements of Moscow coloured their attitude to their Soviet colleagues. An extreme statement of American enthusiasm was that of Averell Harriman, who was to be the new Ambassador in the Soviet Union, in a report to President Roosevelt:

> The Soviet Government [he wrote], before they agreed to the conference had evidently decided that they would take a shot at working together with the British and ourselves in dealing with war and postwar problems. On the whole the Soviets are delighted with the way the Conference went and it has strengthened their tentative decision. It was interesting to watch how Molotov expanded as the days passed. As he began to realize more and more that we had not come with a united front against him and were ready to expose frankly our preliminary thoughts, he showed increased enjoyment at being admitted for the first time into the councils as a full member with the British and ourselves. . . .[157]

This was a point of view which was to have serious consequences before the year was out. The Americans believed that their policy of frankness towards the Soviet Union, coupled with a careful avoidance of prior arrangements with the British, had been the major factor in achieving success at the conference. It was not surprising that they continued this policy when the time came for a meeting of the three Allied leaders themselves.

* See below, p. 347

7 | First Cairo and the Road to Tehran

I

WHILE Mr Hull had been labouring in Moscow, President Roosevelt was planning a meeting with Marshal Stalin. This time it was to be a tripartite affair, and its organization proved a ticklish business. Once again, Anglo-American relations came under stress. The men in the White House were just as eager as the Secretary of State to demonstrate their independence of British influence. At the same time the atmosphere between Britain and America was clouded by many administrative difficulties, most of which were caused by quite genuine and unavoidable domestic problems in London and Washington. Nevertheless, their coincidence with real or suspected American prejudices did not help to reassure the British, who were themselves so eager for an Allied meeting that they were willing to adapt all their plans to ensure its success.

They had very clear ideas about the form this meeting should take. Just as Mr Eden had tried to meet Cordell Hull for preliminary talks before the Moscow Conference, so Mr Churchill wanted a serious Anglo-American discussion on Western strategy before the major Allies finally came together. The Americans, on the other hand, still maintained their desire for a closer association with the Soviet Government. They thought this would not be possible if the Russians felt that the United States and Britain always spoke with one voice. Mr Hull already believed that his personal contacts with Molotov were proving highly successful. The President had always been eager to arrange a *tête-à-deux* with Stalin, and this fact was known in London.*

All through the month of October 1943 coded messages flashed back and forth across the Atlantic registering goodwill but disagreement. On 22 October Roosevelt told the Prime Minister that he did not think the time was ripe for an Anglo-American conference, and added, 'it seems to me that consideration of our relations with Russia is of paramount importance and that a meeting after our special conference with U.J.† would be in order rather than one in early November'.[1] The Prime

---

* See above, p. 81. † 'Uncle Joe', i.e. Stalin.

Minister at once cabled his disagreement, urging that no discussions with Stalin should be arranged without prior agreement on Anglo-American operations.[2]

Meanwhile the meeting with 'U.J.' was not proving at all easy to organize. A long wrangle had developed between the Americans and the Russians about a suitable rendezvous. The Soviet Government firmly stated that Stalin would not be able to travel farther from Russia than Tehran. They argued that the Marshal had to remain in touch with his battle fronts by land communication. There is good reason to suppose that Stalin did, indeed, leave remarkably little room for strategic initiative to his military underlings,[3] but it seems also probable that the Russians did not want to trust themselves to any place where direct ground communications with Moscow were not completely under Soviet control.* For his part Roosevelt genuinely believed that Tehran was an impossible meeting-place for him. Congressional Bills had to be signed personally by the President within a time limit laid down in the American Constitution. He was given to understand that air links with the Persian capital were uncertain, and that land communication was inadequate. It began to seem likely that the Stalin–Roosevelt meeting would once again fail to materialize, and the Americans had to consider a possible substitute. They felt that Russian staff officers should be allowed to participate in the strategic discussions conducted between the Western Powers. The President hoped that this arrangement might be rounded off with a flying visit by Stalin to Basra.[5] On the diplomatic side, Cordell Hull suggested that M. Molotov should go to an inter-Allied conference, and Stalin was ready to consider this. In any case, the Secretary of State was most anxious that closer military and diplomatic consultations with the Russians should be organized, even if Stalin could not be present. On the last day of October he wrote to President Roosevelt stressing Stalin's willingness to participate in the 'forward movement of international co-operation', and suggesting that this hope of co-operation be bolstered by increased military and political contacts. Above all, 'I think it most important that after inviting Stalin and in the event he declines you then invite him to send Molotov and a general of high rank'.[6]

The issue of prior consultation thereupon became confused with the arguments about the feasibility of tripartite staff meetings. The Americans themselves were not clear about what these would entail, but they thought they would be bound to arouse Soviet goodwill. General

---

* Thus when the British offered to lay a land line to Basra the Russians did not respond. The line, which would have been under Russian control, would have passed through British-occupied territory.[4] (See above, p. 118.)

Marshall was not enthusiastic about the idea of a formally combined staff organization, but suggested that an English-speaking Russian staff officer should be given confidential briefings by the Anglo-American Chiefs of Staff. The Western Allies should make at least a small beginning by offering the Russians 'virtually a complete insight into our strategical and logistical doings', whilst making it clear that no information of a similar nature would be required from the Red Army.[7]

Mr Churchill found the idea of Soviet participation in Western military discussions even less attractive than the President's suggested postponement of bilateral talks until after the Big Three meeting. He protested vigorously that the presence of Russian officers would make effective decision-making impossible.[8]

Another cloud on the horizon was the slight and delicate figure of Generalissimo Chiang Kai-shek. The Chinese leader had been discussing his military problems in Chungking with General Brehon Somervell, the Chief of the U.S. Army Service forces, and Roosevelt wished to invite Chiang to meet him if he travelled once more to North Africa. This invitation did nothing to reassure the British about prospects for the forthcoming talks, because they were in a very weak position as far as military operations in the Far East were concerned. The introduction of a Chinese element into the military conversations would not reinforce British demands for more energetic prosecution of the war in the Mediterranean. Furthermore the appearance of Chiang Kai-shek at a major Allied conference would strengthen the impression – already being fostered by the Americans – that China would be the leading Power in the Far East after the war. The future of British possessions in that area was not at all clear in 1943. Mr Churchill knew that neither the Generalissimo nor the President was likely to share his own views on Britain's position as a Power in the Orient.

He therefore welcomed President Roosevelt's invitation to Chiang,[9] but bent his energies to ensuring that he should meet his American partner well in advance of any conference with either the Russians or the Chinese. He sent many messages to Roosevelt about this, suggesting among other things that the two leaders could meet on the way to Cairo in their respective warships – at Gibraltar, Malta or Oran.[10]

President Roosevelt's replies were evasive. This was at least partly due to real administrative difficulties, but it did not improve the general atmosphere. On the home front, the President wanted, quite naturally, to be able to discuss matters with Mr Hull before he himself set out on his diplomatic mission. Mr Hull, however, was a cautious old man, with a sensible regard for his own safety. He was not willing to wait for the President in West Africa for fear of numerous tropical diseases against which he had not been inoculated.[11] Roosevelt thus postponed his own departure so that Mr Hull could return to Washington first, a delay which caused impatience in London.*

The exact date of the rendezvous with the Chinese delegation also caused difficulties. President Roosevelt cabled Chungking that a meeting near Cairo on 25 November would be suitable. On the same day a message had been sent to London estimating that the President's party would arrive in Cairo on 20 November.[13] There seemed to be ample time for the British and Americans to confer before Chiang arrived. But then there came a report from General Somervell that, although the Generalissimo wanted to see President Roosevelt either before or after he met Stalin, if the latter alternative was chosen, the Chinese would prefer to postpone their visit. The President took the hint and decided to make sure that he had plenty of time to see Chiang before his talk with the Russian representatives. So he proposed to invite the Chinese to come to Cairo on 22 November, i.e. at the beginning of the Allied meetings. He assured Mr Churchill – to whom he imparted his decision about Chiang – that he and his staff would have many meetings with the British before either of the other Allied groups appeared. On the face of it this was disingenuous, since Roosevelt and Chiang were now due to arrive in Cairo at virtually the same time, but Mr Churchill did not query it and the President himself may have been quite sincere in thinking that his programme could be arranged in accordance with his message to London.[14]

Meanwhile Mr Churchill and Mr Harriman had been doing research into the Persian weather.[15] Both of them came to the conclusion that the President's earlier doubts about a visit to Tehran had been greatly exaggerated. Land and air communications were not nearly so primitive or hazardous as to threaten the flow of vital documents to the President. When this information reached Washington on 6 and 7 November, Roosevelt at once changed his plans again. He cabled Stalin that he would be able to meet him in the Persian capital after all. Before their rendezvous he would like to see Molotov and a Russian staff party in Cairo on 22 November.

This clearly cut across the arrangements he had made with Mr Churchill. Why? Partly because the visit to Tehran necessitated greater economy of time. The president could not leave Washington for too long. But the main reason was almost certainly because, with a visit to Stalin in the offing, Roosevelt did not want to seem bound to the British. His resolution on this matter may well have been strengthened by a

---

* Mr Churchill proposed that Hull should be allowed to 'rest in the Egyptian sunshine' until Roosevelt arrived at Oran.[12]

dispatch from Mr Harriman in Moscow which arrived on 6 November. In it the Ambassador remarked on the need to build up Soviet confidence in American plans to defeat the Axis. It was, he claimed,

> impossible to overemphasize the importance they place strategically on the initiation of the so-called 'Second Front' next spring. An invitation to the next military conference is, I believe, essential if the seeds sown at this conference [Moscow] are to germinate. It is clear that they never like to be faced with Anglo-American decisions already taken. . . .[16]

When President Roosevelt sent his invitation to Stalin he also intended to inform the British of his decision.* But no message went to London. The President may have been held back by doubts concerning Stalin's reaction. A message from Mr Harriman in Moscow on 9 November seemed to suggest that the Marshal would not even be willing to go as far as Tehran.[18] It was not until a few hours before the Presidential party was about to depart for Cairo that Stalin's telegram of acceptance reached Washington.[19] The delay had not been felicitous. News of the President's offer to go to Tehran and his invitation to M. Molotov had been transmitted to London by the British Ambassador in Moscow. Mr Churchill was piqued by American secrecy and dismayed to learn that President Roosevelt had been suggesting arrangements to Stalin which were incompatible with the plans already made for an Anglo-American meeting.

Just as the President was about to leave the White House for Quantico, Virginia, where his yacht, the *Potomac*, was waiting for him, a 'wounded cable' arrived from London. Mr Churchill pointed out that President Roosevelt had promised him 'many meetings' in Cairo before they were joined by M. Molotov and the Chinese. Now it appeared that M. Molotov would arrive at the same time as the President. The Prime Minister was happy that Roosevelt had decided to meet Stalin, but 'I rather wish you had been able to let me know direct'.[20]

The President at once suspended his departure in order to send a reply. He explained his difficulties with Stalin, but made no bones about his attitude to discussions with the Soviet Government: 'I have held all along – as I know you have – that it would be a terrible mistake if U.J. thought we had ganged up on him in a military action. . . .'[21] The Prime Minister for his part made no bones about his opposition to the injection of a Soviet element into Anglo-American staff talks, but, as things turned out, this argument was unnecessary. Stalin declined to send

---

* The draft of the message to Stalin had the words 'will notify PRIME tomorrow W.B.' These were the initials of Roosevelt's naval aide-de-camp, Admiral Wilson Brown.[17]

M. Molotov to Cairo. Most probably this was because the Russians had learned that Chiang Kai-shek was going to be present. The quest for a senior staff officer fluent in English had also produced no apparent result.[22] What had been conceived as a generous gesture to the Soviet Union had achieved nothing except sourness between London and Washington.

The meeting at Cairo did not promise to be entirely happy from a British viewpoint. If M. Molotov was not going to be present to chaperon the Anglo-Saxons, Chiang Kai-shek would gladly fill the breach. For, at the same time as he had cabled Stalin asking for a meeting at Tehran, President Roosevelt had wired Chungking asking the Generalissimo to be in Cairo by 22 November. The President had arranged the programme to his liking. It remained to be seen how the conferences themselves would conform to his hopes.

II

Shortly after 9 a.m. on Friday, 12 November 1943, a delicate naval manœuvre was being carried out on the smooth waters of the Chesapeake Bay. The U.S.S. *Iowa*, the latest and second largest battleship in the American fleet, with a deck area of $9\frac{1}{2}$ acres and a displacement of 58,000 tons, was riding at anchor. On her starboard side lay a far smaller, but no less distinguished craft, the *Potomac*, Franklin D. Roosevelt's Presidential yacht. On board were the President himself, Harry L. Hopkins and Admiral Leahy. They and their assistants had come down the Potomac river to make a rendezvous with the enormous battleship. The commanders of America's land, sea and air forces were waiting on it to greet them. At precisely sixteen minutes past nine the President left his yacht by means of a special gangway slung between the after sun deck of the *Potomac* and a point on the *Iowa*'s deck just abreast of her number three turret.[23] No honours were rendered as he stepped on board the battleship, nor was his flag broken at the mast-head. Security overruled splendour. This was not a social occasion, nor a time for pageantry. The *Iowa* had become a unique link in the Allied chain of command. For the next eight days it would be the scene of discussions vital for the prosecution of the war. Roosevelt was on his way to his first great conference with Churchill and Stalin. He and his lieutenants were determined that their view of the future should prevail over all obstacles. And for the time being most of those obstacles seemed to them to be manufactured in London.*

* On 14 November an unexpected obstacle appeared in the shape of a torpedo fired at the *Iowa* by one of her escort vessels, the *William D. Porter*. Only an abrupt change of course saved the *Iowa* from being hit, and the torpedo actually exploded a hundred

The Americans had two major purposes as they set out for the Middle East. They wanted to create an atmosphere of trust between themselves and the leaders of the Soviet Union. In particular Roosevelt hoped to achieve a personal *rapport* with Marshal Stalin. They also wanted to ensure that their planned assault against Hitler in the West should not be hampered by secondary undertakings in other spheres. Thus the strategic argument which had been conducted for many months between Washington and London had not been buried at Quebec. It was now being exacerbated by differences of a political nature.

Many of those on board the *Iowa* that day were convinced that some aspects of British policy ran counter to the best interests of the Grand Alliance. This was a view shared by their colleagues ashore. Admiral Leahy, for example, saw British military planning in the Mediterranean and the Far East as a programme for the defence or recapture of Britain's imperial possessions.[25] The Secretary of War, Henry L. Stimson, was consumed with fears about the future of 'Overlord' if the British were allowed to inveigle their allies into activities in the Balkans. He urged steadfast adherence to 'Overlord',[26] and his views were heartily supported by all his professional advisers. At the State Department Cordell Hull was likewise ill disposed towards the British Empire. He and Harry Hopkins felt that British enthusiasm for American schemes of post-war economic co-operation was far too lukewarm.[27] Nor had Mr Hull and Mr Harriman, the American Ambassador to Moscow, made any secret of their belief that they had helped their cause at Moscow by avoiding too close an association with the British.* There were also differences emerging about the correct method of planning the peace settlement. Most important of all were the views of the man who occupied the captain's cabin in the *Iowa*, the President himself. His was a complicated mind to read, but certain general propositions were discernible. He saw the war as a global conflict which had to be succeeded by a global peace. In the establishment of that new order the two most compelling forces would be the United States and the Soviet Union. The President, like most of his subordinates, felt a genuine warmth and sympathy towards Britain, but he envisaged her future as that of a European rather than an imperial nation. In the East new peoples would arise to exercise power and independence. The most important of these would

---

yards astern of her. The firing had been caused by a mistake aboard the *William D. Porter*, but the luckless vessel was placed under arrest and sent back to port. After the excitement died down, General Milton Arnold went up to a furious Admiral King and asked: 'Tell me, Ernest, does this happen often in your navy?' The reply is not recorded.[24]

* See above, p. 121.

be the Chinese, and Roosevelt hoped that China would play a great role in the politics of post-war Asia. At the forthcoming Allied conferences he was determined to stress the importance of the Asian war effort, partly to emphasize the enormous burden which the United States had shouldered in that theatre, and partly to illustrate the Four-Power nature of his prospective peace plans. His concern for events in the Far East had already been demonstrated by his invitation to Generalissimo Chiang Kai-shek to meet him at Cairo.

On the European strategic question, Roosevelt was not inclined to budge from the positions adopted by his Chiefs of Staff, but he did feel the need to offer Stalin the greatest possible help in his offensives. Like Mr Churchill, the President was uncomfortable at the thought of a winter's campaigning conducted entirely by the Soviet armies, and he did not want the British to outbid him by suggesting diversions. He toyed with the idea of an expedition to aid Tito in the Balkans, and, despite the dismay of his associates, persisted in this proposal in Allied counsels until Stalin himself revealed his distaste for it.*

On the main issue, his steadfastness could not be called in question. 'Overlord' came first. The most important task facing the Americans was to establish the unrivalled priority of this operation. To do this they had to be clear how it was to be commanded and by whom. The British Prime Minister was already pressing for a commander to be named,[30] and the Soviet Government also regarded such an appointment as vital if they were to take Western promises seriously.[31]

Unfortunately for the Americans, and perhaps for the whole Alliance, internal political complications had made it difficult for the President to commit himself. In common with Secretary Stimson and most of his political advisers, Roosevelt wanted to give General Marshall the command of 'Overlord'. But his other Chiefs of Staff – and Admiral King in particular – were unhappy at the thought of General Marshall leaving Washington. In October this issue had become further complicated by a partisan smear campaign aimed at the President's chief political lieutenant, Harry Hopkins. It was suggested that Mr Hopkins was intriguing against General Marshall and wanted him sent to Europe as a form of camouflaged demotion.[32] In order to avoid a damaging loss of prestige for America's most gifted general, Roosevelt wanted it made clear that Marshall would be accepting a post in Europe of unparalleled importance. This desire coincided with the American military view that

* The President brought this matter up at a conference of the American Combined Chiefs of Staff on board the *Iowa* on 19 November. Marshall said that air power would be sufficient aid to the Soviet Army if it broke through to the Bug.[28] Then at Tehran Roosevelt again suggested a possible Western assault into the Danube Basin, and Churchill supported him.[29]

there should be a Supreme Commander in the European theatre controlling the entire Anglo-American war effort from the English Channel to the Golden Horn. Admiral Leahy and his colleagues hoped that they would thereby be able to prevent the misappropriation of any Allied forces for operations which might be damaging for 'Overlord'. They were also very eager to place the Western strategic air forces under the Supreme Commander, so as to integrate them into the 'Overlord' strategy. They rightly anticipated bitter opposition from the British to such proposals. A supreme command controlled by the Americans would undermine the British conception of sustained pressure on Hitler from the south as well as the west, and would also threaten the independent strategic role of British Bomber Command in the assault on Germany. The U.S. Chiefs of Staff therefore prepared a reserve programme, according to which there would be a Supreme Commander for the air war who would not immediately be given authority over other operations. A theatre commander for the entire Mediterranean should be appointed – a proposal which Mr Churchill had already been urging from London. However, the British and the Americans were once again at cross-purposes when considering even this obviously necessary step. Mr Churchill wished to instil more life into Mediterranean operations by eliminating the harmful division of command there.* Leahy and Marshall were eager to ensure that the Mediterranean Commander kept a tight rein on Allied activities in that theatre. Thus the Americans were even willing to see supreme command offered to a British general of their choice – Sir John Dill – so long as the Mediterranean Commander was American.[33] None of these proposals turned out to be practicable and within three weeks they had been scrapped. Nevertheless, they contributed to an unfortunate delay and confusion over the 'Overlord' command which did not help the relationships between American and British military authorities. Nor did they assist the presentation of the Western case to Stalin at Tehran.

This question was among the first to be discussed by the President at a conference with his Chiefs of Staff held in his cabin aboard the *Iowa* on 19 November 1943. The conference, which started at 2 p.m., lasted all the afternoon. President Roosevelt made it clear that he would support the Chiefs' demand for an over-all commander in Europe, and was eager to have evidence that the Americans were supporting more troops overseas than the British.[34] He could also not resist giving voice to the belief that British interest in an over-all command for the Mediterranean might have resulted 'from an idea in the back of their

* The Eastern Mediterranean was under the authority of General Sir Henry Maitland Wilson, the Western under General Eisenhower.

heads to create a situation in which they could push our troops into Italy and the Balkans'. His colleagues assured him that such dark designs could be resisted effectively enough, but Roosevelt's tone did not augur well for Anglo-American co-operation in the military sphere.

The discussion then turned to the occupation of Germany. Allied armies were making such progress in the autumn of 1943 that the collapse of the entire European Axis seemed possible. The Allies did not want to be faced with a German capitulation without having made adequate plans for it, and so proposals had been drawn up for a rapid invasion of the Reich in face of small resistance – or of no resistance at all. This operation was described by the code-name 'Rankin'.* Clearly 'Rankin' had to be planned in such a manner that it did not conflict with 'Overlord', but because it envisaged the rapid occupation of Germany it presented a number of very pressing political problems, many of which had not been properly hammered out in Washington, let alone among the three great Allies. It had been settled that Germany should be totally occupied at the end of the war. But how long this occupation should last, what the zones of occupation should be, and in what form Germany should emerge after the occupation had ended was not clear. Cordell Hull strongly believed that the question of partition should not be prejudged, but should be left for the time being to allow for possible developments inside Germany after the war. He had put this State Department view to the President shortly before Roosevelt embarked on the *Iowa*.[35] In the White House there was a greater tendency to regard the permanent partition of Germany as a proper objective for United States policy. The President told his listeners on the *Iowa* that the Russians would not object to breaking Germany up after the war, and that practically speaking there should be three German states, possibly five. Assuming there to be three, the occupational divisions set out in 'Rankin' should, the President thought, conform to the bounds set for them. These would encompass a South German state of Baden, Württemberg and Bavaria, a North-western state extending far enough east to include Berlin, and the eastern part, including West Prussia and Pomerania.[36] These views had been expressed by the President before,† but they now came into uncomfortable conflict with the carefully elaborated plans of the Allied strategic planners.

General Morgan, who had been commissioned to work out the details of 'Overlord' and 'Rankin' as Chief of Staff to a future Supreme

---

* A refinement on this name, 'Rankin C', referred to occupation of Germany if resistance there collapsed completely.

† See above, p. 108.

Commander (COSSAC), had produced a scheme for the movement of Allied forces into Western Europe. It was clear that, from a military viewpoint, the right wing of this gigantic movement should be American and the left British. Logistical requirements, not political ones, necessitated this arrangement. General Morgan was himself the head of an Anglo-American staff organization. Nevertheless, President Roosevelt detected British political interests behind the plan. It would mean that American troops occupied southern Germany, with their lines of communication running through France and Belgium. The British, on the other hand, would take north-western Germany – including the Ruhr – and would have access to Dutch, North German and Scandinavian ports. They would also be well placed if there was a race for Berlin. When this plan had been discussed at Quebec with Mr Churchill, Roosevelt had made no comment except to remark that Western troops should be in Berlin as soon as the Russians.[37] By the time the American party left for North Africa in November, General Morgan had presented the American Chiefs of Staff with modifications to the 'Rankin' scheme which conformed with proposals for German occupation zones drawn up by a committee of the British War Cabinet under Mr Attlee. The modifications were consistent with the military needs of the Western offensive. They created a North-western Zone of Germany under British control and a South-western American Zone. The rest was to be occupied by the Red Army, apart from Berlin, which was to be under tripartite rule, and East Prussia, which, it was assumed, would go to the Poles.[38]

The President did not like this arrangement, and said so to his Chiefs of Staff aboard the *Iowa*. He feared that the United States would have to become involved in the internal affairs of France and Belgium. 'France', he said, 'is a British "baby".' The Americans were unpopular there, and in any case the British and the French ought to handle their own problem together. It was the President's view that, since Britain was the Power interested in restoring France to Great Power status, she should bear the burdens connected with such a reconstruction. He himself believed that France would not become a first-class Power again for at least twenty-five years.[39] Belgium might experience political difficulties, and so the Americans should stay clear of that country.

Roosevelt was also concerned with the question of communications between the United States and her proposed zone of occupation. He thought that, with the Dutch and North German ports available, American troops could be brought to Germany directly from the United States. He expected that about a million men would be needed for this task of occupation, which would last for one or two years.[40] From the political point of view, it doubtless seemed essential for American armies to be able to move easily in and out of Germany, especially since demobilization was bound to cause difficulties and arouse passions at home. The President therefore demanded that the Northern Zone of Germany should be American. Although the 'Rankin' operation pre-supposed a serious German breakdown – Roosevelt himself spoke of a 'railroad invasion of Germany with little or no fighting' – it was clearly going to be very awkward to switch American armies from the right to the left of the Allied assault once they were on the Continent, and the Chiefs of Staff reacted rather cautiously to the President's wishes. But there seemed to be no doubt that British machinations were at work somewhere, and Roosevelt closed his remarks on this point by saying that if COSSAC's proposals were accepted 'the British would undercut us in every move we made in the Southern occupational area proposed for the United States'. He claimed that 'it was quite evident' that British political considerations lay behind the paper.[41]*.

One point on which there was general agreement concerned Berlin. There would be a race for that city, and United States soldiers would have to reach it as quickly as possible.

After a discussion of the war in the Far East, the President turned to another European issue which promised to provide friction between the Americans and their British colleagues. This was the question of Allied activity in the Balkans. Roosevelt stressed that the Americans should not let themselves be 'roped into accepting any European sphere of influence' and did not want to be compelled to keep forces in Yugo-slavia.[42] This was part of a consistent attempt on Roosevelt's part to limit American commitments in Europe to those connected with the occupation of Germany. Otherwise he saw European peace-keeping as an Anglo-Russian matter, with the United States involvement limited to naval or air forces. For his Chiefs of Staff it was more important to reiterate their determination not to undertake activities in the Balkans detrimental to 'Overlord'.

Lastly, the question of co-operation with the Soviet Government and of an institutionalized approach to the settlement of post-war problems in Europe was considered. At the Moscow Foreign Ministers' Conference a number of thorny problems had been referred to the European Ad-visory Commission in London,† and this organization, which Mr Eden had championed with great determination, seemed likely to play a considerable part in the transition from war to peace. Although the

---

* For the outcome of the question of German Zonal boundaries, see below, pp. 267–74.

† See above, p. 118.

Americans at Moscow had not objected to the Commission, there was a strong tendency in Washington to regard it as yet another British scheme aimed at hamstringing military commanders and subordinating them to politicians.

The President seems to have shared these fears. He told General Marshall that the E.A.C. would undoubtedly want a military committee as part of its organization, and Admiral Leahy voiced the opinion that 'the control commission in London will mean nothing but trouble for us'.[43] It was evident that the Americans saw E.A.C. as a possible pawn in the British strategic game, and one which might draw them into Middle Eastern conflicts. The entry of Turkey into the war, for which Mr Churchill had been pressing very urgently, was viewed in the same light.

These discussions, which also ranged over the unsatisfactory nature of Britain's effort in the Far East and the unhelpful attitude adopted by the British Government towards American facilities in the Azores,* had been marked by a sense of frustration towards Mr Churchill and his Government. In a sense, this was to be expected, for the Americans knew that they were due to meet the British Prime Minister before seeing the Russians, and in any closely knit partnership, such as that between Britain and the United States, there were bound to be frictions and clashes of interest. But it was not perhaps entirely fortunate that, as the President crossed the Atlantic for his first meeting with his Soviet allies, so many vexations and difficulties should have come between his party and their colleagues in London.

III

On 20 November the President disembarked at Oran and flew to Tunis. Two days later he landed at Cairo, where Mr Churchill and Generalissimo Chiang Kai-shek were already awaiting him. His aeroplane took him over the Sphinx,[44] a suitable augury for the conferences ahead. The President had no reason to fear it. He could be as enigmatic as any of his partners.

He was taken by car to his villa – that of the American Ambassador, Alexander C. Kirk. Set some distance from Cairo, not far from the pyramids, it was beautifully furnished and had an attractive garden, in which tame gazelles gambolled, and which could be viewed from a patio. The President was guarded by American soldiers. In the kitchens his own personal mess-boys eliminated the possibility of gastronomic

* On 12 October 1943 the Portuguese had agreed to let Britain use the Azores islands as a maritime and air base. The Americans also wanted military facilities on the islands.

disasters. The United States delegation was comfortably placed, physically and politically, for the struggles which lay ahead.

Mr Churchill, on the other hand, had crossed the Bay of Biscay burdened by a feverish cold and the after-effects of various injections. His condition varied in the days which followed, but no permanent improvement took place. Throughout the conferences to follow he was physically below par.[45]

It did not lift his spirits to discover that Chiang Kai-shek was to figure largely on the programme of events in Cairo. The Prime Minister had hoped that the Generalissimo and his formidable consort might be persuaded to 'go and see the Pyramids and enjoy themselves' until after he and the President had been to Tehran.[46] This would have allowed Anglo-American policy to have been planned first, arrangements with the Soviet Union to be settled next and Chinese affairs to take their place firmly at the end of the queue. It was precisely what the wily Chiang had foreseen when he had insisted on being heard before Stalin.*

On the same afternoon that Churchill went to pay his respects to the President, the Generalissimo and Madame Chiang arrived there to greet the Americans. At the dinner and preliminary staff meeting which followed, Far Eastern affairs dominated the discussions. This pattern recurred when the conference itself got under way. The first plenary meeting on 23 November was entirely concerned with the war in Asia.[47] Staff meetings developed into a defence by Admiral Mountbatten of planned operations in the South-east Asian theatre, operations which the British felt to be burdensome and the Chinese inadequate. Chiang's demands for an amphibious operation across the Bay of Bengal, and his insistence on a mathematically convenient but logistically impracticable tonnage of supplies to be flow from India to China,[48] meant that valuable naval and air resources would be diverted from theatres where they could be employed with immediate effect and dropped into the morass of an Asian war in which the United Nations were not ready to take the offensive. Mr Churchill refused to saddle his naval forces with the commitments demanded by Chiang, but President Roosevelt gave the Chinese a promise that the amphibious operations they required would take place within a few months.[49]

The Prime Minister and his staff realized that this would affect the war in Europe, since the landing craft required in Asia were also desperately needed in the Mediterranean. At one moment the British thought that 'Overlord' might be postponed in order to maintain pressure in Italy and carry out the Burmese assault, but in view of the American

* See above, p. 125.

leaders' commitment to 'Overlord' it seems unlikely that they seriously contemplated such a scheme.[50] The vigorously worded demands for a more energetic prosecution of the war in Italy and the Balkans drawn up by Mr Churchill on his way to Cairo[51] were thus overshadowed by discussion of the Chinese story, which the Prime Minister himself described as 'lengthy, complicated and minor'.[52]

This story was by no means just a military one. There was a political side to it, as Mr Eden shrewdly noted when he arrived in Cairo on 23 November. He came to the conclusion that the Americans were 'impressed, almost to the point of obsession, with the merits of General and Mme Chiang Kai-shek'. This boded no good for British interests in the Far East, and the Foreign Secretary sensed that 'even the future of Hong Kong was in question' with the Americans.[53] His fears were well founded. On the evening of Eden's arrival Roosevelt entertained the Generalissimo and his wife to dinner. The only non-Chinese guests were Harry Hopkins and Colonel Elliott Roosevelt.[54] During the discussions after dinner Roosevelt suggested to Chiang that Hong Kong should return to China and might then become a free port. Chiang was reserved in his reply.[55] The President was evidently emboldened to mention this scheme to Mr Churchill himself, proposing that the British should make a *'beau geste'* to China by surrendering Hong Kong. This should at once be followed by a Chinese assurance that property in the city would be restored to its rightful owners and that Hong Kong should be open to international trade.[56]

Mr Churchill gave nothing away, either at Cairo or Tehran.* But the whole course of the conference was sown with dangerous mines for the British. China's claims to Tibet were even raised by Chiang's party, but were met with a steady refusal.[57] It is not surprising that Lord Avon has described this conference as one of the most difficult he ever attended.[58] There was little the British could do except 'hold their end up as best they could, leaving most of the talk and the proposing to others'.[59]

Meanwhile the President and the Generalissimo disposed of the future of Asia. This was done in an informal, almost casual way, perhaps because the two statesmen found themselves so largely in agreement, perhaps because they felt that more elaborate methods might make difficulties with their allies. Both wanted to eliminate European colonialism in the Far East. During the discussions which followed dinner on 23 November, it was settled that China should be given equal status as one of the Big Four Allies, and should join with the United States in controlling the security of the Pacific. American warships

* At Tehran he emphasized to Stalin that Singapore and Hong Kong must return to Britain.

would have facilities in Chinese ports, and Port Arthur was to be put at the disposal of both Powers. China would receive economic aid from the United States. Her four north-eastern provinces should be restored to her, including the Liaotung Peninsula, and Formosa should also be Chinese. Korea and Indo-China would be helped to, and Thailand confirmed in, their independence. President Roosevelt suggested that China should play a large part in the occupation of Japan, and hinted that the Japanese Imperial House might be abolished.* Chiang wisely denied any wish to involve China in these matters, and the catastrophe of a Chinese occupation army in Japan was avoided. The Generalissimo's main concern was for the pacification of China itself, and its establishment as a Great Power after the war. Throughout their stay Chiang and his wife tried to impress President Roosevelt with the progressive nature of the Kuomintang régime, and endeavoured to obtain American help for the creation of a large Chinese Army. After the war Chiang claimed he had been promised arms for ninety divisions by the Americans at Cairo – divisions which, as it turned out, he needed to fight the Communists in his own country rather than the Japanese abroad.[60]

This large programme was not made public at once, and the British found that the final communiqué on China contained little with which they could not whole-heartedly agree. Nothing was said in it about Hong Kong or other ex-European colonial areas invaded by the Japanese. Although the Americans had committed themselves to the independence of Indo-China, for example, the British accepted no such arrangement.[61] The three Allies, whose statement had been seen but not formally approved by the Russians, pledged themselves to wage the war against Japan with due vigour, expel her from the territories she had occupied and restore Manchuria, Formosa and the Pescadores to China. Korea was to be independent. The rest of the Asian map was left a blank.[62]

If the arrangements for the Far East had not been as catastrophic for the British as had at one time seemed possible, the conference as a whole was deeply frustrating for them. Mr Churchill's schemes for intensified activities in the Italian and Eastern Mediterranean sectors, expounded by him with his usual vigour despite the shortage of time at his disposal, were not taken very seriously by the Americans. An argument about the possibility of a combined Commander-in-Chief also proved inconclusive. Militarily the only results of the conference had been plans for South-east Asia in which the British had but a reluctant interest.

The other political problems which the British wanted to bring forward at the conference made no better progress. Mr Eden was

* See below, pp. 386–7.

particularly exasperated with the leisurely pace at which business was conducted, interrupted as it sometimes was by social engagements and photography. Mr Churchill himself described Roosevelt as a 'charming country gentleman' without business methods.[63] It is difficult to find this assessment of so shrewd a politician as Roosevelt very convincing. In fact the Americans were getting what they wanted done at Cairo. Other pressing matters were held over for the meeting with Stalin at Tehran.

For the British Foreign Secretary the most urgent question was the activation of the European Advisory Commission, to which the Moscow Foreign Ministers' Conference had referred a number of important problems.* Although the Soviet Union had evidently accepted the Commission as an organization with an important role to play in the establishment of peace in Europe, the Americans began to react very unfavourably when Mr Eden raised this subject in Cairo.[64]

There was nothing casual or unpremeditated about this attitude. The U.S. Chiefs of Staff had already told the President of their misgivings over E.A.C.† They feared it might undermine the powers of military leaders in their operational spheres. In their view, the administration of conquered territories should in the first instance be the responsibility of the military authorities. They had set up a Combined Civil Affairs Committee in Washington to advise the Chiefs of Staff on economic and political matters connected with liberated or occupied territories. This committee had British as well as American members, but the Foreign Office had never regarded it with much enthusiasm. The Americans believed that pressure from London had caused the complete frustration of the committee, and saw the European Advisory Commission as an attempt to usurp its functions.[65]

At the root of this American distaste for E.A.C. was the suspicion that its creation was a British manœuvre designed to shift the political centre of gravity in the West from Washington to London. Perhaps the most vigorous exponent of this view was John J. McCloy, the United States Assistant Secretary of War. He had formed what might almost be described as an apocalyptic vision of the E.A.C., and the effect it would have on inter-Allied relations. He saw it as a reactionary force calculated to isolate America from Europe. On 25 November 1943 he wrote to Harry Hopkins telling him that the British were going to press the matter of the Commission in discussions with the President. He warned against allowing E.A.C. to control occupied areas in the wake of advancing Allied forces on the grounds that it would increase its powers as it developed and would thus have serious implications for America's

* See above, p. 118.   † See above, pp. 133–4.

post-war policy towards Europe. Mr McCloy saw two dangerous trends appearing which might damage American interests as the war went on. On the North American continent there would be a desire to bring the troops back home and 'liquidate the European involvement'. But elsewhere they could expect 'a tendency on the part of other countries that now that the war is on its way to being won and the invader is no longer at the door, the dependence on the U.S. should promptly be liquidated except in matters of relief'.[66]

Mr McCloy rightly remarked that the development of both these tendencies would be fatal to British and American interests, and he evidently assumed that the Commission was designed to weaken American influence over European affairs. He saw it as an artificial device by which the British were evidently trying to control what he called 'the shift of power'. As such it could not be really effective, but it might frighten American public opinion back into isolationism:

> It is essential [he wrote] that the people of America become used to decisions being made in the United States. On every cracker barrel in every country store in the U.S. there is someone sitting who is convinced that we get hornswoggled every time we attend a European conference. European deliberations must be made in the light of the concepts of the new continent because that continent has now, for better or for worse, become a determining factor in the struggles of the older one.[67]

On the day after McCloy had sent these views to Hopkins, he and Mr Winant, the American Ambassador to Britain, met Mr Eden and Gladwyn Jebb at the British Embassy in Cairo.[68] Mr Winant began by subjecting the E.A.C. to sharp criticism, saying that the Americans were concerned about what he called 'the early introduction of the political aspect into the cessation of hostility planning'. Since all such planning was bound to have a political aspect, it is clear that his real objection was to the political influence of this particular Commission. Mr McCloy followed up quickly with his own views on the damaging consequences which too much decision-making in London might have on American willingness to participate in the post-war reconstruction of Europe. He did, in fact, make it clear that he resented the establishment of an important policy-making body in London and thought that the American people would resent it too.

He can hardly have imagined that Mr Eden would take such views in a meek or conciliatory spirit. E.A.C. had been one of the major achievements of the Moscow Conference, and the British Foreign Secretary was not going to see it eliminated to suit the parochial prejudices of Mid-Western Americans. He pointed out that Mr Hull and the Russians had accepted the Commission and that, to quote Mr McCloy, 'for better or for worse the entire kit and caboodle *had* been referred and it would not do to indicate to the Soviets that any attempt was being made to derogate from the jurisdiction of the Commission now'.[69]

The Americans could not deny this. What they did, however, was to stress the need to subordinate the Commission to the Combined Chiefs of Staff. Its recommendations should be submitted to the military men before being passed on to the Allied Governments. Furthermore, to balance the Commission in London, they demanded that the Combined Civil Affairs Committee in Washington should be revitalized and allowed to function without British obstruction. In return, the Americans agreed – again in Mr McCloy's words – 'to treat the E.A.C. seriously' and to send a strong staff to London as American participants.[70] Mr Eden had had to fight hard for this much progress, and although he had saved the London Commission from extinction the prospect of it emerging as a powerful instrument for the shaping of European peace had become remote.

One aspect of post-invasion planning on which the British and the Americans did share the same views was that of the civilian administration in France. The Americans proposed a joint committee to deal with problems arising out of this, and the reaction on the British side was favourable. De Gaulle's stock stood very low with both the Western Allies in November 1943,* and since Stalin also thought little of him it seemed that the future of the French National Committee was threatened. In actual fact, the Anglo-American preparations for the regulation of France's future proved quite ineffective. De Gaulle was not to be denied his place in the ranks of the conquerors.

All in all, the British had little to show for their stay in Cairo, except to take comfort in the negative belief that it could have been worse. Mr Churchill's sturdy attempts to impress American military leaders with the need for more activity in Italy and the Eastern Mediterranean had been rewarded with the promise to accept action against Rhodes and the attainment of the Pisa–Rimini line as the basis for discussion with the Soviet Government. This was to be a pyrrhic victory.[72] No common policy had been worked out towards the problem of Poland and Eastern Europe. No decision had been taken about the future of Germany, or even about the objectives of the Western Powers there.

---

* The Free French had suspended the Lebanese Constitution after the Lebanese Parliament had voted for independence on 8 November 1943. On 13 November Mr Churchill wrote a furious letter to Roosevelt on this subject, saying: 'There is no doubt in my mind that this is a foretaste of what de Gaulle's leadership in France means. It is certainly entirely contrary to the Atlantic Charter and much else that we have declared.'[71]

The Prime Minister and his Foreign Secretary flew to Tehran on 27 November in a troubled mood. It was not improved by the Prime Minister's sore throat, a recurrent symptom of his steadily worsening condition.

Despite the moral uplift provided by a change of uniform in the aeroplane,* Mr Churchill was not encouraged by his reception at Tehran. He was taken to the British Legation at a leisurely pace in a virtually unprotected motor-car whose route had been well advertised by ineffectually placed Persian cavalrymen strung out along the road. The only attempt at official subterfuge was an arrangement whereby Mr Churchill's car went into the Legation compound by the back way and the Foreign Secretary drove up to the main entrance surrounded by a squadron of cavalry. This simply involved Mr Eden in additional danger, for a donkey was stuck near the Legation gates, and the whole party was forced to halt, a sitting target for assassins. Fortunately there was none present.[73]

The question of security dominated the first hours of the Allied gathering at Tehran. Since Persia had only fairly recently been occupied by the British and the Russians, there was good reason to suppose that German agents were still present in the capital. Neither the Soviet nor the British Government was particularly popular in Persia. The three Allied delegations had decided to live in their respective diplomatic residences, but the American Legation was about a mile from the British and Russian headquarters, which were almost neighbours. On the day of his arrival in Cairo, President Roosevelt had written to Stalin about this, asking whether he could suggest where the Americans ought to live.[74] Both the Soviet and the British authorities thereupon offered him room in their residences, but the President hesitated to accept. His chief Secret Service agent, Michael Reilly, reported that the route from the American Legation to the other Allied quarters presented no security risk.[75] However, the President's special representative in the Middle East, General Patrick Hurley, cabled to say that the Russian Embassy was more convenient, comfortable and secure.[76] Although the Americans did not accept the Soviet offer before they went to Tehran, it is clear that they were already very strongly disposed to do so. When, shortly after they had arrived, Molotov expressed his fears about the President's safety to Averell Harriman, Roosevelt's staff quickly made up their minds to move to the Soviet Embassy.[77]

It is tempting to see this move as an act of great naïveté on the part of

---

* Mr Churchill donned the uniform of an Air Commodore, in which he was later photographed with Roosevelt and Stalin on the portico of the Russian Embassy in Tehran.

the Americans, a move into which they were hustled by an alarmist Russian story about German plots to assassinate members of the conference.[78] There seems no particular reason to believe this. The Americans themselves had always been inclined to accept the Russian offer, and the British expressed relief at the President's final decision.[79] If the Americans were going to move, the Soviet Embassy was their most obvious choice of residence. It offered a self-contained suite under a separate roof from that which sheltered Marshal Stalin. The British could have provided no such suitable facilities.[80] There was certainly a large number of Soviet security agents in evidence at the Embassy when the President arrived, but these rapidly became less conspicuous. In any case, Roosevelt did not lack such protection himself, having brought fourteen Secret Service men with him from Cairo. It is doubtful whether the Soviet authorities gained very much from the opportunity to eavesdrop on their American guests, nor need one imagine that the Americans themselves were unaware of the fact that their new home posed a security risk.

Certainly it all seemed to augur well for the establishment of cordial relations between Roosevelt and the Russians. The President had scarcely arrived in his new and comfortable quarters when he received his first guest. It was Joseph Stalin.

8 | Tehran and Second Cairo

I

THE meeting with Stalin at Tehran on the afternoon of 28 November 1943 was a meeting for which the President had worked unsuccessfully for many months,* and he did not hesitate to remind his Russian colleague of this fact.[1] The Marshal graciously replied that he was to blame for the delay in their meeting, but that military matters had preoccupied his attention. This led on to a discussion of the military situation, which Stalin painted in gloomy colours. The Soviet armies still held the initiative in most areas of the front, but new German divisions were pressing in the Korosten area, and elsewhere the Red Army was finding it difficult to take the offensive. It was natural that the course of the war in Russia should be discussed by the two men, but Stalin's immediate reference to it gave him an advantage over the President. Although both of them were Commanders-in-Chief, Roosevelt had never exercised military command in the way that Stalin had done since 1941. Furthermore, the Red Army's apparent predicament highlighted the failure of the Western Allies to provide a second front, and Stalin's chief concern was to obtain military relief for his forces.

The point had been clearly made and Roosevelt took it. He referred to the hope that a means might be found to draw forty German divisions away from Soviet forces.

He countered Stalin's military remarks by raising the question of economic co-operation, and in particular the possibility of sharing an inflated Anglo-American merchant fleet with the Russians after the war. Stalin seemed favourably inclined to the prospect of increased trade between the Soviet Union and America, Russia supplying the West with raw materials in return for American equipment. The Americans could hope to influence the Soviet Government by promises of economic generosity in the post-war world, and there is no reason to suppose that either statesman was insincere about his desire to co-operate in these matters. The pattern of international affairs after victory had been gained was seen by both as a condominium exercised by their own

* See above, p. 123.

super-Powers. Both were eager that this condominium should be organized as advantageously as possible. Roosevelt was eager that economic co-operation – in which the United States would clearly have the initiative – should be planned out in advance. He was also keen that China's role in world affairs should be given prominence, partly because the Chinese theatre was an area in which the United States was bearing the major part of the military burden, but largely because he saw China as a reliable American ally after the war. Stalin's dry comment on the Chinese front was that the poor fighting qualities of the Chinese were the result of bad leadership – an unfavourable augury for American hopes that Chiang Kai-shek would be afforded the status of a major ally.

On European questions agreement was easier. Both men were willing to see France eliminated as a major power. This became clear from Stalin's characterization of General de Gaulle's political activities as 'very unreal'. For Stalin, 'real' France was Vichy France, which was at that moment helping the Nazis. Roosevelt himself went so far as to suggest that no Frenchman over the age of forty should be allowed to participate in a future administration. Many years of honest labour would be needed before France could be re-established, and 'the first necessity for the French, not only for the Government but the people as well, was to become honest citizens'.

Roosevelt's puritanical attitude towards his French allies chimed in well with Stalin's revolutionary – but historically more defensible – argument that the fault lay with the French ruling classes, who should not be allowed to share in any of the benefits of peace.

In practice these anti-French attitudes amounted to an agreement that Western Europe should be left in a weakened condition after the war, though Roosevelt knew that the British wanted to build up France to her former status.[2] Furthermore his hostility to France was connected with a general desire to liquidate Western European colonial empires. Stalin urged that Japan be fought with political weapons as well as military ones, and for this reason Indo-China must never be returned to France. The President was only too happy to agree, '100 per cent'. He suggested that China be given trusteeship over Indo-China, and Stalin made no demur. Since Roosevelt stressed that America would give the Philippines independence as soon as the war was over, it was hardly to be expected that British colonial possessions would remain unchallenged. Stalin himself did not broach that subject, and when Roosevelt did so agreed that India was a 'sore spot with the British'. The President urged that discussion on the point had better be put off, but made his general view clear by saying that the best solution for India would be to reform from the bottom, 'something on the Soviet line'. Stalin rightly remarked that this would mean a revolution. He had not been Soviet Commissar of Nationalities for nothing, and he knew that Roosevelt's suggestions involved the destruction of the British Empire.

From President Roosevelt's point of view the meeting could not have passed off better. He had been able to find common ground with his Russian colleague on issues which separated them from the British, and which seemed likely to shape a post-war settlement to the advantage of both their own powerful nations. Roosevelt told his host that he was pleased to be occupying the same house as the Marshal himself, because it would enable them to meet informally and frequently.

A few minutes later Stalin, Roosevelt and Churchill met in the conference room of the Russian Embassy. They represented what the British Prime Minister described as the 'greatest concentration of worldy power that had ever been seen in the history of mankind'.[3]

The unparalleled nature of this first tripartite conference impressed itself on many of those present. At one moment even Admiral Leahy, a man not normally given to romantic fancies, remembered the Field of the Cloth of Gold.[4] But, as he himself remarked, there was precious little pageantry at Tehran. The Olympians of the twentieth century conducted their affairs in a drab, businesslike way, largely devoid of pomp and splendour. Secret Service men and military photographers were not an adequate substitute for elephant trains or a retinue of knights. Marshal Stalin, it was true, had done the best he could to enliven the scene by donning a new mustard-coloured gaberdine uniform, resplendent with gold lace, white stars and a thick red stripe down the trousers. Yet even this had only that *ersatz* magnificence normally associated with proletarian dictatorships, and one British observer felt that Stalin had been more impressive in his cloth tunic and knee boots.[5]

From the Western viewpoint, Stalin was the most fascinating figure at the conference. On the whole, he made a good impression, for – unlike his dictatorial ex-ally in Germany – he rarely tried to monopolize a conversation, nor was he given to histrionic outbursts. His manner was patient, his arguments brief and to the point. During conference sessions he sat quietly doodling and smoking cigarettes which he carried loose in his pocket. He was physically more powerful than both his colleagues; Mr Churchill had a cold which was to develop into pneumonia, and the President was already a sick man. What tantrums were thrown at the conference did not come from Stalin. These personal impressions were not unimportant. Both politicians and military men on the Western side felt that they were face to face with a leader of great power and authority, who would not give ground or promises lightly. It was no mean feat to gain the respect, if not always the admiration, of such widely differing personalities as Harry Hopkins, General Marshall, Mr Eden and Admiral Leahy. Even General Sir Alan Brooke, who regarded the Russians with deep suspicion, recognized in Stalin a man of formidable quality.[6]

The first session of the conference began quietly with the President, the youngest of the Big Three, begging leave to welcome his elders. He addressed the Russians as new members of the family circle, stressing the confidential nature of their discussions. The atmosphere at this first meeting, as at those which followed, was calm, and there were fewer outbursts of temperament than would have been expected at a normal Allied staff conference.[7] Discussion was entirely concerned with the conduct of the war.[8] There is little reason to suppose that any one of the three national leaders present had motives other than strategic ones in this military discussion. Before the conference began the Americans were worried that Stalin might demand more action in the Mediterranean, thus threatening the timetable of 'Overlord'.* Mr Churchill evidently felt that the Russians would realize the advantages of putting Allied divisions into action against the Axis – action which would draw Germans from Russia and which could not interfere with 'Overlord' because no shipping facilities existed to bring Allied forces in the Mediterranean back to fight on the Western Front.

The whole question was one of timing: whether the Allies should risk delaying 'Overlord' a month or two in order to exploit favourable opportunities in Southern Europe, or whether they should restrict their Mediterranean activities so as to be sure of starting a cross-Channel invasion on time.[10] Mr Churchill based his pleas for a more active policy on the Mediterranean on two suppositions. The first was that Rome could be taken by January 1944. The second was that Turkey could be pressed into the war on the Allied side. Neither of these hypotheses turned out to be correct. From the historical viewpoint the strategic argument conducted on this occasion was not decisive, since, had Mr Churchill's view prevailed, his hopes would soon have been dashed by political and military failure. †

As it happened, however, Mr Churchill did not win the argument. Marshal Stalin pleased and surprised the Americans by firmly plumping for Western operations rather than more activity in the Balkans or Italy.

---

* On 21 November 1943 Hopkins expected the Russians to side with the British rather than the Americans at Tehran.[9]

† Mr Churchill himself stressed that Turkey's assistance to the Allies was a *sine qua non* of the whole operation. 'If Turkey does not enter the war, that is the end of that', he said.[11]

5 Yalta: Mr Churchill
and President
Roosevelt on arrival
in the Crimea,
3 February 1945.
Admiral Leahy is
behind Mr
Churchill's right
shoulder

6 Yalta: Mr Molotov
greets Secretary of
State Stettinius,
3 February 1945

7 Yalta: A meeting of
the Foreign
Secretaries,
8 February 1945

8   Yalta: The entrance to the
    Livadia Palace, 5 February 1945

9   Yalta: Stalin arrives at the
    Livadia Palace, 7 February 1945

10 Yalta: Stalin visits President Roosevelt at the Livadia Palace, 7 February
    1945

He was very sceptical about the possibility of a Turkish entry into the war. He suggested that Anglo-American forces in Italy would do better to attack southern France rather than pressing on towards the north. He reminded his listeners that the Alps were a formidable barrier, as Suvarov had ruefully discovered.* Stalin's suggestions – although viewed with dismay by the British General Staff[12] – were both politically and militarily sensible as the comments of a sympathetic outsider.

Stalin had already delighted his American allies by stating that Russia would enter the war against Japan as soon as the Germans had been defeated.† This was reassuring to Mr Churchill also, for it meant that the Americans would have less reason to deviate from the Allied principle that Germany should be tackled as first priority. Nevertheless, the manner in which the discussions had developed at this session was important for the future progress of the conference. It set the tone for a situation in which the Russians and Americans seemed to be working in concert, with the British civilian and military delegates in isolation. To a certain extent this had been desired by President Roosevelt before the meeting, but it was also the result of quite unpremeditated alignments during the conference itself.

That evening the three leaders dined in Roosevelt's quarters, and the conversation turned to the situation after the war. Stalin repeated his view that France should be humbled and stripped of her empire. Roosevelt claimed that Dakar and New Caledonia should be taken from her, and Mr Churchill was willing to accept Four-Power‡ control of certain strategic points formerly in the French Empire.[13]

Then Germany was considered. As already noted, both President Roosevelt and Mr Churchill were in favour of its dismemberment and demilitarization.§ But Stalin took a much more savage view. He seemed inclined to be almost racially hostile to the Germans as a people, and felt that the habit of unquestioning obedience was deeply ingrained in their character. He cited the case of German workers in Leipzig in 1907 who failed to appear at a mass meeting because there was no official on the railway station to punch their tickets.

These remarks did not produce a very clear picture of Germany's future as envisaged by the Russian Government. What did emerge was that Stalin wanted the Germans to be permanently degraded. When Roosevelt suggested that the concept of the Reich should be eliminated, and the word even expunged from the German language, Stalin replied that it was not enough to destroy the word; the Reich itself should be

---

* Suvarov was the Russian General who tried to cross the Alps into Switzerland in 1799.
† See below, p. 348.
‡ i.e. Britain, China, the U.S.A. and the U.S.S.R.   § See above, p. 108.

rendered impotent for ever. He discounted any suggestion that the Germans might be reformed, and made dark comments on the inadequacy of Mr Churchill's suggested safeguards against a German *revanche*. His arguments left a deep impression on the President, who was himself inclined to judge the Germans harshly. Stalin's insistence on the ruthless liquidation of Germany's industrial strength almost certainly inclined Roosevelt to accept the 'Morgenthau Plan' for the reduction of the German economy to that of a predominantly agricultural country.* Later on, when Mr Churchill showed uneasiness at these proposals, the President quoted against him words used by Stalin at Tehran.[14]

The question of Eastern European frontiers then arose. Stalin made it clear that Poland's western frontier should be extended to the Oder and that Russia would tolerate no interference with her authority over the Baltic States. This latter assertion was caused by an unfortunate mistranslation when President Roosevelt suggested that the Baltic *Straits* should be put under international control. It was an incident which illustrated how touchy Stalin would be about territories seized by Russia when allied with Hitler in 1939–40. It also embarrassed the Americans, who had no desire to discuss frontier details of this kind.[15] Mr Churchill, on the other hand, was eager to thrash out the settlement of Eastern Europe. At first he was prevented from making very much progress by the condition of his host. The President had gone very pale during dinner, and when the meal came to an end he was forced to retire. Mr Churchill and Stalin continued their discussions on a sofa in the dining-room. The Prime Minister tried to clarify Stalin's views on both the German and the Polish question. Mr Churchill had proposed that the Germans should be denied aviation of any character, that the General Staff system should be abolished and that German industry should be kept under international supervision to prevent rearmament. Stalin gloomily remarked that furniture factories could be transformed into aeroplane works and watchmaking establishments might produce fuses for shells.[16]† When the Englishman tried to make a distinction between the German people and their leaders he found Stalin blankly contradicting him.[17] Mr Churchill then took the bull by the horns and raised the question of Poland. He stressed that Britain had not committed herself to any particular frontiers for a Polish state, but that she had entered the war in 1939 to save Poland and that the re-establishment of a strong, independent Polish nation was one of her war aims. Poland was 'an instrument needed in the orchestra of Europe'.[18] Stalin showed no eagerness to talk about the Poles.[19] He did, however, agree that the Poles

* See below, pp. 174–84.   † See below, p. 179.

had their own language and culture, and that these could not be extirpated. Pressed to be more explicit by Mr Eden, who was also present, the Russian confirmed his willingness to see Poland's western frontier extended to the Oder, and denied any intention of 'gobbling Poland up'. He did, however, express the desire to take a bite at Germany.

The British were determined to follow up any opening on Poland, and although Mr Churchill was careful to point out that he had no authority to make any final commitment he did suggest that the Allied statesmen ought to work out general terms for a Polish settlement at Tehran. He said he would like to see the Polish borders moved westwards rather as soldiers at drill carried out the movement 'left close'. He produced three matches and moved them sideways to demonstrate this idea in dumb show to the Marshal. Stalin was not to be drawn. He seemed ready to agree in principle that the matter should be settled, but remarked that it would still have to be looked into carefully.[20] In some ways it was a repetition of the Moscow conversations between Cordell Hull, Mr Eden and M. Molotov. The evening ended with Mr Churchill and his colleagues little farther forward in their efforts to help the Poles, although Stalin's apparently conciliatory attitude had relieved some of their worst fears.*

The progress of the conference up to that point had not been at all satisfactory so far as the British were concerned. The Prime Minister expressed his views at the end of the first plenary session by telling his doctor that 'a bloody lot has gone wrong'.[22]

Before the meetings had begun Mr Churchill and his party had been able to hope that Stalin might agree with their conception of a vigorously prosecuted war in the Mediterranean, since this would be most likely to give immediate aid to Soviet forces. There was also the point that the British were willing to relegate the war in the Pacific to a very secondary role until after Hitler's defeat, whereas the Americans were refusing to disgorge landing craft needed for their Pacific campaigns and had involved Britain in an unwanted operation against the Andaman Islands. But Stalin's promise of eventual support in the war against Japan, and his openly expressed preference for a second front in the West, had dashed British hopes. The British, and not the Americans, were to be the odd men out at the conference.

* Mr Eden wrote in his diary that during the conversation after dinner Stalin had 'mellowed' and went on: 'The opening moves [about Poland] did not go too badly. If we could get on to the business soon we might be able to hammer something out. A difficulty is that the Americans are terrified of the subject which Harry [Hopkins] called "political dynamite" for their elections. But, as I told him, if we cannot get a solution, Polish–Russian relations six months from now, with Russian armies in Poland, will be infinitely worse and the elections nearer.' Unfortunately Mr Hopkins did not heed this wise advice.[21]

This became even clearer at the meeting of the Allied staffs which began at 10.30 the following morning.[23] Stalin had brought only one military adviser with him to participate in the conference, Marshal Klimenty Voroshilov – a man whose chief characteristic in the view of the British and Americans, appeared to be an unflinching loyalty to Stalin. The British, in particular, held a very low opinion of his strategic abilities.[24] On this occasion he did nothing to raise himself in their estimation. He showed uncompromising preference for 'Overlord' as against all other operations, and at the earliest moment. He put forward Stalin's view that the best diversionary operations should occur in southern France, rather than in northern Italy or the Eastern Mediterranean. General Brooke later ascribed the Marshal's views to folly on his part and unscrupulous political cunning on that of his master, Joseph Stalin.[25] It was an understandable reaction, but not necessarily an accurate judgement. Neither Stalin nor Voroshilov had had to concern themselves with amphibious warfare. They, like the Americans, thought that a Western assault would draw off far more German troops than piecemeal operations elsewhere and they feared further postponements unless a definite promise was extracted from both their allies. Political objectives – and in particular the desire to keep Anglo-American forces away from the Danube – may have been present, but, as with the British, they played a very secondary role in the military argument. In November 1943 the main issue was still that of defeating the Axis; the division of the spoils had not yet really begun.

In one respect the Americans were more concerned than their allies over the question of post-war planning. Just as Mr Hull had been eager to get agreement to Allied participation in a system of international peace-keeping when he met his opposite numbers in Moscow, so the President was quick to press the importance of such a system in Tehran.

Mr Churchill tried at lunch-time to improve his situation by inviting Roosevelt to lunch *tête-à-tête* with him in the British Legation. In conformity with his determination not to arouse Soviet suspicion by any form of Anglo-American collaboration at the conference, Roosevelt refused. It was poor consolation for the Prime Minister to receive a visit from Averell Harriman explaining that Roosevelt did not want Stalin to know that his two colleagues were meeting privately. British isolation was becoming more marked all the time.[26]

Similar dislike for bilateral discussion in no way inhibited President Roosevelt's relations with Stalin. Shortly before three o'clock he welcomed the Marshal to his quarters once again for a private conversation.*

---

* Some accounts suggest that Molotov and Elliott Roosevelt were present. We have taken the Bohlen minutes of the talk as accurate.[27]

After handing Stalin a number of reports concerning the situation in Yugoslavia, the project for shuttle-bombing of Germany and operations in the Far East, he opened a discussion on the future organization of the post-war world. He went on to elaborate his scheme for the United Nations, which was to include a large group of about thirty-five states making recommendations to a smaller body, an executive committee consisting of the Big Four with a number of smaller nations representing the rest,* and finally a body described by the President as 'the four policemen' which would be responsible for direct action to deal with threats to peace. The 'policemen' would of course be the United States, Russia, Britain and China. Stalin's reaction to this was to doubt whether European states would care to have their affairs regulated by a body which included the Chinese. He preferred a European Council on which the United States would be represented. President Roosevelt rather awkwardly pointed out that the American Congress would be unlikely to agree to United States participation in an exclusively European committee, since this might be able to force the dispatch of American troops to Europe. When Stalin asked if these objections would not apply to similar orders being given by a world-wide committee, Roosevelt explained that he only envisaged the use of American aeroplanes and ships in a European conflict; Britain and the Soviet Union would have to supply the land armies.

The inconsequential nature of these arguments cannot have been lost on Stalin. It was clear that the President's major interest in further-ing his scheme was to establish the position of China as a Great Power. Later on in the conversation Stalin remarked that he was dubious about Chinese participation in the small peace-keeping group, and Roosevelt answered that he realized China's present weakness but that 'after all China was a nation of 400 million people, and it was better to have them as friends rather than as a potential source of trouble'.[28] Roosevelt had underlined American reluctance to commit ground troops across the Atlantic by telling Stalin that, without Japanese aggression at Pearl Harbor, it would probably not have been possible for his Government to send forces to Europe at all. By this Roosevelt seemed to imply that Russia would have to face the threat of possible German resurgence with only the British to look to for support. On the other hand, it did not seem that the Soviet Union need fear the United States as a power rival in post-war Europe.[29] It is not possible to know what factors weighed most heavily in the Soviet dictator's mind.

---

* These would be two European countries, one South American, one Near Eastern and one Far Eastern state and a British Dominion. Roosevelt remarked that Mr Churchill thought the British Empire would be under-represented in this arrangement.

But, since he seemed willing to envisage a regional security council for
Europe in which the United States would participate, it seems likely
that he was prepared to see American power in Europe to safeguard a
future peace settlement. Roosevelt's words can only have strengthened
the impression that after the war the Americans would once again
isolate themselves from Europe, devoting their attention to the Far East.
For Russia this was both a danger and an opportunity. Stalin was
determined to secure himself against the former and seize the latter with
both hands.

Stalin's own conception of post-war peace-keeping was partially
illuminated by his remarks on the elimination of the German threat to
Allied security. He expressed the view that Germany could recover her
strength completely within twenty years if steps were not taken to
prevent her from so doing. The Allies should control certain strong-
points either within Germany or on her frontiers, as well as in other
strategically important areas.* The same technique should be applied
against Japan. A peace-keeping commission should have the right to
occupy such strongpoints. The President was able to express his
whole-hearted agreement with this proposal, chiming in as it did with
his own suggestions on the subject. But although it was clear that both
men wanted to see Germany and Japan prevented from renewed
aggression by hedging them about with a ring of strategic bases, the
form which this restriction would take was not specified.

After their private talk, Stalin and the American President went to
participate in the second plenary meeting of the conference. This was
entirely concerned with military questions, and centred on inter-Allied
staff meetings held that morning.[30] Stalin did all he could to encourage
his allies in their efforts to implement 'Overlord'; he embarrassed the
Americans by asking when they would appoint a Supreme Commander
for the operation, and then went on to belittle Mr Churchill's proposed
assaults in the Mediterranean as diversionary operations of secondary
importance. Although Mr Churchill protested that they would not
reduce the effectiveness of the Western assault, Stalin seems to have
come to the conclusion at this meeting that the British, and not the
Americans, were the chief obstacles to the speedy creation of a Western
Front. In this view he was doubtless supported by Marshal Voroshilov,
who had been able to contrast Marshall's optimistic assessment of Allied
chances with the more critical approach of General Brooke.[31]

Stalin therefore turned his attention to the British Prime Minister,
making him the butt of much searching, and often ungracious, criticism.

* Dakar was specifically mentioned – perhaps to play on Roosevelt's prejudice
against the French.

When, later on that evening, Stalin was host at dinner, he lost no opportunity to bait the British Prime Minister, suggesting that Mr Churchill was nursing a secret affection for Germany and wanted to see the war ended with a soft peace.[32] Stalin himself stressed that there must be effective measures taken to control the Germans after the war, and then produced his notorious proposal that at least 50,000 and perhaps 100,000 German officers should be liquidated. Mr Churchill was naturally incensed by this bestial suggestion, and some ill-judged facetiousness on the part of President Roosevelt did not improve the situation.* The Prime Minister was finally driven to lose his patience completely when the President's son, Elliott Roosevelt, rose to declare his enthusiastic agreement with Stalin's plan. Mr Churchill walked away from his colleagues in high dudgeon, and had to be placated by them both before he would return to the dining-room.[34] Stalin also returned to his suggestion that strategic bases should be occupied by the Allies throughout the world to prevent a resurgence of German and Japanese aggression. The President remarked that these bases should be held under trusteeship, and Stalin agreed. The British Prime Minister, however, realized that 'trusteeship' could be simply a convenient camouflage for permanent occupation. He felt that his two allies seemed to be dividing the world up between them in a fashion detrimental to British interests. He declared that Britain did not wish to acquire new territory, although she intended to keep what she had. In this regard he specifically mentioned Hong Kong and Singapore – bases which had fallen to the Japanese, and which might come into the same category as French Indo-China in the eyes of the Americans. If a portion of the British Empire were to be given its independence, this would be in accordance with the moral precepts of the British and not as the result of external pressure. Clearly this warning was aimed as much at Roosevelt as at Stalin. Indeed, the Russian dictator remarked that he favoured an increase in the British Empire, especially in the area around Gibraltar. The Governments of Spain and Portugal ought to be replaced – a suggestion which does not seem to have been taken up by either of his partners.

Mr Churchill did not want to give Stalin an excuse for excessive territorial aggrandizement by laying claims to new benefits for Britain. Instead, he countered by asking what territorial interests the Soviet Union had. It was Stalin's turn to become evasive. 'There is no need to speak at the present time about any Soviet desires', he said, 'but when

---

* The President remarked that 50,000 was really too many, and that perhaps 49,000 would be enough. There is no particular reason to suppose that Stalin was joking. He later returned to the demand that the 'Prussian officers and staffs should be eliminated'.[33] (See below, p. 392).

the time comes, we will speak.' It was not a reassuring answer. With regard to Poland, at least, the time appeared to have come already.

The following day, 30 November, was Mr Churchill's birthday. He celebrated it by redoubling his efforts to achieve his strategic objectives. That morning he was able to meet Stalin privately. It was their first formal bilateral conversation since the Prime Minister's visit to Moscow in August 1942. He wanted to destroy any impression that the British were trying to 'drag their feet' over a second front. Quite the contrary. British planning was aiming at a more effective second front by stretching the Germans to the full in all European theatres. On the other hand, American projects for operations against the Japanese were likely to weaken 'Overlord' by starving Allied forces in the Mediterranean of landing craft.* Mr Churchill also played on Stalin's eagerness for the naming of 'Overlord's' military commander, and stressed his own desire for an early decision on this appointment.[36]

Since the strategic question was always uppermost in Mr Churchill's mind, it is not surprising that he devoted his time with Stalin to discussing landing craft and operation dates, rather than the future of the Poles, the Czechs, the Finns and the Germans. Yet in one way it was unfortunate that he should have chosen to enlist Stalin's support against Roosevelt at this juncture, for it reinforced the impression that Anglo-American solidarity was fragile, and that Stalin's own ambitions for Soviet expansion would not meet serious opposition.

Nevertheless, by the time the three Allied leaders met for lunch, events seemed to have taken a more favourable turn from the British point of view. The strategic arguments between the Western staffs had ended in agreement over the rough timetable of 'Overlord', and Russian suspicions that the project might be put off were stilled. Indeed, it was Mr Churchill who suggested that Stalin be told at once of the projected arrangements. He also volunteered information on the Command structure in the West, about which Roosevelt seemed reluctant to make a decisive statement.† Stalin, for his part, told his colleagues that he approved of the Western communiqué on Far Eastern questions drawn up at Cairo, although he repeated his criticism of the poor fighting efforts of the Chinese Army.

Stalin himself came out of his reserve over Russia's future interests to

* The Prime Minister told Stalin that 'it was not a choice between the Mediterranean and the date of "Overlord" but between the Bay of Bengal and the date of "Overlord"'.[35]

† General Brooke had been successful in getting agreement to 'Overlord' 'during May' – i.e. substantially later than the Soviet suggestion of 1 May.[37] Mr Churchill told Stalin that the 'Overlord' Commander should control operations in southern France, and the Mediterranean Commander those in Italy.[38]

agree with Mr Churchill's suggestion that she would welcome the acquisition of a warm-water port. The Prime Minister was evidently rather put out when Stalin implied that this warm-water outlet should be through the Dardanelles. He expressed the hope that in future Russian fleets would be seen on all seas of the world – a remark which prompted Stalin to remind him that Lord Curzon had had other ideas.* In fact the British Prime Minister had meant to refer to the Far East when suggesting Russia's access to warm water, and he returned to this point later in the conversation. Stalin at once became more cautious, arguing that until Russia entered the war in the Far East it would be better to postpone discussion. This provoked President Roosevelt into proposing that Dairen could be a free port, and Stalin seemed to find this suggestion attractive. It was not clear how attractive it would be to Generalissimo Chiang Kai-shek, but Roosevelt evidently felt that the Cairo talks had given him the right to make offers of this kind.†

While discussing the question of Russia's access to warm water the President had also mentioned the Baltic – a topic which had led to such a regrettable misunderstanding two nights earlier.‡ He wanted to hear Stalin's views on the possibility of a free zone created out of the former German Hanseatic ports of Hamburg, Bremen and Lübeck, together with the Kiel Canal. It was not surprising that Stalin found this proposal perfectly acceptable.

II

While the three leading statesmen in the Grand Alliance were thus disposing of the world, their chief political lieutenants were at lunch in the British Legation. Among Mr Eden's guests were M. Molotov and Harry Hopkins. The British Foreign Secretary was less enthusiastic than his chief for the large-scale proposals of world reorganization which were being bandied about at the conference. He was especially disturbed at the light-hearted way in which French colonial possessions were being auctioned off for the benefit of a shadowy and imprecise peace-keeping organization, and could not but be dismayed at Mr Churchill's evident willingness to grant Stalin substantial concessions on the Polish

* While Viceroy of India from 1899 to 1905, Lord Curzon had done all he could to prevent the expansion of Russian influence towards the Persian Gulf.

† In the Chinese record of the conversation between Roosevelt and Chiang at Cairo on 23 November 1943, the only mention of Dairen asserts that it should be returned to the Chinese. There is some evidence that Roosevelt mentioned the possibility of a free port; the Chinese Director of Government Information told reporters in September 1948 that Chiang had promised to give consideration to such a proposal when it arose and provided that China's sovereignty was not infringed.[39]

‡ See above, p. 148.

issue. His two guests, on the other hand, were all enthusiasm for the turn the conference was taking. They began to enumerate the 'strong-points' to be occupied after the war. M. Molotov suggested that Bizerta and Dakar should be among them, and repeated the fashionable view that France must be punished for her hostile acts. Harry Hopkins seemed to think that special attention should be given to the future defence of Holland and Belgium. Mr Eden gently pointed out that France had not been too well supported by the British when she was trying to resist Hitler; he could have mentioned that British support had at least been more tangible than that of the United States or Soviet Russia. In the British Foreign Secretary's view Pierre Laval and Marshal Pétain were the real enemies. This sophisticated distinction between good and bad Frenchmen did not appeal to Mr Hopkins and did not suit M. Molotov. Nor was Mr Hopkins pleased when Mr Eden suggested that bases in the West Indies leased to the United States should be used as a model for similar arrangements elsewhere. It was clear that both he and Molotov thought in terms of bases being taken from hostile countries – and for this reason 'hostile' was to be interpreted in a very broad fashion. Nevertheless, Mr Eden was able to gain Molotov's agreement to the proposition that bases should not be annexed by the victor Powers themselves, but should pass into United Nations trusteeship.[40] In this respect the remarks of Harry Hopkins – rightly supposed to be the President's *alter ego* – were not without significance. He emphasized that the three major Allied Powers would have to work out a system of security-control points which would guard against the threat of future enemies. It would have to be done in such a way as to prevent the three Powers arming against one another. This was coupled with the remark that bases which the Americans wished to maintain in the Philippines would be under their control, and not that of the United Nations. Island bases taken from Japan were evidently to be treated in the same way, although the United Nations might 'perhaps exercise some protective influence'.[41] From this a clearer picture of American peace plans began to emerge. The Pacific was to be an American lake guarded by American bases and secured by a numerically powerful Chinese satellite. The Soviet Union would be given privileged access to the lake at its north-western end. Britain would no longer play an important role there and France was to be excluded altogether.

The corollary of this Far Eastern situation was that European security should be largely the concern of Britain and the Soviet Union. Hopkins pointed out that the United States was not likely to be faced with any immediate danger from the Germans, and that the difficult problem of imposing peace on Germany would be involved with that of Soviet and

British strongpoints situated near to Germany. Once again, the suggestion was being strongly made that after the war the United States was going to withdraw her physical presence from Europe and leave her two allies to bear the brunt of peace-keeping there.

The conversation then turned to the problem of involving Turkey in the war. Mr Eden was anxious to further this project, since on its success hinged the possibility of major Allied operations in the Eastern Mediterranean. He was not aided by Harry Hopkins's statement that Turkey's entry into the war would probably delay 'Overlord'. M. Molotov seized on this at once, whereupon the American vaguely referred to possibilities that a scheme might be worked out so that action in the Turkish theatre could take place without interfering with the Western offensive.* Harry Hopkins was too astute to imagine that his belated qualification would help Mr Eden. His objective had been gained. It was clear that this exchange would only increase Soviet doubts about Turkey's entry into the war.

For his part Mr Eden was embarrassed by not being able to answer M. Molotov when he asked what Mr Churchill had meant by telling Stalin that Turkey's post-war rights at the Dardanelles might be affected if she did not yield to Allied pressure. This had not been a happy comment by the Prime Minister, and his Foreign Secretary was forced to admit ignorance of Mr Churchill's intentions.

There was another matter about which Mr Eden wished to sound a warning note. He referred to an 'indiscreet conversation' between Stalin and Mr Churchill during which Poland had been discussed. This was clearly the occasion upon which the Prime Minister had made his suggestion that Poland should move 'two paces to the left'.† Mr Eden said that if such territorial steps were to be taken he would like to know how large they were going to be. M. Molotov agreed that the question required careful study, but once more Harry Hopkins hastened to assure his Russian colleague that the President had spoken openly and frankly to Marshal Stalin and had told him all he had on his mind on the Polish question. This put Mr Eden in the position of a doubting Thomas, and diminished the force of his argument. The Foreign Secretary could hardly reckon that his luncheon party had been a great success.

At 4 p.m. that afternoon the conference reconvened for the third and

* In his biography of Harry Hopkins, Robert Sherwood has interpreted these comments as showing Hopkins's indifference to Turkey's entry into the war. In the minutes of the conversation published by the American State Department he did in fact talk at length on this subject, though the point of his remarks – like those of his master – was not entirely clear. Their intention seems to have been to draw from the Soviet Government a statement that 'Overlord' should not be sacrificed to Turkey and in this he was successful.[42]

† See above, p. 149.

last time.[43] Some solid progress had been made, and General Brooke announced to the assembled company that 'Overlord' would take place during May 1944, supported by a campaign in southern France. Mr Churchill urged that 'in closing in on the wild beast all parts of the narrowing circle should be aflame with battle' and referred again to the possibility of Turkish involvement in the war. Stalin, for his part, delivered himself of a famous commitment to launch Soviet offensives on the Eastern Front simultaneously with 'Overlord'. This promise Stalin kept, thereby greatly impressing the military leaders of the Western Powers, who came to regard him as a man of his word.[44]

The formal conference was closed with an enthusiastic discussion of the methods by which 'Overlord' was to be disguised to deceive the Germans.

III

The day ended with a dinner party for the Big Three and their staffs at the British Legation. Mr Churchill was host, an honour he claimed by right of age, Britain's political seniority and the fact that it was his birthday. He presided at table with President Roosevelt on his right and Stalin on his left. The meal was a festive gathering, characterized more by cordial formality than political discussion. Even the droves of Soviet security police and American Secret Service men could not dim the glory of the occasion. The Legation dining-room had originally been built in Oriental style by the Royal Engineers. General Sir Alan Brooke thought it looked like a Persian temple, its walls 'covered with a mosaic of small pieces of looking-glass set at every conceivable angle, the windows with heavy deep-red curtains'. Persian waiters went to and fro 'in blue and red liveries with white cotton gloves, the tips of the fingers of which hung limply and flapped about as they handed plates around'.[45]

During the meal there were many speeches. These took the form of toasts, in conformity with Russian custom, although they were drunk in champagne and not vodka. President Roosevelt set the ball rolling with a graceful tribute to King George VI, whom he described as an old friend. There followed a series of mutually congratulatory remarks in which the three Allied statesmen all participated. Eventually the President gave a toast to General Brooke. Stalin stood with the rest but did not drink. He remained standing after the President had finished speaking, and proceeded to accuse Brooke of being cold and unfriendly to the Russians. He expressed the hope that Sir Alan would 'come to know us better and would find that we are not so bad after all'. Not surprisingly Brooke was very upset by this unexpected attack. Feeling that if he did not answer Stalin he would lose the Russian's respect, he carefully worked out a suitable reply. When the opportunity presented itself he rose to speak. Referring to an earlier discussion on strategic deception and camouflage, he suggested that Marshal Stalin had been deceived by dummy tanks and aeroplanes and had overlooked the real friendship which Brooke felt for his Soviet allies. Unfortunately Sir Alan was not a very glib after-dinner speaker, and the importance of the occasion doubtless increased his diffidence. His manner seemed stiff and his assurances of amity somewhat unconvincing. They were not helped by a series of ironical interjections from Stalin – upon whom the champagne was evidently having a lubricant effect. Sir Alan concluded abruptly with a toast to Admiral Leahy – in itself a miscalculation, since his obvious choice should have been Marshal Voroshilov.[46]

Nevertheless, Stalin shook hands cordially with Brooke once the dinner was over, and Mr Churchill was well pleased with his Chief of Staff.[47]* The speeches, which had already been eulogistic enough, became suffused with the rosiest glow of optimism. Mr Churchill, speaking of changing political attitudes throughout the world, told his audience that Britain's political complexion was turning 'a trifle pinker'. Stalin, who was clearly enjoying himself, rapped out 'That is a sign of good health!' This exchange was not lost on President Roosevelt. When, at the end of the dinner, he claimed the right to have the last word, he returned to the theme of differing political complexions.

I like to think of this [he said] in terms of the rainbow. In our country the rainbow is a symbol of good fortune and of hope. It has many varying colours, each individualistic, but blending into one glorious whole.

Thus with our nations. We have differing customs and philosophies and ways of life. Each of us works out our scheme of things according to the desires and ideas of our own peoples.

But we have proved here at Tehran that the varying ideals of our nations can come together in a harmonious whole, moving unitedly for the common good of ourselves and of the world. So, as we leave this historic gathering, we can see in the sky, for the first time, that traditional symbol of hope, the rainbow.[49]

* Later on in the meal General Brooke was faced with another crisis which required physical dexterity rather than political expertise. A large cream ice was brought round, perched on top of a perforated metal tube in which there was a night light. The ice was therefore illuminated and made a most impressive culinary delight. Unfortunately the tube began to topple as it approached Brooke, and he realized that the whole contraption was about to fall. With great presence of mind he ducked, pulling General Somervell, his American neighbour, down with him. The ice crashed on to the table and struck the Russian interpreter, M. Berezhkov, squarely amidships. He was splashed from head to foot, but since he was at that moment interpreting for Stalin he could not break off his task. Persian waiters wiped him down with towels as he stolidly continued to speak.[48]

It was rhetoric not unworthy of Hollywood, but it suited the mood and the hour.

IV

Although the formal business of the conference was over, some of the more important political issues were still outstanding. So far as the British were concerned, one of the most vital was Turkey's entry into the war. At noon on 1 December the political experts in the Allied delegations met with the Big Three for a working luncheon,[50] and Turkey was the first topic to be discussed. The results were scarcely pleasing for the British, although after his conversation with Harry Hopkins and M. Molotov, Mr Eden can hardly have been expecting much eagerness on the part of his colleagues. The Prime Minister began by stressing that Allied help to Turkey would be restricted to aeroplanes and some anti-aircraft units; the only amphibious assault he envisaged would be an attack on Rhodes in March 1944. This at once aroused American opposition. Harry Hopkins announced that no landing craft were available for such an operation and that no promise of such a move should be made to the President of Turkey. When the Prime Minister suggested that landing craft might be diverted from the Pacific theatre he was promptly contradicted by President Roosevelt. If Mr Churchill hoped that American intransigence over the needs of the Pacific war would draw Stalin into the argument on his side, he was disappointed. The Marshal maintained his customary reserve, although he did agree to declare war on Bulgaria if she attacked Turkey. M. Molotov complicated the issue further from the British viewpoint by returning once again to Mr Churchill's remarks on the future of the Dardanelles. The Prime Minister repeated that in his personal opinion – and he stressed that he was far from his Cabinet and the British Parliament – there should be a change of régime at the Straits if Turkey remained obdurate in her desire to keep out of the war. The position therefore was that Turkey was being urged to enter the war on the grounds that she would thereby gain a position of privilege at the peace-making table; if she remained neutral she might find her international status threatened.

On the whole, the prospects opened up by Mr Churchill's remarks must have seemed more favourable to Russia if Turkey did not enter the war. Her intervention might cause an embarrassment on Russia's southern flank and perhaps complicate arrangements for 'Overlord'. On the other hand her continued neutrality might bring with it political gains for the Soviet Union. Although at the end of the discussion it was agreed that President Ismet Inönü of Turkey should be called to

Cairo to discuss the matter with President Roosevelt and Mr Churchill, it was clear that only one of the Big Three was really enthusiastic for Turkish intervention. It was perhaps not surprising that the Turks were far too wily to let themselves be jockeyed into hostilities by Allied nations who were not themselves united on the issue. Turkey would only come off the fence if the consequences of inactivity were demonstrably more disastrous than those of belligerence. Despite Mr Churchill's eloquence at Tehran and Cairo, the Turks were not faced with a choice sufficiently brutal to force them into the Allied camp.

The next matter to be considered was the future of Finland. President Roosevelt brought this forward, and although he was vague about the American attitude to Finland, his object was evidently to press the Russians into negotiating with the Finns, thereby ensuring Finland's independence whilst removing her from the war. This was probably connected with a general concern for the future of Scandinavia. If Finland could be freed from both German and Soviet domination the fears of the Swedes, in particular, might be stilled. There might even be the prospect of Sweden entering the war. These aspects of the matter remained unspoken, although Mr Churchill did express the hope that Sweden might join the Allies.[51]

Stalin seemed quite amenable to American suggestions about Finnish independence, but he was once again firm in his demand that the western frontier of the Soviet Union should be that drawn in 1940. He was thus unwilling to give up any of the gains Russia had made as the result of the Ribbentrop–Molotov Pact. He also claimed a large reparation from the Finns – 50 per cent of the damage done to the Soviet Union by Finnish aggression. This was another illustration of Stalin's ruthless attitude towards defeated nations, and of his determination to restore the Russian economy by massive reparations. Mr Churchill, in particular, was unhappy about this prospect, not merely because it might give Stalin opportunities for aggressive acts after the war, but also because he remembered the mistakes made by Allied statesmen over reparations in 1919. The differences on this point ran deep and were to bedevil inter-Allied relations until the final division of Germany in 1949. Mr Churchill remembered that during the First World War the Bolsheviks had taken a very different view of peace-making, and slyly remarked to Stalin that in his ears 'there was the echo of the slogan "No annexations and no indemnities"'. The Russian was not put out. He countered by reminding the Prime Minister that he had already admitted to becoming a Conservative. This amusing exchange did not moderate Soviet views on reparations. So far as Finland herself was concerned, the Anglo-American *démarche* may have had some effect.

Stalin was assured by Mr Churchill that Russia would end the war as the leading Power in the Baltic, and Finland's frontiers could evidently be drawn in a fashion generous to Russia. There was no real reason for Stalin to risk a conflict with his colleagues over Finland.

If Finnish prospects seemed less bleak after this lunch-time discussion, those of the Poles were becoming grimmer all the time. From his conversations with both the British and the Americans, Stalin was aware that they were willing to see major Soviet territorial gains in Poland. But there was still some danger that he would be pressed by the Allies into a hard-and-fast agreement which might restrain him from establishing a subservient régime in Warsaw. During the course of that December afternoon this particular danger vanished. Roosevelt had asked Stalin to visit him in his apartments. M. Molotov and Mr Harriman were also present when the two leaders met. The President told his Russian colleagues that if the war went on into 1944 he might be reluctantly forced to run for re-election as President. There were six or seven million Americans of Polish extraction in the United States, and he did not wish to lose their votes. He agreed with Marshal Stalin that the Polish state should be restored, but wished to see the eastern border moved further to the west, and the western frontier shifted to the river Oder.[52] Owing to the political embarrassment which such an arrangement would involve, however, he could not publicly participate in any such arrangement, nor could he subscribe to any decision on Poland taken at Tehran.

Roosevelt's words were of tremendous importance. On the one hand they virtually guaranteed to Stalin the territorial prizes he had been seeking in eastern Poland. On the other hand they removed all necessity for the Soviet Union to make its peace with the Polish Government. Indeed, they made such a *rapprochement* even more undesirable than before, since excessive claims by the Poles for restoration of their eastern territories were evidently not going to be toned down by the Americans. Faced with the prospect of an unattractive and largely unrepresentative Polish Government pressing for a restoration of Poland's pre-war frontiers, Stalin had good reason for preferring to wait upon events. As Mr Eden had already pointed out to Harry Hopkins, the situation would be very much more difficult for the Poles once the Red Army had crossed their frontiers.

Roosevelt went on to explain that the fate of the three Baltic Republics was of internal political significance for the Americans because many citizens of the United States could trace their families back to Latvia, Lithuania or Estonia. If these countries were occupied by Soviet troops, what the President described as 'world opinion' would require some sort of expression of the popular will. He made it clear that such an expression need not take place until after the Russians had been in possession for some time, and he had prefaced his remarks on this point with the jocular comment that he did not intend to go to war about it. Hence it was obvious that the Soviet title to the Baltic States would be acceptable to America provided it were embellished with some suitably attractive political flummery.

Even these modest suggestions produced a very stern reaction on Stalin's part. He retorted that the three Baltic countries had enjoyed no autonomy under the Tsar of Russia when he was in alliance with Britain and the United States. Yet no one had raised the question of public opinion then, and he did not see why it was being raised now. Little demonstrates so clearly the extent to which Roosevelt wished to ingratiate himself with Stalin as his failure to rebut this illogical and historically inaccurate statement.* Stalin was claiming that, by citing the example of Nicholas II, he could ignore the principles of self-determination laid down independently by the American President Woodrow Wilson, by Lenin and by the first Soviet Commissar for Nationalities – who had happened to be Joseph Stalin.†

The President also asked that his proposals for a world-wide peace-keeping body should not be discussed with Mr Churchill at that juncture. He had evidently come to the conclusion that his two allies were lukewarm about this project. He may have feared that Stalin and Churchill would agree to minimize China's role in the new organization, or themselves bring forward plans for regional security systems. Stalin relieved his mind on this score by telling him that, on second thoughts, a world-wide security scheme seemed more attractive. Nevertheless, Roosevelt remained under the impression that his allies were lukewarm and needed more intensive persuasion.‡

The last act – it was not quite the epilogue – of the Tehran Conference began that evening in the conference room of the Soviet Embassy.[54] President Roosevelt initiated the discussion by referring to the two major outstanding issues – Poland and the treatment of Germany at the end of the war. After M. Molotov had rather reduced the effectiveness of this introduction by starting a successful hare about the distribution of the Italian fleet, the President was able to return to the Polish question. He urged a re-establishment of relations between the Soviet and Polish Governments. On the face of it this was a measure of loyal support for both the London Poles and their British hosts.

---

* The United States was never allied to the Tsar.
  † Stalin was appointed Soviet Commissar for Nationalities in November 1917.
  ‡ 'I'll have to work on both of them' were his words to Senator Tom Connally on his return to Washington.[53]

Stalin accused the Polish Government of aiding the Germans. He stressed that the Soviet Government wished to re-establish a Polish state and expand it at the expense of Germany. Only if the Poles in London were willing to co-operate with the partisans* and sever connections with German agents in Poland would the Soviet Government be willing to negotiate with them.

By this time the discussion had become totally unreal. Roosevelt was pressing the Soviet leader to restore relations with the Polish Government in order to placate Polish opinion in America. But he had only just told Stalin in private that no far-reaching settlement about Poland could be accepted by him at Tehran. Stalin could therefore afford to appear reasonable, since he knew that recognition of the London Government was not going to be forced upon him.

The British, of course, were unaware of what had passed between Stalin and the President. They knew of Roosevelt's political worries, but could not imagine that he had opted out of the discussion in advance.[55] Mr Churchill therefore pressed hard for the acceptance of a territorial settlement. He returned to his illustration with the three matches to explain Poland's westward movement, and offered to present any reasonable Soviet formula for new frontiers to the Polish Cabinet. This would be put before them as the best they could hope to obtain; if they refused it Britain would be through with them, and would not oppose the Soviets under any conditions at the peace table. Stalin at once mentioned the Russo-Polish frontier established in 1939. He was nettled when Mr Eden described this as the 'Ribbentrop–Molotov Line'. The situation created by this remark was, indeed, somewhat embarrassing, since the Russian signatory of the notorious Nazi–Soviet Pact – M. Molotov – was himself in the room. He hastened to point out that the 1939 frontier was actually the 'Curzon Line'. This frontier had been proposed by a British Foreign Secretary in 1920,† and therefore seemed less open to objection than that resulting from Hitlerite aggression against Poland. The British and Russian Foreign Ministers began to disagree over frontier delineation, and the statesmen fell to a close examination of maps. Stalin himself took up a red pencil and marked out a number of modifications in the 1939 Molotov–Ribbentrop frontier. These gave Poland a larger area of territory.‡ In return Russia would take part of East Prussia, including Königsberg, Tilsit and Insterburg.

---

* By this, of course, he meant Communist partisans. Both the Poles in London and the Communists accused each other of collaborating with the Germans.

† See above, p. 46 n.

‡ These comprised the region around Bialystock bounded by the Bug in the south and west and extending to Grodno in the east, and a smaller indentation west of and including Przemys.

The Marshal was also happy to agree to an infelicitous suggestion by President Roosevelt that there might be voluntary transfer of peoples from mixed areas. Doubtless Stalin's conception of 'voluntary' differed from that of the President, but since Russian experience of such transfers was far greater than that enjoyed by the Americans each could be pardoned for ignoring the idiosyncratic interpretations of the other.

V

There can be little doubt that it was as the result of this discussion, preceded as it had been by similar proposals from the two Western Powers, that the eastern frontiers of post-war Poland were settled. Over the actual line itself there was comparatively little argument. Mr Churchill wanted to pursue the matter in greater detail, partly because he imagined it to be his task to persuade the Poles to accept the final settlement. Since neither Stalin nor Roosevelt wanted this latter development his concern was largely wasted. So far as Poland's frontiers were concerned, the Western statesmen could feel that Poland had little to complain about. Although Polish nationalists would resist the changes in the east, their country would actually have to surrender few entirely Polish areas.* Poland would, on the other hand, gain very substantially from German dismemberment, and this might well improve her status as a European Power.†

By this time both President Roosevelt and Stalin had good reason to change the subject, although Mr Churchill still persisted in his efforts to dot the i's and cross the t's on a final settlement. Roosevelt suggested that they discuss the partition of Germany, and Stalin willingly agreed. He indicated, however, that the British Prime Minister was not listening, implying that Mr Churchill did not want to see Germany partitioned. This provoked the latter to say that he had not yet left Lwow – one of the chief places in dispute on Poland's eastern frontier.[57] It was to no avail. Roosevelt and Stalin had already ridden off on to another and more congenial topic.

Whatever political difficulties Poland might cause President Roosevelt, and whatever moral obligations Messrs Churchill and Eden might feel towards their gallant Polish allies, Poland lay in Eastern Europe where ultimate decisions lay within the preponderance of the Soviet Union. Germany – the core of the Axis – was of direct concern to all the belligerents. Even for Roosevelt she embodied the magnetic, evil power

---

* The major exception was Lwow, a Polish town with a Ukrainian hinterland.

† Lord Moran quotes Mr Churchill as saying on 29 November 1943 that Poland would emerge from the war more powerful than before.[56]

which had drawn so many of America's sons away from her shores in two world conflicts. The future of Germany was the future of world peace. If it could not be properly controlled, the war would have been waged in vain.

At the start of the discussion it was already clear that all three men believed in the partition of Germany. Mr Churchill still harped on Prussia's separation from the rest of the Reich. Stalin talked grimly of dismemberment, while the President produced his plan for five German successor states with the Ruhr and the Kiel Canal under international control.* This was a radical scheme. As Mr Churchill put it, the President had 'said a mouthful'. The Prime Minister had more modest and perhaps more practical proposals. Apart from Prussia's isolation, a number of South German states should be detached and joined to a new Danubian Confederation.

Such a scheme was naturally most unpalatable to Marshal Stalin. He had no desire to see Britain re-establishing the balance of power in Europe by creating a larger version of the Austro-Hungarian Empire. He argued that German areas within the framework of larger confederations would simply enable the Germans to rebuild a powerful state. In any case he did not believe that there were differences among Germans; all German soldiers fought like devils and the Austrians were the only exception. He was also contemptuous of Presidential suggestions that Germany's armaments industries should be controlled. 'What about the watchmakers and table-makers?' he demanded. Their industries could easily be transformed for military purposes.† He relentlessly dismissed any suggestion that the German economy might have to be reconstructed after the war, or that a healthy Germany was needed for a healthy Europe. 'Re-education' of the German people seemed to have no place in his plans; Germany must be destroyed and the Germans kept weak. On the whole, Roosevelt was eager to fall in with Stalin's views. Mr Churchill put up more resistance. He saw that Stalin's real aim was the Balkanization of Europe. This was made even clearer when the Russian remarked that Austria, Hungary, Rumania and Bulgaria must return to their former status as independent Powers. The Prime Minister promptly asked Stalin whether he wanted to see Europe composed of little states, disjointed, separated and weak. Stalin deftly evaded the question by saying that Germany, and not Europe, should

* Roosevelt's scheme envisaged a small and weak Prussia; Hanover and a north-western section; Saxony and the Leipzig area; Hesse-Darmstadt, Hesse-Kassel and the area south of the Rhine; and Bavaria, Baden and Württemberg. Each of these five areas would be self-governing.
† The President later reminded Mr Churchill of Stalin's words when they met at Quebec on 13 September 1944 (see below, p. 179).[58]

be thus weakened. He saw Poland, France and Italy as strong countries; Rumania and Bulgaria would remain the small states they had always been. He was supported by President Roosevelt, who produced the unhappy comment that Germany had been less of a danger to civilization when divided into 107 provinces. Mr Churchill drily remarked that he hoped for larger units.

It was indeed a bleak prospect for Europe which Marshal Stalin had sketched out. His references to France, Italy and Poland as large states could hardly convince Mr Churchill. He knew how little sympathy either of his allies had shown France; Italy was a defeated nation and Poland had yet to be re-created from the ruins of Nazi rule. Despite these disagreements, one fact had emerged clearly. Germany was to be broken up and kept economically weak. The elaboration of this decision was left to the European Advisory Commission, to which it was formally referred. For the next twelve months the imposition of a draconian peace on Germany was accepted as official Allied policy, although in practice very little was done to work out the details.

Before the discussion ended Mr Churchill made one last determined effort to settle the Polish issue. He repeated his offer to take a formula to the Polish Government. Stalin announced his willingness to accept the Curzon Line as the Polish–Soviet frontier provided that Königsberg and Tilsit went to Russia. President Roosevelt kept silent, and the meeting ended with the general impression having been gained that Mr Churchill would transmit these terms to the Poles in London.[59]

VI

After the Tehran Conference was over Mr Churchill and President Roosevelt returned to Cairo where, from 4 to 7 December, they discussed a number of matters whose resolution was to have an important effect on the outcome of the war.

The strategic decisions taken at Tehran necessitated readjustments in Anglo-American military policy. Of prime importance was Stalin's promise that, once Germany was defeated, he would help to fight the Japanese. Taken in conjunction with the absolute priority given to 'Overlord', this weakened American determination to press on with military operations in conjunction with Chiang Kai-shek. The British had always felt that too much attention was being paid to the Chinese. They doubted the military value of the Chinese Army and disliked Chiang's tendency to meddle with British imperial affairs in India.

In the early days of December 1943 these differences crystallized in an argument over the fate of 'Operation Buccaneer', an amphibious assault on the Andaman Islands which had been promised to Chiang as a support for land operations in northern Burma. Mr Churchill exerted all his efforts to obtain its cancellation, and the British military staffs pressed their American counterparts in the same sense.[60] Roosevelt was unhappy at breaking his pledge to Chiang, but on the evening of 5 December, at a meeting in Mr Churchill's Cairo villa, Harry Hopkins pushed a sheet of paper across to Mr Eden on which he had written: 'It looks as if "Buccaneer" is out and our military plans hence will be agreed tomorrow.'

Eden returned the paper having written: 'If so, you have been very generous, but our chances next year will surely benefit. President has been grand about it all. Note reinforcements (Scotch!) just come in.'[61]

Despite the flippant tone of this exchange, the matter had been fought out in deadly earnest, and the British military staffs, in particular, were delighted with the outcome. By freeing landing craft for operations in Europe the cancellation of 'Buccaneer' undoubtedly helped the Allied war effort. But it also held political implications. It confirmed that China was losing her importance as an ally to the Western Powers. Russia seemed likely to be more effective in finally defeating the Japanese. At the time of the Tehran and Cairo Conferences the war in the Far East seemed to stretch far into the future. One of the strategic plans being considered to crush Japan involved constructing numerous bomber bases on Chinese territory and raising American-trained Chinese divisions to defend them. The plan required an enormous construction effort fed from supply lines in Bengal. Preparations would not be complete until the autumn of 1945 and even then only if the offensives in Europe proceeded favourably. To create the optimum requirements for an overwhelming air assault on Japan a further year's grace would be necessary.[62]* In actual fact many of the projected air bases were overrun during the summer of 1944, when the Chinese proved incapable of defending them. The American air forces began to hope for bases in Russia. When the Japanese were beaten it was as the result of Allied operations in South-east Asia and the Pacific. Chiang Kai-shek played little part in this victory.

China did not, therefore, emerge from the war with the status of a World Power. Yet President Roosevelt's hopes that she could be used as a counterweight to European imperialism in the Far East committed America to support the Kuomintang with financial aid and military assistance. When Roosevelt met Chiang at the first Cairo Conference he encouraged him to apply for a large loan from the United States, and apparently promised to equip a powerful Chinese Army. Chiang's

* The code-name for this operation was 'Drake'.

Government demanded the fulfilment of this latter promise even after the war.[63] Roosevelt's association with the Kuomintang brought America few military advantages. It helped to saddle her with burdensome political obligations in Asia of which she has yet to be relieved.

For his part Mr Churchill was faced with difficulties with allies and associates nearer home. One of his main objectives at Cairo was to bring Turkey into the war. This had been agreed at Tehran, and it fitted in well with the Prime Minister's view that operations in the Mediterranean, the Aegean and the Balkans should be exploited with vigour to disperse German strength before 'Overlord'. He voiced the hope that penetration of Southern Europe would create a vast system of encirclement. If Bulgaria, Rumania and Hungary fell to the Allies the heart of the Axis would be threatened. The next Allied conference, he said, 'might perhaps be held at Budapest'. It was essential that the Germans be held at every point and that the whole ring should close together.[64]

The Americans were not enthusiastic about this concept, but President Roosevelt agreed to help persuade the Turks to join the Allies. Their President, Ismet Inönü, came to Cairo and was subjected to determined pressure by both the British and the Americans. He proved himself a very effective negotiator, who had lost none of the diplomatic adroitness he displayed at the Lausanne Conference of 1923; he gave nothing away. Proposals to move Allied air forces into Turkey were countered with the demand that Turkey's Army should be strengthened to defend her against German attack. Although Inönü was loud in his enthusiasm for participation in the war, it was fairly clear that his conditions would postpone operations *ad calendam*. Turkey remained non-belligerent.

The reluctance of the Turks to fight the Germans was paralleled in the early months of 1944 by set-backs to Allied military policy in the Mediterranean which rendered Mr Churchill's hopes at the Cairo Conference illusory. The Allied offensive in Italy proceeded slowly, and Rome was only captured on 4 June, two days before the second front was opened in France. From the purely military viewpoint it was probably fortunate that the Turkish adventure was never embarked upon, for it might have seriously hampered operations in Italy and France. Nevertheless, the decision to put the major weight of Anglo-American effort into their Western European attack meant that liberation of the Balkans would have to be postponed.

This had political implications for Greece and Yugoslavia. It was the Greek question which was to cause Mr Churchill most difficulty in the months which followed.* Greece was bedevilled with domestic political strife. Her King, George II, had fled from the Nazi invasion to take

* See below, p. 239.

refuge in Cairo. In Greece itself several resistance groups were formed. One of these, ELAS, was under the influence of the Greek Communist Party. It seemed more interested in political victory after the Germans had left than in actually fighting them while they remained. The most effective non-Communist group – known as EDES – was more belligerent towards the Germans.

British officers sent to make contact with Greek partisans did what they could to create unity between the competing groups in an effort to organize an effective struggle against the Nazis. The position of King George was an obstacle to any such unity. He had been associated with the pre-war dictatorship of General Ioannes Metaxas who died in January 1941. Although Greek public opinion was scarcely open to analysis, it was evident that this régime had become discredited. After the fall of Greece to the Germans, King George himself renounced it, but his own future as a monarch was still in question. Politicians in Greece showed reluctance to take him back, and the British were pressed to declare that he would not be imposed upon Greece without an expression of popular support. The Foreign Office in London came round to the view that there was likely to be serious internal conflict unless George agreed to defer returning to Greece until after his people had been given the chance to express their views.

This danger grew more important with the changing strategic situation in the Eastern Mediterranean. Earlier in the war it had seemed possible that King George would be accompanied to Athens by large Allied forces and that he himself would command a liberating army heavily engaged against the Germans. His political stature in Greece would have been immensely strengthened thereby. However, in the late summer of 1943 it had become probable that Greece would remain a military backwater. The Tehran decision in favour of 'Overlord' confirmed that probability. Nazi withdrawal from the country would occur as the result of fighting elsewhere. Allied forces in Greece were unlikely to be numerous. There would be scant protection for the King if his rule were opposed by partisan forces. The British had no desire to waste manpower fighting a civil war. Nevertheless Mr Churchill was determined to establish a stable and friendly Government in Greece.[65]

At the first Cairo Conference Mr Eden had discussed the Greek question with Foreign Office officials and had come to the conclusion that King George ought not to return to Greece until he had been asked to do so by the Greek people. This policy was approved by the British War Cabinet on 22 November, and when Mr Eden returned to Cairo he took the matter up with the King himself. He pointed out that a declaration by the King in the sense suggested might lead the EDES resistance group to put itself under the command of the Greek regular Army, and that this in turn might encourage some ELAS supporters – by no means all of whom were Communists – to accept the authority of the exiled Greek Government.

British policy towards the Greeks received a severe set-back, however, when President Roosevelt intervened. In order to obtain American co-operation for his negotiations with the Greeks, Mr Eden had sent a copy of a Foreign Office memorandum on the subject to Harry Hopkins. Instead of reacting favourably to this gesture the President angrily rejected British attempts to influence the King. His intervention was decisive. On 6 December he told King George that he was under no obligation to make any declaration prejudicial to his own position.[66] The President also instructed Lincoln MacVeagh, the American Ambassador to the Greek Government, to avoid associating himself with any pressure being put on the King.[67]

Two days later Mr Churchill tried to persuade King George that it was in his own interests to make the suggested declaration but, bolstered by Roosevelt's assurances, the King refused to do so. Divisions in the Greek camp grew more serious, and by April 1944 units of the Greek Army in the Mediterranean theatre actually mutinied. On 12 April George II finally declared himself willing to await the results of a free popular vote before he returned to his country. It was a very belated gesture, and although a semblance of unity was created among the Greek resistance groups in September 1944, friction continued and culminated in civil strife. Despite Mr Churchill's attempts to conciliate moderate Greek opinion, it was the British Government which was later to be blamed for supporting 'reactionaries' in Greece.

It is still not entirely clear why President Roosevelt obstructed British policy towards Greece at the Cairo Conference. Most probably it was a reflection of the State Department's obsessive hostility towards spheres of influence – especially British ones. There was also a reluctance to take any step which might offend the Russians. Time was to show that Stalin was happy to accept spheres of influence so long as the Soviet Union received a generous share of them. Nevertheless, Greece remained a source of friction between the British and their allies.

One other issue was touched upon at the second Cairo Conference which was to cloud Anglo-American relations in the following year. This was the problem of finance. Under the Lend-Lease Agreement the British had promised not to build up large-scale reserves of dollars whilst they were in receipt of American aid. A limit had been set at one billion dollars.* Owing to the presence of large American forces in the

* An American billion – actually a milliard or thousand million.

United Kingdom, the British had in fact exceeded this limit. On the
other hand the debts they were incurring as a result of the war far
outpaced their gains in American currency. It was estimated that
Britain would end the war owing five times as much as she had accumulated in dollar reserves. At the second Cairo Conference Mr Churchill
gave Hopkins a Treasury memorandum about this, pointing out that
although the Soviet Government was building up larger reserves than
Britain no restrictions were being placed upon it. If Lend-Lease were
curtailed to the British they would be receiving less favourable treatment
than either the French or the Russians.[68]

This question was related to a larger and more intractable one: how
could Britain remain a World Power after the war, having exhausted
herself economically in order to win it? No effective answer was ever
found. Some of those suggested were of no help to the Allies in planning
a stable European settlement.*

Roosevelt and his staff left Cairo early on 7 December, and the most
important series of conferences which had so far taken place among the
Allied leaders was thereby concluded. Strategically they were very
successful. They laid the foundation for operations against the Axis
which by the end of 1944 transformed the state of the war in Europe and
brought Hitler to the verge of defeat. They also confirmed that, once
the Germans were overcome, the combined power of the Allies would
be turned against Japan.

Politically the results of the meetings were less satisfactory. This was
not surprising. Military issues were rightly treated as paramount. It had
become clear that Germany would be occupied and in some way
dismembered. Poland would be shifted westwards and her Government
would have to be acceptable to the Soviet Union. For the rest, the
settlement of Europe was left open. France's future seemed very
uncertain. It was evident that no other Continental Power would
be allowed to appear which might form a counterweight to Soviet
Russia. The Allies had pledged themselves to support some sort of
peace-keeping organization. Just what its powers would be were still
vague. So far as colonies were concerned, it seemed that the British
would keep theirs as a reward for winning the war. They might even
make some gains.† But American hostility to imperialism and Russian

---

* See below, pp. 178-83.

† See, for example, a memorandum by Charles ('Chip') Bohlen on the attitude of the
Soviet Government on European political questions as expressed by Marshal Stalin
during the Tehran Conference. The memorandum was drawn up on 15 December
1943. It records that 'there should be no reduction of the British Empire, but on the
contrary it should if necessary be increased by turning over to Great Britain on the
basis of trusteeship certain bases and strong points . . .'. France on the other hand was
to become 'a charming but weak country'.[69]

distaste for other Continental Powers suggested that new arrangements might be made in respect of other European colonies, particularly those in the Far East.

The way in which these problems – and especially those concerned with the continent of Europe – were handled would depend on the extent to which the conference decisions could be consolidated at a lower level by patient diplomacy and inter-Allied planning. Since most of the issues open to doubt concerned Britain and America – Russia's position had been made clear at Tehran and her objectives largely accepted – close collaboration between the two Western Allies was especially important. Yet, whereas in the military field Anglo-American planning worked superbly, on the diplomatic front much less progress was to be made. When the Big Three met again – more than a year later – the problem of Europe's future had become acute. But the British and the Americans had still not managed to co-ordinate their policies effectively.

9 | The Morgenthau Plan and JCS 1067

I

THE pattern for the post-war treatment of Germany had been set at Tehran and the architect of it was Joseph Stalin.* Using arguments not unreminiscent of those employed by Georges Clemenceau twenty-five years before at the Peace Conference of Paris, the Marshal demanded Draconian measures against Germany to the end that she might never again be capable of aggression. These measures included complete dismemberment and the prevention of any sort of war-potential remaining in German hands after the Reich had been partitioned. Stalin's interpretation of this latter measure was all-embracing. While President Roosevelt thought in terms of the control of war industries, the Marshal proposed the virtual de-industrialization of Germany, claiming that civilian industries, like watch-making and furniture manufacture, were easily capable of being turned to military production and that the Germans could therefore not be trusted with them.

It is to be believed that Mr Churchill was not receptive to these Soviet proposals. By nature generous, he was unwilling to allow the post-war treatment of Germany to be motivated by pure vindictiveness. Yet he was the last who could be accused of being 'soft' or sentimental about the Germans, though Stalin often made this accusation. Like Lloyd George in 1919, he sought for a formula which would 'contain' Germany without destroying her utterly and completely, believing this, in the light of history, to be virtually impossible.

Not so President Roosevelt; here the parallel with the Paris Peace Conference breaks down, for the President was guilty of none of the humanitarian impulses which had motivated Woodrow Wilson. Roosevelt had his own large-scale plan for the break-up of Germany and he was happy to fall in with the rigorous demands of Stalin. Thus they two overbore the scruples of Mr Churchill, and the Tehran Conference charged the European Advisory Commission with preparing plans and measures for the destruction of Germany.[1] †

* See above, pp. 147–8, 166. † See above, p. 167.

President Roosevelt's motives in thus agreeing with Stalin were complex. In the first place he was anxious to keep on the right side of the Marshal in general furtherance of his dream of a post-war U.S.A.– U.S.S.R. world condominium. Secondly, it was something of a personal conviction with him that Germany should receive harsh treatment. 'There are two schools of thought,' he wrote to Queen Wilhelmina of the Netherlands, 'those who would be altruistic in regard to the Germans, hoping by loving kindness to make them Christians again – and those who would adopt a much "tougher" attitude. Most decidedly I belong to the latter school, for though I am not bloodthirsty, I want the Germans to know that this time at least they have definitely lost the war.'[2] Thirdly, the President appeared to have a hazy, misconceived idea that, by the break-up of the German industrial potential, an economic vacuum would be created which would be filled to Britain's advantage by Britain's exports.

Thus when Roosevelt returned to Washington from Tehran he became a somewhat ready target for the rabid views on Germany propounded by his old friend and Secretary of the Treasury, Henry J. Morgenthau, Jr.

The Secretary of the Treasury ranks next in American Cabinet precedence to the Secretary of State, and Cordell Hull had suffered acutely from this propinquity. A combination of comprehensibly emotional rage at the rise of Hitler and his persecution of the Jews, and a less understandable tendency to act as if clothed with authority to project himself into the field of foreign affairs, not infrequently caused Mr Morgenthau to induce the President to anticipate the State Department or to act contrary to its better judgement.[3] The result was a continuous degree of friction between the two Secretaries.*

---

* Morgenthau's ultimate thinking on the post-war future of Germany originated partly from his own inner consciousness and partly from intimate exchanges of views with his close friend and adviser, Harry Dexter White.[4] White was later indicted before a Senate Committee on a charge of subversive and pro-Communist activities in 1948; he committed suicide shortly after testifying.[5] There have not lacked those who have charged openly that Morgenthau was surrounded at the United States Treasury by a group of Communist sympathizers who were actually guilty of passing Government secrets to Moscow, and the Morgenthau Plan has therefore been formidably attacked as being Soviet-inspired, more especially as it followed so closely the political sentiments of Marshal Stalin. The more recent of these charges has been made in November 1967 by Dr Anthony Kubek, Professor of History at the University of Dallas, Texas, in his historical introduction to the report on the Morgenthau diaries of a subcommittee of the Senate Committee on the Judiciary. His final paragraph runs as follows:

'Never before in American history had an unelected bureaucracy of furtive, faceless, "fourth-floor" officials exercised such arbitrary power or cast so ominous a shadow over the future of the nation as did Harry Dexter White and his associates in the Department of the Treasury under Henry Morgenthau, Jr. What they attempted to do in their curious twisting of American ideals, and how close they came to complete

In the nine months which separated the Tehran and Cairo Conferences from the second Quebec Conference, Morgenthau made frequent representations to the President in respect of the post-war treatment of Germany and redoubled his efforts when, in August 1944, the prospect of a further meeting between President Roosevelt and Mr Churchill became imminent.

Towards the end of this month Morgenthau drew the President's attention to the proof-sheets of a handbook prepared for American officers engaged in training for the Allied Military Government of Occupied Germany, which he considered to envisage an all too lenient line of policy. Roosevelt agreed with him. 'It gives the impression', he wrote to Cordell Hull and to the Secretary of War, Henry L. Stimson, 'that Germany is to be restored just as much as the Netherlands or Belgium, and the people of Germany brought back as quickly as possible to their pre-war state.' The President reiterated the importance of driving home to the German people the fact that they had lost the war and had been engaged in a lawless conspiracy against the decencies of civilization. 'I do not want them to starve to death,' he continued, 'but, as an example, if they need food to keep body and soul together beyond what they have, they should be fed three times a day with soup from Army soup kitchens. That will keep them perfectly healthy, and they will remember that experience all their lives.'[7]*

Shortly thereafter – on 25 August – the President set up a Cabinet Committee composed of the Secretaries of State, the Treasury and War, together with Harry Hopkins, to consider post-war policies for Germany as a preliminary to his discussions with Mr Churchill. In the course of the deliberations of this body it became increasingly apparent that a substantial difference of opinion separated the Secretary of the Treasury from his colleagues. Whereas Hull, Stimson and Hopkins were fully prepared to chastise the defeated Germans with whips, Morgenthau expressed a preference for scorpions, and, what was more important still, it appeared that the President was more closely attuned to his extreme views than to the comparatively more moderate policies advanced by the others.[9]

---

success, is demonstrated in those documents. But that is all which is known for sure. What priceless American secrets were conveyed to Moscow through the tunnels of the Communist underground will probably never be known – and how much actual damage these sinister men did to the security of the United States remains, at least for the moment, a matter of surmise.'[6]

* The President is quoted as saying to Morgenthau: 'We have got to be tough with Germany and I mean the German people not just the Nazis. We either have to castrate the German people or you have got to treat them in such manner so they can't just go on reproducing people who want to continue the way they have in the past.'[8]

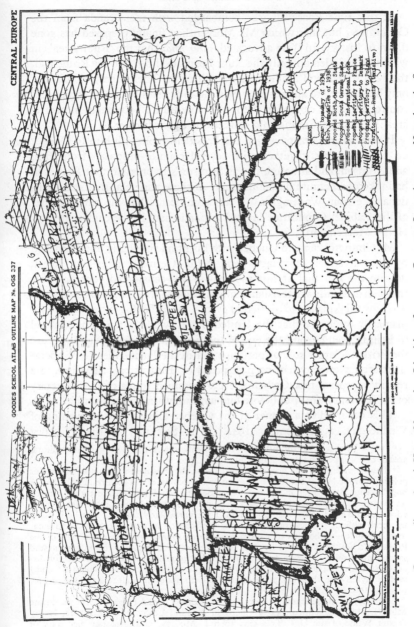

Germany dismembered. Henry Morgenthau Jr's vision of post-war Germany, September 1944. Note that the Saar Basin was to go to France and that the Ruhr was to be internationalized.

At this time Roosevelt was bombarded with memoranda from the Committee, but that which Mr Morgenthau finally prepared has gone down to history. In it he advocated, *inter alia*, that the 'Ruhr Area' (in which he included not only the Ruhr Basin itself but also the Rhineland, the Kiel Canal, and all Germany north of the Kiel Canal) 'should not only be stripped of all presently existing industries but so weakened and controlled that it cannot in the foreseeable future become an industrial area'.[10]* Marshal Stalin could scarcely have gone further.

It was this document which the President took with him to Quebec on 11 September, together with several counter-proposals from Hull and Stimson, and although it was Stimson's impression that Roosevelt had taken no definite decision on any of these papers at the time of his departure from Washington[11] it was significant that the only member of the Cabinet Committee invited to participate in the conference was Henry Morgenthau.†

Mr Churchill came to Quebec with his mind singularly untrammelled by considerations of what should befall Germany after her defeat, despite the fact that at this moment it was considered very probable that German military resistance might collapse in a matter of weeks. He was now thinking ahead of current events. He had come to the conference primarily to ensure that the United States would extend financial aid to Britain even beyond the end of the European war and also to secure for Britain a larger role of participation in the Pacific theatre of operations after Germany had been disposed of. He was not, therefore, in a readily receptive mood when the Carthaginian terms of the Secretary of the Treasury were put before him without warning or preamble.

This occurred at a dinner at the Quebec Citadel on the evening of Wednesday, 13 September 1944.‡ The Secretary of the Treasury

* It is to be noted that the provision for 'grassing down' the Ruhr as an agricultural area does not appear in this memorandum.

† The Secretary of War was concerned about the President's health as well as his policies – or the lack of them. 'I have been most troubled about the President's state of body', wrote Mr Stimson in his diary on 11 September. 'He was distinctly not himself on Saturday [9 September]. He had a cold and seemed tired out. I rather fear for the effects of this hard conference upon him. I am particularly troubled that he is going up there without any real preparation for the solution of the underlying and fundamental problem of how to treat Germany.' Lord Moran confirmed this view of the President's health: 'I wonder how far Roosevelt's health impaired his judgement and sapped his resolve to get to the bottom of each problem before it came up for discussion. At Quebec he seemed to me to have lost a couple of stones in weight . . . and I said to myself then that men at his time of life do not go thin all of a sudden just for nothing.'[12]

‡ There were present on this occasion, in addition to the President and the Prime Minister, Mr Morgenthau, Lord Cherwell, Admiral Leahy, Lord Leathers, Henry Dexter White of the U.S. Treasury, John J. McCloy, U.S. Assistant Secretary of War, H. Freeman Matthews of the State Department, Admiral Ross McIntire, the President's physician and his British counterpart, that inveterate chronicler Lord Moran.

developed his thesis for the destruction of the German economy and the President supported him. Mr Churchill was violently opposed. He was also annoyed. Had he been brought over to Quebec to discuss a scheme such as this, he queried, and added, with a snort: 'England would be chained to a dead body [Germany].' But the President would not recede from his position. He reminded the Prime Minister that Stalin had said at Tehran: 'Are you going to let Germany produce modern metal furniture? The manufacture of metal furniture can be quickly turned into the manufacture of armament.'* Mr Churchill retorted that he was entirely in favour of disarming Germany but not of depriving her of a decent standard of living. There were bonds between the working classes of all countries and the English people would not tolerate the policy which Mr Morgenthau and the President were advocating. 'I agree with Burke. You cannot indict a whole nation.'

The discussion continued with neither side giving way. At one moment one of the Americans suggested that Germany should be compelled to return to a pastoral state with a lower standard of living. The Prime Minister recoiled from this: 'What is to be done should be done quickly. Kill the criminals but don't carry on the business for years.' The meeting broke up with the President's suggestion that the Secretary of the Treasury (and apparently Mr White) should further examine his proposals with Lord Cherwell: 'Let the Prof. go into our plan with Morgenthau.'[13]

There followed a fateful conference. Lord Cherwell entertained an almost pathological hatred for Nazi Germany, and an almost medieval desire for revenge was a part of his character. He was therefore favourably predisposed towards Morgenthau's views. Moreover he saw the matter as somewhat in the nature of a *Kuhhandel* – as he admitted to Lord Brand at Quebec, who chided him for irresponsibility. Mr Churchill very much wanted financial assistance from the United States; Mr Morgenthau very much wanted his document on Germany signed. Though the one was not necessarily dependent upon the other, it was Lord Cherwell's view that Britain would be much more likely to get continued Lend-Lease if Mr Churchill were persuaded to sign the document. 'The Prof.', therefore, joined with Mr Morgenthau in endeavouring to achieve this end. Later, however, on more mature consideration, his natural intelligence and his considerable knowledge of economics convinced him of its folly and he so advised the Cabinet.[14]†

Nevertheless the immediate result was a victory for Mr Morgenthau.

* See above, p. 166.

† 'I can't over-emphasize how helpful Lord Cherwell was because he could advise me how to handle Churchill', Morgenthau reported to his staff on his return to Washington.[15]

Under the force of Lord Cherwell's persuasion Mr Churchill abandoned his opposition, being particularly influenced by the argument that by adopting the Morgenthau Plan Britain would acquire much of Germany's iron and steel markets and would eliminate a dangerous competitor. 'The United Kingdom had lost so many overseas investments that she could only pay her way when peace came by greatly increasing her exports, so that for economic as well as military reasons we ought to restrict German industry and encourage German agriculture', the Prime Minister later wrote in his memoirs. 'At first I was violently opposed to the idea. But the President and Mr Morgenthau – from whom we had much to ask – were so insistent that in the end we agreed to consider it.'[16]

But the Prime Minister did more than consider the Morgenthau Plan. With his usual enthusiasm and ebullience, once the decision had been taken, he threw himself into the affair with great zest. Lord Cherwell and Mr Morgenthau had produced more than one draft of what had been agreed but none of them pleased Mr Churchill. At Mr Morgenthau's suggestion he appears to have consented to write his own draft and, calling in his secretary, dictated the following memorandum of agreement:*

At a conference between the President and the Prime Minister upon the best measures to prevent renewed rearmament by Germany, it was felt that an essential feature was the future disposition of the Ruhr and the Saar.

The ease with which the metallurgical, chemical, and electric industries in Germany can be converted from peace to war has already been impressed upon us by bitter experience. It must also be remembered that the Germans have devastated a large portion of the industries of Russia and of other neighbouring Allies, and it is only in accordance with justice that these injured countries should be entitled to remove the machinery they require in order to repair the losses they have suffered. The industries referred to in the Ruhr and in the Saar would therefore be necessarily put out of action and closed down. It was felt that the two districts should be put under some body under the world organization which would supervise the dismantling of these industries and make sure that they were not started up again by some subterfuge.

This programme for eliminating the war-making industries in the Ruhr and in the Saar is looking forward to converting Germany into a country primarily agricultural and pastoral in its character.[17]†

* The statement that the final text of the 'Morgenthau Plan' was dictated by Mr Churchill – a version which has been accepted by Lord Moran – rests solely on the evidence of Mr Morgenthau himself, as recorded by H. Freeman Matthews of the State Department.

† This final paragraph is an intensification of the Morgenthau–Cherwell draft which Mr Churchill had rejected. This latter text ran: 'This programme for eliminating the war-making industries in the Ruhr and in the Saar is part of a programme looking

There was further consultation along the lines of this text between the two Heads of Government and their advisers on 14 September,[19] and it was on this day that the President gave his assent to financial aid being granted to Britain after the defeat of Germany and while the war against Japan continued, to the tune of $3½ billion for munitions and a further $3 billion for 'other assistance'. Final agreement on Germany was reached on the following day when President Roosevelt and Mr Churchill initialled the text of the memorandum and added 'O.K.' to their initials. Mr Churchill cabled the news of this agreement to Mr Attlee, his deputy in London, and the President informed the Secretaries of State and War of his decision in a memorandum dated 15 September.

Why indeed did Mr Churchill subscribe to the terms of the Morgenthau Plan, a proposition which was manifestly opposed to all his better judgement and his usual wisdom? Was it, as some American historians have suggested, in the nature of a *douceur* to Morgenthau and the President for the continued grant of Lend-Lease?[20] Or was the grant a bribe to Mr Churchill to accept the Morgenthau Plan? John Snell, a reputable historian, rejects this latter theory on the grounds that 'there was no need for Morgenthau to make an offer or for Mr Churchill to accept it'.[21] But this is not quite in accordance with the recorded facts. According to a Presidential memorandum to Secretary Hull dated 15 September, it was specifically stated that 'Morgenthau had presented at Quebec, *in conjunction with his plan for Germany* [authors' italics], a proposal of credits to Britain totalling six and a half billion dollars'. And the Secretary's comment is that 'this might suggest to some the *quid pro quo* with which the Secretary of the Treasury was able to get Mr Churchill's adherence to his cataclysmic plan for Germany'.[22] Point to this view is given by Mr Churchill's own words, that the President and Morgenthau, 'from whom we had much to ask', were so insistent that he abandoned his original opposition to the Morgenthau Plan. Nor is there any real relevance in the emphasis laid by Mr Morgenthau, in reporting on the Quebec Conference to the Cabinet Committee, on the point that the final memorandum on Lend-Lease aid to Britain was not drafted until the final day of the conference and that the Prime Minister had agreed to the policy on Germany prior to this.[23] If the Prime Minister had known from the first – as was asserted by the President though never specifically stated by Mr Churchill – that the two issues were inseparably conjoined, and considered them accordingly, it is of little matter which agreement was accepted first.

There remains one further consideration. *If* the Prime Minister had

---

forward to diverting Germany into largely an agricultural country.'[18] Under the original provisions of the Morgenthau Plan the Saar Basin was assigned to France.

been persuaded by Lord Cherwell into making a *Kuhhandel* with the Americans, how far was he absolutely sincere in doing so? Did he perhaps sense, even at the very moment of agreement, that the disastrous and cataclysmic provisions to which he was assenting were so preposterous that they would prove impossible to sustain after the termination of hostilities, whereas the agreement for Lend-Lease was of a durable value? This is not a hypothesis that can be completely dismissed.

For the counter-attack on the Morgenthau Plan began on the very day it had been accepted (15 September). Anthony Eden arrived on this day from England with his Foreign Office advisers. Sir Alexander Cadogan joined him in Quebec, as did Lord Brand, the representative of the Treasury. The Foreign Secretary had been warned by Lord Halifax from Washington that means to induce a severe post-war inflation in Germany 'might come up at Quebec', but he was wholly unprepared for the *fait accompli* with which he was confronted.

Mr Eden was naturally and justifiably extremely annoyed that an agreement which not only ran counter to the whole principle of the Atlantic Charter but also cut right across the work on which the European Advisory Commission had been engaged for over a year should have been reached without reference to, or consultation with, himself or Cordell Hull. It was particularly ludicrous since the plan produced by the E.A.C. had been approved by Molotov and had received the sanction of President Roosevelt himself. The Foreign Secretary spoke his mind clearly and forcefully in the presence of the President and the Prime Minister, though it is unlikely that he 'flew into a rage' as reported by Lord Moran.[24] Nevertheless his opposition incensed Mr Churchill. 'For the first time', writes Lord Avon, 'he showed impatience with my views before foreign representatives. He resented my criticism of something which he and the President had approved, not, I am sure, on his part, but on the President's.'[25]

The Prime Minister's resentment may have been occasioned by this course, but it is also open to consideration whether Mr Eden's arguments may not have brought him to a realization of the unwisdom of what had been done. The Foreign Secretary may well also have aroused that obstinate streak in Mr Churchill's character which disliked and overran criticism – even when he knew it to be justified. That Lord Avon's account of what occurred is 'underplayed' may be deduced from the record of Mr Churchill's remarks which Mr Morgenthau later gave to his Cabinet colleagues. 'If it is between the British and German people, I am for the British', the Prime Minister is reported to have said, though whether this remark referred to the benefit which the British economy would derive from the execution of the Morgenthau Plan or the advantage secured by its acceptance in respect of continued Lend-Lease is undisclosed. His annoyance with the Foreign Secretary is further shown in his subsequent remarks: 'I don't want you running back to the War Cabinet trying to unsell this proposal before I get there. I want to talk to them first about this.'[26]* Nevertheless Mr Eden's arguments prevailed and, as far as the British Government was concerned, the Morgenthau Plan was 'quietly put away'.

The President also encountered substantial opposition on his return to Washington. On Mr Hull's own admission, 'this whole development at Quebec, I believe, angered me as much as anything during my career as Secretary of State'.[27] Apart from the fact that crucial decisions, which ran contrary to established policy, had been taken, both in respect of German economy and of Lend-Lease, without the aid of any reputable experts or reference to Mr Morgenthau's fellow members on the Cabinet Committee, the Secretary of State was appalled at the sheer irresponsibility of the proceedings. In a personal interview with the President, he gave vent to views which he subsequently supported by a series of memoranda, to the effect that Morgenthau's plan was out of all reason. Its net result, said Mr Hull, would be that nothing would be left to Germany but land and only 60 per cent of the German people could live on the land. This meant that the other 40 per cent would die. If these facts leaked out it might well mean a bitter-end German resistance that could cause the loss of thousands of American lives.[28]

At the hands of Mr Stimson the President received an even rougher passage. The uncompromising integrity of the Secretary of War was deeply shocked by both the vindictiveness and the impracticability of what had been agreed at Quebec. He did not hesitate to say so to the President. Roosevelt essayed his puckish charm. He grinned at the grim-visaged Mr Stimson and 'looked naughty'. Finally he said, 'Henry Morgenthau pulled a boner', and went on to say that all he had wanted to do was to give Britain a portion of the proceeds of the Ruhr; he had no intention of turning Germany into an agricultural state. 'Mr President,' said Mr Stimson, 'I don't like you to dissemble to me', and he proceeded to read to the President portions of the document on which he and the Prime Minister had agreed. Frankly staggered, the President said that he had 'no idea how he could have initialled this'.[29]†

* According to the record of H. Freeman Matthews of the same meeting, Morgenthau expressed surprise at Eden's opposition as he had gained the opposite impression in conversations with the Foreign Secretary in London a short time before. This would presumably refer to a meeting recorded by Harry Dexter White of 13 August 1944.

† To Harry Hopkins the President admitted that he had yielded to the importunities of 'an old and loyal friend' when he affixed his initials to the document.[30]

Under the united pressure of Stimson, Hull, McCloy and Hopkins, the President withdrew his approval for the Morgenthau Plan early in October 1944. There was no communication between him and Mr Churchill on this point, but by common and tacit consent it was allowed to disappear from the field of practical politics.

II

But this was not quite the end of the matter. Mr Hull's fears that the contents of the Morgenthau Plan might become public were realized when that indefatigable and pertinacious journalist the late Drew Pearson gave space to them in his widely syndicated column on 21 September.[31] From whom Drew Pearson had received his information remains a mystery – as was usual with him – but he was certainly well informed. Pearson was followed next day by Arthur Krock in the *New York Times*, and a day later still the *Wall Street Journal* described the main details of the Morgenthau Plan, noting that it was not yet official policy and that there was considerable opposition to it in the Cabinet. Krock followed up on 2 November with more details of the plan and of the *Kuhhandel* of which it had been a part.[32]

These disclosures 'sparked off' considerable comment, mainly adverse, throughout the American Press.* Thence it spread to the European continent and, as Mr Hull had feared, provided excellent ammunition for Joseph Goebbels's propaganda machine.

Ever since the successful landings of D-day, Goebbels had maintained a consistent line of warning to the German people that defeat spelt destruction and that the Allies intended to implement 'a plan of exterminating us root and branch as a nation and as a people'.[34] With this as his theme the Morgenthau Plan came to Goebbels as a godsend. † 'It hardly matters whether the Bolshevists want to destroy the Reich in one fashion and the Anglo-Saxons propose to do it in another. They both agree on their aim: they wish to get rid of thirty to forty million Germans.'[36] The German Ministry of Propaganda continued to pursue this line throughout the winter, declaring, with scant contradiction from London and Washington, that the destruction of German industry

* Mr Stimson was at pains to inform the President that the leak had not occurred in either the State Department or the War Department, indicating that the Government agency which had most to gain from the disclosure was the Treasury, with whom Drew Pearson had close contact.[33]

† It was particularly unfortunate that the publicity given to the Morgenthau Plan coincided with the appearance in the United States of a book by a Dr Kaufman advocating the post-war sterilization of all Germans between the ages of eighteen and sixty in the case of men, forty-five in the case of women – some 48 million in all. This too was grist to Goebbels' mill.[35] See above, p. 176 fn., for Roosevelt's views on this subject.

envisaged by the Allies would be such that 50 per cent of the German population would be faced with the choice between starvation and emigration. 'Germany has no illusions', declared the *Völkischer Beobachter*, 'about what is in store for her people if they do not fight with all available means against an outcome that will make such plans possible. The Quebec decision will serve only to redouble German resistance.'[37] This proved indeed to be the case, as captured letters written by front-line troops were soon to show.*

This would seem to be sufficient comment upon Sir Llewellyn Woodward's statement in his official history that 'the Morgenthau Plan had no effect in prolonging German resistance'.[39]

President Roosevelt sought to redress some of the damage done with a statement in New York on 21 October, in the course of his fourth Presidential campaign. While not officially or explicitly repudiating the Plan, the President asserted that the German people after their defeat would not be plunged into enslavement, but there would be stern punishment for those Germans 'directly responsible for this agony of mankind'.

Indeed the President appeared to undergo a positive revulsion of spirit from the whole idea underlying the Plan. On 20 October he wrote to Mr Hull, 'I dislike making plans for a country which we do not yet occupy'; and five days later he put a comprehensive estoppel on all post-war planning, even questioning the American directive from the Civil Affairs Division which had already been cleared in Washington and circulated to the European Advisory Commission in London.[40] Before the pendulum of President Roosevelt's mercurial genius had returned to a more ordered equilibrium, much valuable time had been lost.

III

Thus should have ended the episode of the Morgenthau Plan – an episode which reflected little credit on the wisdom or the judgement of the two great statesmen participating. And, indeed, in so far as Mr Churchill was concerned, the Plan disappeared from British policy.

In the United States, however, 'the melody lingered on'. When the directive prepared by the Joint Chiefs of Staff – known as JCS 1067 – was promulgated on 22 September 1944, it was found that Secretary Morgenthau had succeeded in injecting a substantial degree of his

* According to Lieutenant-Colonel John Boettiger, President Roosevelt's son-in-law, the Morgenthau Plan was 'worth thirty divisions to the Germans', and General Marshall complained to Morgenthau that, just as the American Army had set up loudspeakers on the frontline urging the Germans to surrender, Krock's article of 2 November appeared and stiffened the will of the Germans to resist.[38]

political thinking into it. JCS 1067 was, in effect, an official but diluted version of the Morgenthau Plan and it remained the cornerstone of American Military Occupation policy until replaced by a new directive in July 1947.

JCS 1067 was intended to punish the German people collectively and indiscriminately by reducing their standard of living to a drastic degree – in accordance with President Roosevelt's memorandum to Secretary Stimson.* No oil and rubber were to be manufactured; no merchant ships built; and all aircraft of any kind were prohibited. The Occupation authorities were specifically forbidden to take any steps to rehabilitate the German economy except to increase to the maximum agricultural production.[41]

To General Lucius Clay, the American High Commissioner, and his chief adviser, Lewis Douglas,† this policy seemed the sheerest lunacy. To create deliberately an unemployment problem in the middle of Europe when nearly every other European country was in dire need of the very necessities of life did indeed seem madness. 'This thing', Mr Douglas declared, on seeing the draft of the directive on 16 April 1945, 'was assembled by economic idiots. It makes no sense to forbid the most skilled workers in Europe from producing as much as they can for a continent which is desperately short of everything.'[42] And General Clay wrote later that 'It seemed obvious to us even then that Germany would starve unless it could produce for export and that immediate steps would have to be taken to revive industrial production.'[43]

General Clay and Mr Douglas agreed that the latter should return at once to Washington, there to consult in Washington with the President, with James F. Byrnes, Director of War Mobilization, and with Robert Lovett, Assistant Secretary of War, to try to obtain some modification of JCS 1067 on lines which should be more realistic in terms of world policy. It was impossible to treat Germany as an isolated factor in a continent which had suffered collectively the horrors and devastation of total war. As Mr Douglas reasoned from his personal observation on arrival in Washington, 'The problem is not a German problem. It is one which embraces a very large part of Europe. It touches France in respect to coal and transportation; Belgium in respect to food and transportation; Holland in respect of food, coal and transportation; Italy, from what I have heard, in much the same manner; and eastern Europe and the Danubian Basin similarly.'[44]

In this reasoning, it is important to remember, there was no thought of a 'soft' peace for Germany. The Morgenthau theory was to treat the

* See above, p. 176.
† Later U.S. Ambassador to the Court of St James's, 1947–50.

German people as a completely separate entity and enact retribution upon them as if they existed in a vacuum. The thought of Mr Douglas and those who shared his views was that the Morgenthau thesis – and, therefore, JCS 1067 – was unpractical for reasons of geography and also undesirable, since a vast pool of unemployed Germans would – and did – create a fertile field for Communist propaganda in the heart of Europe. What they aimed to do was to make the Germans work – in some sense as helots – for the relief and recovery of those countries which had been victims of their aggression and ultimately for their own salvation.*

However, this eminently wise policy was rejected in Washington and Mr Douglas returned dejected to General Clay's headquarters in Frankfurt. An opportunity to facilitate and accelerate the economic recovery of Europe as a whole had been lost for the time being.

* Yet, on 22 July 1945, on the American Broadcasting Company network, Mr Douglas was denounced as 'a believer in a soft peace' by Drew Pearson, who, in terms of some emotion, advocated the policy of Secretary Morgenthau and JCS 1067.

10 | The Road to Yalta

I

THE autumn and winter of 1944 saw a heightening of the tensions which had always been a feature of inter-Allied diplomacy. This was due to the changing military situation and the fact that post-war planning was becoming a more urgent problem as the Nazis were pressed back on all fronts. The differences between the objectives of the various individual Allies – over such matters as the future of Eastern Europe, the treatment of Germany, the nature of the international security organization to be set up after the war, and the restoration of colonial empires – were progressively less easy to gloss over as the time came to take firm decisions. In addition to these fundamental problems there were also important conflicts of opinion within the various belligerent Governments about the nature of diplomacy after the war.

It is difficult to document conflicts of this kind, especially since they often took the form of differences of emphasis rather than open clashes of principle. They were naturally muted when one section of an administration – such as the British Foreign Office or the American State Department – found itself out of sympathy with policies espoused by the great men who were leading the Alliance. Nevertheless, ministries sometimes possess more stamina than individual statesmen, and their views tend to be taken seriously in the long run. Domestic differences of this kind are most easily demonstrable in the case of Britain or the United States, but it is not unreasonable to suppose that they also existed in the Soviet Union. The method of decision-making under Stalin remains something of a mystery; we should not, however, lightly accept the view that Russian policy was simply an expression of his personal whims. When Mr Churchill visited Moscow in October 1944 he formed quite a different view of Stalin's position, and thought that in many matters the Marshal was acting under pressure from others. 'Behind the horseman sits black care' was his comment to his colleagues in the War Cabinet.[1] The Prime Minister undoubtedly exaggerated the extent to which Stalin had to take account of his party apparatus. Nevertheless, arguments over military and political matters went on behind the scenes in Russia as elsewhere, and the significance of such conflicts should not be ignored.[2]

Mr Churchill's comment can serve to illustrate the extent to which the atmosphere at the summit of inter-Allied relations differed from that among the lower echelons of diplomacy and civilian administration. Between the Big Three, whose names were associated with the victorious conduct of the war, there did exist a bond of respect and common endeavour. This by no means precluded mutual suspicion. Mr Churchill feared that post-war Europe might be threatened by Communism, and his fear found expression several times in the summer of 1944.[3]* President Roosevelt, for all his cliché-ridden language, was by no means naïve in his assessment of other men's motives. He calculated that the interests of the United States could best be served by an accommodation with the Soviet Union, and his diplomacy must be judged in the light of this assumption. Stalin's immunity to emotional ties of war-time cameraderie needs no demonstration. Nevertheless, the progress made by the Alliance and the personal communication between its three leaders did incline them towards the idea that major international problems could most conveniently be settled by arrangement between themselves.

Such a point of view seemed less attractive to those diplomats and officials who had to work on detailed problems of international security, territorial apportionment and the future economic health of the victor Powers. They had to plan for a world in which the personal influence of mighty individuals would not always be decisive. It is also important to remember that the issues which most occupied the minds of the Big Three often differed from those engaging diplomats at a lower level. Whereas, for example, the British Foreign Office and the American State Department tended to find themselves more and more in agreement about policies to be pursued over the economic and political future of Europe, their supreme chiefs retained other priorities. For the Big Three the pursuit of victory in the war – the main cohesive factor in their association – was still of overriding importance. True, by the autumn of 1944 victory seemed inevitable, but the speed and the manner of that victory remained undecided. When considering military objectives the alignments which looked natural to diplomats, and which actually did emerge after the end of the war, were by no means self-evident.

From the British point of view a quick victory over Germany was essential. Britain's resources of manpower and money were critically low. So far as Mr Churchill and his service chiefs were concerned the military performance of their Soviet allies was a good deal more

* See below, pp. 290–1.

satisfactory than that of the American-led forces under General Eisenhower. In December 1944 Mr Churchill was dismayed at the failure of the Western armies to achieve their strategic objectives in France and the Low Countries. Field-Marshal von Rundstedt's counter-offensive in the Ardennes seemed for a time to cast even more doubt on the effectiveness of Eisenhower's generalship. At one stage the British tried to interpose an over-all land commander between Eisenhower and his field generals, a proposal which the Americans strongly resented.[4] Stalin's forces, on the other hand, were making much more satisfactory progress. Respect for their achievements deepened when, in January 1945, they responded to appeals from the West and launched powerful new offensives against the Germans.

For their part, the Americans were eager to enlist Russian aid against Japan as soon as they possibly could. Their interest in this was increased by the disastrous collapse of Chiang Kai-shek's Nationalist forces on the Chinese mainland. Although in practice British offensives against the Japanese proved more effective than either Russian or Chinese intervention, the Americans continued to belittle British participation in the Far Eastern War. Mr Churchill was eager to stress the extent to which British naval forces, in particular, would contribute to Japan's defeat, but this was unlikely to make much impression on President Roosevelt. For one thing Britain was engaged against the Japanese already, whereas, though Stalin had pledged his word at Tehran,* Russian help had yet to be secured. For another, Russia's political influence in the Pacific was more welcome to Roosevelt than was that of the British, who might be expected to insist on the re-establishment of European colonial empires in South-east Asia. Above all, the American strategic planners believed that Russian intervention was essential if the Japanese were to be knocked out of the war in 1945.

Under these circumstances Anglo-American displeasure at Soviet excesses in Eastern Europe was often muted by the need to placate Stalin over other urgent matters. The fact that President Roosevelt and Mr Churchill were not always themselves agreed over European problems, such as the post-war treatment of Germany or Allied policies on Greece, Italy and France, did not help to clarify the more fundamental divergences between the Western Powers and the Soviet Union.

II

The most important source of conflict between Stalin and his Western partners remained the Polish question. The nature of this problem was

---

* See above, p. 147.

illustrated in a particularly tragic fashion by the Warsaw uprising of August 1944. In that month the Polish Home Army – whose allegiance was to the Polish Government in London – tried to strike a major blow for independence by liberating their own capital before it was occupied by the advancing Russians. Such a victory for the non-Communist Polish forces would obviously run counter to Soviet plans for the political subjection of Poland. The Home Army therefore received no aid from the Russians. On the contrary, Stalin described them as 'the group of criminals who have embarked on the Warsaw adventure'.[5]

In Britain Mr Churchill and his Air Force chiefs tried to persuade Stalin at least to give the R.A.F. and American air forces the refuelling facilities needed to aid the Home Army. The Russian leader firmly refused. Great bitterness was caused by this incident, especially among those involved in planning the air drop to the Poles. Their service commander, Air Marshal Sir John Slessor, was later moved to write in his memoirs: 'How, after the fall of Warsaw, any responsible statesman could trust any Russian Communist further than he could kick him, passes the comprehension of ordinary men.'[6]*

Although it was difficult to assess the military situation in Poland, it certainly seemed to the British that the Soviet Government, having first broadcast radio messages encouraging the people of Warsaw to risk their lives against the Germans, had then deliberately allowed them to be crushed. Mr Churchill and his colleagues evidently felt that they had not received very warm support from Washington in their efforts to save Warsaw. Although President Roosevelt made sympathetic noises about the Poles and even sent a joint message to Stalin on their behalf, he did not throw himself behind their cause with anything like the vigour shown by his British partner. The President thought that the fate of the Home Army did not warrant a clash with Stalin which might jeopardize prospects for future inter-Allied co-operation.[7] His service chiefs seem to have been lukewarm on the issue; Polish problems did not have the same emotional appeal for them as for the British, who had entered the war to save Poland and had been fighting alongside Polish soldiers ever since.

Nevertheless, the violence and tragedy in Warsaw was simply an illustration of unsatisfactory developments in Eastern Europe which diplomatic circles in both Britain and America could not ignore. While the attention of most military planners in the summer of 1944 was primarily absorbed with details of operations in France, Italy or the Far East, the Foreign Office and, to a lesser extent, the State Department were becoming more and more dissatisfied with Soviet actions in Eastern Europe.

* See below, pp. 288–9.

The problem which faced Western diplomats was the discrepancy between the agreements over Poland reached by the Big Three at Tehran and the desire to prevent Poland becoming a total satellite of the Soviet Union. The Tehran agreements had envisaged the Curzon Line as Poland's eastern frontier and implied that any future Polish Government should be friendly towards the Russians.* Yet the Polish Government in London and the Polish underground movement were both deeply suspicious of Russia, and with good reason. Polish policy before the outbreak of war had been hostile to Soviet Communism and the Russians themselves had a long tradition of repressive and aggressive action against Poland. A settlement of Russo-Polish differences on the basis of the Tehran decisions was almost bound to be unacceptable to the Poles. The thorny task of overcoming their opposition fell to Mr Churchill and the Foreign Office in London. For the Prime Minister, as for President Roosevelt, there could be no question that maintaining the military alliance with Russia took priority over Polish interests, no matter how much sympathy he personally might feel for Poland. The British Foreign Office upheld the Polish cause rather more firmly. Mr Eden and his colleagues had always been alarmed by the dangers which underlay the vague formulations about Poland produced at Tehran. Nevertheless, both Mr Churchill and his Foreign Secretary did their best to press Stanislaw Mikolajczyk, the Polish Prime Minister, and his colleagues to accept the Curzon Line and come to a political agreement with the Soviet Union. They found themselves faced with intransigence in both London and Moscow, for if the Polish Ministers clung to their territorial and political claims with impolitic stubbornness Stalin did nothing to diminish their anti-Soviet suspicions.

In January and February 1944 a lengthy and complex triangular wrangle took place between the British Government, the London Poles and the Soviet authorities in Moscow. The Prime Minister left M. Mikolajczyk in no doubt about the weakness of Poland's position vis-à-vis Russia, and urged him to accept the advantages to Poland offered by annexations from Germany. Only by agreeing to such a settlement could the Poles hope to maintain any sort of independence. If they remained intransigent they must expect their position to get worse rather than better.

For their part M. Mikolajczyk and the Polish Foreign Minister, Tadeusz Romer, appreciated the desperate situation in which they found themselves. But agreement with Stalin – even if that were possible – seemed likely to rob them of all authority over expatriate Poles and the Polish Home Army. One fundamental problem was that the areas in

* See above, pp. 163-5.

dispute between Russia and Poland were those first to be reached by the Soviet Army. The Russians could, and did, simply treat them as Soviet provinces. Knowing that he had Western agreement to the Curzon Line, Stalin was able to ride roughshod over Polish protests. On the other hand the compensations Poland was to be offered in exchange for the Curzon Line all lay deep in German territory. It would not have been acceptable to the Western Allies for a public announcement to be made specifying Germany's territorial losses to Poland, especially since the extent of those losses had not been worked out in detail. Hence the Poles were being asked to give up lands they regarded as theirs by right in return for shadowy promises of compensations in the west. The fact that these promises themselves were not always consistent cannot have helped to reassure them. Stalin cheerfully promised Mikolajczyk the port of Stettin, although the British had not envisaged handing over this purely German city to the Poles.[8]

It will always remain a moot point whether the Polish authorities in London would have been able to come to a lasting agreement with Stalin even if they had been prepared to make the necessary concessions. Given the military position and the obvious political incompatibilities between the two sides, it seems impossible to believe that a compromise between them over the administration of Poland would have been a practical possibility. The existence of a large and strongly anti-Communist Polish resistance movement was unlikely to be tolerated by the Soviet security forces once they had entered the country. On the other hand the ability to make graceful concessions – or to accept them when made by others – was not a characteristic of either the Polish political parties in London or their gallant colleagues in Poland itself. Had a firm and binding treaty been signed between the London Poles and the Soviet Government at a time when German troops were deep in Russian territory it might have been very difficult for Stalin to repudiate. As it was, the time was running out for Poland. Only the most extreme concessions could give the London Poles a chance to influence the administration of their homeland once it had been liberated from the Nazis. Such concessions were beyond the power of M. Mikolajczyk.

Despite Mr Churchill's urgent promptings the Polish Cabinet refused even to accept the Curzon Line as their country's eastern frontier. In any case Stalin was also insisting that the Polish Government in London should be reconstructed in order to make it more acceptable to the Russians. His request could be seen as consistent with the Tehran discussions, since several members of the Polish leadership were very hostile to the Soviet régime. Nevertheless, it was hardly surprising that the Poles resented such a demand. If M. Mikolajczyk and his colleagues rearranged their Ministry to please Stalin they could not retain the confidence of their fellow-countrymen. The Polish Cabinet therefore refused concessions over this, even though Mr Churchill and the British Foreign Office pressed them to change their Commander-in-Chief and drop two Ministers.* On the frontier question Mikolajczyk endeavoured to obtain a compromise whereby administrative demarcation lines should be arranged without fixing a political frontier. The final settlement of the frontier question could then await the peace conference. However, the force of this suggestion was greatly weakened by the refusal of the Polish Cabinet to agree that the demarcation line should be coterminous with the Curzon Line. They seem to have envisaged a compromise position further to the east, and it was obvious that Stalin would never accept that. The most that could be gained was M. Mikolajczyk's personal agreement to a message from Mr Churchill to Stalin saying that the Poles were ready to discuss frontier questions with the Soviet Union, but that they could not publicly agree to cede any Polish territory. If they were allowed to return to Poland as soon as possible they would facilitate collaboration between the Red Army and the Polish underground. Mr Churchill said he had told the Poles that they would not be able to administer areas east of the Curzon Line but wanted to be able to assure them that the area to the west of it would be under their control.[9]

This message did not satisfy Stalin. Indeed, it was scarcely possible that it would in view of his very powerful military position and the promises he claimed to have been made to him at Tehran. The relative vagueness of the Tehran agreements – the very factor which had facilitated their acceptance – was no longer sufficient to camouflage the gulf between Russian and British attitudes towards Poland. From the Soviet viewpoint Russia had been promised the Curzon Line and a friendly Polish Government; the London Poles were now refusing to grant either and the British were supporting them. To the British, on the other hand, the purpose of territorial concessions to Russia agreed to at Tehran had been to establish an independent Poland; if Stalin insisted on setting up a puppet régime the whole basis for the agreement was undermined. The real problem lay in the interpretation of words like 'friendly' and 'independent'. The Soviets could justly argue that by no stretch of the imagination could a Government like that headed by Mikolajczyk be termed 'friendly' to Russia. The British felt that no Communist-dominated régime could be truly 'independent'.

The exchange of messages with Stalin over Poland grew more acrimonious in the spring of 1944. Mr Churchill was ready to argue that

---

* General Marian Kukiel and Professor Stanislaw Kot were particularly repugnant to the Russians.

there had been no firm agreement at Tehran about the Curzon Line, a view which even the British Foreign Office felt could not be sustained and which certainly accorded ill with the records of the conference.[10]* In fact it was the British Government which was in the awkward position of justifying what Stalin characterized as a breach of faith over the Tehran agreements. The British War Cabinet finally sent a statement to Moscow pointing out that, although it had done its best to persuade the London Poles to accept the agreement, it could not jettison them if they refused to do so. If no settlement was possible at that stage the British Government would have to maintain its former position on territorial questions – namely, that they must all be held over for the decision of a peace conference.[11]

There followed a lull in the discussions over Poland, but, as Mr Eden was only too well aware, time was working in favour of Stalin and against the Poles. Matters were scarcely improved in June when Mikolajczyk visited President Roosevelt. The President, who, of course, made no mention of his private talks with Stalin about Poland at Tehran, claimed that only the British and the Russians had accepted the Curzon Line. He gave Mikolajczyk the impression that Poland might, after all, be able to retain Lwow and take Königsberg from the Germans.[12] On 23 June such illusions received a rude shock when the Soviet authorities refused to consider recognizing any Polish Government which had not been reconstructed to suit their taste and which did not recognize the Curzon Line. They also demanded public acknowledgement of Soviet 'innocence' over the Katyn murders. Yet M. Mikolajczyk did not give up hope of reaching an agreement with the Russians. With British encouragement he visited Stalin early in August. Stalin seemed in a benevolent mood, but left the hard bargaining to Polish Communists. Their leader was a sinister figure calling himself Bolcslaw Bierut.† Bierut demanded a reconstructed Polish Ministry dominated by representatives of the Soviet-backed Committee of National Liberation. In view of this, Stalin's assurances to Mikolajczyk that he had no intention of com-munizing Poland rang somewhat hollow.[13]

III

The tragic events which followed in Warsaw underlined the desperate outlook for non-Communist Poles and the threat posed to inter-Allied relations by the Polish question.

* See above, p. 165.

† A Pole who, under the name of Krasnodewski, had been jailed in pre-war Poland as a Soviet agent. In 1927 he was handed over to the Russians in an exchange of agents.

This was not, however, the only problem which arose as Russian troops moved westwards towards their pre-war frontiers. Indeed, even more apprehension was aroused in London by the threat posed by the Red Army to the Danube Basin and the Balkans. Poland was a matter of honour to the British; Bulgaria and Greece had much greater strategic significance. If Greece fell under Communist influence, for example, the fate of other Mediterranean countries, including Italy, might be in the balance. On 3 April 1944 Mr Eden, referring to a Foreign Office memorandum on Anglo-Soviet relations and the Polish question, noted his fear that Russia's aims might include 'the domination of Eastern Europe and even the Mediterranean, and the "communizing" of much that remains'.[14] It was in the early summer of 1944 that Mr Churchill's anxiety about Communist advances into Eastern Europe became especially acute, and he was greatly concerned by the failure of the Italian campaign to carry Western influence more rapidly into the Balkan region.* British alarm was shared in the American State Department, where Secretary Hull had been angered by Stalin's boorishness and expressing himself in favour of a tougher line when negotiating with Russia. This did not mean, of course, that either the British or the Americans contemplated any sort of rupture in their alliance with the Soviet Union. The aim was to impress on Stalin that indifference to Western opinion might bring with it diplomatic and economic disadvantages.

Hull was especially eager to ensure that commercial freedom should be vouchsafed to the states of Eastern Europe. He also retained the view that no binding territorial arrangements ought to be made about liberated territories before there had been time to call a peace conference and consult the populations concerned. In this respect his position vis-à-vis the Soviet Union was actually more unyielding than that of the British, although at the time this fact was obscured by the comparatively weak position of the State Department in American decision-making. The summer of 1944 was, after all, the period in which Mr Morgenthau – with his Germanophobe and Russophil tendencies – was at the height of his influence.†

President Roosevelt was always enigmatic in dealing with his advisers and tended to procrastinate so long as he was able to do so. He was certainly not going to be forced into adopting a reproachful attitude towards Stalin; on the other hand his campaign for the Presidential election in November required him to avoid any commitment which

---

* Mr Churchill's views on this point were essentially defensive. He was less concerned with a breakthrough to Vienna through the so-called Ljubljana Gap than with giving British military influence the chance to establish itself in the Balkan area.
† See above, pp. 174–85.

might upset voters with relatives in Eastern Europe. Hence American policy towards Russia tended to be vacillating and ineffective in 1944. The British response to Communist pressure on Southern and Eastern Europe was more positive, though perhaps less scrupulous. They tried to obtain Russian agreement to a division of spheres of military influence so that Britain's most vital strategic interests would be protected. On 5 May Mr Eden told the Soviet Ambassador in London that Britain would allow Russia to take the lead in policy-making towards Rumania but expected in return that Britain's predominant position in Greece should be recognized by the Soviet Union. The Soviet Government seemed willing to accept this arrangement, but it aroused lively misgivings in Washington. To the Americans, spheres of influence were seen as throw-backs to an older and discredited form of power politics. Mr Churchill always denied any intention of pre-empting a peace conference by such arrangements, but it was obvious that they could be of great importance for the future political complexion of Europe. In any event, American opposition enabled Stalin to evade definite agreement with the British over Greece. Fears of Soviet pressure there were increased when a Soviet mission was sent to liaise with the ELAS forces without the British Government being consulted.

By the autumn of 1944 Russian advances into the Danube Basin were making some sort of agreement about 'liberated' territories essential. The Rumanians signed an armistice on 12 September; the Russians had declared war on Bulgaria a week earlier and quickly invaded that country. The terms of the Rumanian armistice were to be administered by the Red Army, although Rumania had surrendered to the United Nations and not simply to the Soviet Union.

It was against this background that Mr Churchill and Mr Eden, accompanied by their military staff, visited Moscow in mid-October 1944.* In one respect their position vis-à-vis Stalin was stronger than it had been at Tehran; in the intervening months Anglo-American forces had established a powerful bridge-head in Western Europe. Paris and Brussels had both been liberated. There seemed a good chance that General Eisenhower might be able to press on into the heart of Germany before the end of the year. It was no longer likely that the war would end with Central Europe completely in the grip of the Red Army. On the other hand the Prime Minister and his Foreign Secretary could not claim to be representing the Western section of the Alliance in their negotiations with Stalin. President Roosevelt, already concerned about his campaign for the American Presidential election due to take place in November, was not enthusiastic about bipartite meetings from which

* They arrived on 9 October and left ten days later.

he was excluded. On the prompting of Harry Hopkins, he instructed his Ambassador Harriman to keep all options open for the United States, whatever Mr Churchill and Stalin might talk about at Moscow. Mr Harriman was told to impress upon the Soviet leader that 'in this global war there is literally no question, political or military, in which the United States is not interested . . .'. The President wrote further to his Ambassador:

> I can tell you quite frankly, but for you only and not to be communi-
> cated under any circumstances to the British or the Russians, that I
> would have very much preferred to have the next conference between
> the three of us for the very reasons that I have stated to the
> Marshal. . . .[15]

Stalin was not therefore faced with any sort of concerted pressure from his Allies in October 1944.

Nevertheless, the British were well received in Moscow and their talks with the Russians were apparently successful. Mr Churchill arrived at a rule-of-thumb agreement with Stalin about the amount of influence to be exercised by Russia and her Western Allies in the Danube Basin. This was expressed in percentages, and M. Molotov was disposed to haggle over the exact amounts specified for each country.[16] In practice the figures could only act as a rough guide to the amount of influence individual Allies would exercise in the territories concerned. Greece was to be left mainly to Britain, and Bulgarian troops would withdraw from Greek soil. Bulgaria and Rumania were to be predominantly a Russian responsibility, although Western interest in Bulgaria was understood to be greater than in Rumania. Russia was to share responsibility for the control of Hungary and Yugoslavia with the other two allies on a 50:50 basis.[17]

Stress was laid on the temporary nature of such arrangements, which were in any case only to last until the surrender of Germany and the creation of a final peace settlement. Nevertheless, it was obvious that in practice they would be of great importance to the countries concerned, since the type of political life which emerged after the Nazis had been expelled would depend on the attitudes of the liberating Powers. Mr Eden and the British Foreign Office evidently hoped that in Bulgaria and Hungary, at least, the arrangements would allow Western military representatives some say in the way armistice terms were administered. In this they were to be disappointed. On the other hand in Greece the Russians respected their side of the bargain and left the British to settle the complicated and often embarrassing problems of Greek domestic politics without interference from the Soviet side. This alone was worth a great deal to Mr Churchill.

The Polish question was also discussed at Moscow, but no solution was found to it. Leaders of both the London and the pro-Soviet Poles took part in some of the discussions. The atmosphere was not entirely unfavourable and M. Mikolajczyk seemed to be making some progress towards agreement over a Provisional Government to administer Poland. The major obstacle remained the Curzon Line. Despite strong pressure from Mr Churchill, Mikolajczyk was still unable to accept this, and, in particular, he refused to countenance the loss of Lwow. He felt bound by a memorandum issued by the Polish Government on 30 August which had stipulated that Poland should retain 'in the east the main centres of Polish cultural life and the sources of raw materials . . .'.[18] It was, of course, out of the question that Stalin would offer any such concession. M. Mikolajczyk found to his bewilderment that Molotov was referring to American promises made at Tehran to the effect that Russia's frontier should be the Curzon Line. He complained bitterly to Harriman about this, but, of course, the American Ambassador could give him no very reassuring answer.[19] Despite this growing realization of President Roosevelt's duplicity, the Poles adhered to their territorial claims. Mr Eden expressed the tragedy of the situation when, on 16 October, he cabled to the Foreign Office in London: 'and so at this time, after endless hours of the stiffest negotiations I have ever known, it looks as though Lwow will wreck all our efforts'.[20]

It was not so much Lwow as the complete and justified lack of trust between the negotiating parties which rendered the talks over Poland nugatory. Although Mikolajczyk agreed to try to persuade his colleagues in London to show more flexibility towards Soviet territorial claims, he was unable to overcome their intransigence.

The Poles may have still hoped for some help from the United States, but in this they were to be grievously disappointed. President Roosevelt was chiefly concerned with avoiding uncomfortable reactions among the American electorate before it had been given the chance to re-elect him for a fourth term of office. On 22 October he wrote to Mr Churchill expressing pleasure at the progress made in Moscow towards a compromise over Poland. 'When and if a solution is arrived at,' he went on, 'I should like to be consulted as to the advisability from this point of view of delaying its publication for about two weeks. You will understand.'[21] Election day in America was 7 November.

The President had, indeed, been very skilful in his handling of the Polish question. By allowing the British to make the running in seeking a compromise he had encouraged the Poles – and their kindred in America – to believe that he was more sympathetic to Poland than was Mr Churchill, who had to press the London Poles to accept the Curzon

Line. At the same time the President had avoided any serious clash with
the Soviet Union over Poland.

Any lingering hopes that M. Mikolajczyk may have had on the subject
of effective American intervention for Poland must have been dispelled
by an oracular and unhelpful message dispatched to him from Washington on 17 November. In this the President, having remarked that if
Russia, Britain and Poland came to an agreement over frontiers the
Americans would not object to it, added that 'in accordance with its
traditional policy' the United States Government could not guarantee
frontiers.[22] His belief that a future world security organization would
look after this task can have only been of cold comfort to the Poles. At
the end of November Mikolajczyk, still unable to persuade his colleagues
that major territorial sacrifices were necessary, resigned.

The situation worsened still further from the Western viewpoint
when, on 27 December 1944, the Soviet Government recognized the
puppet Communist Lublin Committee as the Provisional Government
of Poland. Mr Eden felt that the British and the Americans should take
a firm and unyielding line over the Polish issue, and it is clear that
opinion in the American State Department also favoured a less com-
plaisant attitude towards Soviet policies in Poland.

However, differences over Poland and other East European areas had
not created any particular feeling of ill-will between the British and the
Russians at Moscow. On the contrary, Mr Churchill and his colleagues
left Russia in a happy mood. The military conversations, especially, had
progressed very satisfactorily. Stalin had even favoured Mr Churchill's
pet scheme for an offensive from Italy into the Danube Basin. The
general tone of the meetings had been friendly, and this seemed to augur
well for the future. Reporting to King George VI on 16 October
Mr Churchill wrote: 'the political atmosphere is extremely cordial.
Nothing like it has been seen before.'[23] On 19 October Stalin even came
to the airport in person to wish the departing Britons *bon voyage*, a
gesture which particularly impressed Field-Marshal Sir Alan Brooke.
Brooke, who was not an unusually optimistic man, noted in his diary:
'We are now in the air heading for the Crimea in lovely sunshine, our
work in Moscow finished and far more satisfactorily than I could ever
have hoped for.'[24]

The fact that hopes raised at Moscow soon began to evaporate was
due to a number of political and military disappointments, only some of
which were connected with the policies adopted by the Soviet Government.

IV

As has been mentioned above, the progress of General Eisenhower's offensive in Western Europe during the late autumn of 1944 proved very disappointing to Mr Churchill.* His tentative hopes for a breakthrough at the so-called Ljubljana Gap were also quickly seen to be quite unfounded. Despite Stalin's encouragement at Moscow the scheme was demonstrated to be impracticable when examined by Mr Churchill's field commander in the Middle East. Hence there once again seemed to be an acute danger that the peoples of Central and South-eastern Europe would owe their liberation from Nazi rule entirely to the Russians. At the same time Soviet policies in Bulgaria, Rumania and Hungary did nothing to reassure the Western Powers. Wherever the Soviet armies established themselves they paid scant attention to the views of their allies when implementing political or economic measures. The fact that the Russians were allowing the British and Americans a fairly free hand in France, the Low Countries, Italy and Greece was not seen as sufficient compensation by the Western Powers.

Soviet political ambitions were particularly worrying to the British Prime Minister and his diplomatic advisers. Mr Churchill's distaste for Communism as a political system had remained unaffected by his enthusiasm for Soviet resistance to Hitler, and in any case British security would be seriously compromised if the European continent were to be dominated by Russia. In America, too, important shifts of opinion about relations with Stalin were beginning to become apparent, although they were slow to affect the White House itself. Whereas President Roosevelt clove to his design for Soviet–American collaboration after the war and tended to belittle problems concerning the balance of power in Europe, many of the officials in the State Department were moving towards a point of view much closer to that of their Foreign Office colleagues in London. This was not a premeditated or deliberate process of change, nor did it produce any very coherent alternatives to Roosevelt's policy. The State Department was itself a very weak element in American decision-making in 1944, although its powerlessness was perhaps exaggerated in later years.†

As we have seen,‡ Mr Hull had always opposed any suggestions by

---

* See above, p. 190.

† George Kennan has argued very persuasively that the State Department was little more than a post office during the war and one which was likely to be by-passed when messages of great importance were involved. He even suggests that Cordell Hull's interest in the United Nations Organization was a compensation for the Department's impotence in questions of power politics. This seems less than just to Mr Hull or his subordinate officials.[25]

‡ See above, p. 114.

the British which might involve the concept of a power balance or spheres of influence. He had placed great emphasis on the prospect of commercial contacts and economic co-operation between East and West after the war, and on the central importance of the international peace-keeping body in any schemes for world security. He had expressed these views at the Moscow Foreign Ministers' Conference in 1943 and maintained them throughout his period of office. Nevertheless, whereas in 1943 he seems to have regarded the British as the most likely obstacles to his policy, by the summer of 1944 he was beginning to find greater fault with Soviet diplomacy, and his eagerness to please the Russians began to lose its intensity.

Early in 1944, for example, the Secretary of State had been against opposing Stalin too strongly over Poland in case this might lessen his willingness to collaborate in wider spheres.[26] However, the experience of Soviet obstructiveness during the rest of the year stimulated Hull, who was in no way an appeaser by temperament, to favour a firmer tone in bargaining with the Russians. He was particularly upset by their attitude at Dumbarton Oaks, where the Soviet negotiators refused to accept a voting procedure which might force Russia to defend her own policies before a world tribunal even if no effective sanctions could be officially undertaken against her.* Hull's disappointment over this issue seems to have caused him to pay more attention to ominous reports which had for some time been coming to Washington from the Embassy in Moscow. Ambassador Harriman, a man of great integrity, did not hide from the President or the Secretary of State the often unsatisfactory nature of Soviet behaviour in matters requiring East–West collaboration. Although President Roosevelt did not always seem to pay very much heed to gloomy reports from Moscow, Secretary Hull and his sub-ordinates in the State Department began to regard Soviet activity in Eastern Europe with a nervous and critical eye. As George Kennan, Counsellor at the American Embassy in Moscow, put it:

> we are being . . . negligent of the interests of our people if we allow plans for an international organization to be an excuse for failing to occupy ourselves seriously and minutely with the sheer power relationships of the European peoples.[27]

At the same time – in the autumn of 1944 – an argument was going on in Washington about the future of Germany and the acceptance of the Morgenthau Plan. Secretary Hull was at first in favour of extremely harsh and even brutal policies towards the Germans, but rapidly came round to the saner views advocated by War Secretary Stimson.[28]

* See below, pp. 543–4.

Although President Roosevelt himself quickly dropped the Morgenthau Plan when he realized how much public opposition it was likely to arouse, he did not lightly give up his desire to be 'tough' towards the Germans, especially because he thought this harsh attitude would find favour with Stalin.* Morgenthau himself had by no means acknowledged defeat in October 1944; his interest in foreign policy questions aroused lively fears in the State Department. On 4 November 1944 Mr Freeman Matthews, the Deputy Director of the Department's Office of European Affairs, reported to Under-Secretary Stettinius that after the American Presidential elections Morgenthau intended 'to get back into the German picture in a big way. I very much fear that he will do just that unless the President calls him off'.[29]

Mr Morgenthau did indeed continue his struggle to impose a Carthaginian peace on Germany and to accompany this with a policy of extreme generosity towards the Soviet Union. In addition to his desire to see Germany reduced to an agricultural nation he also pressed for a scheme of massive dollar credits to the Russians as a means of cementing American friendship with the U.S.S.R. Here again the Secretary of the Treasury found himself in conflict with expert opinion in the State Department.[30] Morgenthau's demand that Nazi leaders should be shot out of hand when captured by the Allies was also opposed by Stimson and by informed opinion in the State and War Departments.

These issues hung together, although no very clear fronts were drawn up in Washington about them. Generally speaking, and bearing in mind many individual differences of emphasis, it can be argued that the Departments headed by Stimson and Hull were moving towards a view of American security and relations with Europe which chimed in better with that of the British Foreign Office† than did those of Mr Morgenthau and his Treasury advisers. However, the crucial factor remained the attitude of the President himself and of his intimate White House advisers. In this entourage there was still a strong tendency to regard European entanglements with suspicion and to stake everything on Russian friendship after the war. Apart from Morgenthau, two of the most powerful voices holding the ear of the President were Harry Hopkins and Admiral Leahy.

Leahy's views on the future role of the United States had been well set out in his famous letter to Mr Hull on 16 May 1944, in which he had stressed that the main danger to peace after the defeat of Germany would lie in a conflict between Britain and Russia. To avoid such a

* See above, pp. 185–6.

† Among the exceptions to this generalization might be counted views on the treatment of war criminals. The British tended for some time to favour summary executions (see below, pp. 398–9).[31]

conflict the United States must prevent these two nations competing to shift the balance of power in their favour on the European continent. By implication this required the United States to abstain from supporting British schemes for European security.[32]

Leahy was, of course, particularly hostile to General de Gaulle, whom he had always disliked. His counsels were reflected in Roosevelt's negative attitudes towards the Free French, whose cause the British Foreign Office was attempting to espouse. On 19 November 1944 Mr Eden gloomily wrote in his diary:

> Three bad messages from F.D.R. These last are unhelpful. Snarky to the French and generally arrogant and aloof, ignoring our invitation to him to come here altogether. I am told that Leahy now has the ear. Whatever the reason the result is a bad augury for new régime.[33]*

Admiral Leahy remained by temperament an isolationist, especially in his attitude towards European politics. He was highly critical of British initiatives in Greece, which were designed to prevent that country falling under Communist control.† Towards the end of 1944, when informed observers were becoming more and more concerned about the situation in Eastern Europe, Leahy had reiterated his isolationist views to Hanson Baldwin, a writer for the *New York Times*. Mr Baldwin believed that the United States should interest itself in the types of governments being established in areas liberated from the Nazis. Admiral Leahy, on the other hand, claimed that America's involvement in European politics would inevitably bring her into another European war. He was determined not to

> sacrifice American soldiers in order to impose any government on any people, or to adjust political differences in Europe or Asia, except when it should be necessary to act against an aggressor with the purpose of preventing international war.[34]

Despite his acknowledged ignorance of – and even contempt for – politics,[35] Admiral Leahy was becoming more important in the President's entourage. President Roosevelt seems to have regarded him as a reliable servant, devoted to American interests, who could help him resist undesirable commitments in the field of foreign affairs.

As for Harry Hopkins, he had always tended to favour a policy of *rapprochement* with Russia, if necessary at the expense of Britain and France. As a politician who had never been burdened with any direct responsibility for making foreign policy, Mr Hopkins, like Admiral

---

* President Roosevelt had just been re-elected for a fourth term of office.
† See below, p. 239.

Leahy and the President himself, sometimes tended to let his prejudices outrun his common sense. To him the old imperialist nations were in decline. The Soviet Union was young, classless and strong. Whatever affections he might feel for the British as individuals, his bias as an American was towards the new force which had arisen in Eastern Europe. At the very least he was determined that the United States should forge its own relations with Moscow and not rely on the British Government as an intermediary. It was Hopkins who had, on his own initiative, held up a Presidential message to Moscow in October 1944 which seemed to him to be too benevolent towards the bilateral Stalin–Churchill meeting and insufficiently concerned to protect American interests. At his prompting Roosevelt cancelled his cable to Ambassador Harriman and substituted the far less enthusiastic message of 4 October.* Although Hopkins was not in the best of health his influence over the President appears to have been reasserting itself in the autumn of 1944.†

Indeed, in the last months of that year American attitudes towards British activities in Greece and Italy were as critical as Mr Churchill's view of American strategy in Western Europe. Matters were not apparently improved from the British viewpoint by the replacement of Cordell Hull at the State Department by his deputy, Edward R. Stettinius, Jr. This appeared to be another step in the emasculation of the State Department, since nobody took Mr Stettinius very seriously as a statesman. He could not compare with his predecessor in intellectual capacity or political stature. A businessman by training, he tended to regard diplomacy as a form of public relations, a mistake all too often to be repeated by his successors in the years which followed. Stettinius was clearly not the man to stand up to President Roosevelt – or for that matter to Mr Morgenthau – in serious clashes over policy. On the other hand there was one sense in which Stettinius's appointment did strengthen the hand of those men in the State Department and its agencies who were having to deal with the day-to-day problems of inter-Allied relations. Mr Stettinius had to rely on their background work when forming his own judgements. Unlike Mr Hull, he had few preconceptions about post-war planning. His contribution to the running of the State Department lay mainly in the sphere of administrative reorganization, and here he seems not to have been entirely ineffective.[37] President Roosevelt doubtless hoped, when appointing

---

* See above, p. 198.

† Robert Sherwood claims that Hopkins had not been politically very active in the summer and autumn of 1944 and that his action over the Moscow telegram brought him back into the field of decision-making.[36]

Mr Stettinius, to maintain his own complete control over foreign policy, but now, with his dynamism at least partly undermined by poor health and inadequately briefed on many of the major issues facing American diplomacy, his sureness of touch was no longer quite what it had been. The State Department was well equipped with facts and figures. Its voice was beginning to be heard more clearly as the platitudes of inter-Allied collaboration lost their power to camouflage conflicts of interest.

V

It should not be imagined from the foregoing that the State Department envisaged adopting an intransigent or even unco-operative policy towards the Soviet Union. Post-war collaboration with Russia was still seen as imperative for the maintenance of peace. But the diplomats had a clearer idea of what such collaboration would involve than some of their political masters. They realized that the West would have to make embarrassing political sacrifices. They also saw that Britain and the United States would have to drive a hard bargain in order to prevent a totally one-sided enlargement of Soviet power on the European continent. Three examples of the kind of advice which both Stettinius and President Roosevelt were receiving from their advisers on Soviet problems throw light on the shifting points of view about Russian–American relations.

The first is a cable from Ambassador Harriman dated 28 December 1944. Referring to the vexed question of the veto over United Nations Security Council debates, Harriman pointed out that the Soviet attitude towards international affairs differed from that prevalent in the West. Having made a dutiful obeisance to Russian feelings of suspicion as the result of the way the revolutionary régime had been attacked and ostracized before the war, Harriman went on to remark that

> The Soviets have definite objectives in their future foreign policy, all of which we do not as yet fully understand. For example, while they have recognized the right of the states bordering the Soviet Union to have their independence, they insist upon 'friendly' governments. From Soviet actions so far, the terms 'friendly' and 'independent' appear to mean something quite different from our interpretation. It is interesting to note that in Iran they appear to justify their recent actions by explaining that they know better what the Iranian people want than the Iranian Government, which does not represent the majority of Iranian opinion.[38]

He went on to point out that the politicians in Persia who opposed the Soviet viewpoint were being dubbed as 'Fascists'. So far as the United

Nations peace-keeping organization was concerned, the Russians regarded this simply as a shield against aggression. They did not want it acting as a court to settle disputes in which they might be involved. These they wanted to deal with unilaterally and in their own interests. Harriman therefore feared that

> we are faced with a very fundamental question of what the effect on the international security organization will be with most of the nations looking to it to develop mediatory or judicial procedures in the advancement of international relations, whereas the Soviet Union appears to view it from a much narrower perspective.

He concluded that the only chance of persuading the Russians to change their minds would be if

> we and the British were prepared to take a firm and definite stand, supported by widespread reluctance on the part of smaller nations to join the organization on the Soviet conditions. It would seem that we should face realistically the far-reaching implications of the Soviet position and adjust our policies accordingly.

This was a very different assessment of Soviet–American relations from that which Harriman had made after the Moscow Conference.* But it represented the experience of a year in Moscow and was not to be ignored. Stettinius passed it on to the President with the recommendation that a very firm stand would have to be taken over the issue of Security Council voting rights.†

The second example of American thinking on the Russian problem comes from within the State Department itself in the shape of a memorandum drawn up by John D. Hickerson, the Deputy Director of the Office of European Affairs. He stressed the urgent necessity of establishing a provisional security council for Europe which could deal with problems arising in liberated territories other an Germany. Hickerson frankly admitted that the Soviet Union would extend her frontiers as the result of the war. This would mean – as indeed it had already meant – the absorption of the Baltic States, territorial gains from Finland, the acquisition of Königsberg and part of East Prussia and the Curzon Line as the Russian–Polish frontier. Bessarabia would also fall to Russia.

Hickerson felt that there was no way in which the United States could resist such changes and that she should be ready to accept them in return for guarantees on the subject of free elections and international peace-keeping. Referring to the Soviet acquisition of the Baltic States, for example, he wrote:

* See above, p. 121.   † See below, p. 545.

... nothing which we can do can alter this. It is not a question of whether we like it: I personally don't like it although I recognize that the Soviet Government has arguments on its side. The point is it has been done and nothing which it is within the power of the United States Government to do can undo it.[39]

The United States had to have the Soviet Union to help to defeat Germany and sorely needed it to defeat Japan. 'The importance of these two things can be reckoned in American lives.'[40]

Towards the end of his memorandum Hickerson made a passionate defence of a conciliatory attitude towards the Russians, saying:

I am willing to sponsor and support the Soviet arguments if it will save American lives in winning the war and if it will save the rest of Europe from the diplomacy of the jungle which is almost certain to ensue otherwise.[41]

Yet Hickerson was not advocating a policy of total capitulation to Soviet demands. He argued that the Americans must accept the territorial *faits accomplis* in Eastern Europe, but should use this conciliatory attitude as a bargaining point with Stalin in order to obtain their own objectives. These were an acceptable and realistic system of international peace-keeping and the safeguarding of democracy on the European continent. To obtain this latter end Hickerson's proposed provisional security council should be able to settle internal problems in liberated territories like Greece and Poland. The Russians might not approve of this but every effort should be made to persuade them.

Hence Hickerson's memorandum contained the traditional American emphasis on international organization as against concern over individual territorial settlements, but it proposed new and apparently practical measures to safeguard popular sovereignty in liberated areas. The concept of a provisional security council was scarcely compatible, for example, with the horror of entanglement in European politics expressed by Admiral Leahy. It was more akin to British schemes for regional security arrangements. In any case it ran counter to Soviet policies in Eastern Europe, and was bound to arouse great opposition in Moscow.

The scheme for a provisional security council – renamed 'Emergency High Commission for Liberated Europe' – was taken up by the State Department and Secretary Stettinius pressed it upon the President as a worth-while objective in tripartite talks with Churchill and Stalin. He also proposed that the Big Three – in association with the Free French – issue a Declaration on Liberated Europe, pledging their determination to give the liberated peoples of Europe the right to choose their own Governments as had been promised in the Atlantic Charter. The High Commission was seen as a piece of inter-Allied machinery to implement this pledge.[42] Unfortunately it was easier to make a declaration than to take the practical steps needed to ensure its fulfilment. Lest it be thought that the Americans were moving towards an acceptance of the conception of 'spheres of influence' which they had found so abhorrent when pursued by the British and the Russians in 1944, it should be pointed out that among the briefing papers available to the President in the weeks before the Yalta Conference there were memoranda which reiterated the American point of view on this question and which even quoted from Admiral Leahy's letter on the subject of May 1944.[43]

One such paper headed 'Liberated Countries' also reflected important American presuppositions about European politics. It expressed anxiety over 'Anglo-Soviet rivalry on the continent of Europe'. It argued that this and 'the resulting power politics scramble for position' was concerned less with territorial questions than with the political character of Governments in various countries beyond the borders of the Soviet Union. Britain and Russia each feared that the other would establish puppet states in the areas it liberated. The paper claimed that these suspicions were probably ill-founded, but that their very existence tended to push the two Allies into opposing attitudes, the British on the right and the Russians on the left. It then expressed the belief that between Communism and reaction lay 'the bulk of the political sentiment of the peoples of Europe',[44]

This statement encapsulated the American view that a post-war Europe could be established in which the moderate Left – Social Democratic perhaps, but not Communist – would hold the reins of power. As a result, countries like Poland, Italy, Yugoslavia and Hungary would possess Governments the 'Left-wing' character of which might be expected to ease the fears of the Soviet Union, yet which would respect democratic political forms and react with enthusiasm to American schemes for free trade and commercial intercourse. This was indeed a noble ideal, and it may well be that, given a free choice, the peoples of Eastern and Central Europe would have welcomed such a development. Unfortunately the concept of free choice in politics was not easily exportable. As War Secretary Stimson wrote in his diary when referring to subsequent proposals for elections in Poland: 'I know very well from my experience with other nations that there are no nations in the world except the U.S. and the U.K. which have a real idea of what an independent free ballot is.[45]

It was certainly true that the moderate Left had never enjoyed much popular support among the nations under discussion. Only in Finland and Czechoslovakia had there been strong and effective democratic systems before the Second World War. The peace-makers of 1919,

influenced by Thomas Masaryk and Eduard Beneš, had placed great
stress on Czechoslovakia's position in Central Europe, and throughout
the inter-war period she had acted as an outpost of Western political
values in an increasingly unfriendly environment. Her betrayal by
Britain and France in 1938 marked the end of any real hopes for
collective security against Fascist aggression. If any nation might have
been thought to fit the American model of a moderately progressive
country willing to act as a bridge between East and West it was Czechoslovakia, especially since President Beneš was busily trying to further
just such a policy from his exile in London.

Yet American plans for collective security after the war did not give
any high priority to the Czechs in Central Europe. When Stettinius went
to the Big Three Conference at Yalta, one of his background documents
contained the recommendation that Hungary should be given territorial
compensations at the expense of the Czechs. It was not clear whether
this strange proposal was the residue of pre-war revisionism, which had
always taken the 'artificial' Czechoslovak state as its chief target, or
whether it was stimulated by American interests in Hungarian oil
companies.[46] It certainly did not reflect any clear-cut conception of a
balance of power in Central Europe.

VI

This was the situation on the eve of the Yalta Conference. Both the
Western Powers were eager for another Big Three meeting. However,
Stalin's reluctance to leave Russia seemed likely to wreck their hopes.
Stalin pleaded bad health and military necessity as grounds for refusing
to travel outside his own country. In fact there is no reason to suppose
that the Soviet leader was any less fit to travel than the President or the
Prime Minister. Nor could it really be claimed that the war situation in
the East was so grave as to demand Stalin's personal presence. Since the
British and the Americans had been forced to travel long distances to
Tehran for the first tripartite conference, it was only reasonable that
Stalin should show reciprocal flexibility about the choice of the next
meeting-place. No such flexibility manifested itself. Instead, the Western
Powers were forced to accept, not only that their leaders should once
again make a long and hazardous journey to the conference, but that it
should be held in the U.S.S.R. itself. It was an immediate and psycho-
logically important victory for Stalin, since it underlined how much
more urgently his partners seemed to need the conference than he did.

Stalin was aided in this preliminary skirmish by the intervention of
Harry Hopkins. He took it upon himself to give the Soviet Ambassador

in Washington a strong hint that the President would be willing to meet Stalin in the Crimea. Once this suggestion had been made it was obvious that Stalin would not budge from Russia. Hopkins justified his action, which naturally aroused great indignation among the President's other advisers, by claiming that the offensives impending on the Eastern Front would demand Stalin's presence in the U.S.S.R. This was a curious argument, since German troops were cleared from Russian soil by the end of 1944 and the Nazis no longer posed any real threat to the security of the Soviet Union.[47] So far as military and political responsibility were concerned, Roosevelt's immediate burdens far outweighed those of his Soviet ally. Stalin pleaded medical advice when refusing to leave Russia, but this was scarcely convincing, especially when the physical handicaps faced by the President were taken into consideration. The fact was, as Hopkins himself put it, that there seemed to be no alternative: 'The all-important thing was to get the meeting. There was not a chance of getting that meeting outside of the Crimea.'[48]

Stalin simply had less need of the conference than President Roosevelt or Mr Churchill. He could feel confident that in a game of international catch-as-catch-can Russia's position on the European continent would enable her to obtain her objectives. It was up to the Western Powers to prove that a policy of collaboration in the post-war world – as well as in the war against Japan – would bring Russia more benefits. Hence the Prime Minister and the President went to Russia in the role – if not with the mien – of suppliants. It was an unenviable diplomatic position.

The site chosen for the Crimean Conference was Yalta. It cannot be claimed that this was a happy inspiration. The whole region surrounding the city had only recently been cleared of German forces and had been severely ravaged by the war. It was thought to harbour malarial mosquitoes, and it certainly provided a plentiful supply of bed-bugs, as some of the Allied visitors were soon to discover. When Hopkins visited London in January 1945 he was told by the Prime Minister that 'if we had spent ten years on research we could not have found a worse place than "Magneto"* but ... we can survive it by bringing an adequate supply of whiskey'.[49]

As in the case of the Tehran Conference, the British were eager to have preliminary consultations with their American colleagues before meeting the Russians. Roosevelt remained reluctant to accept any such arrangements, but it then transpired that medical considerations made

---

* The code-name for Yalta. Mr Churchill had originally suggested 'Colchis' for this purpose, but was over-persuaded on grounds of security lest the German Intelligence should be sufficiently well up in their Greek mythology.

it advisable for him to travel to Yalta by sea as far as Malta, where Mr Churchill eagerly agreed to rendezvous with the Americans.[50]

Although there were many issues on which American and British interests seemed to demand a common front in negotiating with Stalin, Mr Churchill had wider considerations in mind when urging a preliminary meeting. He was very concerned with the need for adequate briefing if the forthcoming conference was to be a success. At one stage he proposed, for example, that Eden, Molotov and Stettinius should spend a week together in Egypt working over the ground for the Big Three conversations.[51]

He pointed to the success of the Foreign Ministers' meeting in Moscow in October 1943 and its value for the subsequent conference at Tehran. The gathering at Yalta was only due to last five or six days and this seemed hardly enough to work out a settlement of world problems. As Mr Churchill put it to the President, 'Even the Almighty took seven'.[52]

Naturally enough, President Roosevelt did not take up Mr Churchill's suggestion. It would have been contrary to his practice to allow Stettinius to participate in a meeting which might develop lines of approach contrary to those favoured by the President. In any case, Stettinius himself did not enjoy the confidence of his principal to the same extent as Eden or Molotov were trusted by Churchill and Stalin respectively. The President must have been aware that his Secretary of State was personally unequal to a full-scale confrontation with his British and Russian counterparts. It was, therefore, only after repeated entreaties from London that the President consented to allow his military staff to fly to Malta on 30 January and agreed that Stettinius should arrive on the following day. He himself would not dock at Malta until 2 February, so that there would be some time for the preparatory staff discussions before he and Mr Churchill had their first meeting. Roosevelt also sent Harry Hopkins to London on 21 January for consultations with Mr Churchill. As the personal representative of the President, Hopkins could be guaranteed to avoid making any undesirable commitments to the British. He seems to have been successful in soothing the rather ruffled feelings of his volcanic host.[53] From London he travelled to Paris, hoping to exercise his charms on General de Gaulle. In this he was far less successful.

The position of France certainly posed an awkward problem for the Americans. Mr Churchill, prodded by the British Foreign Office, wished to give the Free French greater equality of status in the war-time Alliance. He had suggested that de Gaulle might be brought into the later stages of discussions at Yalta, but Roosevelt had steadfastly resisted any such arrangement.[54] In January 1945 de Gaulle got wind of the impending Big Three meeting from speculative articles in the 'Anglo-Saxon' Press.[55] He was quick to voice his displeasure at France's exclusion from it; nor did he have much doubt as to which of the three Allies was chiefly responsible for his missing invitation.[56] He made it clear that the French would not feel themselves bound by any decisions taken in their absence.[57]*

Hopkins's visit did little to ease Franco-American tensions. De Gaulle was not the man to be appeased by ebullient back-slapping or by sweeping statements about the need for post-war collaboration between Washington and Paris. Hopkins suggested that the General might meet Roosevelt after the Crimean Conference. De Gaulle, however, rightly appreciated that absence from this gathering might have its advantages as well as its drawbacks, and that to meet Roosevelt afterwards would simply commit France to decisions taken by others. When, after the Yalta discussions, Roosevelt was unwise enough to summon de Gaulle to Algiers for a meeting, the Frenchman coldly declined. He was not going to allow Americans to play host in part of the French Empire.[58]

It was obvious that France was not going to fit very easily into the auxiliary role envisaged for her by her liberators. It is fair to remember that, however hypersensitive de Gaulle may have been to imagined slights, the attitude adopted towards him by all his allies was decidedly patronising. Few in Roosevelt's entourage were prepared to go very far to meet French claims for equality of status among the Great Powers.[59]

* General de Gaulle had concluded his own Treaty of Alliance with the U.S.S.R. on 10 December 1944.

11 | The Yalta Conference

I

IT was clear, therefore, that, as the political and military leaders of the Anglo-American segment of the Grand Alliance began to foregather at Malta, Western inter-Allied collaboration was not functioning at its most harmonious. Nevertheless, friction over procedure and fears about the ultimate settlement of Europe did not outweigh the general sense of confidence and elation created by the successes of the previous year and the prospect of victory over Germany. By comparison with the mood at later international gatherings, that at Malta and Yalta could be considered optimistic.

The Malta Conference really began at the end of January. On the twenty-ninth of that month Mr Churchill, Mr Eden and Field-Marshall Brooke left London by air with members of their staffs. On the following day the Combined American and British Chiefs of Staff met to consider the final operations to end the war against Hitler. Although there was a good deal of acrimony at these and subsequent military discussions, the matters of substance at issue were not of such crucial importance as those treated at earlier meetings. It was becoming clearer all the time that Germany was beaten and that, after Rundstedt's final fling in the Ardennes, the morale of the Nazi forces was at last beginning to crumble.[1]

The main cause of inter-Allied friction at the military level lay in recriminations over Eisenhower's apparently unsuccessful direction of the Western offensive in the autumn of 1944, and the British fear that he might botch the Rhine crossing by failing to concentrate forces on the northern sector of the front. For their part the Americans not unnaturally resented criticism of their general, and wished to avoid tying his hands by excessively detailed directives. They also suspected the British of wanting to insert an over-all land commander between Eisenhower and the main battle, a suggestion which they refused even to consider in the final proceedings of the conference.[2]* Nevertheless, the British and the Americans were agreed on the objectives of their operations in Europe. Both wanted to see the Western offensive put in train as quickly as

* See above, p. 190.

possible. At this juncture there was no British pressure for any diversion of forces for a thrust into Central Europe via northern Italy and the Balkans. Indeed, five divisions were to be withdrawn from Italy and Greece to strengthen the Western assault. Mr Churchill expressed satisfaction over the transfer of British and Canadian soldiers from the Mediterranean, saying that he was 'anxious that the British contribution to the heavy fighting which would be taking place in North-west Europe should be as great as possible'.[3] It is true that he pressed for a rapid follow-up of any German collapse in Italy because, as he put it, 'it is essential that we should occupy as much of Austria as possible, as it is undesirable that more of Western Europe than necessary should be occupied by the Russians'.[4]

However, this view was in line with the general directives accepted by the Chiefs of Staff. At Malta it was not envisaged that Germany would collapse as quickly as was actually to be the case. The British military leaders thought that the war in Europe was unlikely to be over before the end of June. If, as they expected, the Russian advance was held on the line Landsberg–Riesengebirge, the Red Army would not be able to resume a full-scale offensive before the middle of May.[5] It was therefore not unreasonable for Mr Churchill to hope that the Western Allies might strike into Austria, especially as Stalin himself had seemed to favour this idea during their conversations in Moscow.* Although there was later to be a good deal of argument about the extent to which Anglo-American armies allowed the Russians to advance into Europe, it seems fair to argue that Eisenhower's actual achievement in 1945 did not fall far short of the hopes expressed at Malta, and in some respects – notably the speed of his advance – exceeded them.

It was the political rather than the military problems which promised to cause most difficulty at Yalta and for this reason the British were eager to thrash them out as fully as possible before the two delegations left for the Crimea. Mr Stettinius arrived in Malta on 31 January and it was soon clear that, as the head of the State Department, his thinking was often in line with that of the British Foreign Office. Indeed, on the evening of his arrival Mr Stettinius and Mr Eden found themselves at once in agreement in favour of a firm stand on the question of voting in the United Nations. In this case they differed from Mr Churchill, who was far less enthusiastic about resisting the Russians on that particular issue.[6]

The next day the two Foreign Ministers got together on board the cruiser *Sirius* for longer discussions. As Mr Eden noted happily in his diary, 'We found ourselves in complete agreement on all major points'.[7] There was a difference in emphasis, however, between the American

* See above, pp. 199–200.

and British viewpoints, and this was to be of considerable importance. As Mr Eden went on to say in his private record:

> They seemed to me to give rather too much weight to World Council and too little to Poland, in the sense that unless the Russians can be persuaded or compelled to treat Poland with some decency there will not be a World Council that is worth much.

The American tendency to give priority to the 'World Council' was, of course, consistent with the general line pursued by Secretary Hull during his period of office. It also reflected the views of President Roosevelt and his entourage, who were at this time approaching Malta in the cruiser *Quincy*. Admiral Leahy, for example, remained firmly opposed to any policy which might seem to involve the United States in the politics of other countries.* Leahy was perhaps more important than usual to Roosevelt at Yalta because Hopkins had become ill during his European tour and only rose from his bed to participate in the plenary meetings of the conference.[8]

Mr Hopkins had himself arrived at Malta on the same day as Secretary Stettinius, but was not present at his conversations with Mr Eden. The two Foreign Ministers covered a good deal of ground in their conversations. To begin with, Stettinius raised the question of zones of occupation in Germany over which American procrastination had caused so many delays in the European Advisory Commission. As the result of the morning's work on *Sirius* telegrams were dispatched to the British Foreign Office and the United States Embassy in London indicating the two Governments' approval of the zonal boundaries proposed by the E.A.C.[9] Mr Stettinius also stated that President Roosevelt was willing to give the French a zone of occupation in Germany, and it was agreed that this should be created from the British and American Zones. Both the Foreign Secretaries were in favour of French participation in whatever inter-Allied machinery should be set up to control Germany.

On Poland there was firm agreement not to recognize the Soviet puppet Provisional Government. The two men were prepared for a showdown with the Russians on this issue. They wanted to impress it upon Stalin that the fate of the Poles was so important to American and British public opinion that a serious breach of confidence would result if no solution were found to it. As the record of the discussions put it, 'It was agreed that a deadlock would be bad but that a simple recognition of the Lublin Provisional Government would be even worse'.[10]

Mr Eden felt that it was up to the Americans to press Stalin for concessions over Poland. In his words, '. . . it was their turn to take up

* See above, p. 204.

the burden on this issue. We would back them to the full but a change of the bowling was needed, and we would both have to do all we could.'[11]

The determination of Eden and Stettinius to work together over Poland was consistent with hopes for a common front expressed in State Department briefing documents about this problem.* It was not, however, an aspiration shared with equal warmth by Mr Churchill or President Roosevelt. They were prepared to do their best for Poland so long as they did not damage the fortunes of the Alliance. If that best did not suffice, the Poles would have to be sacrificed.

For the time being it still seemed possible that such unpleasant alternatives might be avoided. To Mr Eden's pleasure, Secretary Stettinius produced a positive proposal which would ensure that the inhabitants of liberated territories should be given the opportunity to choose their Governments in a free and peaceful fashion. This was, of course, the State Department's project for an Emergency High Commission.[12] Since it would apply to Poland it obviously had serious implications for Anglo-American relations with Russia, and this strengthened the impression of Western solidarity over the future of the European continent. The Emergency High Commission represented just the kind of political initiative which Mr Eden wished to see undertaken by the Western Powers and which Admiral Leahy found so unattractive.

If Mr Eden had reason to be pleased by American views of Germany and Poland, the Secretary of State could congratulate himself on having found a willing ally in the American conflict with Russia over voting procedure in the world security organization. The American proposals were expounded at the meeting by Alger Hiss. They distinguished between decisions in the world organization involving discussion of a possible threat to peace and decisions involving action against members of the organization. In the former case the Great Powers would not be able to veto discussion in the Security Council if they themselves were participants in the dispute concerned. In the latter case, however, the right to veto would remain total.† It was agreed to put this proposal to both the President and the Prime Minister and to ask the President to present it to the Russians at Yalta.[13]

There were other issues over which it was felt that Anglo-American solidarity might be needed to squeeze concessions from the Soviet negotiating team. As Mr Eden pointed out when referring to Russian objectives at the Turkish Straits and in the Far East, the Russians

* See above, p. 207.
† The word 'veto' was not of course used in these proposals. It was simply that decisions of the Council had to be unanimous in matters affecting a threat to peace (see below, pp. 543–4).

wanted 'a good many things' from the West and 'we had not very much
to offer them, but we required a good deal from them'.[14] He felt that the
British and Americans should put together all the things they wanted
and set them against what they had to give. He felt, for example, that if
the Soviet Government decided to enter the war against Japan it was
because Stalin did not wish matters in the Far East to be settled by the
United States and Britain alone. Therefore there was no need to offer
Stalin a particularly high price for his co-belligerency. Mr Eden did not
rule out territorial concessions to Russia in the Pacific region, but made it
plain that these should be part of a wider bargain, with the Russians
being expected to make reciprocal concessions. The exact nature of the
Asiatic gains which might be offered to Stalin were left vague, although
it was evident that southern Sakhalin and transit rights through Manchuria were likely to be among Soviet requirements. No mention was
made of the Kurile Islands, although Stalin had already indicated to
Roosevelt that he wanted these.* Expert opinion in Washington saw no
grounds for making over the whole of this island group to Russia, but it
is unlikely that the economic and geographical situation of these Pacific
islands weighed very heavily with either Stettinius or the President at
that moment.[16]

Otherwise Mr Eden was able to assure Stettinius of British support
for attempts to achieve unity between Chiang Kai-shek and the Chinese
Communists. The Americans had received reports that British agents
were sowing dissension in China, reports taken very seriously by those
close to the President.[17] This was symptomatic of the belief in Washington that American interests in the Far East were reconcilable with those
of Russia but that British imperialism was bound to oppose them.
General Patrick Hurley, Roosevelt's representative with Chiang,
claimed that 'British–French–Dutch propaganda' was trying to condemn
American efforts to unite Chinese military forces as interference in
Chinese affairs. The aim was to keep China divided against herself and
to use Chinese and American forces to reconquer colonial empires.[18]

Despite such suspicions, there was agreement between Stettinius and
Eden that their two delegations would find many matters on which they
could present a common front at Yalta, Russia's behaviour towards
Poland and China being only two examples.

* The list of Stalin's demands in the Far East had been cabled directly to Roosevelt
by Ambassador Harriman on 15 December 1944. They were, in fact, very much in
line with the indications Stalin had made to Roosevelt at Tehran. They included the
Kurile Islands and southern Sakhalin, the lease of ports on the southern part of the
Laotung Peninsula and control of the railway lines from Dairen to Manchuli and
Vladivostok. He also required recognition of the *status quo* in Outer Mongolia.[15] There
is no evidence that Mr Stettinius was aware of this telegram when he spoke to Mr Eden,
but its contents would hardly have surprised him (see below, pp. 348–52).

Another was Persia, a state whose strategic position and oil deposits made her of great interest to all three Powers concerned in the Yalta discussions. Both the British and the Americans were apprehensive about Soviet attempts to create a subservient Government in Persia and gain preferential conditions for the exploitation of Persian oil resources. Persia was less vulnerable than Poland in that she was more accessible to Western influence. Two American oil companies had already developed an interest in her future developments.[19] Her strategic position had always aroused the concern of the British rulers in India. British efforts to prevent Russian influence becoming dominant in Persia went back to the turn of the century, when Lord Curzon had repeatedly warned of the dangers of Russian encroachment at Tehran. Mr Eden was aware that similar conceptions of territorial expansion and political domination motivated the leaders of Soviet Russia as had swayed their Tsarist predecessors. It was therefore agreed that the British and Americans should work together at Yalta to obtain the joint withdrawal of all Allied troops from Persia and insist that Persia had the right to refuse the granting of oil concessions while foreign soldiers were on her soil.[20]

A further source of difficulty with the Russians lay in their attitude towards the administration of conquered rather than liberated territories in Eastern Europe. The Western Allies were concerned at the virtual exclusion of their representatives from decision-making in the administration of countries such as Rumania and Hungary. They were also anxious about the fate of their nationals' property in such areas – especially in Rumania, where oil companies owned by Western firms seemed in danger of expropriation by the Soviet authorities. Since the military control commissions in these countries were nominally tripartite in character, the British and the Americans thought they should be consulted over their actions. If it was necessary for the Soviet military rulers to act without prior consultation, the measures taken should be entirely their responsibility.[21]

At these preliminary discussions, therefore, the British Foreign Secretary and the American Secretary of State had found a broad measure of agreement.[22] The extent of Anglo-American preparation for the forthcoming confrontation with Stalin and Molotov was greater than at either the Moscow Foreign Ministers Conference in October 1943, when Mr Hull had avoided Mr Eden on his journey to Russia, or before Tehran, when preliminary discussions at Cairo were dominated by the Chinese issue. The fact that at Malta events had taken a more encouraging turn for the British was largely due to changing attitudes in the American State Department and the obvious community of interest being created as the result of Russian activities in Eastern Europe.

It soon became apparent, however, that co-ordination at the highest level would be little easier than before. On 2 February the President and his party – Admiral Leahy among them – sailed into the Grand Harbour at Valletta aboard the cruiser *Quincy*. They received a tremendous welcome which included a Spitfire escort and several ships' bands playing 'The Star-spangled Banner'. The occasion was, and remained, euphoric rather than businesslike. The President did not seem eager to get down to serious talks about the forthcoming conference. He had held some conversations aboard the *Quincy* with his travelling companions, but since neither Stettinius nor Hopkins nor any members of his military staffs had been present these were not of a detailed character. The State Department had provided complete files of background briefing data for the President on problems to be faced at Yalta, but there is no evidence that he gave them very serious attention.[23] Hence it was not possible to round off the discussions between Mr Eden and Mr Stettinius with an effective top-level meeting at Malta. The President was, in any case, unlikely to desire discussions of this kind since they might undermine what he took to be his own personal *rapport* with Stalin.

Mr Eden was, therefore, once again to be very irritated by what seemed to be the vague attitude of the President towards affairs of state. Neither lunch nor dinner with him produced any diplomatic results. Mr Eden was moved to complain to Harry Hopkins that 'we were going into a decisive conference and had so far neither agreed what we would discuss nor how to handle matters with a Bear who would certainly know his own mind'.[24]

It is difficult to say whether such apparent unwillingness to get down to serious discussion was due to deliberate policy on the part of Roosevelt or whether it was simply the result of Churchillian verbosity on the one hand and Presidential ill-health on the other. The question of Roosevelt's physical condition at the Yalta Conference has been the subject of considerable discussion, and it is still not possible to make a certain judgement about it. Mr Eden thought that the President gave an impression of 'failing powers'.[25] On the American side Admiral King experienced his first feelings of alarm about Roosevelt's health when he greeted him at Malta, not having seen him for two weeks.[26] After the long air journey to the Crimea on 3 February Roosevelt appeared even more jaded. Lord Moran, Mr Churchill's doctor, recorded that the President

> looked old and thin and drawn; he had a cape or shawl over his shoulders and appeared shrunken; he sat looking straight ahead with

his mouth open, as if he were not taking things in. Everyone was shocked by his appearance and gabbled about it afterwards.[27]*

Nevertheless, such impressions were not universal. Admiral Leahy, who was with the President throughout his travels, firmly denied that his Commander-in-Chief showed signs of any serious physical deterioration at Yalta or before it.[29] The President had suffered a heavy cold aboard the *Quincy*, and according to his daughter and his doctor he was suffering from sinus trouble which forced him to sit with his mouth open.[30] James F. Byrnes, who travelled with the President, attributed his apparent failure to pursue State Department background documents prepared for the voyage to the cold which dogged him on the Atlantic crossing.[31] The President was, in any case, physically handicapped and was undertaking a long and demanding journey of historic importance. It would have been surprising if he had not at times shown signs of stress. Even in the relative luxury of his specially appointed Presidential aircraft, flying conditions were still uncomfortable in 1945, especially when, as in the case of the long flight form Malta to Yalta, aeroplanes were forced to reach fairly high altitudes.[32] Hindsight can enable the historian to deduce that the President was already declining in health when he travelled to Yalta, but this does not mean that his actions there were conditioned by physical weakness. The British Foreign Secretary himself came to the conclusion when looking back at the conference that Roosevelt's poor health had not altered his judgement, 'though his handling of the conference was less sure than it might have been'.[33]

II

On 3 February the British and American delegations – a combined total of about seven hundred persons, including the daughters of the two great men concerned† – flew to Saki airfield. After a long drive through the battle-scarred landscape of the Crimea the negotiators arrived at their various headquarters in the neighbourhood of Yalta. The British were housed in the Vorontsov Villa and the President's party occupied the Livadia Palace about twelve miles distant. In between them, though nearer to the Livadia, stood the Yusupov Palace, where the Soviet delegation was quartered.

The environment in which the conference found itself was one

* Lord Moran also claimed to detect 'hardening of the arteries of the brain in an advanced stage, so that I give him only a few months to live'.[28] As a medical man Lord Moran may have been inclined to attach too much importance to physical handicaps in the business of politics.

† Mrs Anna Boettiger and Mrs Sarah Oliver, daughters of the President and Prime Minister respectively.

reminiscent of Tsarist Russia at the turn of the century. The destruction and squalor left behind in the wake of the Nazis was the chief reminder that negotiations were taking place against a background of total war. The Russians had done their best to render the accommodation fit for occupation by their distinguished guests, but they had not been entirely successful. The British, in particular, received an enthusiastic welcome from large numbers of bed-bugs, and although Prince Vorontsov had provided his castle with six marble lions the fact that it possessed only two baths did not make life any more comfortable for its British guests.[34] On the whole the Americans were more fortunate – perhaps because they possessed adequate supplies of DDT.

Both the Western Allies had come prepared with large staffs and their own support systems in the Black Sea. The Americans had a naval auxiliary, *Catochin*, acting as a communications relay ship. They had hoped to be able to moor this in Yalta harbour itself, but the Soviet authorities refused to allow it nearer than Sevastopol, claiming that the waters between there and Yalta were mined. Since two American mine-sweepers had made the journey to Yalta this seems a rather unlikely objection. The Russians may well have preferred a situation in which communications from the conference via *Catochin* had to go by land line to Sevastopol. There was also an air courier service from Saki to Washington which took an average of four days. The British had a daily mail service carried in Mosquito aircraft flying straight from London to Saki.[35] They also had the liner *Franconia* moored in Sevastopol as a headquarters ship in case it was needed. In fact it was simply used as a dormitory and rest centre on the journey back from Yalta after the conference was over. Even then the Russian motorcade could not find the ship and spent an hour wandering through the wrecked streets of Sevastopol before locating it.[36]

The real business of the conference began on 4 February. All formal meetings were held at the Livadia Palace, the headquarters of the American delegation. A former residence of Tsar Nicholas II, it had been constructed in 1911 from white Inkerman granite in mock Renaissance style. One of the two rear courtyards was modelled on the Convent Court of St Mark in Florence; the other was Moorish in appearance. The palace commanded fine views of the sea and of mountains to the east and north. Its grounds were filled with exotic plants and trees collected by the Romanovs. Balmy weather, tactfully attributed by the Russians to the presence of President Roosevelt, added to the attractiveness of the scene.

Roosevelt himself began the day by meeting his diplomatic and military advisers in the palace ballroom. He was given a short briefing by

Secretary Stettinius in which the latter urged him to press the United States scheme for voting in the Security Council, to adopt the proposal for a European Emergency High Commission, to seek agreement on control machinery for occupied Germany, to achieve satisfactory Polish frontiers and to assist the formation of a provisional Polish Government pledged to free elections. Freedom of movement for Allied Control Commissions in Russian-occupied territories and inter-Allied consultation in such areas should also be demanded. The Russians should be asked not to seek oil concessions in Iran until after the war, and both Britain and Russia should be pressed to pledge support for an agreement between the Kuomintang and the Chinese Communists.[37] This was all very much in line with the Secretary's discussions with Mr Eden and the attitudes expressed in State Department background documents.

That it did not entirely coincide with the President's own views quickly became obvious in the Livadia ballroom. Roosevelt reacted very coolly to the idea of an Emergency High Commission, saying that he did not wish to take responsibility for domestic affairs in Europe and that he preferred periodic meetings between the three Foreign Ministers to a permanent Commission. This preference was consistent with his suspicions of the already existing E.A.C., but scarcely compatible with an effective control system in liberated territories. The whole concept of an Emergency High Commission was given a frigid reception at the meeting. Admiral Leahy reiterated the need to remove American troops from Europe as soon as possible. Charles Bohlen, who was special assistant to Mr Stettinius and acted as a liaison officer between the State Department and the White House, claimed that a special American commissioner might be too independent of the State Department and that the Commission itself might become self-perpetuating. Eventually it was decided to redraft the whole scheme as a mere declaration of intent with the possibility of *ad hoc* commissions for individual countries.[38] This would hardly upset the Soviet Union. Nor would it safeguard any of her neighbours. The proposal endorsed by Messrs Stettinius and Eden thereby became a dead letter*

It was also noticeable that the scheme proposed by the President effectively excluded the French from playing a part in shaping the future of Europe. His anti-French inclinations were also reflected in remarks about possible American military action in Indo-China. He was willing to accept this 'so long as it did not involve any alignment with the French'.[39]

Towards the end of the meeting Ambassador Harriman mentioned

---

* Its outcome at the Conference was the 'Declaration on Liberated Europe', which was supposed to govern Allied conduct there. See Document No. 3, pp. 631–2.

among other items the Kuriles, the maintenance of the *status quo* in Outer Mongolia and the control of the railway line to Dairen. These were, of course, more ambitious claims than those which had been envisaged by Eden and Stettinius, but the President, who had already received advance warning of Soviet wishes, seemed quite willing to accept them. He simply remarked that the Outer Mongolia issue would have to be discussed with Generalissimo Chiang Kai-shek. Hence the President clearly indicated that this attitude towards the Soviet Government had not changed since the conference at Tehran.

This point was underlined at 4 p.m., when Marshal Stalin and M. Molotov came to call on their American guests.[40] Apart from mutually flattering – and certainly justified – praise for the military achievements of both countries, two points of agreement emerged from this conversation. The first was that both Stalin and the President were united in a harsh attitude towards the Germans; the second that both were contemptuous of France. If anything, the President was more emphatic in expressing these sentiments than his Soviet colleague. Expressing horror at the devastation he had seen in Russia, Roosevelt said he was feeling 'very much more bloodthirsty towards Germany' than he had done a year ago.

He expressed the hope that Stalin would again 'propose a toast to the execution of 50,000 officers of the German Army'. This sinister remark was a reference to Stalin's suggestion at Tehran that there should be a mass extermination of the German Officer Corps.* At that time Mr Churchill had strongly opposed it and Roosevelt had tried to pass it off with a joke. He may have decided to raise the issue again at this juncture in order to reassure Stalin that the West would not be 'soft' on the Germans at Russia's expense. The specific issue of the treatment of war criminals may also have been in his mind. Since Tehran both the British and the Americans had swung away from the idea of dealing with leading Nazis by judicial process. Summary execution seemed less complicated. Yet when Mr Churchill went to Moscow in October 1944 he had been surprised to find Stalin 'taking an ultra-respectable line' over such executions. At Malta the British view still seems to have been inclined towards summary treatment, although Stalin's opposition was causing Mr Churchill to rethink the whole question.[41] On the American side the Attorney-General (Frank Biddle), War Secretary Stimson and Mr Stettinius sent the President a memorandum on 22 January advising him in favour of an international tribunal to try major war criminals.† The President's remarks to Stalin suggest that he had not fully accepted the advice in favour of a tribunal and would not have been unhappy

* See above, p. 153; and below, p. 392.   † See below, p. 397.

to see his British and Soviet colleagues press him into a more arbitrary course of action. Stalin, however, avoided committing himself.

So far as France was concerned President Roosevelt made fun of de Gaulle, recalling the Casablanca meeting at which, he claimed, the French leader had compared himself with Joan of Arc and Clemenceau. Stalin encouraged him by belittling the French contribution to the war and claiming that de Gaulle, who had recently visited Russia, had declared the Rhine to be the natural boundary of France. According to Stalin the French wanted to stay on it for ever. At this point Roosevelt volunteered to Stalin the 'indiscreet' information that for two years the British had 'had the idea of artificially building up France into a strong power which would have 200,000 troops on the eastern border of France to hold the line for the period required to assemble a strong British Army'. He went on to say that 'the British are a peculiar people and wish to have their cake and eat it too'.*

He complained that the Americans had had a good deal of trouble with the British over zones of occupation in Germany and would have preferred the North-western one so as to be independent of communications through France; 'but the British seemed to think that the Americans should restore order in France and then return political control to the British'. He raised the idea of a French Zone and said he thought this not a bad idea but added that it was 'only out of kindness'. Both Stalin and Molotov heartily concurred with the latter observations. Neither could have left the meeting with the feeling that Roosevelt was enthusiastic about French claims to equality of status with the other Allies. As for the President's views on Germany, these can only have encouraged Soviet hopes for gigantic reparations deliveries from Germany, as well as for a harsh territorial settlement for the Germans in Eastern Europe.

President Roosevelt doubtless hoped to begin the conference by creating an atmosphere of trust between the Soviet and American delegations. He may also have been inclined to torpedo trends of thought on the Anglo-American side which he found distasteful. Like Admiral Leahy he was not interested in a balance of power on the European continent; the global power balance was something which exercised him far more, and in this he sought Russian collaboration.

III

After the talks with Stalin the President and his advisers moved into the Livadia ballroom for the first plenary session of the conference.†

---

* Given in reported speech in the American text.

† The American enumeration has been followed here. Mr Churchill took the meeting of 5 February as being the first meeting.[42]

This was entirely concerned with the prosecution of the war against Germany, and reflected an encouraging sense of optimism on both sides of the East–West alliance. At one point Mr Churchill depressed his own military advisers by raising the possibility that British troops in Italy might be used for an offensive through northern Yugoslavia instead of transferring them to the West. This was due to a suggestion by Stalin, who called on Mr Churchill earlier in the afternoon. The Prime Minister himself did, however, point out to the Russians that the Red Army might not give Anglo-American forces the time to complete a march on Vienna, and in any case the idea conflicted with plans worked out by the Combined Chiefs of Staff at Malta.[43] The chances for an effective thrust into the Danube Basin from Italy were really dead and the Prime Minister knew it.

At a dinner given by President Roosevelt after the plenary meeting the atmosphere was one of cordiality and hope. There was, however, one serious note of disagreement when Stalin made it clear that he was concerned to keep the rights of small Powers restricted to a minimum in the world security organization. Although the President and the Prime Minister assured Stalin that there would be no question of small nations dictating to the Great Powers, the rights of those weaker nations must be respected. As Mr Churchill put it: 'The eagle should permit the small birds to sing and care not wherefore they sang'.[44]* It was a sentiment which did not fit easily into the pattern of Soviet diplomacy.

Mr Churchill himself was not a partisan of the American scheme for voting on the Security Council. After Stalin and the President had withdrawn from the dinner table he told Stettinius and Eden that he was inclined to accept the Russian view on the voting issue because everything depended on the unity of the three Great Powers. Without that 'the world would be subjected to inestimable catastrophe; everything that preserved that unity would have his vote'.[45] Mr Eden warmly opposed these views, claiming that they would dissuade small nations from participating in the organization, and that the British public would also be disillusioned by an international body which was simply a puppet of the Great Powers. The two British statesmen left their American colleagues with this open disagreement still unresolved. It was another example of the way in which agreement between the British Foreign Office and the American State Department was threatened by displeasure from a higher level, this time on the British side. Mr Churchill would probably have preferred to make concessions to Stalin over the United Nations, a body in whose efficacy he can have had but little faith, in order to gain genuine security in Europe. Mr Eden, on the other hand,

* See below, pp. 541–3.

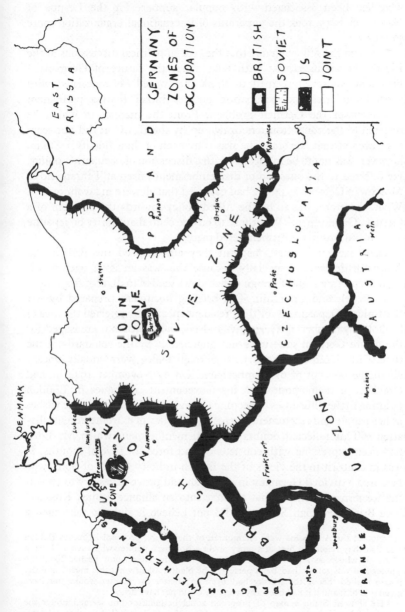

Map of zones of occupation in Germany presented by President Roosevelt to the Yalta Conference on 5 February 1945.

who had been associated with popular support for the League of
Nations in 1935, took the apparatus of international organization more
seriously.*

It was on the following day that the crucial political discussions at the
Livadia began in earnest with talks about the future of Germany.[47]
President Roosevelt seemed to think this would be concerned with
zonal boundaries and occupation policies rather than a permanent
settlement of the German problem. From the manner in which he
referred to the zonal frontiers drawn up by the E.A.C. it did not seem
that, even at that late stage, he was convinced of their finality.† Stalin,
however, was not to be fobbed off with a discussion of occupation policy.
He referred to the question of dismemberment raised at Tehran and at
Moscow in October 1944. He had gathered that all were in favour of this.
What, therefore, was to be the Allied policy towards the problem of a
German Government? Was there to be one central authority or separate
administrations in the dismembered pieces?

These were fair questions, but they embarrassed the British and
American delegates, especially because this was an issue over which
State Department and Foreign Office views tended to diverge from those
of Roosevelt and Churchill. The briefing document prepared by Mr
Stettinius's Department for the President specifically rejected the idea of
forcibly dismembering Germany. Indeed, the frontiers it envisaged for
the future German state were not ungenerous by the standards of the
time.[49] Mr Eden and the British Foreign Office were equally uneasy
about the concept of dismemberment. On 27 November 1944 he had
circulated a memorandum to his Government colleagues in London
pointing to the difficulties of keeping Germany divided against the wishes
of her people and recommending instead a policy of extreme decentralization.[50] This reflected doubts about dismemberment which Mr Eden
had been expressing with consistency and force for several months. It
was in contrast to the views of the British military Chiefs of Staff, who
favoured a divided Germany in case it should prove necessary to recruit
the western portions of that country into an alliance against Russia.[51]
The British Foreign Secretary did not believe it right to take such a

* Not all the Americans were enamoured of their U.N. proposals. Charles Bohlen
said that they reminded him of a story about a Southern planter who gave a Negro a
bottle of whisky as a present. Next day he asked the Negro how he had liked the
whisky and was told it had been perfect. The planter asked what this meant and the
Negro replied that if the whisky had been any better the planter would not have
given it to him and if it had been any worse he could not have drunk it.[46]

† He showed Stalin a map of proposed zonal boundaries but seemed under the
impression that it had been agreed between himself and Churchill at Quebec, whereas
it was in fact a revised version drawn up by the E.A.C. (see Map 2).[48] For zonal
boundaries, see below p. 274.

gloomy view of post-war political developments and strongly maintained his position. For his part, Mr Churchill had recommended to Mr Eden that arguments about the long-term relationship of Germany to Europe should be avoided.[52] President Roosevelt had already shown Stalin that his eagerness for a tough line towards Germany was undiminished.

In fact, both the Western leaders reiterated their commitment to the principle of dismemberment in their replies to Stalin's question. Mr Churchill simply urged that the details of this procedure could not be worked out at Yalta but would need great deliberation and expertise. He repeated his view that the isolation of Prussia and the removal of her might from Germany would eliminate 'the arch evil'. A South German state with a Government in Vienna might indicate the main line of division for Germany. President Roosevelt aired his experiences in Germany forty years earlier and claimed that the country could quite easily be divided into five or seven states – a view which prompted Mr Churchill to interrupt with the words 'or less'.

This discussion set the tone for the consideration of the German problem at the conference. The question was not so much the nature of Allied administration after hostilities ceased but the extent to which dismemberment was to be explicitly agreed upon before Germany surrendered. Stalin insisted that the Germans recognize in their surrender document the determination of the Allies to dismember Germany. Mr Churchill was unhappy with this proviso, but it was accepted in principle and passed to the three Foreign Ministers for consideration. As was to be expected, Mr Eden strove to prevent the acceptance of any formula which would bind the Allies 'hand and foot' to dismemberment before a proper inquiry into the German problem had been undertaken. He was successful in stopping M. Molotov imposing a policy upon the Allies which would have finally committed them to dismemberment.[53] However, the ultimate decision of the conference on this issue was that the Germans would have to recognize in their surrender document that their conquerors were likely to dismember the Reich. All three Heads of Government had accepted some form of German partition, even though the Western Powers sometimes seemed to envisage this as an extreme form of devolution rather than territorial fragmentation. It certainly could not be argued that the division of Germany which appeared after the war ran counter to the intentions of the Allied statesmen at Yalta, even if the circumstances under which it took place were not those they had themselves envisaged. Indeed, had they been able to foresee the fate of Germany in the decades after the war many of them would have felt she had escaped rather lightly.

There then arose the question of French participation in the occupation of Germany. The creation of a French Zone was conceded quickly enough, since this only affected the British and the Americans from whose occupation areas it would be created. Roosevelt openly stated that American troops could not stay more than two years in Europe. But when French participation in the Allied control machinery in Germany was mooted Stalin became very much more obstructive. He claimed that this would encourage other, smaller Powers to want similar rights. Mr Churchill stressed the need Britain felt for a strong France with a powerful army to help hold back a future German attack. At first Roosevelt supported him; then, egged on by Harry Hopkins, he veered against French participation. Stalin concluded that the meeting agreed on a French Occupation Zone but did not desire French membership of the central control council. Doubtless his conversation with Roosevelt the previous day had encouraged him to take an obstructive line on this issue. The solution the conference had come to under his guidance was quite unrealistic; de Gaulle would never have accepted it. Fortunately it was soon to be reversed.

Of greater significance for long-term East–West relations was the question of reparations, which Stalin also insisted on discussing. After the President's 'bloodthirsty' attitude of the previous day he had reason to be hopeful over this. M. Maisky presented the meeting with a report in which he demanded that for a period of two years Germany should be stripped of industrial plant and other movable wealth which would be counted as reparations. This should be followed by a ten-year period of payments in kind.

Germany would be expected to pay reparations totalling $20,000 million, of which 50 per cent should go to the Soviet Union. This was a staggering figure. Mr Churchill told Stalin that Russia would never get anything like so much out of Germany. The President vaguely asserted that America would not lend Germany money or pay to stop Germans starving, but he agreed that German living standards after the war should be no higher than those in Russia.

The Western delegations were haunted by the catastrophic effects of the Allied reparations policies adopted after the First World War. To the Russians these had little significance. Maisky remarked – with some truth – that the problem after 1919 had been one of transfer. Then the Germans had had to make payment in gold or dollars. The Russians were willing to take reparations in kind.

The whole issue was indeed one over which East and West had different but perfectly defensible views. The Russians could not be expected to accept that post-war Germany should have a standard of life superior to their own. Their economy would benefit from a policy of economic looting in Germany. The Western Powers had accepted the premise of a harsh future for Germany but could not bring themselves in practice to face the consequences. They feared that in the long run they would be forced to foot the bill. Within a very few years both these viewpoints had been justified.

The question of reparations for the Soviet Union – for in practice the arguments revolved around that issue – was discussed by both the Foreign Ministers and their principals on several occasions during the conference. On 9 February Mr Stettinius produced a set of proposals which accepted many of the points put forward by the Soviet delegation, including the two-year period of organized looting,* and ten years' payment in kind. However, Stettinius did not set a total figure for payments from Germany. He merely suggested that a future reparations commission, which was to have its headquarters in Moscow, should 'bear in mind' the Soviet proposal of $20,000 million. The Russians demanded a more positive commitment to their suggested figure, and were especially insistent that the commission's terms of reference should include the sum of $10,000 million which they claimed as their share of the German payments.[54]

Mr Eden strongly opposed such demands and the matter came to a head at the seventh plenary session of the conference on 10 February. Stalin declared that if the British did not want Russia to get any reparations they had better say so. Mr Churchill – backed up by a telegram from the British War Cabinet which pointed out that $20,000 million was equal to Germany's yearly export trade in times of peace – refused to budge over the question of a total figure for reparations. The President was also uneasy about this, since he feared that American public opinion would react unfavourably if news of huge reparations demands on Germany leaked out. In the United States it might be assumed that this was a financial burden which the American taxpayers would eventually have to bear.

As the discussion went on and Stalin became more angry, the President received a note from Harry Hopkins which read:

> The Russians have given in so much at this conference that I don't think we should let them down. Let the British disagree if they want to – and continue their disagreement at Moscow. Simply say it is all referred to the Reparations Commission with the minutes to show the British disagree about any mention of the 10 billion.[55]

This, indeed, was the manner in which the final protocol of the conference was worded. It declared that the Soviet and American

* The word 'looting' did not, of course, figure in the memorandum.

delegates had agreed to accept as a basis for discussion the Soviet suggestion for a total sum of $20 billion* dollars and that 50 per cent of it should go to the Soviet Union. The disagreement of the British delegation was duly minuted.[56] Although the Americans could, and later did, argue that the President had committed them to nothing by this concession,[57] it was clear that the Soviet negotiators on the commission would use it as a lever to obtain their ambitious objectives. Had the Three Powers remained united in their post-war treatment of Germany the Soviet–American reparations proposals might have been as fateful for peace as those imposed on the Weimar Republic under the terms of the Versailles Treaty. As it turned out, the Americans and the British were soon to be nursing the German patient back to robust health rather than killing him for the benefit of Soviet Russia.

The issue of reparations was linked with that of German labour being put to work in Allied countries. At the second plenary meeting of the conference President Roosevelt had opened the discussion of reparations by raising this question.[58] Harry Hopkins passed him a note suggesting that all 'Gestapo Stormtroopers and other Nazi criminals' should be sent to Russia for reconstruction work.[59] Stalin, however, brushed the point aside and when Stettinius tried to raise it at a meeting of the Foreign Secretaries M. Molotov said that it was 'very complicated'. The Russians, he added, were not prepared to discuss it at Yalta, though he was willing to see it considered by a reparations commission when one was established.[60]

Soviet caution may have been caused by the desire to obtain a promise of large-scale reparations in kind, irrespective of German labour services. In fact they were able to have a form of words written into the protocol of the conference which accepted that labour services might be considered by the Moscow reparations commission, but that this should not be counted against the sum total of reparations demanded by the U.S.S.R.[61]

The Russians must have realized that formal acceptance of forced labour in the Soviet Union would deepen anti-Soviet feeling in Germany at a time when the Communists hoped to win support from their defeated foes. In any case, the Soviet Government could hope to utilize German prisoners as a work force without any formal agreement. Many Germans and Japanese spent long years in Russia after the war as virtual slaves, a circumstance which did not pass unnoticed in the West.[62]

* U.S. billions.

IV

The next major issue which came before the conference was the method of voting in the Security Council of the world organization proposed at Dumbarton Oaks.* Discussion of this issue laid bare the confusions within the Allied camp over post-war international relations. On the one hand all were agreed that the Big Three Allies should remain united after hostilities ceased. This view had been fervently expressed by Mr Churchill on the evening of 4 February and was reiterated with great force by Stalin at the third plenary session of the conference. His intervention was prompted by Secretary Stettinius's exposition of American plans for voting procedure in the Security Council. These were those agreed upon by Mr Stettinius and Mr Eden at Malta, and were almost identical with American proposals which had already been communicated to the Russians on 5 December 1944. They would enable the Big Three to block any action which might be taken against their wishes or interests, but would not prevent discussion of conflicts in which one of the Allied Powers was actually involved.[63]

Stettinius's statement was backed up by Mr Churchill, who had evidently been persuaded by his Foreign Secretary that support for the Americans on this issue would be of benefit to British interests. The Prime Minister admitted that he had not agreed with the original proposals put forward at Dumbarton Oaks 'since he was anxious that the realities of the situation of the Three Great Powers should be considered'. However, the revised American draft had removed all his anxieties.[64]† He stressed that in the last resort peace depended on the co-operation of the three governments represented around the conference table. Nevertheless, an injustice would be done if small countries were not able to state their grievances freely. In order to avoid the impression that the Three Great Powers were trying to rule the world, they should 'make a proud submission'. To alleviate Soviet anxieties still further he gave an example of the way in which the British felt their interests would be safeguarded in an international dispute to which they were a party. Perhaps for the benefit of President Roosevelt, he selected as his hypothetical case the possibility that China might demand the return of Hong Kong from Britain. Under the American scheme neither China nor Britain could vote on the methods of settlement to be adopted in such a dispute, but Britain could veto any proposal to take measures against her.

At this point Stalin, showing a fine combination of malice and foresight, inquired what would happen if Egypt raised the question of the

Suez Canal. He was clearly unconvinced by the Prime Minister, nor did President Roosevelt's support for the scheme alter his negative attitude. When he began his attack on Stettinius's proposals he covered his rear like the good negotiator he was by claiming that he had not had time to master the details of the Dumbarton Oaks scheme and that he had found difficulty keeping up with the intricacies of Mr Stettinius's oral exposition. This comment strongly impressed James F. Byrnes, who felt that if Stalin had not even read the documents about the international organization sent to him two months previously his interest in it must be rather slender.[65]

Stalin was, in fact, well aware of the issues at stake, as his subsequent statements demonstrated. But by suggesting that Stettinius's scheme was new to him he could imply that it was an Anglo-American product which was in some way discriminatory against Russia. By distorting the sense of Mr Churchill's remark that the Big Three should not appear to be wanting to rule the world, he made it seem that the Soviet Union was being accused of seeking world domination. Stalin went on to repeat his belief in the absolute necessity of preventing quarrels between the Allied Powers, If this could be done there was little chance of the renewal of German aggression. He also pointed out that the question of voting was very important because decisions were made by votes and it was decisions that really counted. He referred to the case of the Russo-Finnish war in 1939, when the League of Nations expelled the Soviet Union at the instigation of France and Britain and world opinion was mobilized against Russia. Although both the Prime Minister and the President tried to reassure Stalin that a world security organization would not be used to pillory the Soviet Union, the Russian continued to express fears about the 'mobilization of opinion against one country'.[66]

The matter was left to rest at that point, but it had been an instructional exchange. In many respects Stalin's doubts about the world organization were justified. All the Big Three leaders expected that international affairs after the war would be dominated by the Great Powers. Roosevelt himself had spoken of the 'four policemen' at Tehran,* and although the fourth policeman – China – hardly seemed fit enough to take his place on the beat, the general lines of this policy remained unaltered. In one sense the future United Nations was to be an exercise in public relations designed to make Big Three domination palatable to the rest of the world. It was also important as a means of involving the United States in overseas security arrangements and preventing her from relapsing into isolationism.

Stalin saw that the Soviet Union would be in a minority position

* See above, p. 151.

among a gathering of predominantly capitalist states. He feared that the United Nations would act as a forum for anti-Soviet views which would render collaboration between the victor Powers difficult once the war was over. There is no particular reason to suppose that he was insincere in this belief: it coincided with his country's own interests. Stalin – like Hitler in 1939 – had no reason to seek a conflict with Britain and the United States so long as they were willing to accept Russia's predominant position in Europe. Stalin's strategic concepts, shared by leaders of the Red Army, were similar to those of Hitler in that he felt that, given control of the continent of Europe, he could allow Britain to develop her overseas Empire and the United States to control the Pacific. Unlike Hitler he had no need to break the power of France; that had already been accomplished by the Germans. He could afford to allow British influence to exist in the western areas of Europe so long as the Soviet Union controlled the main land mass of the continent.

He thought, therefore, in terms of spheres of influence and the balance of power, just as Mr Churchill did. He did not expect states within his sphere of influence to do other than conform to the requirements of Soviet foreign policy; it therefore followed that the British and the Americans would demand the same obedience from smaller nations under their protection.

In some ways both the President and the Prime Minister shared these assumptions, though they did not voice them. But there were very important differences of emphasis. In the first place the Western leaders, having made their careers in a political environment where open discussion and public criticism were accepted facts of life, were willing to tolerate dissentient voices in world councils so long as no effective action could be taken against British or American interests. Secondly, the generous extent of the sphere of influence to which Stalin evidently hoped to lay claim was by no means acceptable to the Western Powers. In this sense there was a link between the status of the smaller powers on the world peace-keeping body and the discussions at Yalta over the territorial settlement in Eastern Europe. If Soviet domination was established east of the Oder, Stalin would have little to fear from the machinery invented at Dumbarton Oaks. A Soviet Poland was worth more to the Soviet Union than the rules of discussion in the Security Council.

V

It was to Poland that the conference next turned its attention. Both the Western leaders began their expositions on this topic by appeals to Stalin for generosity towards the Poles over the matter of their eastern frontier.

President Roosevelt said that there were six or seven million Poles in the United States. It would 'make it easier for me at home' if the Soviet Union could give something to Poland.[67] However, he made it clear that he was simply putting forward a suggestion and would not insist upon it. The Prime Minister described any concession as a 'gesture of magnanimity' by the U.S.S.R. which would be much admired. The tone of these suggestions makes it hardly likely that they were intended to be taken seriously, and they were probably presented more to placate the London Poles than to persuade the Russians. They did, however, form a useful preamble to the main point put by both Roosevelt and Churchill – that the solution of the Polish problem depended on the formation of a representative Polish Government. Mr Churchill expressed this especially forcefully, saying that the British would 'never be content with a solution which did not leave Poland a free and independent state'.[68] Poland must be 'mistress in her own house and captain of her soul'. He hoped that it might be possible to form a Provisional Government at Yalta including men like Tadeusz Romer and Stanislas Grabski.*

Stalin erupted under this pressure with one of his most emphatic statements during the whole conference. Poland, he argued, was a corridor through which Russia could be attacked. As for her frontiers, the Curzon Line had been fixed by Clemenceau and Curzon. Lenin had been dissatisfied with it. He, Stalin, had retreated from Lenin's position, but was he to be less of a Russian than Clemenceau? Poland would receive her compensation in the west even though it would 'cost Russian blood' to wrest lands for her from Germany.[69] Stalin cleverly pointed out that when Mikolajczyk visited Moscow he had been delighted to learn that Poland's western frontier would be extended to the Western Neisse River. Stalin asked the conference to support this western frontier for Poland. As for the suggestion that a Polish Government be created at the conference, Stalin unctiously announced that, though he was called a dictator and not a democrat, he had enough democratic feeling to refuse to create a Polish Government without consulting the Poles. It would be difficult to achieve fusion between the Warsaw and the London Poles. Mikolajczyck had been forced to resign precisely because he wanted an agreement with the Warsaw Government. Arciszewiski had described the Warsaw Poles as bandits† and was against any agreement. Stalin

---

* Polish leaders in London.

† Tomasz Arciszewski was the new Polish Premier in London. On 3 February he had sent a message to Roosevelt protesting over the treatment of Polish patriots by Communist forces in Poland. The term 'Warsaw Poles' – as with the early description 'Lublin Poles' – refers to the pro-Soviet provisional régime recognized by the Russians. Both terms are used in these pages – as they were at the conference.

suggested that the Warsaw Poles might be asked to come to Yalta or Moscow, but gave it as his opinion that they had a democratic mandate 'equal at least to that of de Gaulle'. He complained that agents for the London Poles were stirring up conflicts in Poland and that the Red Army could not afford to have civil war in its rear as it advanced into Germany. He did not mention that most of the tension was due to the aggressive attitude of the Warsaw Poles and the Soviet security forces, which were trying to liquidate anti-Nazi resistance groups unsympathetic to the Soviet Union. Nevertheless, the point Stalin made was a real one; compromise between the rival Polish factions would be difficult to achieve. If left to themselves the Poles would probably plump for an anti-Soviet régime. In that case talk of a Poland as a 'friendly' neighbour to Russia would be meaningless.

All in all Stalin had delivered a powerful broadside over Poland. He had cleverly alluded to the obstinate intransigence of the London Poles, and to the comparative disinterest shown by the Soviet Government in Western countries such as France. He had been quite uncompromising over the territorial issue.

Mr Churchill attempted to reply by casting doubt on Stalin's information about Poland and pointing to the bloodshed and chaos which might ensue if an unpopular Government were to be forced on the Poles. He stressed that the British could not recognize the Warsaw Government, and on this note the discussion ended.

The Western delegations were not disposed to let the Polish issue rest without exerting further pressure on the Russians for concessions. Roosevelt and his advisers drafted a letter to Stalin in which he expressed great concern over the inability of the conference to reach an agreement about Poland. Public opinion in the United States would be very critical over this. He entirely appreciated the Soviet need to secure the Red Army's rear as it went into Germany and took up Stalin's suggestion that leaders of the Lublin Poles should be brought to Yalta. Roosevelt suggested that a number of other named politicians from Poland should be invited to the conference in order to help set up a Provisional Government acceptable to the Big Three. This Government should be pledged to hold free elections in Poland as soon as possible. He felt sure that the Americans and the British would then distance themselves from the London Poles and accept the new régime in Warsaw.[70]

Mr Harriman was sent with this draft to the British headquarters where the Prime Minister and Mr Eden were discussing the need to maintain a hard line about Poland. They approved of the President's letter, but Mr Eden suggested it should be stiffened by some amendments. When the President finally dispatched the letter he included the words 'I have made it clear to you that we cannot recognize the Lublin Government as now composed'. He also remarked that a new Provisional Government would 'no doubt' contain some Polish leaders from abroad like Mikolajczyk, Romer and Grabski.[71]

When the conference met on 7 February it was clear that Roosevelt's initiative had had some effect because Stalin claimed to have been trying – unsuccessfully – to contact the Warsaw Poles by telephone. Towards the end of the plenary session Molotov produced further proposals for the future of Poland. These included details of frontiers suited to Russian interests. In the east this meant the Curzon Line and in the west the Western Neisse. There was also a statement that 'some democratic leaders from Polish *émigré* circles be added to the Provisional Polish Government', which should then be recognized by the Great Powers. This Government should hold elections as soon as possible. The enlargement of the provisional administration should be entrusted to M. Molotov and the Allied Ambassadors in Moscow.[72] Both the President and the Prime Minister reacted unfavourably to the use of the word '*émigré*' to describe the additional members of the Polish régime.

Mr Churchill also objected to the Western Neisse on the grounds that 'it would be a pity to stuff the Polish goose so full of German food that it got indigestion'. He said that, although he would not be shocked if large numbers of Germans were driven out of these areas, many people in Britain would be shocked. Such large numbers of refugee Germans would create great problems. Stalin drily remarked that most Germans in the areas concerned had already fled from the Red Army. The Prime Minister agreed that the Germans had lost from six to seven million casualties in the war and might lose another million before it was over. Stalin interrupted to increase this latter estimate to two million. Mr Churchill continued to express doubts about the practicability of population transfer. He also reiterated his desire to see democratic leaders from within Poland included in the new Government, and with this Stalin concurred.

This was a discussion of major importance, for it set the guidelines for the eventual Yalta Agreement over Poland. The Western Powers had given way over the eastern frontier; that had never really been in doubt since Tehran. The western frontier was still open to argument; it remained undecided at the end of the conference. Stalin had staked out a claim for maximum compensations for Poland, compensations which would involve large-scale deportation of Germans and ensure permanent Polish–German tension. The refugees from these German provinces were in fact assimilated into Western Germany once the British and the

Americans decided to allow their zones to rebuild their economy. This was not foreseen by Stalin in 1945. As for Polish independence, the decision to expand the existing pro-Soviet administration by inviting outsiders to join it meant in practice that the rights of the London Government had been jettisoned. The chances of obtaining a genuine coalition in Poland and genuinely free elections were virtually non-existent. At talks between the Foreign Ministers Mr Eden continued to press forcefully for effective controls over the way in which the elections – which were supposed to take place within weeks of the conference – would be held. His efforts were sometimes successful at the conference table but could have little practical value for the Poles.[73] The elections which Stalin and Molotov promised so quickly did not in fact occur until January 1947, and they were then far from 'free'. Negotiations over Polish affairs conducted in Moscow between M. Molotov, Mr Harriman and Sir Archibald Clark Kerr were nothing but an exercise in frustration, and contributed directly to the ultimate breach between the Soviet Union and the Western Powers.

Yet, in one sense, the Polish question was successfully resolved at Yalta. The primary aim of all the Big Three had been to reach an agreement over Poland which would not create an immediate rift in the Alliance. This they had done. The British Foreign Office and the American State Department had not recognized the Lublin régime, although they had promised to do so once it had been made respectable by the addition of 'democratic' politicians. The Soviet Union retained its grip on the country. After the defeat of Hitler this was seen as a tragedy; at the time it was regarded as a better settlement than might have been hoped for when the Americans and British landed at Saki airfield.

One weakness in the British position when pressing Stalin for concessions in Poland was their own vulnerability to criticism over the British occupation of Greece. As we have seen, Admiral Leahy had described British actions in Greece and Italy as 'active aggression'.[74] The Prime Minister and Mr Eden had spent Christmas in Athens doing their best to suppress a Communist rising there. British troops were still engaged in the task of pacification when the Big Three met.

The British also faced troubles in Yugoslavia, where the chances for a restoration of the Serbian monarchy were rapidly dwindling. The British and the Soviet Governments had agreed to accept a compromise worked out between Tito's partisans – who virtually controlled the country – and the leader of the *émigré* Government in London, Dr Ivan Subašić. Dr Subašić's arrangements were not at all pleasing to King Peter. Encouraged by United States coolness towards them, he rejected the agreement and dismissed Subašić from office.[75] The British Government continued to recognize Subašić as Premier, but the agreement with Tito seemed in danger of collapse. This was the situation when the Allies met at Yalta.

Stalin was too good a negotiator to miss the chance to twit Mr Churchill over his embarrassments in Greece and Yugoslavia. On 8 February, for example, after a particularly emphatic exchange over Poland had ended with no clear result, Stalin introduced the subject of Yugoslavia, saying that he would like to know what was holding up implementation of the Tito–Subašić agreement. He added with ominous diffidence that he would 'also like to know what was going on in Greece. He had no intention of criticizing British policy there, but he would merely like to know what was going on.'[76]

The parallel between the Greek situation and what was happening in Poland must have been uncomfortably obvious to the British delegation. Mr Churchill was moved to remark that they 'had had rather a rough time in Greece and they [the British] were very much obliged to Marshal Stalin for not having taken too great an interest in Greek affairs'.[77] Although the Prime Minister promised a longer statement on Greece at a later meeting, he was not required to do so. Yet the occasional jibe from Stalin reminded the British how vulnerable they were to criticism in this area, and Mr Churchill tended to rise to such bait very easily.[78]

Over Yugoslavia it was the British who were anxious for Soviet help. The Tito–Subašić agreement was in many ways unsatisfactory from their viewpoint because it gave no guarantee that political groups other than those supporting Tito would be allowed to play a part in the political life of the country. Mr Eden asked the Russians to help obtain assurances from Tito that the partisan-controlled Anti-Fascist Assembly of National Liberation of Yugoslavia (AVNOJ) should be expanded to include members of the pre-war Yugoslav Parliament who had not compromised themselves by collaboration with the Germans during the war. He also demanded that legislation passed by AVNOJ be subject to ratification by a constituent assembly.[79] After a good deal of wrangling it was agreed that the conference should accept these amendments and ask Tito to adopt them once the Tito–Subašić agreement was in force. In reply to Stalin's fears that King Peter would still oppose the whole scheme, Mr Churchill and his Foreign Secretary assured him that 'the question of the King had been settled and anyway wasn't important'.

The question was finally resolved at the seventh plenary session of the conference on 10 February, when, supported by Roosevelt, the British succeeded in persuading Stalin to authorize a message to Tito and

Subašić telling them to implement their agreement at once and to accept the British recommendations about AVNOJ.[80] This was a valuable concession from the British viewpoint, but in the long run it made little difference to Yugoslavia. Tito's authority there was too deeply entrenched to be affected by paper agreements. Ultimately it was the nature of his movement and the favourable geographical situation of Yugoslavia which gave Tito the opportunity to establish his independence of Soviet control.

VI

The conference had, indeed, been moving forward on a number of fronts to an extent which surprised and even delighted the Western delegations. On 7 February, after a division of opinion between Mr Churchill and his two allies over French membership of the Allied Control Council to administer Germany, and after initial stages of the discussion over Poland had been completed, M. Molotov announced a major reversal of Soviet policy towards the world security organization. He said that, in view of Mr Stettinius's explanations and Mr Churchill's exposition, the Soviet Union was willing to accept the American proposals for voting in the Security Council. His only proviso was that two or three of the Soviet Republics – the Ukraine, White Russia and Lithuania – should be admitted to the world organization as founder members of the Assembly.[81] He compared these states with the Dominions of the British Commonwealth, a comparison which, though absurd in real terms, looked plausible in theory. The suggestion did not commend itself to President Roosevelt, who, while expressing his genuine delight at the Soviet concession, retired behind a smokescreen of theoretical points concerning the difficulty of deciding on the validity of one state's membership as against another.[82]* If larger states were given more than one vote it might seem to prejudice the whole organization. He stressed that the important thing was to call a meeting to establish the United Nations Organization as soon as possible. He asked that the Foreign Secretaries be asked to implement this demand and suggested that the first meeting of the U.N. might be held towards the end of March 1945 – less than two months away.

Mr Churchill greeted the Soviet announcement even more warmly than the President, and was obviously inclined to favour Molotov's request for extra Soviet votes in the Assembly. On the other hand he was far less eager to see a rapid meeting of the world organization, feeling it

---

* The President had been warned by State Department officials before he left Washington that Stalin would demand votes for the constituent Republics of the U.S.S.R. He told them he would deal with this by asking for a vote for each of the forty-eight states of the U.S.A.[83] See below, p. 547 and n.

would not be practicable in the near future. Mr Eden attributed these objections to the Prime Minister's 'reluctance to see any energies diverted to peacetime tasks'. Nevertheless, the Prime Minister's attitude was not unnaturally resented by the Americans, since Churchill had long ago agreed on such a meeting.[84] The Prime Minister was perhaps betraying his own scepticism about the importance of the world organization. His comments certainly aroused Presidential ire, and in an agitated exchange of notes between Roosevelt and Hopkins it was agreed that the Prime Minister was really worried about domestic politics. Hopkins wrote: 'I am quite sure now he is thinking about the next election in Britain.'[85]

The Dumbarton Oaks issue continued to loom in the minds of the Americans during the rest of the conference. They remained opposed to giving Russia two or three extra votes in the U.N. by accepting the Soviet Republics as voting members. On 8 February Alger Hiss drew up a memorandum setting out the objections to this procedure.[86] Mr Stettinius told a meeting of the Foreign Secretaries that he 'did not see in his own mind' how the Soviet Republics could be acceptable to the organization because the Dumbarton Oaks scheme had specified that each sovereign state should only have one vote.[87] He also argued that only such nations as had signed the U.N. Declaration and formally opened hostilities with the common enemy should be invited to the constituent meeting of the world organization. This was to meet Russian charges that some of the Latin American countries it was proposed to invite to the meeting were not at war with Germany. Several of them had no diplomatic relations with the Soviet Union. Mr Stettinius sent urgent telegrams to the State Department ordering that the Governments concerned be pressed to declare war on Germany before the end of February.[88] It was indeed difficult to explain why the Ukraine should not receive a vote in the U.N. if Haiti was to be thus honoured.

Despite this American move, M. Molotov persisted in his demand for the admission of the Soviet Republics, and Mr Eden expressed sympathy for his view – doubtless because he did not wish to compromise the rights of the British Dominions. On two points, however, the Americans were satisfied. It was agreed that the location of the world meeting should be in the United States and the date was to be 25 April 1945, considerably later than the President had first suggested, but early enough to fulfil his purposes.*

At the Foreign Ministers' conference which saw the resolution of this issue Mr Eden, supported by his American colleague, raised the question of Allied differences in Iran. He urged that no pressure be put on the

* See below, pp. 547–51.

Persians to grant oil concessions and that Allied troops be withdrawn from that country as soon as the overland truck route to Russia became dispensable. Molotov tried to brush this aside, claiming that the problem of oil concessions was dormant at that moment and that the withdrawal of troops was a new issue which the Russians needed time to consider.[89] Attempts by Eden and Stettinius in the next few days to make progress over Iran foundered on M. Molotov's practised obstructiveness. Mr Churchill was reluctant to bring this matter forward in plenary session and the President showed no inclination to do so.

Eventually the British Foreign Secretary decided to go straight to Marshal Stalin for satisfaction. On 10 February he told the Russian leader about the difficulties the Allies were experiencing over Iran. Stalin laughed and explained that Molotov was 'very sore' about Persia because he had experienced a 'resounding defeat' there over the oil issue. Mr Eden said that the time had come to plan the joint withdrawal of Allied troops from Persia, and Stalin seemed agreeable to this. In the summer of 1945 the first steps towards such a withdrawal were taken.[90] However, it cannot be claimed that Persian independence really owed very much to the discussions at Yalta. No formal decision about the future of Iran was taken there. It was a policy of distinctly non-fraternal toughness on the part of President Truman – coupled with the tenacity of the Persians themselves – which kept Iran out of the Soviet orbit after the war.

Despite Soviet hedging on Persia and some embarrassment over the details of the U.N. proposals, the Americans had good reason to be satisfied with the way the conference was developing. For the President, in particular, events were moving in a very encouraging fashion. He had never had any desire to become entangled in the complexities of European politics. On the Polish issue his main concern had been to avoid friction with Russia, and the form of words employed was therefore as important to him as the sense which lay behind them. So far as the U.N. was concerned Stalin had conceded the most serious American demands. On the occupation and treatment of Germany the President and Stalin had no serious grounds for disagreement. There remained the question of Soviet entry into the Japanese war. This matter was first raised in discussions between the Russian and American staffs. On the afternoon of 8 February 1945 Stalin and the President met privately to confer about it.*

Roosevelt began by taking up detailed requests for military co-operation which Stalin's military subordinates had been unable to grant on their own responsibility. He asked for the use of bases in the Far

---

* See below, pp. 350–2.

East and in Hungary, and for permission for American Air Force experts
to assess the extent of bomb damage in those parts of South-eastern
Europe captured by the Russians.[91] To all these requests Stalin graciously acceded, though in practice the Americans were to get no help at
all in their European bombing programme.

Stalin then asked about the possibility of Russia buying shipping
from the United States after the war. The President promised to do his
best to transfer these ships on interest-free credit, remarking that 'the
British have never sold anything without commercial interest but I have
different ideas'.[92] He went on to hope that Russia would 'interest herself
in a big way' in shipping after the war. Roosevelt may have hoped that
his attitude might increase Soviet trust in him and induce a more
flexible Russian policy towards international trade. However, it could
not but encourage Stalin's rapacity towards the Americans and diminish
the chances of wresting concessions from him in return for economic
favours. Stalin certainly made no bones about his requirements when the
talk turned to the Far East. The President told him straight away that
there would be no difficulty over southern Sakhalin and the Kurile
Islands. He also favoured Dairen becoming a free port under international supervision – a method of procedure preferable to a direct
lease to Russia because of the status of Hong Kong, which the President
said he hoped to persuade the British to return to China. On Stalin's
request the President also seemed willing that Russia should acquire use
of Manchurian railways under some scheme of co-ownership with
China. Both men agreed that for security reasons Chiang Kai-shek
should not be told of these arrangements until nearer the time for
Russia to enter the war against Japan. They should, however, be embodied in a written agreement between the Big Three at the conference.

VII

With that the entry of Russia into the Far Eastern War was virtually
settled. A document drawn up over the signatures of Stalin, Roosevelt
and Churchill stated that, two or three months after Germany had been
defeated, the Soviet Union would enter the war against Japan on certain
conditions. These were that the *status quo* in Outer Mongolia should be
preserved and that 'the former rights of Russia violated by the treacher-
ous attack of Japan in 1904 shall be restored'.[93] It was indeed ironical
that Stalin should have gone to such lengths to wipe out a stain on
Russia's honour caused by defeat in a blatantly imperialist war, a defeat
which had, moreover, touched off the 1905 revolution against auto-

cratic Tsarism. Stalin's desire to surpass the imperial glories of Nicholas II was all the more embarrassing because one of his Allies – Great Britain – had actually stood behind Japan in the Russo-Japanese war.

There was, indeed, every likelihood that the British would object to Stalin's arrangement with the President, and Mr Eden was certainly incensed by it. He even went so far as to argue with his chief in front of Stalin and Roosevelt when the matter was put to the British delegation.[94] Sir Alexander Cadogan, formerly British Ambassador in China, was called to give his views, and he too objected to the agreement. Mr Churchill felt, however, that if he failed to put his signature to a scheme which Britain had little power to obstruct British influence in the Far East would suffer. In fact the British lost little by this. Although on the face of it Soviet intervention in the war was a great triumph for the Americans, it very shortly became a great source of bad feeling between the two countries. American pressure on Britain to give up her imperial role in the Far East dwindled. Hong Kong remained British long after Chiang Kai-shek had retired in confusion to Taiwan.

That Mr Churchill was not mistaken in his fear for British influence in the Pacific as the result of American–Soviet arrangements was demonstrated by a further topic of discussion at the private meeting between Stalin and Roosevelt on 8 February. This was the future of Korea. Roosevelt suggested that a form of trusteeship be established for Korea which would be composed of American, Soviet and Chinese representatives. This was a long-term proposal; Roosevelt claimed it would probably take twenty to thirty years before the Koreans were ready for self-government. Stalin did not seem happy about this, and was relieved when the President assured him that no foreign troops would be stationed in Korea. The Russians would have no reason to want American troops stationed on the mainland of Asia.

The President needed to come to some arrangement with Stalin over Korea since it was evident that Soviet troops might occupy the area when Russia entered the war in that theatre. But, as so often in his conversations, Roosevelt expressed his desires in a manner which seemed hostile to his absent partners, the British. The State Department briefing document on Korea recommended a quadripartite administration there under the Americans, British, Chinese and Russians.[95] Roosevelt deliberately omitted the British from his proposal to Stalin and explained that this was a 'delicate' matter, and that the British might resent it. Stalin had no doubts on that score and said that Mr Churchill 'might kill us' if Britain was excluded. He thought she should participate. The President then had to explain that he hoped to establish a similar trusteeship for Indo-China — an idea which the British disliked because they wished that region to revert to France. The British, he said, were themselves worried about the future of Burma.

Roosevelt also touched on the future of China itself and was gratified when Stalin assured him that he favoured a united front between the Kuomintang and the Communists under the leadership of Chiang Kai-shek. The President evidently thought that American interests would be served by collaboration with the Soviet Union in the Far East and by minimizing British – not to mention French – influence there. In this he may well have been influenced by his Ambassador in China, General Hurley. In any case, the displacement of colonial Powers to make way for the so-called 'open door' to American trade was a traditional American policy.

At the plenary session which followed President Roosevelt gained another round, for, after a further period of argument, Stalin gave up his demand that the Ukraine and White Russia – Lithuania had been quietly jettisoned – be invited to the first meeting of the U.N. as founder members.[96] However, he did not give up his proposal that these states should be elected to the U.N. at the earliest possible moment, and it was understood that his Allies would support their election.

Another aspect of international organization which exercised the participants in the Yalta Conference was the question of territorial trusteeships. The old League of Nations had been given authority over former Turkish and German dependencies and, although in practice these areas had been controlled by one or other of the victor Powers, the principle of accountability to an international body was obviously of great importance. After the end of hostilities there would be more enemy possessions – those of Italy and Japan – to dispose of, and trustee-ship seemed the most convenient method of dealing with the problem. The question was made all the more vital and difficult by the severe blow to imperial prestige suffered by the British, Dutch and French when many of their colonies in Asia had been overrun by the Japanese.

The British feared – and with good reason – that the Americans regarded colonial empires as immoral and out of date. They might therefore use the trusteeship system as a means of undermining the authority of the Imperial Powers. From the background documents prepared by the State Department on the trusteeship issue there is little doubt that the Americans hoped that the new U.N. Organization would pursue a much more active policy towards dependent territories than the League had done. They hoped the U.N. would directly administer trust territories instead of handing them over to colonial Powers, and they in-tended that it should at least lay down guidelines 'designed to establish minimum political, economic and social standards for all non-self-governing territories, whether colonies, protectorates or trust territories.'[97]

This clearly implied the possibility of intervention by the U.N. in the colonial policies of Powers like France and Britain. For their part, the British hoped to weaken the influence of the international organization over dependent territories by abolishing entirely the distinction between trusteeships and colonies. Instead they proposed a system of regional advisory commissions which would be of a consultative character and would obviously be able to exert little real authority.[98]

The American position at Yalta was, however, complicated by powerful voices in Washington which were being raised against the whole principle of trusteeship. Foremost among these was that of War Secretary Stimson who was determined that Pacific bases seized from the Japanese should be owned by the Americans in full sovereignty.[99] President Roosevelt was evidently impressed by that argument, despite his hopes that trusteeship might weaken colonialism elsewhere.

At the Yalta Conference there was an informal discussion about trusteeship between Gladwyn Jebb of the British delegation, Alger Hiss of the State Department and James F. Byrnes. Hiss pressed for a discussion of trusteeships and dependent areas at the constituent conference of the United Nations. The British were disturbed about this, but Harry Hopkins advised Eden to wait until the question was raised by the President, hinting that Roosevelt might not be so ambitious in his trusteeship plans as were his subordinates.[100]

However, the British were further disturbed when Stettinius raised the question in the same fashion as Hiss. Mr Eden warned his chief that the matter might come up in plenary session and received a strong minute in return pointing out that the Americans could have any Japanese islands which they conquered 'but "Hands off the British Empire" is our maxim'.[101] In fact Stettinius agreed to drop any mention of trusteeships from the formal invitation to the constituent meeting of the U.N., but it was accepted by the three Foreign Ministers that the five Powers likely to be permanent members of the Security Council should have diplomatic exchanges before the meeting on the subject of dependent territories and trusteeships.

At the sixth plenary session of the conference on 9 February Mr Stettinius read out a report of these Foreign Ministers' discussions. He explained that there should be talks prior to the U.N. Conference on 'providing machinery in the World Charter for dealing with territorial trusteeships and dependent areas'.[102] Before he could continue Mr Churchill exploded in violent wrath, much to the enjoyment of Marshal Stalin, who rose from his chair and applauded at intervals in the Prime Minister's peroration.[103]

Mr Churchill thundered that 'under no circumstances would he ever consent to forty or fifty nations thrusting interfering fingers into the life's existence of the British Empire. As long as he was Prime Minister, he would never yield one scrap of their heritage.'[104] Stettinius hastened to explain that he was only referring to the administration of dependent territories taken from the enemy. As a result of Mr Churchill's outburst the section of the final conference protocol dealing with future discussion of trusteeships made it clear that only enemy dependencies or territories formerly under the mandate of the League of Nations would come under the category of trust territories.[105]

This was certainly a triumph for the British Prime Minister, since Britain had seemed vulnerable on this issue. Within a very short time, however, it proved a pyrrhic victory. Mr Churchill's hope of maintaining a huge colonial empire was as illusory as Roosevelt's faith in a friendly Chinese Government. Looking back on the incident in later years the British Foreign Secretary regretted the pleasure it had given to Stalin.[106] He had enjoyed seeing the Western Powers fall out. Mr Churchill's point also reinforced the principle that the Allies should not interfere in each others' spheres of influence. What the British could do in Africa the Russians could do in Poland.

If Mr Churchill was unnecessarily obsessed with trusteeships, the President remained preoccupied with the United Nations. His colleagues in the American delegation were deeply worried about his apparent willingness to concede extra votes in the U.N. Assembly to the Russians. This was obviously implied by the promise that White Russia and the Ukraine be elected to membership of the international organization. Byrnes and Leahy were among those who warned their chief of the difficulties which might arise with Congress over a situation in which it could appear that the U.S.S.R. had three votes and the United States only one. Roosevelt was therefore moved to write to both Stalin and Churchill asking that they agree to an arrangement whereby the United States might increase her voting rights to three also.[107] Stalin and Churchill agreed immediately. However, it soon became clear that such a horse-trade would be publicly embarrassing for the American Government. The final protocol of the Yalta Conference included the statement that, at the constituent conference of the U.N., the British and the Americans would support Russia's proposal to elect the two Soviet Republics as founder members of the organization.[108] The American Government was so unhappy about the outcome of this that they even tried to claim that the wording of the relevant report of the Foreign Ministers' conference had been changed without reference to them.[109]

This claim, firmly denied by Mr Eden, smacked of desperation. It also demonstrated the exaggerated priority given to the U.N. by both the State Department and American public opinion.

One beneficiary of this American concern about the U.N. at Yalta may have been General de Gaulle. As we have seen, President Roosevelt was initially opposed to British attempts to include the French in the Allied Control Council for Germany. But, as the conference progressed, the Americans saw that French co-operation might be useful to 'sell' the U.N. to smaller Powers, without whose ready acceptance the whole scheme would be doomed. The Declaration on Liberated Europe would also seem more impressive if the French Government acceded to it. Mr Hopkins had received a message from Georges Bidault in Paris that made him think that de Gaulle would meet the President after the conference, and it was hoped that he would agree to support American views on international organization.

The President and his advisers therefore agreed to change their attitude to French participation in German occupation machinery. Roosevelt passed word to Stalin through Ambassador Harriman that he had decided it would be best to accept France as a partner in the control machinery. On 10 February, at the seventh plenary meeting of the conference, Roosevelt formally announced his change of heart and Stalin accepted it. Thus the French were to become partners in the administration of Germany as well as simply receiving a zone.[110] The decision came as a great relief to the British, who had realized that de Gaulle would not accept one without the other. Although the French did not prove easy partners in Germany, it was well for the Western Powers that this decision was taken at Yalta.

One other question raised at plenary meetings was that of the treatment of German war criminals.* Mr Churchill opened the discussion of this point on 9 February by saying that the Declaration on War Crimes issued by the Moscow Foreign Ministers' Conference in 1943 had been 'an egg he had laid himself'. Referring to the section dealing with the main culprits whose crimes had no geographical location, Mr Churchill suggested that a list of such people be drawn up, and that after their identity had been definitely established they should be shot. This was in conformity with British fears that if Hitler, for example, were to be subjected to a formal trial it would be difficult to frame charges which would conform to accepted international law, despite the obviously criminal nature of his activities. Lengthy judicial proceedings would give leading Nazis the chance to strike martyred attitudes and, even if they were found guilty, it would be claimed that judicial processes

* See below, pp. 396–7.

held in such circumstances had no real validity. Summary executions would be much more easily understood. The British Prime Minister did not go into detail over this because it was clear that neither the President nor Marshal Stalin wanted to discuss it, although Stalin voiced what were evidently lurking Soviet suspicions about British relations with Hess.[111] No decisions were taken about the trial of war criminals at Yalta.

Nor did the British obtain any concrete guarantees when they tried to press the Russians about the unsatisfactory nature of developments in South-eastern Europe with the advance of Soviet armies there. Mr Eden bitterly upbraided M. Molotov over the conclusion of a pact between Yugoslavia and Bulgaria – the latter a former member of the Axis. He also criticized Russian violation of Anglo-American property rights in Rumania and the lack of consultation between the Red Army and the Western Allies in occupation policies throughout the Danube Basin.

M. Molotov proved unyielding on all these points and Mr Stettinius was not able to give his British colleague much support. No decisions emerged from the conference on these points and the final protocol spoke merely of 'an exchange of views'. It was, however, agreed that the question of the Yugoslav–Bulgarian treaty should be taken up with Molotov by the British and American Ambassadors in Moscow.

All that emerged from Western efforts to ameliorate the situation in Eastern Europe was a 'Declaration on Liberated Europe' pledging the Allies to work for the establishment of democratic institutions in the territories they freed from the Axis. It was to prove valueless as an instrument of policy, but Russian disregard for it was to have a bad effect on inter-Allied relations.

Despite their disappointments the Western delegates left Yalta in a cheerful frame of mind. The Alliance had emerged strengthened from the conference. The Polish issue had not resulted in the complete deadlock foreseen by Eden and Stettinius at Malta. The Russians had promised to enter the war against Japan and had accepted the American proposals for U.N. voting – the concessions the Americans had most wanted from them. As for the British, they were apprehensive about Poland but had gained their objectives over French participation in the occupation of Germany, the Tito–Subašić agreement, and the avoidance of anti-colonial commitments in the U.N. They had also evaded any Soviet interference with their activities in Greece. As Mr Eden wrote later, 'At Yalta the Russians seemed relaxed and, so far as we could judge, friendly.' There was no evidence that this state of affairs would change. But it did, and with rapidity.[112]

12 | Unconditional Surrender of the German Armed Forces

I

THE primordium of Unconditional Surrender lay in the principle enunciated by President Roosevelt – seemingly in the form of 'throw-away line' – at the Casablanca Conference of January 1943.* Mr Churchill at once concurred and Marshal Stalin shortly thereafter signified consent. It was apparent from the first that Unconditional Surrender had two meanings: a military capitulation in the field and an unequivocal acceptance of defeat and surrender by the Axis régimes. This latter meaning, President Roosevelt had been careful to assert, did not comprise the destruction of the German and Italian peoples, but the destruction of the philosophies in those countries based on fear and hate and subjugation of other peoples.

It was clear therefore that Unconditional Surrender had both a military and a political significance. It might be applied in one or both of these aspects, but in many respects a greater importance was attached to the latter than the former.†

The tempo of events overran Allied preparations in each of these fields when the principle of Unconditional Surrender came to its first practical application in the case of Italy in September 1943.‡ While the Foreign Office was still engaged in drawing up an extensive and complicated set of terms for the Italian surrender it became necessary for reasons of grand strategy to get the Italians out of the war as soon as possible, and the instrument signed on 3 September was of the briefest nature; it accepted the Unconditional Surrender of the Badoglio Government in Rome, interpreting it to mean that this Government placed itself

* See above, p. 60.
† The principle of Unconditional Surrender had already been applied in its purely military sense by the Japanese at the capitulations of Hong Kong, Singapore and Corregidor. The first large-scale surrender on these terms on the part of an Axis army was that of Stalingrad on 1 February 1943; this was followed on 13 May of the same year by the Unconditional Surrender of General Sixt von Arnim and Marshal Giovanni Messe to General Eisenhower at Tunis.
‡ See above pp. 64–78.

unreservedly under the orders of the United Nations as represented by the Supreme Allied Commander.

Thereafter it was felt necessary to make full and adequate preparation for the day on which the principle of Unconditional Surrender should be applied to Germany and, by inference, to Japan also. These preparatory measures had been included among the tasks assigned to the European Advisory Commission by the Tehran Conference of November–December 1943* and had been completed in time for the Yalta meeting of the Big Three in February 1945.† The documents prepared by the Commission for the military and political capitulation of Germany were accepted at Yalta with the added amendment to Article 12:

> The United Kingdom, the United States of America and the Union of Soviet Socialist Republics shall possess supreme authority with respect to Germany. In the exercise of such authority they will take such steps, including the complete disarmament, demilitarization and the dismemberment of Germany, as they deem requisite for future peace and security.[1]

Scarcely had the ink dried upon the Yalta Agreement than the principle of Unconditional Surrender was called into pragmatic operation. By the beginning of 1945 it had become fully apparent to many Nazi leaders – though not to Hitler – that the war was lost and that the time had come to cut the losses of the Reich and explore the exact meaning of Unconditional Surrender. In so doing those who contemplated a surrender did so in terms only of the Western Powers. The idea in their minds was, presumably, to avoid a capitulation which would include surrender to the U.S.S.R., or, if they failed in this, to sow such dissension between the Western Allies and the Soviet Union as would greatly impair the prosecution of the war to a complete annihilation of Germany.

In accordance with these precepts a move was made in late February 1945 by Heinrich Himmler, *Reichsführer* of the S.S., through the intermediary of his sometime Chief of Staff, Karl Wolff, now Chief of S.S. in Northern Italy. Using a trusted member of the Office of Strategic Services as his contact, Wolff conveyed to Allen Dulles, Head of the O.S.S. office in Berne, a willingness to negotiate for the ending of German resistance in northern Italy and the surrender of Field-Marshal Albrecht Kesselring's army to the Supreme Allied Commander. It was made clear that Wolff was acting on his own responsibility but with the tacit approval of Himmler. He did not have, at that moment, the authority or consent of Kesselring.‡

---

* See above, p. 167.   † See above, p. 216.
   ‡ Mr Dulles has written a detailed and vivid account of these negotiations in his book *Secret Surrender*.

Allen Dulles relayed this information to Washington and London and also to Field-Marshal Sir Harold Alexander (SACMED) at his Caserta headquarters. In so reporting he emphasised that no negotiations had been entered into with Wolff, who had been told that the Allies were only interested in Unconditional Surrender.

Field-Marshal Alexander grasped willingly at a possibility of thus speeding the favourable conclusion of hostilities on his front and, while not evincing too great optimism, sought permission on 11 March from the Combined Chiefs of Staff in Washington to send his Deputy Chief of Staff, Major-General Lyman L. Lemnitzer, and his Chief of Intelligence, Major-General Sir Terrence Airey, to Switzerland to make contact with Wolff and to hear what he had to say, even though, as yet, he was unauthorized to speak for Kesselring. The Combined Chiefs agreed to this but warned SACMED that the Russian Government should be advised of the whole operation before these officers entered Switzerland.* Sir Archibald Clark Kerr and Averell Harriman, British and American Ambassadors in Moscow, accordingly informed Molotov on 12 March and obtained from him a statement that the Soviet Government 'did not object' to the proposed conversations but requested that three Soviet general officers should accompany Field-Marshal Alexander's representatives. In transmitting this message to Washington Mr Harriman also sent a strong recommendation from Major-General John R. Deane, Head of the United States Military Mission in Russia, to the effect that Molotov's request be disallowed as it would constitute 'an act of appeasement which will react against us in future negotiations'.[3]†

It was accordingly pointed out to Molotov on 13 March that the representatives of SACMED were only empowered during their talks in Berne to arrange for a German plenipotentiary to go to A.F.H.Q. at Caserta, where terms of surrender could be discussed with Field-Marshal Alexander. As the proposed surrender was only operable on an Anglo-American front he alone would be responsible for the negotiations. Nevertheless, the presence of Soviet military representatives at Caserta would be welcomed.

This communication occasioned a furious and discourteous response from Moscow in London and Washington. Molotov refused to accept

---

* The American Chiefs of Staff had favoured an immediate dispatch of the two officers to Switzerland, but the British Chiefs held out for a previous notification to Moscow and an invitation for Soviet participation. Compromise was reached on notification only. Field-Marshal Alexander's officers did not, however, enter Switzerland until after Soviet approval had been obtained.[2]

† General Eisenhower held a similar view and advised Mr Churchill that, if the Russians were brought into a question of the surrender of Kesselring's forces, what could be settled in an hour might be prolonged for three or four weeks.

the facts as stated by the two Ambassadors and demanded that 'the negotiations already begun in Berne be broken off'. A further attempt to explain and pacify him succeeded only in adding fuel to the flames. On 22 March, Molotov in a written Note to the two Embassies declared that

> In Berne for two weeks, behind the backs of the Soviet Union, which is bearing the brunt of the war against Germany, negotiations have been going on between the representatives of the German military command on the one hand and representatives of the English and American commands on the other.[4]

Molotov went on to infer that the purpose of these negotiations from which the Soviet Union had been purposely and specifically excluded, was aimed not only at a cessation on the northern Italian front but also at a separate peace with Germany, which would leave Russia alone to finish the war.

The effect of Molotov's two insolent missives was to provoke President Roosevelt to elevate the exchange of Notes to summit level. He cabled Stalin, reiterating the innocence of the Berne meeting, and received in reply an open accusation of treachery:

> My military colleagues [cabled Stalin on 3 April] . . . do not have any doubts that the negotiations . . . have ended in an agreement with the Germans, on the basis of which the German Commander on the Western Front, Marshal Kesselring, has agreed to open the front and permit the Anglo-American troops to advance to the east, and the Anglo-Americans have promised in return to ease for the Germans the peace terms. . . . As a result of this at the present moment the Germans on the Western Front have in fact ceased the war against England and the United States. At the same time the Germans continue the war with Russia, the ally of England and the United States.[5]

Shocked and affronted by this monstrous charge and with the dawn of disillusionment beginning to break regarding his ultimate beliefs in American–Soviet political co-operation, President Roosevelt replied in bitterness on 5 April. He repudiated the Soviet impeachment, reiterated the good faith of the Western Allies and did not hesitate to add in conclusion:

> Frankly I cannot avoid a feeling of bitter resentment toward your informers, whoever they may be, for such vile misrepresentation of my actions and those of my trusted subordinates.*

* President Roosevelt's message of 5 April was drafted by Admiral Leahy, his Chief of Staff, and General George Marshall, the United States Chief of the General Staff, since his health did not permit him to prepare his own text. Mr Churchill was, however, convinced that this final paragraph was the President's own.[6]

Mr Churchill also remonstrated strongly with Stalin and cabled sympathy and support to the President. Thus, faced with Anglo-American solidarity against a hectoring attack, the Marshal retreated from his abusive attitude. This was not an issue of integrity and trustworthiness, he asserted on 7 April. 'Neither I nor Molotov had any intention of "blackening" anyone. It is not a matter of "blackening" anyone, but of our having developed differing points of view as regards the rights and obligations of our ally.'[7]

Thus did this remarkable display of international pyrotechnics peter out in the mutterings and gruntings of a Soviet face-saving formula.* But the incident had a deep and vital significance. It had revealed the utterly ephemeral nature of the atmosphere of co-operation and accord which had seemed to be achieved at Yalta only a few weeks earlier. The insulting Notes of Stalin and Molotov had disclosed a complete distrust of the motives and promises of the British and Americans and also the long-festering Soviet suspicion that the Western Allies might make a separate peace with Germany – a suspicion which ignored the fact that Stalin had not been above using this political warfare technique in the earlier stages of the war when Russia was in a greater degree of dependence upon Anglo-American support than in 1945, when his armies were racing through eastern Germany. The Russian reaction to the approaches of Karl Wolff, coupled with their intransigence in the conduct of Polish and Rumanian affairs, and the treatment of liberated prisoners of war, was a clear indication of their belief that, since Yalta, they could force their will upon Britain and the United States on any issue by means of threats and blackmail. 'The arrogant language of Molotov's letter, I believe,' Ambassador Harriman cabled to President Roosevelt, 'brings out in the open a domineering attitude toward the United States which we have before only suspected',[8] and Henry Stimson noted in his diary 'a spirit in Russia which bodes evil in the coming difficulties of the post-war scene'.[9]

Both Mr Churchill and the President were reluctant to admit this patent threat to their war-time tripartite solidarity, though the disillusionment was certainly more painful for the ailing President who had entertained hopes of a post-war world dominated by America and Russia in collaboration. The final paragraph of his Note to Stalin of 5 April had all the bitterness of a friend betrayed. The last days of his life were darkened by this revelation of Soviet duplicity.†

---

* A certain *détente* in Allied relations had been created by the denunciation on 5 April by the Soviet Union of its treaty of neutrality and non-aggression with Japan (see below, p. 356).

† President Roosevelt died suddenly of a cerebral haemorrhage at Warm Springs, Georgia on 12 April 1945, and was succeeded by Vice-President Harry S. Truman. For further evidence of Roosevelt's disillusionment, see below, pp. 298–9.

To Mr Churchill, who had but briefly entertained any such delusions, holding Marshal Stalin in personal respect as a war-time ally of proven courage, there was no question of what course to adopt. 'If they [the Russians] are convinced that we are afraid of them and can be bullied into submission, then indeed I should despair of the future relations with them and much else', he had cabled to the President.[10]

Though the immediate acerbities were tided over, they were not forgotten and, when the three Great Powers met again at Potsdam later in the year, the rift in the lute was highly discernible.

II

Meanwhile the contact with Karl Wolff, which had produced such violent repercussions, had resulted in exactly nothing. Field-Marshal Alexander's staff officers had met Wolff abortively in Berne on 19 March. Kesselring had been recalled from Italy to become over-all Commander-in-Chief of the German armies on the Western Front, and his successor in Milan was Colonel-General Heinrich von Vietinghoff. The Allied officers tried to persuade Wolff to come at once to A.F.H.Q. at Caserta, there to arrange the surrender, but he refused to comply without further consultation with Kesselring and Vietinghoff; he therefore returned to Germany for this purpose. When nothing further had been heard from Wolff by the end of the month, Field-Marshal Alexander recalled Generals Lemnitzev and Airey to Caserta, having so arranged matters that the door was not closed to further approaches should these be forthcoming.

Wolff had been having his own troubles in Germany. Though Himmler had known of his original venture, the *Reichsführer* S.S. was notoriously suspicious, even of those nearest to him. He cross-examined Wolff on the latter's return to Berlin but was apparently satisfied with what his former Chief of Staff reported – though how much Wolff actually told him is unknown. However, by 24 April Wolff was back in Switzerland with full powers from Vietinghoff to make preliminary arrangements for a capitulation of the German armies in northern Italy and Austria, and in order to avoid all possible danger of omission and commission Mr Churchill at once informed Stalin of this fact, asking him to send Russian representatives to Caserta to be present at the surrender. 'Field-Marshal Alexander', he told the Marshal, 'is free to accept the unconditional surrender of the enemy on his front, but all political issues are reserved to the three Governments.'[11]

The Russians duly arrived, as did Vietinghoff and Wolff, and the formal surrender to Field-Marshal Alexander took place at A.F.H.Q. on

29 April, just twenty-four hours before Adolf Hitler's suicide in the *Reichskanzlei* bunker in Berlin.[12]

Before the final communication at Caserta of Karl Wolff's original approaches, Himmler had made his own bid to achieve Unconditional Surrender. Devious as ever, at the very moment that the *Reichsführer* S.S. was cross-examining Wolff on the progress of his contacts with the Allies, he was himself engaged in similar negotiations but on a larger scale.

Himmler had for some considerable time been playing a double role in the Third Reich. There had been a moment, at the time of the threatened military collapse before Moscow in November 1941, when Himmler, sensing defeat, had toyed with the idea of an S.S. *coup d'état* on his own, with the object of reaching a negotiated peace with the Allies before Germany sustained a major military disaster. His apprehensions, and also his intentions, remained unfulfilled because of Hitler's ruthless and demoniac energy in meeting the immediate calamity and restoring the situation. Yet a year later, in December 1942, Himmler, who again saw further than most concerning the ultimate outcome of the war, had given tacit approval to the tentative 'peace soundings' which his lawyer, Carl Langbehn, had held with a British official in Zürich and with Professor Bruce Hopper of the O.S.S. in Stockholm. Later still, Himmler had been drawn, by the offices of the ever obliging Karl Wolff, into closer contact with the conspiracy against Hitler and in August 1943 had authorized the further mission of Langbehn to Berne where he had held discussions with Allied Intelligence officers.[13]

When, however, the Generals' Conspiracy of 20 July 1944 failed, it was Himmler who had assumed command of the situation, ultimately becoming Commander-in-Chief of the Army of the Interior, and had hunted down those implicated in the plot earning the publicly expressed gratitude of the Führer.

But by the beginning of 1945 Himmler was again a prey to the dread of defeat and the nightmare of the Reich delivered over to the Russians. He condoned (if he did not actually authorize) the meetings of Karl Wolff with Allen Dulles and the representatives of Field-Marshal Alexander, and placed himself in touch with the representative of the Swedish Red Cross, Count Folke Bernadotte.

Himmler and Count Bernadotte had held secret meetings in Berlin in February and again early in April 1945. Very tentative talks had resulted. Himmler was not yet ready to take the final step. His loyalty to the Führer, which had been half-hearted for some years, was weighed in the balance against his hatred and dread of the Russians. He waited in vain for some gesture by Hitler which might facilitate the termination of hostilities, but his patience was rewarded by the Führer's proclamation of 22 April, calling for a last desperate defence of Berlin – a *Götterdämmerung* of the Third Reich.

Himmler now hesitated no longer. On the evening of 23 April he met Count Bernadotte very secretly at Lübeck and there proposed that he, Himmler, acting on behalf of the Führer, now *non compos mentis*, should proceed to the headquarters of General Eisenhower and negotiate the surrender of all German forces on the Western Front – it being implied that resistance to the Russians would continue. Would the Swedish Government give them assistance in making the necessary arrangements?

Count Bernadotte suggested that the Western Allies would not entertain a proposal of surrender which did not include the German forces in Denmark and Norway, and to this objection Himmler acceded, also including Italy and Yugoslavia. Count Bernadotte also asked what Himmler would do in the event of the British and American Governments' refusal to accept a German surrender without Russian participation. Himmler replied that, in this case, he would take command of the Eastern Front and die in battle.[14]

Armed with this intelligence, Count Bernadotte returned to Stockholm and informed his Government. The S.S. General Walter Schellenberg was designated as the channel of communication with Himmler, and waited at Flensburg near the Danish–German frontier. The British and American Ministers* were summoned to the Swedish Foreign Ministry around midnight on the twenty-fourth and informed of the turn of events. The Foreign Minister was frankly suspicious of the whole affair, sensing in it an attempt by Himmler to sow dissension among the Allies. Yet he recognized the fact that a 'package surrender' in the West would greatly assist the Allies, including Russia. He advised that Count Bernadotte's news should be relayed to London and to Washington and expressed no objection, so far as his Government was concerned, to it being sent to Moscow also.

Of the wisdom of this advice Mr Churchill was fully and immediately aware. The memory of the recent exchanges with Stalin was too new to be forgotten, and on receipt of Sir Victor Mallet's report early on the morning of 25 April, he first informed the War Cabinet, which at once agreed to inform Moscow forthwith, and then telegraphed to President Truman asking him to do likewise. When no reaction was forthcoming from Washington, Mr Churchill telephoned to the President and

---

* The British Minister in Stockholm at this time was Sir Victor Mallet, about to depart for Madrid where he had been appointed Ambassador; his American colleague was the Hon. Herschel V. Johnson.

discovered that, owing to an unexplained breakdown in communications, neither the American Minister's message from Stockholm nor the Prime Minister's telegram from London had reached Washington and, as a result, President Truman was entirely unaware of what had taken place. In a lengthy telephone conversation Mr Churchill put the President 'in the picture'. Together they agreed that Stalin must be informed at once, first that no surrender could be considered unless it were unconditional and to all three of the Great Allies, and secondly, that if such terms were accepted by the Germans the surrender should take place at once on all fronts to local commanders in the field.[15]

Stalin's reply was immediate and friendly; he too had learned something from the earlier exchanges. He acknowledged warmly the loyalty of his Allies in informing him of the Himmler approaches, concurred in the terms which they had proposed and added in his reply to Mr Churchill: 'Knowing you as I do, I had no doubt that you would act in this way.'[16]

The news of tripartite Allied solidarity was passed via Schellenberg to Himmler, who failed to carry out his threat to die fighting on the Eastern Front and was next heard of as a prisoner in British hands. He surrendered to a British control post on the Lüneburg Heath on 23 May, and committed suicide by taking poison during medical examination. He was unrecognized by his captors

III

In the welter of chaos which surrounded the final plunge into the abyss of the Third Reich, the Nazi hierarchy had been much thinned. Hitler and Goebbels had sought a suicide's grave; Göring, Himmler and Ribbentrop were in disgrace. The torch of succession, now barely burning, passed, by virtue of Hitler's last will and testament, into the hands of Grand-Admiral Karl Doenitz, who thus became the second, and last, of the German Führers. Being himself in the frontier town of Flensburg, near the Danish border, and close by the once mighty naval base of Kiel, Doenitz made shift on 1 May to form a Government which might hold together, at least for the moment, the crumbling remnants of the Reich.

To Doenitz, Hitler had sent instructions for the composition of such an administration, but the Grand-Admiral wisely refused to be bound by this or any other external influence. Within the first few hours of his régime he had rejected in quick succession the services of Himmler, Ribbentrop and Dr Arthur Seyss-Inquart. The latter had been designated by Hitler as the new Foreign Minister, but Doenitz, realizing the evil reputation which Seyss-Inquart had achieved abroad, chose a former Rhodes Scholar and Reich Finance Minister, Count Lutz Schwerin von Krosigk, to preside over the demise of Germany's foreign relations.

By 3 May Doenitz had decided to effect, if possible, the surrender to Field-Marshal Sir Bernard Montgomery of the three German armies withdrawing in front of the Russians between Berlin and Rostock. Doubtless he intended by this means to save his troops from Russian imprisonment and to cause dissension among the Allies, hoping also perhaps thereby to purchase a little more worthless time. Accordingly Field-Marshal Wilhelm Keitel sent to the headquarters of 21st Army Group on the Lüneburg Heath a delegation composed of Doenitz's successor as Commander-in-Chief of the German Navy, General-Admiral Hans von Friedeburg, General Kinzel, Chief of Staff of Field-Marshal Ernst Busch, Rear-Admiral Wagner of the Naval Staff, and two staff officers from O.K.W. They tried at first to parley with Field-Marshal Montgomery but found him in no receptive mood. Acting on the instructions of General Eisenhower, he rejected out of hand their suggestion for the surrender of the three German armies on the Eastern Front, and when Admiral von Friedeburg appealed to him on humanitarian grounds on behalf of refugees and troops alike, saying that they would, if they fell into Russian hands, be condemned to the horrors of work camps in the Soviet Union, the Field-Marshal replied that the Germans should have taken these things into consideration before they began the war and more particularly before they attacked Russia in June 1941. Under questioning by Field-Marshal Montgomery, the Germans admitted that they were not empowered to discuss the surrender of their troops on his front. The Field-Marshal then crystallized the situation by offering to accept the Unconditional Surrender on a tactical basis of the troops on 21st Army Group's front and in Denmark; should this be refused he would be delighted to continue the battle.

Von Friedeburg was at first disposed to reject this proposal and to attempt further parley but, during the luncheon interval, his nerve broke; he wept, and at the conclusion of the meal agreed to recommend to Keitel all Montgomery's demands. These were incorporated in a paper to which the British Field-Marshal and the German Admiral later put their signatures.* The Admiral returned to Flensburg but was

---

* It is a somewhat melancholy fact that of these principal German signatories of the instrument of surrender of 4 May 1945, two, von Friedeburg and Kinzel, committed suicide, the first by poison, the second by shooting. Major Friedel, one of the O.K.W. staff officers who accompanied them, was killed in a motor accident. Admiral Wagner lived to hold high command under the Bonn Government.

back at Tactical Headquarters on the afternoon of 4 May, armed with full plenipotentiary powers from Keitel to surrender unconditionally all German forces in Holland, Friesland (including the islands and Heligoland), Schleswig-Holstein and Denmark. The instrument of surrender was signed at 6.30 on the evening of 4 May. The cease-fire order became operative at eight o'clock on the following evening.[17]

Thus ended, in so far as British armies in Europe were directly concerned, the war which had begun on 3 September 1939. The early inertia, the later disasters, the still later victories were over, and within the last three days over two and a half million German soldiers had surrendered to British commanders. But there remained Japan.

IV

This series of spectacular surrenders had been purely tactical. The moment had now come for the final burial of Nazi brutality and Prussian militarism in a common grave with the stone of Unconditional Surrender rolled against the mouth of it. To this end had the war been fought to a finish; to this end had the European Advisory Commission laboured so diligently.

And yet when the moment actually came it found the preparations of the Allies in a sad state of unreadiness. This was certainly not the fault of the E.A.C. which, under the able and indefatigable chairmanship of Sir William Strang, had worked early and late to meet just this eventuality. The decision of the Big Three in November 1944 to admit France to equal partnership in the Commission had necessitated a certain amount of amendment to the basic documents on surrender, then already in draft, and a further complication had arisen from the decision of the Yalta Conference to dismember Germany, while excluding France from the Allied committee on dismemberment appointed to draw up plans for this purpose.

By March 1945 the final text of the Instrument of Unconditional Surrender had been completed by the Commission, approved by the Allied Governments and dispatched to SHAEF for safe-keeping against the coming of the day so long desired. No sooner had this been done, however, when the situation became more fluid and consequently changed completely. In the agreed text the original concept had been followed of demanding surrender in the names of both 'the German Government and the German High Command', but as the pace of both the advance of the Allied armies and the disintegration of the Reich accelerated, it became increasingly evident that there would be no German Government to make a formal surrender, nor even a central

German civilian administration claiming to possess authority over the whole country. The agreed text already in the hands of SHAEF would therefore no longer serve, and some new provision was required whereby the Allied Governments would themselves proclaim the final defeat and Unconditional Surrender of Germany and the assumption by themselves of the sovereignty of the Reich. The E.A.C. therefore concentrated on this task. A British draft 'Declaration regarding the Defeat of Germany and the Assumption of Supreme Authority with respect to Germany' was completed by the end of March but did not come up for discussion by the Commission until the beginning of May, by which time events had far outpaced their deliberations.*

The news on 1 May of the death of Hitler and the fact that American and Russian forces had already linked arms at Torgau convinced General Eisenhower that he would very shortly be faced with the final emergency. He therefore took stock of his position and consulted his chief of Post-Hostilities Planning Section, Lieutenant-Colonel John Counsell, in civilian life a distinguished member of the British theatrical profession on the managerial side.† Colonel Counsell's advice was based on the known facts, namely that, though an Instrument of Unconditional Surrender as prepared by the E.A.C. existed, it was already out of date and inappropriate for use by reason of the fact that it envisaged the existence of a 'German Government' and the Allies had not recognized the Doenitz régime at Flensburg as such. Moreover the Supreme Commander had not at that date received any authority from either the Combined Chiefs of Staff or the Heads of Government to sign. The advice tendered by Colonel Counsell to General Eisenhower and to his Chief of Staff, General Walter Bedell Smith, was to use a much simpler document saying in so many words that the German High Command unconditionally surrendered the forces under their authority. This, it was urged, would save lives through hastening the German signature and ending German resistance by German military order.

The Supreme Commander and his Chief of Staff had themselves argued in favour of a simple form of surrender in the case of Italy; they were therefore well disposed to this proposed course of action and a text was accordingly prepared. It was sent for approval on the evening of 4 May to the Combined Chiefs of Staff in Washington, to the British Chiefs of Staff in London and to the Allied Military Missions in Moscow.‡

Meanwhile in London there was continued hesitation. On 1 May the

---

* The final text of the Declaration was not agreed by the E.A.C. until 12 May. It was eventually signed at Soviet headquarters at Berlin on 5 June 1945.

† Now Director of the Theatre Royal, Windsor.

‡ The draft of the signal which was sent is in the possession of Colonel Counsell.

E.A.C. had signed a protocol making the textual changes necessary for the inclusion of France among the signatories of the Instrument of Unconditional Surrender, but there was still complete lack of agreement as to whether the word 'dismemberment' should be included or not. In a desperate effort to meet the emergency, two sets of documents, one including the word and one omitting it, were prepared, on the initiative of Philip Mosely, of the American delegation to the Commission, in English, Russian and French, with an agreed German translation, and these were held ready for immediate use.

On the evening of 4 May the American Ambassador, John Winant, discussed the question of surrender with General Bedell Smith by telephone from London. By this time the matter had become fiercely practical, as the final tactical surrender of Admiral von Friedeburg to Field-Marshal Montgomery had been completed that afternoon and the Admiral was preparing to proceed to Rheims on the following day, there to discuss a general surrender. General Bedell Smith reiterated that SHAEF had received no authority to sign the E.A.C. document, nor had they an authoritative text of it. Winant telephoned at once to Washington (taking advantage of the time difference) and begged that the necessary authority to sign the E.A.C. document be wired to SHAEF immediately.

On the following day, 5 May, news of the fact that SHAEF was preparing its own instrument of surrender caused repercussions in London. Mr Churchill summoned Sir William Strang from a meeting of the E.A.C. to discover the existing position. The news was not encouraging. There was the original E.A.C. draft, already obsolete; there were Mr Mosely's alternative drafts, and there was the Declaration on which the Commission was earnestly engaged. The Prime Minister said that time pressed. It was essential to get a military capitulation by Germany as soon as possible. To do this he was disposed to agree with General Eisenhower's proposal for a short and simple document.

John Winant was less happy and less pliable. He foresaw difficulties with the Russians – difficulties which certainly subsequently arose – and the inherent danger which would occur unless the degree of Allied agreement, which had been reached after months of wearisome negotiation, were not somehow safeguarded in whatever instrument of surrender was eventually signed. He presented these views to Mr Churchill and by telephone to General Bedell Smith and, by his own personal insistence, was successful in getting inserted into the surrender document a new Article 4, in the form of a general enabling clause leaving the way open for imposing on Germany the additional military and political conditions which had been embodied in the original E.A.C. document and had now been transferred to the draft Declaration which the Commission had currently under discussion. With this somewhat tenuous authority General Eisenhower proceeded to receive the representatives of the German High Command.[18]*

When Admiral von Friedeburg left Field-Marshal Montgomery's headquarters on 5 May he proceeded to SHAEF at Rheims and at the same time Field-Marshal von Kesselring asked permission to send a representative to arrange terms of capitulation for the remainder of the Western Front. To both of them General Eisenhower replied that he would consider no further arrangements for surrender that did not involve all German forces everywhere and, in passing this information to Moscow, he asked for a general officer to be assigned to his headquarters to participate in any negotiations that the Doenitz Government might propose. The Soviet Government assented.†

The terms of surrender had how, therefore, been defined not only as unconditional but also as total. There must be no more piecemeal capitulation. The German Admiral relayed these tidings to Flensburg and received the reply that General Alfred Jodl was on his way to Rheims. He arrived on 6 May. Sensing that the Germans were even now playing for time and might attempt any devious subterfuge, the Supreme Commander instructed his Chief of Staff to inform Jodl and von Friedeburg at the outset that, unless they were prepared to abandon, once and for all, all pretence and delay, he would consider the truce at an

* This account, which is based on the works of Lord Strang, Professor Philip Mosely, John Counsell and Major-General Deane, differs substantially from that of General Bedell Smith in *My Three Years in Moscow* (Philadelphia, 1950) p. 20, and is at complete variance with that of Robert Murphy in *Diplomat Among Warriors* (London, 1964) pp. 296–7. The facts are simply not as Mr Murphy states them. It was not a question of General Bedell Smith having forgotten the existence of the E.A.C. document, but of a too great awareness of it, which caused him to advise General Eisenhower to decide in favour of a short and simple document of surrender. As has been seen, Bedell Smith was discussing the E.A.C. document with Mr Winant in London on 4 and 5 May, and therefore could not have 'forgotten it', as Mr Murphy alleges. Whatever the wisdom of the decision may have been, it was taken after due deliberation. There remains the mystery of the SHAEF signal of 4 May to London, Washington and Moscow. It certainly reached London on the fifth, for it was on the basis of it that Mr Churchill summoned Sir William Strang. Yet by 9 May neither the State Department nor the War Department in Washington had any news as to the origin of the text of the surrender used in Rheims and Berlin on 7 and 9 May, and after the first of the ceremonies the Soviet Government protested violently at the substitution of the shorter instrument of surrender for the E.A.C. agreed text. This, however, was less a matter of holding the E.A.C. sacrosanct than a last and smouldering suspicion in Moscow that General Eisenhower was preparing to make a separate truce. Russian suspicions had been allayed in time for the later 'formalization' in Berlin of the Rheims surrender.

† The Russians appointed Major-General Ivan Suslaparov Head of the Russian Military Mission to SHAEF. General de Gaulle also appointed General François Sevez to represent General Alphonse Juin, the Chief of Staff.

end and prevent by force any more refugees from entering his lines. In view of this stern attitude the Germans, after some demur, cabled Flensburg asking for authority to make a surrender, unconditional and total, to become effective forty-eight hours from midnight on that day. Doenitz at last complied and the surrender was signed by a weeping Jodl at 2.41 a.m. on 7 May 1945.[19]*

'So this is at last the end of the war', Field-Marshal Sir Alan Brooke wrote in his diary that evening. 'It is hard to realize. I can't feel thrilled; my sensation is one of infinite mental weariness.'[20]

The war in Europe was over. The Semblance of Peace was beginning.†

* The Rheims surrender was formally ratified at Russian headquarters in Berlin on the afternoon of 9 May.

† The most authoritative account of the Unconditional Surrender of the German Armies is that given by Major-General Sir Kenneth Strang (then General Eisenhower's Chief of Intelligence) in his book, *Recollections of an Intelligence Officer*.

13 | Germany Divided: the Zones of Occupation

I

AT this point it is necessary to digress somewhat in order to explain to the reader the development of Allied policies towards Germany, and to describe the circumstances under which the division of that country – foreshadowed at Tehran and Yalta – became a reality. As we have seen, such a division would have come as no surprise to Allied leaders in 1943 and 1944, although some of them would have regarded it with more enthusiasm than others.* Indeed, the existence of two German republics, both enjoying a relatively strong position within their own power blocs, was a remarkably favourable outcome for the Germans by comparison with the grim schemes for dismemberment and economic impoverishment bandied about in Allied capitals when Hitler's armies were still powerful enough to command fear and respect.

For a number of reasons the enthusiasm for dividing Germany which had existed among the Big Three – albeit with reservations on the part of the British Prime Minister – quickly evaporated after the Crimean Conference. On the one hand, as we have already seen, neither the British Foreign Office nor the U.S. State Department was keen on dismemberment, and their doubts about it increased as time went on. It was becoming clear that post-war Europe would be faced with tremendous economic problems and social upheavals, and the permanent disruption of Germany as an industrial, agricultural and commercial unit would make the achievement of stability there very difficult. Both the Western Allies feared that they would be asked to shoulder huge financial burdens as the result of Hitler's defeat; the Americans were especially determined not to pay Germany's reparations bill to Russia – as they claimed they had subsidized reparations in the 1920s. For their part the British were worried about the effects a policy of dismemberment might have on the costs of occupying Germany.

On 7 March 1945 the British Treasury presented a memorandum to the War Cabinet pointing to the dangers of a situation in which the British

* See above, pp. 147–8, 174–87, 228–9.

Zone of Occupation – the industrial north-western area of Germany – might be asked to make heavy reparations payments whilst at the same time being unable to feed its own population, 'let alone the hordes of refugees already known to be moving westwards across Germany to avoid capture by the Russians. It would be intolerable if the British had to pay for food imported into their zone to help the inhabitants make reparations to Russia.[1] Dismemberment, designed as it was to render Germany permanently weak, would also have the effect of making her less capable of meeting her post-war obligations, and in this way she might become a liability to her British and American occupiers. It might also have been remarked that the Soviet Union would have no such problem since it claimed the lion's share of reparations, it would occupy a zone more capable of feeding its own population and would in any case be less likely to feel scruples about starving the Germans.

The situation seemed especially serious in the region to be occupied by the British, where social disturbances might result from steps taken to impoverish German industry. If the British had to enforce prohibitions on Germany's administrative and economic unity, the difficulty and danger inherent in their position would be greatly increased. Although Mr Churchill and his Foreign Secretary were not as firmly opposed to the idea of partition as the Treasury, Mr Eden too made it clear to his Cabinet colleagues that he had serious doubts about dismemberment.[2]

In Washington the State Department had really won its battle with Secretary Morgenthau over his scheme for a Carthaginian peace settlement with Germany, despite President Roosevelt's recurrent inclination to be 'tough' with the Germans, and his belief that such toughness would cement American–Soviet relations after the war. Neither Secretary Hull nor his Department had ever been enthusiastic about dividing Germany. As the fear of Nazi power diminished, so the problems which dismemberment would create became more obvious. Shortly before President Roosevelt went to Yalta the State Department had prepared a briefing paper which recommended against a forcible partition of Germany, though it did urge decentralization.[3] When, in July 1945, his successor went to the last great Allied conference at Potsdam the State Department's recommendation – which Roosevelt had ignored at Yalta – was once more reinforced. The partition of Germany might, it was argued, create a condition of permanent German resistance against any settlement, and the 'result of such a state of affairs might be a Germany unable to make war but nonetheless a Germany able to keep the world in lasting perturbation'.[4]

President Truman was much more inclined to be influenced by such expert advice than his predecessor. In addition, by July 1945 the problem of occupying and administering a beaten Germany had passed from the realm of theory and had become an urgent problem requiring immediate decisions. Earlier in the war vague schemes for partition tossed in the air by Allied leaders could be divorced from the problems which were actually to face Allied military administrators when they took over a devastated country. Agreements to divide Germany would affect the manner in which the country was administered while under occupation, even if the final confirmation of such a division was left to a peace conference. Yet both the British and the Americans were agreed that the welfare of Western Europe would be damaged if the German Reich was not treated as an economic and administrative unit while under occupation. The State Department was most insistent that President Truman should press this point home at Potsdam, and it was supported by his military advisers.[5]

Perhaps more surprising, though in the event quite as easily explicable, was the change of attitude apparent on the part of the Soviet Government. At Yalta Stalin had been anxious to commit the Allies to a policy of dismemberment and it was largely as the result of Soviet pressure that a tripartite committee* was established to determine how this policy might be implemented. At the committee's second meeting, on 11 April 1945, it agreed to consider proposals put forward by any of the three Allies. No such proposals were made and the committee never met again. Some two weeks earlier, on 26 March, the British Foreign Office had been informed that the Soviet Government no longer considered the decision on dismemberment at Yalta to be 'an obligatory plan'. When, on 9 May, Stalin issued a statement celebrating victory over Germany, he expressly disclaimed the intention of dismembering or destroying that country.[7]

It is difficult to be certain of the motives behind this *volte-face*, but there were obvious reasons why the Russians should wish to discard dismemberment in 1945. Perhaps it would be best to consider some of the least plausible first, since chronologically they were among the earliest to be advanced. When Harry Hopkins flew to Moscow at the end of May 1945† he saw it as his purpose to save the special relationship he believed had been created between Roosevelt and Stalin. One of the

---

* It met in London and was chaired by Mr Eden or his deputy, Sir William Strang. The Soviet and American Ambassadors in London acted as their countries' representatives – in effect it was the E.A.C. without French representation. In fact the question of dismemberment had been referred to the E.A.C. after the Tehran Conference, but in January 1944 the Soviet representative said he had no instructions and the matter was dropped.[6]

† See below, pp. 305–7, 358–60.

issues on which the two statesmen had found it easiest to agree had been that of Germany. Mr Hopkins therefore queried the Soviet declaration renouncing dismemberment and took it upon himself to claim that President Truman 'was inclined towards dismemberment' himself, and in any event wanted the Saar, the Ruhr and the Rhineland detached from Germany.[8] Stalin promptly put the blame on the British, claiming that in the tripartite committee they had interpreted the Yalta Agreement on dismemberment as a threat to hold over the Germans' heads rather than as a positive commitment, and that United States Ambassador Winant had accepted this view. The Russians had therefore not bothered to pursue the matter.[9] This was clearly a half-truth. Mr Eden would have had every reason to water down a policy he and the British Foreign Office felt to be misguided, and Ambassador Winant undoubtedly appreciated the British view, the more so since it chimed in with that of the State Department. During the period of executive torpor after President Roosevelt returned from Yalta and before President Truman took up office, the problem of dismemberment does not seem to have been followed up at the highest level in Washington.* Nevertheless, this does not explain why the Russians failed to exploit the advantage Stalin had gained at Yalta over the dismemberment issue. There were evidently other reasons behind the cooling of Soviet enthusiasm.

Two factors seem to have been most important in contributing to the change. The first was the hope that conditions in Germany after Hitler's fall might enable pro-Soviet forces to dominate political life there. Circumstances seemed particularly favourable to this development since the Russians would control some of the main food-producing areas of Germany in their zones, whereas, as we have seen, the bomb-devastated Ruhr area was to be administered by the West. Hence fear of German power in Russia gave way to an appreciation of the political advantages which might be gained from a Communist – at least a neutral – Germany.

Stalin had always been eager to let the Western Powers bear the responsibility for vengeful policies towards the Germans even when he was their main instigator.† He was far too shrewd a politician to saddle the Russian occupation forces with the odium of dismembering Germany, and in practice most German attention was concentrated on the 'beastliness' of the American Morgenthau Plan.

As early as 1943 Stalin had encouraged pro-Russian elements among

* When the President's Map Room in the White House prepared an appreciation of this problem at the beginning of July 1945, it had no information about the meetings of the tripartite committee with the exception of Hopkins's account of his talk with Stalin.[10]

† See above, p. 174.

the *Wehrmacht* forces captured in Russia to align themselves with the Soviet Union, tempting them with hints of a Russo-German alignment after the war. The League of German Officers (*Bund Deutscher Offiziere*) and the Free Germany Committee (*Kommittee Freies Deutschland*) were two organizations sponsoring an apparently broadly based 'anti-Fascist' front among captured Germans. In addition the Russians had at their disposal a number of German Communists who – unlike many of their comrades – had survived Stalin's purges and the dangerous situation created by the Nazi–Soviet Pact. They could now form the nucleus of a pro-Soviet political front in Germany. Only a few weeks after the Yalta Conference had ended, the guiding lines of Soviet occupation policy in Germany were set out. Every effort was to be made to win the Germans over by presenting Russia as the friend of a unified, centralized Germany ruled by a 'democratic' coalition dedicated to social reform – not proletarian dictatorship.[11]

When Marshal Grigory Zhukov, the Soviet Commander in Germany, began to issue orders for the administration of the occupied zone he disclaimed any intention of dismembering the country and quickly encouraged the formation of 'democratic' and 'anti-Fascist' political parties – a move designed to endear the Soviet régime to the Germans whilst enabling German Communists to establish themselves as the decisive force in a confused situation.

Soviet policy towards Germany was also affected by a second factor, namely the desire for reparations. This had already come into the open at Yalta, and indeed after the terrible losses inflicted on Russia during the war it was only natural that Stalin should put Soviet claims for restitution high on his list of priorities. The nervous reaction of both the British and the Americans at Yalta to the enormous reparations claims put to them by their Soviet colleagues made it more difficult for the Russians to press for policies towards Germany which might hopelessly compromise any chance of large-scale reparations deliveries. The fact that the Soviet Government was eager to obtain much industrial plant from the Western-occupied zones of Germany meant that some form of centralized administration would be of advantage to the Russians, whereas dismemberment might encourage the British and Americans to 'go it alone' in the areas they controlled.*

Hence by the spring of 1945 the long-standing policy of dismemberment was proving unable to resist the stress of competing interests and

---

* No such desire existed at this time among the political decision-makers in London and Washington, but the British defence chiefs were more inclined to envisage the possible incorporation of West Germany into a Western defence scheme.[12] For this reason they had been better disposed towards dismembering Germany when the subject was under discussion in Britain in the autumn of 1944.

the pressure of expert opinion. Furthermore it was clear that, whatever the ultimate fate of Germany might be, the immediate problem of occupation called for decisions which would inevitably affect that country's future. These decisions had actually been taken by the time Allied soldiers entered Germany, albeit at a level of authority sometimes regarded with scant respect by the principals at Tehran and Yalta.

II

The allocation of the zones of occupation in Germany had resulted from careful planning by military and civilian staffs, occasionally interrupted by arbitrary and often confused directives from their political superiors – particularly President Roosevelt.[13] Since most of the disagreements which arose over occupation zones concerned the disposition of British and American forces, arguments about zonal boundaries tended to be conducted between London and Washington. The problem had arisen first of all in connection with plans for a second front drawn up by General Morgan (COSSAC) and his staff in London in 1943. In the event of a sudden German collapse enabling Anglo-American forces to launch a rapid cross-Channel attack, it was obviously necessary to decide which parts of Germany should be designated to which armies. For reasons of geographical convenience – American bases in Britain being in the western part of the country – it became clear that the easterly or left-wing section of the assault should be British and the right wing American. From this it followed that the Americans would liberate France and Belgium and occupy the southern part of Germany, whereas the British would move through Holland, into the Ruhr and Scandinavia.

Meanwhile Mr Eden had proposed to the British Cabinet that Germany be divided into three zones and totally occupied at the end of hostilities. A committee of the Cabinet chaired by Mr Attlee reported in the late summer of 1943 that the British should control the North-western Zone, the Americans the South-western Zone and the Russians the Eastern Zone. Berlin was to be under joint occupation. The frontier drawn up by Mr Attlee's committee as the western boundary of the Russian Zone was that which was finally accepted by the Allies, and to this day it marks the eastern limit of the Federal German Republic. It was a frontier which put 40 per cent of pre-1937 German territory and 36 per cent of German population under Soviet control. The British hoped thereby both to ensure Soviet co-operation and to limit the cost to themselves of the occupation.[14]

The British plan was communicated by General Morgan to General

Marshall in Washington in October 1943, and was discussed by President Roosevelt on his way to the Cairo Conference aboard U.S.S. *Iowa*. Roosevelt disliked the British plan and stressed that the Americans must occupy northern Germany so as to control the German ports. The Americans must also occupy Berlin. One reason for the President's attitude was his peculiar aversion to any involvement in French politics, which he described as 'a British baby'.* He also feared that the United States would become involved in 'local squabbles in such a place as Yugoslavia' if the Americans were given the Southern Zone. Turning to a National Geographical Society map he drew his own version of the zonal boundaries – a version which gave the United States a very large area in the north-west of Germany, including Leipzig and Berlin (see map, page 227).[15]

When the American delegation reached Cairo, discussions were held with the Prime Minister and his staffs on this question. Although the British pointed to the logistical difficulties involved in this scheme, and apparently persuaded Roosevelt that Berlin, at least, should be under tripartite control, they did not press their objections to an American-occupied zone, and a directive was issued to General Morgan to revise his plan 'on the basis of the new allocation of spheres of occupation'. The General was so put out by this instruction that at first he thought it must be a practical joke.[16] When his staffs investigated the military implications of the proposal they found it was quite unworkable and reported as much to their superiors. Meanwhile the British Government blandly ignored the American plans and went ahead in advocating their own. They were aided in this enterprise by the lack of co-ordination which existed between the various executive departments in the United States – and in particular by the strange isolation of the State Department, which was ill-informed about much of what had transpired at Cairo and Tehran.

President Roosevelt's casual method of doing business led to a confused situation over Germany which was to last for several months. Officially the surrender and occupation of Germany were on the agenda of the European Advisory Commission, the body established largely as the result of Mr Eden's labours at the Moscow Conference of Foreign Ministers in October 1943.† When this body came together for its first working meeting on 14 January 1944, the British representative, Sir William Strang, produced his Government's proposals for zonal boundaries in Germany – proposals which had already been shown to the American military authorities at Cairo but about which the American diplomats on the E.A.C. – Ambassador Winant and his political adviser,

* See above, pp. 131–2.   † See above, pp. 113–14.

George Kennan – knew nothing at all. When the Americans cabled Washington for instructions they received no answer. Their position became very embarrassing after 18 February 1944, because on that day the Soviet representative at E.A.C. declared that his Government would accept the zonal frontiers set out in the British plan.

While the American delegation at E.A.C. was waiting in suspense for instructions, the State Department had been vainly, if not very decisively attempting to pierce the fog of Presidential intentions towards Germany. Roosevelt made it plain that he rejected the British plan, but no clear alternative was produced. At the same time the President was conducting a campaign by cable to persuade Mr Churchill that the United States should have the North-western Zone.[17] Eventually the State Department did receive a directive from the American War Department which was to be passed to E.A.C. without discussion, and was duly sent to Winant on 8 March.

It was described by George Kennan as 'a most curious communication', and consisted of a single sentence describing an American Zone in northern Germany. Its eastern frontier cut, in Kennan's words, 'apparently without rhyme of reason across geographic and administrative boundaries.'[18] Although the frontier was very imperfectly defined, it was evidently intended to include a considerable part of what the Russians and the British had already accepted as the Soviet Zone. Indeed it was calculated that the zone Washington was proposing the Americans should occupy would contain 46 per cent of Germany's pre-1937 territory and 51 per cent of its population. This whole scheme was, of course, the President's own brainchild which he had drawn up aboard the *Iowa*, but the directive to Winant did not make this clear.

Needless to say, some cogent and well-presented arguments would be necessary if the British and the Russians were to be brought to accept a scheme which differed so drastically from the one they had been using as the basis of discussion for two months. Since the American directive was accompanied by no explanatory material, Mr Kennan took it upon himself to fly back to Washington to obtain clarification. There he found neither help nor encouragement at the State Department, where a general air of apathy seemed to prevail over the whole question. It was becoming clear that only the President himself could unravel this peculiarly absurd tangle and Mr Kennan insisted on seeing him. When he showed Roosevelt the instruction setting out the eastern frontier of the American Zone the President laughed gaily and said, 'Why that's just something I drew on the back of an envelope'.[19] He raised no objections to the boundaries of the Soviet Zone as set out in the British proposals to E.A.C. On 1 May Winant was authorized to accept this and he did so a month later, after further discussions with Roosevelt. It is fairly clear that the President's casual manner hid a change of policy towards the Russian presence in Germany: his confidence had been increased by the Tehran Conference and he believed that Soviet–American co-operation would succeed after the war. The frontier between the Western and Soviet Zones had, therefore, been arrived at as the result of very careful study and negotiation – at least on the British and Soviet side. So far as the Western Powers were concerned it represented a favourable division, since at the time it was accepted that there were no Anglo-American forces in Northern Europe and it seemed most unlikely that Western troops would beat the Red Army to the Elbe. In any case, at that juncture in the war the needs of the Alliance against Hitler were paramount; a scheme for zonal administration which gave one of the Allies an inordinately large share of Germany could only have created suspicion – especially in Moscow. It was assumed by the E.A.C. planners that tripartite co-operation would continue after hostilities had ceased and for this reason Berlin was to be jointly occupied by all three Powers. No provision was made, however, for Western access to the capital, which would lie deep in Soviet territory. Its control would be of great political value in any future battle for German allegiance.

Despite agreement on the Soviet Zone, the occupation problems of the Western Powers were not yet solved because President Roosevelt still hankered after the northern of the two Western zones. It was not until September 1944, when the President and the British Prime Minister met at Quebec to discuss military strategy in the final stages of the war,* that Roosevelt finally agreed to accept the Southern Zone. Even then the exact boundaries between the zones were left undecided, and there was still opportunity for wrangling. In particular the Americans wanted to control the ports of Bremen and Bremerhaven, and this involved working out a scheme for American enclaves in the British Zone. From the Western viewpoint the delays involved in this zonal settlement were very unsatisfactory because unless watertight agreements were reached before the Red Army pressed into Germany there was always the chance that the Soviet Union might want to reconsider its own zone. In fact the final decision to agree on the zonal boundaries was only reached when Mr Eden and Mr Stettinius met at Malta on 1 February 1945.† The official protocol confirming this was signed by the American, British and Soviet representatives at the E.A.C. on 6 February.[20] It had also been agreed by Messrs Eden and Stettinius that the French should be given a zone of occupation carved exclusively

* See above, pp. 178–84.   † See above, p. 216.

11 Victory: British
    paratroops greet a comely
    Russian ally near Wismar,
    May 1945

12 Partners in victory:
    Russian and American
    officers celebrate at
    Torgau, 27 April 1945

13   Victory: The Americans prepare to welcome Soviet allies, 25 April 1945

14   Victory: Field-Marshal Montgomery and Marshal Rokossovsky (*centre*) meet near Wismar, 11 May 1945

out of the Western zones. At Yalta Stalin agreed to this arrangement, albeit with ill grace. The British aim in establishing a French Zone was not simply to increase French influence in European affairs, but also to put some of the burdens of occupation on to French shoulders. This seemed especially necessary in view of President Roosevelt's proclaimed desire to remove American troops from Europe within two years.

Although the geographical boundaries of the occupation zones seemed thereby to have been settled – at least so far as the three main Allies were concerned – one more series of alarms and excursions was to put them at risk again. This time it was Mr Churchill who attempted to upset the apple-cart so carefully put together by E.A.C.

During March and April 1945 Anglo-American forces were advancing with surprising rapidity into the heart of Germany. The British Prime Minister was alarmed beyond measure at the intransigent attitude being adopted by the Russians in Poland and other parts of Eastern Europe, and anxious lest the Red Army should establish itself with massive force along a 'Russianized frontier running from Lübeck through Eisenach to Trieste and down to Albania'.* He urged Generals Eisenhower and Montgomery to establish themselves as far to the east in Germany as they could in order, as he put it, 'to head our Soviet friends off'.[22]

In the event Anglo-American forces were able to advance substantially farther to the east than the Soviet zonal boundary. They crossed the Elbe and the Mulde, liberating Wittenberg and Magdeburg. Leipzig and Erfurt were well behind the Western lines. All these cities had been designated for the Soviet Zone. On the other hand the Russians had occupied Berlin and Vienna and there seemed some doubt whether they would accept zonal arrangements suggested for the occupation of Austria. Mr Churchill therefore urged President Truman that Anglo-American forces should remain where they were and not retire to the zonal frontiers set down in the E.A.C. agreements until the Soviet authorities had met Anglo-American requirements in Austria and had accepted a Western presence in Berlin. In addition he hoped for Soviet agreement to arrangements for provisioning the Western zones of Germany with food supplies from the agricultural east.[23]

He therefore produced a rather curious interpretation of the zonal arrangements in Germany, telling President Truman that they had been decided 'rather hastily at Quebec' at a time when nobody had foreseen the speed of the American advance.[24] This was hardly an accurate description of decisions which had been worked out after a long period of tedious tripartite negotiations and had been formally agreed upon

* These words were used in a message to Stalin on 23 June 1945.[21]

little over three months previously. The fact that the boundary of the Soviet Zone was that suggested by a committee of the British Cabinet did not make Mr Churchill's argument any easier to sustain.* President Truman, a man accustomed to reading carefully the documentation referring to any political problem, was not very impressed by Mr Churchill's gloss on the zonal agreements, though he did take a strong line with the Russians over the occupation of Austria. On 12 June he cabled to London that American forces would be ordered to withdraw to the zonal boundaries in Germany, and the British had no option but to follow suit. The work of the E.A.C. had at last borne one small – if somewhat bitter – fruit.

Mr Churchill later recorded that President Truman's message 'struck a knell in my breast. But I had no choice but to submit.' Nevertheless, he denied the intention of going back on agreements already arrived at, and indeed it would have been virtually unthinkable to do so. For one thing public opinion in the West was quite unprepared for a sudden switch of policy towards the Soviet Union. General Eisenhower, who would have had to carry through such a scheme on the ground, subsequently stated that it would have been 'indefensible' to renege on the zonal agreements, and there is little doubt that he was right.[26] Mr Churchill's own fears of Soviet policies were very powerful in the spring of 1945, and his warnings on the subject are well documented. Yet it is scarcely conceivable that he thought a standstill order to Western forces in Germany would transform the situation. His main objectives at the time were to strengthen the Western position at the forthcoming Potsdam Conference and to ensure the recognition of Anglo-American rights in Berlin and Vienna.[27] Although he failed to obtain the first of his aims, his extreme fears about Austria and Berlin proved unfounded. The Russians did accept an E.A.C. zonal agreement over the former country, and a Western presence was soon established in both Vienna and Berlin.

III

Two further problems remained to be solved in connection with the German zones – the position of the French and the exact status of Berlin. As we have seen,† Messrs Churchill and Eden had successfully prevailed upon their reluctant allies at Yalta to give the French a zone of occupation and allow them to participate in the Allied Control Council for Germany. The French Zone had to be drawn up rather hastily and

---

* In his account of the Second World War, Mr Churchill admitted to the British authorship of the boundaries but dismissed the work of Mr Attlee's committee as 'purely theoretical'.[25]

† See above, p. 249.

Western Germany under Allied occupation

consisted of the south-western corners of the American and British Zones. Owing to its suggestive shape it was sometimes referred to as the 'brassière' in Anglo-Saxon circles. It comprised the Saar Basin, the former Bavarian Palatinate, part of the former Prussian Rhineland and the south-western parts of Baden and Württemberg.

The French were also to be involved in the inter-Allied occupation of Berlin. The Russians insisted that, here too, all the French sector must come out of the areas assigned originally to the Americans and British. When challenged about this – since it was not specifically referred to in the Yalta Agreement – they produced the obviously bogus argument that their sector of Berlin was so seriously devastated that none of it could be surrendered.[28] Since the Russians occupied Berlin, and since more important issues were at stake in July 1945, the Western Powers gave way.[29] General de Gaulle's sector in Berlin, like his zone in Western Germany, was given to him by the grace of the Anglo-Saxons. He did not show any marked appreciation of either favour.

The second unsolved problem was that of access to Berlin itself. Although it had been agreed by the E.A.C. – and confirmed by the Big Three at Yalta – that the occupation of Berlin should be an inter-Allied affair, no arrangements had been made about the way in which Western troops would be able to move between their zones and the German capital. President Roosevelt, who in 1943 had been very eager to see American forces reach Berlin before anybody else,[30] had evidently lost interest in this city after his meetings with Stalin. The Americans seemed more concerned about access routes through the British Zone to Bremen and Bremerhaven than they did about Berlin. After the Yalta Conference a staff paper drawn up in Washington and approved by the British was sent to the Russians proposing free transit by all occupation forces throughout Germany and Austria. There was never any reply to it. Further attempts to obtain a Soviet commitment to the principle of free access to Berlin were fruitless.

It was left to the American and British Commanders sent to Berlin to come to an agreement on 29 June 1945 with the Soviet Marshal Zhukov. He agreed that Western forces could travel to the city unhampered by Soviet interference, though their access routes were restricted by Soviet logistical problems. This agreement was verbal and unspecific. General Lucius D. Clay, who had been appointed to administer military government in the American Zone of Germany,* thought it unwise to set out precise rules for access since this would seem to accept limitations on Western rights. As a result no treaty over access routes existed apart

---

* He was officially American Deputy Governor in Germany. He became Governor in March 1947.

from an agreement over air lanes concluded in September 1945. General Clay is almost certainly correct in arguing that, though unfortunate, this omission was not crucial.[31] The Russians' geographical position made it easy for them to obstruct land and water routes to Berlin simply by inventing 'technical' problems. This was, in fact, the technique they later used when imposing a blockade upon the city. In any case in June 1945 collaboration between the Western Allies and the Germans against Russia seemed quite out of the question. Whatever doubts were being felt at a political level, the military leaders of the Alliance were well pleased with Soviet collaboration.

Germany, indeed, was seen as the testing-ground for inter-Allied relations, the opportunity to demonstrate that an alliance forged in war could last into the peace. When, in September 1944, Robert Murphy was appointed political adviser to General Eisenhower on German affairs, he was told personally by President Roosevelt that the primary objective of United States policy after the war was co-operation with the Soviet Union and that Germany would be the place where such co-operation could be put into practice.[32] The arrangements for governing Germany after her surrender had been worked out by the E.A.C. and were confirmed at Potsdam.* The supreme authority in the country was to be an Allied Control Council (A.C.C.), representing the Four Powers who, under the Instrument of Unconditional Surrender, had assumed the sovereignty of Germany. No German Government was to exist at all, though provision was made in the Potsdam Protocol for State Secretaries – executive administrators – who might head the main departments once a centralised administration was established. They would, however, have been entirely dependent on the Control Council. The A.C.C. was to issue regulations affecting the whole country and hence was a quadripartite instrument of government. At the same time the Potsdam Protocol on Germany stressed that she should be treated as an economic unity.[33] It therefore seemed that Anglo-American and Russian policies were firmly set against any permanent division of the Reich.

At first relations between the military men in charge of these arrangements seemed to be developing favourably, and Western commanders were optimistic that the splendid achievements of war-time collaboration could be emulated in the occupation. As a gesture of good faith towards the Russians the Western command structure, SHAEF, was abolished in June 1945, and the three Western contingents in Germany became independent of each other. This certainly worked to the advantage of the Soviet cause in Germany, though how much it imbued the

---

* On 5 June 1945 the Allies issued a declaration on Germany at Berlin in which they assumed supreme authority over the country.

Russians with feelings of trust is very doubtful. General Eisenhower took a distinct liking to his Soviet opposite number, Marshal Zhukov, and felt he had established a relationship of personal confidence with him. Similarly his deputy, General Clay – at the outset – enjoyed friendly relations with the Soviet Commander in Berlin, General Vasilid Sokolovsky.[34]* The Allied Control Council, which met in Berlin and had its first session on 30 August 1945, functioned fairly smoothly at first, mainly because it was issuing orders of a negative character eliminating all traces of National Socialist rule from Germany. It was a honeymoon period which was to be only temporary, and which did not reflect the increasingly embittered relationships between the four Allied Governments. When the divergent nature of the various Allied interests in Germany – which had already become apparent at Potsdam – manifested themselves in occupation policy, there was bound to be some sort of confrontation.

This deterioration of relations between the Allies in Germany was paralleled – and indeed preceded – by a marked cooling of the enthusiasm felt by ordinary soldiers in the Western armies for their Soviet colleagues. The Red Army had been very popular in the West before the two sides joined forces in Germany, and when the junction took place it occasioned great rejoicing. The victors embraced each other in rapturous – if often alcoholic – euphoria. But when British and American forces made closer acquaintance with Soviet troops – especially the occupation units which replaced front-line Red Army fighters after the war had ended – their feelings towards them began to change.† Nevertheless, it should be stressed that most of the civilian and military administrators on the American and British side in Germany at that time still felt loyalty to the war-time alliance and hostility to the Germans. When General Clay and his political adviser, Robert Murphy, itemized the major problems facing them, relations with the Soviet authorities did not figure prominently on their lists.[36] They were far more worried about the difficulties involved in carrying out secret and contradictory sets of Allied occupation instructions. These commanded them to behave sternly to the Germans on the one hand, whilst restoring the German economy enough to make it self-sufficient on the other.‡ If trouble was anticipated with any of their co-occupiers, it was the French and not the

---

* These relations deteriorated progressively and swiftly with the passage of time.

† Lord Moran was told in Berlin in July that the 11th Hussars – whose ballot papers had been mislaid in the General Election – demanded the right to vote again because they wanted to change from Labour to Conservative after seeing the state in which Soviet troops had left their barracks.[35]

‡ The instructions concerned were the American occupation order JCS 1067 and the Potsdam Protocol. See above, pp. 184–6, for the origins of JCS 1067.

Russians who seemed likely to be obstructive. Initially the Americans and the British pursued policies of non-fraternization towards the Germans and were alert to any attempt by their conquered foes to divide the Western Allies from the Soviet Union.[37]

The Allied occupation staffs were seriously short of trained personnel and faced herculean tasks in a country devastated by aerial bombardment and land fighting, with its cities in rubble and its transport in chaos. Conditions were made worse by the large numbers of refugees and displaced persons – some fleeing the Red Army and others victims of the Nazi terror. There was little time for ideological speculation on the political future of Germany as a whole.

Yet despite conditions which seemed both to favour and to demand inter-Allied co-operation, conflicts between Soviet and Anglo-American policies in Germany soon came to the surface. At Potsdam the three Allies had agreed that Germany should be treated as an economic unity, although the Russians had simultaneously undermined the purpose of this provision by handing over important eastern areas to the Poles.* Even at that juncture the motives of the various Allies in seeking such unity were diverse.

The Soviet authorities wanted to ensure they would obtain reparations deliveries from the Western zones – especially the Ruhr. At the same time they established in Berlin a very effective foundation for a centralized German administrative machine which might be expected to form the basis of a nation-wide executive. They did this by encouraging 'anti-Fascist' elements among the population in their zone to come forward and collaborate with them. This line of policy had been prepared in Moscow in February 1945 and was put into effect after the conquest of Berlin in May. On the first of that month Walter Ulbricht and a group of German Communists flew in from Russia to begin establishing a pro-Soviet political front. On 10 June Marshal Zhukov issued an order authorizing the establishment of anti-Fascist political parties.[38] The Communist Party was naturally one of these, although it was careful to stress its desire for social reform rather than revolution. The Soviet authorities deliberately refrained from giving much prominence to Communists when selecting Germans for administrative posts. Their German-staffed administration in Berlin was organized departmentally so that it might be able to extend its authority over the whole country – albeit under the authority of the A.C.C. The impression was given that professional expertise rather than party affiliation was the decisive factor when making appointments, but appearances were somewhat deceptive. Of twelve departmental heads in the central administration

* See below, pp. 334–6.

only three were Communists. But of their seventeen deputies – responsible for the key areas of personnel and organization – no less than ten were in the party. The same tendency could be detected at other levels of civic and political life. The Communists remained unobtrusive but they wielded great influence. As Walter Ulbricht is reported to have said at the time, 'It's quite clear – it's got to look democratic but we must have everything in our control.'[39]

Had Germany been administered in the manner envisaged at the Potsdam Conference, Soviet influence over its central bureaucracy would have been disproportionately large. The same calculation could be made about German political life, the revival of which was at first given less encouragement by the Western Powers than by the Russians. Berlin was the obvious centre for German political parties and the Russians were confident that they controlled the capital – which was, in any case, the headquarters of the Russian zonal administration. The Russians could hope that anti-Fascist organizations developed under their influence would extend their authority throughout the whole of Germany. That, at any rate, was the intention of Herr Ulbricht and his colleagues when they began their operations in Berlin.[40]

Against this well-planned and ruthless kind of campaign the Western occupiers were sadly confused in their policies, and the conditions under which they were operating handicapped their capacity to counter Soviet moves. Although they were represented on the A.C.C. in Berlin and on the Four Power *Kommandatura*, which was responsible for administering the capital itself, their own zonal headquarters lay in Western Germany – and were widely separated from one another. As we have seen,* SHAEF had been abolished, and the French in particular showed no interest in co-operating with the British and Americans. They took rapid steps to seal their zone off from the others and were obstructive on the A.C.C. Indeed, it was French intransigence which was to prove the first – if unintentional – stumbling-block to Soviet plans in Germany.

When the A.C.C. began to function, the Americans, British and Russians were eager to establish joint administrative machinery covering the whole country in accordance with the Potsdam Protocol. But the French had not been invited to Potsdam. General de Gaulle made it only too clear that he did not regard the decisions taken there as binding on him. Under the rules of the A.C.C. – established by the Potsdam agreements – its decisions had to be unanimous. The French opposed any measures which might restore a centralized German administration. They saw this as the first step to a revival of German power, and firmly

* See above, p. 279.

vetoed their colleagues' efforts to establish central German agencies, even for such matters as transport and communications.

De Gaulle's policies, which were of course motivated by fear of the Germans rather than hostility to the Soviet Union, also had serious effects on the economic front. He and his successors* wanted to see the Saar coal-mines and the Rhineland go to France and the Ruhr area put under international control.† The latter idea had, of course, been aired at war-time conferences between the major Allies, but the British and Americans were rapidly becoming opposed to it. They were more and more concerned with the need to restore the German economy to a level at which their zones would cease to be a burden to them. Hence they wished the country to be treated as an economic unity – as had been agreed at Potsdam.

Soviet policy on this point was confused and often contradictory. Whilst laying claim to reparations from the West, the Russians progressively sealed off their own zone and refused any arrangement whereby food supplies or export surpluses from it might be used to benefit Germany as a whole. Meanwhile Soviet agencies independent of their own military occupation authorities moved into Russian-controlled areas and began an orgy of indiscriminate dismantling. All kinds of equipment were uprooted and transported back to Russia, where much of it rusted away through lack of use. Such activities, combined with the brutal behaviour of Red Army troops during their march across Germany, did not encourage the Germans to regard Soviet rule with enthusiasm.

It also aroused indignation on the Anglo-American side. It had been accepted at Potsdam that the Russians could take reparations from Germany in the form of industrial plant, but the scale of the dismantling seemed seriously to compromise any hope of Germany becoming

* He resigned as French Premier on 20 January 1946.

† An interesting light was cast on French attitudes to the occupation of Germany in a conversation between Georges Bidault, the French Foreign Minister, and Secretary of State Byrnes in Washington on 23 August 1945. Bidault claimed that, under decisions taken at Yalta and Potsdam, it had been agreed that Germany should be 'whittled down in the east on a basis officially temporary but probably permanent in actual fact. Nothing like that had been done in the west.' Secretaries of State established for the whole of Germany would have authority over the country up to the French frontier, and they would be sitting in Berlin under Soviet influence. It would be easy for the Russians to exert influence through propaganda using the administrative systems of the other zones. Byrnes pooh-poohed these fears, saying that German families who were better treated in the Western zones than in the Soviet Zone would be unlikely to be very influenced by 'Soviet political philosophy'. M. Bidault then shifted his argument somewhat, stressing that the centre of gravity of Germany had been moved towards the west by the Potsdam and Yalta agreements, and claiming that 'to have Saarbrücken regarded as forming part of Germany and administered by a German, while this was not the case in Königsberg and Danzig, was an impossible situation'.[41]

economically self-supporting. The Russians were also taking reparations deliveries from current industrial production in their zone. The British and the Americans, who faced heavy expenditure maintaining the areas they controlled, contended that under the Potsdam Agreements such surpluses should first be used to pay for necessary German imports of food and raw materials. These arguments went unheeded. The Russians were only interested in economic unity so far as it applied to Soviet reparations from the Western zones. The economic and political future of Germany looked bleak indeed.

14 | The Road to Potsdam

THE morrow of the termination of the war in Europe found the counsels
of the Grand Alliance in considerable disarray and the cause of this
disconsonance lay in the altered policy of the Soviet Union. At Tehran
and at Yalta Marshal Stalin had been in a position to chaffer and he had
driven a hard bargain. Though the way had been made easy for him by
President Roosevelt's determination to develop a special relationship
with the Soviet Union, Stalin had impressed the Americans at Yalta by
his apparent willingness to make concessions, but most of these related
to such matters as the United Nations and the Far Eastern War and did
not affect the sensitive issues involved in Eastern Europe. On those
questions Stalin had given nothing away, and platitudinous formulas
like the Declaration on Liberated Europe – so dear to Mr Stettinius –
could but disguise the fact that the Russians had obtained virtually all
they required. Indeed, Stalin had some reason to suppose that his allies
were really resigned to the inevitability of Soviet domination in Eastern
Europe, since both his 'percentage' arrangement with Mr Churchill in
Moscow in October 1944 and his private conversations with Roosevelt –
not to mention General de Gaulle – seemed to point in that direction.
The British were clearly concerned about the Poles, but it was also
evident that Polish representatives in London were beginning to
exasperate the British Government. As for the large phrases about free
elections which had been bandied about at Yalta, they could hardly be
taken seriously by a man of Stalin's kidney.

It was here that the conflict between words and deeds which was so
obvious in the Soviet treatment of areas occupied by the Red Army
began to erode the mutual enthusiasms – which had never been more
than skin-deep among many of the political leaders – engendered by the
war-time alliance. The fact was that, although the British and the
Americans realized Soviet influence would inevitably be very important
in Eastern Europe after the war, they were not prepared for a situation in
which the independence of such countries as Poland, Hungary, Czechoslovakia and Rumania was completely extinguished. Having returned

from Yalta confident that they had achieved a businesslike – if scarcely very palatable – compromise with Stalin, they found themselves up against a Russian policy which, based as it was on the manifest power of the Red Army, seemed to be bent on achieving the wildest dreams of the imperial Tsars, dreams which envisaged the authority and domination of Russia over those European areas which had once formed the Habsburg and Hohenzollern˙ Empires, together with *their* territorial ambitions – a dominion reaching as far westward as the Elbe (and potentially to the Rhine) and from the Baltic to the Aegean and the Mediterranean.*

Broadly speaking, the objectives of Soviet policy were the nullification of the provisions of the Treaties of Portsmouth (1905) and Brest-Litovsk (1918). In Asia this involved the re-establishment of Russian influence in Manchuria, Mongolia and Korea, the return of South Sakhalin and the occupation of Dairen and Port Arthur. In Europe it meant the re-establishment of Russian power in Finland and the Baltic States, in eastern Poland, in northern Bukovina and Bessarabia. It meant too a Soviet protectorate over Bulgaria, Yugoslavia and western Poland and an outlet to the Baltic Sea in East Prussia.

These European intentions might be explained by a desire both to fulfil Lenin's pledge that the provisions of the 'robber peace' of Brest-Litovsk would one day be redeemed and revenged, and also for a wider protective glacis against an attack from the West. This explanation, however, would not suffice in regard to Russia's Asiatic expansion. This was dictated certainly by an urge to undo the results of a humiliating defeat by Japan but also by a desire for economic advantage and a domination in the Pacific.

But in addition to this there was manifested in Soviet policy an 'imperialist itch' for further and wider spheres of influence. The disappearance of France and Italy as Mediterranean Powers left Britain without rivals in that area and also in the Middle East. It was soon apparent that Russia intended to fill the role of active competitor, and the passage of the Dardanelles again reappeared as a traditional issue of policy.

To fulfil these terms the Soviet leaders were prepared to employ all means ready to their hand – conquest, malfeasance, duplicity, mendacity, obstruction, cajolery and intimidation. For the moment they relied on the

* The sentiments uttered by the chauvinist Pan-Slav poet, F. I. Tyutchev in the 1860s might easily have been written in 1971 as the ultimate aims of Russian power:

> Seven inland seas and seven mighty rivers
> From the Nile to the Neva
> From the Elbe to China
> From the Volga to the Euphrates
> From the Ganges to the Danube
> Such is our Empire to be.[1]

sheer numerical and geographical advantage of the Red Army, pushing forward with amazing speed and establishing satrapies in their wake. Their object was clearly to be in possession of as much territory as possible in the shortest possible time so as to be able to confront Russia's allies with a declaration of '*J'y suis, j'y reste*'.

That Russia's allies were not immune from her brutality of conduct had been demonstrated even before the final conclusion of the hostilities in Europe in her unseemly and unfounded accusations against Britain and the United States on the occasion of the preliminary secret negotiations for the surrender of the German armies in northern Italy,* and in her high-handed attitude towards the Allied protests in connection with the repatriation of their prisoners of war.† The terms of the Declaration on Liberated Europe were being blatantly disregarded by the Soviet Government – indeed it would probably be fair to say that they had never imagined they were to be taken seriously. In Hungary, Rumania and Bulgaria there had appeared régimes which, though not formally Communist in character, were clearly subservient to the Soviet Union and were preparing the ground for further Sovietization. All the evidence available in the West suggested that these régimes lacked wide popular support, but Russian obstructiveness made it very difficult to discover what was actually going on. The great danger which faced the Western Powers in Europe in the spring of 1945 was that, under cover of a verbal commitment to democratic processes at some ill-defined stage in the future, provisional arrangements would be made which would secure Russian control over an area stretching from Lübeck to Albania, and from the Elbe to the Pacific.

This danger was well expressed in a report from the American Embassy in Moscow dated 19 May 1945. The report, in which the elegant hand of George Kennan was detectable, pointed out that

> It can safely be said that no group of people anywhere are more conscious of the critical quality of the post-hostilities period, of its dangers and possibilities, than the leaders of the Soviet Union. Themselves the bearers of a régime forged in the chaotic aftermath of

---

* See above, pp. 254–5.
† On 11 February 1945 analogous agreements were reached at Yalta between the Soviet Union and Britain and the Soviet Union and the United States for the protection, maintenance and repatriation of Allied prisoners of war and civilians liberated by Allied troops. Both the British and American Governments had substantial grounds for complaint in respect of the physical treatment of those of their prisoners of war liberated by the Russians in Poland and also the dilatoriness of their repatriation. This led to an acrid correspondence between Marshal Stalin on the one hand and President Roosevelt and Mr Churchill on the other, the Marshal alleging that the British and American prisoners liberated by the Russians had received far better treatment than that accorded to the Russian prisoners released in Germany, who had been 'ill-treated and beaten' by the Americans and British.[2]

the last war, they are keenly aware that it is in this period of civil and social confusion following on the heels of general military conflict that the lines are drawn which congeal into permanency and determine the overall pattern of the future. They attach even greater importance to the decisions of the next few weeks than to the decisions of possible future peace conferences. For these later decisions, in the Soviet view, will be largely the products of the actual blows that will have been struck while the iron was hot.[3]

From the Western point of view the most painful example of Soviet expansionism was to be seen in Poland. There was, of course, nothing new in this. It had been a problem exercising Western, and particularly British, statesmen since 1941. In a situation bedevilled by traditional Russian acquisitiveness towards Poland, Soviet suspicions of post-war Polish politics and the embarrassing lack of realism shown by Polish leaders in London, the task of those who sought a Soviet–Polish compromise was virtually doomed from the outset. Stalin's intentions towards Poland were always fairly clear, though agreements settled during the period of Soviet weakness might have salvaged something from the wreck of Polish independence.*

From their initial cynical invasion of Poland in September 1939, thereby inflicting a stab in the back to a country with which they were officially on friendly terms and with whom they had contractual obligations in respect of mutual non-aggression and neutrality, it had become increasingly apparent that the Soviet Government was determined to be possessed of Poland, lock, stock and barrel, in some form or another.

As has already been recorded, by December 1944 the tragedy of the gallant Warsaw Rising had so envenomed relationships between the London Poles and the Soviet Government that – despite the efforts of Messrs Churchill and Eden – the prospects for any acceptable settlement became totally bleak. On 27 December 1944 the Soviet Government recognized the so-called Committee of National Liberation at Lublin, composed of Communist Poles who had in many cases been resident in Moscow for a number of years, as the legitimate Government of Poland, under the leadership of the distinguished Communist leader, Boleslaw Bierut. It was this body which Mr Churchill at Yalta had sought to have abolished and replaced by a Polish National Government composed, 'on a broader democratic basis', of an equal number of the Lublin Poles and of those represented by the Polish Government-in-exile in London. To this Stalin had agreed in principle and, as an integral part of the Yalta Agreement, a commission had been established consisting of the

* See above, p. 93.

Soviet Foreign Minister, Molotov, and the British and American Ambassadors in Moscow, Sir Archibald Clark Kerr and Averell Harriman, to work out the details, in terms of personalities, by which such a Government might be formed.*

Again the deliberate bad faith of the Soviet Government was in evidence. Not only were the meetings on the commission during the spring of 1945 reduced to a farce of procrastination and equivocal wrangling, but in the midst of them the Soviet military authorities in Warsaw at the end of March suddenly arrested the sixteen remaining leaders of the Polish Home Front who had survived the Warsaw Rising, including General Leopold Okulicki, who succeeded General Tadeusz Bor-Komorowski as the Commander-in-Chief of the Underground Army, and held them in secret confinement.†

The Soviet attitude towards Poland and, incidentally, their treatment of the Home Front leaders was protested against by Mr Churchill and by President Roosevelt and President Truman in an exchange of messages with Stalin remarkable for their increasing acerbity.[4] As a result, a nominally joint representative Government was formed in Poland, including (from London) both Mikolajczyk and Stanislas Grabski, which was recognized by the United States and Britain. It proved, however, to be of but brief duration. By the time the Potsdam Conference opened in mid-July it was clear beyond peradventure that Stalin's line of country was to be, in Mr Jorrocks's immortal words, 'Where I dines I sleeps"

II

Of the leaders of the Western partners in the Grand Alliance only Mr Churchill was vividly aware of the danger which menaced from the East. When Russia became an ally, *malgré lui*, in June 1941, he did not hesitate to hail her warmly as a sharer in the battle against Nazi aggression and tyranny. In the years which followed he was staunch in his support of the Russian war effort, as the gallant story of the Arctic convoys can bear witness. When the tide of battle turned and the German armies were thrown back from Russian soil he applauded the amazing achievements of the Soviet armed forces, congratulating them on the defeats which they inflicted on the common enemy. Throughout he was a faithful and loyal ally, but equally he was never without realization and apprehension of the terms which the Soviet partner in the Grand Alliance would ultimately exact as the price of that partnership.

* See above, pp. 238–9.
† The Polish Home Front leaders were placed on trial and sentenced on 21 June 1945. General Okulicki received ten years' imprisonment and died in the course of it.

With the analytical percipience of the historian, combined with the wealth of wisdom derived from half a century's experience of politics, domestic and foreign, Mr Churchill resolutely put 'first things first', but never did he lose sight of what the next 'first thing' might be. Accustomed to wide horizons and largely untrammelled by illusions, he was able to see further and more distinctly into the future than – for example – his great colleague Franklin Delano Roosevelt.

To Mr Churchill it was crystal-clear as early as 1943. *En route* for the conference at Tehran, where for the first time the three great architects of victory were to meet together, he voiced his anxieties to Harold Macmillan. He could not, he said, persuade the Americans to take a sufficiently long view on post-war problems, and then he added:

> Cromwell was a great man but he had one failing. He had been brought up in the tradition of the Armada to believe that Spain was still a great power. He made the mistake of supporting France against Spain and thereby establishing France as a great power. Do you think that that will be said of me? Germany is finished, though it may take some time to clean up the mess. The real problem now is Russia. I *can't* get the Americans to see it.[5]*

Throughout the Tehran Conference Mr Churchill's depression increased. He was distressed at the all too apparent rapacity of Soviet claims, at the degree of acquiescence with which these were received by the President and at his own dilemma. For, although he alone realized the magnitude of the danger involved, he knew too that alone he was powerless to avert it. Committed by inclination and policy to maintaining a solidly unified Anglo-American front, he was faced with a situation in which American policy chimed in more often with that of Stalin than with his own. He was thus compelled, usually against his better judgement, to concur in decisions which he felt to be inimical to the interests of Europe in general and Britain in particular.†

He returned to London cast down and unresilient, altogether unlike himself. He could not shake off the awareness of lowering danger. 'I realized at Tehran for the first time what a small nation we are', he confessed to Lady Violet Bonham-Carter.‡ 'There I sat with the great Russian bear on one side of me, with paws outstretched, and on the other the great American buffalo, and between the two sat the poor little British donkey, who was the only one, the only one of the three, who knew the right way home.'[7]

---

* It is of interest to find corroborative opinion of this view from so distinguished a historian and diplomatist as Lord Strang who, in enumerating the defects of Cromwell's policy, lists among them that he 'allied himself with a rising power, France, against a declining power, Spain'.[6]

† For the story of the Tehran Conference, see above, pp. 143–67.

‡ The late Baroness Asquith of Yarnbury.

Cartoon by Cummings for the *Daily Express*, 28 January 1952

During the months which followed, the British Prime Minister essayed with every means within his power to create a settlement in Europe which would not involve the domination of that continent by the Soviet Union. He did this in various ways – by urging the Americans to pass on into Germany as fast as possible and to stay there once they had arrived, by taking pains to persuade Stalin to make compromise arrangements over Eastern Europe and by putting pressure on the Poles and Yugoslavs in London to accept them. But he was not successful. There followed the Yalta Conference, about whose outcome he felt even less enthusiasm.* It can be argued that, by accepting the decisions taken at Yalta, Mr Churchill shouldered some of the odium which was later attached to them. Yet these decisions reflected a changing world situation in which British – and for that matter European – power counted for far less than before.

And this he knew. He returned from Yalta in sombre mood, as is recorded by his devoted Private Secretary and shrewd chronicler John Colville, voicing grave doubts:

> The shadows of victory were upon us. In 1940 the issue was clear, and he [Mr Churchill] knew what was to be done, but when Sir Arthur Harris [G.O.C. Bomber Command] had finished the destruction of Germany, 'What will lie between the white snows of Russia and the white cliffs of Dover?' Perhaps, however, the Russians would not want to sweep on to the Atlantic, or something might stop them as the accident of Genghis Khan's death had stopped the horsed-archers of the Mongols. Be that as it might, there was an unspoken fear in many people's hearts. After this war we should be weak; we should have no money and our strength would have been drained away. We should lie between the two great powers of the U.S.A. and the U.S.S.R.[8]†

With the aftermath of Yalta the irrefragable pattern of Soviet policy became clear for all to see. The suspicions which Mr Churchill had entertained for so long, the doubts which he had expressed so consistently, now became certainties. The truculence and discourtesy, the lack of good faith, displayed by the Soviet leaders, caused him to write to President Roosevelt in April 1945: 'If they [the Russians] are convinced that we are afraid of them and can be bullied into submission, then indeed I should despair of the future relations with them and of much else.'

The close of hostilities in Europe increased rather than diminished the

---

* For the story of the Yalta Conference, see above, pp. 221–50.

† Mr Colville also records that in February 1945 Mr Churchill told President Beneš of Czechoslovakia that a small lion was walking between a huge Russian bear and a great American elephant, but that perhaps it would turn out to be the lion that knew the way.

gravity of the situation. The arbitrary behaviour of the Russians in the Eastern Zone of Germany which they occupied and their evident determination to maintain massive armed forces both there and in the satellite states, coupled with the declared intention of the United States to withdraw virtually all their troops from Europe within two years, occasioned Mr Churchill the liveliest anxiety. 'I could only feel the vast manifestation of Soviet and Russian imperialism rolling forward over helpless lands', he has written.[9] The one slender hope of salvation before the chasm opened irrevocably between East and West seemed to him to be to call together again the three leaders of the Grand Alliance so that together they might assail the problems arising from victory. It was essential to do this, he considered, before Soviet control became ineradicably rooted in Europe and before the withdrawal of American troops left the British and the Russians in single and unequal confrontation.

He approached President Truman on this score, proposing a joint invitation to Stalin to a tripartite conference in July 'in some agreed unshattered town in Germany' and also suggesting a preliminary meeting between themselves. This proposal received but scant encouragement. The new President of the United States, so recently and tragically elevated to this high office, was feeling his way with caution, seeking to maintain an independent stand between the sharply conflicting views of Britain and Russia, above all anxious to avoid giving the impression to Stalin of 'ganging-up' on the Soviet Union. He said as much.

It was then that Mr Churchill sent to the President his now historic telegram of 12 May:

> I am profoundly concerned about the European situation. I learn that half the American Air Force in Europe has already begun to move to the Pacific theatre. The newspapers are full of the great movements of the American armies out of Europe. Our armies also are, under previous arrangements, likely to undergo a marked reduction. The Canadian Army will certainly leave. The French are weak and difficult to deal with. Anyone can see that in a very short space of time our armed power on the Continent will have vanished, except for moderate forces to hold down Germany.
>
> 2. Meanwhile what is to happen about Russia? I have always worked for friendship with Russia, but, like you, I feel deep anxiety because of their misinterpretation of the Yalta decisions, their attitude towards Poland, their overwhelming influence in the Balkans, excepting Greece, the difficulties they make about Vienna, the combination of Russian power and the territories under their control or occupied, coupled with the Communist technique in so many other

countries, and above all their power to maintain very large armies in the field for a long time. What will be the position in a year or two, when the British and American Armies have melted and the French has not yet been formed on any major scale, when we may have a handful of divisions, mostly French, and when Russia may choose to keep two or three hundred on active service?

3. An iron curtain* is drawn down upon their front. We do not know what is going on behind. There seems little doubt that the whole of the regions east of the line Lübeck–Trieste–Corfu will soon be completely in their hands. To this must be added the further enormous area conquered by the American armies between Eisenach and the Elbe, which will, I suppose, in a few weeks be occupied, when the Americans retreat, by the Russian power. All kinds of arrangements will have to be made by General Eisenhower to prevent another immense flight of the German population westward as this enormous Muscovite advance into the centre of Europe takes place. And then the curtain will descend again to a very large extent, if not entirely. Thus a broad band of many hundreds of miles of Russian-occupied territory will isolate us from Poland.

4. Meanwhile the attention of our peoples will be occupied in inflicting severities upon Germany which is ruined and prostrate, and it would be open to the Russians in a very short time to advance if they chose to the waters of the North Sea and the Atlantic.

5. Surely it is vital now to come to an understanding with Russia, or see where we are with her, before we weaken our armies mortally or

---

* This telegram is the first recorded occasion on which Mr Churchill used the phrase 'an iron curtain', but it was not the first time that it had been in use during the war. On 25 February 1945 Joseph Goebbels wrote in *Das Reich*: 'Should the German people lay down its arms, the agreement between Roosevelt, Churchill and Stalin would allow the Soviets to occupy all Eastern and South-eastern Europe together with the major part of the Reich. An iron curtain [*ein eiserner Vorhang*] would at once descend on this territory which, including the Soviet Union, would be of enormous dimensions.' This is probably the first time that the phrase was used in print. The first mention of 'iron curtain' in the spoken word occurred on 2 May 1945, when in a broadcast to the German people from Flensburg, Count Schwerin von Krosigk, who had just been appointed Foreign Minister in the Government of Grand-Admiral Doenitz, said: 'In the East the iron curtain behind which, unseen by the eyes of the world, the work of destruction goes on, is moving steadily forward.'[10]

Mr Churchill repeated the words in a further telegram to President Truman on 4 June, in which he begged for a halt to the withdrawal of American troops in the Control Sector. This, he said, would bring 'Soviet power into the heart of Western Europe and the descent of an iron curtain between us and everything to the eastward'.[11] He came very close to using the words to Stalin's face when, in the course of the Potsdam Conference, he spoke of the 'iron fence' which had come down on the British Mission in Bucharest, a statement which the Marshal dismissed as 'all fairy tales'.[12] Mr Churchill's first public use of the term was of course in his famous speech at Fulton on 5 March 1946.

It is perhaps of interest to find Mr Macborrowdale, in *Gryll Grange* saying: 'I detest and abominate the idea of a Siberian dinner, while you just look on fiddle-foddles, while your dinner is behind a screen and you are served with rations like a pauper.' To this an editor, David Garnett, has appended: 'The practice of carving at a side-board behind a Russian screen (or iron curtain) was called dining *à la Russe*. Mr Macborrowdale called it Siberian as the joint had been sent into exile.'[13]

retire to the zones of occupation. This can only be done by a personal meeting. I should be most grateful for your opinion and advice. Of course we may take the view that Russia will behave impeccably, and no doubt that offers the most convenient solution. To sum up, this issue of a settlement with Russia before our strength has gone seems to me to dwarf all others.[14]

It was of this message that Mr Churchill wrote his own comment: 'Of all the public documents I have written on this issue I would rather be judged by this.'

It would, however, be entirely erroneous to convey the impression that Mr Churchill was entirely consistent in his attitude towards the Russians. Indeed consistency had never been among his virtues or his failings. As he himself has admitted, 'During my life I have often had to eat my own words and I have always found them a wholesome diet'.

Though his fundamental hostility and distrust of Communism remained unshaken, he would not permit this to impinge upon or interfere with the successful progress of what he regarded as the two most vital issues current at that moment, namely, the victorious outcome of the war and the smooth confluence of Anglo-American relations. In the great triumvirate of Western leaders, his was, indeed, the role of Lepidus.

Thus, though Mr Churchill, in his famous broadcast of 22 June 1941, welcomed the Soviet Union as an ally against Hitler, he withdrew nothing of what he had said and professed about Bolshevism in the previous decades. On the other hand, he would disregard, or deliberately neglect, the warnings of Anthony Eden before Yalta, against the danger of appeasing the Russians without getting something from them in exchange,* and would follow, if reluctantly, the lead of President Roosevelt in making wholesale concessions, because he believed in Anglo-American unanimity of thought as transcending all else in importance. And though he might assure the Spanish Ambassador in October 1943 that 'I am still as anti-Communist as ever and if Communism should be a danger for Europe I shall fight against it, as I have done all my life with all my strength',[15]† he was not entirely proof against that animal, brigand charm which Stalin knew so well how to use and exploit. 'I *like* that man', he is recorded as saying to Anthony Eden of

---

* See above, p. 215.

† This is an interesting contrast to the official British line which Sir Samuel Hoare had communicated to General Franco's Foreign Minister, General Count Jordana, only eight months before: 'The victory at the end of this war will be an Allied, not a Russian victory, namely a victory in which the British Empire and the United States of America will exercise the greatest possible influence. Moreover, Mr Stalin declared on 9 November 1942 that it was not the future policy of Russia to interfere in the internal affairs of other countries.'[16]

Stalin on returning from one of the sessions of the Potsdam Conference.*

His basic suspicion of Communism – and therefore by definition of Russia – combined with his natural percipience, caused Mr Churchill to sound the tocsin of alarm to the post-war world at Fulton, Missouri, on 5 March 1946, wherein he declared the real design of the Kremlin to be 'the fruits of war and the indefinite expansion of their power and doctrine'.† Yet this did not deter him in 1955 from making a final effort to reach a formula of agreement with Moscow.[17]

Both the strength and the weakness of Mr Churchill's statesmanship lay in the pliancy of mind.

III

President Roosevelt approached the problem of the Soviet Union in a different manner and from a different angle. From the earliest period of the war, when neither the Soviet Union nor the United States was a belligerent, he had visualized an American–Soviet partnership for peace in the then uncertain shaping of the post-war world. When later they became comrades in arms, this concept increased rather than diminished. Russia and America were to be cast in the role of two super-policemen, supervising East and West, under the aegis of the United Nations. Not until just before his death did the President abandon the belief that it was possible to work out a post-war partnership with the Russians on a common basis acceptable to both parties. Until that moment of enlightenment came, however, President Roosevelt was immutably convinced that he, and he alone, could bring about this unlikely miracle.

This was an illusion which had afflicted Neville Chamberlain in his personal dealings with Hitler. When reminded of the fact, on his return from the Munich Conference, that the Führer had made other previous promises and had broken them, the then Prime Minister replied: 'I know, my dear fellow, I know. But this time, you see, it is different; this time he has made them to me'. It was in this same vein of euphoric vanity that President Roosevelt had written to Mr Churchill as early as 18 March 1942: 'I know you will not mind my being brutally frank when I tell you I can personally handle Stalin better than either your Foreign Office or my State Department.'[18]‡

---

* See below, p. 338.   † See below, p. 561.

‡ Ambassador William C. Bullitt (perhaps not the most objective of sources!) records a conversation with President Roosevelt (the date is not given but is certainly after Pearl Harbor) in which he [Bullitt] expatiated on the inherent danger of trusting the Russians. At the close of the conversation the President said: 'Bill, I don't dispute the logic of your reasoning. I just have a hunch that Stalin is not that kind of a man. Harry [Hopkins] says he's not and that he doesn't want anything but security for his country, and I think that if I give him everything I possibly can and ask nothing in

Nor did the President fully understand or appreciate the full motives behind Mr Churchill's fears. 'The trouble is the P.M. is thinking too much of the post-war world and where England will be. He's scared of letting the Russians get too strong', President Roosevelt observed to his son Elliott at Tehran.[20] But it was not for England alone that Mr Churchill feared; it was for the whole western world, of which he looked to the United States to become the strongest bastion.*

That Stalin was himself aware of this difference of attitude, though in a cruder vein, may be believed from his remarks some time later to Milovan Djilas, while the latter was on a mission to Moscow from the Yugoslav Government. 'Churchill', said the Marshal, 'is the kind who, if you don't watch him, will slip a kopeck out of your pocket.... And Roosevelt? Roosevelt is not like that. He dips in his hand only for bigger coins.'[22]

The President's hopes for a special relationship with Russia were not dimmed by the Yalta Conference, despite the storm warnings which Averell Harriman continued to send him from the United States Embassy in Moscow. Messages from London critical of Soviet policy seemed only to arouse in the Presidential mind a sense of irritation that the British were trying to embroil him with his Russian allies. On 16 March 1945 he told his Cabinet colleagues in a 'semi-jocular' manner that he was 'having considerable difficulty in his relations with the British', who were 'perfectly willing for the United States to have a war with Russia at any time' and that in his view 'to follow the British programme would be to proceed towards that end'.[23]

Doubtless this remark was meant more as a warning to his subordinates than as an analysis – however jocular – of the international situation. The President must have been aware that some of his colleagues were nervous of Soviet power in the post-war world. These included the Secretaries of War and the Navy, as well as the redoubtable Admiral Leahy who, although isolationist by tendency, admitted preferring White to Red Russians.[24] Harry Hopkins, the most enthusiastic supporter of the President's pro-Russian policy, was a sick man. In addition to these internal pressures, the President was faced with an unmistakable hardening in Soviet attitudes after the Yalta Conference, a change which manifested itself in truculent communications and

---

return, *noblesse oblige*, he won't try to annex anything and will work with me for a world of democracy and peace'. When Bullitt expressed the opinion that Stalin was 'a Caucasian bandit whose only thought when he got something for nothing was that the other fellow was an ass', the President replied with irritation: 'It's my responsibility and not yours; I'm going to play my hunch.'[19]

* 'You will find us lining up with the Russians', said Harry Hopkins to Lord Moran as they journeyed together to Tehran.[21]

obstructive policies. This was most obvious in the accusations of bad faith levelled against the President by Stalin and Molotov over the tentative German surrender negotiations in Switzerland, to say nothing of Soviet intransigence over the Polish issue.

It is difficult to say how far the President was affected by these developments. In March 1945 his health was obviously deteriorating and many of those who saw him at that time recorded their sense of shock at his enfeebled appearance. Mr Churchill later recorded that messages he received from the President had in fact been drafted by General Marshall. Marshall himself was naturally preoccupied with the need to cement Soviet–American relationships in order to secure Russian participation in the war against Japan. In the spring of 1945 the Japanese seemed far from beaten and the American military staffs did not expect peace in the Far East for one or two years to come.

It is fruitless to speculate how President Roosevelt would have handled relations with the Russians when the need for their military help against the Japanese became less pressing in the summer of 1945 and when the unacceptable nature of their policies in Eastern Europe had become impossible to overlook. There is some evidence to suggest that his attitude towards Stalin was already shifting shortly before he died, and he certainly expressed feelings of disenchantment to some of those around him. On 24 March, Anna Rosenberg,* an old and valued friend, lunched 'off the record' at the White House. A cable from Harriman was brought to the President at the table. He read it and became angry and agitated. Banging the arms of his wheelchair he cried: 'Averell is right, we can't do business with Stalin. He has broken every one of the promises he made at Yalta.'[25] On the following day he left Washington for the last time. He went to the Little White House at Warm Springs, Georgia, where, on 5 April, in his penultimate message to Stalin, he spoke of 'bitter resentment' and 'vile misrepresentations'.[26]† Seven days later President Roosevelt died.

Of his Vice-President, Harry S. Truman, the world knew little as yet. It knows considerably more today. President Truman may well be numbered among the great leaders of the United States. He differed from his predecessor in background, character and approach. President Roosevelt's ancestry was that of the aristocratic patrician families; President Truman came of virile, pioneer stock. President Roosevelt had reached the White House through the Governor's chair in Albany, New York; President Truman had begun his political career in the

---

* Now Mrs Paul Hoffman.

† See above, p. 254. This spirited riposte resulted in a grudging and ungracious apology from Stalin and the President's last message to the Marshal (sent on the day of his death) was a somewhat cool acceptance.[27]

Pendergast machine in Kansas City, Missouri. Without the subtlety and agility of mind and the blinding charm of Roosevelt, Truman matched him in courage, in vision and in bulldog determination and, when necessary, excelled him in ruthlessness. Their principles and precepts were identical, but whereas Roosevelt arrived at his uncanny understanding of American public opinion by means of an almost feminine intuition, Truman derived his own keen perception of the views of his countrymen from within himself, through an upwelling of his own inner consciousness. Truly the comment of a New York weekly magazine that 'President Roosevelt was *for* the people; President Truman *is* the people' was not far off the mark.*

The thirty-second President of the United States personified that combination of fundamental toughness, commonsense and goodness of heart which comprises the average American. He was more forthright, less devious, than President Roosevelt and by his very forthrightness he prevented the American people from slipping back into that myopic self-righteous isolationism which had afflicted them after the First World War.

President Truman differed radically from President Roosevelt not only in character but also in his working methods. He was a man who rose early and applied himself to his official papers. When making up his mind about international problems – upon which he had never been briefed by his predecessor – he turned to the expert advice provided for him by the State Department. His first official business as President on 13 April 1945 was an interview with Mr Stettinius, from whom he demanded a report on American relations with foreign countries. This report was sent to him the same day. It claimed that Anglo-American understanding was good, although Mr Churchill tended to be rather stern towards Russia and to adopt an attitude of 'unnecessary rigidity as to detail'. On the other hand the Soviet Government had taken up a 'firm and uncompromising' stand on nearly every major question that had arisen in its relations with the United States.[28] These comments were not lost on the new President, who was quite capable of being firm himself – as M. Molotov was soon to discover.

It should not of course be imagined that the change at the White House in April 1945 immediately heralded a more negative policy towards the Soviet Union or a clear line in favour of hard bargaining. President Truman sincerely wanted to continue the policies of his great predecessor, who he knew had gained enormous international stature for his leadership in peace and war. As we have seen, President Roose-

---

* A less kind version of this remark was contained in the bitter jest: 'For the last twelve years we have had the champion of the common man in the White House; now we have the common man himself.'

velt's own confidence in Soviet–American accord was wavering before his death, and the views of his diplomatic advisers had hardened even before the Yalta Conference.* Nevertheless, the appearance of a lively and vigorous chief executive on the bridge of the American ship of state at a moment when its course had been dangerously unsteady was of great importance to the Western Powers in 1945. There was – and this was inevitable and understandable – a period of vacillation and uncertainty while the new captain got his bearings. The whole problem of American–Soviet relations was very complicated and the President was not at all clear what President Roosevelt's policy had actually been on this issue. The new President was, moreover, at the mercy of conflicting counsels.

The problem was essentially complicated and difficult of solution. Against the menace of Soviet policies in Europe had to be considered the agreed necessity of Soviet participation in the Pacific War, and against this, in turn, the repercussions of such participation on the future of the Far East.

These factors weighed heavily upon the President and he discussed them with Harry Hopkins during their journey from Hyde Park to Washington after the funeral of Franklin Roosevelt on 15 April and tentatively mooted to him an idea which had been taking shape in his mind – an attempt, by contact through a personal envoy, to re-establish good personal relations between himself and Stalin. Would Hopkins consider going to Moscow? Would his health permit him to assume such a mission? Hopkins was indefinite. He would have to consult his doctor, he said, and anyhow, why didn't the President send his message through Averell Harriman; after all, he was the American Ambassador to Moscow? Because, Truman replied, Hopkins, by reason of his close friendship with Roosevelt, represented a continuing link between the old Administration and the new, and could impress upon Stalin the determination of the President to carry on his predecessor's policies.†
Hopkins said he would think about it.

Averell Harriman himself arrived within a matter of hours, having

---

* See above, pp. 206–7.

† President Truman later recorded in his diary for 22 May that he had invited Harry Hopkins to undertake this mission 'because I trusted him and because he had been Roosevelt's messenger to Russia on a previous and similar occasion, that Hopkins was a noted and advanced "Liberal" but not a professional one (I considered the latter a low form of politician), that he had horse sense and knew how to use it'.[29]

Hopkins himself was eager to ensure that President Truman did not fall under the influence of those critical of Soviet policies – especially Winston Churchill. For this reason he was alarmed by suggestions that the Prime Minister might come to Washington during or soon after President Roosevelt's funeral. He told Anthony Eden and Lord Halifax that Truman, who knew nothing of world affairs, 'would have been terrified . . . had the Prime Minister come'.[30] The picture of a 'terrified' President Truman is not wholly in character!

posted from Moscow to Washington in record time, and on 20 April he conferred with the President. He had been alarmed lest Truman did not realize, as the late President had only belatedly realized, that Stalin was breaking all his Yalta promises. He was anxious to give the President the true picture. But by this time President Truman had done his homework. He had read the full record and documentation of the Yalta Conference, together with all Harriman's messages to Roosevelt and all those which the late President had sent to Stalin. He was in full mastery of the situation, somewhat to the amazement of the Ambassador.*

Briefly and succinctly, Harriman gave the President 'a real pitch on the developments of the situation'. He emphasized that Stalin was pursuing two policies concurrently – one, that of co-operation with Britain and the United States, the other of extending Soviet control over neighbouring states by independent action. Generosity and co-operation on the part of the Western Powers in respect of the first policy were misinterpreted as an indication of softness and an unwillingness to offer a challenge to the second. He added that, in his opinion, the world was faced with a 'barbarian invasion of Europe'. Where Soviet control was established in any country the foreign relations of that country became at one subservient to Moscow and the Soviet system of secret police and control of expression or opinion became paramount. The United States must make up its mind to face facts and, having done so, must decide on what attitude they should adopt. It should be, in his view, an attitude of firmness.†

The President replied that he was not afraid of Russia and that he intended to be firm but fair. He sounded Harriman on the idea of sending Hopkins to Moscow as a special envoy and the Ambassador was enthusiastic in his approval.[33]‡

---

* 'That was the first time I realized what an extraordinary faculty Mr Truman had of reading all of the documents', Mr Harriman later told a Congressional Committee. 'I found as I worked for him more and more it became even embarrassing.'[31]

† Five days later, Ambassador Harriman gave his views to the United States delegation to the San Francisco Conference in even more emphatic terms: 'Since the Yalta Conference our relations with Russia had taken a very different turn. The relations of war-time were developing into the beginning of the relations of peace-time, which might in part explain the change in our relations. All men who have dealt with Russia knew of the Russian attempt to chisel, by bluff, pressure and other unscrupulous methods to get what they wish. We also recognize that they wish to have as much domination over Eastern Europe as possible, and that as the Red Army has advanced, governments in Eastern Europe have tended to come under the domination of the army. While we cannot go to war with Russia, we must do everything we can to maintain our position as strongly as possible in Eastern Europe. Russia is building a tier of friendly states there and our task is to make it difficult for her to do so, since to build one tier of states implies the possibility of further tiers, layer by layer. . . . Our whole position, the one advantage we had, was to stand firm in our position in Eastern Europe.'[32]

‡ Mr Harriman told the Congressional Committee on 6 June 1967: 'I got him [the President] to send Harry Hopkins to Moscow.'[34]

In the meantime Mr Churchill was desperately endeavouring to bring about a conference of the three Allied leaders in two stages: first a meeting between himself and President Truman and then a full-dress confrontation with Stalin. This idea was broached to President Truman by Mr Eden and Lord Halifax on 16 April (the day after Roosevelt's funeral) and was repeated by the Prime Minister himself in a cable to the President on the twenty-fourth. At first it seemed as if Truman was half inclined to accept the invitation; at least he did not dismiss it out of hand. But it was noticeable that, as Mr Churchill waxed more emphatic on the need for the two meetings, so the President's enthusiasm waned. On 9 May he accepted in principle the desirability of a tripartite meeting but expressed a strong preference that the initiative should come from Stalin and not from the Western Allies, and two days later he finally disposed of the idea of a previous meeting with Mr Churchill in order to avoid any suspicion of 'ganging up' arising in the so-sensitive mind of Joseph Stalin.[35] It was at this point that Mr Churchill sent his 'iron curtain' message,* but to no avail.

Throughout this correspondence with Mr Churchill the President had not mentioned his own plan of a unilateral approach to Stalin. Whether he deliberately kept the Prime Minister in ignorance of his hopes on this point or whether he did not wish to inform him of the project until it was fully matured, it is difficult to say, but his preparations were going forward throughout this period and Harry Hopkins's influence became evident in the formulation of policy.

For the President had now made up his mind. He was aware of the danger which Soviet policy presented and was desirous of countering it – but in his own way, and not Mr Churchill's. President Truman descried in the Prime Minister's attitude towards Russia a degree of danger to the tripartite solidarity which he himself was anxious to restore and maintain. He shared Mr Churchill's wish for a new meeting of the Big Three but he did not share the other's feeling of urgency. He therefore rejected the suggestion of an Anglo-American invitation to Moscow and also the proposal of a meeting with Mr Churchill before such a conference was held. He gambled heavily on the success of his plan to send a personal envoy to Stalin.

Harry Hopkins came again to the White House on 4 May and the President took occasion to renew his invitation to go to Moscow on a personal mission. Sick man though he was, Hopkins was also a man of courage, devoted to the fulfilment of Roosevelt's policies as he saw them, dedicated to the service of his country. He gave his final acceptance on the following day.

* See above, pp. 293–5.

The President's advisers were divided on the choice of Hopkins as an envoy. Harriman and Hull warmly favoured him, but the Secretary of State, Edward Stettinius, backed by the Department and also by James F. Byrnes, was opposed both to the idea of a personal mission and to the selection of Hopkins to undertake it.* The President, however, over-ruled them.[36]†

Having taken this decision, the President sought Stalin's agreement on 19 May to a visit by Hopkins accompanied by Harriman, and received a warm reply on the following day. The date of their arrival in Moscow was agreed as 26 May.[40]‡

There remained the problem of how to explain all this to Mr Churchill. The President and Hopkins were at one in their unwillingness to accept the Prime Minister's warnings about Russian ambitions at their face value. Hopkins frankly admitted to James Forrestal, the Secretary of the Navy, on 20 May that he was 'sceptical about Churchill, at least in the

---

* This is as stated by President Truman, but it would appear that later Mr Stettinius changed his mind (see note below).

† The President does appear to have wavered in his choice at one subsequent moment. According to his diary entry for 22 May, he asked Joseph E. Davies, a former Ambassador to Moscow and a fervid supporter of American–Russian amicable relations, to undertake the mission which he had apparently already offered to Hopkins; Mr Davies declined for reasons of health.[37]

The above account of the origins of Harry Hopkins's last mission is taken from President Truman's own records, including his diaries and memoirs written in 1954. There is, however, a curious discrepancy between this account and that of Hopkins's biographer, Robert Sherwood, who, writing in 1947 (and presumably without full access to documentation), has a different story to tell. According to this the initiative to send Hopkins to Moscow lay with Averell Harriman and Charles Bohlen who, on their return to Washington from the San Francisco Conference 'less than a week after V.E. Day' (8 May), called upon Hopkins in Georgetown and proposed the idea to him. After initial reluctance, Hopkins accepted in principle but 'expressed the despondent conviction that Truman would never send him on this mission'. Harriman then went to the White House and put the suggestion to the President, who, though favourably impressed, said that he 'would need some time to think it over'. Several anxious days followed with Hopkins fearing that 'it would all come to nothing, but then Truman sent for him and asked him if he felt capable of making the long journey'.[38]

This account is at great variance with that of President Truman in that it omits any mention of his conversations with Hopkins on 15 April and 4 May, and of Hopkins's acceptance on 5 May. By V.E. Day the whole thing was settled, and it is difficult therefore to claim that it had been initiated 'less than a week after V.E. Day'.

President Truman never minimized the part which Averell Harriman played in this matter. He told Joe Davies on 22 May that he had sent Hopkins to Moscow 'at Harriman's suggestion and after consultation with Hull, Byrnes and others'.[39] But in this he did himself an injustice. It was he who first broached the idea to Hopkins on 15 April and he did not see Harriman until 20 April.

‡ Apparently President Truman's approach to Stalin was taken without the knowledge of the State Department, who were not informed until 21 May. The Acting Secretary of State, Joseph Grew, telephoned the news to Stettinius (then at the San Francisco Conference) that afternoon. The Secretary of State is recorded as saying that 'he thought it was an excellent arrangement and definitely the right thing to do', a somewhat different view from that which he had expressed when first canvassed on the subject of the Hopkins Mission some two weeks previously.[41]

particular of Anglo-American-Russian relationship'; to him it was of vital importance that America should not be manœuvred into a position 'where Great Britain had us lined up with them as a bloc against Russia to implement England's European policy', and the President himself believed that 'Stalin already has an erroneous opinion that we are ganging up on him'.[42]

Yet the President did not wish to forfeit the confidence of Mr Churchill, whom he much admired, and was at pains to find some means o avoid so doing. He sought advice from Joe Davies on the night of 21 May (the day after he had received Stalin's agreement to receive Hopkins) and that ardent protagonist of Soviet–American amity suggested that 'if he could talk to Churchill he could make him see the light'.[43]

If Mr Hopkins was the man to send to Stalin, Mr Davies was decidedly not the man to send to Mr Churchill. Indeed a worse envoy could scarcely have been chosen.

Mr Davies's brief record as Ambassador to Moscow had been one of unalloyed placation of Stalin. In his approach to Mr Churchill he disclosed himself as a 'vain amateur' who, in the opinion of Anthony Eden, was 'a born appeaser and would gladly give Russia all Europe, except perhaps us, so that America might not be embroiled. All the errors and illusions of Neville C[hamberlain] substituting Russia for Germany.'[44]

During the meetings held at Chequers on 26 and 27 May and later at No. 10 Downing Street, Mr Davies made an impassioned plea for confidence in Stalin and suggested to the Prime Minister at the outset that the President and the Marshal should meet privately before any formal conference of the Big Three and that British representatives should be invited to join these conversations 'a few days later'. In effect, far from the Americans and the British 'ganging up' on the Russians, the Russians and the Americans should 'gang up' on the British. Mr Churchill reacted violently against such a proposal and it would appear that Mr Davies had put it forward on his own authority and not that of the President. When Mr Churchill cabled his views on such a plan to the President on 31 May, the latter was utterly amazed. 'I had at no time proposed seeing Stalin alone at any separate conference', he records.[45]

After this inauspicious beginning it is not surprising that little profitable came of the conversations. Provoked by Mr Davies's almost fanatical espousal of Soviet policies, the Prime Minister was at his most eloquent and robust in his rebuttal. Indeed Mr Davies was shocked and appalled. If, he declared, it were known to the Russians that such views were held by the British Prime Minister, it would be more than a sufficient explanation for their actions in Europe during the past several weeks. Was the Prime Minister now willing to proclaim to the world that he and Britain had made a mistake in not supporting Hitler, for, as it seemed to Mr Davies, he was now expressing the doctrine which Hitler and Goebbels had proclaimed and reiterated for the past four years. Mr Churchill replied that he was not essentially opposed to the American policy, though he was prepared to take the risk of a much tougher line, and it was with this somewhat cold comfort that the President's envoy returned to Washington. He brought back a disconcerting report to President Truman; he left behind him a thoroughly unsalutary impression with all who had met him.*

IV

'So I have sent Hopkins to Moscow and Davies to London. We shall see what we shall see . . .', wrote President Truman in his diary on 22 May.

> I told Hopkins what I had in mind. He said he would go, said he understood my position and that he would make it clear to Uncle Joe Stalin that I knew what I wanted – and that I intended to get it – peace for the world for at least 90 years. That we have no territorial ambitions or ulterior motives in Poland, Rumania, Bulgaria, Czechoslovakia, Austria, Yugoslavia, Latvia, Lithuania, Estonia or elsewhere, and that our only interests concern world peace.[47]

Though one of his doves of peace had returned to the ark with its plumage somewhat ruffled, it was to the success of the other that the President attached a greater importance, and it is clear from this epitome of his thinking that he had given Hopkins very wide terms of reference which amounted to a virtual recognition of Soviet claims in the countries which he enumerated.

Hopkins left Washington on 23 May and, flying via Paris, arrived in Moscow on the evening of the twenty-fifth. On the following day he began a series of conferences with Marshal Stalin which continued until 6 June; he was accompanied on these conversations by Averell Harriman and Charles Bohlen, the State Department's brilliant Soviet expert.†

In the opinion of Mr Harriman they found the Marshal uneasy and clearly worried at the deterioration which had developed in Soviet–American relations since the Yalta Conference. The firm attitude which

---

* Mr Davies reported orally on his mission to the President and to Admiral Leahy at dinner on the evening of 5 June, and subsequently sent two written reports, both dated 12 June. Mr Churchill wrote a formal minute of their conversations and states that a copy of it was given to Davies. This Davies categorically denies.[46]

† Mr Bohlen kept the minutes of these conversations in considerable detail, and Harry Hopkins himself sent a daily cable to the President at Washington.[48] An excellent account of the Hopkins Mission has been written by Dr Herbert Feis.[49]

President Roosevelt had taken before his death, and which had been maintained on various occasions by President Truman, was believed by the Ambassador to have had its effect.[50] Whether this was the case one cannot in fact tell, but it is true that, after some initial sparring and bluster, Stalin assumed an almost genial attitude towards his visitor. Butter, it appeared, would not melt in the Bear's jaws and on paper Harry Hopkins could reckon a remarkable record of achievement.

Stalin agreed to the proposal of a meeting of the Big Three and Hopkins at once telegraphed this welcome news to the President who began his preparations forthwith. By the close of the conversations it had been arranged that the Three should meet in Potsdam on 15 July.

The Marshal also agreed to a compromise on the issue of the voting procedure in the Security Council which had paralysed the San Francisco Conference and endangered the birth of the United Nations Organization.* In addition he had given satisfactory assurances on future Soviet participation in the war against Japan in accordance with his promise given at Tehran† and on the Soviet attitude towards China in the post-war period.‡

It was, however, in the matter of Poland that Hopkins seemed to have achieved his greatest measure of success. He appeared to have struck a bargain with Stalin which held within it the germ of a viable compromise. Hopkins agreed to Stalin's claim that only those Poles who accepted the Yalta Accord on Poland could be considered as eligible for co-operation and that the Warsaw Poles (who had been the Lublin Poles) were to have a majority of the new reorganized Government. In return Stalin conceded that the Soviet Government would abstain from interference in Polish affairs once the new Government had been formed and had assumed office, and that it would not object to the inclusion of independent political Poles in the composition of the Government. He also accepted the provision of free elections and the respect of individual rights and liberties. The Soviet Union, he said, would co-operate with the British and American Governments in the organization of these elections.

On paper this agreement had favourable aspects, but only on paper, and indeed it may have been that Hopkins himself was not too confident about it.§ There were certainly lacunae in its provisions and at least two debatable points had been swept under the carpet. It remained inherent

---

* See below, pp. 548–51.   † See above, p. 147.   ‡ See below, pp. 358–9.

§ There was at least one dissentient voice among Hopkins's advisers. That prescient observer of Soviet affairs, George Kennan, when informed by Hopkins of the terms of the tentative agreement, urged him not to accept it. 'I thought', he writes, 'we should accept no share of the responsibility for what the Russians proposed to do in Poland.' Hopkins replied: 'I respect your opinion but I am not at liberty to accept it.'[51]

15   Cecilienhof, 13 July 1945

16 Potsdam: Mr Churchill meets President Truman for the first time,
16 July 1945

in what Hopkins had agreed that the Soviet Union retained the power of domination as regards the ultimate outcome of the negotiations, since all the members of the Polish Commission, as constituted under the Yalta Accord, would have to approve its conclusions, thus giving the Soviet Government a virtual power of veto. Moreover, in the event of no agreement being reached on the formation of a new Polish Government, the Red Army and the puppet Bierut régime would simply continue to extend their control. And furthermore, the Soviet unilateral acts of handing over part of its zone of occupation in Germany to the Bierut Government and of signing a formal treaty with it, had gone unchallenged in the discussions.

As a result of this Stalin–Hopkins agreement, a new Polish Government, which included representatives of the London Poles as well as of Bierut's group, was formed and received British and American recognition on 5 July. It was of but brief duration.

On one point Stalin remained adamant – he would not release the sixteen leaders of the Polish Home Front arrested in March by the Soviet military authorities in Warsaw.* All that he would concede was the principle of a fair trial and lenient sentences. In effect, General Okulicki was sentenced to ten years' imprisonment and died in captivity, and only two of the original sixteen succeeded in escaping from Poland to the West.

Nevertheless Hopkins's mission was hailed as a spectacular success by Averell Harriman in his telegram to the President on 8 June and he himself was greeted as a diplomatic victor on his return to Washington. Less than a year later he was dead.†

Thus was the way cleared for the meeting of the Big Three. Though Mr Churchill, once Stalin's acceptance in principle had been obtained, strained every effort to arrange the meeting in June or early July, he was obstructed by both the President and by Stalin and it was not until 15 July that the leaders of the Grand Alliance began to gather in Potsdam.

---

* See above, pp. 288–9.

† Harry Hopkins was admitted to the New York Memorial Hospital in November 1945 and died there on 29 January 1946.

15 | San Francisco and Potsdam

BEFORE the three major Allies came together for what proved to be their final conclave at Potsdam, their deputies, Messrs Eden, Molotov and Stettinius, had an opportunity to exchange views in the United States. The occasion for these contacts was the United Nations Conference held at San Francisco.* Stalin's willingness to accept United States proposals about this conference, and to concede some ground on the issue of U.N. voting procedures, had been a source of great satisfaction to the Americans at Yalta.† But in the increasingly gloomy atmosphere of Western–Soviet relations which followed the Crimean Conference, doubts appeared about the whole-heartedness of Soviet participation in the United Nations Organization. In March 1945 negotiations over Poland were deadlocked, Soviet intervention in Rumania's domestic affairs had become quite blatant and Russian pressure on Turkey had added a new and unwelcome factor to the politics of the Eastern Mediterranean.‡ It was also announced that M. Molotov would not attend the proposed U.N. Conference at San Francisco, even though both his Western colleagues were clearly pledged to do so.

It was when faced with this deterioration in relations with the Soviet Union that Mr Eden wrote in his diary on 23 March: 'Altogether our foreign policy seems a sad wreck and we may have to cast about afresh.'[1] The road to post-war inter-Allied understanding had always been stony. It now seemed to be running into impassable obstacles.

The death of President Roosevelt served, in one sense at least, to bring the Eastern and Western halves of the Alliance momentarily closer together. When news of this event was brought to Stalin he asked Ambassador Harriman what step the Russians might take to cement American friendship at such a moment of stress. Acting on his own initiative, Mr Harriman suggested that M. Molotov's presence at San Francisco would be greatly appreciated as a gesture of goodwill and as an aid to the success of the U.N. Conference. Stalin, who never allowed

* See below, p. 544.   † See above, pp. 241–2.   ‡ See below, pp. 557 ff.

himself to be inhibited by respect for his Foreign Minister's *amour-propre*, promptly agreed. Thus it was that on 22 April 1945, ten days after taking up his unexpected responsibilities as President of the United States, Mr Truman found himself face to face not only with Mr Eden, whom the British Prime Minister had already sent to represent him at President Roosevelt's funeral, but also with the redoubtable M. Molotov, whose toughness and skill as a negotiator had impressed friend and foe alike.

At the time of the Soviet Foreign Minister's arrival relations with the Soviet Union were clouded by a number of issues, of which the Polish problem seemed the most serious.* Despite firmly worded representations from the President and Mr Churchill, Stalin had gone ahead with his plan to conclude an alliance with the provisional Polish Government, whose composition was the subject of such wearisome wrangling between the Allied Powers. The alliance had actually been signed on 21 April, the day before M. Molotov arrived in Washington. It was an act denounced by the British Foreign Office as totally incompatible with the spirit of the Yalta Declaration. Messrs Stettinius,† Harriman and Byrnes, with all of whom Mr Eden had been in consultation since his own arrival in Washington on 14 April, entirely agreed with this viewpoint, and President Truman accepted the need for a firm stand on the Polish issue.[3]

He did not wish to raise contentious questions during his first meeting with the Soviet Foreign Minister, but reiterated his desire to stand by the commitments agreed upon by President Roosevelt. When M. Molotov mentioned the Yalta agreements, however, the President promptly stressed the urgency of a solution to the Polish problem because of its effect on American public opinion.[4] The tone of this first confrontation was friendly, but M. Molotov proved much less amiable when, shortly afterwards, he and the British Foreign Secretary were present at a discussion in the State Department. The Russian's attitude over Poland was entirely negative and his temper was probably not improved by the realization that Mr Stettinius was acting in close harmony with Anthony Eden. M. Molotov particularly depressed his listeners by affecting not to know the contents of a joint message about Poland sent by President Truman and Mr Churchill to Stalin on 15

---

* See above, pp. 288–9.

† Secretary Stettinius's position had been called in question by the change in the Presidency, although Mr Truman had asked him to stay on at least until after the San Francisco Conference. Mr Eden was sorry to contemplate the Secretary's retirement, doubtless because he had established such a powerful influence over his intellectually lightweight colleague. As he wrote of Mr Stettinius at the time, 'He is not brilliant, but he is a good friend of our country and easy to work with'. It was a somewhat ambiguous compliment.[2]

April.[5] He also demanded that the Warsaw Government should be offered a seat on the U.N. Organization at the San Francisco Conference. This would have precluded any further Western attempts to change the character of that Government, and was obviously unacceptable.

The President himself was furious at M. Molotov's demands. On 23 April he told a gathering of his advisers – who included Messrs Stettinius, Stimson, Leahy, Marshall, King and Harriman* – that American agreements with the Soviet Union 'had so far been a one-way street and this could not continue'.[7]

The Secretary of State and Ambassador Harriman joined with the Secretary of the Navy, Forrestal, in urging a confrontation with the Russians over Poland, even if this meant M. Molotov's withdrawal from the San Francisco Conference. Secretary of War Stimson and General Marshall were far more cautious. For them Soviet military co-operation had proved itself in action, and the need for Soviet help in the Far East seemed as great as ever if countless American lives were not to be sacrificed in long campaigns against the Japanese.† General Marshall and Mr Stimson were, in any case, not very interested in Polish politics, the latter remarking that his experiences in Nicaragua had taught him to expect the ruling party in such places to win elections.

Perhaps more interesting were the comments of Admiral Leahy, who had attended the Yalta Conference as President Roosevelt's closest political adviser. He remarked that 'he had left Yalta with the impression that the Soviet Government had no intention of permitting a free government to operate in Poland and that he would have been surprised had the Soviet Government behaved any differently than it had'. He also shocked Mr Stettinius by claiming that the Yalta Agreement on Poland was capable of two interpretations – a claim firmly denied by the Secretary of State.[8]

Admiral Leahy was faithfully representing the isolationist view of European affairs which had undoubtedly played a part in shaping American policy at Yalta. He knew that President Roosevelt had not given high priority to Polish independence as an Allied objective and had set greater store by post-war collaboration with the Russians. In the

---

* It was typical of the change in political style of the Truman Administration that the President discussed important matters formally with his senior departmental heads and military chiefs, and kept them informed of events in the diplomatic field. President Roosevelt had not done this. One result of the change was to make the advice of the State Department weigh more heavily in decision-making. Informal arrangements of the kind Roosevelt had preferred tended to undermine collective wisdom. It is interesting that, when Harry Hopkins went to Moscow towards the end of May 1945, it was alleged that his reports were not referred to other senior members of the Administration. Secretary Forrestal complained to Mr McCloy that this was Hopkins's own doing and that it marked a relapse into old, bad methods.[6]

† See below, pp. 356–8.

months which had followed the Crimean Conference, however, irritation at Soviet pin-pricks and abhorrence of the methods adopted by Soviet occupation authorities in parts of Eastern Europe had created a changed atmosphere. As a result American leaders – and especially the new President – were more inclined to give weight to the advice of those who, like Ambassador Harriman, were dealing with the Russians professionally and expressing warnings about their policy.

The problem which faced President Truman, however, was not simply one of whether to be 'hard' or 'soft' with the Russians over Poland. There was also the question of relative priorities. Mr Stettinius – though he agreed with Ambassador Harriman's gloomy analysis of Soviet policies in Eastern Europe – seems to have been chiefly worried that M. Molotov's intransigence might threaten the success of the San Francisco Conference. The failure of that conference would jeopardize the future of the U.N. Organization, that international Eldorado which had been sought so hard by the State Department throughout the war. For Secretary Stimson, on the other hand, the U.N. had a very much lower priority. He thought it absurd to weaken the victorious American–Soviet alliance just to win public acclaim at San Francisco. As he recorded in his diary:

> Contrary to what I thought was a wise course, they [the State Department] have not settled the problems that lie between the U.S. and Russia and Great Britain and France, the main powers, by wise negotiations before this public meeting in San Francisco, but they have gone ahead and called this great public meeting of all the United Nations and have got public opinion all churned up over it and now they feel compelled to bull the thing through. . . .[9]

This was, of course, an easy and perhaps justified criticism to make. It was less easy to envisage what negotiations, however wise, could have settled inter-Allied problems in the spring of 1945.

There was, therefore, considerable confusion of purpose among President Truman's advisers, but they seemed generally in agreement that firmness towards the Russians would be a good thing, even if they were by no means clear what they should be firm about.

President Truman himself needed no special encouragement to take a stern tone with M. Molotov. He had never been a man to mince words and he did not intend to change his character as chief executive.

Later that same day there occurred the now famous interview between the President and the Soviet Foreign Minister in which the latter experienced what may well have been the most uncomfortable few minutes of his diplomatic career. The President flatly stated his dissatisfaction over the lack of progress in broadening the provisional Polish

Government, and immediately linked Poland to the prospect of American economic aid for Russia after the war. President Roosevelt had earlier pointed out to Stalin that no policy could succeed in the United States unless it had public support. This applied, said President Truman, 'in the field of economic as well as political collaboration'. He went on to remark that 'legislative appropriations [are] required for any economic measures in the foreign field, and I [have] no hope of getting such measures through Congress unless there [is] public support for them'. To M. Molotov's pleas that the Soviet Government stood by the Crimean decisions and was confident that all difficulties would be overcome, the President reiterated that an agreement had been reached over Poland and 'there [is] only one thing to do and that [is] for Marshal Stalin to carry out that agreement in accordance with his word'.[10] The United States wanted friendship with Russia but not 'on the basis of a one-way street'. This was too much for M. Molotov. 'I have never been talked to like that in my life', he expostulated. 'Carry out your agreements and you won't get talked to like that', was the reply. It was hardly a cordial note on which to end an interview, but nobody could complain that the President had been ambiguous or dissembling with his difficult ally.

His bluntness could not, however, save Poland from Stalin. It was too late for that. The Yalta agreements over Poland were too unrealistic to be taken seriously even if the Soviet Government had ever had any intention of diluting its control over that country.* The question at issue was really how far Stalin was prepared to make even token concessions to the Western viewpoint so that the façade of inter-Allied unity could be maintained throughout the period of German surrender, Japanese defeat and the establishment of the United Nations.

During the San Francisco Conference, which followed M. Molotov's abrasive session with the President, the United States delegation was in some confusion about its attitude towards the Soviet representatives. It was not entirely clear whether its aim should be to use American consent for Soviet desires at the conference as a lever for obtaining concessions for Poland, or whether the success of American plans for the U.N. should be given the highest priority. Mr Eden would doubtless have preferred the former, but not even Mr Harriman on the American side could bring himself to advise any steps which might make M. Molotov leave the conference except on a matter which could be grasped by all as a cardinal issue of principle.[11] As it was, the Russians embarrassed their American hosts by demanding that the Polish Government be elected to the U.N., whilst opposing the election of Argentina – whose candidacy

---

* See above, pp. 238–9.

was warmly supported by the Latin American countries. It was indeed awkward for the Americans to have to support the Argentine, a country with obviously pro-German sympathies which had earned the hearty dislike of Allied leaders during the war. President Truman himself was among those who regarded its Government with contempt. Nevertheless, American interests in the Latin American hemisphere and the need to keep the large bloc of Latin American votes in line at San Francisco made it necessary for the United States to vote for Argentine admission to the U.N. It was not an edifying spectacle and the Russians made the most of it, despite the fact that Latin American co-operation had been essential to seat the two dubious-looking Soviet *protégés*, the Ukraine and White Russia.*

The arguments about Polish admission to the U.N. and M. Molotov's behaviour over this at San Francisco made it apparent that there was very little to hope for in this sphere of inter-Allied relations. It was not until Mr Hopkins's mission to Moscow, from 26 May to 6 June 1945,† that any further progress – if such it could be called – was made on the Polish question. At his first meeting with Stalin Mr Hopkins laid great stress on the importance of this issue for American public opinion and for the future of Soviet–American relations. He strongly denied any intention of using Poland to re-establish a *cordon sanitaire* around the borders of Russia – a desire which Stalin attributed to 'British Conservatives' who did not want to see Poland friendly to the Soviet Union.[12]

Nevertheless, Hopkins hammered home the American belief that a solution to the Polish problem had to be worked out between the Allied Powers and that there must be free elections in Poland. Stalin must have considered this to be an almost farcical suggestion, but he smoothly replied that there was no question of Sovietizing Poland, which would live under the parliamentary system 'like Czechoslovakia, Belgium and Holland'.[13] However, he did agree that four posts in the Polish Government might be given to suitable men proposed by the Western Powers, and indicated that these could include M. Mikolajczyk, who had been persuaded by Mr Churchill to agree to the Curzon Line as Poland's eastern frontier. Since M. Mikolajczyk had been accepted by Stalin as long ago as 25 April, there was nothing very new in this statement.[14] Nevertheless it was the extent of Russian concessions. Mr Hopkins was, for example, unable to obtain the release – or even the rapid trial – of the Polish resistance leaders seized by the Soviet authorities.‡

At his last meeting with Stalin, Harry Hopkins attempted to clarify the American position over Poland by lecturing his Soviet host on the

---

* For the founding of the United Nations, see below, pp. 528–53.
† See above, pp. 305–7.   ‡ See above, p. 307.

nature of democracy. This entailed, he said, free speech, freedom of expression for political parties and the rights of public trial and habeas corpus. A lesser negotiator than Stalin might have shown signs of irritation at such forthright language, but the Russian contented himself by remarking that the principles of democracy were well known and would find no objection from the Soviet Government.[15] By referring to the danger of Fascism and the question of military security, he effectively blocked Mr Hopkins's idealized demands, which did indeed bear little relationship to conditions in Poland. Messrs Hopkins and Harriman went away feeling that something had been achieved, and if the intention had been to work out a face-saving formula over Poland – which was probably true so far as Mr Hopkins was concerned – then some results did emerge. Shortly afterwards M. Mikolajczyk went to Moscow, and on 21 June an agreement was reached there over the composition of a Polish National Council. Its Presidium would be headed by M. Bierut, but it would include two non-Communist Polish leaders, Wincenty Witos and Stanislas Grabski. A Government was established on the twenty-eighth with three Poles from abroad among its twenty Ministers. These included M. Mikolajczyk. Such measures could not prevent the consolidation of Soviet influence throughout the country. They did, however, enable the British and Americans to recognize the new régime and thus eliminate this particular diplomatic difficulty before the Big Three met at Potsdam.

II

Poland was probably a lost cause from the Western viewpoint by the beginning of 1945. This was due mainly to the presence of the Red Army, although due regard has to be paid to the state of Polish politics both before and during the war. The same could not be said about Czechoslovakia. It was during the period of the San Francisco Conference that crucial decisions were taken affecting the fate of that country. Czechoslovakia had not played the central role in Allied war-time diplomacy occupied by Poland. At first sight this was curious, since the Czechoslovak state had been the most successful experiment in parliamentary democracy in Central Europe between the wars, and throughout its short life it had been the corner-stone of the post-Habsburg peace settlement in the Danube Basin. Only its betrayal by the Western Powers at Munich in September 1938 had delivered the country up to Hitler and destroyed its political freedom.

During the war Czech soldiers and airmen had fought alongside the British, although they were naturally fewer in number than the Poles. A provisional Czechoslovak Government existed in London, headed by

President Beneš and with Jan Masaryk as Foreign Minister, and in December 1943 it prudently concluded a treaty of mutual assistance and guarantee with the Soviet Union. Hence the Czechs had apparently secured themselves against the vicissitudes of war-time politics so long as the Germans could be driven from their country. It was still curious, however, that neither the British nor the Americans seem to have devoted a great deal of attention to Czechoslovakia in their plans for the liberation of Europe. President Beneš's very success in negotiating with the Russians may have damaged his own cause in this respect, for the Czechs always seem to have been suspected of pro-Soviet sympathies, and they never managed to attract the same emotional commitment in London or Washington which was aroused by the more flamboyant – if politically less mature – Polish exiles.

One reason for this was the awkward fact that in 1939 Poland had been invaded not only by Germany but also by the Soviet Union. The frontiers of that country had thereafter provided an extremely difficult problem for inter-Allied diplomacy. The same was not true of Czechoslovakia, although the Russians were known to be interested in the province of Ruthenia, situated at the eastern extremity of the country. But the future of Czechoslovakia as an independent state, and the procedure by which it was to be liberated by the Allies, had not been a serious issue for discussion at the meetings of the Big Three.

The Czechs made their own preparations for the liberation of their country when, on 8 May 1944, they signed a civil affairs agreement with the Soviet Government, allowing Czech authorities to take over the administration of liberated territory as soon as military circumstances permitted. At this time it was assumed that the Red Army would be first into Czechoslovakia, and no such agreement was concluded with the Western Powers. One factor which seemed likely to cement Czech–Soviet co-operation was the Czechs' desire to expel the German minorities from their country. This was understandable in view of the excuse which that minority had provided for Hitlerite aggression. Nevertheless the Western Powers were more likely to feel scruples about this than the Russians, for whom population transfers were nothing new and who themselves envisaged removing the Germans from regions of the German Reich east of the Oder–Neisse line.

Towards the end of March 1945 Dr Beneš went to Moscow to negotiate the return of his Government to those parts of Czechoslovakia liberated by the Red Army. Stalin went out of his way to be gracious to the Czech President. He gave a dinner in the Kremlin at which he denied the intention of pursuing the old Tsarist policy of Pan-Slavism. Nor, he said, was there any desire to Bolshevize Europe, despite some suspicions on this subject. Stalin also told Dr Beneš privately that Czech Communists who had spent the war in Moscow were 'good, patriotic men but wore "blinkers"', and he suggested that Dr Beneš should undertake 'to broaden their outlook'.[16]

This masterly piece of hypocrisy did not entirely erase President Beneš's anxiety about Soviet influence in his country. Negotiations between the Communists and the parties involved in the London Government culminated in the formation of a new Cabinet headed by Zdenek Fierlinger, the Czech Ambassador to Moscow. M. Fierlinger was described by George Kennan in the American Embassy as 'to all intents and purposes a Soviet agent',[17] and there was no doubt where his sympathies lay. Indeed, Stalin made a show of regret to Dr Beneš about the choice of Premier, saying that it might seem – erroneously of course – to indicate a Soviet intention to influence the internal affairs of Czecho-slovakia.[18]

Stalin's avowal of disinterest hardly seemed convincing when set against the composition of the new Czechoslovakia Ministry or the behaviour of Soviet occupation forces in Czechoslovakia. When the régime was finalized there were six known Communists among the twenty Ministers – a high proportion in relation to the pre-war voting strength of the Czech Communist Party. More important was the nature of the posts they held. Two were Deputy Premiers, one the Minister of the Interior and another Minister of Information.* In addition three important 'non-party' Ministers were described by the American Embassy in Moscow as being 'thoroughly Sovietized'. These were Prime Minister Fierlinger himself, Defence Minister General Ludvik Svoboda† and Minister of Education Zdenek Nejedly.

The Communists also made much of Soviet control in Slovakia. A Slovak National Council had been established headed by a Communist called Gustav Husak,‡ and in April this was given control over civilian affairs throughout the Slovakian region. Dr Beneš and his Government had moved to Košice in eastern Slovakia, but despite his own expressed desires and strong pressure from the Western Powers neither Britain nor American diplomats were allowed access to him. It was not until the end of May – by which time the war had been over several weeks and the Czech Government had re-established itself in Prague – that Western diplomats were allowed access to the Czechs.

Meanwhile military decisions had been taken which surrendered

---

* The others were the Ministers of Labour and Agriculture.
† Now President of the Czechoslovak Socialist Republic.
‡ Who became leader of the Czechoslovak Communist Party after the country had been invaded by the forces of the Warsaw Pact in August 1968.

Czechoslovakia to Soviet influence. At the end of April 1945 American forces were advancing very rapidly towards the former German–Czech frontiers of 1937. By 4 May strong American armoured units were within sixty miles of Prague, whereas Soviet forces were still a hundred miles distant. This was a situation which had been foreseen in London and Washington, though different conclusions were drawn from it. As early as 13 April Mr Eden sent a message to Ambassador Winant urging the Americans to liberate Prague before the Red Army got there. The message was only slowly relayed to Washington, and at San Francisco on 28 April Mr Eden took the matter up personally with Mr Stettinius. He gave the American Secretary of State a memorandum in which he pointed out that Czech politicians in London were delighted with the arrival of American soldiers in their country and that the Communists 'were correspondingly depressed'. He went on:

> In our view the liberation of Prague and as much as possible of the territory of western Czechoslovakia by United States troops might make the whole difference to the post-war situation in Czechoslovakia and might well influence that in nearby countries. On the other hand, if the western Allies play no significant part in Czechoslovakia's liberation that country may go the way of Yugoslavia.[19]

Mr Churchill, with whom the British Foreign Secretary was in close contact, repeated the same message to President Truman, who was also advised by Mr Stettinius that American forces should press forward into Czechoslovakia with all haste. General Marshall and the U.S. Chiefs of Staff had other ideas. They set their faces firmly against operations conducted with a political rather than a military purpose and were in any case reluctant to take steps which might upset their Soviet allies. On 5 May the Soviet Chief of Staff, General A. I. Antonov, asked General Eisenhower to halt his forces along a line running through Plzen (Pilsen) and Karlovy Vary (Karlsbad) – well to the west of Prague. The Americans duly halted.

It is difficult to estimate what effect an American liberation of Prague would have had. As recorded above, Soviet influence over the Czech authorities was very strong. However, if President Beneš and his colleagues had been able to operate in a capital free from the presence of the Red Army, it would almost certainly have been easier to mobilize support for political groups uncommitted to Moscow. Czechoslovakia was a country with a genuine parliamentary tradition and a relatively well-educated electorate. The fact that in its formative stages after the war the Czech Republic was under Soviet domination played an important part in its descent into satellite status three years later.

General Eisenhower's decision was therefore of considerable importance. General Bedell Smith told Robert Murphy that American forces would have had no difficulty in reaching Prague before the Red Army had they been instructed to do so.[20] That was certainly the view of the hard-bitten Commander of the U.S. armoured forces in the Plzen area, Major-General 'Hell-on-wheels' Ernest N. Harmon. It is difficult, however, not to sympathize with the view expressed at the time by General Marshall that 'I should be loath to hazard American lives for political purposes'.[21] The fact that the German High Command was urging the Americans to advance on Prague could not have made the prospect any more attractive to honourable soldiers who did not wish to betray the trust of their Soviet allies. Above all, there was no clear political directive which bound the military leaders to act.

Although at the time this decision to halt before Prague did not seem too serious, since Czechoslovakia was apparently soon to be independent of all liberators, in retrospect it appears as one of the most tragic errors of American military-political strategy during the post-Roosevelt era. Poland was by this time a lost cause; the occupation arrangements in Germany could hardly be altered;* but no agreements had been made about Czechoslovakia and the ability of the politically sophisticated Czech people to direct their own affairs depended not a little on the nature of the administration imposed upon them by their liberators. As it was, the Communists in Beneš' Government could rely on Soviet support in closing their grip on the Czech security forces and propaganda media, with results which became apparent less than three years later.[22]

III

One other important issue which arose while the San Francisco Conference was in session was that of the future of Lend-Lease, and in particular of its continued application to the Soviet Union. Ambassador Harriman was eager to use the flow of American supplies to Russia as a weapon with which to bring Stalin into a more malleable frame of mind. On 22 March he cabled Secretary Stettinius that to stop shipments of food to the U.S.S.R. would have 'a salutary effect on our relations with the Soviet Government'.[23] As we have already seen, President Truman was well briefed by Mr Harriman on Soviet–American matters, and he seems to have accepted the idea of economic pressure as a possible option to use against Russia. Certainly he gave this impression when berating M. Molotov about Poland.†

The question of aid to the Soviet Union was in any case complicated by the restrictions placed upon the American executive by Lend-Lease

* See above, pp. 275–6.   † See above, p. 312.

legislation. President Truman – as a former Vice-President – was keenly aware of the feelings in Congress about such matters. Lend-Lease supplies could only be provided if they contributed directly to the Allied war effort. Once Germany was defeated, shipments to Russia could only be justified under Lend-Lease if they were designed to help the Soviet build-up against Japan. Yet it was obvious that the Russians were using Lend-Lease programmes to construct industrial plant which could hardly come into operation in time to affect the war. This was understandable in view of the economic distress suffered by the Soviet Union during the war. It had been assumed in both Washington and Moscow that some sort of arrangement would be made to continue American supplies to Russia after the war was over. The difficulty arose over the method by which they were to be financed.

As early as May 1944 the Americans had made proposals for an agreement under which the Soviet Union might receive supplies on credit from the United States once Lend-Lease ended, but no arrangements about payment were ever concluded. Instead the Soviet Government put forward ambitious claims for long-term post-war credits totalling $6,000 million on very favourable terms of interest. Mr Harriman had been scandalized by these proposals and thought they reflected the Armenian background of the chief Soviet negotiator, Anastas Mikoyan.[24] Although the Secretary of the Treasury, Henry Morgenthau, favoured a generous credit settlement with the Soviet Union, the State Department resisted him and no firm decision was taken before President Roosevelt died.

During the spring of 1945 the problem became acute, since with the end of the war in Germany the legal basis for most Lend-Lease shipments to Russia would be undermined. The officials directly connected with Lend-Lease were clearly irritated by Soviet unwillingness to come to terms over the post-war credit problem, as well as by some unauthorized transfers of Lend-Lease equipment to other countries – especially Poland.[25] This coincided with a growing tension in Soviet–American relations and a not unnatural tendency to exploit American economic power for diplomatic advantage.

Nevertheless, it was not as the result of any clear-cut policy decision to squeeze the Russians that the State Department and the Lend-Lease administrators agreed that shipments to the Soviet Union should be suspended. Rather it seems to have been an action designed to meet a particular problem but sanctioned the more readily in view of existing difficulties with the U.S.S.R. It certainly proved to be one of President Truman's less happy executive decisions.

Early in May a memorandum had been drawn up by the State

Department and Lend-Lease administrators urging the immediate adjustment of Lend-Lease to the U.S.S.R. following the end of hostilities in Europe. Supplies needed to complete industrial plant under construction should be continued, but all other deliveries were to be cut off and shipping diverted to countries in Western Europe with which arrangements for post-war aid had been agreed upon. The Assistant Secretary of State for Economic Affairs, William L. Clayton, and the Foreign Economic Administrator, Leo T. Crowley, were very eager that this policy should be implemented with firmness and dispatch. For this reason they were determined that it should receive the personal support of the President. As Mr Crowley put it in a telephone conversation with the State Department:

> ... he wanted to be sure that the President thoroughly understands the situation and that he will back us up and keep everybody else out of it ... he [Crowley] would be having difficulty with the Russians and he did not want them to be running all over town looking for help.[26]

The memorandum was presented to the President on 11 May by Messrs Crowley, Clayton and the Acting Secretary of State, Joseph C. Grew. President Truman himself claims that he listened to their arguments but never bothered to read the memorandum and simply signed a note authorizing action.[27] The Lend-Lease authorities promptly suspended shipments to Russia and even ordered some ships in transit to return to the United States. Russia was not the only country to suffer by this abrupt action, but her Government not unnaturally drew the worst conclusions from it.

President Truman quickly regretted the step he had taken and tried to rectify it. On 23 May he explained that what was intended was not so much a cancellation as a gradual adjustment.[28] It seems possible that the President was impressed by Mr Crowley's arguments without realizing exactly in what form he proposed to implement his action.

Whatever the reason for the sudden interruption in Lend-Lease, its results were most unfortunate from the point of view of inter-Allied amity, which was already under strain. The Soviet Government immediately reproached the Americans with an act of bad faith, and President Truman's withdrawal of his order merely gave an impression of indecision and divided counsels. When Mr Hopkins went to Moscow at the end of May he was forced to blame the affair on a subordinate agency – a difficult excuse for what had clearly been a high-level decision. He stressed to Stalin that there was no intention on the American side to use Lend-Lease as a 'pressure weapon'. 'The United States', he said, 'is a strong and free power and does not go in for these methods'.[29]

Mr Hopkins was almost certainly sincere in this statement, but elsewhere in the United States Administration the idea clearly existed that a tough line on Lend-Lease would teach the Russians a salutary lesson. This was almost certainly mistaken. The Soviet Government did not need American aid so desperately that it could be deflected from its policies in order to obtain it. The pin-prick of curtailed shipments fitted in well with Russian views about the nature of capitalist Governments and the sort of response they might offer to Soviet pressure. It was not a response likely to worry Stalin.

The whole incident put the United States Government in a weaker position than it might otherwise have occupied in the more serious argument over post-war credit arrangements with Russia. During the months which followed, Washington and Moscow became embroiled in a bickering dispute about this problem, in which recriminations over the cancellation of Lend-Lease played their part.[30]

IV

By now the time had come for a renewed confrontation between the leaders of the three major Allies. The military problem in Europe had been temporarily solved, but the civilian problems connected with liberation and conquest were proving very damaging to inter-Allied solidarity. Former conferences had been mainly concerned to further the war effort; the next one was to pave the way for peace. At Yalta the final toast had been to a victorious meeting in Berlin. Berlin lay in ruins, but the site chosen for the next conference was not far distant. It was the summer residence of the Hohenzollern monarchy in the days of the German Empire – Potsdam. A garrison town since the days of the Great Elector, Potsdam had been elevated to glory by Frederick the Great, who had endowed it with many fine buildings, including the famous rococo palace of Sonssouci. The city had been severely damaged by bombing but was not in a state of such total devastation as Berlin. All things considered, it was a very suitable meeting-place.

The Potsdam Conference differed in several ways from those at Tehran and Yalta. In the first place the purpose of the war-time Alliance, the military defeat of Germany, had been achieved. Although Japan still remained in arms against Britain and the United States, Russia was not at war with her when the conference convened but had pledged herself to enter the Pacific War shortly.* Military planning for Soviet participation in the Far Eastern conflict did of course take place at Potsdam, and the American delegation regarded the confirmation of such participation

* See below, p. 358.

as a primary objective of the conference. Nevertheless, the pressing needs of war were not felt so strongly at Potsdam as at earlier Allied meetings. Stalin told Harry Hopkins on 26 May 1945 that the purpose of the discussions at Potsdam would be to pave the way for a peace conference. It was therefore the divisive issues of post-war politics rather than the cohesive designs of war which set the tone of discussions at Potsdam.

It was also clear that since the Crimean Conference shifts had occurred in the attitudes and objectives of the various delegates, particularly on the Western side. At Tehran and Yalta President Roosevelt had tried to win Stalin's confidence by implying that the United States and the U.S.S.R. had more in common with each other than with the British. By the opening of the Potsdam Conference possible friction between Great Britain and the United States was receding in importance. At San Francisco it had been the Soviet delegation which had proved most obstructive, whereas Anglo-American collaboration had on the whole been smooth. The question of trustee-ships which had so disturbed Mr Churchill at Yalta* had not led to a major confrontation over colonialism. At the same time there appeared a sudden flush of alarm in some sections of the American leadership about Soviet policies – an alarm which sometimes seemed to verge on para-noia.† At the root of this anxiety lay events in Eastern Europe. President Roosevelt's assumption that Soviet aims in Eastern Europe need have no damaging impact on American–Soviet relations elsewhere was proved to be mistaken.

There was still confidence in the Russians in the military field, where General Marshall and his colleagues were rightly satisfied with the enormous contribution to the defeat of Nazism made by the Red Army, and were eager to ensure that Soviet forces played their full part in defeating Japan. In this there was little difference of opinion between the British and American delegations. Nor did the status of China provide any stumbling-block to Anglo-American relations as it had at Cairo and Tehran, for example. The Americans had become seriously disillusioned with their Chinese ally, especially after his poor showing in the war. They still hoped that the Chinese would play an important role in the Far East once Japan was beaten, but they were less inclined to damage relations with France and Britain in order to please Chiang Kai-shek. The future of Hong Kong, for example, was not an issue raised at Potsdam.

* See above, pp. 247–8.

† Secretary of the Navy Forrestal, for example, was very concerned over reports of Soviet espionage activity in Mexico, and Mr Harriman was in the United States hammering home the message that Russia was not to be trusted.[31] (See above, p. 301 n.)

It was true that President Truman had angered the British by his attempts to hold a private meeting with Stalin before important discussions began, and that the usual British efforts to obtain a preliminary Anglo-American meeting were unsuccessful.* There was to be no equivalent of First Cairo or Malta. This may have weakened the Western delegations vis-à-vis Stalin on matters about which they wished to present a united front, but on the whole it was probably fortunate that, in the phrase favoured by the Americans, the Russians could not claim that their allies were 'ganging up' on them before the meeting. As it was, a full exchange of views took place in Potsdam between representatives of the British Foreign Office and the American State Department on 14 July 1945, the day before the conference was due to open.[32]† The Americans had also circulated their proposed agenda to both their allies well in advance of the first meeting.

So far as the composition of the Western Allied delegations was concerned, the situation had also changed considerably from that at the Crimean Conference. The most obvious contrast was in the leadership of the American contingent, where the inexperienced but energetic and businesslike figure of Harry S. Truman had replaced President Roosevelt. At Yalta Roosevelt had certainly not been in good physical shape, however exaggerated later reports of his feeble appearance may have been.‡ President Truman, on the other hand, was certainly the fittest of all the Big Three at Potsdam, and his capacity to master a brief was demonstrated beyond doubt. His party left the United States aboard the cruiser *Augusta* on 7 July and spent over eight days at sea before docking at Antwerp. During that period he had intensive discussions with Admiral Leahy and the new Secretary of State, James F. Byrnes, who had succeeded Mr Stettinius on 3 July. The President was more inclined to give weight to expert advice from the State Department than his predecessor had been. It followed that the Secretary of State became more important in his system of government. This was one reason why he decided to drop the photogenic but not especially gifted Edward Stettinus.§ Mr Byrnes – who was present at the Yalta Conference – had been a very successful Director of the Office of War Mobilization and was a man of considerable political skill. Unlike Mr Stettinius, however, he was less likely to follow the path set out for

* See above, pp. 301–2.

† The officials concerned were Sir Alexander Cadogan and Joseph Dunn. In fact Stalin's late arrival delayed the conference.

‡ See above, pp. 220–1.

§ Another reason may well have been President Truman's possible apprehension lest, in the event of his own death, the United States should be saddled with President Ed. Stettinius, Jr. At that time the Secretary of State was the next in line for the Presidency should the President die without a Vice-President to succeed him.

him by strong-minded advisers or persuasive allies – such as Anthony
Eden. He was not possessed of any very clear conceptions about international politics, although he was determined to protect American
interests from rapacious foreigners. In negotiation he tended to be
devious and to rely on his ability 'to play it by ear'. The results were not
always entirely happy.

Nevertheless, there was no doubt that by the time the American
party on the *Augusta* reached Europe it had thoroughly covered the
issues it expected to deal with at Potsdam. The party President Truman
headed at the conference was probably better prepared for its task than
any of those headed by President Roosevelt.

On the British side the situation was in some ways less satisfactory
than at Tehran or Yalta. The timing of the Potsdam meeting meant that
it followed quickly on the British General Election, voting in which
took place on 5 July 1945. The British Coalition Government had
broken up, and in its place there was a 'caretaker' Conservative Ministry
waiting to know its fate at the hands of the electorate. Owing to the
amount of time needed to count the votes of servicemen in various
theatres of war, the results of the election would not be known until
26 July. Needless to say, this encouraged an atmosphere of uncertainty
in the British delegation, an uncertainty which deepened as doubts about
the result seeped into the initially confident entourage of the Prime
Minister. So that there should be continuity in British foreign policy
if the Conservatives were defeated, Clement Attlee accompanied the
British delegation to the conference. But Mr Churchill fully expected
to see the discussions at Potsdam through to the end because, even if the
electorate rejected him, he was not expecting to have to give up his post
until Parliament reassembled.[33]

The Prime Minister himself was not quite on the top of his form at
Potsdam. The physical strain of his office was beginning to tell on him.
As we have seen,* he was emotionally burdened by his fear of Communist expansion in Europe as well as by the realization that Britain
could no longer hold her place in the front rank of World Powers.
Furthermore he had devoted a great deal of energy to a rumbustious
election campaign which had included a 'victory drive' through Britain.
Exhausted after these domestic preoccupations he repaired to Biarritz,
where he attempted to forget his electoral worries, but he does not seem
to have applied himself very intensively to the problems of the forthcoming conference.[34] When he began work at Potsdam some of his
assistants described him as seeming poorly briefed, tired and inclined to
procrastinate.[35] Often he would make long speeches setting out the

* See above, pp. 289–96.

British position on a particular point and then finish by accepting Soviet and American proposals. Stalin twitted him on this, saying 'Why don't you agree? The Americans agree and we agree. You will eventually, so why don't you do it now?'[36] President Truman thought that the Prime Minister's purpose was to state Britain's argument for the record in case of dispute later, but such long-windedness irritated the President, who wanted decisions rather than discussion. It should not be thought, however, that Mr Churchill was a spent force at Potsdam; his speeches were often powerful and he impressed his new American colleague in a favourable way. Neither the Americans nor the Russians seem to have thought that the Conservatives would lose the British elections. Nevertheless, Potsdam was not Mr Churchill's best conference.

His Foreign Secretary was also feeling jaded and depressed. Mr Eden found electioneering much less to his taste than did his chief. In any case he had been laid low for most of June by an internal ulcer. When he resumed Foreign Office work at the end of that month he was, as he himself put it, 'haggard in fact as well as looks'. On 5 July he noted in his diary: 'Am beginning seriously to doubt whether I can take on F.O. work again. It is not the work itself, which I could handle, but racket with Winston at all hours. . . .'[37]

The Soviet delegation at Potsdam presented its usual well-drilled exterior, but even here there were problems. Stalin's arrival was delayed for medical reasons – it later transpired that he had suffered a slight heart attack. This did not prevent the Marshal from giving his usual masterly performance at the conference table, and M. Molotov, as well briefed as ever, was always ready to split hairs on the wording of any document which did not please him.

Stalin's position was indeed a strong one at Potsdam, even if his policies in the preceding months had aroused hostility in the West. At the time of the conference no Soviet troops were in action anywhere, and the Soviet Union had apparently defeated all its enemies. Anglo-American forces, on the other hand, were still deeply committed in the Far East and their troops were being rapidly redeployed into that theatre. Stalin had established his position in Eastern Europe and had prevented Western interference in Soviet policies towards Bulgaria, Finland, Hungary and Rumania. The Yugoslav Government seemed entirely under his influence. His designs were going forward well in Czechoslovakia. The Western Powers had finally recognized his favoured régime in Warsaw, albeit with some face-saving adjustments. The Russians wanted to use the Potsdam Conference to ensure the final liquidation of the former Polish régime in London, from which the British Government had already withdrawn recognition. Otherwise they needed to do little about Poland; it was less of an embarrassment than at Yalta.

There was, however, the question of Germany – now occupied according to the zonal arrangements worked out in E.A.C.* The Russians wanted to establish occupation arrangements which would ensure them the largest possible amount of reparations, maximum freedom of action in their own occupation zone and maximum political influence in Germany as a whole. At the same time – and this was a very contentious question – they wished the conference to recognize their transfer of territory up to the line of the Oder and the Western Neisse rivers from Germany to Poland. This meant not only that the western frontier of Poland – left open at Yalta – should be recognized along lines which were extravagantly generous to Poland, but also that the area of occupied Germany should be at once diminished, and in such a way that it lost important food- and coal-producing areas. The strength of the Russians' position here was once again their opportunity to present the Western Powers with a *fait accompli*. If no positive steps were taken by the conference, the Oder–Neisse territories would be administered by the Poles.

In other spheres Stalin had ambitions which were less easily accomplished without at least the connivance of the Western Powers. These could perhaps be lumped together as part of a 'warm water' complex which Stalin seems to have shared with the Tsars.† They included penetration of, and influence over, Manchuria, the furtherance of territorial demands on Persia and Turkey and revision of the Montreux Convention affecting the passage of naval vessels from the Mediterranean into the Black Sea. Involved in the latter ambition was the intention of establishing a Soviet naval base on the Straits. The Soviet Government was also determined to claim one-third of the German merchant and naval fleets – most of which had been captured by the British.

So far as the Western Powers were concerned, they both agreed on a firm line with Russia, but their views differed upon which issues needed the greatest firmness. The American's first concern was to obtain Soviet aid in the Far East without paying Stalin a higher price than he had

---

* See above, pp. 266–84.

† One curious feature of this concern with 'warm water' was Stalin's use of it to justify Soviet annexation of Königsberg in East Prussia. This had been accepted by Stalin's allies at Yalta, but he wanted it confirmed at Potsdam, and stressed that Russia needed it because it was 'ice-free'. This piece of special pleading enraged Mr Kennan at the American Embassy in Moscow, since he was well aware that Königsberg 'lies forty-nine kilometres from the open sea at the end of an artificial canal which is frozen several months of the year'. On the other hand the Baltic Republics – which Stalin had annexed – possessed ice-free ports with better harbours than Königsberg.[38]

already exacted at Yalta. Mr Churchill was less enthusiastic about Soviet participation in the Oriental war, and he certainly urged President Truman to reconsider the Unconditional Surrender formula for Japan if it might shorten the conflict.[39]*

Early in the proceedings at Potsdam the Americans received renewed assurances from the Russians that they were going to take up arms against Japan, and indeed the Americans realized that Stalin was anxious not to be robbed of the gains President Roosevelt had promised him in the Far East. On the other hand the Americans never altered their views on the desirability of Soviet participation in the defeat of Japan. The fact that on 16 July President Truman was brought news of the successful testing of the atomic bomb in New Mexico did not alter American policy in any fundamental way. There were still doubts about the weapon's practical application – Admiral Leahy, for example, was most sceptical – and, even if it were successful operationally, it would be no more devastating than the mass fire-bomb raids already being mounted on Japanese cities.[40] Mr Churchill certainly hoped that possession of the bomb would strengthen the Western position at the conference and reduce the American eagerness to bring Russia into the Pacific theatre.[41] Yet it is difficult to see quite how the bomb could have been used as a diplomatic weapon at the conference, and indeed the Western delegations were considerably embarrassed by the problem of communicating news of it to Stalin without arousing too much Soviet curiosity[42] Eventually, on 24 July 1945, President Truman gave Stalin a brief account of the new weapon. To his relief, and to that of Mr Churchill who was watching, the Russians showed no great interest in this information.† Soviet Intelligence was already well acquainted with the nature of the atomic project; whether Stalin appreciated its massive implications is a matter of doubt.[43]

Over Eastern Europe the Americans were indignant at the non-fulfilment of the Declaration on Liberated Europe, and wanted to make the Allied Control Commissions in Soviet-occupied areas more effective. This applied to former German satellites – Finland, Hungary, Bulgaria and Rumania. The British Foreign Office was at first inclined to give up these states as a bad job and simply conclude peace treaties with their Governments. However, Mr Eden was prepared to support the American proposals on Eastern Europe and felt that American insistence on refusal to recognize satellite régimes was correct.[44] He and his colleagues were also very worried about Soviet pressure on the Eastern Mediterranean, and were not inclined to surrender a large part of the German fleet to the Soviet Union, since this could only strengthen the Russian threat to British interests in the Near East.[45] Mr Eden was especially disquieted to discover that the Russians were adding matters like the international control of Tangier and the situation in Syria and the Lebanon* to the conference agenda, as well as the question of trusteeship over Italian colonies. He saw this as another example of the way in which, 'on any and every point, Russia tries to seize all that she can and she uses these meetings to grab as much as she can get'.[46] He went on to suggest to Mr Churchill that Soviet interest in the Lebanon was the first stage 'to an interest in Egypt, which is quite the last place we want them, particularly since that country with its rich Pashas and its impoverished fellaheen would be a ready prey for communism . . .'.†

President Truman and his colleagues were not so concerned about the Near East as were the British, though the Americans were ready to resist Soviet pressure on Persia and Turkey. They were, however, concerned that peace should be made as quickly as possible with Italy and that she should be admitted to the United Nations. The British Foreign Office accepted the necessity of a peace treaty with Italy,[47] but were not eager to rush things. The interests of Dominion countries had to be consulted and there was a good deal of resentment in Britain – shared by Mr Churchill – about the behaviour of the Italians during the war.

On the whole it is fair to say that Western policies were closer to one another at Potsdam than at earlier meetings, but that there were still important differences of emphasis. In any case, as Mr Eden ruefully admitted, the Western Powers did not have many cards in their hand.[48] Potsdam was not destined to be a very happy conference for them.

V

The British and American leaders reached Potsdam on 15 July. Stalin was prevented by his illness from arriving until two days later. On the whole living conditions were better than at Yalta. The delegations were housed in comfortable villas in Babelsberg, a smart residential area and recreational resort on Lake Grebnitz, some twelve miles out of Berlin. It was a thickly wooded region and made an attractive setting in midsummer, even if mosquitoes tended to be troublesome. The houses assigned to the delegations were large and in good repair, though they had been stripped internally and had to be refurnished by the Russians. The first contact between principals at the conference took place when Mr Churchill visited President Truman on the morning of 16 July. Both men evi-

---

* French attempts to re-establish their political control over this area had led to bloodshed and had forced the British to intervene.

† Stalin mentioned at Potsdam that Russia might be interested in administering Tripoli.

dently formed a good impression of one another, although no serious business was discussed.[49] On the following day Stalin arrived and also visited the President. Messrs Byrnes and Molotov were present, and this in itself was something of a breach with past practice, since President Roosevelt had not been in the habit of meeting Stalin in the presence of his Secretary of State. Stalin was prevailed upon to stay for lunch in the American villa, and the meeting seemed to be a success.* However, it was noticeable that President Truman, whilst trying to make a good impression on his guest, did not seek to imply any common interest which the two countries might share to the exclusion of the British. It was left to Stalin to comment that Britain was unlikely to pursue the war in the Far East very whole-heartedly with Germany beaten, a remark which would have angered the British delegation, and especially Mr Eden, whose son had just been killed flying the supply route into Burma. If the Soviet leader's aim was to play on American anxiety to obtain Soviet aid in the Far East, his gambit misfired. President Truman simply remarked that his country was not in the same dire straits – vis-à-vis Japan – as Britain had been when facing Germany earlier in the war.[50] In general the meeting – which was largely devoted to Far Eastern affairs and Soviet negotiations with China – went off cordially enough, but Stalin must have appreciated the difference in style between his new American partner and President Roosevelt. The fact that Secretary Byrnes had pressed home the point that Russian gains in the Far East were not to be in excess of those agreed at Yalta added to the impression that bargaining with the Americans might have its difficult side.

The formal business of the Potsdam Conference commenced on 17 July. It was conducted in the Cecilienhof Palace, a curious mock-Tudor construction – complete with decorative beams – built for the German Crown Prince Wilhelm during the First World War. Its four wings encased a courtyard or quadrangle in the middle of which the Soviet authorities had thoughtfully planted a large red star of geraniums, roses and hydrangeas. The conference itself was seated at a round table in the palace's former reception room. President Truman, who took the chair, began the proceedings in a businesslike fashion with the American proposals for the conference agenda, which had already been circulated to the other delegations.[51]

The first of these was a scheme for a Council of Foreign Ministers which should prepare peace treaties with the German satellites and eventually with Germany herself.[52] On the whole there was not much objection to this proposal, since all agreed that careful preparation was necessary when drawing up the peace treaties – the difficulties experi-

* See below, pp. 369–70.

enced by the peace-makers in Paris in 1919 were not forgotten. The British were eager to see regular consultative machinery established which might keep an eye on European problems, and although they regretted the demise of E.A.C. – a natural consequence of the American proposal – they hoped that the new body might function as effectively. The Russians also concurred in the plan, although M. Molotov did his best to reduce the role of France* in the new Council.[53] Eventually it was decided that only those members of the Council who had signed the documents of surrender with former enemy states should participate in the preparation of the relevant peace treaties, although special arrangements were made for the French to be consulted on an Italian treaty.[54]

The Americans regarded the Council of Foreign Ministers as a major achievement of the conference, and in theory it made good sense. In practice, however, it was to demonstrate the maxim that institutions are only as useful as the participants wish to make them.†

President Truman's other items for the agenda concerned the administration of Germany, the application of the Declaration on Liberated Europe to Greece, Rumania and Bulgaria, and the question of facilitating peace with Italy.

As has been mentioned above, the British were willing to accept an Italian treaty provided that its terms could be agreed between the Allies and the British Dominion countries. But on 15 July the American Secretary of State had suddenly informed the British Foreign Office that the President would also press for Italian admission to the United Nations. The excuse for this precipitate act was Italy's intended co-belligerency in the war against Japan, although this intention had been known for some weeks. Foreign Office officials in London protested that, with their principals on the way to Potsdam, they could hardly agree to such a suggestion, especially since it would be thought to compromise the terms of the Italian peace settlement. Mr Byrnes promised to postpone this proposal but, not for the last time in his relations with the British Government, failed to keep his promise.[55] When President Truman raised the Italian question on 17 July he proposed that the Allies support Italian membership of the U.N.

Not surprisingly there was an immediate objection from Mr Churchill, who referred to President Roosevelt's 'stab in the back' phrase describing Italian aggression in 1940,‡ as well as to British efforts against Italy in North Africa.

Mr Churchill's outburst was understandable but not entirely well

---

* All three Allies agreed that China would not be involved in discussions not connected with the Far East.

† See below, pp. 420–64.   ‡ See above, p. 32 n.

judged, since it appeared to create a division between the British and the Americans where fundamentally none existed. The British were certainly determined that the Italians should not regain their colonial Empire, but it was in Britain's interest to accept a treaty with Italy and to align her with other Western European nations. The Cabinet in London had already discussed preconditions for such a treaty.[56] Had the Americans co-ordinated their action more effectively with the British delegation and not faced Mr Churchill with an abrupt and unpalatable demand for Italian membership of the U.N., this awkward *contretemps* could have been avoided. As it was, Stalin did not fail to take advantage of the opportunities offered to him. He was able to exploit Mr Churchill's apparently stern views on Italy by presenting himself as a champion of tolerance and reconciliation. He admonished his British colleague that 'it would be incorrect to be guided by injuries or feelings of retribution'.[57] At the same time he linked discussion of Italy with references to the Governments of Bulgaria, Finland, Hungary and Rumania, régimes which might well benefit if Allied policies towards former German satellites followed the pattern foreshadowed in American policy towards Italy.

Hence the Italian question became closely enmeshed with American efforts to implement the Declaration on Liberated Europe, and in particular to ensure Allied access to territories which had formerly been Nazi – and were now rapidly becoming Soviet – satellites. President Truman showed himself a tough negotiator in resisting Stalin's attempts to undermine the American position on this issue. When, for example, on 21 July, Stalin attempted to insert an amendment to American proposals which would have involved recognition of the East European satellite Governments, the President firmly rejected it, saying that 'when these countries [Bulgaria, Finland, Hungary and Rumania] were established on a proper basis, the United States would recognize them and not before'.[58]

He was supported by Mr Churchill, just as Mr Byrnes enjoyed firm backing from the British Foreign Secretary at their daily meetings with M. Molotov. When the latter insisted that the Eastern satellites had done more to help defeat the Germans than Italy, Mr Eden replied that their Governments were not regarded as representative, being 'mainly composed of communists'. M. Molotov was quick to deny this, and pointed to the fact that in Rumania the King had appointed the Cabinet. 'With a little help from Vyshinsky perhaps?' asked the British Foreign Secretary, a rejoinder made none the less telling by the presence of M. Vyshinsky* at the meeting.[59]

---

* On 26 February 1945 Andrei Vyshinsky had arrived in Bucharest to supervise the appointment of a pro-Soviet Government there.

The main American demands, which were fully supported by the British, were for inter-Allied supervision of elections in former satellite countries, free movement of observers there and full freedom of the Press and political activity. Stalin and Molotov countered by suggesting they might demand similar rights in Italy and Greece, but this misfired because they were willingly offered reciprocity.[60] Nevertheless, the Russians refused to consider supervised elections and whittled down proposals for guaranteed political freedom until they were worthless.

Typical of the disgust felt by American participants in these negotiations was the record of a subcommittee meeting on the subject which included the comment:

> Gromyko came up with a weasel-worded statement on assuring correspondents the right to report out of these countries. He still insisted on military censorship and admitted this could cover political censorship of certain stories. Would not agree to affirmative declaration against political censorship and freedom of press in these areas. Meeting adjourned with no agreement.[61]

The latter phrase summed up a good deal of the work at Potsdam. So far as the Declaration on Liberated Europe was concerned the best that could be obtained was a Russian promise that facilities for the joint Allied Control Commissions should be improved.[62] The Americans were able to gain recognition of the special position of Italy in the Potsdam Protocol, since it was agreed that preparation of a peace treaty with that country was to be the first task of the Council of Foreign Ministers. On the other hand it was also accepted that Bulgaria, Finland,* Hungary and Rumania should be next in the queue, although treaties were to be concluded with 'recognized democratic governments' in those countries.[63] This was hardly a very effective safeguard and was of no practical importance.

All in all, the wrangling over Italy and the other former Axis satellites did little except move the Allies towards a formal acquiescence in the *status quo*. Italy was in the Western orbit and the rest fell under Soviet influence. The British had hardly expected anything better, but the negotiations may well have added to the growing anti-Soviet feeling among American officials. The idealism about the shape of post-war international relations which still characterized some American thinking was beginning to crumble in the face of that outmoded concept, the sphere of influence.

It was with exasperated indignation, for example, that on 30 July 1945 the American representative in Sofia reported on the Bulgarian Prime Minister, Kimon Georgiev:

---

* Finland was in fact the only satellite country in which elections had been held. They were conducted fairly.

He sees the world as largely divided between three great powers and their respective spheres of influence. It is his belief Balkans fall squarely within Russian sphere. . . .

To him world-wide co-operation in interests of world security is a formula designed only to dupe people who react against war and who are not sufficiently realistic to accept his estimate of forces that really shape destiny of world.[64]

It might have been an epitaph on the policies of Cordell Hull.

It should not be thought that even these modest Soviet concessions over Italy and the German satellites were written into the Potsdam Protocol without protracted bargaining. It was a recognized technique of Soviet diplomacy to maintain a negative attitude on all questions at issue until the last possible moment, and they were able to carry this through at Potsdam since the timetable of the conference was not so tight as at Tehran or Yalta. Hence when the leaders of the British delegation left Potsdam on 25 July to discover their fate at the hands of the electorate, the conference still seemed in a state of virtual deadlock. It was only after the Americans produced a 'package' compromise which involved not only the arrangements described above but also a formula on two of the major issues to divide the conference – German reparations and the Oder–Neisse line – that agreement became possible.

The reparations problem was one of the most worrying for the Western delegations at Potsdam. The absurdities of the reparations settlement with Germany after the First World War had been a major reason for the failure of the Versailles Treaty, and had involved the victor Powers – particularly the United States – in financial difficulties of a long-term character. When, at Yalta, the Soviet Government had presented a scheme whereby Germany should pay $20,000 million, of which half should go to Russia, the British and the Americans had reacted very coolly.* A reparations commission established to discuss the question had made no progress, largely because there was complete disagreement about the amount of reparations Germany could be expected to pay without becoming a burden on her Western occupiers. The Russians kept harking back to their figure of $20,000 million despite the fact that this had never been accepted as more than a basis for discussion. As the facts about the devastation of Germany became more obvious, the British and the Americans absolutely refused to countenance this figure as a practicable possibility. Indeed, the Western Allies wanted any reparations agreement to be based not on absolute figures but on percentages of available plant or surpluses, and they wanted the whole scheme linked to an exchange of food and raw materials between the Eastern and Western zones of Germany.

* See above, pp. 230–1.

On 23 July Secretary Byrnes suggested to Molotov, and repeated his suggestion at a plenary meeting, that in lieu of an over-all agreement each Ally might simply take reparations from his own zone.[65] This suggestion was unpalatable to the Russians because they looked to the British sector – especially the Ruhr – for a large proportion of their payments. The Americans claimed that by their calculations such Russian hopes were not only unrealistic but unjustified, since 50 per cent of Germany's resources lay in the Soviet Zone, 30 per cent in the British Zone and 20 per cent in the American Zone respectively.* Doubtless these figures were open to question, but they did underline the fallacy of assuming that the Ruhr in its devastated condition could be regarded as the treasure-house of the German economy.[66] The whole question of food and raw materials was closely bound up with that of the Oder–Neisse frontier, since the physical size of the Soviet Zone was bound to affect the amount of supplies which could be provided from it.

Soviet occupation forces were already treating the territories east of the Oder–Neisse line as though they no longer belonged to Germany. At the second plenary session of the conference on 18 July, Mr Churchill interrupted a discussion on German occupation to inquire what the term 'Germany' actually meant. He was prepared to accept American proposals for the control of that country only if they referred to the pre-war frontiers of the Reich. President Truman agreed and in the face of Soviet hair-splitting said that the German frontiers should be those of 1937. Stalin was unhappy about this, claiming that the Polish–German frontier should be settled at once and remarking that if a German administration appeared in Königsberg 'we should expel it'.[67] Nevertheless, the 1937 frontiers were accepted, at least as a starting-point for discussions.

The Polish question itself was soon to be raised – the Russians taking the initiative in demanding that all relations with the former London Government should be served and all assets and armed forces transferred to the new Warsaw régime. Mr Churchill pointed to the debt Britain owed to Polish servicemen in the West, but could do no more than express the hope that conditions in their country would soon become attractive enough to pesuade them to return to it. The recognition of the broadened Warsaw Government by the Americans and British had made it impossible for the Prime Minister to press for a change in domestic Polish affairs. Indeed he declared his satisfaction at the settlement of Polish differences – a satisfaction which all the Powers expressed formally in the communiqué at the end of the conference.[68]

The nature of the Polish régime was, however, to impinge upon the

* The French Zone was counted as part of the American Zone for this calculation.

conference because Stalin ingeniously used it as an excuse for his demand that the line of the Oder and Western Neisse should be recognized as the Polish frontier. By claiming both that there were no longer any Germans east of this line* – a claim that caused Admiral Leahy to whisper 'The Bolshies have killed them all' into President Truman's ear[69] – and that the Polish Government was demanding this territory for its own country, he forced the Western Powers into a position where it was deemed necessary to invite representatives of the new Polish régime to the conference.[70]

On 24 July a number of Polish leaders – including M. Bierut and M. Mikolajczyk – appeared before the daily meeting of Foreign Ministers at the conference. The Poles put forward a series of statements demanding the line of the Oder and the Western Neisse for Poland. It was perhaps embarrassing for the British and the Americans that the most sophisticated – if hardly the most convincing – arguments were expressed by M. Mikolajczyk, their own nominee in the Polish Ministry. He contended that the large area Poland was claiming would weaken German capacity to commit aggression by depriving her of two-thirds of her supplies of zinc as well as of the important coal deposits in Silesia† – deposits which Poland needed far more than Germany. It was important that Stettin should be taken from the Germans because it provided the best outlet for exports from Eastern European countries and these had previously been channelled through Germany. If Stettin were to be Polish, the whole of the Oder–Neisse river system had to go to Poland also because 'In view of the fact that the supply of water is found between the Oder and the Lausitzer Neisse, if the Oder's tributaries were controlled by someone else the river would be blocked'. He concluded by pointing out that Germany was still losing less than Poland 'on a percentage basis', since Poland would be 20 per cent smaller than before the war whereas Germany would be only 18 per cent smaller.[72] Later that day M. Bierut put the same case to President Truman.[73]

No immediate progress was made. On 25 July – the day the British leaders left Potsdam – both the President and the Prime Minister stressed at the plenary session that they could not tolerate a situation in which the Poles were administering part of one of the German occupation zones and expelling millions of people from it into other areas – mostly those administered by the Western Powers.[74] Stalin, who had

---

* Later the Russians admitted to about a million Germans remaining in the area.

† There was, for example, an argument between Stalin and Mr Churchill about whether Berlin's coal supplies came from Silesia or Saxony. Later, Mr Churchill complained that Silesian coal was being sold by the Poles to Sweden at a time when the British were forced to provide coal for Western Europe out of their depleted stocks.[71]

BALTIC SEA

Danzig
(Gdańsk)

FREE CITY
OF
DANZIG

EAST
PRUSSIA

Köslin
(Koszalin)

Swinemünde
(Swinoujście)

Stettin
(Szczecin)

Bydgoszcz
(Bromberg)

Frankfurt

Poznań
(Posen)

POLAND

Łódź
(Lodz)

Fürstenberg

Crossen
(Krosno Odrzańskie)

Sagan (Żagań)

Vistula (Wisła)

GERMANY

Görlitz

Liegnitz
(Legnica)

Breslau
(Wrocław)

Lauban
(Lubań)

Zittau

Brieg
(Brzeg)

Oppeln
(Opole)

Katowice
(Kattowitz)

Glatz
(Kłodzko)

Glatzer Neisse

Neisse
(Nysa)

Prague
(Praha)

Ratibor
(Racibórz)

CZECHOSLOVAKIA

Ostrava

**CONSIDERATION OF THE WESTERN FRONTIER OF POLAND
AT THE BERLIN CONFERENCE**

——·——·—— 1937 International Boundaries

●●●●●● Western Limit of Polish Administration Pending the
Final Determination of Poland's Western Frontier
at the Peace Settlement

28776 3-60

previously been so sanctimonious about not allowing vengeance to govern the policy of the victors,* simply claimed that the Poles 'were taking revenge for the injuries which the Germans had caused them in the course of centuries', to which Mr Churchill retorted that this revenge 'took the form of throwing the Germans into the American and British zones to be fed'.[75]

The British Prime Minister went on to take the bull by the horns and announced that the Polish frontier question 'lay at the root of the success of the conference'. If their discussions ended with no agreement on this frontier, with the Poles virtually admitted as a fifth occupying Power of Germany and with no arrangement made for equitable food distribution in that country, then 'this would undoubtedly mark a breakdown in the conference'.[76] The result might be that – as the American Secretary of State had already suggested† – the occupiers would simply have to hold on to what they had in their own zones. This was Mr Churchill's final blast before leaving Potsdam, and he later averred that he would not have accepted the Polish–German frontier arrangements eventually agreed to by the conference.[77] It is a claim of which one historian has written 'it is magnificent but it is not history'.[78]

The fact was that the British Prime Minister was leaving for London on 25 July having kept his bargaining position intact and having maintained the apparent support of President Truman. Although many of the wrangles over Poland and Germany had been bitter, Mr Churchill was not entirely displeased with the way the conference had been developing or with his own performance at it. He was not sorry to see the business of negotiation proceeding slowly, since he obviously wanted to await the outcome of the British elections before bringing matters to a head.[79] It should also be remarked that he was being well managed by Stalin, who always tried to put the British on the defensive in plenary meetings by references to such matters as the German fleet, Greece or the Levant, and yet who still managed to persuade Mr Churchill that – despite political differences – a personal bond existed between the two men which enabled them to work well together.

On 18 July the Prime Minister had dined with Stalin, who warmed his guest's heart by assuring him that he would win the British elections. Communists and other Soviet informers in Britain forecast a comfortable Conservative majority. This was quite probably true; Soviet assessments of Western politics were notoriously faulty. When Mr Churchill ventured to express his own doubts about the servicemen's vote, his host pointed out that the Army preferred a strong Government[80] – a belief which the Prime Minister shared and which had indeed influenced his decision to call an early election. Mr Churchill came away from the meeting in expansive mood enthusing about Marshal Stalin's amiability and apparently feeling he had made a good impression on the Soviet leader. He was especially pleased with a phrase he had used to Stalin in which he described Russia as 'a giant with his nostrils pinched' – referring to the Baltic and the Black Sea.[81] By assuring Stalin that Britain had no objection to Russia becoming an important sea Power, he had compromised British resistance to handing over part of the captured German fleet to the Soviet Navy. Mr Eden was not unnaturally a little exasperated by this sort of thing, especially when – even before his *tête-à-deux* at dinner – the Prime Minister was to be heard repeating 'I *like* that man' with reference to Stalin. The Foreign Secretary remarked how much he admired the way Stalin was handling Mr Churchill, a comment which was not lost on his chief, though Mr Eden feared it had little lasting effect.[82]

On the whole Stalin did not exert such a strong influence over President Truman who, in his impatience to get things done, was irritated by both Soviet obstructiveness and Churchillian rhetoric. He did share one bond with his Soviet partner, however, which was a taste for classical music. A keen pianist himself, President Truman had arranged for a Chopin piano recital to entertain his guests at their first tripartite dinner party on 19 July. When it was the Russians' turn to entertain at dinner, Stalin sent to Moscow for Russian musicians – including two heavyweight lady violinists who, in Admiral Leahy's words, 'made up in musical ability what they lacked in looks'.[83] The President was delighted, but his sturdy Admiral and Mr Churchill found the entertainment less to their taste. At 1 a.m. the Prime Minister glumly went over to the President and asked him when he was going to leave, only to be told that his American colleague was enjoying the music and would stay to the end. Mr Churchill pronounced himself bored to tears and retired into a corner to commiserate with the equally unenthusiastic Admiral Leahy. It was one of the few occasions when the British Prime Minister wanted to be the first to break up a diplomatic evening. He did not, however, take this reverse lying down. On 24 July it was his turn to play host to his colleagues, and when they arrived at the British headquarters they found themselves confronted with an orchestral section of the band of the Royal Air Force. It played vigorously throughout the meal and continued its performance until 2 a.m. As Admiral Leahy – no music-lover it is true – rather grimly remarked, the Potsdam Conference certainly set at least one record: it was the most musical of all Allied war councils.[84]

All the convivial scenes at the conference, and these included the spectacle of Marshal Stalin taking round his menu to be autographed by those present at the British banquet, could not disguise the fact that, by the time the British leaders left Potsdam on 25 July, very little had been accomplished. The opposing sides had established their positions on such matters as Italy, the German satellite countries, the Oder–Neisse frontier and German reparations, but the real bargaining had yet to begin. Mr Churchill was confident that the battle over these issues would be resumed with full vigour and some prospect of success when he returned.

He did not return. Overwhelmingly defeated in the British election, he resigned on 26 July and his office was taken over by Clement Attlee. As Foreign Secretary Ernest Bevin replaced Anthony Eden. On 28 July these new British representatives took their seats at the conference table. Mr Attlee drily expressed regret that 'domestic occurrences in Great Britain had interfered with the work of the conference'.[85] He was, of course, no stranger at Potsdam since he had accompanied Mr Churchill in the earlier meetings. However, he had been remarkably taciturn during that period and neither the American nor the Russian delegations seem to have taken him very seriously. Yet as Deputy Prime Minister in the British War Cabinet he was well briefed on foreign policy. His Foreign Secretary was new to the business of diplomacy but not to the craft of negotiation, and as Minister of Labour in the war-time coalition he was informed on the general issues facing the conference. In addition the permanent Foreign Office officials – led by Sir Alexander Cadogan – stayed at their posts, and had indeed held the fort in Potsdam while their political superiors were learning the secrets of the ballot-boxes in Britain. This was an impressive demonstration of continuity in British politics which may have surprised the Soviet – and indeed, the American – representatives at the conference. Mr Attlee thought that the Russians were very suspicious of his own failure to forecast the election result before it was announced.[86]

There were no major differences between the Conservative and Labour Ministers over issues before the conference, although Mr Attlee took a more hostile view of the Spanish Government than did his predecessor.* As democratic Socialists both Mr Attlee and his Foreign

---

* Stalin had raised the question of Allied attitudes towards Spain at the conference, urging that there should be some sort of rejection of the Franco régime. Mr Attlee made one of his rare comments in the presence of Mr Churchill when he associated himself with Stalin's proposal that this matter should be considered at the conference. Mr Attlee had been a staunch supporter of the Republican Government in Spain before the war. The Potsdam Protocol did contain a negative reference to the Spanish Government, but it was of no importance.[87]

Secretary had every bit as much distaste for Soviet policies in Eastern Europe as their Conservative opponents. Yet the new British leaders were bound to lack that confidence in their own prestige which Mr Churchill had carried with him as the veteran of inter-Allied diplomacy. It was difficult for them to adopt an intransigent stance at the outset of their mission in foreign affairs, and such a position would have been highly unpopular with their supporters at home. If the American delegation decided that it was ready to make concessions to Stalin in order to produce at least some results from the conference, then there was little that Messrs Attlee and Bevin could do about it.

President Truman was indeed losing patience with the Potsdam negotiations. He was irritated with Soviet obstruction, but he saw no point in dragging the proceedings out for the sake of objectives which had little chance of attainment. For him the war against Japan was still of primary importance, and a breakdown of the conference might still jeopardize Soviet participation in it.

Before their first appearance at a plenary session of the conference on 28 July, Mr Attlee and Mr Bevin visited President Truman and Secretary Byrnes to discuss the working of the conference. The Americans evidently proposed a compromise over the German–Polish frontier and the reparations question. Mr Bevin objected strongly to Soviet demands, especially so far as the Oder–Neisse frontier was concerned.[88] Admiral Leahy found the new Foreign Secretary's attitude rather disconcerting, remarking that he was 'gruff and tough' and 'did not know too much about Poland'.[89] The fact was that the compromise package which the Americans adumbrated to their British colleagues was regarded by the British as conceding too much to the Soviet Union, and Mr Bevin wished to press the Western case with more vigour than Secretary Byrnes seemed willing to do.

The American 'package' was put to the Russians on 29 July. The President, Secretary Byrnes and Admiral Leahy received M. Molotov at their villa, Stalin having excused himself on the grounds of a cold. Mr Byrnes told M. Molotov that two main questions were still outstanding at the conference: the western frontier of Poland and German reparations. If they could reach agreement on them the proceedings could be concluded. The American delegation was prepared to concede that the area east of the Oder and the *Eastern** Neisse should be administered by Poland and should not be considered part of the Soviet Zone of occupation.[90] In return they asked for Soviet agreement to a reparations plan according to which each Power would take reparations from its own zone, but the Soviet Union would in addition receive

* Author's italics.

25 per cent of the total equipment available as reparations from the Ruhr.[91] As a shrewd negotiator, M. Molotov showed no great enthusiasm for these proposals, and in particular denied that the Poles would accept the Eastern Neisse as a boundary. Nevertheless that same evening Stalin suggested to M. Bierut that, in view of the American concessions, the Poles should accept the line of the Kwisa (Queiss) instead of the Western Neisse. The Polish Ministers actually agreed to accept the watershed of the Queiss and the Western Neisse – a concession of no great value, but a concession just the same[92] (see map, page 336). Yet even this minor reduction in Polish demands proved unnecessary. The next day Secretary Byrnes told M. Molotov that the Americans were willing to concede the Western Neisse.[93]

At the Foreign Secretaries' meeting which followed, Secretary Byrnes announced the American compromise 'package'. He claimed that it represented 'a sacrifice of the views held and expressed by the United States delegation'.[94] It certainly represented a sacrifice of the views held by the British delegation. Mr Bevin and his colleagues had agreed to accept the American proposals – if without enthusiasm – on the understanding that the Eastern Neisse would be the limit of Polish expansion. It was Mr Bevin's intention to try for concessions over internal political conditions in Poland – and particularly a promise of early elections – in return for any acceptance of the Western Neisse frontier for the Poles. He had been putting strong pressure on a surly M. Bierut about these problems – as indeed had Mr Churchill before he left Potsdam.[95] Mr Byrnes's precipitate concession undermined the British position. At the plenary meeting on 31 July, Mr Bevin objected to the Western Neisse and put awkward questions to Stalin about the nature of the Russian presence in Poland.[96] But there was no longer any question of effective resistance to the territorial settlement and no real safeguards could be obtained for constitutional freedoms in Poland.

Despite irritation over Mr Byrnes's handling of this issue – and it was not the last occasion upon which Mr Bevin was to suffer cavalier treatment at his hands – there was much in his compromise arrangement to attract the British. In their critical economic situation the burden of occupying Germany was a much more urgent problem than a territorial adjustment between the Soviet Zone of Occupation and Poland. It would have been inconceivable to break up the conference because of a discrepancy between the Western and Eastern Neisse rivers – especially since the Soviet Union already controlled the whole area in one way or another. It is, however, just possible that Mr Churchill's presence at the conference might have extracted a minor territorial or political concession on this issue.

The Western acceptance of the Oder–Neisse frontier* had, of course, been part of a wider proposal which included both a statement on the future of Italy and the former German satellites† and the question of German reparations. Needless to say, the Soviet delegation was not satisfied with Byrnes's offer to Molotov on reparations; they still demanded more deliveries from the West, but were ready to accept less than they had originally asked for. On 30 July Byrnes explained that the Americans envisaged a scheme under which 15 per cent of capital equipment from the Ruhr designated as unnecessary to the peace-time economy should be made over *gratis* to the Russians and 25 per cent on receipt of equivalent amounts of food and raw materials from the Soviet Zone. Mr Bevin was not at all pleased with this offer. It seemed over-generous at the expense of the British Zone, even though the Americans suggested compensating the British for excessive losses.[97] He proposed a figure of 10 per cent of industrial plant from both Western sectors, providing that arrangements were made for supplies of food and materials from the East. There followed, on 31 July, a period of haggling better suited to a bazaar than an international conference.

Mr Bevin was ready to offer the Russians 10 per cent of dismantled plant from both Western sectors *gratis* and 10 per cent in exchange for supplies. Mr Byrnes suggested $7\frac{1}{2}$ per cent and 12 per cent. The Russians asked for 10 per cent and 15 per cent, together with $500 million worth of shares in industrial concerns in West Germany and 30 per cent of Germany's gold and foreign investments. The latter items were evidently bargaining counters; Mr Byrnes rejected them and Stalin promptly said that the 'percentages' would have to be raised. In the end Mr Bevin, after a verbal dual with Stalin about the burden being placed on the British Zone, agreed to accept the *gratis* transfer of 10 per cent of plant earmarked for dismantling in the Western zones and the exchange of a further 15 per cent in exchange for supplies of food and raw materials.[98]

The British were unhappy about this arrangement but it was probably more favourable than any scheme which might have tied them to fixed totals of reparations in return for supplies from the East. By establishing the principle that in general the victors should take reparations‡ from

---

* This frontier was, of course, theoretically provisional and would have to be confirmed in a peace treaty with Germany. No such treaty was ever signed and the West Germans and their allies refused to give the frontier final recognition. However, on 18 November 1970 a treaty was initialled in Warsaw between the Poles and the West Germans which affirmed that the frontier set out in the Potsdam Agreement was the western frontier of Poland.

† See above, p. 332.

‡ And those of smaller Allies: Poland in the case of Russia, Holland and Belgium in the case of Britain.

their own zones, the British and the Americans shielded themselves from the worst excesses of Soviet rapacity. Industrial dismantling went on for Soviet benefit long after relations between the occupying Powers had begun to deteriorate,* but as the split between the two halves of Germany widened, so the transfer of plant was halted.

The Potsdam Conference ended on a sour note. Although the final communiqué, issued on 2 August, seemed to show an impressive list of achievements concerning the frontiers and administration of Germany and the preparation of future peace treaties, the compromises which had been accepted satisfied neither the British nor the Americans. The façade of inter-Allied solidarity had to be maintained, and the final communiqué spoke of the conference as having 'strengthened the ties between the Three Governments and extended the scope of their collaboration and understanding'.[99] There was little substance in this statement. The British delegation had not made much impact on either of its allies, and Mr Bevin in particular had not found much common ground with either Mr Byrnes or M. Molotov – the former he disliked for his inconsistency and the latter for his political record.[100] As for Soviet–American relations, it was clear that the warmth of the Roosevelt era was a thing of the past. On 30 July President Truman wrote to his mother and sister: 'You never saw such pig-headed people as the Russians. I hope I never have to hold another conference with them – but of course I will'.[101]

In fact the President's hopes were justified. He never met Stalin again. The Potsdam Conference marked the end of the war-time alliance in Europe. Hostilities there had ceased but the peace settlement was still a long way off.

* See above, pp. 282–4.

16 | The Unconditional Surrender of Japan

I

FROM the first, the war against Japan in the Pacific – as distinct from the South-east Asia Command – was an American war. This was, perhaps, both natural and inevitable. The humiliation of the Pearl Harbor disaster stirred America more deeply than any happening in Europe could possibly have done. Whereas the Allied cause in the West, represented by a beleaguered Britain and a beset Soviet Union, was a source of interest, sympathy and alarm to the eastern seaboard of the United States, it had no hold upon the imagination of the Pacific coast and met with positive hostility from the embattled strongholds of isolation in the Middle West, where in 1940 and 1941 the propaganda of the 'America First' movement exercised a powerful influence.

Japanese aggression, however, was a different thing altogether. It struck at the very heart of American security. The disaster at Pearl Harbor, the crushing defeats in the Philippines, the ultimate capitulation at Corregidor, the loss of Wake Island, culminated in a wave of fear in the State of California, which considered itself under direct danger of attack and invasion. Throughout the country as a whole there was a vast reaction of dedication and devotion to national unity and to the ultimate defeat of the aggressor. This was America's war. American lives had been lost, American ships had been sunk; America's pride had been humbled; American hatred had been aroused.

In the light of historical hindsight one stands amazed at the ineptness of the Axis grand strategy. It was really quite unnecessary for them to have brought America into the war at all at this juncture, though it is improbable that she would have been able to avoid eventual participation at a later date. But had Japan directed the full force of her attack in the Far East against the British positions of Hong Kong and Singapore, leaving the American possessions and bases untouched, it is not to be doubted that the Government of the United States would have continued its policy of neutrality until it became more imminently menaced. Not all the persuasiveness and far-sightedness of President Roosevelt, it is believed, could have led Congress into a declaration of war. Girdled and folded within her defences, America would have waited for an attack upon herself.

This was the first Axis mistake, and the second was similar to it. Had Hitler not declared war upon the United States on 11 December 1941, it is to be greatly doubted whether Congress would have taken the initiative in this respect. Great pressure would have been brought to bear upon the President and legislators to concentrate all America's vast war-potential on waging war upon Japan. In this, it is believed, the forces of 'America First' would have taken the lead. The isolationists, whose anti-belligerence was directly against involvement in Europe, might well have seen in a Pacific 'one-front' war a challenge to America's liberty and independence. The war would have been brought to them and they would have accepted the challenge with that dramatic self-centred courage which has often characterised American policy. As a result, the cause of Britain would inevitably have suffered. The invaluable, indispensable aid which flowed to her through the supply line of Lend-Lease would have dwindled and perhaps dried up altogether. And the same would have been true of Russia.

While America was battling victoriously against Japanese aggression in the East, the resistance to Nazi aggression in Europe might have been arrested by a creeping paralysis of famine and deprivation. Nor is this picture merely a nightmare figment of the imagination. It could have come dangerously near reality. The United States was desperately anxious not to become involved in the European War, and we know that von Ribbentrop had urged the Japanese Foreign Minister, Baron Yosuke Matsuoka, in the spring of 1941 to assault Singapore while leaving the United States unattacked.[1]

Providentially, however, these strategic blunders were committed by Tokyo and Berlin. Mr Churchill, who on 10 November 1941 had declared at the Guildhall Banquet that 'if the United States became involved in war with Japan . . . the British declaration will follow within the hour', made good his promise on the very morrow of Pearl Harbor, when on 8 December Parliament declared war upon Japan.[2] To make the picture complete, Hitler, who had received no forewarning of the attack on Pearl Harbor, which came as a complete surprise to him, maintained Axis solidarity by declaring war on the United States on 11 December. Italy followed suit on the same day.* Well might Mr

---

* The sequence of events was as follows: Japan declared herself at war with the United States and the United Kingdom as from 8 December 1941. On the same day (taking into consideration the time factor) Britain declared war on Japan; the United States, more equivocally, declared that a state of war existed with Japan, thereby evading an actual declaration of war. On 11 December Germany and Italy declared

Churchill, who had welcomed the German attack on Russia for similar reasons, now exclaim, 'The war is won'. At last the limitless spiritual and material strength of the United States was enlisted, without let or hindrance, reservation or parsimony, on the side of the Allies.

Yet though the Allies entered upon the Pacific War in a general spirit of mutual comradeship, it was still to be America's war for some long period of time. Driven from their naval bases at Hong Kong and Singapore, the British were fighting for their lives in Burma, where one of the great defensive battles of the war was fought by General Alexander to deny the Japanese complete success in their invasion operation. By the end of May 1942 his army was out of danger, and though, in the words of General Joseph V. ('Vinegar Joe') Stillwell, he had taken 'the hell of a beating',[3] Alexander, though losing heavily in equipment, had succeeded in saving the bulk of his valuable manpower, in a superbly conducted retreat from Rangoon to the Indian border. Thus the British continued to maintain a containing operation until the time came for the great events in the closing years of the war which drove the Japanese from Burma. No British manpower could be spared from the vitally important campaigns in Africa and Italy and the build-up for the opening of a British front in Normandy. For practical purposes the Pacific was America's war.

Nor must it be forgotten that the relations between America's other great partner, Russia, and Japan were controlled by the treaty of neutrality which both states had concluded in April 1941, for their mutual protection from a 'two-front' war.*

While the bulk of the American people still felt that their major commitment was to the Pacific War, the Administration in Washington was by no means exclusive in its concept of partnership. In 1940 Britain had been undeniably proud of 'standing alone' against the might of Nazi Germany, yet she was indisputably relieved when a year later Hitler's invasion of Russia took some of the burden of resistance from her shoulders. So now the United States, though assuming the major share of the war-effort in the Pacific, was by no means averse from the prospect of Russian support in this theatre of war.

Such an intervention on the part of Russia was adumbrated to Maxim

---

war on the United States and on the same day Congress responded with a formal declaration of war. Germany, Italy and Japan also concluded a pact on 11 December whereby no one of them would enter into a separate peace with the Allies.

* It was believed in some German official circles that Baron Matsuoka, the travelling Japanese envoy, was forewarned during his visit to Berlin in the spring of 1941 of the German intention to attack Russia later in the year and had divulged this secret to Stalin as the price of the neutrality treaty. This is categorically denied by the subsequent Foreign Minister, Mamoru Shigemitsu, in his memoirs.[4]

Litvinov, the newly arrived Soviet Ambassador in Washington, by both President Roosevelt and Secretary Hull on 8 December, immediately after Pearl Harbor,* and, two days later, General Douglas MacArthur made strong recommendations to General George Marshall to this same effect.

The President specifically invited Stalin to call an Allied Conference in Moscow to discuss possible joint action. The Marshal, beset by the German armies, replied that he would prefer to wait until spring before making a decision. Neither then nor for some time later was any reaction available as to Soviet participation in the Pacific War.[5]

But the need for Soviet participation continued to occupy the thoughts of American military planners. When Harry Hopkins came to the first Quebec Conference in August 1943, he brought with him a 'high-level' strategical memorandum, entitled 'Russia's Position', which frankly declared that

> With Russia as an ally in the war against Japan, the war can be terminated in less time and at less expense in life and resources than if the reverse were the case. Should the war in the Pacific have to be carried on with an unfriendly or a negative attitude on the part of Russia, the difficulties will be immeasurably increased and operations might become abortive.[6]

The author of this memorandum remains unidentified, but it was generally assumed to represent the agreed opinion of the higher echelon of military planning, and the estimate which it made was of considerable importance as indicating the policy which guided the President and his advisers and his ally, Mr Churchill, in making subsequent decisions at Tehran and at Yalta.

So far Stalin had remained silent and sphinx-like on this issue, but towards the end of the Quebec Conference it was learned that he would welcome a meeting of the three Foreign Secretaries in Moscow in the following October. This duly occurred, and it was in the course of one of the banquets which played so important a part in Soviet diplomatic hospitality that Stalin unexpectedly showed his hand. To the astonishment and delight of Mr Hull the Marshal declared, 'clearly and unequivocally', that, upon the defeat of Germany, Russia would join in defeating Japan.† The Secretary of State recorded that this promise was 'entirely unsolicited' and, as far as he could divine, 'had no strings attached to it'.[7] A hint in more guarded language but of a similar character was vouchsafed by the more secretive M. Molotov to Anthony Eden.[8]

---

* Similar approaches to the Soviet Government were also made by General Chiang Kai-shek in Chungking on 8 December.

† See above, p. 121.

These Russian assurances were repeated to President Roosevelt and Mr Churchill at Tehran in November 1943, but they had become somewhat more definite and certainly less 'stringless'. Stalin was now evincing a definite interest in Dairen and the Soviet use of the Manchurian and eastern Chinese railways. The pattern of things to come was clearly taking shape and President Roosevelt was not averse to granting Soviet claims in China.*

A year later, at the Moscow Conference of October 1944, the British and Americans attempted to persuade the Russians to be more specific as to their intentions towards Japan. To Anthony Eden and to Averell Harriman Stalin repeated his previous assurance that Russia would take the offensive against Japan about three months after the defeat of Germany, but on two conditions. The necessary stocks of weapons must be built up and the political terms clarified.⁹

So far these Soviet assurances had been only oral, and it seemed to Mr Eden that it would be as well for him and Mr Harriman to put down on paper a clear and unequivocal statement of their understanding of what the Russians had agreed to do and to present this to Molotov. This they did, with the result that Stalin was furious. This, he declared, was a further example of the lack of secrecy among the Western Powers; the slightest leak of Russian intentions would be sufficient to invite a Japanese invasion. 'I am a cautious old man', he added, and he refused to consider the paper.¹⁰

It was not until the Big Three met at Yalta in February 1945 that Stalin became specific in the matter of his demands and conditions for a Russian entry into the war against Japan, or that these were embodied in the form of a written commitment. When this was in fact accomplished it constituted one of the great centres of dispute in respect of the 'Betrayal of Yalta'. This must be viewed against the facts as they were known at the time.

At the beginning of 1945 the nuclear researches which some six months later were to alter the course of history were far from being in their final stage; the bomb itself, wrote Mr Churchill, was an unknown quantity and could under no conditions be regarded as a military or a political factor.¹¹† The near-defeat inflicted on the Americans by

---

* See above, p. 155.

† On 30 December 1944 Major-General Leslie R. Groves, head of the 'Manhattan District' atom-bomb project, notified General Marshall that his project should have 'sufficient material for the first implosion-type bomb sometime in the latter part of July' (1945); that the first 'gun-type' atom bomb 'should be ready about 1 August 1945; the second one should be ready by the end of the year and succeeding ones at . . . intervals thereafter'. The Chief of Staff passed the Groves Report to President Roosevelt and to Secretary of War Stimson on the same day and minuted on it that both had 'read and approved it'.¹² Secretary of State Stettinius was informed of these facts in the

Field-Marshal von Rundstedt's Ardennes offensive in the previous December was still fresh in their memories. The Anglo-American armies had not yet crossed the Rhine and no one knew how long the war in Europe would last or what the casualties would be. When that had ended, the Allied planners estimated that Operations 'Olympic' and 'Coronet', which were to be launched against the homeland of Japan, would entail at least eighteen months' hard fighting, with casualties to the invading forces amounting to half a million at the very minimum – even with Russian assistance on the mainland of Asia.[14]

Aware of all these facts, the President's military advisers brought immense pressure to bear upon him to bring Russia into the Pacific War as soon as possible after the conclusion of the war in Europe, a view which was crytallized in a memorandum sent by the Joint Chiefs of Staff to the State Department shortly before the departure of the United States delegation for the Crimean Conference: 'We desire', they wrote, 'Russian entry at the earliest possible date consistent with her ability to engage in offensive operations and are prepared to offer the maximum support possible without prejudice to our main effort against Japan.'[15] General Douglas MacArthur, Commander of the United States forces in the Far East, and Admiral Ernest King, Commander-in-Chief of the United States fleet, also shared this imperative view.

President Roosevelt himself was anxious to achieve two objectives: to hasten the end of the war, and to obtain British and Russian co-operation in establishing the United Nations Organization. Moreover, he had not yet abandoned his hope for an American–Russian overlord-ship in the post-war world and still cherished his belief that he and he alone could come to terms with Stalin. In addition, he had to contend with the problems inherent in his decision to run for a fourth term as President of the United States.

Mr Churchill too was concerned with the possibility of hastening the end of the war in Europe and in the Orient. Alone of the Big Three he was acquainted at first hand with the horrors of war* – had he not taken part in the historic charge of the 21st Lancers at the Battle of

course of the Malta Conference (31 January–2 February 1945) by Colonel William S. Considine, of General Groves's staff.[13] Thus when the Yalta Conference met on 4 February all the principal American representatives were in possession of information that by the beginning of August 1945 the United States would have at its disposal an atom bomb 'capable of wrecking a large city'. There is no evidence available to indicate that this knowledge materially affected their political thinking or that it was imparted to, or discussed with, the British at Malta, or either the British or the Russians at Yalta.

* It is true that Stalin had seen combat during the Russian Civil War and had given his name to the town of Stalingrad in memory of an engagement there in which the White armies had been defeated. It was evident, however, that his somewhat limited military experiences had not affected him as deeply or as similarly as those of Mr Churchill.

Omdurman in 1898 and had he not commanded, briefly but gallantly, a battalion of Royal Scots Fusiliers in Flanders during his political eclipse in 1916 – a year in which British casualties amounted to 60,000 in one day? Though he had not blanched or wavered in the great ordeal of leadership with which he had been confronted since 1940, the carnage and waste of war were fully apparent and abhorrent to him.

When therefore he was warned by Mr Eden, before they left for Yalta, that Stalin would ask a considerable price for his participation in the Pacific War, Mr Churchill replied that he would not be prepared to resist Russian demands for the freedom of the Straits in Europe and for substantial territorial concessions in the Orient if granting them led to a quick end to the war against Japan.[16]

Marshal Stalin was fully aware of the anxieties of his Allied colleagues. He had done his homework well. He had his shopping-list prepared. Most of his demands had at least the virtue of being for territory which had at one time or another been Russian or Russian-controlled. Much of it had been taken from Russia by Japan as a result of the war of 1904–5. It had therefore the appearance of being Japanese territory, though the fact remained that most of it had been originally ceded to Russia or to Japan by a reluctant but helpless China. Russia, who as a result of her pact with Hitler in 1939 had won back all, and more, of the territory which she had lost under the Treaty of Brest-Litovsk in 1918, was now demanding from the Western Allies all, and more, that she had lost under the Treaty of Portsmouth in 1905.

On arrival at Yalta President Roosevelt held private conversations with Stalin from which Mr Churchill was excluded,* on the subject of the Japanese War. The Marshal stated his terms and refused to make any major modification in regard to them. The President agreed to all the Russian demands. On 10 February, after two days of secret negotiation with the President, Stalin had a private conversation with Mr Churchill and, without disclosing the full details of the terms which he had virtually agreed with President Roosevelt, secured the Prime Minister's approval of Russia's losses in the Russo-Japanese War being made good. Final agreement was reached on 11 February, when Mr Churchill was presented with the full text for the first time. He signed it.[17] These were the terms:

(a) The preservation of the *status quo* in Outer Mongolia.
(b) The restoration of the Russian rights lost in the year 1904, viz:
　(i) Recovery of southern Sakhalin and the islands adjacent to it.
　(ii) Internationalization of the commercial port of Dairen with safeguards for the pre-eminent interests of the U.S.S.R. and

* See above, p. 243.

the restoration of the lease of Port Arthur as a Soviet naval base.

(iii) Joint operation by the Soviet–Chinese company of the Chinese Eastern Railway and the South Manchurian Railway, providing an outlet to Dairen, on the understanding that the pre-eminent interests of the U.S.S.R. will be safeguarded and that China will retain full sovereignty in Manchuria.

(c) Acquisition by the U.S.S.R. of the Kurile Islands.[18]

Thus President Roosevelt had conceded – and Mr Churchill had condoned in the concession – all that Stalin had demanded, regardless of the fact that it constituted a flagrant violation of the principles of the Atlantic Charter and an abandonment of the agreement reached with Chiang Kai-shek at Cairo in 1944.* They recognized the re-establishment of Russia as an influential Power in the Pacific, replacing Japan and paving the way for the destruction of the Nationalist régime in China.

Though President Roosevelt could not have foreseen the latter event, he equally could not have been ignorant of the former fact. Yet he undertook to be the intermediary between Stalin and Chiang Kai-shek in communicating the terms of the Yalta Agreement.

Indeed the President's conduct appears to have been remarkable in the extreme. It has become axiomatic to excuse him on the grounds of political pressure – 'He did not dare face American mothers and tell them that their sons had to die because he would not allow Stalin the Kurile Islands in order to get his help', one American historian has written[19] – and of ill-health. There is little evidence to prove that the President's declining health altered his judgement. In the words of Lord Avon:

> For those who attributed Roosevelt's decisions to illness, it must be remembered that, though the week of the Conference was strenuous enough to keep a man even of Churchill's energy occupied, Roosevelt found time to negotiate in secret, and without informing his British colleague or his Chinese ally, an agreement with Stalin to cover the Far East. This document was, in my judgement, a discreditable by-product of the Conference.[20]

Nor was this the end of this crepuscular episode. The Far Eastern Agreement found no mention in the protocol of the Yalta Conference. The text was handed to Admiral Leahy for safe-keeping in the secret files of the White House. The State Department, other than Edward Stettinius and Averell Harriman, were not informed of its existence, which was hidden from all but the President's closest advisers. It was

* See above, p. 136.

feared that if too many people were privy to it information would leak
out in Washington or in Chungking and that Japan might hear of it.
She might then, it was thought, upset the Allied plans by denouncing
the Soviet–Japanese pact of neutrality and non-aggression and launching
an attack on the Soviet Union before Russian troops could be transferred
from Europe to the Far East. It was agreed privately between Roosevelt
and Stalin that only after the troop movements were completed would
the President inform the Chungking Government of the terms of the
Yalta Agreement.[21]

It is possible that, under the circumstances, some at least of these
provisions for security were justified, but it cannot be denied that it is
necessary to go back to the days of secret diplomacy, of Kaunitz and
Talleyrand and Metternich, to find a parallel for such duplicity of
conduct among allies.

II

Just as what is now known as the 'pre-emptive strike' had become an
accepted opening of hostilities in Japan's conduct of war, so had an
almost immediate beginning of the consideration of peaceterms. 'A
swift war and a swift peace' had been as axiomatic in Tokyo as in
Berlin as an ideal pattern for hostilities, it being considered that a gesture
of peace made when the tide of victory was running favourably was worth
much more than if made at a disadvantage after defeat.

This technique was practised in Japan's earlier wars with China in
1894–5 and with Russia in 1904–5. In both cases the Japanese Government and the Emperor's personal advisers were on the alert from the
first to recognize and to grasp the psychological moment to end the war.
An envoy, Count Kaneko, was dispatched to the United States shortly
after the outbreak of the Russo-Japanese War to pave the way for
American mediation for its conclusion and it is a significant fact that
no sooner had the decisive defeat been inflicted on the Russians at
Mukden on 10 March 1905 than the Chief of Staff of the victorious
Army in Manchuria, General Count Kodama, was posted home with the
advice that this battle should be the last and that tentative preliminaries
for peace should be begun forthwith. As a former Japanese Prime
Minister, Shigeru Yoshida, has written: 'It was largely because of this
degree of foresight and clear thinking on the part of those in power in
Japan in Meiji times that a small island nation in the Far East came in less
than half a century to rank among the five Great Powers of the world.'[22]

For various reasons, notably because she was part of a great world
alliance, Japan employed neither her habitual military nor her diplomatic policies during the First World War, but she returned to the use

of both in the Second. The technique of the 'pre-emptive strike' was employed against the Americans on 7–8 December 1941 at Pearl Harbor and against the British at Kota Bahru and Hong Kong; in the first week of February 1942, before even the great British fortress of Singapore had surrendered, the Keeper of the Privy Seal, the Marquess Kido, had advised the Emperor 'to grasp any opportunity to bring about the earliest possible termination of the war'. The Emperor had passed on this advice, with his own favourable endorsement, to the Prime Minister, General Hideki Tojo – but Tojo did nothing.[23]

This was to prove to be the high tide of Japan's military success, for four months later, on 7 June 1942, she sustained defeat at the Battle of Midway – now regarded as a turning-point in the Pacific War. Four days later Shigeru Yoshida called upon Prince Konoye – who, with Prince Higashikuni, was interested in negotiating for peace – with a plan that the Prince should go at once to Switzerland, there to provide an agency through which such Powers as might be so disposed might discuss peace and its possibilities. Though the Prince was himself not unfavourable to the suggestion, and was in fact prepared to undertake the mission, he was already under suspicion by General Tojo as being 'politically unreliable' and was kept under close official surveillance. Yoshida's proposals, therefore, came to nothing.[24]

The year 1943 was climacteric in respect of both the war as a whole and of Japan in particular. As a result of the Casablanca Conference in January, the Emperor and his advisers, both military and political, found themselves confronted with an Allied demand for their Unconditional Surrender, to be followed in November, at the Cairo Conference, by an Allied declaration of intention that, once conquered, Japanese territory was to be reduced to that held before the Treaty of Shimonoseki, which terminated the Sino-Japanese War in 1895. In other words, all that Japan had taken by conquest from China and from Russia was to be surrendered.*

Even more gloomy than this spectre of defeat was the reality of defeat itself. In the second half of 1943 the tide of war ran heavily against Japan. The Japanese detachment in Attu, in the Aleutian Islands, was annihilated, Imperial forces in Guadalcanal and Bougainville were wiped out, and New Britain and the Admiralty Islands were recaptured by the Americans, whose submarines and aircraft menaced the Japanese lines of communication, inflicting shattering losses on the enemy's fleet and air arm.

At a Crown Council on 30 September 1943 the Chief of the Naval General Staff, Admiral Osami Nogano, could give little hope that the

* See above, p. 137.

Imperial Navy could hold the new line which it had established in the Pacific – which, it nevertheless declared publicly, 'must be held to the death'. The Premier, General Tojo, remained optimistically belligerent, but the Emperor was sufficiently discouraged to announce to his people late in December: 'The situation is the most critical in the long history of the Empire.'[25]

Those who had earlier been active in the course of a negotiated peace became yet more ardent in their urging. Yoshida revived his plan for a mission to Switzerland by Prince Konoye and offered to go with him, but this project was found to lack practicality when it was discovered that the only way of getting to Europe was by submarine![26] The Prince, however, was engaged in his own activities. Taking the initiative, he formed a group of like-minded men of high standing and desirous of peace, who maintained indirect contact with the Emperor through his most intimate adviser, the Marquess Kido. The Konoye group aimed primarily at planting their own representative in the Tojo Government, with the object of mitigating the general belligerency of his policies. Their choice was Admiral Mitsumasa Yonai, who had been Prime Minister in 1940 and whose Government had fallen because of his reluctance to support the Imperial Army's projected alliance with Germany. In effect they failed to achieve their purpose, but in April 1943 Mamoru Shigemitsu, who, as early as a year before, had advocated recognition of China's sovereignty and independence and giving back China to the Chinese, was appointed Foreign Minister on the specific condition that he should be free to inaugurate his 'new China policy'.[27] The course of peace was thought to have been benefited thereby. This proved to be illusory.*

* There were, however, two abortive attempts, one official and one unofficial, to come to terms with China for a separate peace. In September 1943 Wang Ching-wei, head of Japan's puppet Chinese Government in Nanking, reported to Tokyo that Sun Fo (son of Sun Yat-sen and nephew by marriage of Generalissimo Chiang Kai-shek, in whose Government at Chungking he held office) had made tentative gestures for a negotiated peace. To this approach General Tojo replied that peace could only come about if the Nationalist Government at Chungking severed relations with Britain and the United States. If this were done, Japan might consider withdrawing her troops from China.[28] The second attempt, which took place a year later in the winter of 1944, was initiated by Prince Konoye and his friends, who employed the Prince's younger brother as their envoy. A tentative agreement was reached between the Konoye group and the Nanking and Chungking régimes for the overthrow of the existing Government in Tokyo by a *coup d'état* and the establishment of a 'Badoglio Government' with Prince Higashikuni at its head and with the benign approval of the Emperor. Such a régime would terminate hostilities with China, undertake to punish those guilty of 'war crimes' and negotiate a permanent settlement on the basis of the Cairo Declaration, though omitting the process of Unconditional Surrender. For a variety of reasons nothing came of these proposals which were rejected in both Japanese and Chinese Government circles, but those concerned continued to maintain contact and exchange views through the agency of the Institute of International Problems in Shanghai until the final Japanese surrender.[29]

Throughout the year 1944 the fortunes of war were steadily adverse to Japan, and they continued so into 1945. Saipan, the keypoint of the Marianas, surrendered in June 1944, to be followed by Tinian, Guam and Kwajalein. The Japanese fleet was badly mauled and was practically destroyed in the Battle of Leyte in October 1944. The recapture of the Philippines began in the same month with the landings on the island of Luzon. Further landings in the Lingayen area began on 9 January 1945; by February General MacArthur had returned to Manila, and the disasters of Bataan and Corregidor were avenged. On 1 April thousands of American, British and Australian troops landed on the western beaches of Okinawa, an operation which was ultimately to open up a strategic gateway to the heartland of Japan. And throughout the period the American air offensive against the Japanese mainland increased in volume and fury.

Against this background of disaster the political tide of battle in Tokyo ebbed and flowed. The Tojo Government fell on 18 July 1944, to be succeeded by that of the less belligerent but equally less efficient General Kuniaki Koiso. Shigemitsu remained Minister of Foreign Affairs and continued to pursue his tentative 'new policy' towards China. He also entertained hopes – pale though they may have been – of negotiating a separate peace between Germany and the Soviet Union, but these were effectively extinguished when, on 7 November, Marshal Stalin openly denounced Japan as an aggressor state on a par with Nazi Germany. Moreover, shortly after the conclusion of the Yalta Conference in February 1945 rumours became current that new decisions had been made there by the three Allied leaders with regard to Japan and the Far East, though no word, of course, reached Tokyo of the magnitude of these decisions.

The Axis sun was sinking. Germany, apparently at her last gasp, still refused to sue for peace, but it was increasingly apparent in Tokyo that if Japan were to survive, and if the Imperial régime were to be preserved, she must adopt a less intransigent attitude to fate than that displayed by her ally. Shigemitsu looked desperately around him for an intermediary through whom he might make a direct appeal to the United States and Britain. He toyed with the idea of Spain and of enlisting the good offices of the Papal Delegate to Japan, but neither of these agencies seemed willing, or indeed entirely desirable. Finally his choice fell upon the Swedish Minister, Widor Bagge, a good friend of Japan, who was about to go on leave to Stockholm.[30]

Toward the end of March 1945 Shigemitsu approached Bagge in terms which convinced the Swede that he was prepared 'to do everything in his power to end the war as soon as possible, even at great sacrifice to his country'.[31] Bagge responded warily, but before he could make his departure for Stockholm two major events took place on the same day. On 5 April the Government of the Soviet Union abruptly abrogated their pact of neutrality with Japan, and the Government of General Koiso collapsed.

Koiso was succeeded in the premiership by the aged Admiral Baron Kantaro Suzuki, who, as President of the Privy Council, had been an outspoken critic of the war policies of General Tojo. Realizing at once that the new Soviet *démarche* was surely but a prelude to the entry of Russia into the war against Japan, he was fully aware of the necessity of making peace as soon as possible. His Foreign Minister, Shigenori Togo, urged upon M. Bagge the necessity of speeding his mission. The Swedish Minister left Tokyo on 13 April, but owing to the conditions of travel in war-time it was not until 10 May that he was able to make contact with the Japanese Minister in Stockholm, who to Bagge's disappointment and chagrin, had received neither information nor guidance concerning his mission.

But in the meantime an event of infinitely greater importance had occurred. On 7 May General Eisenhower had received the Unconditional Surrender of the German armies. It was now a case of Nippon *contra mundum*.

<h2 style="text-align:center">III</h2>

In speaking to the British nation and people on 12 May 1945, at the height of their celebrations of the Unconditional Surrender of Germany, Winston Churchill, while sharing in the general jubilation, did not hesitate to remind his hearers that the end was not yet. 'I wish I could tell you tonight', he said, 'that all our toils and troubles were over. . . . But, on the contrary, I must warn you, as I did when I began this five years' task – and no one knew then that it would last so long – that there is still a lot to do, and that you must be prepared for further efforts of mind and body and further sacrifices to great causes if you are not to fall back into the rut of inertia, the confusion of aim, and the craven fear of being great.'

> We must never forget [the Prime Minister went on to say] that beyond all lurks Japan, harassed and guilty, but still a people of a hundred millions, for whose masses death has few terrors. I cannot tell you tonight how much time or what exertions will be required to compel the Japanese to make amends for their odious treachery and cruelty. . . . I should be unworthy of your confidence and generosity if I did not still cry: Forward, unflinching, unswerving, indomitable, till the whole task is done and the whole world is safe and clean.[32]

A few days earlier, on 8 May, President Truman, in language less eloquent but more specific, had stated in unmistakable terms just what the Japanese could expect:

> The Japanese people [he warned] have felt the weight of our land, air and naval attacks. So long as their leaders and the armed forces continue the war, the striking power and intensity of our blows will steadily increase, and will bring utter destruction to Japan's industrial war production, to its shipping, and to everything that supports its military activity.
>
> The longer the war lasts, the greater will be the suffering and hardship which the people of Japan will undergo – all in vain. Our blows will not cease until the Japanese military and naval forces lay down their arms in *unconditional surrender*. [33]

The President went on to define with some clarity what Unconditional Surrender did and did not mean for the Japanese people. It meant the end of the war and also of the influence of the military leaders who had brought Japan to the brink of disaster. It meant provision for the return of members of the armed forces to their homes, their families and their jobs. Above all, it did not mean the extermination or the enslavement of the Japanese people. No mention was made of the future, positive or negative, of the Emperor and of the Imperial régime.

In these two statements the leaders of the Western Powers had made clear their intention of pressing to ultimate victory their conduct of the war against Japan, but they knew that an unspoken but major factor in their calculation was the willingness of the Soviet Union to make good her promises given at Yalta – and at what a price! – to participate in the Pacific War.

In the months which had elapsed since the Yalta Conference the solidarity of the Grand Alliance had been badly shaken. Both Mr Churchill and President Truman were anxious to restore it. Each, however, favoured his own method, and they were not entirely the same. The Prime Minister saw a new and early meeting of the Big Three as the only hope of salvaging the already severely damaged barque of Allied mutual trust. He believed it to be a matter of direct urgency, that no time should be lost. But, as we have seen, he could not strike a fully responsive chord in President Truman.*

The President, somewhat awed but no whit dismayed by the grave responsibilities which he had so suddenly and so recently assumed, was moving with a cautious circumspection which might well, as Mr Churchill had diagnosed, have been at variance with his natural in-

---

* For a description of Mr Churchill's attempt and failure to achieve an early meeting of the Big Three, see above, p. 302.

stincts. He had inherited from President Roosevelt a policy of friendship, and virtually of appeasement, towards Russia, although there had been signs of a belated disillusionment on the part of the late President shortly before his death. President Truman was under as great pressure as his predecessor had been to achieve some major degree of Soviet military participation in the Pacific War as soon as possible now that German Unconditional Surrender was an accomplished fact, and this achievement presupposed the fulfilment of the Far Eastern Agreement signed at Yalta.

It is to be believed that when, shortly after his assumption of office on 12 April 1945, President Truman had been made cognizant of the contents of this agreement, he had been startled by the scope of its commitments and the lack of clarification as to what these really implied. Nevertheless he had committed himself to the continuation of the Roosevelt policies, at home and abroad, and when ten days later, on 22 April, Molotov called upon him at the White House and inquired, *inter alia*, as to whether the Yalta agreements in regard to the Far East still stood, the President replied that they certainly did.[34]

As has been shown, the President decided to send a personal envoy to Moscow in the person of Harry Hopkins, charged with the task of achieving a 'meeting of minds' with Marshal Stalin.* Hopkins left Washington on 23 May and arrived in Moscow, where he was joined by Harriman, on 25 May. Their talks with Stalin began on the following evening and continued until 6 June. Far Eastern affairs were not reached in the discussions until the third day (28 May) when it became clear that although Stalin envisaged participation in the Pacific War against Japan – he specifically stated that his troops would be ready to attack by 8 August – he had no intention of taking any action in the matter until the Chinese Government had accepted the terms of the agreement reached at Yalta.

This attitude did not come as a surprise to either Hopkins or Harriman. What did surprise them, and very favourably, was the manner in which the Marshal was prepared to interpret the terms of the Yalta agreement vis-à-vis the Nationalist régime. He acquiesced willingly in Hopkins's statement that America was gravely concerned for the maintenance of the unity of China. The U.S.S.R. too desired a unified and integrated China – 'We should all occupy ourselves with helping China to achieve unity'. Indeed, Stalin went a good deal further and declared that 'the United States must play the largest part in helping China to get to their feet; the Soviet Union would be busy with its own internal reconstruction and Great Britain would be occupied elsewhere'.

* See above, pp. 305–7.

Nor was this all. It seemed that sweet reasonableness permeated the Marshal's every thought and motive. Catechized by Harriman as to his future policy towards Manchuria, Stalin replied, without hesitation, that the Soviet Union did not propose to alter the sovereignty of China over Manchuria or any other part of China and had no territorial claims upon her, and added for good measure that wherever Soviet troops went in China the civilian administration would be made responsible to Chiang Kai-shek, who would be free to send in his representatives to establish the régime of the Kuomintang Party. Of the Generalissimo himself, Stalin said that Chiang was 'the best of the lot and would be the one to undertake the unification of China. He said he saw no other possible leader and that, for example, he did not believe that the Chinese communist leaders were as good or would be able to bring about the unification of China.' It was indeed Harry Hopkins who expressed the view (with which Stalin not unnaturally agreed) that Chiang would have to take certain steps and make certain reforms if he was to be successful in bringing about the unification of his country. In addition, the Marshal agreed unreservedly to the American proposal for a Four-Power trusteeship for Korea, in which China should participate.[35]

What then was behind this extraordinary performance of Joseph Stalin? Was it his intention to 'make a monkey' out of Hopkins and Harriman; to deceive them deliberately and, through them, the President of the United States and the American people? Did he really believe that he and Chiang Kai-shek could work together for the liberation and ultimate unification of China, or indeed that Chiang was the Chinese leader who could accomplish this? Or was he already privy to the plans which even then were in formulation by Mao Tse-tung and Chou En-lai for the overthrow of the Chinese Nationalist Government and the Kuomintang, and the establishment of a Communist régime in China? Was he in effect duping Chiang Kai-shek as grossly as Hopkins and Harriman and, withal, using the Americans to do his duping for him?

In the light of hindsight there is little doubt that Stalin was in process of playing the greatest game of bluff and deception of even his remarkably devious career, and in doing so he was greatly aided by the willingness of Hopkins – and in some degree of Harriman – to be deceived. Even in the light of what had happened in the case of Poland and of the long stretch of broken Soviet pledges in this regard, Hopkins himself was heartened by the mere fact that Stalin had repeated to him all the promises which he had made at Yalta in respect of the future of China. 'We were very encouraged by the conference on the Far East,' he cabled to President Truman at the conclusion of his talk on 28 May.[36]

Yet is all this so hard to understand? Harry Hopkins had shared to the full Franklin Roosevelt's dreams of an American–Soviet partnership in the post-war world. He may even have dreamed more extravagantly than his chief and friend. He had not, however, shared that bitter disillusionment which had clouded the last weeks of the late President's life. In Hopkins's mind the ideal of a world condominium of the two Great Powers was still cherished. And, in view of this, it is not so difficult to understand the degree of self-deception which, either consciously or unconsciously, he practised vis-à-vis Stalin.*

Indeed, as a distinguished and gifted American historian, Herbert Feis, has written:

> Who except the most unbelieving would have doubted promises so frontal and so explicit? They were deemed to be of enough value to China and the Kuomintang Government to warrant them in concurring in the Yalta accord, thus rewarding the Soviet Union for entering the Pacific War. Would these promises not enable China to regain possession of Manchuria and Formosa? Would they not mean that China would be protected against superior Soviet force? Would they not influence the Chinese Communists to come to terms with the National Government, accepting a conjunctive political and military place?
>
> If such boons would follow Chiang Kai-shek's assent to the Yalta accord, why continue to hesitate to carry it through? What reason was left for seeking thereby to make sure that the huge Red Army would crush the Japanese in Manchuria, and leave the American combat forces free for other attacks, and bring the war to an end sooner?[38]

Such at any rate was the reaction of President Truman on the receipt of Hopkins's report on 28 May. In it he said Stalin had repeated that, although he was ready to make the break with Japan, his actual declaration of war would depend upon China's definite acceptance of the Yalta Agreement; for this purpose, and in the light of the recent conversations, the Marshal urged that President Truman should persuade T. V. Soong,† who was then attending the San Francisco Conference, to come to Moscow not later than 1 July, for the purpose of clarifying the provisions

---

* At the time the Hopkins Mission was hailed as a diplomatic victory. 'Harry did a first-rate job in presenting your views and in explaining the most important matters . . . which were giving us concern', Averell Harriman reported to the President on 8 June after Hopkins's departure from Moscow for Washington. 'The talks about the Far East, I feel, were of real value, particularly Stalin's agreement to take up with Soong in the first instance the political matters affecting China in the Yalta Agreement, and also his agreement to allow Generalissimo's troops to go into Manchuria with the Russian troops to set up Chinese National Government Administration.'[37]

† T. V. Soong, Prime Minister and Foreign Minister in the Nationalist Government of China, was the brother of those three redoubtable sisters who, each in her own way, played so important a part in the history of modern China – Mme Sun Yat-sen, Mme Chiang Kai-shek and Mme H. H. Kung.

of the Yalta Agreement and of negotiating a definite accord with the Nationalist Government. Hopkins cordially recommended that this course of action be pursued, and on 31 May the President cabled his agreement. He added: 'At the time of Soong's arrival in Moscow I will take up with Chiang the conditions stated at the Yalta Conference.'[39]

From this it will be seen that President Truman had jettisoned his original intention to postpone any attempt to obtain Chiang Kai-shek's approval of the terms of the Yalta Agreement until after he was aware of the success or failure of the atom-bomb test or until he had had a personal meeting with Stalin.* Under the joint persuasion of Stalin and Hopkins the President was now prepared to arrange a meeting between Stalin and Soong for the implementation of the Yalta terms before either Soong (in San Francisco) or Chiang (in Chungking) had been informed of what those terms consisted. It is somewhat of an understatement to say that this conduct of affairs disclosed considerably less than usual of the President's customary acumen.

Nor did the President allow the grass to grow under his feet. With characteristic energy and initiative, he invited T. V. Soong to Washington on 9 June and there made him acquainted with the terms of the Yalta Agreement, with the substance of the Stalin–Hopkins conversations and with Stalin's desire for the immediate opening of negotiations in Moscow. Soong was not unnaturally perturbed. He attempted to elicit some interpretation from the President and from Acting Secretary of State Joseph Grew, who had accompanied him from San Francisco and attended the meeting at the White House. No such interpretation was forthcoming, and the Chinese Premier was urged not to quibble but to accept the joint assurance of the United States and the Soviet Union. Speed, Soong was told, was of the essence of the contract, for until Chinese acquiescence with the Yalta Agreement had been achieved the Soviet Union would make no move to join in the Pacific War. A further attempt at elucidation on 14 June was equally unsuccessful and Soong departed for Moscow on 15 June with a heavy heart.† On this same day

---

* See above, p. 302.

† T. V. Soong's discussion with Stalin, which subsequently developed into negotiations for a 'pact of friendship and alliance', began on 30 June. These negotiations were interrupted on 14 July by Stalin's departure for the meeting of the Big Three at Potsdam. Following the conclusion of the Potsdam Conference on 2 August, the negotiations were resumed in Moscow, but by this time Wang Shih-chieh had replaced Soong as Foreign Minister. A pact was signed by him and Molotov on 14 August 1945 and ratifications were exchanged on 24 August (for text see Document 5, pp. 646–57 below). In all respects the terms of the Yalta Agreement were generously interpreted. Both parties agreed to give mutual assistance in military operations against Japan and in the work of economic rehabilitation after the war; the Manchurian Railway and the Port of Dalny (Dairen) were to be operated jointly for thirty years, after which they were to revert to Chinese ownership without payment; Port Arthur was to be converted into a

Chiang Kai-shek was informed by the American Ambassador in Chungking, General Patrick J. Hurley, of the details of the Yalta Agreement and of Soong's mission to Moscow. This done, President Truman informed Mr Churchill by cable of all that had been done, to which, the President records, the Prime Minister replied: 'I entirely agree and welcome these arrangements.'[40]*

---

purely naval base for the use of Chinese and Russian warships and merchantmen only, its actual defence being entrusted to the U.S.S.R. A Soviet declaration pledged that the Government 'had no intention of interfering in Chinese internal affairs', while the Chinese Government undertook to recognize the independence of Outer Mongolia if a plebiscite resulted in a manifestation of such a desire on the part of the inhabitants. The Soviet Union had, of course, declared war on Japan on 8 August, as promised, but subsequent to the dropping of the first atom bomb on Hiroshima on 6 August.

* The relations between Stalin and the Chinese Communists on the one hand and the Chinese Nationalists on the other is far from clear. Neither historians of Communist sympathies nor those of hostile views have succeeded in penetrating the full mystery of that enigmatic mind. This ambivalence of attitude dates back certainly to the early contacts with Moscow which Sun Yat-sen had established on behalf of the Kuomintang in 1922. These continued until 1927 when, following the Nationalist–Communist split within China, the Soviet advisers to the Canton Government, including Borodin and Galen, were forced to leave the country and the Chinese Communist Party was driven underground. Tentative relations were maintained between Moscow and Mao Tse-tung throughout the 1930s and 1940s, but there is no unassailable evidence of Russian interference in the internal affairs of China during this period. Indeed the climate of ideas surrounding official Sino-Soviet relations improved to a state of warmth once China had become the victim of Japanese aggression in 1937. Chiang Kai-shek had long entertained the hope of reaching a lasting agreement with Moscow and, as the war progressed to its close, there were indications that Stalin himself was not averse to this – or at least not apparently. On 15 April 1945 General Hurley, passing through Moscow, was received by both Stalin and Molotov. He reported to President Truman that, as a result of these conversations, he believed the Russian attitude to be: 'The Soviet Union is not supporting the Chinese Communist Party. The Soviet Union does not desire internal dissension or civil war in China. The Government of the Soviet Union wants closer and more harmonious relations with China.' This, in effect, as we have seen, was what Stalin told Harry Hopkins on 28 May and, according to the authorized biographer of Marshal Tito, Vladimir Dedijer, he repeated these sentiments to a delegation of top-ranking Yugoslav Communists in 1948. 'We told them [the Chinese Communists] bluntly', Stalin is reported to have said on this occasion, 'that we considered the development of the uprising in China had no prospect and that the Chinese comrades should seek a *modus vivendi* with Chiang Kai-shek, that they should join the Chiang Kai-shek Government and dissolve their army.' He repeated this to Milovan Djilas at the same period.

There did not lack those at the time who viewed these assurances of Stalin's with considerable lack of confidence. George Kennan, the American Minister in Moscow, cabled on 23 April to his superior, Averell Harriman, then in Washington, certain comments on Hurley's interpretation of Stalin's views: 'Stalin is, of course, prepared to affirm the principle of unifying the armed forces of China. He knows that unification is feasible in a practical sense only on conditions which are acceptable to the Chinese Communist Party. Actually I am persuaded that in the future Soviet policy respecting China will continue what it has been in the recent past: a fluid resilient policy directed at the achievement of maximum power with minimum responsibility on portions of the Asiatic continent lying beyond the Soviet border.' To this Harriman added his own independent warning. Hurley's report, he said, gave a 'too optimistic impression of Marshal Stalin's reactions', which were in reality much less sanguine. In Harriman's view, Stalin would not co-operate indefinitely with Chiang Kai-shek but would, if and

IV

The outcome of the Hopkins Mission, in respect of the prospects of Russian intentions to enter the Far Eastern War, was of undoubted satisfaction to President Truman.

> I was re-assured [he wrote later] to learn from Hopkins that Stalin had confirmed the understanding reached at Yalta about Russia's entry into the war against Japan. Our military experts had estimated that an invasion of Japan would cost at least five hundred thousand American casualties even if the Japanese forces then in Asia were held on the Chinese mainland. Russian entry into the war against Japan was highly important to us.[42]

This was the figure which had been given to President Roosevelt prior to his departure for Yalta,* and it still represented the military thinking of the American High Command. General Marshall repeated this figure to the President in the middle of June,[43] and Mr Stimson, as a result of assessments presented to him as Secretary of War, was thinking in terms of half a million to a million casualties.[44]† It was natural for the President and his military advisers to favour any reasonable policy which might diminish this appalling figure.

Yet at this moment the higher councils of the United States Supreme Command were divided. General MacArthur still ardently desired Russian intervention. He had a pretty good idea of what the price of this would be and was prepared to pay it.[45] On the other hand, Admiral Leahy took a jaundiced view of Russia going into Manchuria,[46] and Admiral King declared that in his opinion the Russians were not indispensable 'and he did not think that we should go so far as to beg them to come in'.[47] From Moscow General Deane advised that 'military collaboration with the Soviet Union was no longer vital to the United States'.[48] In view of this diversity of advice the President made up his own mind. He came down on the side of enlisting Russian aid in order to

---

when the Soviet Union entered the Far Eastern War, make full use of the Chinese Communists even to the point of setting up a puppet Government in Manchuria and possibly within China.

In effect, these negative warnings came very close to accurate prophecy. Whatever Stalin may have said – and meant – when he talked to Hurley and Hopkins and the Yugoslav Communists, the fact remains that he gave material assistance to the Chinese Communists during 1945–6. Immediately after Soviet troops had entered Manchuria and a part of Inner Mongolia, the Communist Party leadership shifted an important part of its armed forces to these regions where they received extremely valuable assistance from the Soviet Union in their revolutionary struggle.[41]

* See above, p. 190.

† The discrepancy between the Marshall and the Stimson figures may have been covered by the fact that the Chief of Staff was speaking of lives lost and the Secretary of War was thinking of total casualties – killed, wounded and taken prisoner.

lessen American casualties. At a meeting at the White House on 18 June, at which his chief military advisers were present, he announced that 'one of his objectives in connection with the forthcoming conference [Potsdam] would be to get from Russia all the assistance in the war that was possible'.[49]

It has been said that this decision of the President's was taken under pressure from his new Secretary of State, former Supreme Court Justice James F. Byrnes.[50]* If this was so it merely indicates that Mr Byrnes shares responsibility for this momentous step. It does little or nothing to mitigate its unwisdom.

In taking this decision the President disregarded the reports of American Intelligence to the effect that the Japanese Air Force had been virtually eliminated as a military factor, partly because of shortage of planes and partly from lack of fuel. He also ignored the information which Harry Hopkins had cabled him from Moscow on 28 May after his third meeting with Stalin, telling him of the imminent collapse of Japan and of certain tentative peace approaches made by Japanese would-be negotiators. He had cabled on this occasion:

1. Japan is doomed and the Japanese know it.
2. Peace feelers are being put out by certain elements in Japan and we should therefore consider together our joint attitude and act in concert about the surrender of Japan.[51]

It is probable that Hopkins was referring here to the secret conversations in Tokyo which the Japanese Foreign Minister, Shigenori Togo, had authorized between his personal representative, Koki Hirota, a former Foreign Minister and Prime Minister, and the Soviet Ambassador, Jacob Malik. Malik reported fully on these discussions to Moscow, but it was soon evident that the 'moment of truth' had not arrived and the talks proved abortive.[52]

The direful 'fire-raids' of the American B-29s on 10 March and 25 May had reduced at least half of Tokyo to ashes and rubble and several million people had been evacuated from the capital. The Emperor was profoundly moved and greatly discontented with the failure of his advisers to reach a unified policy. At a Crown Council on 8 June, while the leaders of the country wrangled and failed to agree, he remained 'furiously silent'; his desire to end the war became daily intensified. He

---

* Mr Byrnes did not take office officially until 3 July 1945, but he had been very much in President Truman's confidence since the latter's assumption of office in April. His predecessor as Secretary of State, Edward R. Stettinius, was appointed head of the United States delegation to the San Francisco Conference. During Mr Byrnes's absence in Europe at the Potsdam Conference, Joseph C. Grew, the veteran Ambassador to Japan and Far Eastern expert, served as Acting Secretary of State (see below, p. 367).

approved the peace 'feelers' which had been put out to Moscow for transmission to the Allies. He urged his advisers to hasten the means of ending the war. On 18 June he informed the members of the War Council of his desire for peace and demanded urgency. Two and a half weeks later, on 7 July, when little or no progress had been made, he again emphasized the need for haste.[53]

Certain facts now became known and clear to the Japanese leaders. T. V. Soong was in Moscow in secret negotiations with Stalin and Molotov. A new meeting of the three heads of the Grand Alliance was recognized to be imminent. It was now an indisputable fact that only Japan's Unconditional Surrender would end the war. The Navy accepted this as inevitable; the Army refused to countenance it. Faced with an *impasse*, the Emperor decided to appoint a special envoy, Prince Konoye, to bring a personal letter from the Emperor to the Government of the Soviet Union requesting their mediation with the Western Powers. This decision was communicated to Naotake Sato, the Japanese Ambassador in Moscow. on 12 July, and he at once informed the Soviet Foreign Ministry. Molotov replied that as he was about to leave with Stalin for the Allied Conference at Potsdam (they left on the fourteenth) he could not receive Prince Konoye. The matter of Japan's immediate future was now in the hands of the Great Powers who were about to discuss their own plans for forcefully prosecuting the war in the Far East.[54]

Nor were these the only Japanese approaches. Once again, as in the case of the preliminaries to the surrender of the German armies in northern Italy,* Allen Dulles's office of the O.S.S. in Berne became the centre of clandestine activity. This time the issue was complicated by the fact that both the Japanese Naval Attaché and the Military Attaché were engaged in parallel, though uncorrelated, efforts to bring about peace. Of these, those of the latter were the more serious. Lieutenant-General Seigo Okamoto had contacts in Zürich with the Japanese representatives in the Bank for International Settlements. Through them he enlisted the good offices of the Bank's Swedish adviser, Per Jacobsson, as a go-between with Allen Dulles. This contact was established in mid-May and the General made clear the bases of the peace which he desired to see brought about. These included the retention of the Imperial institution, no revision of the Japanese Constitution, the internationalization of Manchuria, and Japan to retain both Formosa and Korea.

A less promising set of proposals could scarcely be imagined, but Allen Dulles played his fish with care. In replying to Jacobsson, he made a Japanese surrender the basis of any negotiation. He hedged on the

* See above, pp. 252–3.

question of the retention of the Emperor (which was then under hot discussion at a high level among the Allies*), saying that it was possible that this might be achieved in the event of surrender. The Constitution, he said, would certainly have to be radically amended. He refused to comment on the future of Japanese territorial possessions, and he added, for good measure, that if Jacobsson's friends did not succeed in persuading Japan to open peace negotiations officially before the Soviet Union entered the war, their efforts were doomed to failure.[55]

Word of these discussions was reported to Washington in mid-June, while Allen Dulles was in the capital preparatory to going to Potsdam to make a personal report to Secretary Stimson.† Admiral Leahy, the President's Chief of Staff, sent for Dulles and questioned him about the rumours. Dulles was not disposed to enlighten him. The O.S.S. had well-established channels to both the Combined Chiefs of Staff and the Joint Chiefs of Staff. It was highly desirable that this system of 'command channels' should not be further complicated by bringing in the Admiral, who would undoubtedly have thought that 'he would have to do something about it'. This was the last thing that Dulles wanted and he did not hesitate therefore, under the circumstances, to deny that the O.S.S. was engaged in any such negotiations with the Japanese.[56] An additional reason for this action was his imminent departure for Potsdam to report to Stimson; moreover, at that moment, he did not know whether he had 'a fish on the line' or only a nibble.[57] In point of fact the Okamoto–Jacobsson approaches, like the Konoye Mission, were overtaken by events.

President Truman and his advisers sailed for Europe in the U.S.S. *Augusta* on 7 July. Because the American cipher experts had succeeded in cracking the Japanese codes early in the Pacific War, it is presumable that the President was informed during the voyage of the exchange of telegrams from 11 to 13 July between the Foreign Ministry in Tokyo and the Japanese Embassy in Moscow on the subject of the projected Konoye Mission. It came to him therefore as no surprise when Stalin gave him information of these peace manœuvres at their meeting *à deux* on 18 July. Similarly, when a second desperate effort was made by the Tokyo Government between 17 and 21 July to secure Soviet mediation before Unconditional Surrender became unavoidable, President Truman was fully informed of it considerably before Stalin saw fit to disclose the fact on 28 July.‡

---

* See below, pp. 367–9.   † This report was made to Mr Stimson on 20 July 1945.
‡ President Truman landed at Antwerp on the morning of 15 July; thence he motored to Brussels and flew to Berlin. According to Secretary Forrestal, the first news of the Japanese peace feelers became known in Washington on 13 July, through intercepted messages.[58] This information was relayed to the President at once and was

V

When the Presidential party sailed on 7 July, the vitally important question of what to do with the Emperor of Japan remained unresolved. Indeed the highest counsellors of the Administration were divided on it. Joseph Grew, for example, the veteran Far Eastern statesman, had consistently advised throughout the war that the United States should refrain from directing any of its propaganda against the person of the Emperor, and that no attempt be made to bomb the Imperial Palace. His experienced view was that not only would such action defeat its own ends,* but, if successful, would eliminate the one person who, when the time came for Japan's surrender, could bring it about by issuing an Imperial Rescript, a document held sacred by all Japanese which the Emperor alone could promulgate. This was of vital importance since the Japanese militarists, who considered themselves superior in all respects to civilian Ministers, and of whom, in the last analysis, they would and could hold themselves independent, would bow in obedience to commands from such a source of divine authority.[60]

The views of Cordell Hull and the State Department as a whole had been embodied in memorandum to the President, dated 9 May 1944. This paper recognized the probable ineffectiveness of any attempt to abolish the Imperial Institution in view of the 'almost fanatical' devotion of the Japanese people to their Emperor. On the other hand, the Imperial institution had been made an instrument of the Japanese military and, since the object of Allied military victory was to wipe out Japanese militarism, all connection between this and the Emperor must be severed. In any case it was assessed as *conditio sine qua non* of Japan's surrender that the ultimate and supreme authority must be the Allied Military Government.

Without definitely recommending the retention of the Imperial institution, the memorandum, by process of analysis and elimination, did indicate that this would be inevitable, whether it was desirable or not. In this case it was urged that a formal cession of over-all authority to the Allied Military Government should be made by the Emperor and that certain of his functions should be re-delegated to him by the Supreme

---

made generally available to the American delegation at Potsdam on 16 July. The President disclosed to members of his staff and to State Department historians at a meeting on 24 January 1956 that he had known of both sets of Japanese peace approaches in advance of the information vouchsafed by Stalin on 18 and 28 July.[59]

* The wisdom of Mr Grew's advice is borne out by the psychological effect upon the British people of the bombing of Buckingham Palace in 1940 and on the Norwegians and Dutch by the attempts to kill or kidnap their sovereigns. In a country where the ruler was regarded as semi-divine this would be even more true.

Allied Commander. Such action, it was believed, would assure the good behaviour of the Japanese people and would keep in office the maximum number of Japanese officials willing and acceptable to serve directly under the supervision of Allied Civil Affairs officers'[61]

Of the other major partners in the Grand Alliance, the British Government concurred in all basic essentials with the view of the United States,[62]* but both the Soviet and the Chinese Governments held somewhat contrary opinions. Generalissimo Chiang Kai-shek had told President Roosevelt frankly that 'all the Japanese militants must be wiped out and the Japanese political system must be purged of every vestige of aggressive elements. As to what form of government Japan should adopt, that question can better be left to the awakened and repentant Japanese people to decide for themselves.'[64] This, in theory at least, left the matter open and implied that should the Japanese people elect to return to the Imperial form of government, Nationalist China would not oppose such a decision.

Stalin, however, had been more definitely negative. In conversation with Harry Hopkins on 28 May 1945, he had expressed the view that it would be better to do away with the office of Emperor of Japan, since 'while the present incumbent was not an energetic leader and presented no great problem he might be succeeded at some time in the future by an energetic and vigorous figure who could cause trouble'.[65]

Such was the situation in the summer of 1945 when the swift passage of events translated the question of the retention of the Imperial institution in Japan from academic discussion to the realm of stern reality. It will be recalled that, in making his broadcast address on 8 May, President Truman had made no reference at all, either positive or negative, to the future position of the Emperor of Japan.† Since that time, however, he had come under severe pressure from Mr Grew, who had rallied to his policy of retention the support of Secretaries Stimson and Forrestal,[66] but there were powerful forces at work within the State Department which were strongly hostile to any pre-surrender pledges being made in respect of the future of the Imperial insti-

---

* This policy, originally initiated by Mr Churchill and Mr Eden, was adhered to by Mr Attlee and Mr Bevin when the Labour Party assumed office after the General Election. In a conversation with Secretary Forrestal in London towards the end of July, Mr Bevin stated that, in his opinion, there was no sense in destroying the instrument through which we might have to deal in order to establish effective control of Japan. He then added: 'It might have been far better for all of us not to have destroyed the institution of the Kaiser after the last war; we might not have had this one if we hadn't done so. It might have been far better to have guided the Germans to a constitutional monarchy rather than leaving them without a symbol and therefore opening the psychological doors to a man like Hitler.'[63]

† See above, p. 357.

tution.* It was held by some that if the Emperor were to be retained at all in any capacity it must appear to be as an act of grace on the part of the Allied occupation authorities and not as a bait to the Japanese Government to surrender. This view was also expressed by former Secretary Hull, when he was consulted.[68]

From this mass of advice proffered to him the President had evolved his own decision before he sailed for Europe on 7 July. He agreed that a proclamation should be made to Japan urging her to surrender. He rejected the advice of Mr Grew that this should be made from Washington prior to the opening of the Potsdam Conference. It should be made, in his opinion, as a declaration from the conference itself, thus demonstrating to the Japanese people and Government, and to the world at large, that the Allies were united in their purpose. He also postponed, for discussion at the conference, the vexed question of the future of the Emperor.

In reaching this decision President Truman had applied the test of practical common sense. He now knew that the atom bomb would receive its first test in mid-July, that is to say during the course of the conference. If the test were successful the whole of the thinking of the Allies would have to be reviewed; if it failed then Allied unity in persuading the Japanese to surrender before the hazardous procedure of invasion was embarked upon would be all the more essential, and the question of the future of the Emperor must necessarily be left open for discussion between himself, Churchill and Stalin.[69]

VI

The gathering of the eagles at Potsdam was scheduled for 15 July. President Truman and Mr Churchill arrived punctually, but Marshal Stalin's arrival was delayed for twenty-four hours by a mild heart attack – a state secret of considerable importance which was well kept.[70] The first contacts were therefore between the President and the Prime Minister on the sixteenth. This was a purely social event and no conference business was discussed. On the following day President Truman met Stalin for the first time. The impact was friendly; a good impression seemed to be made on both sides. Stalin and his companions† accepted a spontaneous invitation to lunch informally.

* For an illustration of the discord within the State Department on this issue, see the Minutes of the 133rd Meeting of the Secretary's Staff Committee held on 7 July 1945, at which the Acting Secretary of State, Joseph Grew, and the Under-Secretary of State, Dean Acheson, found themselves at variance.[67]

† According to most accounts of this meeting, including that of President Truman, Stalin was accompanied only by Molotov and his interpreter, Pavlov. It is on record, however, that the President's diary entry for the day mentions that Vyshinsky was also present.[71]

The Marshal himself introduced the subject of the Japanese War. He had not, he said, been able to make as rapid progress with T. V. Soong as he had wished and an agreement with China on the basis of the Yalta Agreement was still a prerequisite of his entry into the war against Japan.* However, he would resume the negotiations on his return to Moscow and was confident that Russia would declare war by the middle of August.[73] The questions of Japan's surrender and the future of the Emperor were not mentioned.

Churchill and Stalin also met on the seventeenth in the evening and the Marshal informed the Prime Minister of the Japanese peace feelers which he had received immediately before his departure from Moscow.[74] At luncheon with the President on the following day Mr Churchill repeated this information (which Truman already possessed†) and stated that, while Britain was determined to prosecute the war against Japan as long as the United States thought fit, the price of enforcing Unconditional Surrender upon Japan would be a very costly one. He favoured exploring the possibility of finding some means of bringing the war to an end, assuring at the same time the essentials for future peace and security and also leaving the Japanese some show of saving their military honour and some guarantee of their national existence after they had complied with all safeguards necessary for the conquering Allies to assume control. Whether or not President Truman was momentarily disturbed by the comparatively 'soft' line of argument is unknown, for he countered by saying that in his opinion Japan had forfeited her military honour after Pearl Harbor. Nevertheless he spoke with feeling of the terrible responsibilities that rested upon him in regard to the unlimited shedding of American blood.[75]

There would appear to have been a certain degree of reticence, amounting almost to 'blind man's buff', in this conversation of the eighteenth, since both participants were in possession of knowledge which was cognate and vital to the subject under discussion.

On the evening of 16 July at Babelsberg, a suburb of Potsdam, Secretary Stimson had received from Washington a telegram in 'gobble-degook' language, which informed him that the atomic-bomb test at Alamogordo had been made and that, though a final report was not yet available, the 'results seem satisfactory and already exceed expectations'.[76] Stimson at once took this cable to the President and Secretary

* American Intelligence sources in Chungking were reporting to Secretary Byrnes that Soviet demands upon China went considerably further than the terms of the Yalta Agreement. With the approval of the President, Byrnes accordingly sent to Chiang Kai-shek a message on 23 July to the effect that the United States was not urging any agreement with Russia in excess of the Yalta Agreement.[72]

† See above, p. 366 n.

Byrnes at the former's lodging, No. 2 Kaiserstrasse, which had been christened 'the Little White House'.* On the following morning (17 July) Stimson gave Byrnes a memorandum, which he had completed the previous night after the receipt of the news from Alamogordo, suggesting that, in view of the Japanese peace feelers in Moscow and of the new potential weapon to their hand, the conference should issue a direct warning to Japan urging their surrender and backing it with threats of the possibility of the entry of the Soviet Union into the war and 'the power of the new forces'.[78] That same afternoon the Secretary informed Mr Churchill, by the simple sentence 'Babies satisfactorily born', that the New Mexico tests had been successful.[79]

Thus, when President Truman and Mr Churchill met at luncheon on 18 July, they were both in possession of the same facts, and indeed the President brought with him the second – 'most enthusiastic and confident' – report on the Alamogordo experiment which had been received from Washington that morning.†

Yet it is curious that neither of them appears to have discussed its significance with reference to the ending of the Japanese War. What had exercised their minds was whether or not this new and vital information should be communicated to Stalin, and it was agreed between them that the President should communicate to the Marshal the bare and simple fact that the United States possessed this great and powerful weapon, but refuse at all costs to divulge any particulars.[81]

On 21 July there arrived at Potsdam by special courier General Groves's detailed report, giving a full and eloquent account of the tremendous success achieved.[82] It was an illuminating document of the greatest political and historical significance, and President Truman at once realized the importance of sharing its contents with Mr Churchill. Accordingly, that same afternoon, Stimson and Harvey Bundy, the Secretary of War's special assistant, took the report to the Prime Minister whose reading of it was disturbed and therefore renewed on the following morning,[83]‡ when, in the presence of Stimson and Bundy, he exclaimed: 'This is the Second Coming in Wrath'.[85]

* In one of the rare errors in his memoirs, President Truman states that the first report on the A-bomb tests was 'flashed to me in a message from Secretary of War Stimson on the morning of 16 July. . . . Stimson flew to Potsdam the next day to see me and brought with him the full details of the test.'[77] It is clear from the documents, however, that the sequence of events was as stated above.

† Lord Avon in his memoirs states that it was the President who on 17 July told the Prime Minister of the success of the experiment at Alamogordo,[80] but this is not so. The first intimation of the successful explosion of the atom bomb was given to Mr Churchill by Mr Stimson on the seventeenth, as stated above.

‡ This statement, which is taken from Mr Stimson's diary, would seem to dispose of Robert Murphy's assertion that 'the full report of the test explosion was also read by Stimson personally to Churchill'.[84]

Immediately thereafter, at the invitation of the President, Mr Churchill and he conferred together for an hour at Truman's lodging. At this meeting it was agreed between them that an atom bomb must be dropped on Japan if she did not accept Unconditional Surrender.*

The final decision as to when and where to use the bomb remained inevitably in the hands of President Truman, but neither he nor Mr Churchill had the slightest qualms on the essential rightness of such a use. 'The historic fact remains', writes Mr Churchill 'and must be judged in the after-time, that the decision whether or not to use the atomic bomb to compel the surrender of Japan was never an issue. There was unanimous, automatic, unquestioned agreement around our table.'[92]

This decision having been taken, there remained two specific but uncorrelated corollaries: to inform Stalin of the existence of the bomb and to acquaint the people of Japan with the terms of their fate. The first of these actions was taken by President Truman two days later, on 24 July, at the close of a plenary session of the conference, when he 'casually mentioned' to the Marshal that the United States possessed 'a new weapon of unusual destructive force'. Stalin, according to the President's observation, displayed 'no special interest'. He replied that he was glad to hear it and hoped that good use would be made of it against the Japanese.[93] According to James Byrnes, who was next to the President on this occasion, the Marshal smiled blandly and replied briefly,[94] but to Mr Churchill, standing some five yards away, it seemed that Stalin was delighted. 'I was sure that he [Stalin] had no idea of the significance of what he was being told.' Mr Churchill adds, 'If he had had the slightest idea of the revolution in world affairs which was in progress his reactions would have been obvious',[95] and with this view James Byrnes agreed.

In actual fact, however, it is more than likely that, in the light of hindsight based on later information, both Mr Churchill and Mr Byrnes were wrong. We now know that the Soviet intelligence service in the

* Apart from those of the two participants,[86] no record of the substance of this epoch-making conversation and decision appears to exist, and there is even some confusion as to who else was present. Mr Churchill asserts that the President had with him General Marshall and Admiral Leahy, but the latter makes no mention of this in his chronicle of the day's events.[87] It would also appear from the Prime Minister's account that he was alone, but Lord Avon states that he was present at the meeting but that the President was accompanied by Secretary Byrnes; he makes no mention of either Marshall or Leahy.[88] No official minute of the meeting seems to have been made by either side.[89] It should be remembered, however, that on 1 June the President's Interim Committee had recommended the use of the bomb against Japan and Truman had accepted their advice.[90] Mr Churchill's assent in this decision had been given on behalf of Britain by Field-Marshal Sir Henry Maitland Wilson as early as 4 July, before the Alamogordo test had taken place.[91]

United States and in Canada had been in possession of an increasing volume of information regarding the bomb for the last three years. Professor Klaus Fuchs later confessed to passing to the Russians details of the Anglo-American atomic research as early as 1942 and to have continued doing so until 1949,[96] and it was disclosed at the official inquiry in Canada that Dr Alan Nunn May had also been reporting on the project by March 1945.[97]

Thus Stalin, like President Roosevelt,* could have been aware of the potential of the bomb long before the Yalta Conference, and whereas neither of them apparently used their knowledge at this time in reaching their vital decisions,† it is altogether improbable that by the time the Potsdam Conference assembled Stalin had not been made aware of the tremendous outcome which was imminent. He may well have found confirmation of this knowledge in the toughening of President Truman's attitude towards him after the receipt of General Groves's final report on 21 July. This had been apparent to Mr Churchill, who had remarked on it to Secretary Stimson.[99] If Stalin had made similar deductions – and there is no good reason why he should not have done so – this would surely have substantiated the information already available to him. Verification of his knowledge and confirmation of his suspicions may well have accounted for the comparatively phlegmatic reception which Stalin gave to President Truman's guarded disclosure. ‡

Developing, perhaps, from his observation of the President's stiffening attitude towards the Russians, subsequent to his knowledge of the success of the Alamogordo tests and of his talks with Secretary Byrnes, who told him of his advice to T. V. Soong not to give way on any point to the Russians but to keep on negotiating pending further developments, Mr Churchill reached a further conclusion. 'It is quite clear', he minuted to Mr Eden on 23 July, 'that the United States do not at the present time desire Russian participation in the war against Japan.'[101] To the Prime Minister it appeared that all occasion for the necessity of Russian participation in the Pacific War had disappeared. There was no further need to ask favours of them since, with the possession of the bomb and the agreed intention to make use of it, the end of the Japanese

* See above, p. 348 n.

† That President Roosevelt had, however, appreciated in full the information which was transmitted to him on 30 December 1944 may be believed from General Groves's disclosure that, at a conference at the White House shortly before his departure for the Crimea, the President stated that if the European War was not over before the first bombs were completed, he wished the General to be ready to drop them on Germany.[98]

‡ This view is also held by Herbert Feis on the basis of the description given him by Averell Harriman of the latter's first meeting with Molotov after their return from Potsdam. In this conversation Molotov spoke with such sneering emphasis of President Truman's revelation to Stalin that Harriman inferred that the Marshal had known much, if not everything, about the bomb project beforehand.[100]

War was no longer dependent upon operations for invasion, with their attendant hideous toll of slaughter.

Mr Churchill's confidence that these views were shared by at least some of his American colleagues was to some degree justified. Secretary Byrnes was certainly 'most anxious to get the Japanese affair over with before the Russians got in',[102] and on 23 July President Truman, in response to a somewhat pathetic message from T. V. Soong to the effect that China had 'gone as far as we possibly could' to meet the Russian demands,[103] which appeared to be ever widening, had replied that, while he had asked Soong to carry out the Yalta Agreement, he had at no time desired him 'to make any concession in excess of that agreement'.[104]*

From this it would appear that, although the Americans were in fact 'dragging their feet' in respect of Russian participation against Japan, this reluctance did not extend quite as far as Mr Churchill hoped and believed. When, at a meeting of the Joint Chiefs of Staff on the afternoon of 24 July, General Antonov formally confirmed the statement already made by Stalin to President Truman on the seventeenth,† namely that Soviet troops would be ready to begin operations by the middle of August but that the actual date depended on the results of the negotiations with China,[105] this assurance was received with satisfaction and there was little doubt that the Chinese representatives would be encouraged to comply.

Moreover, President Truman's most intimate advisers were divided on the efficacy of the bomb, even after the reports of the success of the Alamogordo experiment. General Marshall, it is believed, was reserved in his estimate of the new potential, whereas Admiral Leahy was among the declared unbelievers. 'This is the biggest damn-fool thing we have ever done', he told the President. 'The bomb will never go off, and I speak as an expert on explosives.'[106]‡ There were others who urged upon the President the continuing necessity of getting Russia into the Pacific War, and some were not particular as to how high a price was paid to achieve this.

As against this, General Eisenhower besought the President not to give anything away to secure Russian participation in the Pacific theatre of war. In his view the Soviet Government was desperately anxious to get into this theatre, and there was no question but that

---

* See above, p. 361.   † See above, p. 370.

‡ The Admiral was at least consistent, if rooted, in his disbelief. When, on 2 August 1945, King George VI and President Truman met in Plymouth Sound in *Renown* and *Augusta*, there was much talk of the new atomic weapon. Admiral Leahy was the only open sceptic. 'It seems like a professor's dream to me', he said. 'Would you like to lay a little bet on that, Admiral?' King George asked, and the Admiral later recorded with honesty: 'Events shortly were to prove that in this respect I was very much in error.'[107]

Japan was already thoroughly beaten.[108] Ambassador Harriman corroborated this from another angle. To him it was abundantly clear that the point of no return had already been passed in so far as the Russians were concerned. The United States had for three years been urging Stalin to declare war and had already agreed to a substantial price for this. It was impossible now to ask him to remain neutral. Moreover, as Harriman pointed out, there was no way of keeping the Russians out, even if there had been a will to do so. Russia, he had told Admiral Leahy, would come into the war, regardless of what we might do; and he added for good measure the opinion that, in the end, Moscow would exercise control over whatever Governments might be established in Manchuria and Outer Mongolia.[109] General Douglas MacArthur had changed his opinion and was now in consonance with General Eisenhower. Whereas in 1941 he had urged Soviet participation in the Pacific War, by 1945 he regarded such intervention as 'superfluous', and he was amazed at the 'apparent deal with Soviet Russia against already near-defeated Japan.'[110]

It was to this somewhat fatalistic inevitability that President Truman's own thoughts tended. The possession of the bomb and the readiness of the United States and Britain to use it against Japan could not carry as a corollary the exclusion of Russia from the Pacific theatre of war – however desirable this prospect might be! The President, therefore, decided to continue his policy of endeavouring to secure Russia's entry on the limited terms of the Yalta Agreement, while at the same time demanding the surrender of Japan.

On 17 July Mr Churchill and Marshal Stalin had met for a private conference with only their interpreters present, and it was then that the Marshal had told the Prime Minister of the Konoye approaches to Moscow to the effect that Japan wished to bring hostilities to an end but was determined to fight on to the death so long as Unconditional Surrender was demanded. With Stalin's approval, Mr Churchill passed on this intelligence to President Truman on the following day. Later, at dinner that same evening (18 July), Stalin further informed Mr Churchill of Molotov's reply to Tokyo that, since their communication was couched in general terms and contained no concrete proposals, the Soviet Government could take no action.[111]

President Truman was, as we know, already informed of these peace feelers.* He was unimpressed by them in so far as they sought to evade Unconditional Surrender, but, under the influence of the arguments of both Mr Churchill and Secretary Stimson, he was prepared to lay down certain 'conditions for Unconditional Surrender' by publicly defining more precisely the treatment intended for Japan and for the Japanese

* See above, p. 366 n.

people after they had surrendered unconditionally. He had brought with him to Potsdam the draft of an ultimatum to Japan, which had already received the concurrence of Stimson, Forrestal and Grew and was designed for joint sponsorship by the United States, the United Kingdom and China, and also by the Soviet Union if she had entered the war by the date of its publication.[112]

This paper the President gave to Mr Churchill on 24 July, desiring him to read it and, if in agreement with its contents, to concur in its dispatch to Chiang Kai-shek.[113] After study by the British delegation the draft was returned to the Americans on the same day with certain small but important amendments, all of which were marked for acceptance,[114] and the amended document was radioed that evening to Chungking.* On the twenty-fifth, the day of his departure to London in order to be present at the result of the British General Election, Mr Churchill gave his formal assent and his willingness to sign.[116] There was a certain technical delay in receiving the Generalissimo's reply, but it finally arrived from Chungking on the twenty-sixth containing agreement with one minor amendment.[117] At 9.20 (Western European time) on the evening of 26 July 1945 – by which time the British electorate had rejected Mr Churchill by a substantial majority – the joint proclamation in its final form was issued by President Truman from Potsdam:†

26 July 1945

We, the President of the United States, the President of the National Government of the Republic of China, and the Prime Minister of Great Britain, representing the hundreds of millions of our countrymen, have conferred and agree that Japan shall be given an opportunity to end the war.

2. The prodigious land, sea, and air forces of the United States, the British Empire, and China, many times reinforced by their armies and air fleets from the West, are poised to strike the final blows upon Japan. This military power is sustained and inspired by the determination of all the Allied nations to prosecute the war against Japan until she ceases to resist.

3. The result of the futile and senseless German resistance to the might of the aroused free peoples of the world stands forth in awful clarity as an example to the people of Japan.

* That admirable and meticulous historian John Ehrman, writing in 1956 (before the publication of the *Potsdam Papers* by the United States State Department in 1960), says that the text of the Potsdam Declaration was sent to Chungking for approval 'probably after 18 July', and while this statement is factually correct it is now possible, from Mr Stimson's diary entry and from the text of the radiogram itself, to pin-point it definitely as the twenty-fourth.[115]

† Since the Soviet Union had not declared war upon Japan by 26 July, she could not be a signatory of the Declaration. The text was not officially communicated to Marshal Stalin in advance, therefore, but President Truman informed him of its contents privately, and a copy was sent to the Soviet delegation after its announcement. Neither Molotov nor Stalin was best pleased at this lack of prior consultation.[118]

The might that now converges on Japan is immeasurably greater than that which, when applied to the resisting Nazis, necessarily laid waste the lands, the industry, and the methods of life of the whole German people. The full application of our military power, backed by our resolve, will mean the inevitable and complete destruction of the Japanese forces, and just as inevitably the utter devastation of the Japanese homeland.

4. The time has come for Japan to decide whether she will continue to be controlled by those self-willed militaristic advisers whose unintelligent calculations have brought the Empire of Japan to the threshold of annihilation, or whether she will follow the path of reason.

5. The following are our terms. We shall not deviate from them. There are no alternatives. We shall brook no delay.

6. There must be eliminated for all time the authority and influence of those who have deceived and misled the people of Japan into embarking on world conquest.

7. Until such a new order is established and until there is convincing proof that Japan's war-making power is destroyed, points in Japanese territory designated by the Allies will be occupied to secure the achievement of the basic objectives we are here setting forth.

8. The terms of the Cairo Declaration shall be carried out, and Japanese sovereignty shall be limited to the islands of Honshu, Hokkaido, Kyushu, Shikoku, and such minor islands as we determine.

9. The Japanese military forces after being completely disarmed shall be permitted to return to their homes, with the opportunity of leading peaceful and productive lives.

10. We do not intend that the Japanese shall be enslaved as a race nor destroyed as a nation, but stern justice will be meted out to all war criminals, including those who have visited cruelties upon our prisoners. The Japanese Government shall remove all obstacles to the revival and strengthening of democratic tendencies among the Japanese people. Freedom of speech, of religion, and of thought, as well as respect for fundamental human rights, shall be established.

11. Japan shall be permitted to maintain such industries as will sustain her economy and allow of the exaction of just reparations in kind, but not those industries which would enable her to rearm for war.

To this end access to, as distinguished from control of, raw materials shall be permitted. Eventual Japanese participation in world trade relations shall be permitted.

12. The occupying forces of the Allies shall be withdrawn from Japan as soon as these objectives have been accomplished, and there has been established, in accordance with the freely expressed will of the Japanese people, a peacefully inclined and responsible Government.

13. We call upon the Government of Japan to proclaim now the unconditional surrender of all the Japanese armed forces, and to

provide proper and adequate assurances of their good faith in such action. The alternative for Japan is complete and utter destruction.[119]

The Potsdam Declaration is a document of great importance. It departed significantly, as may be seen, at the last moment and for the first time, from the bare formula of Unconditional Surrender which, according to the Mikado's message to Stalin in proposing the Konoye Mission, was apparently the main obstacle to peace. It represented, therefore, a success for the more moderate of the President's counsellors,[120] but it still omitted any definite statement as to the future of the Emperor or of the Imperial institution.*

VII

The text of the Potsdam Declaration was picked up by the Japanese radio monitoring service at six o'clock in the morning of 27 July by Tokyo time, and immediately a battle of wills began. The first reactions were divided between acceptance and refusal of the Allied terms.[126] Admiral Toyoda, the Chief of the Imperial Naval Staff, favoured a statement by the Government that the Declaration was absurd and impossible of consideration. Most of the high military commanders, except the Navy Minister, Admiral Mitsumasa Yonai, were advocating

* Meanwhile, before the Potsdam Declaration had been proclaimed, the question of Unconditional Surrender had become an issue of the political warfare campaign waged by the Office of War Information against Japan. The American naval expert on Japanese affairs, Captain Ellis M. Zacharias, had been making a series of broadcasts directed towards convincing the Imperial Government of the necessity of Unconditional Surrender. The twelfth broadcast in this series was scheduled for 21 July, but was preceded, as a part of the campaign, by the publication of an open letter by Captain Zacharias in the *Washington Post*, stating that Unconditional Surrender on the part of Japan must be understood to be within the terms of the Atlantic Charter, whose provisions stated that the victors sought no territorial aggrandizement and that the vanquished would be permitted to choose their own form of government.[121] The letter received considerable publicity and was followed in the same vein by the broadcast of 21 July, the text of which was made public by the O.W.I.[122] The fact that Zacharias had been described over the air without any justification as an 'official spokesman of the United States Government' gave his words an added importance, and both Press and public interpreted his reference to the Atlantic Charter to indicate the formulation of United States policy towards the Emperor. The State Department hastened to deny any direct responsibility for 'clearance' of the broadcast and Elmer Davis, head of the Office of War Information, declared that no specific significance need be attached to the fact that the text of this particular broadcast had been released to the press whereas the others in the series had been withheld.[123] The Japanese reaction to the broadcast was not without interest. In a telegram to Ambassador Sato in Moscow on 25 July, Foreign Minister Togo, while dismissing it as a whole as 'simple propaganda strategy', conceded that special attention should be paid to the fact that this was the first time that reference had been made to the Atlantic Charter, to a peace based on which 'we have no objection'.[124] The reply to Captain Zacharias, broadcast on 24 July by a Professor Kiyoshi Inouye (formerly of the University of Southern California), declared that if an offer of peace were made on the basis of the Atlantic Charter – 'excepting its punitive clause' – the Japanese nation and military 'would automatically, if not willingly, follow in the stopping of the conflict'.[125]

an out-and-out immediate rejection. The Foreign Minister, Shigenori Togo, however, was less violent in his reaction, though he was puzzled by certain discrepancies which he descried between the terms of the Declaration and the phraseology of Captain Zacharias's broadcast. The invocation by the O.W.I. of the Atlantic Charter had succeeded in confusing the outlook not a little, more particularly with regard to the Potsdam territorial provisions for surrender which, Togo considered, 'I did not deem, in the light of the Atlantic Charter, to be fitting'.[127]

Nevertheless, when compared with the terms of Unconditional Surrender imposed on Germany, the Potsdam Declaration seemed to the Foreign Minister to provide a not unattractive basis for the opening of discussions with the Allies, either directly or through the medium of the Soviet Government, which was still at this moment neutral. At this moment the long-anticipated reply from Moscow about the proposed Konoye Mission had still not arrived and Togo therefore advised the Prime Minister, Admiral Suzuki, that until this was received no reply should be sent to the Allied ultimatum, and the statement which the Admiral made in Cabinet that same morning gave Togo to understand that he had won his point.* In publishing the terms of the Declaration, however, the Imperial Government gave to the Japanese people a very 'bowdlerized' version, toning down the original text to make it appear more lenient and attractive than in effect it was.

Unfortunately the Prime Minister met later that evening with the reactionary die-hards of the military High Command.† Admiral Suzuki was old and very tired and he had never been a very forceful man. He was among his service comrades who were fierce and adamant in their arguments and unyielding in the pressure which they brought to bear upon him. They demanded of him – Admiral Yonai dissenting – that he come out strongly and in unequivocal language rejecting the ultimatum. In a moment of weakness, and almost certainly against his better judgement, he consented to do so. At a Press conference held at 3 p.m. (Tokyo time) on the following day (28 July) he informed the journalists that 'the Government does not find any important value in it [the Potsdam Declaration] and there is no other recourse but to ignore it entirely and resolutely fight for the successful conclusion of this war'.[128]

---

* Instructions were immediately sent to Ambassador Sato in Moscow to press for an early reply on the Japanese request for mediation. He was unable to make any contact with the Soviet Foreign Office, save with Vice-Commissar S. A. Lozovsky, until, on 6 August, he got word that Molotov would receive him at 5 p.m. Moscow time (11 p.m. Tokyo time) on the eighth.

† There were present at this meeting, among others, the two Service Ministers, General Koreihika Anami and Admiral Mitsumasa Yonai, and the two Chiefs of Staff, General Yoshijiro Umezu and Admiral Toyoda.

This statement in itself was blind enough, but its effect was further complicated by the use of the word *mokusatsu* in describing the intention of the Imperial Government regarding the Declaration. Forthwith there arose one of the bitterest controversies of the war, which still remains unresolved.

The American translators rendered *mokusatsu* as 'ignore', but it is in dispute whether Suzuki really meant to use it in this sense. A Japanese–English dictionary offers alternative meanings, namely 'to take no notice of', 'to treat with silent contempt' and 'to ignore'. Shades of meaning creep in here and it has been argued by some Japanese protagonists that, for example, 'to ignore it should have meant simply that we refrained from commenting on it'[129] – thus implying neither contempt nor rejection – and another writer goes so far as to conjecture: 'Who knows but that save for the fateful word *mokusatsu*, Japan might have been spared the horrors of the atomic bomb.'[130] Foreign Minister Togo, however, does not question the meaning of *mokusatsu* as understood by the American translator,[131] and there is evidence that the War Minister, General Anami, was working to persuade the newspapers to interpret the term *mokusatsu* as 'rejection by ignoring'.[132]

Appalled and amazed at what he read for the first time in the newspapers, Shigenori Togo could only deplore an action which he understood as 'most disadvantageous for Japan'. He essayed redress and failed to achieve it; he sought comfort and found none.[133] For at Potsdam the Suzuki announcement had been interpreted, not altogether unnaturally, in its crudest and worst aspect. As Secretary Stimson has noted grimly:

> In the face of this rejection we could only proceed to demonstrate that the ultimatum had meant exactly what it said when it stated that if the Japanese continued the war, the full application of our military power, backed by our resolve, will mean the inevitable and complete destruction of the Japanese armed forces and just as inevitably the utter devastation of the Japanese homeland.[134]

VIII

At Potsdam the conference continued in a strangely unreal atmosphere. The Japanese response to the Declaration came as something of a surprise, but there was no wavering in President Truman's mind as to the necessity of using the new weapon. Agreement on this point had been reached between himself and Mr Churchill, but Britain's chief representative at the conference was now Mr Attlee, whom the President proceeded to 'put in the picture'. On 1 August he wrote to the new Prime Minister informing him of the latest weapon and of the agreement for its use. To this Attlee replied with warmth and gratitude, saying that he would come to see the President that afternoon.[135]*

The atmosphere was now one of rising tension. All was ready for the use of the bomb, but not even President Truman knew exactly when the drop would be made. As early as 24 July (i.e. two days before the Potsdam Declaration was issued) the President had sent an order to General Carl Spaatz, commanding the Strategic Air Services, alerting him to 'deliver its first special bomb as soon as weather will permit visual bombing after about 3 August 1945 on one of the targets: Hiroshima, Kokura, Niigata and Nagasaki. . . . Additional bombs will be delivered on the above targets as soon as made ready by the project staff.'[137]

With this order the President had taken his decision; on the same day he sent instructions to Secretary Stimson (who had returned to Washington ahead of him) that the order to Spaatz would stand unless the President notified him that the Japanese reply to the Potsdam Declaration was acceptable.

The declaration of the Suzuki Government that the Japanese Government had decided to treat the Allied ultimatum with *mokusatsu* had become known at Potsdam late on the evening of 28 July. The conference dispersed on 2 August, and after a historic meeting and luncheon with King George VI in Plymouth Sound the U.S.S. *Augusta* and *Philadelphia* set out upon their return journey that same afternoon.[138] Four days later, on 6 August, as the President and Secretary Byrnes were lunching with the crew of *Augusta*, the message arrived for which all had been waiting with varying degrees of excitement. The first atomic-bomb attack in the history of the world had been successfully carried out on Hiroshima.[139]

IX

At the close of a meeting at Potsdam between President Truman, Secretary Byrnes and Molotov (Stalin was absent owing to a slight indisposition) on Sunday, 29 July, the Soviet Foreign Minister put forward the suggestion that in order to provide 'an immediate cause' for Russia's entry into the Far Eastern War, the British, American and Chinese Governments should send a formal request to the Soviet

* Unfortunately there exists no copy of President Truman's original letter, which was handwritten, nor does the log of his movements show any record of a meeting between himself and the Prime Minister. Lord Attlee, however, subsequently wrote that though he knew that the 'Tube Alloy' project existed 'the first news I had of it [the bomb] was from President Truman at Potsdam, when he told me of the successful explosion in New Mexico. Agreement for the dropping of the Bomb by the United States had already been given by Sir Winston Churchill on behalf of Britain. I was, therefore, not called upon to make a decision, but if I had been I should have agreed with President Truman. . . . His was the decision and courageously he took it.'[136]

Government asking them to declare war on Japan. The basis for such a request might, he suggested, be the failure of the Japanese to accept the Allied ultimatum and the desire to shorten the war and save loss of life. Of course, he added, it was assumed that the Sino-Soviet Agreement would be signed before any such declaration of war took place.[140]

This Soviet manœuvre came as a surprise to President Truman, and an unpleasant one at that. He played for time, saying that he must give it careful consideration, and at once consulted with the British delegates, Mr Attlee, Mr Bevin and Sir Alexander Cadogan, and with Secretary Byrnes and Admiral Leahy. The President, with his admirable pragmatic commonsense, saw in this new move from Moscow a cynical attempt to make the Soviet entry into the Pacific War appear to be the decisive factor in the defeat of Japan. The Western Allies were under no obligation to give the Russians a pretext for breaking with Japan, since at Yalta (reaffirmed at Potsdam) Stalin had agreed to enter the war in the East three months after V.E. Day, provided that the Sino-Soviet Agreement implementing the Yalta Far Eastern Accord had been concluded. 'I was not willing', he wrote later, 'to let Russia reap the fruits of a long and bitter and gallant effort in which she had had no part.'[141]

Nor was Secretary Byrne less disturbed. He did not wish the United States to be implicated or in any way responsible for the denunciation of the Soviet–Japanese non-aggression pact, which would have to be illegally terminated by the Russians, since it did not expire for nearly a year.[142]

The truth of the matter was, or course, not so much the high moral considerations adduced by President Truman and his Secretary of State as the fact that, with the imminent dropping of the atomic bomb, they were hoping for a speedy Japanese surrender which would render the Soviet entry into the war unnecessary.

This attitude represented a marked reversal of the policy followed at Yalta and also at the beginning of the Potsdam Conference, when no sacrifice appeared to be too heavy, no price too great, and no third party's interests too sacred, to bring the Soviet Union into the war against Japan. Now it seemed that no manœuvre was too devious to keep her out.

Byrnes and his legal adviser, Benjamin Cohen, thereupon drafted for the President's signature a statement of such sophistry that the mind boggles at its achievement. The object of the exercise was to find a means of avoiding a definite rejection of the Soviet request without committing the United States Government and its allies, and they succeeded to a fantastic degree. They recalled that in the Moscow Declaration of October 1943 the Soviet Government and the Western Allies had agreed 'to consult with each other . . . with a view to joint action on behalf of the community of nations', and that in Article 103 of the United Nations Charter it was provided that 'in the event of a conflict between the obligations of the Members of United Nations under the present Charter and those under any other international agreement, their obligations under the present Charter shall prevail'. Disregarding the fact that the Charter, though signed at San Francisco, had not been formally ratified, the drafters of this statement would have President Truman say: 'It seems to me under the terms of the Moscow Declaration and the provisions of the Charter, above referred to, it would be proper for the Soviet Union to indicate its willingness to consult and co-operate with other great powers now at war with Japan with a view to joint action on behalf of the community of nations to maintain peace and security.'[143]

With this communication, which was handed unofficially and unsigned to Marshal Stalin on 31 July,[144] there was a covering memorandum to say that this letter, duly signed, would be sent formally to the Marshal by the President 'at your convenience after you notify me you have reached an agreement with the Government of China'.[145]

In considering this episode it is impossible to disagree with the verdict of Herbert Feis: 'All the citations around which this sophistical statement was woven were taken out of context, it may be said bluntly. Yet the President approved it, and Attlee concurred in it.'[146]

In effect, however, this document was not given official being. The tempo of events became so swift that, like Alice through the Looking-glass, the Soviets were kept busy running fast to stay where they were and not to be left behind. The negotiations with T. V. Soong and Wang Shih-chieh were resumed on the return of Stalin and Molotov to Moscow from Potsdam on 6 August and, in order to delay matters until they had reached a satisfactory conclusion, the Soviet Government continued to procrastinate in their dealings with the Japanese Ambassador, who was pressing for Soviet intervention with the Allies in an effort to mitigate the formula of Unconditional Surrender. On 30 July, and again on 2 August, Sato, under pressure from Tokyo, begged the Soviet Foreign Office to obtain approval for the dispatch of Prince Konoye on a mission of peace. He besought the Deputy Commisar, Lozovsky, not to regard the Potsdam Declaration and its reception by the Suzuki Government as a final episode, for, despite appearances, it was still hoped that, once Prince Konoye had arrived in Moscow, the Declaration might be used as the basis of the study regarding definite peace terms.[147] He received no scintilla of satisfaction from Lozovsky.

Molotov pursued his delaying tactics – for Lozovsky was clearly acting under instructions – until suddenly confronted with the amazing news of the attack on Hiroshima on 6 August. Thereafter he acted very quickly. Jettisoned was the *conditio sine qua non* that a Sino-Soviet Agreement must precede a declaration of war on Japan. The negotiations were indeed resumed, but they were relegated now to a place of secondary importance.* The vital thing was to get into the Pacific War as soon as possible lest it should end too precipitately and Russia be cheated of her share of the spoils.

Forthwith the luckless Sato was summoned to the Foreign Office on 8 August to be told by Molotov that a state of war existed between the Soviet Union and Japan as from the following day as a result of the rejection of the Potsdam Declaration, in response to the request of the Allied Powers, in order to 'deliver the people from further sacrifices and suffering and to enable the Japanese people to avoid those dangers and destruction which Germany had undergone'. He thus used a 'bowdlerized' version of the Byrnes–Cohen letter which President Truman had given to Stalin on 31 July. Soviet armies swept into Manchuria at once and encountered little resistance.[148]†

As Senator Alexander Wiley of Wisconsin remarked on hearing the news: 'Apparently the atomic bomb which hit Hiroshima also blew "Joey" off the fence.'[150]

X

By mid-morning on 6 August it was known in Tokyo that a strange bomb of stupendous force had obliterated the city of Hiroshima, a naval base and also Western Army Headquarters. The civilian casualty toll was immense; the Provincial Governor perished with the citizens, the Commander-in-Chief escaped unhurt.[151] The full hideous gravamen of the report received by the Vice-Chief of the General Staff, General Toroshiro Kanabe, was contained in one terrifying sentence: 'The whole city of Hiroshima was destroyed instantly by a single bomb.'[152]

No meeting of the Cabinet took place on that day and even on the seventh no decision was reached, pending the result of the investigation which the Army had ordered. But the Supreme War Council met on the seventh and listened to fantastic and benighted arguments on the part of the Army, who were not prepared to accept the Potsdam Declaration, even as a basis for negotiations, unless serious counter-conditions and reservations were put forward. Unreality could not go further.[153]

---

* The Sino-Soviet Agreement was eventually signed on 14 August 1945 and ratified ten days later (see above, p. 361 n.).

† Molotov informed Averell Harriman and Sir Archibald Clark Kerr of the Soviet action on the evening of 8 August. 'This move did not surprise us' is President Truman's comment.[149]

Meanwhile the Allies were far from inactive. Millions of leaflets were showered upon Japan by the American Air Force urging capitulation in order to avoid further devastation, and intensified radio propaganda was carried on. By night the arguments became more forceful. 130 B-29s raided the Japanese homeland on the seventh and on the eighth the Twentieth Air Force reported 420 B-29s in day and night sorties.[154]

The Foreign Minister, Togo, now assumed personal responsibility for informing the Emperor of the catastrophic situation. On the afternoon of 8 August he was received in audience in the Imperial air-raid shelter. The Mikado quickly grasped the necessity for immediate measures, realizing that 'since bargaining for terms had little prospect of success at this stage, measures should be concerted to ensure a prompt ending of hostilities'.[155]

On receiving the Foreign Minister's report of his audience, the Prime Minister summoned a further meeting of the Supreme War Council for the following morning (9 August), but before they could convene news reached them in the early hours that the Soviet Union had declared war on Japan. It was therefore under this additional shadow of calamity that the Supreme Council met at eleven o'clock, and before it adjourned two hours later came the further tidings that a second bomb had demolished Nagasaki.

Yet even this stark and terrifying evidence could not bring Japan's rulers to a sense of reality and of the inevitable. The military reactionaries and 'last-ditchers' opposed resolutely the acceptance of the Potsdam Declaration without conditions. For hours they argued and blustered, refusing to face facts, thundering of national honour and prestige, and of forlorn hopes and last stands. Neither could the Imperial Cabinet reach a conclusion, for here again the War Minister, General Anami, continued to reject the counsels of reason.

All day was consumed by futile wranglings while the sands of Japan's destiny ran out and the horrid expectation of a third nuclear bomb hung above them.* Finally, shortly before midnight on 9 August, the issue was referred by Admiral Suzuki to Imperial arbitration and decision. The Supreme War Council met in the Emperor's presence. Once more the conflicting forces deployed their arguments; once more they failed hopelessly to convince each other. Despairingly the Prime Minister placed the responsibility for a final decision upon the Emperor, humbly begging his adjudication.

Hirohito responded with calm courage and wisdom. The confidence of the armed services – and particularly the Army – could not be relied

---

* There was in fact no third bomb at the immediate disposal of the American Air Force, though others even more powerful were on the way.[156]

upon, he said, their earlier forecasts having often been at variance with
the realities. Therefore he gave his approval to the course advised by the
Foreign Minister. He would submit to the terms of the Potsdam
Declaration as they stood. Under his Imperial prerogative he took the
final overwhelming decision to end the war.

This Imperial mandate had been given at about half past two on the
morning of 10 August. Within half an hour the Cabinet was in session.
By seven o'clock identical messages had gone out to the Japanese
Legations in Berne and in Stockholm for transmission to Washington.
The message was clear and unequivocal. The Japanese Government
were ready to accept the terms of the Potsdam Declaration, with but one
reservation – 'that the said declaration does not comprise any demand
which prejudices the prerogatives of His Majesty as a Sovereign
Ruler'.[157]

XI

Meanwhile in Washington – whither the President and his advisers had
returned from Potsdam on the evening of 7 August – there was some
disappointment that the dropping of the first atomic bomb on Hiroshima had not evoked some definite and positive reaction from the
Japanese Government.[158] It was decided to give the enemy three days'
grace while maintaining an inexorable 'conventional' air bombardment
and propaganda offensive.

On 8 August, early in the afternoon, President Truman received
notification from Moscow of the Soviet Union's declaration of war on
Japan. He at once called a Press conference and disposed of this momentous news in five sentences, surely the most terse welcome which any ally
has ever been accorded! After four preliminary and explanatory
remarks, the President said: 'Russia has declared war on Japan, that is
all.'[159] President Coolidge could scarcely have been briefer.

But here indeed was irony. That which President Roosevelt had so
long sought for, that for which he had pursued so doggedly a policy of
appeasement and concession, had been achieved at last and it was but
Dead Sea fruit, hailed with reluctance and brevity by his successor.
The whole course of the world's history had changed since 18 June when
President Truman had announced to his advisers that, at the coming
Potsdam Conference, one of his objectives would be to get from Russia
'all the assistance in the war that was possible'.* That brilliant blinding
flash at Alamogordo, that mushrooming cloud above Hiroshima, had not
only ushered in a new and uncharted era, but had rendered Soviet
assistance in the Pacific War altogether unnecessary, and President

* See above, p. 364.

Truman would have given much at this juncture to keep the Russians out. Yet such was the momentum of Fate that Russia's entry could not be prevented and, with the melancholy of hindsight, one can now see that within this action lay the kernel of the Korean War some five years later.

The second bomb was dropped on Nagasaki on 9 August, and on the following day there followed the Japanese acceptance of the Potsdam Declaration as a basis for surrender, with the one reservation safeguarding the person and authority of the Emperor. Because of the vagaries afforded by the International Date Line and general difference in time, the text of the Japanese acceptance arrived in Washington on the same day and date, and approximately at the same hour, as it left Tokyo, and straight away President Truman went into conference with his closest advisers, Byrnes, Stimson, Forrestal and Leahy. The discussion was long and lively, for now at last the issue of the Emperor and of the Imperial institution – that issue which had been so carefully avoided in previous discussions and in the Potsdam Declaration itself – had been brought into the open. The time for the final crunch had arrived. The question was clear. Were the Allies to accept the one Japanese reservation to Unconditional Surrender? Were they to continue the Pacific War indefinitely in order to accomplish the dethronement of the Emperor, with the consequent chaos which would inevitably occur within the Japanese Empire itself and among her armies abroad?

Stimson, Leahy and Forrestal were for immediate acceptance of the Japanese offer to surrender, together with its reservation. Though Stimson had disagreed with Joseph Grews' desire for an earlier statement by the Allies safeguarding the Emperor's authority and excluding him from indictment as a major war criminal, he had now changed his mind. In order to end the war in the shortest possible time and to avoid enormous loss of life, both Allied and Japanese, he counselled using the Emperor as their instrument to command and compel his people to stop fighting. Both Leahy and Forrestal supported this view – not, as the Admiral wrote later, 'that I favoured the Emperor retaining all his prerogatives. I had no feelings about little Hirohito, but was convinced that it would be necessary to use him in effecting the surrender.'[160]

Opposition to this view came from Secretary Byrnes, who felt that, cogent though these arguments were, they did constitute a divergence from the agreement which had been reached at Potsdam and embodied in the Allied Declaration, to which Russia had now adhered. This had called for Unconditional Surrender without stipulation. It would not therefore be correct to accept the Japanese reservation immediately without prior consultation with the other Allies involved. He won his way and he was deputed by the President to draft the reply to the Japanese. This was completed by noon (Washington time) and was a masterpiece of hedging. It said that the Emperor's authority and that of his Government to rule would, from the moment of surrender, be subject to the authority of the Supreme Allied Commander and that the Emperor personally should sign the surrender document. It added that the future government of Japan would be left to the freely expressed will of the Japanese people.[161]

This text was dispatched for consideration to London, Chungking and Moscow. Chiang Kai-shek accepted it as it stood.[162] The British, replying within six hours, made, according to Secretary Byrnes, one modification, namely that the Emperor's agents, and not the Emperor himself, should sign the terms of surrender. This was, in effect, not the case. What the Government did suggest was that the surrender should be signed not only by the Emperor but also by the Japanese Government and by the Japanese military authorities.[163]* In the final text, which was somewhat hurriedly prepared, it was demanded that 'The Emperor will be required to authorize and ensure the signature by the Government of Japan and the Japanese Imperial General Headquarters of the surrender terms necessary to carry out the provisions of the Potsdam Declaration'.[165]

The Russians were more obstructive. With an eye on extending the area of occupation effected by their armies in Manchuria, they proposed a delaying course of action. This was opposed by Averell Harriman and after some argument the Soviet conditions were withdrawn.[166]

The Allied views having been collated, the reply to the Japanese offer was dispatched from Washington, through Berne, on the morning of 11 August.

The Allied reply was received in Tokyo at a quarter to one in the morning of 12 August (Tokyo time) and at once there developed a heated discussion both in the Supreme War Council and in the Cabinet. The service representatives, with the exception again of the Navy Minister, Admiral Yonai, demanded the rejection of the Allied terms on the grounds that they infringed the Imperial authority and institution, by virtue of paragraph 5 – namely, that the Japanese people would be permitted to decide, by their freely expressed will, their ultimate form of

---

* The impression left in London by the precipitancy of the American approach was that they had behaved in a very high-handed manner, since the British amendment, though accepted, was not acknowledged, and the final reply was dispatched by Byrnes without further notification. 'It was cool of the Americans to go ahead without consulting us or the other two', Pierson Dixon wrote in his diary on 11 August, 'but it is characteristic of their healthy aggressive mood to wish to take the lead and be the spokesman.'[164]

government. Against them was the Foreign Minister, Togo, supported by the Marquess Kido, Keeper of the Privy Seal, and the Navy Minister. Togo maintained that paragraph 5 contained no real infringement and that any attempt by the Japanese Government to advance further conditions of surrender might well result in the Allies abolishing the Imperial House altogether. Between these two groups of contestants the aged Prime Minister, Suzuki, wavered and fluctuated like a distracted hen.

For nearly two mortal days the argument continued, while Allied patience neared exhaustion and unrest was being fomented by the War Minister within the armed forces.* Finally, at 10.50 on the morning of 14 August, the matter was again referred to the Emperor for a final decision. He listened patiently while both sides stated their case, severally and in detail. Then very calmly and serenely he gave his command. On the vital point of paragraph 5, he said: 'I agree with the Foreign Minister that it is not intended to subvert the national polity of Japan; but, unless the war be brought to an end at this moment, I fear that the national polity will be destroyed, and the nation annihilated.' He therefore commanded that an Imperial Rescript be prepared forthwith, declaring the acceptance of the Allied terms and the end of the war.

It was undoubtedly a noble performance and one which deeply affected all those present. We 'wept at these reasoned and gracious words, and at conceiving the Emperor's emotions', wrote Shigenori Togo. 'It was an inexpressibly solemn and moving scene.' As the last 'Council before the Throne' in the history of Japan dispersed and he drove to a Cabinet meeting: 'each of us in his thoughts wept again'.[168]

That night the text of the Japanese acceptance of Unconditional Surrender was handed to the Swiss Minister in Tokyo. It was received in Washington at 4 p.m. (Washington time) on the same day. The Imperial Rescript was duly issued and on 15 August the Emperor broadcast directly to the people of Japan announcing the end of the

---

* General Anami's activities were in part successful. On the night of 14–15 August a *coup détat* was attempted in Tokyo by officers of the Imperial Garrison, who sought to seize the person of the Emperor and arrest prominent members of the peace party. This was put down with some bloodshed and after the homes of Foreign Minister Togo and the Marquess Kido had been destroyed by fire. As late as 20 August there was a second abortive attempt by Army officers to seize the Palace, while officers of the Air Force dropped leaflets urging the population to continue the war and to rally to a 'Government of Resistance'. General Anami committed suicide on 15 August after the failure of the first *coup*, and Admiral Onishi, Vice Chief of the Naval Staff and himself a distinguished air pilot, after the second.[167]

It is of interest to note that whereas on 20 July 1944 Army officers in Berlin sought to assassinate Hitler and to overthrow the Nazi régime in Germany in order to bring about peace, these Japanese military risings were attempted in order to remove the Emperor from the influence of his pacifist advisers and to continue the war.

war and the defeat of Japan, and ordering all Japanese armed forces to cease fighting.

General Douglas MacArthur, as Supreme Commander of the Allied forces in the Pacific theatre of war, had been appointed by President Truman to organize and to receive the Japanese surrender, and for this purpose preliminary discussions opened at his headquarters at Manila on 19 August with a delegation headed by General Torashiro Kanabe, Vice-Chief of the General Staff. As a result of the orders then given by the Supreme Allied Commander, the way was made clear for the final act of the drama of surrender.

On the quarter-deck of U.S.S. *Missouri*, one of America's most powerful ships of war, riding at anchor in Tokyo Bay, on the morning of 2 September 1945, General MacArthur received the Unconditional Surrender of the Japanese Empire. He did so in the presence of representatives of those other Allied Powers who had borne the brunt of Japanese aggression – Britain, China, Australia, New Zealand, the Netherlands and France – and of the Soviet Union. And there were others – wasted and recently liberated figures from the past. General Jonathan M. Wainwright, hero of the gallant defence of Corregidor and Bataan, was there, and with him General Arthur Percival, whose defence of Singapore had been even more tragic. These two watched the Unconditional Surrender of those who had exacted similar humiliation from themselves.*

The Supreme Commander was under no instructions as to procedure. He was on his own – 'with only God and my own conscience to guide me'[169] – and he was sombre of utterance and severe of mien. In a slow clear voice he addressed the Japanese representatives, Mamoru Shigemitsu, the Foreign Minister in the new Government of Prince Higashikuni, the Emperor's cousin, and General Yoshijiro Umezu, Chief of the Imperial General Staff. He spoke for only a few minutes and then invited the Japanese to sign. It was just nine o'clock. First the Foreign Minister wrote his name followed by the Chief of the General Staff. There was a measured pause and then General MacArthur added his name, to be followed by the Allied representatives.[170]

It was all over. The greatest, most ghastly war in history had been fought and won. The victory had taken just six years to achieve – six years filled with suffering and heroism, courage and destruction, gallantry and endurance, of hope now realized, of hope deferred, and the tragic loss of many millions of lives.

---

* Another spectator of the surrender on board U.S.S. *Missouri* was a young lieutenant in the British Navy then known as Prince Philip of Greece, who some years later was to marry Princess Elizabeth of England.

17 | The Trial and Punishment of the Nazi War Criminals

I

THE trial and punishment of Axis war criminals did not become an act of faith for the Allied Powers until the Conference of Foreign Ministers held in Moscow in October 1943.* On 13 January 1942, a Nine-Power Conference, sitting in London, had adopted a Declaration on the subject, calling Germany to book for acts of aggression, imposition of régimes of terror and other acts of violence and oppression, and warning that she must ultimately answer for these crimes 'in order to satisfy the sense of justice of the civilized world'. Some months later, in August 1942, President Roosevelt had warned the Axis Powers that 'the time will come when they will have to stand in the courts of law in the very countries they were oppressing and answer for their acts',[1] and the Declaration of the Moscow Conference went no further than this, save that it gave official recognition to the principle.

It was, however, at the Moscow Conference that divergent views first appeared among the Allies as to how the punishment of war criminals should be effected. M. Molotov was in favour of 'stern swift justice'. Mr Eden argued that all the legal forms should be observed. Mr Hull put his view forthrightly: 'If I had my way,' he said, 'I would take Hitler and Mussolini and Tojo and their accomplices and bring them before a drumhead court-martial and at sunrise on the following day there would occur an historic incident.' This speedy action, he contended, would make certain the prompt disposition of world gangsters who were worse in their methods and purposes than a million mad dogs let loose on every centre of population.[2]

In the early years of the war the British had been too vitally concerned with their struggle for survival to evolve a definite plan for retribution for war crimes, and the same was true of the Americans. As Secretary of War Henry Stimson wrote later:

> We did not ask ourselves in 1939 or in 1940, or even in 1941, what punishment, if any, Hitler and his chief assistants deserved. We asked

* See above, p. 119.

simply two questions: How do we avoid war, and how do we prevent this wickedness from overwhelming us? These seemed larger questions to us than the guilt or innocence of individuals.[3]

Thus, when the Big Three of the Grand Alliance met for the first time in Tehran, in November 1943, the Allied policy on war criminals had not progressed further than the punishment of those imbrued (Mr Churchill's word) by atrocities and had not so far concerned itself with those who had been engaged in crimes on a grander scale. Nor was it greatly clarified as a result of the Tehran Conference. Relegated to the tail of the agenda, it was not discussed until the dinner party on the evening of 29 November, and then only – in so far as Marshal Stalin and President Roosevelt were concerned – in a jocular manner which shocked Mr Churchill.*

The Marshal, with grim humour, declared that at least 50,000 of the German General Staff must be physically and summarily liquidated, and the President, in a similar mood, suggested that the number be reduced to 49,000. The Prime Minister was revolted both by the levity and the philosophy of his colleagues. He took strong exception to the cold-blooded execution of soldiers who had fought for their country. Those who had committed atrocities should be tried in the countries in which these acts had been committed, but he was vehemently opposed to execution for political purposes. The British people, he declared, would never stand for such mass murders and he reiterated that no one, Nazi or no, should be summarily dealt with before a firing-squad without proper legal trial. 'I would rather', he said, 'be taken out into the garden here now and be shot myself than sully my own and my country's honour by such infamy.'†

It is not impossible that the Prime Minister also had in mind the circumstances which had prevailed at the end of the First World War. Then there had been a strong popular demand for the punishment of those who had perpetrated crimes and atrocities during the war and, in addition, for the indictment of the ex-Kaiser as the individual most responsible for the war. The matter was the subject of careful discussion

* See above, p. 153.

† According to the version of this conversation as given by the British Ambassador, Sir Archibald Clark Kerr, to Lord Moran, Mr Churchill said: 'I will not be a party to any butchery in cold blood. What happens in hot blood is another matter. . . . I would rather be taken out now and shot than so disgrace my country.' He did not make any reference to the trials of those who had committed atrocities. According, however, to Mr Churchill himself, to Charles Bohlen, who kept the minutes for the dinner-table conversation for the State Department, and the President's son, Elliott Roosevelt, who was also present, the conversation went as recorded above. Mr Churchill sent a minute to Sir Alexander Cadogan on the subject on 19 April 1944 but, as will be seen (see below, p. 398), he changed his view somewhat at a subsequent date.[4]

among the Allies immediately after the signature of the Armistice. M. Clemenceau favoured a trial of the Kaiser, with a sentence, in the event of a verdict of 'guilty', of condemnation to international outlawry, 'so that there should be no land in which he could set his foot'.[5] Mr Balfour wished to take administrative action, as had been done in the case of Napoleon, rather than a legal trial, in the course of which the arguments of lawyers 'would draw attention off the main fact that this man was the ringleader in the greatest crime against the human race on which the eyes of the whole world ought to be fixed'.[6] The Italians, while in accordance with the general principle of bringing the Kaiser to justice, warned against the danger of martyrdom and cited the subsequent value of the 'St Helena legend' to the Bonapartist cause, culminating in the establishment of the Second Empire.[7] In America, President Wilson did not commit himself definitely before the Armistice, but neither his 'Texas Talleyrand', Colonel Edward House, nor his Secretary of State, Robert Lansing, were enthusiastic advocates of trying the Kaiser, which they feared would militate against the creation of an 'enduring peace'. In Britain, Mr Lloyd George was firmly in support of a trial.[8]*

The outcome of these varying views, which were forcefully pursued throughout the relevant committees and subcommittees of the Paris Peace Conference, was the provision in the Treaty of Versailles (Article 227) for the arraignment and trial of the ex-Kaiser, 'for a supreme offence against international morality and the sanctity of treaties', before a specially constituted tribunal comprised of five judges, appointed respectively by the United States, Great Britain, France, Italy and Japan. It would be the duty of the tribunal 'to fix the punishment which it considers should be imposed'. Under Articles 228 and 229, the German Government undertook to surrender to the Allies for trial before military tribunals 'persons accused of having committed acts in violation of the laws and customs of war'. In addition, by Article 231, which was the introduction to the reparation clauses (Part VIII) of the Treaty, the Allies affirmed and Germany accepted the responsibility of Germany and her allies for all loss and damage incurred 'as a conse-

---

* In fairness to Mr Lloyd George it must be recorded that he never did use the words 'Hang the Kaiser' which have frequently been attributed to him. What he did say in his famous Bristol speech on 9 December 1918 was that 'The Kaiser must be prosecuted' and that 'Germany would pay to the utmost limit of her capacity'.[9] It was George Barnes, the Labour member of the War Cabinet, who declaimed on 30 November 1918 'I am for hanging the Kaiser', and Sir Eric Geddes, then a Conservative candidate for the Borough of Cambridge, who said on 9 December: 'I have personally no doubt that we will get everything out of her [Germany] that you can squeeze out of a lemon and a bit more.'[10] On this the Press added the gloss of 'Squeeze them till the pips squeak'.

quence of the war imposed by the aggression of Germany and her allies'.

This was indeed a formidable reckoning, but it was virtually without result. Protected by the robust and adamant refusal of Queen Wilhelmina to extradite him in the face of strenuous Allied pressure, the German Emperor remained in exile in Holland until his death in June 1941.[11] Though the Allies presented to the German Government in Weimar a comprehensive list of war criminals, beginning with the names of the German and Bavarian Crown Princes and ending with those of 'other ranks', it persistently refused to surrender them and professed itself helpless in the matter of bringing them to trial. After months of wrangling the Allied Governments agreed to a test case of twelve obscure men who were brought before the Supreme Court of the Reich at Leipzig. The accused at once became popular heroes in Germany, where they were portrayed as martyrs rather than criminals. Six were acquitted outright; the remainder received sufficiently trifling sentences as to be farcical. Thus ended the punishment of war criminals.[12]

The Allied Governments clung to the war-guilt clause of the Treaty (Article 231) as the basis of the reparation claims, and successive German Chancellors sought anxiously to achieve its repeal. Gustav Stresemann in 1925 very nearly wrecked the whole basis of the Locarno Agreement by refusing to allow Germany to enter the League of Nations until a formal recantation of the war-guilt clause had been made by the Allies. To this demand Aristide Briand replied with one of the briefest Notes in diplomatic history. It consisted of two sentences:

1. The question of German guilt was settled at Versailles.
2. It only depends on Germany to hasten the evacuation of the Cologne Zone.*

Foiled of this intention, Stresemann, two years later, persuaded President von Hindenburg to pronounce a solemn disavowal of war guilt on the occasion of the dedication of the Tannenburg Memorial (17 September 1927):

The accusation that Germany was responsible for this greatest of all wars we hereby repudiate. Germans in every walk of life unanimously reject it. It was in no spirit of envy, hatred or lust of conquest that we unsheathed the sword.... With clean hearts we marched out to defend the Fatherland and with clean hands did we wield the sword. Germany is ready at any moment to prove this fact before an impartial tribunal.[13]

* The evacuation of the three zones occupied by Allied troops in accordance with the provisions of the Treaty of Versailles was made dependent on the fulfilment by Germany of her obligations incurred under the Treaty – notably in respect of reparations and disarmament.

The egregious Franz von Papen also sought a similar end at the Lausanne Conference in 1932. Arguing that since Article 231 was the first article of Part VIII of the Treaty of Versailles which was abrogated by the Conference in respect of reparation payments, von Papen maintained that the whole contained the part and sought to have a formal declaration to this effect included in the Final Act of the conference. But to this neither Ramsay MacDonald nor Édouard Herriot would agree, and von Papen had to satisfy himself with making a public – but unilateral – statement on 11 July 1932 that 'The war-guilt clause has been removed from the Treaty of Versailles with the lapsing of Part VIII'.[14]

It was inevitable that the subject of war guilt should figure largely in the campaign of the Nazi Party against the Treaty of Versailles, both before and after the Revolution of 1933, which brought them to power in Germany. It was a sure means of rallying popular support against the Reich Government when in opposition and against Britain and France when in power. The final repudiation of Article 231 was made by Adolf Hitler in a speech before the Reichstag on 30 January 1937:

> I solemnly withdraw the German signature from that declaration which was extracted under duress from a weak government, acting against its better judgement, namely the declaration that Germany was responsible for the war.[15]

Thus ended the second attempt in history to bring war criminals to justice. In the first attempt the Powers first declared Napoleon to be an outlaw and then implemented this declaration by executive action in exiling him to St Helena. The result had been to remove the immediate cause of disturbance to a safe distance, but also to perpetuate the Napoleonic legend in France. In their second attempt the powers had been more ambitious. They had arranged to bring the Kaiser to trial 'for a supreme offence against international morality and the sanctity of treaties'; to execute justice on those who had committed violations of the laws of war and of humanity; and they had endeavoured, by extracting a declaration of responsibility for the war, to instil some sense of political war guilt into the German people.

For a variety of reasons they failed to achieve any of these objectives, and yet the efforts which they made to attain them were not entirely wasted. For, just as in 1815 the decision of the powers to fasten the responsibility of war guilt upon the person of the Emperor Napoleon constituted a new departure in the Law of Nations and a precedent for future generations, so the labours of the Allied Governments after the First World War carried the process a step further, strengthening the precedent already established and creating other prototypes (and

warnings) for the benefit of those who came after. By their very failure
they made a valuable, if negative, contribution, and their errors were
not neglected by those who in later years were called upon to face
similar problems.*

The dangers and difficulties inherent in these historical precedents
did not escape the careful notice of the leaders of the Western democracies and their advisers during the Second World War. Nor were
they unaware of the depth of feeling and the consequent imperative
demands for retribution which had been stirred within the countries
occupied by Axis troops and reflected in the views of their Governments-
in-exile in London, where a United Nations War Crimes Commission
had been operating since 1943, and had prepared a long list of Nazis
who were suspected of criminal activities.

It had been the general intention of the Big Three at Tehran that
legal clarification of their expressed policy as regards the trial and
punishment of war criminals should go forward forthwith and should
have taken some definite and positive form before their next meeting.
In fact, because of the rapidly increased tempo of hostilities and the
concurrent pressure of affairs at a high level, nothing of the sort was
set in train until the beginning of 1945, when it became evident that
the leaders of the Grand Alliance would have to meet again in the
imminent future. Even then the preparation was greater in the United
States than in Britain, where the War Crimes Executive, under the

---

* In the years between the wars efforts were made through the machinery of the
League of Nations and by separate acts of diplomatic initiative, such as the Locarno
Agreement and the Kellogg–Briand Pact, to circumscribe and reduce the risks of war by
emphasizing the criminal aspect of aggression. At the same time much attention was
given towards the regulating and humanizing of the conduct of war, should that
calamity again occur. The First World War had disclosed many gaps in the existing
rules of war and the introduction of new weapons of destruction, unimagined at the
time of the Hague Conferences of 1899 and 1907, made it evident that new international
legislation was required. The Geneva Protocol of 1925 prohibiting the use of poisonous
gases and the Geneva Convention of 1929 which sought to ensure the fair and proper
treatment of prisoners of war were achievements in this field, and there were significant
efforts made to enact and enforce laws governing the conduct of war at sea, especially of
U-boat warfare. The Washington Disarmament Conference of 1921–2 sought to
clarify the question of criminal responsibility in this respect. The conference failed,
largely owing to the opposition of the French delegation, to achieve its wider aim of the
abolition of submarines altogether, but by Resolution 3 it proclaimed 'the valid law in
respect of attacks on commercial vessels' and also that 'any person in the service of any
Power, who may infringe any of these regulations, independently of whether that person
is subordinate as a government official or not, shall be considered as a violator of the
rules of war, and will be subject to trial by the civil or military authorities of the Power
within whose jurisdiction he may be'.[16] This is the first provision in an international
instrument for penal action against any international law-breaker, and though a
resolution of a conference has not the same binding validity as a signed and ratified
convention, the Washington Resolution is sufficiently definite to be recognized as
binding on its signatories.

chairmanship of the Attorney-General, Sir David Maxwell Fyfe,* was not established until June 1945.

II

Early in January 1945 President Roosevelt had instructed his personal legal adviser, Judge Samuel Rosenman, to co-ordinate the efforts of the Departments of State, Army, Navy and Justice on the subject of war criminals to the end that the mistakes made after the First World War, when, through procrastination on the part of the Allies and duplicity on the part of the Germans, virtually every war criminal escaped justice, should not be repeated. 'This time', said the President, 'let's get the trials started quickly and have the procedures all worked out in advance. Make the punishment of the guilty swift.'[17] As a result of these discussions, a memorandum initialled by Edward Stettinius, Henry Stimson and the Attorney-General, Francis Biddle, was presented to the President on 22 January for his consideration during his journey to the Crimea.

This document, a comprehensive analysis of the whole problem, contained succinct advice:

> After Germany's unconditional surrender, the United Nations could, if they elected, put to death the most notorious Nazi criminals, such as Hitler or Himmler, without trial or hearing. We do not favour this method. . . . We recommend the following: The German leaders and the organizations employed by them, such as those referred to above (S.A., S.S., Gestapo), should be charged both with the commission of their atrocious crimes, and also with joint participation in a broad criminal enterprise which included and intended these crimes, or was reasonably calculated to bring them about.

The memorandum further recommended that the major war criminals – 'to a number fairly representative of the groups and organizations charged with complicity in the basic criminal plan' – should be brought before an international military tribunal, which should be empowered to make findings as to the nature and purposes of the criminal plan, the identity of the groups and organizations involved in it and the acts committed in its execution. The tribunal should also have power to pass sentence upon the individual defendants whom it might convict.[18]

This memorandum is of the utmost historical importance since it provided the basis of all subsequent American thinking on the subject of war crimes. It also contains the basic groundwork of what ultimately became the Charter of the International Military Tribunal and of the indictment which was later served upon the accused at Nuremberg,

* Later the Earl of Kilmuir and Lord Chancellor.

with its much debated provision for the charge of 'criminal conspiracy'. It will be noted also that the views of President Roosevelt's advisers, as expressed therein, ran completely counter to those which the President himself had shared with Marshal Stalin at Tehran, namely for the summary execution of Hitler and his associates.

Unfortunately this extremely valuable contribution was not communicated to the British delegation at Yalta, nor did it form the basis of any discussions between the Americans, the British and the Russians. No agreement on war crimes had been reached between the Allies before the conference and no action was taken by them at Yalta other than to refer it to some later meetings of the three Foreign Ministers. No such meeting, however, took place until the international conference for the setting-up of the United Nations Organization had convened in San Francisco in April.

One of the last acts, however, of President Roosevelt before his death on 12 April was to dispatch Judge Rosenman to Europe, there to pursue in London discussions with the British for the speedy trial of war criminals.* Here he found as great a change of opinion from that held by Mr Churchill at Tehran as had occurred in the thinking of the President. Whereas the Prime Minister had been horrified by the willingness of President Roosevelt and Marshal Stalin to eliminate the Nazi leaders by summary execution and had declared that the British people 'would never stand for it', he now warmly espoused just these views, and his antagonism to trials and tribunals was reflected in the opinion of his Cabinet colleagues.†

Judge Rosenman, in his conversations with Mr Churchill at Chequers and with the Lord Chancellor, Lord Simon, with Anthony Eden, and with the Attorney-General, Sir David Maxwell Fyfe, in London, found a marked preference for the disposal of the Nazi leaders without trial. They were particularly averse to a trial of Hitler which, in their view, would inevitably be a long-drawn-out process, impossible to curtail, perhaps even missing the point that his guilt lay in the totality of his offences against accepted international standards. Though Judge Rosenman repeated the dictum of President Roosevelt, after his own conversion to legal processes, that 'If those men are shot without trial, there'll soon be talk stimulated by Nazi adherents about whether they were really guilty of any crimes at all', and reiterated that instead of being recognized as criminals they might be ultimately mourned as

---

* Judge Rosenman was subsequently confirmed in his mission by President Truman.[19]
† In April 1945 the British Cabinet was presented with a memorandum from the Lord Chancellor advocating summary executions. Mr Churchill favoured an Act of Attainder declaring named Nazi leaders subject to the death penalty.[20]

martyrs, he was unable to shake the British in their adamant opposition.[21]*

Matters might well have remained indefinitely in this state of dead-lock but for three important events. On 1 May came the news of Hitler's and Goebbels's suicides in the Berlin Bunker. The possibility, therefore, of the Reich Chancellor's appearance as a prisoner in the dock was thus eliminated. On the following day came word from Sir Alexander Cadogan at San Francisco that Secretary of State Stettinius proposed to hold a meeting of the four Foreign Ministers on the following afternoon and that Mr Eden desired to know the views of his colleagues in the War Cabinet. On this same day, 2 May, President Truman, in a sense, 'jumped the gun' by issuing an Executive Order appointing Supreme Court Justice Robert H. Jackson as Chief Counsel for the United States in the process of preparing and presenting charges of atrocities and war crimes 'against such of the leaders of the European Axis Powers and their principal agents and accessories as the United States may agree with any of the United Nations to bring to trial before an international military tribunal'.[23]

Thus when the Foreign Ministers met on 3 May to receive Judge Rosenman's report, there had already been, willy-nilly, a progression towards common agreement. The talks continued until the tenth in an informal manner, but they resulted in the complete acceptance by all parties of certain general principles which governed their subsequent course of action. In the first place they agreed that the major war criminals should be placed on trial before an international military tribunal and not be disposed of 'politically'; to this end each Government should appoint a Chief of Counsel who, acting together as a committee, should prepare the indictment and manage the prosecution. It was also agreed that those criminals whose crimes were of a fixed geographical character should be returned to the countries where their crimes were committed.

In the course of the San Francisco Conference the American delegation completed its draft, prepared by Judge Rosenman, for an Executive Agreement for the organization and conduct of the International Military Tribunal. This was presented to Mr Eden and Messrs Molotov and Bidault and, apart from certain minor amendments agreed between the British and Americans in London on 28 May, it became the basis on which the four Governments accepted the plan for a trial.[24]†

---

* When Judge Rosenman returned to England in 1947 Mr Churchill said to him: 'Do you remember our talk at Chequers when I argued so strenuously against trying those Nazi war criminals? Now that the trials are over, I think the President was right and I was wrong.'[22]

† On 29 May Mr Churchill announced in the House of Commons that the Attorney-General, Sir David Maxwell Fyfe, had been appointed Chief of the British Prosecution

The matter of the trial of major war criminals was carried considerably further along the road to practical achievement in the course of a Four-Power Conference of Jurists held in London from 26 June to 8 August 1945, under the chairmanship of Sir David Maxwell Fyfe.* This was a remarkable, even a unique, gathering. Its object was to prepare the machinery and the procedure of the first International Military Tribunal in the history of law. To achieve this purpose it was necessary first to reconcile into a working entity the legal codes of the four Powers concerned – in itself no mean task. It is not surprising, therefore, that there ensued certain stresses and strains born of suspicion and misunderstanding. That it eventually succeeded in forging an instrument of international justice at all was something of a miracle, but that the instrument should prove effective and should preserve the principle of quadripartite solidarity long after it began to crumble elsewhere was truly miraculous.[25]

While the discussions in London were in process the subject of the disposal of major war criminals came under consideration elsewhere at a higher level. As soon as the surrender of Germany had been accomplished, preparations were set on foot for the convening of a further meeting of the Big Three. At the end of May the British Government submitted to the State Department in Washington a list of subjects for inclusion in the agenda of the forthcoming conference. The subject of war criminals was not among them.[26] A month later, however, on 29 June, Lord Halifax informed the Acting Secretary of State, Joseph Grew, that the British Government were now desirous of including the matter of war criminals on the conference agenda, despite the fact that the Conference of Jurists had opened in London three days before.[27]

before the International Military Tribunal. Subsequent to the change of Government after the election of July 1945, this arrangement required revision. The Labour Attorney-General, Sir Hartley Shawcross, became the Chief of the British Prosecution team. In this capacity he exercised complete control of everything that took place up to and until the opening of the trial, where he made the opening speech for the British Prosecution. Thereafter the day-to-day direction of the British team was in the hands of Sir David Maxwell Fyfe, but Sir Hartley retained the general direction in the sense that if any matter which was out of the ordinary routine course arose, he was at once communicated with in London and took whatever policy decision was necessary. He visited Nuremberg on several occasions when there was need for discussion on general policy and also made the closing speech for the British Prosecution. Both these speeches were feats of great oratory, remarkable alike for their restraint, their legal wisdom and their depth of feeling.

The Soviet and French Governments subsequently appointed General A. R. Rudenko and François de Menthon to lead their respective Prosecution teams.

* With the change of Government in Britain after the General Election, Sir David Maxwell Fyfe was replaced as British representative by the new Lord Chancellor, Viscount Jowitt. However, he presided over all sessions of the conference except the last. For details of the American, Soviet and French delegations, see below, p. 404.

Justice Jackson, when he learned in London of this request, confessed to being 'rather appalled' at the idea of a discussion by the Big Three of such an involved and technical subject, but the Foreign Office and the War Cabinet were looking further ahead. Mindful of how prone Marshal Stalin and his colleagues were to suspicion of the Western Allies' intentions to thwart the designs of the Soviet Union at every turn, they had visualized the possibility of a secret Russian belief that the British, and even the Americans, would attempt some evasion of the prosecution of the Nazi war criminals. This then was the root of the British desire to include the matter on the conference agenda – not for the purpose of a detailed discussion but to allay any possibility of Soviet suspicions.[28]

Nor were they ill-advised in so doing. This particular item on the agenda of the Potsdam Conference was not reached until after the result of the British General Election. Mr Churchill and Mr Eden had been replaced by Mr Attlee and Mr Bevin as the leading British delegates. However, during the closing days of the conference (30 July – 1 August) it was discussed at considerable length both in the Committee of Foreign Ministers and in the sessions of the Big Three. There was a marked difference of opinion, though all parties agreed that, in view of the great and growing public interest in the matter, some statement on the bringing of war criminals to justice should be included in the final statement of the conference.

The Russians favoured a definite announcement to the effect that in the near future a Four-Power International Military Tribunal would be established with power to try, condemn and execute the leading Nazi leaders, whom the conference should name.[29] When Justice Jackson in London became aware of this proposal he was deeply dismayed. It happened to coincide with a moment in the deliberations of the London Conference of Jurists when the Russians had become most obstructive and intransigent, refusing to accept any but their own definitions of such vital items as a 'war crime' and other equally important matters.

So bitter did the atmosphere of the London Conference become that Justice Jackson told Judge Rosenman on the telephone on 1 August that he had almost abandoned any hope of agreement on a joint tribunal because of the impossibility of working with the Russians, and was contemplating the establishment of a tripartite tribunal, from which the Russians would be excluded. He therefore begged Rosenman to advise President Truman very strongly against committing the conference to the setting-up of a Four-Power tribunal and equally emphatically against naming any of the war criminals, since this would weaken his hand in dealing with the Russian delegation in London.[30]

Doing his best to calm his brilliant but certainly erratic and explosive colleague,* Judge Rosenman, nevertheless, passed on to the President this advice from Justice Jackson, shortly before the last session of the Potsdam Conference was to convene. A further wrangle occurred in which Marshal Stalin again demanded the inclusion of names and Mr Attlee as adamantly refused, though he did suggest, unexpectedly enough, that the name of Hitler might be included, to which the Marshal replied acidly that they did not have a Hitler at their disposition but that he had no objection to naming him.[31]†

A compromise formula put forward by the British, expressing confidence in the efforts of the London Conference to provide proper means to bring the Nazi leaders to speedy justice, was accepted by the Russians, and the Americans and British agreed to a proposal by Stalin that the first list of war criminals should be published within one month of the conclusion of the Potsdam Conference.[33]

Thus, when the Protocol of the Potsdam Conference was signed by President Truman, Marshal Stalin and Mr Attlee at about midnight on 1–2 August 1945, it contained the following proviso:

> The three Governments have taken note of the discussions which have been proceeding in recent weeks in London between the British, United States, Soviet and French representatives with a view to reaching agreement on the methods of trial of those major war criminals whose crimes, under the Moscow Declaration of October 1943, have no particular geographical localization. The Three Governments reaffirm their intention to bring these criminals to swift and sure justice. They hope that the negotiations in London will result in speedy agreement being reached for this purpose, and they regard it as a matter of great importance that the trial of these major criminals should begin at the earliest possible date. The first list of defendants will be published before 1st September.[34]‡

There would seem to be little doubt that, having to some extent gained his point at Potsdam, Marshal Stalin sent word to his representatives at the London Conference that an agreement on the establishment of a Four-Power Military Tribunal was desirable and that they should

---

* Judge Rosenman told Justice Jackson that in his opinion the exclusion of the Russians from the tribunal would constitute a slap in the face which would lead to recriminations, whereas it would not be quite so bad, if it was decided that each nation would try its own war-criminal prisoners.

† It was at this session that Mr Bevin, addressing Marshal Stalin, declared that if there were any doubt about Hess [as a war criminal] he could give an undertaking that Hess should be handed over and, he added, the British could also send along a bill for his keep.[32]

‡ The subject of the trial and punishment of major war criminals was included in almost identical wording in the final communiqué of the conference issued on 2 August.[35]

therefore adopt a less obdurate attitude. Within a week of the conclusion of the Potsdam Conference a solution to all differences of opinion had been found in London, and the agreement incorporating the Charter of the International Military Tribunal was signed on 8 August 1945.[36]

The Charter provided, *inter alia*, a definition of what a war crime actually was. Three categories were defined (Article 6).

Crimes against Peace: The planning, preparation, initiation or waging of a war in violation of international treaties, agreements, or assurances or participation in a Common Plan or Conspiracy for the accomplishment of any of the foregoing.

War Crimes: violations of the laws of war or customs of war. Such violations to include murder, ill-treatment or deportation to slave labour or for any other purpose of civilian population of occupied territories or of prisoners of war or persons on the seas, the killing of hostages, plunder of public or private property, wanton destruction of cities, towns or villages or desolation not justified by military necessity.

Crimes against Humanity: murder, extermination, ill-treatment etc. of or against any civilian population, before or during the war, or persecution on political, social or religious grounds in execution of any crime within the jurisdiction of the Tribunal.

Thus arraigned on these charges the major war criminals, whether as individuals or members of organizations, were to be tried and, if convicted, sentenced to punishment by the Tribunal, which itself was to consist of four Judges, one each appointed by the Governments of the four Contracting Powers, and four Alternate Judges, similarly appointed (Article 2).

Steps were at once taken to fill these offices, and certain somewhat bizarre effects resulted. President Truman, having appointed an Associate Justice of the Supreme Court as the American Chief Prosecutor, now offered the senior position on the Tribunal to the Hon. Francis Biddle, a Philadelphia lawyer who had served briefly as Attorney-General in President Roosevelt's Administration but had not survived President Truman's reshuffle of his Cabinet in June 1945. He accepted the President's offer and proved a highly valuable member of the Tribunal. The American Alternate was Judge J. Parker of North Carolina, presiding judge of the United States Circuit Court of Appeals for the Fourth Circuit. A Republican by politics, he had been nominated in 1930 by President Hoover to a vacancy in the Supreme Court, but the Senate had refused by a tied vote to confirm him. For fifteen years he had been a disappointed man.[37]

In Britain there had also been heart-burning. In an excess of zeal the Lord Chancellor, Lord Jowitt, offered at the end of August the position of Judge on the Tribunal to Mr Justice (Sir Norman) Birkett, who accepted with gratification. Shortly thereafter, however, the Foreign Secretary, Mr Bevin, desired the Lord Chancellor to reconsider the appointment. It had become known that a strong possibility existed that the British Judge would become President of the Tribunal and it was therefore considered desirable, by the Foreign Office, that someone of greater legal hierarchic status, preferably a Law Lord, should fill the position. No Law Lord, however, was available and the Lord Chancellor turned to the Court of Appeal, inviting Lord Justice du Parcq, then on the point of retirement. At the same time the Prime Minister, Mr Attlee, wrote to Sir Norman Birkett asking him to go to the Tribunal as the British Alternate. Again Birkett accepted, but with 'secret anguish', as he recorded in his diary, at having been selected as Member and then asked to become Alternate 'merely because of the absurd snobbishness of the Foreign Office'.[38]*

As it happened, Lord Justice du Parcq refused and the appointment went to Lord Justice (Sir Geoffrey) Lawrence,† who gave to the Tribunal, over which he presided, much of its dignity, wisdom and impartiality.

The French Government, whose representation made little impact on the proceedings of the Tribunal, either on the Bench or on the Prosecution, nominated Professor Donnédieu de Varbres, a recognized authority on international law, as their Judge and Judge Roland Falco, of the Court de Cassation, as his Alternate. The Soviet Union was powerfully represented by I. T. Nikitchenko, Vice-Chairman of the Soviet Supreme Court, and A. F. Volchkov of the Soviet District Court. It is probable that the Russians experienced the greatest surprise of any nationals present as the course of the Tribunal subsequently unfolded. From a grim and saturnine air of hostile suspicion they came to display human traits of humour and amiability. Never, however, did they abandon their meticulous passion for detail and their logical approach, which caused them, as members of an International *Military* Tribunal, to sustain the role of soldiers – a Major-General and a Lieutenant-Colonel respectively – and to appear always in uniform despite the fact that their colleagues elected to wear 'black Geneva gowns'.‡

Since the Tribunal had been established on a special relationship to the Allied Control Council for Germany, it was deemed proper that it

* In fairness to the Foreign Office it must be said that the intervention of the Foreign Secretary was made with some reluctance, and without any consultation with the officials of the Foreign Office.

† Later Baron Oaksey and Trevethin.

‡ Similarly, the Soviet Chief Prosecutor, M. Rudenko, later Procurator-General of the U.S.S.R., sported the rank and uniform of a general.

should hold its first session in Berlin.* This took place on 18 October with General Nikitchenko in the chair. Its principal function was to receive from the Chief Prosecutors the text of the indictment lodged, in accordance with Article 14 of the Charter, against a specific list of defendants[39] comprising the names of Göring, Hess, von Ribbentrop, Ley, Keitel, Kaltenbrunner, Rosenberg, Frank, Frick, Streicher, Funk, Schacht, Krupp von Bohlen und Halbach, Dœnitz, Raeder, von Schirach, Sauckel, Jodl, Bormann, von Papen, Seyss-Inquart, Speer, von Neurath and Fritzsche.†

An examination of the list recalls some notable absentees in the upper echelons of the Nazi hierarchy. Hitler was of course dead and for him there was no substitute. But Goebbels and Himmler were also dead and in their place the Russians had insisted upon substituting members of the 'second eleven', namely, for Goebbels, Hans Fritzsche, who had been a senior official of the Ministry of Propaganda, and for Himmler, Ernst Kaltenbrunner, who, as chief of the Security Police and the *Sicherheitsdienst* and Head of the Reich Security Office (R.S.H.A.), might well have qualified in his own right for a place among the accused.

Before the trial opened, moreover, the list of twenty-four accused had been reduced to twenty-one. Martin Bormann had never been in Allied hands and had completely disappeared; Robert Ley, the Nazi Labour Front leader, had hanged himself in his cell and Gustav Krupp was adjudged too ill and senile to stand his trial.‡ In this case it was the American Prosecution who wished to enter a substitute in the person of Krupp's son Alfried, but the Tribunal, led by Norman Birkett (though the Alternates had no vote), decided against this view.

Having received the indictment and ordered that it be served on the defendants, the Tribunal adjourned after directing that it should reconvene on 20 November at Nuremberg which, by Article 22 of the Charter, had been designated as the scene of the trial. The Tribunal also elected Lord Justice Lawrence as its President.§

Nuremberg had occupied an important place in German history.

* This meeting was also attended by Sir Hartley Shawcross, the British Attorney-General.

† In addition, the Reich Cabinet, the Leadership Corps of the Nazi Party, the S.S. and S.D., the S.A., the Gestapo and the General Staff and High Command of the German Armed Forces were also indicted as criminal organizations.

‡ A similar attempt on the part of Rudolf Hess's defence counsel to have him declared unfit to stand trial failed in its purpose.

§ It had originally been intended that the Presidency of the Tribunal should go by rota among the four Judges, each occupying the chair for a month. At the close of the first month, however, so admirably had Lord Justice Lawrence discharged the office of President that his colleagues unanimously requested him to continue to do so. This he did for the remainder of the trial.

Though in modern days it ranked only as the second city of Bavaria, it had once held the proud status of a Free City, a favourite place of residence of the Holy Roman Emperors and guardian of the Imperial Regalia. Hitler had been fully conscious of the historical connections of Nuremberg and had given it a definite place in the organism of the National Socialist Party. While Munich remained the headquarters of the Nazi movement, Nuremberg became the national showground of the party. From there Julius Streicher had published in the *Stürmer* his odious and obscene libels against the Jews. There was the centre of those vast pageants at which the Führer spoke *ex cathedra, urbe et orbe*, to his followers. Where the narrow streets and ancient walls of the city had once re-echoed the sweet voices of Hans Sachs and other Meistersingers, there had resounded the fierce chorus of the 'Horst Wessel Lied', cacophonously roared with fanatical fervour by the S.A. and S.S. Here had marched in serried ranks the sun-tanned paladins of the Labour Service battalions and the glowing faces of the Hitler *Jugend*. Here, in the gigantic arena, which Albert Speer had erected to the greater glory of National Socialism, Hitler had given to Germany the infamous laws of anti-Semitism; here he dangled before his cohorts the bright prizes of ultimate *Lebensraum* in the Ukraine and beyond the Urals; here too he had threatened Czechoslovakia with extinction and the world with war.

It was widely believed that this close association with the zenith of National Socialist triumphs had actuated the London Conference in its selection of Nuremberg as the seat of the trial before the International Military Tribunal. Indeed this had been among the considerations of their choice, to the end that Germany and the world should witness the Nemesis of their evil exultation. But what induced them as much – and even more – in their preference was the fact that, in a Reich which had been 'scourged from end to end' by Marshal of the Royal Air Force Sir Arthur Harris and Bomber Command, it was almost alone in possessing a large jail in a fair state of repair, a court-house of requisite size and a witness-house capable of housing the many who would be called to testify. Added to these facilities was the need for adequate accommodation for the members of the Tribunal, the prosecution teams, the defence counsel, the court staff, the hosts of Pressmen and the considerable number of distinguished visitors who descended upon the city, not to mention the large force of American troops and military police attached for guard duty.

Not that Nuremberg had escaped bombing. When troops of the U.S. Seventh Army finally captured it on 20 April 1945 it was pronounced by experts to be '91 per cent dead'. Nevertheless, 'the capabilities' existed and, though the decision to hold the trial there was not taken until July, thus giving only four months to make it ready for this purpose, the miracle was accomplished and its achievement constituted an outstanding tribute to the energetic resourcefulness, organizational skill and improvising genius of the United States Corps of Engineers.*

III

Thus, on 20 November 1945, the Great Nuremberg Trial began.† It was to last for all but a year and in its course there was to be exposed to the shocked and horrified world a pageant of infamy and brutality, of 'man's inhumanity to man' and of man's capacity for dishonour and perfidy as was to make the Third Reich a stench in the nostrils of the civilized universe and of which the stigma will remain for generations. A veritable 'Procession of Protracted Death', it was a withering away of the very soul of Germany. Names such as Belsen and Auschwitz, Buchenwald, Ravensbrück and Dachau, flamed across the Court-room; crimes of genocide and of wholesale slavery, such as had been unknown in Europe since the Middle Ages, were bared to view. Often those present in court were physically sickened by the bestial details of atrocities and appalled by the evidence of betrayal of a nation's pledged word.

The course of the trial also witnessed a remarkable display of brilliance and efficiency on the part of the British representatives on both the Tribunal and the Prosecution. The fact that the trial throughout was conducted with great dignity and decorum owed much to the presiding ability of Lord Justice Lawrence. Firm and fair, distinguished alike for discipline and for understanding, Sir Geoffrey kept effective control of the proceedings throughout, earning the respect and admiration of his colleagues, and of the Prosecution and Defence.

Equally, an ascendancy was established by Sir David Maxwell Fyfe, who became the acknowledged leader of the Prosecution, more especially in view of the dwindling of Justice Jackson's reputation and leadership after he had been disastrously defeated by Göring during the latter's cross-examination. It was from this dilemma that he had to be rescued by Sir David, whose subsequent effective handling of the exultant

---

* For those interested in statistics, it has been computed that from 22 August to 1 December 1945, 157 American soldiers put in a total of 83,396 man-hours. German civilians worked 143,000 man-hours and 717 German prisoners of war were used on an average day. 500 bags of cement, a quarter of a million bricks and 100,000 board-feet of timber and more than six tons of paint went into the work of reconstruction. Seven generators were installed to supply electricity, and more than a million feet of wire and cable were used.[40]

† That which follows is written from notes made at the time by Sir John Wheeler-Bennett, who was attached to the British Prosecution.

Göring by the brilliance of his cross-examination laid the foundation of legal promotion which led him ultimately to the Woolsack.*

1 October 1946 was the last day of the Nuremberg Trial – the day of reckoning. For nearly eleven months the Tribunal had heard argument and counter-argument, examination and cross-examination, the unfolding of a mass of evidence, sometimes nauseating in its revelation of barbarous cruelty, and at all times shocking in its record of intrigue and infamy. For eleven months the defendants had listened to the testimony of their crimes and one by one they had sought to mitigate the damning case against them; some had behaved with great dignity, some had blustered; some had wept, others had confessed; nearly all had lied. Now the hour of Nemesis was approaching and, for the last time as a group, they sat in the dock to hear judgement and sentence.

No one who was present on that occasion can ever forget the experience. There was an electric tension throughout the court-room, palpable alike in the body of the court, in the Press seats and in the visitors' gallery which was crowded with distinguished persons as never before since the beginning of the trial. The suppressed excitement extended even to the tables of the Prosecution where, behind a mask of professional impassivity, all waited with anxiety and suspense to hear the results of their great indictment.

On the previous day the Tribunal had begun the delivery of its judgement and this was now completed before the rendering of the verdict and sentences. It was for these that we all waited.

The Tribunal found all the accused guilty, with the exception of Schacht, von Papen and Fritzsche, who were acquitted and discharged from the court. Of these, the latter's verdict was almost a foregone conclusion, for Hans Fritzsche was but a pale shadow of his master, Goebbels. But the acquittal of Schacht and von Papen sent a momentary wave of incredulous surprise over the court-room after the announcement of each verdict. There was, of course, no audible discussion, but it was as if the collective shock which many present had sustained manifested itself in an almost visible manner. Von Papen gave his habitual vulpine grin – the Silver Fox had given the hounds the slip; Schacht, the picture of smug complacency, had never doubted the

---

* The British Prosecution team was indeed a forcing-ground for genius. Sir David Maxwell Fyfe became, on the return of the Conservative Party to power in 1951, first Home Secretary and later Lord Chancellor. Of the remainder, Colonel Henry Phillimore became a Judge of the High Court, Elwyn Jones Attorney-General in Mr Wilson's Labour Government, Mervyn Griffith-Jones Common Serjeant of the City of London, and Patrick Dean, the Foreign Office representative on the team, became Ambassador in Washington.

verdict for a moment. Had he not cynically affirmed even before the trial opened that 'You can't hang a banker'?

The reading of the verdicts ended and the court adjourned for lunch. In the dock there was an unwonted stir and conversation. The defendants were about to separate for the last time and ere they passed one by one into the steel lift which communicated with the cells, they spoke together for a moment. The three acquitted men received the congratulations of their counsel and in some cases of their co-defendants. Schacht received a number of handshakes, but none from Göring, and a few moments later was auctioning his autograph for bars of chocolate in the court-house canteen. Fritzsche received somewhat perfunctory congratulations. No one, save his counsel and his son, shook hands with von Papen.

When the Tribunal reconvened for the final afternoon session, they confronted for the first time in eleven months an empty dock. The eighteen remaining defendants must now appear one by one to hear their doom. There was an awed hush, a constrained silence, in the court-room as we waited; a silence broken at length by the sound of the opening of the back panel of the dock, and Göring, standing between two guards, appeared framed in the dark aperture.*

In the next twenty minutes we heard twelve men individually condemned to death † The atmosphere within the court had grown tense and ghoulish. No one of those present had listened before to such a mass condemnation to the ultimate penalty, and it was almost with relief that we heard Lord Justice Lawrence sentence Dœnitz to ten years' imprisonment, Raeder and Hess to imprisonment for life and Baldur von Schirach to twenty years; then followed sentences on Speer for twenty years and von Neurath for fifteen years,‡ and then the final

* Goring's hands were free during the pronouncement of his sentence. Hess and all the subsequent defendants were handcuffed.

† These were Göring, von Ribbentrop, Keitel, Kaltenbrunner, Rosenberg, Franck, Frick, Streicher, Sauckel, Jodl, Seyss-Inquart and Bormann, who had been tried, convicted and sentenced *in absentia*. Of these Göring cheated the hangman by committing suicide in his cell on 15 October. All the other ten were hanged on the following day, 16 October.

‡ Of those sentenced to imprisonment at Nuremberg and all subsequently lodged in the Spandau Jail, only Hess remains in custody. In August 1967 his son Wolf-Rudiger Hess, began an agitation for his release in a statement to the effect that Rudolf Hess had been exonerated by the International Military Tribunal and that 'the maintenance of a political prison by four major Powers for the single purpose of watching the slow death of an old man is not in keeping with the spirit of this age', and that his continued imprisonment was 'a flagrant defiance of human feelings'. This statement Wolf-Rudiger Hess sent to Francis Biddle, asking him to endorse it publicly. Mr Biddle consulted with Lord Oaksey (formerly Lord Justice Lawrence) and on 12 October 1967 he himself issued a statement, with which Lord Oaksey concurred. After saying that many of the younger Hess's claims on behalf of his father were either fallacious or nonsense, Mr Biddle concluded: 'But both Oaksey, the presiding member of the

death sentence on the absent Bormann pronounced to an empty dock brought the grim succession to a close.[42]*

In the moment of hushed silence which followed the pronouncement of the last sentence, it was as if there echoed through the court-room the last eloquent appeal of Sir Hartley Shawcross in his closing address for the Prosecution:† 'These are our laws – let them prevail.' The judgement of the civilized world had been visited upon those who had dared, in the full knowledge of the penalty of failure, to attempt to substitute the reign of terror and oppression for the rule of justice and law. It was a moment in which one hoped – and almost glimpsed – a new order, in which the solidarity of comradeship among the Four Powers who had dealt out justice at Nuremberg should lead the suffering, yearning peoples of the world to a happier way of life.

But all prospect of the realization of this vision, together with that fine display of quadripartite solidarity and co-operation which had been so salient and inspiring a characteristic of the trial, was shattered by the closing statement of Sir Geoffrey Lawrence: 'I have an announcement to make', he said in those grave tones that had not once lost their firm dignity throughout the trial.‡

Tribunal, and I think that Hess has served long enough and, that he should now be released'. This proved to be but a fruitless appeal for clemency, for, while the American, British and French Governments favoured the release of Hess, the Government of the Soviet Union remained adamant.[41] Raeder was released from life imprisonment, on account of age and ill-health, on 26 September 1955 and died on 11 November 1960, von Neurath was also released on 6 November 1954, before the completion of his sentence, and died on 14 August 1956. Doenitz was released at the end of ten years' sentence, on 1 October 1956, and Speer and Baldur von Schirach completed their sentences on 30 September 1966.

* In addition to these sentences, the Tribunal pronounced the upper echelons of the Leadership Corps, the Gestapo and the S.D. and the S.S. to have been members of criminal organizations. The Reich Government, the S.A. and the General Staff and High Command were acquitted of criminal charges.

† See above, p. 399 n.

‡ The dignity of Lord Justice Lawrence was proof against any emergency. On a warm August afternoon during the trial, in the somnolent air of a post-luncheon session, he had dozed behind his hand as has many another great legal luminary under similar circumstances. In the witness box was an S.S. Judge who was being examined by defence counsel on behalf of that organization. The witness was at pains to deny the existence of horrors in the concentration camps, in which, he said, the aim was to give the inmates an existence 'worthy of human beings'. Every facility was afforded them. 'They had' said the S.S. Judge, 'regular mail service. They had a large camp library, even books in foreign languages. They had variety shows, motion pictures, sporting contests. They even had a bordello.' At this moment Sir Geoffrey Lawrence came to full consciousness. With grave interest he asked the witness: 'What was it they even had?' His friend and colleague Francis Biddle sought to enlighten him. 'Brothels', he interpolated, not realizing that the public announcement system on the bench was 'live'. 'What did he say?', asked the now thoroughly aroused President. 'Bordello, whore-house', thundered Mr Biddle, and suddenly noticed from the rising tide of amusement in the court-room that they were overheard. 'I see', said Sir Geoffrey Lawrence, with immense dignity. 'The witness may proceed.'[43]

The Soviet Member of the International Tribunal desires to record his dissent from the decisions on the cases of the Defendants Schacht, Papen and Fritzsche. He is of the opinion that they should have been convicted and not acquitted. He also dissents from the decisions in respect of the Reich Cabinet and the General Staff and High Command, being of the opinion that they should have been declared to be criminal organizations. He also dissents from the decision in the case of the sentence on Defendant Hess, and is of the opinion that the sentence should have been death and not life imprisonment.[44]

As we passed out of the shadow of the court-house into the crisp sunlit October air, much of the sense of achievement had departed, to be replaced by infinite sadness.*

IV

The authors of the Nuremberg Judgement did not escape criticism. These critics were informed and uninformed, ignorant and learned, political and legal.

It was said of the Tribunal that it should not have included representatives of the Soviet Union, which was itself not free from charges of aggression and annexation in respect of Poland and the Baltic States. To this the obvious answer was that the Russians, as partners in the Grand Alliance which had won the war and reduced the Germans to Unconditional Surrender, had been corollarily and inevitably party to all the preparation and planning for the trial and punishment of the German war criminals, and that without them it would have been impossible to have a trial at all. Moreover the fact was cited that, both on the level of the Tribunal and of the Prosecution, the Russians had been good and co-operative colleagues until the last moment of dissent over the judgement.

It was alleged that the Tribunal had no foundation in law, but this was manifestly not so since it had been created by the international agreement concluded between the Four Powers on 8 August 1945, and a treaty is a legal document. The Tribunal also claimed jurisdiction

---

* There is good reason to believe that General Nikitchenko, who throughout the trial had shown the same spirit of co-operation and compromise which had characterized the relations of all members of the Tribunal, had not himself differed from the views of his colleagues. When the text of the Judgement had been agreed by the Tribunal while it was in process of translation, the word had gone round Nuremberg that unanimity had been reached on all points. It was not until the Tribunal had reconvened on 30 September that a rumour began to circulate concerning a Soviet dissenting opinion. In the interval, it would appear, General Nikitchenko, unlike his colleagues on the Tribunal, had communicated the text of the Judgement to his Government and that he acted on instructions to enter a dissenting opinion which reached him after the text had been examined in the Kremlin.

from the sovereignty of the Allied Powers over Germany which they had assumed under Unconditional Surrender.

Another common misunderstanding was that the trial involved the principle that soldiers might be executed for obeying the orders of their superiors. This is, of course, a vexed question, but it certainly did not arise at Nuremberg. Keitel and Jodl were not executed for *obeying* orders but for *giving* them. They were a part of the military and political hierarchy of the Third Reich carrying out by personal orders the ruthless and barbarous programme and policy of their Führer. Other German generals, such as Ludwig Beck, Chief of the General Staff of the Army until 1938, had objected and had been permitted to retire. There was no evidence that either Keitel or Jodl had ever expressed a single objection or exercised the slightest resistance to the formulation of inhuman policies. In addition, it may be said that even the farcical proceedings against war criminals of the First World War before the Leipzig *Reichsgericht* in 1921 had held that obedience to superior orders was not a valid defence.

And there was the accusation of *ex post facto* law. It was claimed by both the informed and the misinformed that certain of the most important charges contained in the Nuremberg Indictment, and thus consequently reflected in the verdict of the Tribunal, were based on law which made criminal that which was not a crime when committed, and the legality of the Tribunal's judgement was challenged on these grounds. It was learnedly contended, both before the Tribunal and outside it, that, on the basis of the maxim *nullam crimen, nulla poena, sine lege*, the defendants could not be punished for acts which had not been specified as being criminal by legislation. However, according to the proponents of the judgement, this rubric ignored the existence of international law. It did not mean that a case had to be defined and its punishment fixed by statute before the offender could be tried, but that some law must exist before it could be said to have been violated. Thus the Kellogg–Briand Pact of Paris in 1928 – an international instrument signed, ratified and adhered to by sixty-three nations – had condemned recourse to war as an instrument of national policy and had expressly renounced it. It is true that the treaty did not explicitly state aggression to be a crime, nor did it consequently provide a clear definition of aggression, but it could very well be argued that since war itself was outlawed as an instrument of national policy this automatically included any aggression which might lead to war – and also the planning of it. Similarly it must be emphasized that the Hague Convention of 1907 and the Geneva Convention of 1929 outlawed certain acts and methods of war, without specifically stating that they were crimes or imposing any penalties. Nevertheless a breach of them has always been regarded as criminal, and violators of these rules of warfare had been tried frequently by military tribunals and, where found guilty, punished.[45]

What then had the Great Trial of Nuremberg achieved?

It had achieved certain vitally important precedents, not the least of which was the establishment in international law of the principle of responsible government declared some three hundred years ago by Chief Justice Coke to his sovereign, King James I, proclaiming that even a king is still 'under God and the Law', and consequently that, in the terse dictum of Secretary of State James Byrnes, 'It would take some of the joy out of war if the men who started one, instead of a halo around the head, got a rope around the neck'.[46]

The agreement of 8 August 1945 establishing the Tribunal had constituted a basic charter in the international law of the future. Its principles had been incorporated into a collective judicial precedent. The Judgement rendered by the Tribunal shifted the power of the precedent to the support of the rules of war. No one could thereafter deny that the principle on which the Nazi leaders were adjudged to forfeit their lives constituted law – and law with a sanction.*

What may be termed a 'fringe benefit' of the Nuremberg Trial is the inestimable boon which it conferred on students of the history of the inter-war and war years. Virtually the whole of the archives of the Third Reich, and much of those of the Weimar Republic, had fallen into Allied hands shortly before or after Unconditional Surrender, and the Prosecution had made full use of them during the trial. Indeed not the least impressive aspect of the proceedings was the extent to which the Nazi leaders were convicted on the evidence of their own documents. Those documents which were used in evidence or in the preparation of cross-examination were made publicly accessible when the proceedings of the trial were published at its conclusion,† and the effect was as if the cream of the secret registries of Whitehall had suddenly been made accessible to scholars – without the restriction of the thirty-year rule! Without the circumstances of the Nuremberg Trial this would never have happened. The proceedings of the International Military

---

* The same was made clear in respect of the Japanese war criminals as a result of the proceedings of the International Military Tribunal of the Far East which sat in Tokyo from 19 January 1946 to 12 November 1948 (see below, pp. 492–9).

† Of the 42 volumes of the Record of the Nuremberg Tribunal, 17 are devoted to documents. A further windfall for historians was afforded by the agreement, reached in 1946, by the British and American Governments (to which the French Government subsequently adhered) for the editing and publication of the archives of the German Ministry of Foreign Affairs. Of this project, which has now produced some 17 volumes, Sir John Wheeler-Bennett was British Editor-in-Chief from 1946 to 1948.

Tribunal gave to historians what a quarter of a century of research could not have accomplished.

There is a modern tendency among some British and German historians to jeer at the Nuremberg documentation.

A. J. P. Taylor, for example, warns historians against the danger of using it and adds that 'even lawyers must have qualms about the evidence at Nuremberg'. He also continues to cast doubt upon the validity of the famous Hossbach Protocol as a record of what Hitler told his lieutenants on 5 November 1937; this he stigmatizes as 'a hot potato'.[47] Historians of the period will naturally apply to the Nuremberg documents those acid tests of scholarship which are essential in the use and evaluation of all such material. The important thing is that, thanks to the existence of the International Military Tribunal, *we have the documentation to which to apply the tests*. This is all that is claimed for them and it is sufficient. They provide the most important contribution to source material in this century.

As to the Hossbach Protocol itself, it was used at Nuremberg – and subsequently – as the best available illustration of the Führer's intentions. It was his 'blueprint' though not his 'timetable', for aggression. Many other documents exist, however, which gave an equally damning and convincing picture of Nazi foreign policy. For example, among the most valuable discoveries to be found in one of the recent volumes of the *Documents on German Foreign Policy* is one produced by the defence counsel of Dr Schacht at Nuremberg, consisting of a memorandum written by Hitler in September 1936 (more than a year *before* the events recorded in the Hossbach Protocol) embodying his decision to override all objections from Schacht and his fellow economists, to make Germany as self-sufficient as possible and to have both the German Army and the German economy ready for war in four years' time (i.e. by 1940).[48]

It was President Truman who was responsible for projecting the Law of Nuremberg into a further state of development. On 23 October 1946, just three weeks after the Judgement of Nuremberg had been delivered, the President of the United States, addressing the opening meeting of the second part of the first session of the United Nations General Assembly, referred to the Charter as pointing 'the path along which agreement may be sought, with hope of success', among the peoples of all countries 'upon principles of law and justice'. On the following day the Secretary-General of the United Nations, Trygve Lie, in presenting his report, advanced the suggestion that the Nuremberg principles should be made a permanent part of international law. 'From now on', he said, 'the instigators of new wars must know that there exist both law and punishment for their crimes. Here we have a high inspiration to go forward and begin the task of working toward a revitalized system of international law.'[49]

A similar line of approach had been made by Francis Biddle in his report to President Truman on the work of the Nuremberg Tribunal. On 9 November he proposed that the United Nations should reaffirm the principle of Nuremberg and that the time had come to set about drafting – most cautiously – a code of international criminal law. The President assented to both suggestions,[50] and a few days later, on 15 November, a resolution to this end was formally introduced by the United States delegation.[51] The Assembly finally adopted a resolution on 11 December, affirming the Nuremberg Principle of International Law and directing its committee on the codification of international law to treat as a matter of 'primary importance' plans for an International Criminal Code embracing these principles.[52]

By the following year the euphoric climate of ideas which had predominated in the months following Unconditional Surrender had considerably diminished. The United Nations Assembly of 1947 merely reiterated its instructions to the International Law Commission to pursue its labours. These labours eventually bore fruit in 1950 when the Commission presented its findings on the Nuremberg Principles to the Fifth General Assembly. A draft statute for an International Criminal Court was presented to the Assembly in 1953.[53]

The appalling atrocities and barbarities which had been disclosed in the proceedings of the Nuremberg and Tokyo Tribunals had highlighted the need to assert and safeguard human rights. The realization of this need had been a progressive feature of the Second World War. The Atlantic Charter of 1941 had called for a peace in which these rights would be reiterated and extended.* The Dumbarton Oaks Conference of 1944, which had prepared and co-ordinated plans for a new international organization,† had included in its proposals the phrase 'to promote respect for human rights and fundamental freedoms'. In the Preamble to the United Nations Charter, as it emerged from the hand of General Smuts at the San Francisco Conference on 26 June 1945, the members undertook to reaffirm their faith in fundamental human rights and in the dignity and worth of the human person, and these rights are referred to subsequently in six individual articles.‡ Nevertheless it was the disclosures at the International Tribunals which gave grim and pragmatic point to the tragic necessity for such preservation, and it was with the revelations of Nuremberg and Tokyo in mind that the United Nations subsequently established its Commission on

* See above, p. 42.   † See below, p. 542.   ‡ See below, p. 548.

Human Rights and in 1948 adopted its Declaration.* The international convention forbidding genocide was also adopted and signed on 9 December 1948.[55]

More practical and, it may be believed, more successful was the outcome of a further aspect of the Law of Nuremberg. From April to August 1949 there sat in continuous session at Geneva a diplomatic conference charged with the task of revising the instruments already existing for the protection of war victims. The sessions of the Tribunals of Nuremberg and Tokyo had disclosed the necessity for such action and, as a result of the conference, there emerged conventions which 'constituted both an emphatic vindication of humanitarian principles and a noteworthy contribution to the volume and appearance of the modern laws of war'.[56]

The existing conventions, the violation of which had formed the basis of the Nuremberg Indictment, were the Geneva Convention of 1929 for 'the Amelioration of the Conditions of the Wounded and Sick in Armed Forces in the Field', the Tenth Hague Convention of 1907 for the Laws of Maritime Warfare, and the 1929 Geneva Convention relative to the Treatment of Prisoners of War. These were all revised in the light of the experience of the Second World War. The conference also framed and adopted a new Convention, perhaps the most important of all, for the Protection of Civilian Persons in Time of War,[57] – a further manifestation of the desire to safeguard human rights.†

Taken as a whole these four Conventions, which are binding on more than sixty states and will eventually, when full adherence and ratification have been completed, be binding upon every civilized nation, are a unique contribution to the modern law of war and an emphatic avowal before the world that the humanitarian principles of justice and compassion must govern and determine the treatment of man by man if civilization is to be worthy of the name – or indeed endure at all.

* Here United Nations profession may have outrun performance. One distinguished commentator has written: 'When in 1948 the General Assembly gave endorsement without dissentient voice to the Declaration of Human Rights, words came as near to being emptied of meaning as at any time in the history of the Organization. When verbal promissory notes had to be changed into harder legal currency of conventions some healthy misgiving appeared, but too late to save years of verbiage to which no end is in sight.'[54]

† The Geneva Conventions were formally signed on 12 August 1949. British ratification was delayed until 1957. The Geneva Convention Bill received the Royal Assent on 31 July 1957 and the Instrument of Ratification was deposited at Berne on 23 September.

PART TWO

NO WAR—NO PEACE

18 | The Paris Peace Conference and the Five Peace Treaties

I

ONE of the by-products of the Yalta Conference had been a provision (included in the final Protocol of 11 February 1945) for meetings of the Foreign Ministers of the three Great Powers 'as often as may be necessary, probably about every three of four months' in rotation in the three capitals.[1] There had been no opportunity for such meetings between the dispersal of the Yalta Conference and the forgathering of the Big Three at Potsdam five months later, but at this latter meeting the machinery for consultation between Foreign Ministers was given definite and formal shape.*

By the Potsdam Protocol of 2 August 1945 – and largely due to the initiative of Secretary Byrnes – there was established a Council of the Foreign Ministers of the United Kingdom, the United States and the Soviet Union, together with those of France and China, each of whom was to appoint a deputy for purposes of continuing the work of the Council between sessions. The Council would meet 'normally' in London, where its secretariat would be housed.[2]

What the Protocol described as the 'immediate and important task' of the Council of Foreign Ministers was to be the preparation and drafting of treaties of peace with Italy and with the four other minor satellites of Germany – Bulgaria, Finland, Hungary and Rumania. These when ready were to be submitted to the United Nations, though whether the approval of that body was to be sought before or after signature was not made clear. However, it was specifically stated that the conclusion of these treaties with the Governments of the ex-satellite states 'will make it possible for the Three Powers to fulfil their desire to support an application from [each of the five ex-enemy states] for membership of the United Nations'.[3]

Of secondary, but no minor, importance was the second task laid upon the Council, namely that it should be 'utilized' for the preparation

* See above, p. 329.

of a peace settlement for Germany 'to be accepted by the Government of Germany when a Government adequate for the purpose is established'.[4] It is not without interest that today – some quarter of a century later – no such German Government has been established and no treaty has been drafted, accepted or signed.

The position of the two newcomers, France and China, which was to prove so bitter a cause of contention, was not considered a controversial issue at Potsdam, where the Big Three had issued a 'cordial invitation' to the two Governments to join in setting up the Council of Foreign Ministers, attaching 'much importance' to their participation.[5] No restrictions were placed upon the degree of such participation, but specific steps were taken to make completely clear the position of France. Since she had been a party and a witness to the Unconditional Surrender of Germany, her status in respect to a treaty of peace with that country was fully established. Her position vis-à-vis Italy was, however, not so legally viable, since she had had no part in the conclusion of hostilities with the Royal Government of Marshal Badoglio. In order to regularize this, therefore, a certain *ad hoc* legality had to be employed, and the Potsdam Powers declared formally that 'for purposes of the peace settlement for Italy, France shall be regarded as a signatory to the terms of surrender for Italy'.[6]

The interval between the adjournment of the Potsdam Conference on 2 August and the convening of the Council of Foreign Ministers in London on 11 September had been fraught with events of the first importance. The first and second atomic bombs had been dropped on Japan, and between these events Russia had entered the Pacific War. Japan had surrendered, and the arrangements for her occupation had been put in train. There had been an intensified effort to bridge the gap between the warring factions in China. Throughout her policies in Europe and in Asia there had been manifest and unmistakable evidence of Soviet expansion.

The Council convened at Lancaster House on 11 September in a spirit of restrained optimism on the part of the British and the Americans, of enigmatic hostility on the part of the Russians and of anticipatory goodwill on the part of the French and Chinese, but from the opening session it was clear that M. Molotov and his colleagues were going to be difficult in every possible way. The tolerably good *rapport* which had existed at Potsdam between him and Mr Bevin and Secretary Byrnes had to a great extent evaporated in the intervening forty days, and was extended in no measure at all to Georges Bidault and Dr Wang Shi-chieh.*

---

* Both Prime Minister T. V. Soong and that redoubtable veteran of Chinese diplomacy, Dr Wellington Koo, took part in the discussion on various occasions. John Foster Dulles accompanied Secretary Byrnes in an advisory capacity.

Such good relations as did exist originally had completely disappeared by the adjournment on 2 October.[7]

From the outset the Russians were on the offensive. Sensing that the French and Chinese votes would be against them in the majority of cases, they attempted to have France and China virtually excluded from all major decisions on the grounds that at Potsdam it had been agreed that these should be taken by the Big Three alone. Molotov therefore proposed that France should be allowed to participate only in the discussion of problems affecting Western Europe, and that China should be excluded from European discussions altogether. The object of this manœuvre was to ensure that, in the drafting of the treaties with those former Nazi satellites who fell within the Russian sphere of influence, the Soviet representatives would have to contend with two opponents and not four.

In the ensuing discussions M. Bidault and Dr Wang stood aside, but Mr Bevin and Secretary Byrnes spiritedly contested the Soviet thesis and to such good effect that M. Molotov conceded the point and, by the so-called Agreement of 11 September, accepted his French and Chinese colleagues as full participants in the work of the Council without reservations.

But this spirit of concession was short-lived. A series of wrangles, in which a varying element of acrimony obtained, culminated on the fourteenth in a Soviet demand for an individual trusteeship over the former Italian colony of Tripolitania. This revived the similar bid which Stalin and Molotov had made at Potsdam and which Churchill and Bevin had successfully resisted.*

The Soviet proposal was now opposed by Secretary Byrnes, on the grounds that all the Italian colonial possessions should be placed under the joint trusteeship of the United Nations. With this proposal Dr Wang agreed, but M. Bidault argued in favour of making Italy herself the trustee for her own former colonies, a proposition which was unacceptable to the British, who had promised the Senussi tribes, in recognition of their assistance to British arms during the desert campaigns, that under no circumstances should Italy be placed in control of their territory or their people.† Both Britain and France, however, were at one in their opposition to the Soviet Union acquiring a foothold in the Mediterranean area, either in the Middle East or on the coast of North Africa, and both therefore became aligned in supporting the United States proposal.

---

* See above, p. 328.
† This pledge was given by Anthony Eden in the House of Commons on 8 January 1942.[8]

A lengthy and fruitless altercation ensued, enlivened by the introduction by M. Molotov of a letter sent to him by Edward Stettinius
during the San Francisco Conference (April-June 1945) which the then
Secretary of State had written in general terms, expressing the view that
the Soviet Union was 'eligible' to receive territory for administration
under trusteeship. M. Molotov now asserted that this constituted a
pledge that the United States would support the Soviet claim to
Tripolitania and professed grave suspicion of their refusal to do so. An
insoluble deadlock was established.

A congeries of sessions followed on the Balkan peace treaties. Each
displayed an increasing acrimony, since the British and American
representatives refused to recognize the régimes in Bucharest and Sofia
until these had been broadened on a basis 'representative of all democratic elements in the populations and pledged to the earliest possible
establishment, through free elections, of a government responsive to the
will of the people'. In return Molotov attacked the United States
support of Fascist régimes in Spain and the Argentine. Recriminations
followed and multiplied until, on 22 September, the Soviet Foreign
Minister precipitated what proved to be a 'terminal crisis'.

On this day M. Molotov sought to jettison the so-called Agreement of
11 September and reverted to his thesis that France and China should
become virtually 'second-class' members of the Council. He proposed to
exclude China from discussion on all the European treaties and France
from all except the German and Italian treaties. Mr Bevin and Secretary
Byrnes both asserted their clear understanding that the decision at
Potsdam had been that, while France and China could not *vote* on any
proposals under the circumstances cited by the Soviet Government,
they could most certainly *participate* in the discussions which preceded
the taking of a vote. This had been accepted by M. Molotov at the time
and had been reaffirmed by the Agreement of 11 September. To ask the
French and Chinese Foreign Ministers to withdraw now would be to
inflict unnecessary humiliation upon them and, at the same time, make a
nonsense of the Council.

Molotov remained adamant, however, in the face of these Anglo-
American arguments and, in an attempt to save the meeting from
immediate collapse, Secretary Byrnes telephoned to President Truman
on the twenty-second urging him to appeal directly to Marshal Stalin to
agree that France and China could continue to participate in discussion
on all treaties but could vote only on treaties with those countries with
whom they had signed armistice terms. After consultation with Molotov,
Stalin replied on the twenty-fourth giving his full support to the stand
which his Foreign Minister had taken.

The Council had reached an *impasse* and, though its sessions lingered on for a further week in a state of vitriolic bickering, during which Mr Byrnes, supported by Mr Bevin, put forward three separate formulas of compromise, all of which were stolidly rejected by M. Molotov, the conference was formally adjourned on 2 October and the deputies were instructed to collate the meagre and unimportant results of its labours.

These indeed were distinguished only for their insignificance, yet they shed a certain pale effulgence of insincerity. It was, for example, ironic that among the major decisions of the Council was that the treaties of peace with Italy and the satellites should include a Declaration of Human Rights under which the five defeated nations would guarantee their citizens freedom of speech, religious worship, political belief and public assembly. This decision was taken in accordance with the agreement reached by the three Foreign Ministers in Moscow in October 1943.* Of the five states concerned, only Italy and Finland have been permitted to implement its provisions.

Of the remaining decisions, most of them concerned Italy who, on the conclusion of the treaty, would have her sovereignty restored to her. She was to lose her colonies to the trusteeship provisions of the United Nations Charter and the islands of the Dodecanese to Greece. The question of the amount of her reparation was left unresolved, as was the form of trusteeship to be applied to her African colonies. Somewhat cryptically, it was agreed that she should rely on the United Nations for her protection and devote her resources to the needs of her civilian economy instead of engaging in competition in armaments.

No decision was reached on the future of the treaties. The Soviet Union favoured keeping the power of drafting and completing them in the hands of the Big Three, in accordance with the general view expressed at Potsdam, whereas the United States felt that a conference was necessary in order to permit the peace-making participation of other nations who would be vitally concerned in maintaining and enforcing the provisions of the treaties. No solution was found for this deadlock.[9]

Somewhat sadly, Secretary Byrnes remarked in his report to the American people on 5 October on the first session of the Council of Foreign Ministers: 'Experience reveals that a certain degree of understanding among the major powers is essential to secure general agreement among many nations.'[10] Such degree had not been apparent during the Lancaster House discussions. Indeed the complete reverse had been the case. 'The depressing thing is the utterly realistic and selfish approach

* See above, p. 120 n, and below, p. 542.

of the Russians and the complete absence of any wide considerations in the interests of peace for the benefit of all', Pierson Dixon wrote in his diary on 4 October.[11]

II

The course and collapse of the Lancaster House meeting of the Council of Foreign Ministers had gone far to convince Ernest Bevin of the futility of the search for an East–West *détente*. His scepticism was largely based on pragmatic common sense and it is interesting to note that, starting from this premise, he arrived at much the same conclusions as that expert and brilliant American analyst George Kennan in his famous 'long telegram' of 22 February 1946.[12] This, however, was far from true of Secretary Byrnes.

Mr Byrnes had been largely influential at Potsdam in getting the idea of a council of Foreign Ministers accepted. His personal 'image' was therefore closely associated with its success or failure and he was appalled at the ignominious conclusion of its first session. On his return to Washington he embarked almost immediately on a policy directed towards persuading the Russians to resume the meetings of the Council at the earliest possible moment, in the course of which he adopted the line of whole-hearted appeasement of Moscow, of complete disregard of his allies and of such independence of thought and action as to bring him on to a direct collision course with the President of the United States.*

On his own showing Secretary Byrnes determined to break the deadlock with Moscow by demonstrating the fact that, under circumstances which indicated an observance by the Soviet Union of the terms of the Yalta Declaration on Liberated Europe, the United States would not withhold recognition of the new régimes. Thus the United States joined Britain in recognizing the Provisional Government of Austria on 20 October, and the Provisional Government of Hungary two weeks later, on 2 November. In addition, the United States Government took the initiative in implementing a provision of the Potsdam Agreement

---

* President Truman wrote of Mr Byrnes at this time: 'In his executive position during the war years Byrnes had enjoyed unprecedented freedom of action. . . . It caused him to believe that, as an official of the executive branch of the Government, he could have a completely free hand within his own sphere of duty. In fact, he came to think that his judgement was better than the President's. More and more during the fall of 1945 I came to feel that, in his role as Secretary of State, Byrnes was beginning to think of himself as an Assistant President in full charge of foreign policy. Apparently he failed to realize that, under the Constitution, the President is required to assume all responsibility for the conduct of foreign affairs. The President cannot abdicate that responsibility, and he cannot turn it over to anyone else. A Secretary of State should never have the illusion that he is President of the United States.'[13]

which envisaged the revision of the Montreux Convention of 1936 for the Control of the Straits. On 7 November it was stated officially that the United States would join in a multilateral guarantee of free access to the Straits and their opposition to a settlement confined to the Black Sea Powers.

At the same time the Secretary of State adopted a British suggestion and dispatched the editor of the *Louisville Courier-Journal*, Mark Etheridge, a leader of liberal political thought, on a personal fact-finding mission to Rumania and Bulgaria. In order that Mr Etheridge should bring an unprejudiced mind to his assessment of the facts, the State Department was specifically directed to withhold official information from him.

Having struck a balance between demonstrating American willingness to recognize national régimes which appeared to satisfy their conditions of freedom and to withhold such recognition in cases where these conditions did not apply, Mr Byrnes sought to draw the attention of Marshal Stalin to this moral example. The United States Ambassador, Averell Harriman, was instructed to seek an audience of Stalin and to emphasize and explain the difference between the United States policy as applied to Austria and Hungary on the one hand and Rumania and Bulgaria on the other, and to urge him to remedy the situation in respect of the two Balkan states. Stalin's response caused consternation in the State Department. The Marshal was clearly unimpressed and uninterested by the vagaries of the United States policy of recognition. He knew where his strength lay and where he could flout the United States with impunity. He dismissed the European aspect of the conversation with brusqueness and at once directed it to the control of Japan, an area where American and not Russian influence was paramount.[14]

A more experienced statesman than Mr Byrnes might well have taken warning from Stalin's attitude, but the Secretary of State was seemingly myopic – and certainly persistent.

Thursday, 29 November 1945 was Thanksgiving Day in the United States. Despite the holiday, Mr Byrnes was in his office, deep in cogitation of the many problems which assailed the Department of State – viewing them in the light of past experience, exploring possibilities of exploiting this experience for the future. Suddenly he bethought him of that provision of the Yalta Agreement which called for personal consultation between the Foreign Ministers, if possible, every three or four months. True, they had met in London only two months ago under singularly difficult circumstances, but this had been by virtue of the machinery created by the Potsdam Conference (albeit under the inspiration of Mr Byrnes himself) and in company with their French and Chinese colleagues. A meeting of the Foreign Ministers of the Big Three would satisfy the strongly expressed desire of the Soviet Union to keep the ultimate decision of peace-making in the hands of Russia, the United States and Britain. Agreement on basic principles might be reached under such circumstances and such an agreement could later be submitted to the French and Chinese for their concurrence.

So reasoned the Secretary and, with him, to reason was to act. After a somewhat perfunctory consultation with the President and with the Department, where considerable opposition was encountered, a telegram was dispatched to Harriman without further ado, and before the weekend was over Russian acceptance for a meeting in Moscow had been obtained.[15]

The reaction in Whitehall at being thus by-passed and confronted with a *fait accompli* was not altogether favourable. Mr Bevin was not unnaturally displeased at the discourtesy implied by this lack of consultation between allies, a further demonstration of Mr Byrnes's consistent neglect of British feelings and lack of concern for Anglo-American relations. But, apart from this sense of personal slight, he was inimical to a meeting at which, he feared, Russia would almost certainly be the major gainer, Britain would gain nothing and the Americans would give away British interests to the Russians for the sake of a settlement.[16] However, he accepted the inevitable and went to Moscow on 15 December, the eve of the conference.

There his worst fears were realized. Mr Byrnes had come to Moscow determined to achieve some sort of an agreement. He did not much care what kind of an agreement it was and he certainly considered Anglo-American relations as expendable if, by sacrificing them, he could make a compact of some sort with the Russians. Thus he needlessly offended the British by giving a copy of the Etheridge Report to Molotov but not to Bevin, although Mark Etheridge had undertaken his mission largely at British initiative and the British Embassy in Moscow had opened its files to him.[17]

Infinitely more serious, however, was the Secretary's conduct in respect of the field of atomic energy. On 15 November, as a result of several days' negotiation between President Truman, Mr Attlee and the Canadian Prime Minister, Mr Mackenzie King, at Washington, a tripartite agreement was reached on the need for international action under the auspices of the United Nations for the provision of controls over atomic energy to ensure its use for peaceful purposes only; to outlaw atomic weapons and other major weapons capable of mass destruction; and to provide for effective safeguards through inspection.

They also agreed that there should be full and effective co-operation in the field of atomic energy between the United States, the United Kingdom and Canada. This much had been announced to the world by President Truman, but in the course of the discussions preceding the agreement there had been exchanges of a confidential character the gist of which the President had reported to his Cabinet.[18]

On the eve of his departure for Moscow, Secretary Byrnes conferred (on 10 December) with Senators Vandenberg, Connally and McMahon, who constituted the Atomic Bomb Committee of the Senate, and also certain other members of the Committee on Foreign Relations, to whom he disclosed his intention of suggesting, in the course of his forthcoming conversations with Stalin and Molotov, first, an exchange of atom scientists and scientific information between Russia and the United States, and then that the Soviet Union should join with the United States in setting up an Atomic Commission under the auspices of the United Nations. In other words, Mr Byrnes was proposing to make the Soviet Union privy to, and participant in, the agreement which had been concluded less than a month before with Britain and Canada without even the courtesy of informing his allies of his intention to do so; furthermore, he left the Senators with the impression that he might turn over to the Soviet Government certain atomic energy information even before there had been an agreement on safeguards and inspection.

So disturbed were the Atomic Bomb Committee by these tidings that they sought immediate audience of the President who received them next morning, by which time the Secretary of State was already airborne. As a result of their report they found that President Truman shared their anxiety, but an examination of the directive which Mr Byrnes had caused to be drawn up by the State Department on his own instructions made it possible for him to discuss any portion of the proposal independently of other sections. This came as a surprise to all and the Committee respectfully suggested that the directive should be immediately amended and the Secretary informed by radio. The President hastened to reassure the Senators that no such action as appeared to be meditated by Byrnes had been discussed with him or had received his approval, and forthwith he instructed the Under-Secretary, Dean Acheson, to enjoin Byrnes that no atomic information was to be given to the Russians and that his activities were to be confined to securing Soviet support for the establishment of the United Nations Commission. The Secretary replied on the seventeenth that he did not intend to put forward any proposal 'outside of the framework of the three-power declaration'.[19]

Arrived in Moscow, Byrnes informed Bevin of his intention to present his memorandum on atomic energy to the Russians and, when the Foreign Secretary protested against any such action being taken without the cognizance, if not the concurrence, of the British and Canadian Governments, Byrnes ignored him and sent the papers to Molotov without further reference. It was not surprising that Bevin regarded this as an instance of direct bad faith and discourtesy, or that he was furious.[20]

Nor is it surprising that under the influence of Mr Byrnes's blandishments the Soviet Government acquiesced in a series of meaningless commitments. M. Molotov accepted the principle of the Three-Power Declaration, placing atomic energy under the control of the United Nations, and at the first session of the General Assembly in London a month later the Soviet delegation joined the unanimous-vote approval on 24 January 1946 which adopted the British resolution establishing the United Nations Atomic Energy Commission with the powers delegated to it by the Washington Declaration. Thereafter, however, the policy of the Soviet Union was directed towards nullifying the work and objectives of this body, a feat in which it was singularly successful.

The Soviet Union, after a certain amount of 'shadow-boxing', conceded the right of the British and Americans to send representatives to Rumania and Bulgaria in pursuit of the establishment of democratic Governments, yet, in effect, no such Governments were ever established.

Finally, a Three-Power decision was reached on the various phases of peace-making, a decision which conceded virtually everything to the Soviet preference. There were to be six stages. First, the preliminary terms of peace with Italy and the four satellites were to be drawn up by the Council of Foreign Ministers, as the principal Powers which had signed the respective armistices; secondly, these preliminary terms were to be submitted to a conference called by the United States, Britain, the Soviet Union, France and China (as representing both the Council of Foreign Ministers and the permanent members of the Security Council of the United Nations) and to which would be invited all those states which had been actively engaged in war with substantial force against the European members of the Axis; thirdly, at this conference, which would be held in Paris not later than 1 May 1946, the representatives of each of the five ex-enemy states would be permitted to discuss the terms of the peace treaty to be concluded with each respective nation; fourthly, the conference would consider the drafts prepared by the Council of Foreign Ministers and would formulate its recommendations for the final texts; fifthly, the Council would, in the light of these recommendations, prepare the final texts; and sixthly, these final texts of the five treaties would be signed by all the states represented at the Peace Conference.[21]

The Moscow Conference dispersed on 26 December, and on the following evening the State Department issued Secretary Byrnes's communiqué on its results. The communiqué had been released without previous reference to the White House and indeed it constituted the first information which the President had received on the final decisions taken at the conference. On reading it President Truman was unfavourably impressed. 'I did not like what I read', he recorded. 'There was not a word about Iran or any other place where the Soviets were on the march. We had gained only an empty promise of further talks.'[22]

Forthwith he summoned the Secretary of State to report to him on board the Presidential yacht *Williamsburg* in the Potomac and there, on 29 December, he administered personally an imperial rocket, which he followed up on 5 January with a withering, swingeing letter, of which the final paragraphs contained the kernel of his new policy:

> I do not think we should play compromise any longer [wrote the President]. We should refuse to recognize Rumania and Bulgaria until they comply with our requirements; we should let our position on Iran be known in no uncertain terms and we should continue to insist on the internationalization of the Kiel Canal, the Rhine–Danube waterway and the Black Sea Straits, and we should maintain complete control of Japan and the Pacific. We should rehabilitate China and create a strong central government there. We should do the same for Korea. Then we should insist on the return of our ships from Russia and force a settlement of the Lend-Lease debt of Russia.
>
> I'm sick of babying the Soviets.[23]

Mr Byrnes accepted this master ruling apparently without demur.* He did not resign or give warning of resignation, but this was the beginning of his decline and of President Truman's intention to redeem one of his most disastrous mistakes in appointment. Thenceforward there was no further doubt as to who formulated the foreign policy of the United States.† 'My memorandum to Byrnes', wrote the President, 'not only clarified the Secretary's position, but it was the point of departure of our policy. "I'm sick of babying the Soviets", I had said to

* In his second book of memoirs, Mr Byrnes asserts that his conversation with President Truman on the *Williamsburg* was friendly and that the President had said that 'he understood and expressed pleasure at the progress we had made'. Mr Byrnes does not mention, even to deny, the President's letter. In statements to Professor Herbert Drulls, in the course of his researches, President Truman, Ambassador Harriman and Judge Rosenman all asserted that Secretary Byrnes behaved in so high-handed a manner because he was jealous of the President, who, Byrnes believed, had stolen the Presidency from him.[24]

† Mr Byrnes gave no sign of departure until April 1946 when he suggested, both personally and in writing, that his health would be the better for a rest. He agreed to continue in office during the negotiation of the peace treaties which grew out of his Moscow commitments and finally left the State Department on 20 January 1947, to be succeeded as Secretary of State by General George Marshall.

Byrnes, and I meant it.' It was the premonitory symptom of the Truman Doctrine and the Marshall Plan. It was in effect the first American riposte in the Cold War.

III

The Moscow Conference of the Big Three had agreed on 26 December 1945 that the Peace Conference should meet in Paris not later than 1 May 1946, by which time the Council of Foreign Ministers should have agreed among themselves upon the texts of the five draft peace treaties. By the beginning of April 1946, however, there had been no move to reconvene the Council and Secretary Byrnes called the attention of his colleagues to the passage of time. When they finally met in Paris on 25 April two things were apparent: in the first place there was no hope of meeting the scheduled date for the opening of the Peace Conference. In the second, Secretary Byrnes, chastened by his passage of arms with the President and ably supported by Senators Tom Connally of Texas, chairman of the Senate Committee on Foreign Relations, and Arthur Vandenberg of Michigan, the ranking Republican member of that body, had shed his proclivity towards appeasement of Russia and was now a protagonist of a robust policy of resistance. When President Truman had said he was 'sick of babying the Soviets' he had meant it, and so now did his Secretary of State.

Much credit must be given to the great amount of drafting and preparation which had been achieved by the deputies in their sessions at Lancaster House between the breakdown of the first session of the Council of Foreign Ministers in October 1945 and the beginning of its second session the following April. Working together on a professional basis, which removed them from the considerations of a political level, these four men – Gladwyn Jebb (U.K.), James Dunn (U.S.A.), Messrs Vyshinsky or Gusev (U.S.S.R.) and Roger Couve de Murville (France), all of whom attained great eminence and distinction in their later careers* – performed prodigies of work in drawing up the preliminary drafts of the treaties for their masters' consideration. That the Paris meetings of the Council achieved anything at all was largely due to their labours.

The second session of the Council of Foreign Ministers, though it did not break up in such complete confusion and dissidence as the first, was

* Gladwyn Jebb became British representative on the U.N. Security Council and Ambassador to Paris, being raised to the peerage as Lord Gladwyn; James Dunn served as American Ambassador to Rome, Paris, Madrid and Rio de Janeiro; Vyshinsky and Gusev both served as Soviet representatives on the Security Council and as Deputy Foreign Ministers; and Couve de Murville became General de Gaulle's Foreign Minister and Premier.

no feast of amiability.[25] Where the Russians could be obstructive they obstructed; where they could see a means to improve their advantage in the Mediterranean area or in Eastern Europe they essayed to take it; where the British and the Americans could prevent this accretion of Soviet power they did so. On the issues of Italian reparation payments, of Italian colonies, or of the dispute over Trieste, of the government of Germany and the future of Austria, deadlock followed deadlock, *impasse* gave place to *impasse*; and the date of the opening of the Peace Conference became indefinitely postponed.

After nineteen days of virtually inconclusive discussion on the major aspects of the proposed treaties, Secretary Byrnes, on 14 May, asked for a month's recess of the Council meeting and for once his colleagues were in unanimous agreement with him. The meeting adjourned on the seventeenth.

In these sessions Secretary Byrnes had been at his best. 'Appeasement simply feeds the hazard from which it seeks to escape', reflected Senator Vandenberg. 'Paris was Munich in reverse. We now know that Munich was a ghastly mistake. This at least suggests that "Munich in reverse" was wise at Paris. I may be wrong but I think Byrnes did a magnificently courageous and constructive job.'[26] More detached but no less accurate was the British assessment of Pierson Dixon. 'Byrnes is an admirable representative of the U.S.', he wrote in his diary on 14 May, '[he is] weak when the American public is weak, and tough when they are tough. At present they are tough.' And he added three days later: 'People at home seem depressed at the failure of the Conference to settle; but it is better to disagree than to give way.'[27]

Once again the deputies, on the instruction of their principals, performed prodigies and with such effect that, during the interval of recess, real progress was made towards the penultimate stages of the peace treaties.

When, however, the Council of Foreign Ministers reassembled on 15 June it was in atrociously cold midsummer weather, and the atmosphere within the Luxembourg Palace appeared to be as glacial as the temperatures without. Yet, in contrast with the meetings before the recess, the Council was able by 12 July, when it concluded its session, to reach sufficient agreement on the draft treaties with Italy and the four satellites to justify the calling of the plenary Peace Conference on 29 July. But they failed in their efforts to agree upon draft treaties with Germany and Austria.

There was a common form in the five draft treaties which emerged from the Council of Foreign Ministers for the consideration of the Peace Conference.[28] Each of the treaties contained provisions on which the

Council had reached agreement or, in cases where no agreement had been found possible, alternative proposals. The four members of the Council were pledged to support at the conference those provisions on which they had agreed.

In addition to clauses relating to territorial adjustments, which necessarily varied in each case, the five draft treaties had certain major provisions in common. Thus, each of them contained undertakings for the protection of human rights, the prevention of the revival of Fascist-type organizations and the apprehension of war criminals and traitors. There were, furthermore, stipulations for the limitation of armaments and armed forces, the payment of reparations and compensation and also for restitution.*

IV

The Peace Conference which opened on 29 July 1946 in Paris was extremely unlike that which had framed the settlement after the First World War. In one respect it adhered to the original planning of 1918 more closely than had the first Peace Conference. It had been at first intended in 1918 to hold a preliminary conference which should draw up terms of peace with Germany and her former allies and that these should then be discussed with the representatives of each of the ex-enemy states. This course of action was in effect abandoned in 1919; it was followed in 1946.

In other respects, however, the two conferences differed. The representatives of the twenty-one states gathered in July 1946 in that lovely Palace of the Luxembourg, which Henri Quatre's widow and neice, the Queen-Regent Marie de Medici, had built in 1615 and which throughout the Third, Fourth and Fifth Republics has housed the Senate, were strangely different and yet not unlike those delegates who had come together in the Quai d'Orsay's Salle de l'Horloge in January 1919. In the first place the calibre of the delegates was different and, it is believed, of a lesser quality in 1946 than in 1919. At that first Peace Conference there had been the then giants of the world – Wilson, Clemenceau, Lloyd George – and other great figures who would mould, or had moulded, the destinies of their nations: Paderewski, Venizelos, Masaryk, Pašić and Smuts. Of these only Field-Marshal Smuts remained a living bridge across the time-gap of the two world wars.†

There was one other link with the past. Harold Nicolson, who had

* The peace settlement with each of the five countries, together with its political background, is treated later in this chapter; see sections VI–X below.

† There was, in point of fact, one very old member of the Brazilian delegation at the Peace Conference of 1946 who had also been a delegate in 1919.

been a junior member of the British delegation in 1919, attended the conference of 1946 as a commentator for the British Broadcasting Corporation. From his comparative recollections he wrote, somewhat sourly:

> Our delegation does not look impressive. Attlee, so small, so *chétif*; A. V. Alexander, sturdy but scrubby; Hector McNeil, Scotch and dour; Glenvil Hall, a secondary school teacher.* How insignificant they look there in their red plush stalls! How different from Lloyd George and Balfour, how terribly different from Winston.[29]†

The outstanding difference between the two conferences was, of course, the presence of the delegation from the Union of Soviet Socialist Republics. Though the shadow of Bolshevism, then a new and unknown menace to world society, had been a not insignificant factor in Paris in 1919, it had been a factor *in absentia*; in 1946 the Soviet delegation was a very present cause of conflict, alarm and disunity.

The twenty-one national delegations‡ which assembled in the Luxembourg Palace on 29 July were almost immediately plunged into a maelstrom of disagreement on the issue of procedure. The Council of Foreign Ministers, acting on Soviet initiative, had recommended, among the rules of procedure, that on the various commissions which the conference might set up§ a two-thirds majority would be required for a recommendation, but the minority also would have the right to express its views. The smaller nations, under the Antipodean leadership of

---

* Ernest Bevin was prevented by ill-health from attending the opening of the conference and the delegation was led by the Prime Minister. Alexander was First Lord of the Admiralty, McNeil Under-Secretary of State for Foreign Affairs, and Hall Financial Secretary to the Treasury.

† With that puckish sense of humour which was not always appreciated by Americans (for whom he had neither a basic liking nor understanding), Nicolson gave to the representative of the *New York Times* a very different point of view. The correspondent had said that necessarily there was a difference of personalities in the make-up of the two conferences; in 1919 they had been giants. 'Nonsense', replied Nicolson, 'don't you believe it. Mr Byrnes, to my mind, is more effective that President Wilson; Bevin is certainly a stronger and finer character than Lloyd George; old Orlando cannot be compared for force and capacity to Molotov; and in the circumstances Bidault is a far more suitable person than Clemenceau could ever have been.' Nicolson records that his interlocutor was 'distressed'.[30]

‡ The twenty-one nations represented were the United Kingdom, the United States, the Soviet Union, France, China, Australia, Belgium, Byelorussian Soviet Socialist Republic, Brazil, Canada, Czechoslovakia, Ethiopia, Greece, India, the Netherlands, Norway, New Zealand, Poland, Ukrainian Soviet Socialist Republic, Union of South Africa and Yugoslavia.

§ The conference set up ten such bodies, viz.: a General Commission (which never met), a Military Commission, a Legal and Drafting Commission; these consisted of representatives of the twenty-one nations participating. In addition there were five Political and Territorial Commissions varying in composition in that they consisted of representatives of the four sponsoring members of the Council of Foreign Ministers, plus those of the states which had been at war with each individual ex-enemy state, and also an Economic Commission for Italy (from which only Norway was excluded) and an Economic Commission for the Balkan States and Finland.

Dr Herbert Evatt and Dr William Jordan (respectively Australian and New Zealand Ministers for External Affairs), opposed this proposal and marshalled the arguments in favour of a democratic process of majority decision. M. Molotov defended the original ruling of the Council; Mr Byrnes supported the minor Powers; the British delegation eventually offered a compromise formula which, after more than a week of lively discussion, was finally adopted on 9 August, to the effect that those proposals on the peace treaties which received the votes of a simple majority of the members of the conference would be received by the Council.[31] The conference also agreed to draw up its own rules of procedure as a whole.[32]

Having extricated itself from its procedural morass, the conference devoted six days (10–15 August) to hearing the representatives of the five ex-enemy states, who were permitted to make their comments and observations on their respective treaties.[33] This was among the great contrasts between the two Paris Conferences and was productive of some emotional moments. Alcide de Gasperi, for example, was deeply moved. The Italian treaty, he said, was extremely harsh and did not conform to earlier Allied declarations. It left Italy in a defenceless condition, with both her western and eastern frontiers wide open. There was no recognition of the part she played as a co-belligerent after the fall of Fascism, nor of the fact that she was the first Power to break with Germany.* (She had, of course, been the first Power to ally herself with Hitler's Reich.) He criticized the provisions of the draft treaty which dealt with Trieste and with reparation payments but asked for no special concessions. 'Only', he said, 'that the peace be framed within that wider peace which men and women of all countries who fought and suffered for an ideal are wanting.'

In the main, de Gasperi's performance had been one of dignity and even nobility, but it was received in cold and hostile silence – with one exception. As the Italian Prime Minister passed him, Mr Byrnes stood up and shook his hand. 'It was', Harold Nicolson commented, 'an occasion not unworthy either of the conquerors or the conquered.'[35] Byrnes himself says that he thought de Gasperi 'had suffered enough at the hands of Mussolini and the Nazis without the Allies inflicting further suffering on him', but he goes on to add a somewhat Machiavellian gloss

---

* The Potsdam Protocol of 2 August 1945 had made recognition of the fact that 'Italy was the first of the Axis Powers to break with Germany, to whose defeat she has made a material contribution and has now joined with the Allies in the struggle against Japan. Italy has freed herself from the Fascist régime and is making good progress towards re-establishment of a democratic government and institutions. The conclusion of such a Peace Treaty with a recognized and democratic Italian Government will make it possible for the Three Governments to fulfil their desire to support an application from Italy for membership of the United Nations.'[34]

17 Potsdam: The Big Three on the steps of the Prime Minister's residence, 25 July 1945

18 Potsdam: Mr Attlee with Mr Joseph E. Davies (wearing hat) and Mr J. C. Dunn

19 Potsdam: *l. to r.* President Truman, Ernest Bevin and Clement Attlee, 30 July 1945

in that he sought by this gesture 'to win the confidence and friendship of the new Italy' against the Soviet Union.[36]

The representatives of the lesser satellites followed, each making his excuse, seemingly using the defence of the housemaid who, on being discovered in delivery of an illegitimate baby, pleaded that it was only a little one. M. Tartarescu said that Rumania had not become a satellite until 1941 and had risen 'sword in hand' against the Axis in 1944. Her treaty, he complained, contained no provision for compensation from Germany and Hungary for the great damage and losses they had caused.

M. Kulichev, the Bulgarian Foreign Minister, repudiated unreservedly the moral responsibility of his people and had the effrontery to demand access to the Aegean 'by the restitution of western Thrace'. He too claimed reparations from Germany to compensate for goods taken without payment and also the rank of co-belligerent for Bulgaria similar to that of Italy.

On behalf of Hungary, M. Gyöngyösi, her Foreign Minister, sought to obtain the return from Rumania of certain areas in Transylvania and for a restraint to be placed upon Czechoslovakia to prevent her expelling Hungarians from Slovakia. He claimed to represent 'a new and democratic Hungary'.

The Finnish draft treaty had been written in virtual entirety by Russia, with but scant reference to Britain, the only other Power whom Moscow would even admit to the negotiations. When Carl Enckell, the Foreign Minister, sought to obtain mitigation of the terms, saying that Finland's policy was now based firmly upon a lasting co-operation with Russia, he was sternly taken to task by M. Molotov, who warned him never to permit Finland to lend herself to plans for disrupting the three Great Powers.

The conference then passed into its committee stage where progress was painfully slow, and at the end of August the Council of Foreign Ministers held a session to decide on measures for speeding up the proceedings. After consultation with Dr Wang Shih-chieh and Paul-Henri Spaak, Belgian Foreign Minister and President of the United Nations Assembly, it was agreed on 8 September to postpone the forthcoming session of the Assembly from 23 September to 23 October. This imposed a final date-line for closure on the Peace Conference and it was decided that its last meeting should take place on 15 October.

After further tireless work on the part of the deputies, who examined the host of amendments submitted to the draft treaties, agreement was reached on those which could command general support in the conference. The commissions completed their work on 5 October and their reports were considered by the conference as a whole for two days. Two further days were devoted to the Italian treaty, and voting on the satellite treaties took place on 10–13 October.[37]* The recommendations were then formally submitted to the Council of Foreign Ministers for their consideration before the final texts were prepared for signature. It was agreed that at this same meeting the Council should begin their consideration of the terms of a German peace treaty. After much discussion and disagreement it was finally decided that they should meet in New York on 4 November.[38]

Thus ended the curious non-Peace Conference of Paris. It had been unique in that though it had sat for the better part of three months, and had heard the views of both the smaller Allied Powers and of the satellites themselves, it had adjourned without having agreed upon the final texts of the treaties on which they had deliberated. The ultimate form of the treaties remained the responsibility of the four Great Powers, and though they were morally bound to adhere to the recommendations of the conference there was no legal obligation binding upon them to do so and little legal redress if they did not. It may be said, therefore, that whereas the Treaties of Versailles, St Germain, Trianon, Neuilly and Sèvres, which emerged from the 1919 Peace Conference of Paris, were, in a sense, dictated to the enemy, the treaties which were discussed at the Peace Conference of 1946 were virtually dictated by the Great Powers to their enemies and minor allies alike – a new aspect in diplomatic history.†

V

The Council of Foreign Ministers had met in London, in the Palladian elegance of Lancaster House, and in Paris, in the seventeenth-century grandeur of the Palais du Luxembourg; it now gathered in New York,

---

* When the Peace Conference finally adjourned on 15 October it had passed fifty-three recommendations by two-thirds majorities and forty-one recommendations by simple majorities.

† A further complication to the work of the conference was the challenge presented to Secretary Byrnes's bipartisan policy, and indeed the solidarity of Anglo-American relations, by the bitterly pro-Russian and anti-British speech on 12 September at a Madison Square Garden meeting of Henry A. Wallace, President Truman's Secretary of Commerce and the leader of the Russophil element in his Cabinet. Wallace denounced the 'get tough with Russia' policy agreed upon between the President and his Secretary of State. He proposed that Russia be given a free hand to 'socialize' Eastern Europe in return for the United States receiving an equally free hand to democratize Western Europe, the Western Hemisphere and Japan. China was to work out her own salvation. From Paris, Mr Byrnes protested and was supported in his protest by Senators Connally and Vandenberg, the latter saying that he wished to co-operate with the Truman Administration but could only co-operate with 'one Secretary of State at a time'. After some prevarication the Secretary said bluntly that either Wallace must cease to speak on foreign affairs or he, Secretary Byrnes, must resign. On 20 September President Truman asked for and received Secretary Wallace's resignation.[39]

in the comfort and luxury of an Age of Affluence. The session which opened on 4 November 1946 was held in an exotic room on the thirty-seventh floor of the Waldorf-Astoria Towers in the heart of Manhattan Island. The Ministers,* Pierson Dixon wrote in his diary, sat 'round a circular table of maple wood, the central space being filled with Braque-like flowering plants, and the eau-de-nil walls covered with rather unmodern pictures'.[40] But, though the setting might differ, the pattern scarcely varied, and on the second day of the conference Dixon was recording 'a head-on collision between Byrnes and Molotov.'

The goal which the Council had hopefully set for itself was the settlement of those issues emerging from the five draft treaties which had not yet been accorded agreement by the Four Powers, and in this connection the United States had committed itself to support the fifty-three recommendations from the Conference of Paris which had received a two-thirds majority. The other three Governments were not so committed. It was the hope of, at any rate, the Western Europeans that their labours would be completed within three weeks and that they could all then begin the discussion of a peace treaty with Germany, which was rightly regarded as the crux of the problem of European peace.[41]

The now customary and inevitable clash between United States and Soviet policies began at once and continued throughout. Byrnes was ready to accept the progress made at the Paris Conference as represented by the fifty-three two-thirds recommendations; Molotov was prepared to jettison them altogether and to revert to the position which he had taken up before the conference opened. Byrnes at length declared that, rather than become involved in a further bout of acerbic and interminable debate, he would recommend to his colleagues that they admit defeat and abandon all attempt to reach agreement on the treaties. M. Molotov thereupon, with characteristic Soviet unpredictability, completely reversed himself and accepted almost immediately forty-seven of the fifty-three conference recommendations which had been adopted by a two-thirds majority and twenty-four of the forty-one which had received a simple majority.[42]† Those recommendations which Molotov could

---

* Georges Bidault, at that time Prime Minister and Foreign Minister of France, was prevented by national domestic problems from attending the New York meeting, where France was represented by M. Couve de Murville.

† It was, of course, a matter of fact that the Soviet Union had much to gain by getting the treaties into operation. For example, British and American troops would then withdraw from Italy, thereby giving more scope to the Italian Communist Party. On the other hand there was no such provision for the withdrawal of Russian troops from Rumania and Hungary since, so long as the Austrian issue was unresolved, Russia needed them for the maintenance of her lines of communication with Austria. The same applied to Soviet troops in Poland so long as there was no peace settlement

not, or would not, accept were simply dropped, and as a result of this sudden – if temporary – break in the Soviet ice-flow it was made possible for the final texts of the five treaties to be finally agreed on 6 December.*

Before the Council dispersed on the twelfth it had been agreed that, in order to give the deputies the requisite time to complete the final drafting, the treaties should be formally signed on 10 February 1947. This involved some unusual problems of logistics. Mr Byrnes signed the five treaties in Washington, as his last act as Secretary of State, on 20 January. They were then flown to Moscow, where M. Molotov signed them on 29 January, and to London for Mr Bevin's signature on 4 February. At a somewhat unimpressive ceremony in the Salle de l'Horloge at the Quai d'Orsay – the same room in which the Covenant of the League of Nations had been adopted in 1919 and the Kellogg–Briand Pact renouncing war as an instrument of national policy had been signed in 1928 – the peace treaties of the Second World War were finally signed by M. Bidault on behalf of France and by representatives of all the other Allied and ex-enemy states on 10 February.†

There was no sense of finality about these peripatetic treaties; no real belief that they ushered in a new world or a new age. Already there hung above Europe a premonitory cloud of conflict and of the denial of the very principles which were supposed to be enshrined within these agreements. Irony and cynicism were more justifiably the transcendent sentiments of the hour, rather than hope and optimism. The treaties were nominally to deny the use of force and to ensure the liberties of man. Yet, in little more than a year from the time of their signature, one man among those present in the Salle de l'Horloge had been hounded to death by acts of force and the denial of such liberties. Jan Masaryk, Czechoslovakia's Foreign Minister, that most lovable and human of men, met his death on 10 March 1948.

---

with Germany, and the Finnish treaty provided for permanent Soviet garrisons in Finland. The treaties also provided for the withdrawal of Allied Control Commissions from the Eastern European states, and though Russia never had the least intention of taking seriously the treaty provisions for civil liberties she preferred to have no Allied witnesses to this fact. It was in order not to be baulked of these manifest advantages that Molotov performed his *volte-face*.[43]

* The New York meeting of the Council of Foreign Ministers began its preliminary discussion on treaties for Germany and Austria on 9 December. No progress was made and it was decided to postpone these two questions to a further meeting of the Council to be held in Moscow in March 1947 (see below, p. 471).

† The House of Commons accepted the five treaties on 28 March 1947 and the British ratification was deposited on 15 September 1947. The United States Senate rejected, by 67 votes to 22, a motion by Senator William Fulbright to defer the Italian treaty for fuller consideration and accepted four of the five treaties (not having been at war with Finland) on 5 June. President Truman formally ratified them on 14 June.

VI

In April 1934 one of the authors of this book was discussing with Major-General Walther von Reichenau, then a departmental head in the *Reichskriegsministerium* in Berlin, the shape of things to come in the event of a Second World War. The talk turned to allies and political alignments, notably that of Italy. Hitler's future Field-Marshal was disdainful of allies in general – 'In the last war we were tied to a lot of rotting corpses' – and for Italy he entertained that contempt which the Teuton has felt for the Latin since the days when Arminius the Cheruscan overwhelmed the legions of Quintus Varus. 'Mark my words', he said. 'It does not matter on which side Italy begins the war, for at its close she will be found playing her historic role as "the Whore of Europe".'[44]

Without giving complete endorsement to General von Reichenau's thesis of Italian political fidelity, it must be admitted that – especially from the German point of view – there is a strong substratum of truth to it. In 1914 the Kingdom of Italy was a partner of the Triple Alliance, together with Germany and Austria–Hungary, to whose alignment she had adhered in 1882. In the crisis which followed the assassination at Sarajevo she shared the initiative with Britain in searching for a peaceful solution, but when this proved impossible and Britain stood with her allies Italy declared her neutrality. Her reasons given for so doing were that the terms of the Triple Alliance provided for common action only in the event of an attack upon one of its members, and it was the Austrians who had sent an ultimatum to Serbia; that Italy had not been consulted before such action had been taken; that she was not in a sufficient state of preparedness to make war; and that, in any case, the treaty of 1882 'was not directed against England'.

There followed some eight months of equivocal diplomatic activity, during which the major Allies, Britain, France and Russia, endeavoured to lure Italy on to their side and Prince von Bülow, that egregious Imperial Chancellor who had incurred his Kaiser's undying enmity and whose memoirs are so misleading as to have been adjudged by some to be positively mendacious, sought desperately on behalf of Germany to keep her in a state of neutrality amicable to the Central Powers. Both sides enjoyed some lack of inhibition since neither was bargaining with their own territory. Italy's demands were upon Austria-Hungary, with whom Britain, France and Russia were at war and whose territorial possessions were regarded by Germany as being, although those of an ally, supremely expendable in persuading Italy not to desert to the Entente Powers.

Placed in this favourable position, Italy certainly made the most of it. Her original demands upon Austria, made in the autumn of 1914, were rejected by Vienna as unacceptable even for consideration. They were promptly bettered by the Allies and, though Prince von Bülow succeeded in persuading the Imperial Government in Vienna to make very considerable modifications in its original adamantine attitude, Allied diplomacy won the day and on 26 April 1915 the Treaty of London, a secret agreement between the four contracting Powers, opened up before Italian eyes a glowing vista of future conquests. All the Trentino was to be hers, together with the Isonzo Valley, Rhodes and all the Dodecanese islands; if an Albanian state were created after the war it was to be within Italian control, and meanwhile Italy would have the Albanian port of Valona for herself outright; she was promised a share in the projected partition of Turkish possessions in Asia Minor, and by the subsequent Agreement of St Jean de Maurienne in April 1917 the Smyrna region of Anatolia was allocated to her. In return, Italy denounced the Triple Alliance on 3 May 1915, and declared war on Austria-Hungary on 24 May of that year and on Germany on 27 August 1916.

With the collapse of the Central Powers in the autumn of 1918 and the consequent ending of the war, leaving a virtual vacuum in Central Europe, Italy was suddenly projected into an international position incommensurate with her war effort or her political capacity. With the disappearance of the Hohenzollern, Habsburg and Romanov Empires, the Kingdom of Italy became a ranking Great Power in Europe and as such, with the United States, Britain and France, one of the Big Four arbiters of the fate of the world at the Peace Conference of Paris. But her position was by no means an easy one. She was a bigger claimant of territory and therefore a less detached participator than any of the other Big Four Powers. She had received lavish promises of territorial acquisitions on the fulfilment of which she had every intention of insisting. She was also aware of the possibility of further 'soft pickings' if the cards were well played.

But here a further difficulty arose. President Wilson, on bringing the United States into the war in April 1917, had been made aware of the secret treaties entered into among the various Allied Governments in the years prior to American belligerency as guiding principles in the future treaties of peace. He had been appalled by them. He had announced that he would have none of them and had publicly substituted his own basis of peace as formulated in the Fourteen Points (January 1918), of which one of the salient was the principle of self-determination. Thus at the outset of the partnership for peace there was a cleavage of outlook, approach and principle between the Old World and the New.

The Italian representatives at the Peace Conference, Vittorio Orlando and Sidney Sonnino, pursued a course of conduct similar to that which, in English law, is known as 'pleading inconsistent defences'. For example, they claimed northern Dalmatia, overwhelmingly Slav by race, by virtue of the Treaty of London, which President Wilson had repudiated, and also demanded Fiume by virtue of the Wilsonian principle of self-determination, by reason of its being predominantly (and recently) Italian-speaking, although the Treaty of London had specifically recognized it as being part of Croatia and had therefore awarded it to the newly created state of Yugoslavia. Moreover, the Italians refused to yield a scintilla of their claim, despite the blandishments, cajoleries and minatory admonishments of President Wilson.

There followed the extraordinary gesture of the American President's appeal on 23 April 1919 to the Italian people over the heads of the Government and accredited representatives, to modify their national attitude and to abandon their claim to Fiume. The effect of this lunatic action was to solidify the Italians behind their Government, and Orlando and Sonnino withdrew from the conference in a not very dignified huff. This did them little good since during their absence the remaining Big Three agreed to set aside the 1917 Agreement of St Jean de Maurienne in so far as Italy was concerned and to award the Smyrna area of Anatolia to Greece. When the Italian representatives, having got over their sulks, returned to the Peace Conference on 7 May, it was with their prestige diminished.*

Thus Italy entered on the post-war period in a state of semi-frustration. Though she had increased her Dalmatian and Aegean holdings considerably, she did not obtain control of the new Albanian state and she had made no accretion of territory in Africa or in Asia Minor, where she had been superseded (to her infinite benefit if she had but known it) by Greece. Nor did she even become a mandatory Power, as did Britain and France – and even Belgium – when the African and Asiatic possessions of Germany and Turkey were thus distributed. She regarded herself as having been 'let down' by her allies and this feeling of resentment, together with the itch of national expansion and ambition which had manifested itself during the war, undoubtedly contributed to the

* There followed on 12 September 1919 the *opéra-bouffe* episode of Gabriele d'Annunzio's seizure of Fiume and his establishment of it as a minuscular state, an action which, if it was not connived at, was certainly condoned by the Italian Government. D'Annunzio remained in unchallenged occupation of Fiume until January 1921 when, consequent upon a tentative agreement between Italy and Yugoslavia in the Treaty of Rapallo (November 1920), he was forcibly evicted by Italian military and naval forces. Fiume was finally recognized as Italian territory by the Italo–Yugoslav Treaty of Rome on 27 January 1924.

rise and success of the Fascist movement which Mussolini finally brought to power in 1922.

The stark brutality, which came to be a recognized characteristic of Fascist and Nazi foreign policy, was first made manifest in the Italian attack on Corfu in 1923, to be followed by naked aggression against Ethiopia in 1935 and Albania in 1939. Italy became the joint sponsor of Germany in the Rome–Berlin Axis, a co-partner of the Anti-Comintern Pact (1936) and a signatory of the Pact of Steel (1939). She took avidly all that was to be gained from membership in the 'Dictators' Club'.

Yet Mussolini shrank from the ultimate responsibilities of a Second World War, to which he correctly judged that Italy's economic stability and military potential were unequal. In the Czech crisis of 1938 and the Polish crisis of 1939 Italy made frantic efforts to avoid a general con-flagration and, when her efforts failed in the second event, she repeated her manœuvre of 1914 and declared her neutrality in September 1939.

There is reason to believe that Hitler would have infinitely preferred to have his 'ally' as a neutral rather than a belligerent. His contempt for the warlike qualities of the Italian armed forces was coupled with a recognition of the advantages which a 'friendly' neutral could afford him in eluding the rigours of the British naval blockade and also of the disadvantages presented by the vulnerable position which Italy would present on Germany's southern flank if she became an active participant in the war.

The lure of 'soft pickings' proved, however, to be too strong for Italy. With the collapse of France in the summer of 1940, and the seemingly imminent defeat of Britain, she hastened to make a hyena-like entry into the war on 10 June, thus earning for herself President Roosevelt's well-merited scorn in his 'stab in the back' speech at the University of Virginia on the same day.*

Not content with riding to the kill in France on the coat-tails of the Germans, Italy embarked on an attack of her own on Greece on 28 October 1940, and was so soundly trounced by the Greek armies that she had to be rescued from a débâcle by the *Wehrmacht*. Thereafter she sustained a series of crippling defeats at the hands of the British, American and French armed forces, being hustled out of North Africa at the surrender of Cape Bon on 13 May 1943 and out of Sicily, together with the Germans, by the end of August. The Allies bombed Rome on 19 July, and on 3 September British troops landed on the mainland of Italy, north of Reggio, while less than a week later General Mark Clark's Fifth Army effected a landing in the Gulf of Salerno, south of Naples.

Meanwhile the more moderate and clear-sighted among the Fascist

* See above, p. 32 n.

leaders had overthrown the Duce at the historic session of the Grand Council on 25–6 July, and the King of Italy had resumed his full powers and prerogatives. The Government which he appointed under the leadership of Marshal Pietro Badoglio at once began secret negotiations through Lisbon for Unconditional Surrender and signed a preliminary armistice at Supreme Allied Headquarters in Sicily on 3 September, the full and formal surrender ceremonies taking place on board H.M.S. *Nelson* in Malta Harbour on 29 September.[45]*

Thereupon the Badoglio Government, representing the newly liberated Italy, proceeded to *voler au secours de la victoire*. Anxious to be found on the winning side at the close of the war and to be numbered as being among the angels of democracy – although having served a term among the 'fallen' – Italy declared war on Germany on 13 October 1943,† and thereby passed from the status of a conquered enemy who had surrendered unconditionally to that of a 'co-belligerent'.‡ An Italian corps fought with credit in the Eighth Army under the command of Field-Marshal Alexander, and the various resistance groups of partisans in northern Italy surpassed themselves in ferocity in sabotaging German military activities and in settling private scores of their own among the former supporters of Fascism.

But if these tergiversations were expected to result in a 'special relationship' for Italy in the peace settlement, such hopes were woefully disappointed. When the final accounting came, Italy was called upon to meet the full score of the misdemeanours of her Fascist past, despite the able and forceful arguments of Signor de Gasperi as to her new demeanour as a reformed character.

When the Treaty of Peace with Italy was finally signed on 10 February 1947[46] it came as a bitter disappointment to the de Gasperi Government and, moreover, membership of the United Nations, which Italy had been led to believe – or had certainly assumed – would follow automatically after the ratification of the treaty, was denied her by the Russian veto until 1955.

Italy was spared little. The record of her past, good and bad, was set out in the Preamble and there followed provisions for the limitation of her armed forces and for her reparation payments. She was forbidden to possess certain categories of weapons such as tanks, submarines and bombers, her Army was limited to 250,000 men, her Navy to 25,000 and a total tonnage of 67,500 tons and her Air Force to 25,000 men, flying 200 fighters and 150 transport planes. In so far as the economic

---

* See above, pp. 66–73.   † And upon Japan on 14 January 1944.
‡ The term 'co-belligerent' was invented for this purpose by Harold Macmillan.

clauses were concerned the Western Allies renounced all claims to reparations, but the Soviet Union demanded the surrender of specified Italian vessels and the payment of $100 million in reparations.* Italy's neighbours and the former victims of her aggression, Greece, Yugoslavia, Albania and Ethiopia, received a further $260 million between them.† Compensation for damage to property in Italy belonging to member states of the United Nations was to be paid at the rate of two-thirds of the agreed value and Italian assets in Allied countries were to be impounded, retained or liquidated, though here again some countries agreed not to press their claims in this regard.

It was, however, in the territorial and political clauses of the treaty that the knife cut deepest. Italy was shorn not only of her predatory annexations under the Fascist régime, but also of her earlier-acquired colonial possessions. The independence and sovereignty of both Ethiopia and Albania were reaffirmed and, in addition, Italy was required to renounce proprietary rights in the colonies of Libya, Eritrea and Italian Somaliland, disposal of which was to be made by the four Great Powers, within one year of the signing of the treaty. In fact it took rather longer than this, the delays being due partly to Soviet obstruction and partly to the chronic and inveterate irresponsibility of the General Assembly of the United Nations.

The final dispositions were as follows: it was agreed in the autumn of 1949 that Libya (including Cyrenaica) should be placed temporarily under the aegis of the United Nations and should achieve full independence on 1 January 1952. This was duly done and Libya accordingly became a member of the United Nations.‡ In November 1949 it was also agreed that Italian Somaliland should be placed under Italian trusteeship for ten years, at the conclusion of which time the General Assembly would review the situation with a view to eventual independence. This form of government continued in effect until 1 July 1960, when Italian Somaliland was united with the British Somaliland Protectorate in the independent Republic of Somalia, which duly became a member of the United Nations. The fate of Eritrea, Italy's oldest colony, was finally disposed of by the General Assembly in December 1950 when a plan for a federal union with Ethiopia was approved, Eritrea being assured of full domestic autonomy.[47] This arrangement came into operation on 15 September 1952 and continued

---

* An Italian–Soviet agreement for the regulation of payment was signed on 11 December 1948.

† The awards were as follows: to Albania $5 million, to Ethiopia $25 million, to Greece $105 million and to Yugoslavia $125 million.

‡ The actual date of Libya's independence was 24 December 1951. She was admitted to the United Nations on 14 December 1955.

until 14 November 1962 when, as a result of the federation becoming a unitary state, Eritrea became fully integrated with Ethiopia.

Within the continent of Europe, Italy was called upon to surrender territory to France, Greece and Yugoslavia, though, somewhat unexpectedly, she retained the much disputed districts of the Alto Adige. Four small frontier areas went to France; Rhodes and the Dodecanese islands to Greece; and the Adriatic islands and most of Venezia Giulia to Yugoslavia.

In her retention of the Alto Adige lay Italy's one material success under the peace treaty. Acquired from Austria by virtue of the Treaty of St Germain-en-Laye of 1919 (Article 27, section 3) and in consequence of promises made under the Treaty of London of 1915, the province of the South Tyrol was among the last of Italian claims for *terra irredenta* which dated back to the *Risorgimento*. The Fascist régime had subjected the province to an intensive process of Italianization which had evoked strident protests from Austrian sources, both locally and in Vienna. When Italy declared war on Germany in October 1943, the Reich had annexed the provinces of Bolzano, Trento and Belluno and had incorporated them into the governmental structure as the zone of Alpenvorland. Thus at the close of hostilities, when Austria declared the resumption of her independence,* these territories were actually in her possession.

The Conference of Foreign Ministers, and subsequently the Paris Peace Conference, awarded the areas to Italy partly on ethnic and partly on economic grounds. Their decision was also strongly influenced by the fact that the Austrian and Italian Governments had themselves reached a mutually satisfactory agreement which, signed by Alcide de Gasperi and Dr Karl Gruber, was actually annexed to the Italian Peace Treaty. This provided for complete equality of cultural and economic rights for the German-speaking inhabitants of Bolzano and the bilingual areas of Trento. Opportunities were thus afforded for elementary and secondary education in both languages, equal right of entry into public services and a measure of local autonomy, a provision which became an established fact with the coming into force of the Regional Statute for Trentino–Alto Adige on 29 January 1948.

As a well-informed commentator has written: 'The Austro-Italian treaty was regarded as an outstanding example of the way in which agreement could be achieved in difficult circumstances given the good will of both sides.'[48] On the whole the Regional Statute has worked very well.

But by far the most difficult problem arising out of the territorial adjustments under the Italian Peace Treaty, and one which defied

* See below, pp. 468–9.

solution for nearly a decade, was that of Venezia Giulia. Here again were echoes of the First World War, of promises made to Italy in 1915 by the secret Treaty of London and their fulfilment at the Peace Conference of Paris in 1919. By the Treaty of St Germain, Italy had acquired among other booty the Istrian Peninsula. This territory, which juts south from the head of the east side of the Adriatic, approximately opposite Venice, has the great port of Trieste as its chief city and the former Austro-Hungarian naval base of Pola (Pula) at its southernmost tip. Its acquisition by Italy meant the transfer to Italian nationality of some half a million Slovenes, who felt the full weight of oppression under the Fascist régime. The memory of these years was fresh in the mind of the Yugoslav General Yovanović when he occupied and liberated Trieste and Venezia Giulia in the spring of 1945, ousting the Nazis and Fascists and substituting a Communist form of government in their place.

When New Zealand troops entered Trieste in May 1945 the Yugoslavs had been in possession for some forty-three days – a fact which doubtless contributed considerably to the warmth of the welcome given by the Triestini to the New Zealanders – and were singularly ill-disposed to any idea of surrendering control to the Allies. However, thanks to the good relations which Field-Marshal Alexander's Chief of Staff, General Sir William Morgan, succeeded in establishing with General Jovanović, a temporary line of demarcation (known as the 'Morgan Line') was agreed to, behind which the Yugoslav troops withdrew. This placed Trieste, together with a narrow corridor embracing the railway running north through Gorizia to Carinthia, under Allied Military Government, which also assumed authority over Pola and the anchorages south of Trieste.

All the remainder of Venezia Giulia remained under Yugoslav occupation, and whereas there was never any doubt in the minds of the Great Powers that the 'Morgan Line' was anything more than a *pis-aller*, it was never regarded as anything but permanent by the Government of Marshal Tito in Belgrade, the more so on the principle that possession constitutes nine points of the law.

This then was the position at the moment when the preparations for the Italian Peace Treaty began, both Italy and Yugoslavia tenaciously claiming the whole area of the Istrian Peninsula. A Four-Power boundary commission dispatched in March 1946 to make demarcation recommendations *in situ* resulted, as occurs not infrequently on such occasions, in the submission of four disparate solutions. Of these, that of the French representatives was, after long dispute among the Conference of Foreign Ministers, adjudged to be the most practical in character, since it approached as nearly as possible an ethnic frontier, and it was this solution, with modifications, which was eventually incorporated in the peace treaty.

The result was a compromise which, from the first, gave great dissatisfaction to both parties. The treaty provided for the creation of a Free Territory, stretching from Duino in the north to Novigrad in the south, and including a hinterland to a maximum depth of about ten miles. The integrity of this latest on the list of ill-fated Free Zones and cities placed under international protection was guaranteed by the Security Council of the United Nations. The area east of this territory was awarded to the Yugoslavs, who had an overwhelming ethnic majority there.

The Governor of this strange new political entity was to be appointed by the Security Council with the concurrence of the Four Powers, and until this appointment had been made the Free Territory was temporarily divided into two zones, 'A' and 'B', very much on the principle of the division made by the 'Morgan Line'. The northern zone, 'A', was placed under the joint administration of the British and the Americans, leaving Zone 'B' to the Yugoslavs. It was a temporary expedient which was to last for seven years.[49]

The Free Territory of Trieste was thus virtually stillborn and remained in a state of inanition from which various attempts to revive it proved fruitless. When the deadlock had endured for more than a year the Big Three of the Western Powers allowed themselves to be stampeded into action remarkable both for its unwisdom and its subsequent results. On 20 March 1948 the Three Powers issued a Declaration recommending the return of the whole Free Territory to Italy.

The motives behind this action were varied. The first was certainly one of frustration. Throughout the previous twelve months every attempt to appoint a Governor for the Free Territory had failed. The Soviet Union would agree to no candidate put forward by the Western Powers who, in their turn, found the Soviet nominees equally unacceptable. A subcommittee of the Security Council had been no more successful, and the Italian and Yugoslav Governments, when appealed to by the Council to consult together and produce a nominee, had also failed to reach agreement.

However, in addition to a desire to break the deadlock, there were two other considerations: first, the manifest attempts of the Yugoslavs to assimilate Zone B into their national territory, and secondly the growing danger of a notable success by the Communist Party of Italy in the general elections which were to be held in April. The Allied Declaration of 20 March 1948, therefore, was intended as much to bolster the

Christian Democratic Party of Signor de Gasperi as to defeat the annexationist tendencies of Marshal Tito.

The immediate result of the Declaration was its emphatic rejection by Moscow and Belgrade, and this put an end to any slim chance which might have existed for an agreed solution of the Trieste tangle. As might have been expected, however, it was immensely popular in Italy where the Christian Democrats won a sweeping victory at the polls. Confirmed by the French Government at the Franco-Italian conversations at Santa Margherita in February 1951 and by Britain during the visit of Signor de Gasperi and Count Carlo Sforza to London in March of the same year, the Declaration of 20 March 1948 became the basis of all subsequent Italian policy concerning Trieste.

The Declaration had, of course, no legal substance without Soviet approval, which it never received, and had, at best, only a measure of short-term tactical success. Its long-term value was both compromised and complicated by the events which took place in Yugoslavia within the next three months where, on 28 June 1948, the Government of Marshal Tito was expelled from the Cominform on charges of ideological heresy, and hence Yugoslavia was automatically deprived of Soviet support in her foreign policy. Thus the Western Powers, having recommended the restitution of Venezia Giulia to Italy in order to forestall a Communist electoral victory, now found themselves in need of making a gesture of support to Yugoslavia, which, though not by any means a capitalist state, was at least in schism from Moscow.

It necessitated the diplomatic skill, the negotiating patience and the long experience of Anthony Eden to resolve the Trieste problem.* When the Conservative Party returned to power and Mr Eden to the Foreign Office in October 1951, the deadlock still obtained. But the British Foreign Secretary, as a part of a closer co-operation with the United States, paid a visit to Marshal Tito in September 1952 and at the same time opened up conversations with the Italians. As a result he became convinced that, since nothing could be hoped for from the way of negotiation, whatever solution was to be forthcoming for the Trieste problem must be imposed from without, and this became the basis of his planning.

Forthwith, after consultation with the American Secretary of State, John Foster Dulles (whom Mr Eden found less *gemütlich* than his predecessor Dean Acheson), an Anglo-American plan was announced

---

* Mr Eden, with considerable foresight, had raised the question of Trieste at the Yalta Conference. In a paper submitted to the Foreign Ministers' Committee on 10 February 1945, he described Venezia Giulia as a 'potential powder magazine' and outlined a plan to deal with it. Unfortunately this important matter did not receive decisive attention at the conference's highest level.[50]

on 8 October 1953, awarding Zone A to Italy (with the termination of Allied Military Government) while Yugoslavia remained as administrator of Zone B. Though not very original in concept, the Anglo-American plan was a revision of the Three-Power Declaration of March 1948, but it pleased nobody. The Italian Government openly stated that the acquisition of Zone A was but a *sakushka* for the absorption of Zone B, while the Yugoslavs threatened that any movement of Italian troops into Zone A would be regarded as an act of war. Both contestants joined in vilifying Anthony Eden, who was rightly considered to be the author of this plan. The British Embassy in Belgrade was attacked by mobs of infuriated Yugoslavs, while '*Porco Eden*' joined the graffiti decorating the walls of Rome.

Despite these inauspicious beginnings, the way towards a solution had actually been opened. Much, however, remained to be done, but Mr Eden remained unrepentant in the face of criticism, confident that he was on the right track and untiring in his patience and pertinacity. Under his over-all direction, negotiations of the greatest secrecy began in Vienna between the American Ambassador and High Commissioner Llewellyn Thompson, and Geoffrey Harrison, a Deputy Under-Secretary for Foreign Affairs (both of whom were later to become their respective countries' Ambassadors in Moscow), aided materially by the Italian and Yugoslav Ambassadors in London, Manlio Brosio and Dr Vladimir Velebit.[51]*

For nearly a year these five men laboured patiently. Little by little and bit by bit, as men of goodwill working together in complete secrecy, they approached an agreed formula whereby, in effect, with minor frontier rectifications and population adjustments, Italy received Zone A and Yugoslavia Zone B. Italy undertook to maintain Trieste as a free port and Yugoslavia received $20 million from the United States and £2 million from Great Britain to help her in the construction of a new port at San Nicola in Zone B, south of Trieste. Final agreement was reached in the autumn of 1954 and the various documents were duly initialled in London on 5 October.[52]†

The problem of Trieste had been solved by what Lord Avon has called 'a classic example of the true function of diplomacy, an open agreement secretly arrived at . . .'. Peace, he has added, is not just

---

* In the final stages of the negotiations Robert Murphy, of the State Department, played an important part.

† Because it was legally impossible to make changes in the Italian Treaty of Peace without the approval of the Soviet Union – which was not forthcoming – it was held to be expedient to emphasize the 'provisional' nature of the solution. For this purpose the document was designated a 'Memorandum of Understanding', the word 'Agreement' being deliberately omitted.

something that happens. At times it is necessary to take risks and even to increase the immediate danger to win a lasting agreement. Trieste was one of these occasions.'⁵³

The conclusion of the Trieste dispute in 1954 marked the final stage of Italy's post-war rehabilitation. By this time she had been accepted back into the European polity. She had become a signatory of the North Atlantic Treaty of 1949, a partner in the stillborn European Defence Community in 1952 and ultimately a charter member of the Western European Union of 1954.* She had 'worked her passage home'.

VII

The settlement in Eastern Europe was effected under very strong Soviet influence. This was both understandable and inevitable since all the countries concerned – Rumania, Hungary, Bulgaria and Finland – had been in active belligerency in alliance with Germany against the Soviet Union. None of them had participated in hostilities against the Western Allies, and the United States had never declared war on Finland. The outstanding feature of the settlement, however, was the decline and fall of Rumania, and here again were echoes of the First World War.

Rumania had come into existence with the union of the Principalities of Moldavia and Wallachia in 1861.† Fifteen years later Prince Carol, of the Catholic branch of the House of Hohenzollern (Hohenzollern-Sigmaringen), was recognized as Prince of Rumania and the country achieved its complete independence in 1878 as a result of the Congress of Berlin. Carol proclaimed himself King of Rumania in 1881 and two years later entered into a secret alliance with Austria-Hungary and Germany.

The outbreak of the First World War in 1914 found Rumania divided in sentiment. The country as a whole was pro-Ally, but the aged King and the court were pro-German and the Government was hampered by the secret treaty of 1883. The British, French and Russian Governments offered Transylvania, Bukovina and the Banat if Rumania would join the Entente. The Central Powers promised her the Russian province of Bessarabia if she would either join them or remain neutral.

Rumania was in a mood for expansion. She had already forced Bulgaria to cede the southern Dobrudja in 1913 as an outcome of the Second Balkan War and her ambitions now centred on further accretion of territory. But while King Carol I sat upon the throne he would not

---

* See below, pp. 598–9.
† The Paris Peace Conference of 1856 had guaranteed the autonomy of the two provinces.

Eastern Europe: territorial changes, 1939–47

desert his allies in Vienna and Berlin; he remained neutral, with the promise of Bessarabia.

On 10 October 1914, however, he died and was succeeded by his son, Ferdinand, a man largely dominated by the flamboyant and ambitious personality of his beautiful British wife, Marie, a daughter of the first Duke of Edinburgh and of the Grand-Duchess Maria Feodorovna of Russia, and a granddaughter of Queen Victoria. Queen Marie was passionately pro-British and she carried her husband and his Government with her. Rumania declared war on the Central Powers on 27 August 1916. Disastrous defeat followed almost at once and she was compelled to sign a humiliating peace with Germany, Austria-Hungary, Bulgaria and Turkey at Bucharest on 7 May 1918, by which she was forced to return her possession of southern Dobrudja to Bulgaria. The Treaty of Bucharest was, however, never ratified by Rumania, who again took up arms against the Central Powers, and it was formally abrogated by Germany under the terms of the armistice agreement of 11 November 1918.*

By the Treaties of Trianon and Neuilly Rumania received complete fulfilment of all that had been promised to her by the Allies. Transylvania and Bukovina were ceded by Hungary and the southern Dobrudja was restored by Bulgaria. Moreover, for good measure, the Allies presented Rumania with the Russian province of Bessarabia, originally promised to her by the Central Powers, on the grounds that, historically, ethnographically, geographically and economically, 'the re-union of Bessarabia to Rumania is fully justified' and further, that the population of Bessarabia had given proof of its desire for such a reunion. This award was made by a separate treaty between the Powers and Rumania, signed at Paris on 28 October 1920, by Article 9 of which Russian adherence was invited 'as soon as a Russian government recognized by them [the Powers] should be in existence', but, the Article continues, 'it is understood that the frontiers defined in the present treaty, as well as the sovereignty of Rumania over the territories comprised cannot be called in question'.[54] Russia, however, at no time abandoned her claims upon Bessarabia.†

---

* This was confirmed by Articles 259 and 292 of the Treaty of Versailles.

† The fate of the treaty of 28 October 1920 and the legal position of Bessarabia remained uncertain. Of the Big Four who signed it, only two ratified: Britain on 1 January 1921 and France on 20 April 1924. Of the remainder, Italy made no move at all and it was believed that some secret understanding between the U.S.S.R. and Japan was reached at the time of their treaty of 1 January 1925, whereby Japan undertook to delay her ratification indefinitely. Abortive Russo-Rumanian negotiations took place in Vienna during March 1924, during which the Soviet delegation offered to forgo the former rights of Imperial Russia over Bessarabia but refused to recognize the treaty of 28 October 1920. The conference broke up inconclusively on 2 April 1924. No

Thus Rumania emerged from the First World War more than doubled in size and in population,* and King Ferdinand and Queen Marie were crowned sovereigns of Greater Rumania, with great pageantry, at Alba Iulia on 16 October 1922. Rumania at once essayed to play a role in Eastern and Central European affairs. She established an alliance with Poland on 8 March 1921, based on a common fear of Russia and some degree of distrust of Hungary; in the same year she aligned herself with Czechoslovakia and Yugoslavia in the formation of the Little Entente in order to protect the succession states against the threat of a Habsburg restoration and against the resurgence of German nationalism;[57] accepting French leadership in Europe, she, with the other members of the Little Entente, together with Poland and Belgium, constituted that *cortège habituel* of France, which strengthened the hand of French policy in the Council and Assembly of the League of Nations. †

Moreover, Queen Marie of Rumania spun a network of marriage contracts throughout the Balkans to fortify and bolster the monarchy by means of dynastic alliances.‡

As the new menace of National Socialism arose in Germany and the reins of leadership in Europe fell from the nerveless grip of France, Rumania found herself in an exposed and vulnerable position. Surrounded by neighbours from all of whom she had acquired territory and who were consequently avidly awaiting an unfavourable turn in her fortunes, Rumania also believed herself to be directly threatened by the forces of the Third Reich and sought to reinsure accordingly. This was

---

diplomatic relations existed therefore between Bucharest and Moscow, and the Rumanian Government was at pains to strengthen its defensive pact with Poland by a supplementary treaty signed on 8 February 1926. Both the U.S.S.R. and Rumania, however, were signatories of the Pact of Paris (Kellogg–Briand Pact) of 27 August 1928 and, after long and tortuous discussions, Rumania adhered to the Moscow Protocol of 9 February 1929, which reaffirmed the provisions of the Pact renouncing the use of war as an instrument of national policy among the Soviet Union and her neighbours. But the issue of Bessarabia prevented Rumania from participating in the network of treaties of neutrality and non-aggression which Maxim Litvinov concluded during the years 1931 and 1932.[55] It was this omission to which, as will be seen, M. Molotov drew attention in the spring of 1940.

* According to the census of 1912 Rumania's population was just over 7½ million and her area at the outbreak of the First World War was 53,489 miles. After the Peace Conference of Paris her population increased to 17,393,149 and her area to 122,282 square miles.[56] As a result of the Second World War, Rumania's area decreased to 91,071 sq. miles but her population, according to the census of 1956, was in excess of 18½ million.

† The Franco-Rumanian Treaty of Alliance was signed on 10 June 1926.

‡ Of Queen Marie's children, one daughter, Elizabeth, became the wife of King George II of Greece (1921), and the other, Marie, married King Alexander of Yugoslavia (1922). Her son, King Carol II, married, as his second wife, Princess Helen of Greece (1921). Both the Greek marriages ended in divorce.

the object of King Carol II's* state visit to London in 1937, his desperate appeals for support in March 1939 after the Nazi occupation of Prague and his immediate acceptance, on 13 April of the same year, of the Anglo-French guarantee of assistance in the event of Rumania's choosing to resist Nazi aggression.

There followed that marriage of incompatibles, the Nazi-Soviet Pact of 23 August 1939, and a year later the direful summer of 1940. On 27 June the Soviet Union, drawing attention to the fact that she had no non-aggression pact with Rumania, demanded the immediate cession of Bessarabia and northern Bukovina and occupied both territories two days later. Carol appealed to Germany, and as an earnest of change of heart renounced the British guarantee of April 1939. Hitler was unimpressed by this death-bed repentance. Not only did he refuse any support to Rumania in respect of Soviet aggression, but he ordered her to comply with the demands now made on her by Bulgaria and Hungary. Thus on 21 August she ceded the southern Dobrudja to Bulgaria and on the thirtieth, by the Second Vienna Award, she lost the whole of northern Transylvania to Hungary, at the dictation of Germany and Italy.

Thus, stripped of all she had gained after the First World War, Rumania passed under the dictatorship of Marshal Ion Antonescu, who demanded the abdication of Carol II. The King departed with his mistress, the celebrated Hélène Lupescu, into exile in Portugal, leaving his thorny heritage to his son Michael, who became King for the second time on 6 September 1940.

Carol was basically an Anglophil, proud of being a great-grandson of Queen Victoria and a Knight of the Garter. His sympathies were with the West and his flirtation with Hitler had been prompted by expediency rather than conviction. Not so Antonescu. Like many another political leader, great and small, on the continent of Europe during that Black Summer of 1940, he embraced the illusion that the *Wehrmacht* was invincible and the Thousand-Year Reich an established fact. As a member of Hitler's New Order in Europe, Rumania might regain some of the territory of which she had recently been deprived, more especially Bessarabia and Bukovina, since Hungary and Bulgaria would also be satellite followers of Hitler. Antonescu therefore adhered to the Anti-

* Before his death in 1927 King Ferdinand had exiled his eldest son Prince Carol from the country and had compelled him to renounce his rights of succession to the Rumanian throne. These passed to his son, Prince Michael, who succeeded, at the age of six, on the death of his grandfather, under a Council of Regency. In 1930, however, Prince Carol took advantage of the political complications in Rumania to make a dramatic return by air to his country where, displacing his son (who became Crown Prince), he was acknowledged as King.

Comintern Pact on 23 November 1940 and, when the Führer invaded Russia on 22 June 1941, he declared war on the Soviet Union. Rumanian troops reoccupied the lost provinces and took part in the operations on the Eastern Front until many of them were captured at Stalingrad on 1 February 1943.

As the tide of battle turned in the East, King Michael, who had inherited his father's partiality for Britain and things British, attempted with considerable courage to redress the errors of Antonescu's policy. On 23 August 1944 he master-minded a *coup d'état* in Bucharest, personally arresting the Marshal during an audience at the Palace, and declared war on Germany and her allies. On 12 September he concluded an armistice with the Soviet Union.

This *volte-face*, however, brought to Rumania only very limited advantages. When the Peace Treaty came to be signed on 10 February 1947,[58] she received back from Hungary about two-fifths of Transylvania, while Bessarabia, Bukovina and the southern Dobrudja remained permanently lost to her.

Under the military clauses of the treaty Rumania's land forces were limited to 120,000 men, together with a 5,000-strong anti-aircraft defence force. Her naval forces were restricted to 5,000 men and a total tonnage of 15,000 tons. She was permitted an Air Force of 8,000 personnel, with 150 aircraft, of which only a hundred might be of combat type.

In addition she was required to pay in reparations to the Soviet Union $300 million, over a period of eight years beginning from the date of the armistice, in commodities (oil products, grains, timber, seagoing and river craft, etc.).

Thus concluded the attempt of Rumania between the wars to assume a leading role in Balkan affairs. It had profited her nothing.

VIII

The case of Hungary was at once similar to, and different from, that of Rumania. Between the two countries there flourished a glowing contempt and a bitter hatred, deriving from the remote feudings of the Huns and the Dacians and, more modernistically, from the termination of the First World War when Rumanian troops had invaded Hungary and established a brief occupation. Moreover the Treaty of Trianon had awarded Transylvania to Rumania. In addition, Hungary represented to Rumania, as well as to all the succession states, the embodiment of Habsburg reaction. Had she not declared herself a kingdom, with a Regent on the vacant throne? And was it not to Hungary that the Emperor Karl had directed his steps in the attempted restorations of

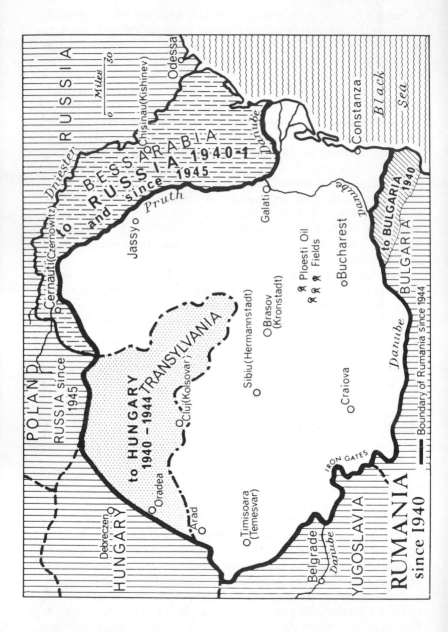

1921? Although the Regent, Admiral Nicholas Horthy,* had refused to permit the Emperor Karl to assume the Crown, the intentions of Hungary as a revisionist state were still suspect and the Little Entente had been formed for common defence against her.

When the unity of the Little Entente began to diminish in the 1930s, as French influence waned in Central and South-eastern Europe, so Hungary pursued a cautious pro-German policy. She was not at first assured that Hitler's outrageous conduct in international affairs would be successful and, though harbouring definite territorial designs upon both Czechoslovakia and Rumania, Hungary refused the offer of a millitary alliance with Germany in the spring of 1938. When, however, it became clear, in the course of the Czechoslovak crisis, that Britain and France were infinitely reluctant to oppose Hitler, the Hungarian Government began publicly to assert their claims against the Czechs and to bicker with the Poles as to a subsequent division of the spoils.

As a part of the Anglo-French plan for the solution of the Czech problem, which had been proposed to President Beneš by Mr Chamberlain and M. Daladier on 19 September 1938 after the former's return from Berchtesgaden, the two Governments had offered a guarantee of the frontiers of the Czechoslovak state as they would emerge after the proposed cessions of territory to Germany had been made. This guarantee had been specifically reaffirmed in an annex to the Munich Agreement of 29 September, in which it was further stated that Germany and Italy would also join in the guarantee 'when the question of the Polish and Hungarian minorities in Czechoslovakia has been settled'; a declaration annexed to the Agreement stated that, if within three months of the signature of the Agreement the Polish and Hungarian Governments had not settled the question of their minorities, the four Munich Powers would meet together again and make a decision.[59]

These provisions were of as ephemeral value as the rest of the Munich Agreement. On 2 November 1938, there having been no decision reached on the matter of the Czech minorities, the German and Italian Foreign Ministers met at Vienna and handed down what became known as the First Vienna Award, which gave to Hungary the Hungarian-speaking part of Slovakia.

The fact that this constituted a flagrant breach of the Munich Agreement, since it was made without consultation or the approval of the other two Munich Powers, was totally ignored by the British and French Governments. Indeed they actually went so far as to express relief at

* Nicholas Horthy de Nagybanya, last Commander-in-Chief of the Austro–Hungarian fleet, was elected Regent of Hungary in 1920 and continued in that office for the next twenty-four years.

having been freed from considerable embarrassment which might have involved 'a definite danger'.[60] The value of their own guarantee of Czechoslovak territorial integrity was manifested some five months later when, in March 1939, Hitler stated in Prague that 'Czechoslovakia has ceased to exist'.

For her co-operation and complicity during the successive Czech crises, Hitler awarded to Hungary the Carpatho-Russian province of Ruthenia, which became effective on 16 March 1939.

Having thus shared in the humbling of Czechoslovakia and the disintegration of the Little Entente, Hungary, two years later, performed the same office for Rumania when, by the Second Vienna Award of 30 August 1940, she received back the whole of northern Transylvania.* Not content with these acquisitions, she allowed herself to be inveigled, by promises of further spoils in the Ukraine, into joining in Hitler's crusade against Russia, on whom she formally declared war in June 1941. Hungarian troops shared the fate of their German and Rumanian comrades in the débâcle of Stalingrad.

With the triumphal advance of the Red Army westwards, Admiral Horthy sought desperately to dissociate himself from the Axis Powers, only to find them too strong for him to oppose. He himself was arrested at Hitler's order in October 1944, but on 28 December the new Hungarian Government of General Bela Miklós withdrew from the Axis and declared war on Germany. An armistice was signed with the Soviet Union on behalf of the Allies on 20 January 1945.

By the Peace Treaty of Paris on 10 February 1947,[61] Hungary met with her deserts. Her frontiers with Austria and Yugoslavia were confirmed as those of 1 January 1938 (i.e. as laid down by the Treaties of St Germain and Trianon). But the decisions of the two Vienna Awards of 1938 and 1940 were declared null and void. Hungary, therefore, ceded two-fifths of northern Transylvania to Rumania and resumed with Czechoslovakia the frontier of 1 January 1938, save for additional concessions to the Czechs of three small areas.

As to Ruthenia, this territory was lost to Hungary but did not return to Czechoslovakia. Its destiny had already been settled by an agreement signed on 25 June 1945 whereby Czechoslovakia, while momentarily reassuming sovereignty over Ruthenia, thereupon at once ceded the province to the Soviet Union.[62] Thus for the first time Russia obtained a common frontier with the Czechoslovak Republic, a matter of later ominous significance.

Hungary undertook certain reparation obligations and military restrictions. To the Soviet Union she covenanted to pay $200 million,

* See above, p. 454.

and to the Czechoslovaks and Yugoslavs $100 million apiece, all to be paid over a period of eight years and in kind. Hungary's armed forces, including anti-aircraft and frontier troops and her river flotilla, were not to exceed 65,000 men, and her air force was confined to 5,000 personnel and 90 aircraft, of which not more than 70 should be fighters.

IX

The case of Bulgaria was again different and also found its origin in earlier peace settlements. She had been assigned historic boundaries under the Treaty of San Stefano in March 1878, whereby the Russians had concluded bilaterally their successful war against the Turks. In the course of the Congress of Berlin, later in the same year, these boundaries were severely curtailed and Bulgaria had been avid to achieve their original limits ever since. The First Balkan War had brought her parts of Thrace and Macedonia but the Second, in which she was disastrously defeated, resulted in her losing southern Dobrudja to Rumania under the Treaty of Bucharest (10 August 1913). Persuaded by promises of rewards at the expense of Turkey, Greece and Serbia to renounce her neutrality and join the Central Powers in 1915, Bulgaria was again overwhelmingly defeated and by the Treaty of Neuilly (27 November 1919) not only lost all that she had gained since 1913 but was also compelled to cede certain areas to Yugoslavia and the whole of her Aegean coastline to Greece.

Bulgaria was therefore susceptible and vulnerable to Nazi blandishments, as a result of which she entered readily into the German economic orbit. During the early part of the Second World War she remained neutral and received tempting offers from both sides. But Hitler was in a stronger position as a dispenser of spoils and, while Britain condoned the loss of the southern Dobrudja by Rumania to Bulgaria* and even let it be known in Sofia that this would be confirmed in Bulgaria's favour in the final peace settlement, Germany was able to dangle prizes to be earned at the expense of Britain's allies, Greece and Yugoslavia.

Bulgaria therefore joined the Axis on 1 March 1941 and declared war on Britain (and subsequently on the United States) a month later, granting the full use of her Black Sea ports to Hitler and providing a staging-ground for the German invasions of Yugoslavia and Greece. In return she was permitted to annex western Thrace and part of eastern Macedonia from Greece, and Macedonia and the Morava Valley from Yugoslavia, thus achieving – though very briefly – her full San Stefano boundaries.

* See above, p. 454.

She did not, however, declare war on Russia or supply a contingent for Hitler's armies on the Eastern Front, and it was even believed in some circles that her sovereign, King Boris, who was torn between his natural Anglophil sentiments and his equally natural national desires, was contemplating an approach to the Western Allies with a view to defection from the Axis at the time of his death in mysterious circumstances on 28 August 1943.* However, if this was his intent, it proved fruitless and did not save Bulgaria from a declaration of war by Russia on 5 September 1944, to be followed some seven weeks later by an armistice, on 28 October.

Under the Treaty of Peace of 10 February 1947,[63] Bulgaria's frontiers were confirmed as of 1 January 1941; that is to say, she retained the cession of southern Dobrudja from Rumania but none of her temporary conquests in Greece and Yugoslavia. Her land forces were not to exceed 55,000 men, with a permissible addition of 1,800 anti-aircraft troops. Her Navy was restricted to 3,500 men with a total tonnage of 7,250 tons, and she was permitted an air force of 5,200 men with 90 aircraft, of which only 70 might be combat types. Moreover she was prohibited from building permanent fortifications or military installations on her frontier with Greece where weapons capable of firing into Greek territory could be emplaced.

In addition, by way of reparation, she was required to pay $45 million to Greece and $25 million to Yugoslavia, the payments to be made in kind over a period of eight years.

X

There remained Finland, a country unique in two respects in that it is the only state to have won its freedom from Soviet Russia and remain independent and the only state to have discharged its indebtedness in full to the United States after the First World War. These achievements redounded both to her credit and her advantage.

In the welter of chaos which followed the Russian Revolution, Finland declared her independence from Russia. All Finns were agreed on this step but, having taken it, there developed a cleavage of opinion so irreconcilable that it led, in the winter of 1917–18, to civil war. The Left desired a close affiliation with Russia, the Right a complete break with the Russian tradition and an orientation towards Scandinavia. In

---

* Prince Ferdinand (1861–1948), fifth son of Prince Augustus of Saxe-Coburg-Gotha, was appointed Prince of Bulgaria by the powers in 1887, and proclaimed himself King in 1908, together with the independence of Bulgaria. He abdicated after the First World War and was succeeded by his son Boris, who married the youngest daughter of the King of Italy, Princess Giovanna of Savoy.

the course of the civil war the Reds were openly backed by the Soviet Government and the Whites by Germany. The forces of the Right under General Baron Carl von Mannerheim eventually triumphed and the Republic of Finland was established.

Finnish independence was recognized by Russia in the Treaty of Dorpat on 12 October 1920, whereby the historic frontiers of Finland, including the port and province of Petsamo, were affirmed. Thereafter Finland pursued a circumspect and peaceful policy. She was recognized as a 'model state' and a dependable member of the League of Nations. She adhered to the Kellogg–Briand Pact of August 1928 and to the subsequent Moscow Protocol, which Maxim Litvinov conjured into being to re-emphasize and reinforce the provisions of the Pact between the Soviet Union and her neighbours. In the general epidemic of 'pactomania' which afflicted Europe in the late 1930s, Finland entered into a non-aggression pact with Russia on 21 January 1932 but refused to enter into a similar agreement with Germany in the summer of 1939. As the storm clouds gathered over Europe she declared her intention of remaining neutral in conformity with the general policy of the Scandinavian states.

She was not, however, permitted to do this. Having concluded the non-aggression pact with Nazi Germany on 23 August 1939 and thereby neutralized German interests, Soviet Russia turned towards strengthening her defensive position in the north. She made severe demands on Finland to cede part of the Karelian Isthmus and to permit the construction of a Soviet military base on Finland's southern coast in order to assure the greater security of Leningrad. When the Finns refused their compliance the Soviet Government denounced the Soviet-Finnish pact of non-aggression and on 30 November attacked her neighbour without declaring war, an action which resulted in her expulsion from the League of Nations a fortnight later, on 14 December.

There followed the Winter War in which the Finns, under Marshal von Mannerheim, fought with great skill and gallantry, earning the moral support and admiration of the world but very little else. Overwhelmed by the superiority in equipment and manpower of the Russians, Finland was compelled to admit defeat and suffered the harsh peace of 12 March 1940, whereby she surrendered the whole of the Karelian Isthmus, together with the strategic strongpoint of Viborg (Viipuri), and also all Finnish holdings on the shores of Lake Ladoga. Russia also received a lease of the peninsula of Hangö (Hankö) for thirty years at a rental of eight million Finnish marks per annum.

These demands by the Soviet Union were considerably in excess of those originally put forward before hostilities began, but Finland, despite her courageous resistance, was not in any real position to argue. She prudently acquiesced, thinking herself fortunate that the Russian depredations did not embrace Petsamo.

In the months which followed the Finns licked their wounds and nursed their hatred. The old feelings of friendship and gratitude towards Germany, which had cooled somewhat as a result of the Nazi-Soviet Pact, were now renewed, and propaganda from Berlin was rife. When Hitler invaded the Soviet Union on 21 June 1941 and invited Finland to join him, with a view to recouping herself for her losses, she readily assented and declared war on Russia on the same day. The Finnish Army won numerous successes and rapidly regained all that had been lost to Russia in the previous years. In mid-August the United States Government transmitted an offer on behalf of Russia to restore the old frontiers if Finland would make peace. The United States expressed hope that the offer might be accepted but, under German pressure and not without certain national ambitions, the Finnish Government rejected it and proclaimed their intention of fighting on until they had achieved an assured strategic position of security against Russia. By so doing Finland forfeited American goodwill and sympathy, which had been greatly in her favour, and brought upon herself a declaration of war by Great Britain, somewhat under Soviet pressure, on 5 December 1941.*

The Finnish Army did not advance very far beyond its historic frontiers once these had been reconquered. Despite German appeals they did not participate in the advance on Leningrad but 'abode within their borders'. This merely alienated the Nazis and made no impression whatsoever on the Russians. When the tide of victory overwhelmed the Axis Powers in the East, Finland broke off relations with Germany on 4 September 1944 and signed an armistice with the Soviet Union on the nineteenth.

When the Peace Treaty came to be signed,[64] it was found that this time the Soviet Union meant to have Petsamo, which Finland duly ceded, together with the peninsula of Poskkala (which was returned by the Russians in 1956). In other respects the terms of the treaty of 12 March 1940 were reaffirmed, and it was commonly agreed that the Åland Islands were to remain demilitarized.

Finland's Army, all inclusive, was limited to 34,000 men, her navy to 4,500 men and a total tonnage of 10,000 tons, and her air force to 60 aircraft, of which none might be bombers, and 3,000 men. A reparation

---

* The United States was never at war with Finland but, as a result of a further abortive attempt to persuade her to make peace with Russia in the summer of 1944, broke off diplomatic relations with Finland on 30 June of that year.

payment was imposed of $300 million over eight years, beginning from the date of the armistice, and payable in commodities.

The terms were hard but Finland could count herself lucky that she had kept more than the semblance of her freedom. Though the menace of Soviet Russia loomed at her across the Gulf of Finland, she did not experience the clanking domination suffered by Hungary, Rumania and Bulgaria, nor the deceptive strategy and pressure applied later to Czechoslovakia.

XI

Article 2 of each of the treaties signed on 10 February 1947 contained a formal affirmation of the inviolability of human rights and fundamental freedoms, in accordance with the Declaration on Liberated Europe, promulgated by the Big Three at Yalta two years previously. From the first there was little evidence that the Soviet satellite states of Bulgaria, Rumania and Hungary showed any inclination of observing their undertakings.

In Bulgaria a referendum declared in favour of a 'People's Republic' on 8 September 1946 and ousted the ten-year-old King Simeon II from his throne. In the general election for a National Assembly, held on 27 October, the Communist-dominated coalition, the Fatherland Front, obtained 366 seats, of which 277 went to the Communist Party, and the Opposition 99 seats. On 26 August 1947 the leading Opposition party, the Agrarian Union, was declared dissolved and its leader hanged. Thereafter the other Opposition parties either prudently dissolved themselves or merged with the Fatherland Front.

King Michael of Rumania was compelled to abdicate on 30 December 1947 and a 'People's Republic' was proclaimed. In the general election held on 28 March 1948 for the Grand National Assembly, the largely Communist Popular Democratic Front captured 405 of the 414 seats.

In Hungary the 'People's Republic', proclaimed on 1 February 1946, passed speedily under the control of the Communist Party, into which other political parties were forcibly merged to make the Hungarian People's Independence Front, which later became the Patriotic People's Front.

All these states had concluded treaties of friendship with the Soviet Union, as their only international ties.

During the years which followed the signing of the peace treaties political conditions within these states appreciably worsened, and at the second part of its third regular session, in April 1949, the General Assembly of the United Nations expressed 'deep concern at the grave accusations made against the Governments of Bulgaria, Hungary and

Rumania regarding the suppression of human rights and fundamental freedoms in those countries'. The Assembly drew the attention of those Governments to their obligations under the peace treaties, including the obligation to co-operate in the settlement of all these questions.

The Governments concerned paid no attention whatsoever to the admonitions of the United Nations. They neither mended their ways nor made any attempt to co-operate in the efforts of the U.N. to examine the charges brought against them. The Assembly, therefore, at its fourth session in October 1949, took cognizance of the accusations brought against the three Governments by the Allied and Associated Powers which had signed the peace treaties, and turned to the International Court of Justice for an advisory opinion. Did a dispute exist between Bulgaria, Hungary and Rumania and certain Allied and Associated Powers in accordance with the provisions of the peace treaties? And further, if a dispute did exist, were the three states obligated to nominate their representatives to the commission for the settlement of disputes for which provision was made under the peace treaties?*

The International Court rendered its opinion on 30 March 1950 by eleven votes to three, to the effect that a dispute did exist and that the answer to the second question was in the affirmative.[65] It then, on 5 May 1950, set a time limit of thirty days for the three states concerned to comply with this opinion.[66]

The states concerned did nothing of the sort, whereupon the Court turned its attention to two further questions referred to it by the Assembly: (1) Did the refusal of the three states to comply with the Court's opinion authorize the Secretary-General of the United Nations to appoint the third member of each commission as provided in the peace treaties? (2) Would a commission of two members in each case, one appointed by the Secretary-General and the other by a party to the dispute (i.e. the Allied and Associated Powers), be competent to make a definite and binding decision?

To these questions the Court replied on 18 July 1950, by eleven votes to two, that the answer to the first was in the negative, and that as the second question, therefore, did not arise an answer was not necessary.[67]

No further efforts were made to enforce the human rights provisions of these treaties.

* Article 36 of the treaty with Bulgaria, Article 30 of the treaty with Hungary and Article 38 of the treaty with Rumania.

19 | The Austrian State Treaty

I

IT is given to few men to found two republics in a lifetime. It is even more rare for the same man to survive the downfall of the first and to know for certain, at the time of his death, that the second would endure. The story of the birth of the two Austrian republics is the story of that Grand Old Man of Austrian Socialism, Karl Renner, and the success of the second of these republics is his enduring monument.

At the time of the death of the Emperor Francis-Joseph in November 1916, Karl Renner was the leader of the Socialist Party in the Austro-Hungarian *Reichsrat*, and thereafter he sought for the reconstruction of the Empire on lines which would have turned it into a federation of autonomous states such as was, too tardily, proclaimed by the Emperor Charles shortly before the collapse in the autumn of 1918.

When all hope of salvaging the Empire disappeared, Renner proclaimed the Republic and became its first Federal Chancellor, continuing in office until his retirement in October 1919. After a succession of increasingly feeble governments, a semblance of stability was achieved by that astute and perspicacious cleric, Monsignor Ignaz Seipel. Before resigning Renner had fathered the Constitution of the Republic and had accepted its founding principle of mutual desire for union with Germany.*

In March 1933 Chancellor Engelbert Dollfuss tore up the Republican Constitution of 1920 and replaced it in the following year by a Corporative Constitution on semi-Fascist lines. Renner, then President of the National Assembly, protested so vehemently against this rape of the Republic that he was arrested on a charge of high treason and imprisoned, spending several months in jail. On his release he resumed his

---

* One of the first acts of the Austrian Republic was to declare itself, on 12 November 1918, an integral part of the German Reich. When the Weimar Constitution was adopted by the German National Assembly on 31 July 1919, provision was made under Article 61 for the union of German Austria with the Reich and her representation in the *Reichsrat*. The Allied Powers, however, annulled these provisions and, by Article 80 of the Treaty of Versailles and Article 88 of the Treaty of St Germain, forbade the *Anschluss* between Austria and Germany.

opposition both to the Government of Chancellor Kurt von Schuschnigg and to the growing menace of the Austrian Nazis. The final annexation of Austria by Germany in March 1938 resulted in his rearrest and detention in a concentration camp for some years. When he emerged from his ordeal he retired to Gloggnitz, a small township at the foot of the Semmering Hills, where he remained throughout the war.*

When Hitler annexed Austria he did so in open and intentional violation of the Treaties of Versailles and St Germain and also in complete disregard of the Anglo-French-Italian Declarations of 17 February and 27 September 1934 and that of 14 April 1935, at Stresa, whereby the Three Powers reaffirmed their assertion that the maintenance of the independence and integrity of Austria was of paramount importance in their policies. There was, moreover, the Führer's own agreement with Austria of 11 July 1936 in which Germany recognized the full independence of Austria and undertook not to interfere with her internal affairs. Thus Hitler had been consistent alike in flouting the Paris peace terms, in ignoring the somewhat half-hearted declarations of the Western Powers and in jettisoning his own pledged word.

'Hitler was heir to the ambitions and animosities of the Pan-German nationalists of the old Monarchy', Alan Bullock has written in his brilliant and penetrating analysis of the Führer. 'He saw himself as the man destined to reverse the decision, not only of 1918 but of 1866. Born on the frontiers of Germany and Austria, he felt . . . called upon to reunite the two German States which had been left divided by Bismarck's solution of the German problem.'[1] This end transcended all other considerations. To achieve it, no means was deemed too devious, too ruthless or too brutal.

The *Anschluss* was generally approved by the denizens of the Third Reich, except perhaps in extreme Lutheran circles where the influx of some six million additional Roman Catholics into Germany was frowned upon. In Austria also it was not entirely unwelcome, except to the Communists, the Social Democrats, the Jews, a few ultra-nationalists and a handful of monarchist supporters. Had the idea of union with Germany not been overshadowed by the menace of National Socialism, had it come about under almost any other auspices, it would have been greeted with even greater acclaim.

For this reason it was with the greatest reluctance that even some of

* During his exile Dr Renner wrote a *magnum opus*, a study of the past, present and future of social organization, into the composition of which went all the experience of a strenuous career. The manuscript was successfully hidden from the Nazi authorities, who periodically searched his dwelling, but was destroyed in an Allied bombing raid towards the end of the war.

20 President Truman with
Secretary of State James
F. Byrnes after the latter's
return from the Paris
Peace Conference

21 General George C.
Marshall in 1947

22   President Truman proclaims the NATO Treaty to be in effect, 24 August 1949. He is watched by diplomatic representatives of NATO states. Third from right is Mr Acheson and fourth from left Mr L. Johnson, United States Secretary of Defence.

the conspirators against Hitler relinquished the idea of a de-Nazified Germany's retention of Austria in any post-war settlement.* There were, moreover, those in Britain who, as late as 1940 and 1941, still thought that Austria, and even the Sudetenland, should form a part of post-war Germany.

It was not indeed until the Conference of Foreign Ministers in Moscow in October 1943 that the position was definitely established and clarified.† Mr Eden, Mr Hull and M. Molotov declared the *Anschluss* 'imposed on Austria by Germany on 13 March 1938 as null and void', and that they wished to see the re-establishment of 'a free and independent Austria'. At the same time Austria was reminded that she had 'a responsibility which she cannot evade for participation in the war at the side of Hitlerite Germany and that in the final settlement account will be taken of her own contribution to her liberation'.⁴‡ It was this last sentence that was later to give rise to Soviet demands on Austria.

It had been hoped that the Austrians would themselves assist in the overthrow of the Nazi régime. These hopes, however, were doomed to disappointment. Neither in Austria nor in Germany was there effective opposition, let alone resistance, to the tyranny of Hitler. Not until the advent of the Soviet armies did Austrian leadership assert itself.

By the end of March 1945 the Russians had crossed the Austrian frontier. On 4 April came news that their armoured units had advanced to within twelve miles of Vienna and on the fifth they were in the suburbs. Heavy street fighting in the city followed, though Vienna did not suffer the same degree of destruction as did Budapest. On 13 April the occupation and subjugation of the city was completed.

It was now that Karl Renner made his reappearance. His first contact was with a local Soviet commanding officer, with whom he came to intercede on behalf of the people of Gloggnitz. Quickly recognizing in the veteran Socialist leader a tool of possible value, the General sent him to Marshal Ivan Koniev's headquárters, whence he emerged, on 27 April, as head of a Provisional Government.§

Renner's anti-Fascist and anti-Nazi record and his distinction in

---

* For example, when Ulrich von Hassell, the former German Ambassador to Rome, was preparing a secret memorandum of peace terms in February 1940, for submission to Lord Halifax, he laid it down as a necessity that Germany should retain both Austria and the Sudetenland.² (See above, p. 19.) On the other hand, another group of conspirators, operating through the Vatican about the same time, specifically stated that they desired to see Austria granted self-determination as to her future status. This provision was included in the famous X-Report of October 1940.³

† See above, p. 114.

‡ On 13 November 1943 the French Committee of National Liberation issued a statement corroborating the terms of the Moscow Declaration of 3 November.

§ The provisional Government consisted of 10 Socialists, 9 People's Party representatives, 7 Communists and 3 Independents.

Socialist circles in Europe rendered him an almost perfect candidate, from the Soviet point of view, for the leadership of a provisional Government. The exiguous degree of authority with which Marshal Koniev invested him was bestowed in the full expectation that he would be a willing puppet for Soviet policies. In fact he adroitly avoided becoming this. Though he would doubtless have preferred fewer Communists among his colleagues, he bowed to Soviet pressure in this matter because of the importance, as he saw it, of forming a Provisional Government with the minimum of delay and, furthermore, because he confidently believed that his Government would soon be replaced by a duly appointed Federal Cabinet following a general election, on the results of which he based all his hopes. Pliant, polite and charming, he employed every artifice to persuade the Russians to permit the people of Austria to go to the polls in freedom, and when this privilege was granted towards the end of the year, his confidence in the good sense of his countrymen was fully justified.*

Before this was achieved, however, the political structure of the Austrian state had to be built anew. The first act of Renner's Provisional Government was to ratify the Declaration of Austrian Independence which had been adopted by the three political parties on the same day that the Provisional Government was formed (27 April). By its provisions the *Anschluss* of March 1938 was declared to be abrogated and the democratic Republic of Austria re-established 'in the spirit of the Constitution of 1920'. This was significant in that it assured the repudiation not only of Hitler's predatory action but also of Dollfuss's Corporative Constitution of April 1934, making of Austria an authoritarian rather than a parliamentary state.

At the same time the Provisional Government, in deference to the final sentences of the Moscow Declaration of 1943, undertook 'without delay' to contribute in every way possible to the liberation of Austria, but felt 'prompted to note that this contribution, in view of the debilitation of our people and the pauperization of our country, to her regret, can only be a modest one.'[5]

The Provisional Government was, at the outset, recognized on 29 April by the Soviet Union only. The British, United States and French Governments agreed in withholding their recognition on the grounds that the organization of any Austrian Government was the concern of all four occupying Powers and not of one alone, more especially when that one Power, Russia, was still excluding the other three from partici-

* When, on 25 November 1945, the Russian occupation authorities, misled as to the strength of the Communist Party, permitted an election, the results were far from agreeable to them. In an Assembly of 165 members, the People's Party won 85 seats, the Socialists 76 and the Communists but 4.

pation in that joint occupation of Vienna which had been previously agreed upon.[6]

On 4 July 1945 the European Advisory Commission, sitting in London, completed and signed an agreement on the Allied administration of Austria, establishing an Allied Control Council in which all decisions were to be unanimous; this meant that each of the Four Powers had the right to veto. The immediate tasks of this body were to effect the separation of Austria from Germany and to assure that the provisions of the Declaration of 5 June 1945 regarding the defeat of Germany* were complied with by Austria; to establish a central Austrian administration; and to pave the way for the foundation of a freely elected Austrian Government. Five days later on 9 July, the E.A.C., in a further agreement, recognized the frontiers of Austria as those of 31 December 1937 and delimited the four Allied zones of occupation. The writ of Dr Renner's Provisional Government still did not run beyond the Soviet Zone.

This somewhat anomalous state of affairs continued to exist until, on 20 October, as a part of Secretary Byrnes's programme of indicating to the Soviet Government the willingness of the Western Powers to recognize Governments in ex-enemy states which were demonstrably in accordance with the letter and spirit of the Yalta Declaration on Liberated Europe, the British, American and French Governments recognized the Provisional Government, which had been broadened as to its basis,‡ and authorized the extension of its authority to the whole of Austria.

As a result of the success of the People's Party at the general elections of 25 November, its leader, Dr Leopold Figl, became the first Federal Chancellor of the Second Republic in a Government consisting of 8 of his own followers, 6 Socialists, 1 Communist and 2 Independents. When the Federal Assembly, consisting of the National Council and the Federal Council sitting together, met for the first time on 20 December, it elected Karl Renner the first President of the reconstituted Federal Austrian Republic.

It remained now to prepare a treaty of peace with Austria, and here the prevailing obstacle was one of interpretation of the final provision of the Moscow Declaration of 1943. At the Potsdam Conference it was agreed to waive any payment of reparations by Austria,[7] save in the case of 'German assets' in Austria, and of these the conference failed to provide any hard and clear definition. Tentative attempts were made at

---

* See above, p. 279 n.

‡ On 25 September 1945 the Provisional Government was reorganized on a broader basis. It now comprised 13 People's Party, 12 Socialists, 10 Communists and 4 Independents.

the meetings of the Council of Foreign Ministers at Paris during the early summer of 1946 to make a start on the drafting of an Austrian treaty and to appoint deputies for this purpose. On each occasion these efforts were baulked of success by the intransigence of the Soviet Union, who insisted upon an agreement on 'German assets' as a preliminary to any discussion of peace terms.[8]

However, at the meeting of the Council in New York in December 1946, agreement was reached that at its next meeting, which was to be held in Moscow in March 1947, the discussion of an Austrian treaty should receive first priority and that special deputies, meeting in London, should begin the work of drafting in January.[9]

These persons* duly began their work at Lancaster House and at once encountered an unexpected frontier problem in the claim of Yugoslavia for the cession by Austria of Slovene Carinthia and part of Styria, amounting to some 3,000 kilometres with 200,000 inhabitants in all. This claim might have been dismissed somewhat summarily – for it had little to support it – had not the Soviet Union backed the Yugoslav demands. The result was the inevitable deadlock, and neither could the deputies agree on a definition of 'German assets'.

Yet, though they disagreed on eight clauses, they agreed on seven, among which were a reiteration of the provision of the Treaties of Versailles and St Germain that Austria should never join Germany, and also the limitation of Austria's army to 55,000 men and her air force to 90 fighters, served by 5,000 men.[11]

'Thus the peace-making machinery rumbled along', wrote one commentator, 'the ruts in the road making its springs screech and squeak, its wheels causing a dust-storm of propaganda from the corners of the world. Half drowned by contradictory reports, the four Foreign Ministers were to assemble in Moscow, hoping to complete the Austrian treaty and to lay the basis for a German settlement.'[12]

II

From mid-January to mid-March 1947 the deputies continued their labours and made very little progress. There was, however, agreement on what the Austrian treaty was to be called. Great importance was attached to the title by the Austrian Government itself since it was anxious to establish the fact that it was not a peace treaty which was being negotiated because Austria had never, of her own will, been at

* The deputies were the Hon. Robert Murphy and General Mark Clark for the United States, Sir William Strang and Viscount Hood for the United Kingdom, M. Gusev for the U.S.S.R., and M. Couve de Murville for France. Mr Murphy and General Clark have left brief accounts of their work as deputies in their memoirs.[10]

war save as the *Ostmark* of the German *Reich*, an allegedly unwilling vassal of Berlin. In Vienna the Federal Government was careful always to refer to the proposed treaty as a *Staatsvertrag*, a State Treaty, by which was indicated that its purpose was to restore the sovereign state of Austria, which had been liquidated by the *Anschluss* of 1938. This same intent was reflected in the title finally agreed upon by the deputies, namely 'A Treaty for the Re-establishment of an Independent and Democratic Austria'.

It was at the meeting of the Foreign Ministers at Moscow in March 1947 that the Russians put their cards finally on the table. The climate of ideas as between Moscow and Washington had been steadily worsening. When President Truman had said a year earlier that he was 'sick of babying the Soviets'* he had meant it, and throughout the ensuing twelve months the tension between East and West had grown appreciably greater. President Truman was determined to make a major challenge to Communist expansion and it was not a happy augury for the outcome of the Moscow Conference that the President allowed it to synchronize with his announcement that the United States would assume the obligations towards Greece and Turkey – which Britain had just jettisoned – in opposition to Communist activities in those two countries, an act which became known to history as the Truman Doctrine.†

Nor were the chances of success – however tenuous they may have originally been – greatly enhanced by the fact that the new American Secretary of State, General George C. Marshall, had but very recently assumed his office. He succeeded to this formidable task under grave difficulties. As Ambassador to China since December 1945 he had been completely out of touch with European affairs for many months, and because this, his first major confrontation with the Russians, took place only shortly after his appointment he had not had time to master the details of many of the issues under discussion. 'This probably was the only occasion when the General, celebrated for his retentive memory, ever was in such an embarrassing position', one of his staff has written. 'It must have been galling to his pride to lead debates in which it was evident to everybody that he was unfamiliar with relevant facts.'[13]

It is, however, improbable that, had the United States Secretary of State been the Archangel Gabriel himself in place of General Marshall, the outcome of the Moscow Conference of 1947 would have been any different, for by this time the Cold War was being fought in the open. If General Marshall went into battle unprepared, he emerged from this experience very clearly informed, and from this ordeal by fire he evolved

* See above, p. 429.   † See below, p. 565.

that cerebral chain-reaction which resulted in the Marshall Plan.*

Beginning on 12 March, the Moscow Conference continued for nearly six weeks. From the opening session the Soviet representatives left no doubt that there was no real basis for an agreement with the Western Powers on a German and, therefore, on an Austrian treaty. They also made it abundantly clear that, in challenging the Anglo-American position in Germany and in Austria, they were confident that Russia could thwart all Western plans for the re-establishment of the national economies of those two countries and could thereby jeopardize the rehabilitation of non-Communist Europe.

Such discussion of Austrian affairs as was permitted centred around the Yugoslav claims for the cession of territory in southern Carinthia and Styria and also for the payment of reparations, despite the Potsdam decision not to exact reparation payments from Austria. This, the Yugoslavs blandly asserted, did not apply to them as they were not a party to it. Both these claims were supported by the Soviet Union and opposed by the Western Powers, and no decision was reached on either of them.

The main bone of contention, however, was the definition of the terms 'German assets' in the Potsdam Agreement. Some eight months before, on 6 July 1946, the Soviet Government, through its Commander-in-Chief in Austria, General Kurasov, had made a unilateral inter-pretation of the term as including all property on Austrian soil belonging to Germans before the *Anschluss*; all property brought into Austria by Germans after the *Anschluss*, as well as all factories built with German capital after 13 March 1938; and all property purchased by Germans after the *Anschluss* for which the purchase price represented the property's real value and was not the outcome of a fixed sale.

At Moscow the Western Powers proposed that the term 'German assets' should apply to all property, rights and interests possessed in Austria by Germany or by German citizens on 7 May 1945 (the date of Germany's Unconditional Surrender), with three exceptions: property acquired under Nazi legislation or by force or coercion or confiscation; property belonging to the Austrian Federal State before the *Anschluss*, or acquired after it, and being used for the purpose of normal govern-mental administration; property in which non-Germans also had a share or interest.[14]

After what seemed like endless discussion, the only ground gained was a concession by the Soviet representative in respect of property acquired by force. Otherwise there was agreement on no other facet of the Austrian problem. In view of this General Marshall announced

* See below, p. 563.

that the question of Austria must be submitted to the United Nations under Article 14 of the Charter* as a situation deemed likely to 'impair the general welfare or friendly relations among nations', unless the Foreign Ministers could find a basis for agreement before their next meeting in London in November. It was therefore decided to refer the matter once again to deputies who should examine the outstanding points at issue *in situ* and draft a solution.

Apart from this the conference, when it closed on 24 April, was virtually abortive, and the Austrian Foreign Minister, Dr Karl Gruber, who had come hopefully to Moscow in the expectation of signing a *Staatsvertrag*, returned to Vienna a depressed and disappointed man.

The Commission of Deputies† met, as instructed, in Vienna from 12 May to 10 October 1947. Austria was not represented, and after a procedural dispute, which occupied several weeks, the deputies settled down to the usual futile and bootless wrangle. In the course of seventy-nine meetings they achieved no more than Omar Khayyam: 'but ever-more came out by the same door as in I went'.

When they met for the eightieth time on 8 October, the French member of the Commission, General Cherrière, presented a compromise formula. The essence of what came to be known as the 'Cherrière Plan' was that, in disposing of German assets in Austria among the Allies, part should be made over in rights or ownership of physical property and part be commuted into a cash claim. The tentative figure given as the total redemption sum was $100 million.[15] The Soviet member of the Commission, M. Novikov, showed interest in General Cherrière's proposal and promised to study it 'carefully'. As, however, it went beyond the terms of reference of the Commission, the members merely attached the 'Cherrière Plan' as an annex to the summary of their record of failure. This they presented to the four Governments on 11 October.

At the London meeting of the Council of Foreign Ministers – which opened in gloom on 25 November 1947 and broke up in despair and frustration on 17 December – General Marshall and Mr Bevin, while not wholly endorsing the 'Cherrière Plan', agreed to accept it as a basis of negotiation. M. Molotov, however, pronounced it totally inadequate

---

* Article 14 of the United Nations Charter reads: 'Subject to the provisions of Article 12, the General Assembly may recommend measures for the peaceful adjustment of any situation, regardless of origin, which it deems likely to impair the general welfare or friendly relations among nations, including situations resulting from a violation of the provisions of the present Charter setting forth the Purposes and Principles of the United Nations.'

† These deputies were Sir George Rendel for the United Kingdom, Joseph Dodge for the United States, General Paul Cherrière for France and K. V. Novikov for the U.S.S.R.

and demanded a sum nearly twice as large as that put forward in the Plan. Despite the efforts of the Austrian Foreign Minister, Dr Gruber, and the manifest goodwill of the Western Powers, no sort of progress was achieved in respect of the Austrian treaty at the conference, on the agenda of which, at the insistence of M. Molotov, it had been placed last (presumably so that he could hold yet another bargaining position in readiness for the end of a long series of meetings). All seemed lost in the shipwreck of the London meeting of the Council of Foreign Ministers.

III

Contrary to all expectations, the deputies charged with the problem of the Austrian treaty were enabled to meet again in London on 20 February 1948, and on the initiative of the Soviet Government. Now, however, M. Koktomov met his match in his American and British colleagues, Samuel Reber and James Marjoribanks, who showed that, when occasion demanded, they could be as obstinate and intransigent as the Soviet deputy.

For the better part of eleven weeks they sat and haggled over the question of 'German assets' as defined in the 'Cherrière Plan'. The British and Americans held to the original figure of $100 million; the Russians demanded $200 million. By the third week in March M. Koktomov had reduced his figure to $175 million and General Cherrière had increased his to $115 million. On 1 April the Russians said they were prepared to accept $150 million to be spread over six years, but they still supported the Yugoslav claim for a similar figure of $150 million and for the cession by Austria of Slovene Carinthia. Since the Western deputies took a firm stand on the Potsdam principle of 'no payment of reparations by Austria' and the frontiers of 1938, the usual *impasse* ensued and the meeting adjourned *sine die* on 6 May.

They did not meet again that year, but on 6 December the Austrian Government, frustrated, humiliated and wellnigh desperate, appealed to the Big Four to resume the negotiations for a *Staatsvertrag*. Moscow raised no objections, and wearily the West agreed. Once more the deputies assembled in London on 9 February 1949,* but it was soon apparent that no change of heart had taken place, and after a fruitless reiteration of arguments, from which neither side retreated, they 'agreed' – *mirabile dictu* – on 10 May to adjourn until 25 June.

In the meantime a new session of the Conference of Foreign Ministers opened in Paris on 23 May, the first since the débâcle of December 1947.

* Georgi Zarubin, Soviet Ambassador in London, replaced M. Koktomov on this occasion, and M. Berthelot succeeded General Cherrière for France. The American and British deputies remained the same.

Now Mr Bevin was the one surviving veteran of Potsdam. Dean Acheson, that brilliant, inspired legalist, sat in the chair of General Marshall, Robert Schuman in that of M. Bidault, and Andrei Vyshinsky in the place of M. Molotov who, in contradiction of his Party nickname of 'stone bottom', had become temporarily unstuck from the Soviet Ministry of Foreign Affairs.

In so far as Austria was concerned, while M. Zarubin had little new to propose on behalf of his own country, the rift in the international Communist lute, consequent upon the rejection by Marshal Tito's Government in June 1948 of the authority of the Cominform, resulted in the abandonment of Soviet support for Yugoslav territorial and financial claims. Somewhat to the surprise of his colleagues, M. Vyshinsky announced suddenly and without preliminaries that he would accept Article 5 of the draft treaty – to which successive Soviet representatives had consistently over the last four years refused to give assent – namely: 'Austria's frontiers shall be those of 1 January 1938.'*

But the price which Russia exacted for her concession was high. While accepting the Potsdam principle in waiving all claims to 'German assets' (a step which the Western Powers had taken three years earlier), Russia demanded – and the Western Powers agreed – that exception should be made in the case of her oil claims, which amounted to 60 per cent of oil production, concessions and refineries in eastern Austria, and of the Danube Shipping Company and that she should receive $150 million, payable over six years. It was further conceded that, in addition to the assets of the Danube Shipping Company in the Eastern Zone, those in Rumania, Bulgaria and Hungary should become forfeit to Russia.[16]

The cynical nature of this agreement is apparent. Russia was to receive $150 million payable over a period of six years, in a freely convertible currency, that is to say in dollars. This payment was to be considered as being made in place of 'German assets' in Austria which, by the same agreement, Russia now renounced. Since all concerned knew that Austria could never possibly pay this amount without the support of an American dollar loan, it meant, in the final analysis, that the United States would be paying the Soviet Union for property of which Nazi Germany had robbed Austria![17]

As usual the deputies were accorded the task of 'tidying up' the situation which the Foreign Ministers had left and of producing a draft treaty by 1 September. But though they laboured unremittingly from 4 July onwards there were still nine articles in dispute when the deadline

* Austria, for her part, was to undertake to guarantee the rights of her Croat and Slovene minorities.

of 1 September was reached and, on the suggestion of Mr Reber, they adjourned to New York to reconvene on 22 September. When this was done, however, it proved as sterile a process as before, and although the Western Powers were ready to make minor concessions it was evident that Moscow's interpretation of the agreement reached in Paris in June was so rapacious as to be aimed at establishing a complete Soviet domination of Austria's economic structure.

Though the matter of the Austrian treaty was discussed sporadically by the Council of Foreign Ministers and their deputies throughout the years 1950, 1951 and 1952, they produced no tangible results whatever, and it was not until February 1953 that negotiations were resumed on a semi-constructive basis.

IV

The failing health of that courageous man, Ernest Bevin, which finally brought about his resignation in March 1951, weakened his hold on policy during the latter months of his term of office. British foreign policy lacked that initiative and energy which had characterized Mr Bevin's earlier years at the Foreign Office and it certainly gained neither wisdom nor initiative under the leadership of his successor Herbert Morrison, surely among the most obscure and least distinguished of Britain's Foreign Secretaries.

The failure to resume negotiations on the Austrian treaty for so long a time was due in part to the immobility of Soviet policy, partly to the sense of disillusioned frustration in Washington and partly to the lack of initiative in London. It required that touch of professional genius and long experience, which returned to the Foreign Office with Sir Anthony Eden, to stir again the half-smothered embers into life. *

As in the case of the Trieste problem,† Sir Anthony pursued a careful line of approach and, having studied the issue from all angles, moved his allies to exploratory action on a new and somewhat more hardy course. On 13 March 1952 the three Western Powers, acting on the suggestion of the Austrian Ambassador in Moscow, who believed that the Soviet Government might be acquiescent, and on the initiative of the British Government, presented to their Russian ally a 'shortened' draft of an Austrian State Treaty. 'Shortened' it certainly was, for instead of the

---

* Mr Bevin resigned as Foreign Secretary on 9 March 1951 and was succeeded by Mr Morrison, who continued in office until the General Election of the following October, as a result of which Sir Winston Churchill returned to office. Sir Anthony Eden became Foreign Secretary for the third time on 28 October 1951 and so continued until he succeeded Sir Winston as Prime Minister on 6 April 1955, when Harold Macmillan became Foreign Secretary.

† See above, pp. 448–9.

fifty-three articles which had been so laboriously hammered out by the deputies, and then batted to and fro like a shuttlecock between the Foreign Ministers, there now appeared a treaty of no more than eight articles containing the meat of the matter at issue.

Among the forty-five articles thus jettisoned as constituting, in the view of London, Washington and Paris, an infringement of Austrian sovereignty, were those dealing with the limitation of armaments and the guarantee of democratic rights. The vexed question of 'German assets' was relegated to a new article which merely stated that the Four Powers waived their claims in this matter. No mention at all was made of the lump-sum payment of $150 million to the Soviet Union.

It is not clear what reaction the Western Powers hoped to produce from the presentation of the 'shortened' treaty: whether they hoped that it would be accepted as a basis of discussion and negotiation or whether they merely desired to prick the Government of the Soviet Union out of its Achillean moroseness. If the first, then they were more than naturally naïve; if the second, they certainly achieved success.

The Moscow Government exhibited every kind of annoyance and surprised petulance. They demanded the immediate withdrawal of the new treaty, characterizing it in unequivocal terms as wholly unacceptable, and essaying at the same time to couple the whole Austrian issue with that of Trieste. When the Western Powers suggested that the 'shortened' text might be referred to the deputies for further discussion and ultimate redrafting, their proposal met with the firmest of rejections. By the autumn of 1952 this particular gambit had been concluded and Austria remained the victim of treatment more severe than that which had been accorded to other liberated countries or even meted out to countries which had fought on the side of the Axis.*

Yet, though nothing positive had emerged from the manœuvre of the 'shortened' treaty, it had not been completely worthless nor unduly time-consuming. It had succeeded in effecting a slight thaw in the glacial conditions which had obtained for over two years, during which period neither side had achieved any communication at all. At least the Russians had been persuaded to resume intercourse, if it was only to reiterate their persistent use of the word '*niet*'. In diplomacy even negative discussion is better than no discussion at all.

And wearisome negative stuff it was, with precious little about it to encourage even the trained optimism of Anthony Eden. But when, on 9 February 1953, the Foreign Ministers' deputies met for the two hundred and sixtieth time to discuss the Austrian treaty and adjourned

---

* The Austrian Government drew attention to this fact in a Note circulated on 31 July 1952 to all the Powers with whom Austria had diplomatic relations.

indefinitely because of Soviet insistence on the withdrawal of the 'abbreviated' treaty and the refusal of the Western Powers to do so, Sir Anthony was not discouraged. Nor was he disheartened by a further refusal of the Soviet Union on 25 May to hold any further discussions on Austria, either directly through the Foreign Ministers' Council or at the professional level of the deputies, as long as the 'shortened' treaty lay upon the table.

By a curious quirk of fate the kernel of a solution was about to be discovered, though it was yet to be some years before it germinated successfully. The ingenious and indefatigable brain of Dr Karl Gruber was actively employed in finding some new avenue of approach. Refusing to accept failure in deadlock, he hit upon the hardy plan of introducing an entirely new factor into the Austrian treaty discussions, that of a diplomatic mediator.

In their Note of 25 May the Soviet Government had stated that, in their view, there was no future in further discussions among deputies but that the whole question might be examined through diplomatic channels. Though this might well have been understood to restrict such diplomatic contacts to the representatives of the Powers concerned, there was no specific statement to this effect, and in the absence of such provision Dr Gruber was quick to take the initiative. On 25 June he met at Burgenstock, near Lucerne, with the Prime Minister of India, Jawaharlal Nehru, and Krishna Menon, then Indian Ambassador in Moscow, and requested their good offices on behalf of the restitution of a free and independent Austria. In the course of the conversation Dr Gruber reverted to an idea which had originally been adumbrated by Karl Renner as early as December 1945, namely that the newly resurrected Austria should adopt a policy of complete neutrality on the model of the Swiss Republic.[18] This idea had been adopted into the programme of the Austrian Socialist Party in 1947 and had been formally affirmed in a Government Declaration two years later. Now the idea of utilizing this principle of Austrian military neutrality as a lever in the negotiations for a State Treaty was put forward by the Foreign Minister in his talks with the Indian statesmen.

Pandit Nehru was intrigued with the idea. He accepted the office of mediator and shortly thereafter Krishna Menon, in conversation with Molotov in Moscow, advanced the proposal – as coming from himself and without committing the Austrian Government – that an undertaking by Austria not to allow foreign military bases upon her territory or to adhere to any military alliance of alignment with a foreign Power might form the basis for the conclusion of a *Staatsvertrag*. To this Molotov is said to have replied that, though such a declaration on the part of Austria would be of 'undoubted value', it would still be inadequate unless accompanied by other guarantees which he did not specify.[19]

Though without apparently direct results, the Indian proposals, fostered by Dr Gruber, were not without their indirect repercussions. On 30 July the Soviet Government itself took the initiative. In identical Notes to the three Western Powers M. Molotov intimated that the withdrawal of the 'shortened' treaty would permit of the resumption of negotiations for a State Treaty, and followed this up with a tentive proposal for a meeting of the four Foreign Ministers to consider the German question and therefore, by definition, the Austrian question. The Western Powers replied that they were prepared to withdraw the 'shortened' treaty on condition that the Russians, for their part, would refrain from dragging such red herrings as the Trieste question or the conclusion of a German peace treaty into the Austrian negotiations and were ready to sign a treaty which would ensure the political and economic independence of Austria. On this basis, among others, the Conference of Berlin opened on 25 January 1954.

The British Government approached the conference with a triple objective: to avoid becoming bogged down in the morass of haggling which had become so repetitive a pattern of previous discussions; to make at least some slight progress towards the conclusion of a treaty of peace with Germany; and to sign – almost at any cost – a *Staatsvertrag* for Austria. To attain the first and last of these objectives the Western Allies leaned over backwards to accommodate the Russians, but all to no purpose.[20]

For the purposes of the Austrian discussions the conference co-opted the Foreign Minister, Leopold Figl, and his State Secretary, Bruno Kreisky, into their midst. The Austrians reiterated their willingness to accept a status of neutrality on the Swiss model and, at the suggestion of Sir Anthony Eden, the Western Powers agreed to accept the Soviet interpretation of the five articles of the original draft text of the Austrian treaty[21] which still remained outstanding. This offer took M. Molotov somewhat aback and nearly surprised him into some degree of affability. Hitherto he had run true to form, but such willingness on the part of the Western Powers to meet him more than half-way was almost embarrassing. '[It is] the same old gramophone record with scarcely a variant', Anthony Eden wrote in his diary on the evening of 25 January. 'Austria the only faint suggestion of one.'[22]

Molotov really does appear to have been a little rattled. He had no desire at all to sign an Austrian treaty – even on his own terms as then disclosed. He therefore shied away from compliance to the Western proposals and startled the conference on 12 February by putting forward completely new and unacceptable terms. By virtue of these a new and supplementary article (Article 4 *bis*) would be inserted in the draft, which would require of Austria that she should undertake not to join any bloc or military alliance, not to permit foreign bases on her territory or to engage the services of foreign military advisers; that, in order to preclude any attempt to renew an *Anschluss* with Germany, the withdrawal of the Allied troops occupying Austria should be delayed until the conclusion of a German treaty, though they should not interfere in the public and political affairs of the country; and, furthermore, that the Austrian question should be linked with that of Trieste. The only concession offered was that payment by Austria for 'German assets' should be in goods and not in cash.[23]

After this *démarche*, though the conference continued to linger on in desultory activity and deepening gloom until 18 February, there was no real hope that an agreement on the Austrian treaty was possible, let alone the other issues with which the conference was engaged. Even if the Western Powers had been disposed to accept the Soviet proposals (which they were not), it would have been impossible for the Austrian Government to have accepted them. 'I ask you, gentlemen,' Dr Figl demanded of the conference, 'which of you would take the responsibility, if he were in my place, of appearing before the Parliament of his country with a proposal of this nature?'[24] As Sir Anthony Eden pointed out, the Russian demand that occupation troops should remain in Austria until a peace treaty had been signed with Germany was tantamount to condemning Austria to an indefinite occupation, since the Russians were doing their best to hold up the conclusion of such a treaty.[25]

Moreover, the Soviet demands on Austria in respect of her international status made a humiliating mockery of the Austrian offer to accept neutrality voluntarily, as had Switzerland, while retaining an honourable position in the family of nations. In Sir Anthony Eden's words, 'Molotov behaved with callous brutality'.

The Foreign Ministers and their Austrian colleagues dispersed on 19 February in dejection and exasperation, having rejected Dr Figl's final appeal 'not to permit this conference to go down to history as a proof that the great ones of this world were incapable, in the middle of the twentieth century, of bridging world tension or of fulfilling the promise that full freedom would be restored to our native land'.[26]

V

All hopes for an Austrian State Treaty seemed to have disappeared in the ashes of the Berlin fiasco. For nearly a year no move was made in this particular aspect, but on the wider stage of international affairs a prolonged series of shifting personalities and policies was in progress and was to have its cumulative effect. The signature, on 4 April 1949, of the North Atlantic Treaty marked a new milestone in the history of the Cold War which, taken in conjunction with its natural corollaries, the European Defence Community (of ill-fated memory) of 1952 and the Western European Union of 1954, had not failed to have its effect on Soviet political thinking,* and at the same time there had been a change of cast.

On 4 November 1952, in a landslide Republican victory, General Dwight D. Eisenhower was elected to succeed Harry Truman as President of the United States and, which was perhaps even more significant, this resulted in John Foster Dulles becoming Secretary of State. In March of the following year Marshal Stalin died, thereby terminating a dictatorship of nearly thirty years. Two years later, in April 1955, Sir Winston Churchill concluded his third administration and retired from office, leaving the succession to Sir Anthony Eden, who appointed Harold Macmillan as his Foreign Secretary. In France the Fourth Republic lurched forward upon its turgid and tortuous career, displaying little distinction in either internal or foreign affairs.

Thus, in the space of less than three years, a new group of actors had appeared on the stage giving, by the very fact of their neoteric nature, fresh impetus to the efforts to conclude treaties with Austria and with Germany. The first step was taken by Edgar Faure, the French Prime Minister, who, in a public speech on 25 March 1955, advocated a further meeting of the Big Four. Sir Anthony Eden at once agreed, having arrived independently at the same conclusion. After preliminary discussions between themselves, the three Western Governments invited Russia to join in an effort to remove the sources of conflict which had arisen between them.

In so far as this concerned Austria, it was agreed among the Western Governments, on the suggestion of Sir Anthony, that they should take their stand on the proposal which they had made to the Russians in Berlin, namely that they would accept the Soviet versions of the five outstanding articles of the treaty. If the Russians were prepared to conclude a treaty on these terms, the Western Allies might go further and agree to consider the military and political neutralization of Austria.[27]

Meanwhile events were moving with surprising and unaccustomed speed on a bilateral Russo-Austrian level. On 14 March the Austrian Government, through its Ambassador in Moscow, had once again reiterated its intention to join no military alliances or to permit the

* See below, pp. 595–600.

establishment of foreign military bases on Austrian territory and had renewed their willingness to accept a status of neutrality. Ten days later, on 24 March, Molotov replied accepting these declarations as a basis on which a State Treaty might be signed, expressing a desire for the convening of a special Four-Power Conference for such a purpose and inviting the Austrian Chancellor, Julius Raab, to Moscow for preliminary discussions.

The Chancellor, accompanied by his Vice-Chancellor, Dr Adolf Schärf, and his Foreign Minister, Dr Leopold Figl, went to Moscow on 12 April and three days later there emerged the so-called 'Moscow Memorandum'. In this bilateral agreement the Russians offered to sign an Austrian treaty without delay and even agreed to the withdrawal of all occupation forces not later than 31 December. The long and dreary argument on 'German assets' was brought to an end by a final payment of $150 million in Austrian goods to the value of $25 million a year. The Russians also made some important concessions, including the renunciation of their claims to Austrian oilfields and refineries, and the return to the Austrians of the Danube Shipping Company, against a cash payment of $2 million. All Austrian prisoners still in Soviet hands would be repatriated by the date on which Soviet troops left Austria.

In return Austria renewed her proposals for adopting permanent neutrality and undertook to do all things possible to elicit international support for this declaration. She would, in addition, welcome a guarantee of the independence, inviolability and integrity of Austrian territory.[28]

Not the least significant aspect of the 'Moscow Memorandum' – apart from the unwonted speed with which agreement on it was reached – was the fact that it succeeded in obtaining for Austria far more favourable terms on a number of important points in the *Staatsvertrag* than had been achieved in the course of the previous long-drawn-out negotiations between the Soviet Union and the Western Powers.

Following on the announcement of the Russo-Austrian agreement, the Soviet Government, pursuing its precipitant path of unaccustomed expedition, proposed to the Western Powers an immediate conference of the four Foreign Ministers for the purpose of concluding and signing a State Treaty. The Western Powers naturally agreed but suggested that some preparatory work was needed – with the lapse of time it was found necessary to make over one hundred amendments to the 'agreed' draft – and suggested that a preliminary conference of the four Ambassadors should meet in Vienna for this purpose on 2 May.

With what Harold Macmillan has justly termed 'their usual calm effrontery', the Soviet Government, after a policy of procrastination which had lasted a good eight years, now complained about ten days' delay.[29] However, with much bad grace they eventually assented, and on 12 May the Four Powers agreed upon the so-called 'Vienna Memorandum',* which reconciled the terms of the 'Moscow Memorandum' with the existing draft of the treaty and became the final basis for the *Staatsvertrag* which was formally signed on 15 May 1955 by the five Foreign Ministers – Harold Macmillan, John Foster Dulles, Vyacheslav Molotov, Christian Pinay and Leopold Figl.†

The Austrian State Treaty was signed, with much flourish and *panache*, in the Marmorsaal of the magnificent Palace of the Belvedere. This splendid residence, with its gardens and lawns, had been given by the Holy Roman Emperor to Prince Eugene of Savoy in recognition of his victories, just as Queen Anne had bestowed Blenheim upon the Duke of Marlborough. Later the Belvedere had become the town house of that ill-fated couple, the Archduke Franz-Ferdinand and his morganatic wife, Sophie Chotek, Duchess of Hohenberg, who perished at Sarajevo.

No imperial ghosts, however, cast their gloom over the ceremonies of signature on 15 May 1955. The event was one of jubilation and enthusiastic celebration. 'A lot of champagne was drunk *inside* the Belvedere, and the crowd was intoxicated with joy in the gardens *outside*', wrote Harold Macmillan in his diary.[31]

This remarkable display of warmth and amity had not been achieved without some difficulty. The treaty contained no stipulation as to Austrian neutrality, though, under Article 2, 'The Allied and Associated Powers declare that they will respect the independence and territorial integrity of Austria'. It had been Molotov's intention too that the treaty should be accompanied by a declaration on Austrian neutrality, and he went so far – after the treaty had been signed – as to read out a draft of such a document. Not unnaturally his colleagues from the West protested, first, that they had not been furnished with the text of the Soviet proposals, and secondly that the treaty must first be approved by the Austrian Federal Government and National Assembly before there could be any question of a Four-Power guarantee. After some discussion Molotov, in the prevailing urbanity of the moment, withdrew his proposal and assented to the view of the majority.[32]‡

The ball was therefore in Austria's court, and she was speedy in

---

* On the same day a separate Memorandum was signed on behalf of France and Austria comprising similar terms to the Four-Power Memorandum.[30]

† The State Treaty was subsequently adhered to by Czechoslovakia, Yugoslavia, Poland, Mexico, Brazil, New Zealand, Canada and Australia.

‡ All five signatories having ratified the State Treaty, it came into effect on 27 July 1955.

returning it. By 8 June both the Austrian Government and the two chambers of Parliament had accepted the principle of a neutral status for their country and had authorized the enactment of constitutional legislation to this effect. The law came into force on 5 November and ten days later the text was communicated to the Governments of all those countries with whom Austria had diplomatic relations, asking for its due recognition. This was accorded on 6 December by the Four Powers in identical Notes,* and on 14 December Austria was admitted to membership of the United Nations, thereby indicating that her declaration of neutrality did not prevent her joining non-military international organizations and associations.

Thus ended, in what Harold Macmillan has termed 'an agreeable interlude in our relations with Russia',[33] an episode which was among the strangest in this shadow world of 'no war, no peace'. For ten years the Russians had blocked and obstructed the conclusion of a treaty with Austria only to adopt at the end a policy of rush and bustle and almost querulous allegations of delay. There were those who read into the ultimate Soviet contribution to the solution of the Austrian treaty problem a good augury for the future, but they were doomed to disappointment.

VI

The *volte-face* of March 1955 in Russian policy vis-à-vis Austria presents a mystery as impenetrable as it is tantalizing. Why, it is asked, after ten years of opposition and the farcical exhaustion of some four hundred fruitless meetings of Foreign Ministers, deputies and experts, should the Soviet Government suddenly reverse itself, agree to the conclusion of a *Staatsvertrag* within a period of two months, and fleetingly present itself to Europe in a not unfavourable light?

The unravelling of this mystery will remain incomplete and maddeningly elusive until such time as the Soviet state archives are made available to historians, and even then the whole truth may not be known. Until such millennial prospects have been realized, however, one is dependent upon half-knowledge and intelligent conjecture to create some darkling picture of what occurred. For what is very certain – and what has been made abundantly clear in the circumstances of the Czechoslovak crisis of August 1968 – is that we do not know what is going on in the Kremlin. Let us surmise then as best we can.

* On 20 June, at San Francisco, the Four Powers had agreed that when it became necessary for them to make a statement on an Austrian declaration of neutrality they would all use the same text. By March 1957 sixty-one states had recognized the neutral status of Austria.

It is at least an acceptable thesis that Stalin, very much a man of his own generation, emerged from the Potsdam Conference of 1945 with a rooted conviction that sooner or later a third European war would take place in circumstances not unlike the first and second wars of this century. Despite his knowledge of the capabilities of the Bomb as a weapon and of its subsequent progress and development, Stalin had not grasped the total difference which nuclear weapons could and would bring to land battles, and he may have believed that in the final upshot they would not be used. On the basis of such a confidence in war of a conventional character, it clearly mattered very greatly whether or not Russian troops remained stationed right up to the boundary of the Soviet Zone in Austria, and it would clearly have been of material military disadvantage to have withdrawn them to Hungary or East Germany, which were then the only alternatives, since Czechoslovakia was still, at that time, a free country and unoccupied by Soviet divisions.

It was for this reason therefore, according to our surmise, that Stalin issued his directive of '*niet*' to the Soviet representatives who attended the discussions on the Austrian treaty from 1945 onwards and that this monosyllabic negative remained the root of Soviet policy until his death in 1953. In adhering to such a policy Stalin would certainly have had the support of Molotov, a sincere revolutionary of the old type, cleaving to the stern, orthodox, puritanical line that good Communists must not be contaminated by contact with the West.

Such was not the view of Khrushchev, who had a wider and less rigid – if more complicated – approach to international affairs. Thus, when the dust of the battle which followed the death of Stalin and the struggle for power among his successors had settled and Khrushchev, early in 1955, emerged as the victor, it became apparent that the views formerly held by Stalin were now defended only by Molotov and that Khrushchev's policy was to be very different.

Khrushchev, with his more agile mind, understood about nuclear capability and went, it may be believed, on the assumption that if a Third World War did break out in Europe nuclear weapons would of a certainty be used. If this were so, it would be almost wholly irrelevant whether Soviet troops remained in Austria or were withdrawn* and, if their withdrawal could be turned to the advantage of Russia, then let them be withdrawn by all means.

The question then resolved itself into one of what advantage Russia might gain in return for her agreement in the conclusion of an Austrian

---

* It should be remembered also that by this time Czechoslovakia had finally passed behind the Iron Curtain.

treaty. It was here that long-term and short-term planning appeared to overlap.

The primary short-term consideration for Russia was the problem of Germany, and if the example of Austrian neutrality, with its consequent advantage of the evacuation of occupying troops, could be dangled before Germany it might well succeed in persuading her to pursue a similar course and not become wholly integrated into the Western European bloc. This thesis was one good reason for agreeing to the formula recently put forward for an Austrian treaty.

A second reason, of equal plausibility and attraction, was Khrushchev's long-term objective of achieving a summit meeting with his peers which might even result in some sort of over-all *détente* with the United States, on the strength of which he could take up the question of Germany – and especially of Berlin – in a manner more favourable to Russian interests. To achieve such an end Russia must present herself in a good light, and Khrushchev was certainly well aware that both Sir Winston Churchill and President Eisenhower had often repeated that they would not agree to a summit unless there were not only promise but also performance of good behaviour by the Soviet Union in some way such as an Austrian treaty.

An additional argument in favour of greater pliability was Khrushchev's known desire to restore a good relationship with Yugoslavia. The conclusion of an Austrian treaty would – and did – certainly give important reassurance to Tito with regard to Soviet military intentions in that part of the world.*

Taken all in all, therefore, it is believed that Khruchshev was confident that he had nothing to lose and, indeed, perhaps much to gain from abandoning the consistent course of intransigence with regard to Austria. Two factors now remained for consideration: to establish the exact Soviet price for acquiescence and to overcome the opposition of Molotov. Khrushchev would appear to have decided to settle for the neutralization of Austria and for compensation – the famous $150 million – and this he ultimately achieved. As for Molotov, he would seem to have 'dragged his feet', as long as this was possible in the Soviet ambiance, fighting a rearguard action in defence of orthodox Communism. He is said to have capitulated in the face of a direct order from Khrushchev, but it was the beginning of his downfall. He was finally removed from his position as Soviet Foreign Minister on 1 June 1956.

* It was precisely the opposite in August 1968, when the Soviet occupation of Czechoslovakia caused the liveliest apprehension in Belgrade.

20 | The Japanese Peace Treaty

I

OF all the defeated Axis nations in the Second World War, Japan was unique in that her conclusion of hostilities and subsequent return to the status of normal diplomatic relations followed the accepted conventional and traditional processes of an armistice, involving Unconditional Surrender, followed by a period of occupation, followed by a formal treaty of peace. In the case of Italy the situation became somewhat confused by reason of her temporary excursion into the ways of 'co-belligerency', which permitted her defection from the Axis to the Allied camp to assume a legal aspect, while with Germany, as of this year of 1971, no peace treaty has yet been signed and, in so far as both Germanys are concerned, their official status is one of 'non-belligerency'.

As the war in the Pacific had been primarily a war conducted under the direction of the United States, so was the first phase of peace largely an American operation. Both the reason and the wisdom of this circumstance were soon self-evident. In Europe the brunt of the war had been borne by Britain and by Russia before the United States entered hostilities, and both had immense armies in the field at its close, whereas Japan had been defeated largely by American arms. While it was true that both Germany and Japan had surrendered to an American Supreme Commander acting in each case on behalf of the Allied and Associated Powers, the immediately subsequent events were different in both countries. The Grand Alliance, as represented by General Eisenhower, dissolved into disunity almost immediately, while its power and prestige, as represented by General MacArthur, were maintained intact; indeed, the image of the Supreme Commander became so inflated as to necessitate his ultimate dismissal by the President of the United States.

Moreover, the very nature of the relationship between the Allies and the defeated nation differed materially. The sovereignty of Germany had been placed in commission. The country had been divided into four parts, each controlled by a victorious Power, and the supreme dominion stemmed from an Allied Control Council, in which all four Powers were equal in standing and authority.* Because of this equality of status and also because of the difficulties inherent in government by commission, agreements entered into between the Allies for their mutual co-operation soon broke down and within three years the situation had so deteriorated that one of the occupying Powers was blockading three out of the four sectors of Berlin and two of the other three occupying Powers were employing their air forces to break this operation of investment. †

Very different was the situation in Japan. In planning for the future the United States Government had learned its lesson from the early difficulties in the occupation of Germany. 'On one thing', Dean Acheson has written, 'we were determined: there would be no zones of occupation.'[1]

It had therefore been agreed – as we have seen, not without a struggle ‡– to retain the Emperor, subject to certain modifications in his personal status whereby he ceased to be regarded as a deity and became a ceremonial monarch.§ He and his Government were subject to the orders of the conquering Power by the mouth and hand of its proconsul and Supreme Commander, General Douglas MacArthur. These orders, purely American in their concept and execution, were contained in a directive prepared in great measure by Secretary of War Stimson and Under-Secretary of State Joseph Grew. The document was approved by President Truman on 6 September 1945.[2]‖

* See above, pp. 279–80.
† See above, pp. 280–4, and below, pp. 580–1.
‡ See above, pp. 387–8.
§ The whole issue of the Imperial status in Japan is frought with nuances almost incomprehensible to the Western mind. Briefly it may be simplified in these terms: up to the beginning of 1946, the Emperor was *less* than a deity; under the new constitution, when he renounced his 'divinity', he became *less* than a constitutional monarch.

The word for 'deity' in Japanese is *kami*, and it is used for God, for the gods, for superior beings, for very gifted or powerful people or for 'spirits'. It may also apply to any kind of charismatic personality, or even substance. In the case of the Emperor, he was particularly and deeply revered as a descendant, 'through ages eternal', from the mythological goddess of the sun. But he was not, in the Western sense, 'divine' and had never been regarded as such either by himself or his people. When, therefore, he was ordered by General MacArthur to disclaim his 'divinity', the idea seems to have struck him as absurd.

On the other hand, the Constitution of 1946 stripped the Emperor of all power and sovereignty, rendering him less than any constitutional monarch in the Western sense. His consent is not required for acts of the Diet to become law; he does not even have the right to see state papers or to advise or to be kept informed. He has no rank or status in respect of the Self-Defence Force, nor does the oath taken by members of this Force even mention his name. His function is purely ceremonial, opening the sessions of the Diet, and receiving heads of foreign diplomatic missions and visiting Heads of State. It is not surprising, therefore, to find many reputable Japanese constitutional lawyers claiming that, legally speaking, their country is a republic.

The substance of this document was sent by radio to General MacArthur on 29 August and in full by messenger after the President's approval on 6 September.

From the first the position of the other Allied Powers was recognizably subordinate both in the military occupation and in the administration of Japan. It was understood that troops from these countries would be both welcome and acceptable, always provided that they were unequivocally under the authority and orders of the Supreme Commander. Troops from Great Britain, Australia, New Zealand and India participated on these lines. The Soviet Union refused to accept them and was not represented in the forces of occupation. Moreover, when the Soviet Military Mission, led by General Kusma Durevyanko, truculently threatened to send a Russian force into Hokkaido whether General MacArthur liked it or not, the Supreme Commander replied that if one Russian soldier entered Japan without his authority he would arrest General Durevyanko and all his Mission and hold them in jail indefinitely. And the Soviet General admitted that he recognized that MacArthur meant what he said.[3]

That the United States was equally determined to maintain ultimate authority over the control policies for the occupation of Japan is clear from the wording of its original directive, which stated unequivocally that

> Although every effort will be made, by consultation and by constitution of appropriate advisory bodies, to establish policies for the conduct of the occupation and the control of Japan which will satisfy the principal Allied powers, in the event of differences of opinion among them the policies of the United States will govern.[4]

Thus, from the first, it was made evident that the Americans were prepared to stand no nonsense or misunderstanding in respect of the occupation and control of Japan. While not wishing to exclude their allies from participation, the United States had stated their position clearly from the outset. Such participation, while welcomed, was to be in a purely advisory capacity. The operation as a whole was to be essentially American in character.

II

It was as a result of its insistence upon the advisory nature of its Allies' participation in the occupation of Japan that the United States Government first met with difficulty. As early as 21 August 1945 (that is to say, before the formal signature of the instrument of Unconditional Surrender), an invitation had proceeded from Washington to London and Moscow and to Chungking to join with the United States in setting up an international body, to be known as the Far Eastern Advisory Commission (F.E.A.C.), to assist the Supreme Commander in the execution of the aims of the Potsdam Declaration and the terms of surrender.[5]* Of the three recipient Powers, China and Russia accepted at once, the first unreservedly, the second with an expressed desire, which later became a precondition, for the establishment of a Control Council consisting of the four Great Powers concerned.[6]

Mr Bevin raised objections on behalf of Great Britain on the grounds that, by definition, the proposed Commission would have only advisory powers; Britain also inclined towards the Soviet proposal for a Control Council, though with far less sweeping powers than those envisaged in the Russian demands. In addition both Australia and New Zealand desired a more decisive share in participation.

When the Conference of Foreign Ministers met in London for its first session in September 1945 it was evident that the Russians were proposing to include Japan in their general field of obstruction. When the conference closed the British Government had accepted the American proposal of 21 August but objected to the original draft terms of reference and had submitted an alternative draft.[7] The Soviet Government, on the other hand, had virtually withdrawn its original acceptance and it was evident from Molotov's remarks and the subsequent comments of Marshal Stalin to Ambassador Harriman at the celebrated Sochi (or Gagri) conversations of 24–26 October that their attitude was one of 'high dudgeon'.

In consonance with their policy of not allowing Russian obstruction and sulks to prevent progress, the United States reached agreement with Britain and China for an enlarged membership of the F.E.A.C. Invitations were issued to Australia, Canada, France, India, the Netherlands, New Zealand and the Philippine Commonwealth to be added to the composition of the Commission, which held its first session on 30 October under the chairmanship of a distinguished American, General Frank McCoy.†

The Soviet Union refused, however, to take any share in the work of the F.E.A.C., and her participation in the moulding of policy for Japan was only secured by a compromise arrived at during the second session of the Conference of Foreign Ministers held in Moscow in December 1945. In the course of these meetings concessions were made by both the Soviet Union and the United States. Stalin had told Averell Harriman at Gagri that he was willing to concede a dominant American position in Japan, but he insisted on Russia having a real

---

* The invitation stated that 'the membership of the Commission may be increased, as conditions warrant, by the addition of representatives of other United Nations in the Far East'.

† General McCoy had been a member of the Lytton Commission which had inquired into the Mukden Incident in 1931 under the auspices of the League of Nations.

share in the formulation of policy and in the control and administration of Japan. He was not willing, he said, for the Russian representative to be merely 'a piece of furniture'. He was apprehensive lest American policies should result in the development of a Japan capable of becoming a threat to the Soviet Union.

The United States went a long way towards meeting the expressed desires of the United Kingdom and the Soviet Union for the establishment of a Four-Power body in addition to the Ten-Power organization.

The compromise was given effect in the Three-Power Agreement of 26 December 1945, whereby the life of the F.E.A.C. was terminated and in its place were established a Far Eastern Commission (F.E.C.) and an Allied Council for Japan (A.C.J.).[8] Of these the first was composed of the representatives of those countries which had been members of the F.E.A.C. Its duty was to provide for 'full and adequate consultations, as occasion may require, with representatives of the United Nations not members of the Commission in regard to matters before the Commission which are of particular concern to such nations'– a masterpiece of diplomatic drafting obscurity. The task of the Commission was more clearly defined. It was 'to formulate the policies, principles and standards in conformity with which the fulfilment by Japan of its obligations under the terms of surrender may be accomplished'. Operating out of Washington, the F.E.C.'s decisions reached Japan by way of the United States Government which was charged under the December agreement with 'preparing directives in accordance with policy decisions of the Commission and shall transmit them to the Supreme Commander'.

As to the Allied Council for Japan, this was composed of the Supreme Commander, or his deputy, as chairman and United States member, and one representative each from the British Commonwealth, the U.S.S.R. and China. Its seat of operations was in Tokyo and its function was to consult and advise the Supreme Commander. In addition:

> If, regarding the implementation of policy decisions of the Far Eastern Commission on questions concerning a change in the régime of control, fundamental changes in the Japanese constitutional structure, and a change in the Japanese Government as a whole, a member of the Council disagrees with the Supreme Commander (or his deputy), the Supreme Commander will withhold the issuance of orders on these questions pending agreement thereon in the Far Eastern Commission.

This provision was virtually the equivalent of the introduction of the veto, and indeed the whole of the compromise of 26 December 1945 marked a significant retreat from the original principle enunciated by President Truman: 'The experience of Potsdam now made me determined that I would not allow the Russians any part in the control of Japan.'⁹ It soon became a source of grave indignation, first between the President and his Secretary of State, who President Truman was convinced had lost his nerve in dealing with the Russians and had wallowed in appeasement,¹⁰ and then between the Supreme Commander and the State Department.¹¹ It was a part of that general agreement conceded by Secretary Byrnes in Moscow and denounced by the President in his historic phrase: 'I'm sick of babying the Soviets.'*

As matters turned out, however, the decision of Moscow did not constitute a grave menace to American supremacy in the occupation of Japan. The international bodies created in December 1945 soon wrought their own negation. 'The very nature of its composition and procedures eventually made the Far Eastern Commission ineffective', General MacArthur has written. 'All four major powers had a veto. It took time for the commission members to convene, and it took an even longer time for them to make a decision once they had convened.'¹² In its climate of ideas the sessions of the Commission were unusually amicable for a post-war international body on which the Soviet Union and the Americans were represented, and the veto was only infrequently used. It soon settled down 'to a genteel position of pompous futility', as Ambassador Edwin O. Reischauer wrote subsequently. The case of the Allied Council for Japan was even sadder. It became first a place for 'acrimonious argument', and then 'lapsed into a moribund state'.¹³

Though the F.E.C. possessed powers which made it difficult for the United States to modify in any great degree on its own initiative the nature of the occupation or to terminate it, the Commission never had the capacity to control the occupation or to formulate basic policies for it. Despite appearances, neither the United States nor her allies harboured any misunderstandings as to the essentially American nature of the operation, which was frankly recognized as an American undertaking.

III

If there was some degree of dissension among the Powers as to the conduct of the Japanese occupation and the degree of their participation therein, there was a remarkable unity of thought as to the punishment of war criminals. The devious policy which had culminated in the infamy of Pearl Harbor, together with the Rape of Nanking, the Death-March of Bataan, and the 'Railway of Death' in Siam, the

* See above, p. 428.

horrors of Changi Jail, of the camp at Bandung and the Victoria Hospital at Hong Kong, as well as a host of other flagitious cases of brutal cruelty in individual and less-known concentration centres, had rendered it imperative that – like those held ultimately responsible for the perpetration of the atrocities of Auschwitz and Buchenwald and Ravensbrück – these people must be brought to justice.

The Allied intention to visit retribution on those persons had been first announced at the Conference of Foreign Ministers in Moscow in October 1943,* and a few weeks later the three Powers most concerned, the United States, Britain and China, had proclaimed at Cairo at the end of November that they were 'fighting this war to restrain and punish the aggression of Japan'.† This point was reaffirmed by the United States and Britain in the Potsdam Declaration of 26 July 1945, whereby notice had been served that 'There must be eliminated for all time the authority and influence of those who have deceived and misled the people of Japan into embarking on world conquest . . . stern justice will be meted out to all war criminals, including those who have visited cruelties upon our prisoners.'‡

As soon as the processes of Unconditional Surrender had been completed and the full authority of the Allied occupation established, General MacArthur as Supreme Commander took the first steps to transform this policy into performance. Liberated Allied prisoners of war were interviewed by Allied intelligence officers and the Japanese Government was required to deliver accused war criminals to the Supreme Commander (S.C.A.P.) for imprisonment. As a result, by the end of 1945, some six hundred Japanese, ranging from the Marquess Kido (the Emperor's most intimate counsellor) to 'Tokyo Rose' (the famous radio broadcaster) had been arrested and were awaiting trial.

These *détenus* were divided into three classes: first, the major war criminals charged with 'the planning, preparation, initiation or waging' of aggressive war; secondly, those high-ranking military officers charged with command responsibility for troops who had committed atrocities;§ and thirdly, those smaller fry who stood accused of ill-treatment or execution of prisoners of war and civilians.‖ The accused

---

* See above, p. 119.   † See above, p. 136.   ‡ See above, p. 376.

§ Of these 'Class B' prisoners, two distinguished commanders, Generals Yamashita and Homma, held responsible respectively for atrocities on citizens of the Philippine Commonwealth and on American and Filipino prisoners of war, of whom some 70,000 had died, were tried by *ad hoc* military courts at Manila and convicted. Yamashita was hanged, Homma shot.

‖ A number of these 'Class C' criminals were tried locally by British, Australian, Chinese and other Allied military authorities. Most of them, however, were tried at Yokohama. Of the 4,200 in this category, 400 were acquitted, approximately 700 were sentenced to death, and 3,100 to varying terms of imprisonment.[14]

in these three categories were to be tried in accordance with the new concept of international law first used at Nuremberg.* Now, for the second time, this new concept would bring before the bar of justice persons who, in public or private life, had pursued policies of aggression which the military had put into effect against other peoples.

Those arraigned in 'Class A' numbered twenty-seven of the highest ranking members of Imperial Japan's military and political leadership.† They were as follows:

General Sadao Araki, Minister of War 1931–4.

Colonel Kenji Doihara, 'the Lawrence of Asia'.

Colonel Kingoro Hashimoto, participant at the Rape of Nanking, 1937.

Field-Marshal Shunroku Hata, Commander-in-Chief, Central China, 1938.

Baron Kiichiro Hiranuma, President of Privy Council 1930–9; Prime Minister 1939.

Koki Hirota, Foreign Minister 1933–6, 1937–8; Prime Minister 1936–7.

General Seishino Itagaki, War Minister 1938–9; C.-in-C. Korea 1941–5.

Okinari Kaya, Minister of Finance 1937–8; 1941–5.

Marquess Koichi Kido, Keeper of the Privy Seal 1940–5.

General Heitaro Kimura, Vice War Minister 1941–4; C.-in-C. Burma 1944.

General Kuniaki Koiso, C.-in-C. Korea 1935–6; Governor-General, Korea, 1942; Prime Minister 1944–5.

General Iwane Matsui, C.-in-C. Central China 1937–8, at the time of the Rape of Nanking.

Yosuke Matsuoka, President of the South Manchurian Railway 1935–9; Foreign Minister 1940–1.

General Jiro Minami, War Minister 1931; C.-in-C. Kwangtung Army 1934–6; Governor-General, Korea, 1936–42.

* See above, Ch. 17.

† There should have been twenty-eight defendants, but Prince Fumimaro Konoye, the former Prime Minister, successfully committed suicide, by taking poison (as was his right as a member of the *kuge* order), before the opening of the trial. General Hideki Tojo also attempted to perform the traditional *hara-kiri*, but failed. There were two other defendants who died between arrest and indictment before the Tribunal. These were Yosuke Matsuoka, the Foreign Minister who had negotiated the pact of non-aggression with Stalin in 1941, and Admiral Osami Nogano, who as Chief of the Naval Staff had cast the decisive vote in the War Council for the attack on Pearl Harbor. In addition there was the chauvinist writer Shumei Okawa, who was originally included among the accused. He enlivened the proceedings of the opening day of the trial by slapping the bald head of General Tojo, who sat immediately below him in the dock. Okawa was then declared to be too mentally unbalanced to stand his trial and was committed to an institution for the insane.[15]

General Akira Muto, C.O., 2nd Guards Division, Sumatra, 1943; Chief of Staff, 14th Army, Philippines, 1944.

Admiral Osami Nogano, Navy Minister 1936–7; C.-in-C. Combined Fleet 1937; Chief of Naval General Staff 1941–4; Supreme Naval Adviser 1944–5.

Vice-Admiral Takasumi Oka, C.-in-C. Korea Naval Station 1944–5.

Shumei Okawa, organiser of the 'Mukden Incident', 18 September 1931.

Hiroshi Oshima, Ambassador to Germany 1938–9, 1941–5.

Lieutenant-General Kenryo Sato, Chief of Military Affairs Section, Military Affairs Bureau, War Ministry, 1941–2; Chief of Bureau 1942–4.

Mamoru Shigemitsu, Ambassador to U.S.S.R. 1936–8, to Great Britain 1938–41, to Nanking 1941–3; Foreign Minister 1944–5.

Admiral Shigetaro Shimada, C.-in-C. China Fleet 1940; Navy Minister 1941; Chief of Naval General Staff 1944.

Toshio Shiratori, Ambassador to Italy 1939.

Major-General Teiichi Suzuki, President, Cabinet Planning Board, and Minister without Portfolio 1941–3; Cabinet Adviser 1943–4.

Shigenori Togo, Ambassador to Germany 1937, to U.S.S.R. 1938; Foreign Minister 1941–2, 1945.

General Hideki Tojo, War Minister 1940–1; Prime Minister, War Minister and Chief of General Staff 1941–4.

Yoshijiro Umezu, C.-in-C. China 1934; C.-in-C. Kwangtung Army and Ambassador to Manchukuo 1939–44; Chief of General Staff 1944–5.

Whereas the Nuremberg Tribunal was established by the international legal Conference of London during July 1945, and derived its authority from the Allied Control Council, to whom the sovereignty of Germany had been confided by the Four Great Powers who had received her Unconditional Surrender,* the circumstances vis-à-vis Japan were quite different. The Three Powers represented at the Moscow Conference of December 1945, together with China, had designated the Supreme Commander in the Pacific as the authority charged with the implementation of the terms of Japan's surrender. It was therefore on his order, dated 19 January 1946, that an International Military Tribunal for the Far East was constituted and approved for the 'prompt trial and punishment of the major war criminals in the Far East'. It consisted of not less than six and not more than eleven members appointed by the Supreme Commander from a list of names nominated by the

* See above, pp. 402–3.

signatories of the Instrument of Surrender, plus India and the Commonwealth of the Philippines.* The Supreme Commander also appointed
the President of the Tribunal,† but thereafter had nothing further to do
with its proceedings until called upon to pass its final judgements and
to enforce its sentences.[16]‡

'The Case of Hideki Tojo and Others' – as it was officially termed –
was tried by Anglo-Saxon law. The trial began in the auditorium of
the former Imperial War College on 19 January 1946 and continued
for nearly three years. In the course of the proceedings, as the Prosecution and the Defence counsels deployed their arguments, displayed
their evidence and examined and cross-examined their witnesses,§ the
whole pageant of Japanese aggression and overseas conquest, from the
original planning in the 1920s and the Rape of Manchuria in 1931 to
the final humiliation of Unconditional Surrender on 2 September 1945,
was passed in review in sombre legal fashion. Often the long story of
this vastly crowded period of Oriental history became, despite its
horrors and its infamy, incredibly tedious. Not infrequently the wranglings of the attendant legal luminaries seemed pettifogging and picayune,
and it would appear that the Tokyo Tribunal lacked both the dignity
and the precision of that of Nuremberg.[18]‖

At last the wearisome business began to draw to a close. Testimony
and argument were completed in April 1948, and the Tribunal then
adjourned to write its Judgement. It was now that the question of the
Emperor reappeared as a political factor. Among the many witnesses
summoned by the Prosecution had been Henry Pu-yi, sometime
Emperor of China and later of Manchukuo. His appearance on the

* In effect there were eleven judges, representing Australia, Canada, China, France,
India, the Netherlands, New Zealand, the Philippines, the U.S.S.R., the United
Kingdom and the United States.

† Sir William Flood Webb, K.B.E., then Chief Justice of Queensland, now a Justice
of the High Court of Australia.

‡ General MacArthur's own views on the trial of war criminals were expressed as
follows: 'I had approved penalties adjudged against enemy field commanders or other
military personnel who had permitted or committed atrocities against soldiers, and
civilians who had fallen under their custody during the war, but the principle of holding
criminally responsible the political leaders of the vanquished in war was repugnant to
me. I felt that to do so was to violate the most fundamental rules of criminal justice. I
believed, and I so recommended, that any criminal responsibility attached to Japanese
political leaders for the decision to wage war should be limited to an indictment for
the attack on Pearl Harbor, since this act was effected without a prior declaration of
war as required by international law and custom.'[17]

§ A total of 419 witnesses gave their evidence during the trial and a further 779
persons provided depositions and affidavits. The full transcript of the trial ran to
48,412 pages of indifferent paper with limp covers, in marked contrast to the record of
the Nuremberg Tribunal which was admirably bound and printed.

‖ For example, the Nuremberg prisoners were permitted to wear their own clothes or
uniforms, though without insignia of rank, and consequently maintained a quite smart
appearance. The Tokyo prisoners, on the other hand, wore ill-fitting prison garments.

stand had been the occasion for a demand by General Durevyanko, the Soviet representative on the Allied Council, that the Emperor of Japan be also subpoenaed to give evidence. This demand was opposed by the Chief Prosecutor, Joseph Keenan, and disallowed by the Supreme Commander.[19] This grant of immunity, however, was not approved by the President of the Tribunal, Sir William Webb, who made no secret of the fact that, in his view, the Emperor should have been prosecuted, and he ultimately appended a separate opinion to this effect to the Tribunal's Judgement.

Now, during the months in which the members of the Tribunal were in the throes of composition of their Judgement, the rumour became current that the Emperor would abdicate once that Judgement had been rendered. It was, so ran the rumour, the Emperor's desire to share responsibility with his subordinates, and moreover he could not suffer the loss of face if officers were executed for actions committed in his name. This prospect was received with considerable alarm and despondency in the entourage of General MacArthur. Most of the success of the Allied occupation depended upon the close co-operation of the Emperor with the Supreme Commander. Abdication, it was felt, would not only raise an already tense situation to boiling-point but would also undermine the discipline of the Japanese nation vis-à-vis the occupation. By every means possible, therefore – including, it is said, the personal intervention of the General with the Emperor* – the Mikado was advised that his abdication would be a grave disservice to his people and, indeed, politically disastrous. It would appear that this counsel had influence with the Imperial decision – always supposing that the rumours of abdication had ever had any basis of reality.[20] It is a fact that now, over twenty years later, the Emperor still occupies his throne.

It took nearly seven months for the Tribunal to agree upon its Judgement and nine days to deliver it in open court. They began on 4 November 1948 and ended on the twelfth. Command with the Nuremberg Judgement it was a somewhat rambling document but, whether heard or read, it is an impressive and terrifying account of the determination of an ambitious military clique to capture all the organs of the state, to prepare the Japanese mind for military conquest and military rule and, in so doing, to entwine their tentacles so inseverably about the body politic of the nation as to strangle little by little public opinion, parliamentarianism and all sense of international decency. Again and again the Judgement demonstrated with manifest authority the spiritual and moral deterioration of Japanese policy and of its formulation during the two decades which preceded Pearl Harbor, a deterioration which

* There is no mention of such intervention in the Supreme Commander's memoirs.

not surprisingly resulted, once war was declared, in the pattern of cruelty followed in widely separated areas which originated from an authority superior hierarchically to that of field commanders.* It was a grim record of aggression and bullying and brutality, of maltreatment and malfeasance, shot through with assassination, duplicity and deceit. There were few extenuating circumstances.

After the Judgement came the sentences. These were pronounced on 12 November. Unlike Nuremberg, there were no acquittals. Of the twenty-five defendants, seven were condemned to death. There were six generals – Tojo, Itagaki, Doihara, Matsui, Muto and Kimura – and one civilian, Koki Hirota. Of the remainder, sixteen were sentenced to life imprisonment; one, Shigenori Togo, to twenty years' imprisonment and one, Mamoru Shigemitsu, to seven years; it being generally believed that he had only been included among the accused at Soviet insistence, having been Ambassador in Moscow.

The sentences were reviewed by the Far Eastern Commission on 24 November and were upheld in their entirety by a majority vote.† They were then confirmed by the Supreme Commander on 23 December 1948, and the death sentences were carried out on that day. The Great Assize of the Orient was finished.‡

The various criticisms and justifications of the work and circumstances of the International Tribunal of Nuremberg were reiterated in respect of the International Tribunal of Tokyo. The long-range effect

---

* In the opinion of some Far Eastern experts, cruelty in the Japanese armies of occupation originated much more from local commanders and their juniors than from superior authority. One of the paradoxes of the Japanese military machine was the way that discipline was *not* enforced. The War Ministry sent orders to theatre commanders to treat prisoners of war correctly – the official position being that, although Japan was not a party to the Geneva Convention, its provisions would be respected. However, no effort was made by the Ministry to see that these superior orders were obeyed. Nor were theatre commanders any more scrupulous in the matter of supervision; hence many of the atrocities committed on prisoners of war and others.

It would seem that there was no deliberate policy of terrorism or brutality handed down by the 'top brass'. Cruelty was strongest at the lowest level. Terrorism in Japan always came from below. It was not, as in Germany, a situation in which a group of criminals constituted the Government of the country.

For a brilliant analysis of this whole matter of the thought and behavioural patterns of Japan's war-time leaders, see Masao Maruyama's *Thought and Behaviour in Modern Japanese Politics* (Oxford, 1963) pp. 83–134.

† The French representative, General Pechkoff, made a personal appeal for clemency, the Indian, Dr Chakravarty, asked that all death sentences should be commuted to life imprisonment, and the Netherlands representative, Baron Lewe van Aduard, asked for a certain mitigation in the prison sentences of Umezu, Hata, Shigemitsu and Togo, and that Hirota's death sentence should be commuted to life imprisonment.[21]

‡ In February 1949 the Far Eastern Commission announced that no further sessions of the International Military Tribunal would be held and that no further 'Class A' criminals would be tried, it being held that they could be more usefully indicted on 'B' and 'C' charges.

upon international law and international deliberation was much the same in both instances, though Nuremberg, coming first, had the greater impact.

As to the effect upon the Japanese people, it is doubtful whether this was either deep or lasting. The trial was too long and too boring to hold the attention of a people who were virtually struggling to make an existence. Most Japanese were at first glad enough to see brought to justice those leaders whom yesterday they had acclaimed but with whom today they had become disillusioned. But most also were annoyed at having the dishonour of Japan thus dragged into the public domain. Moreover, in view of the pre-war governmental and political structure and the divine nature of the Emperor, the man in the street found no cause to blame himself or to feel the least guilt for the crimes for which his leaders were arraigned and punished. The concept of a people sharing ultimate responsibility for the actions of their leaders was as utterly alien to the minds of the Japanese people as it had been to the Germans. Tojo's open assumption of full responsibility for the war, thereby absolving both the Emperor and the people of Japan from guilt, raised him – with national relief – to a position of a national hero and man of loyalty. Moreover, the fact that certain members of the Tribunal entered dissenting opinions from the majority findings, amounting in the case of the Indian representative to basic disagreement, either bewildered the general public or left it with an impression of cynicism.[22]

Again, as at Nuremberg, one of the greatest assets of the Far Eastern Tribunal was the boon which it conferred on scholars and historians of the period, by reason of the vast bulk of documentary material which it made available and of the research which was accomplished by the Prosecution. Over 4,300 exhibits were admitted in evidence, and this by no means exhausted the treasure trove of new material.

A great experiment in international law had been made and justified. Its long-range value has yet to be assessed.

IV

The Allied occupation of Japan was a phenomenal administrative triumph. The fact that it was, though nominally Allied, in effect virtually an American operation, preserved it from the difficulties which beset similar régimes in Germany and elsewhere in Europe, but the fact that it was largely a 'one-man show' gave it a character and a personality of its own, which was lacking in the European occupation régimes, and also contributed greatly to the success of its achievements.

The presiding genius of the administration was, of course, General Douglas MacArthur, and if there had been any doubt as to the extraordinary nature of this unique individual during the war, his remarkable characteristics were even more brightly illumined in this latest aspect of his highly unusual career.

Probably the most outstanding of the Allied Supreme Commanders in military genius, General MacArthur now revealed himself as that rare figure in our modern world, a conventional concept of a proconsul on the pattern of Imperial Rome and 'an American version of a traditional British grandee'.[23] He was, as it were, a curious amalgam of Lord Kitchener and Lord Curzon in the days of their Indian splendour. But, while he excelled 'K.' in military ability, and vied with him in Olympian detachment, he had all Curzon's vanity and sensitivity – and some of his intellectual gifts also – while lacking his brilliance of mind and his incessant, indomitable capacity for hard work over a prolonged period. No Indian Viceroy in the most effulgent days of the role of the British *raj* had indulged a more complacent self-dramatization than did Douglas MacArthur in these years of occupation. Like Kitchener, he enjoyed the attentions of sycophants. A little group of devoted *claqueurs* had collected about his several war-time headquarters, following him from Manila to Alice Springs and to Tokyo. Some of these obtained posts in the upper echelons of the occupation hierarchy and they saw to it that only the most roseate picture of the General and his régime was transmitted to the outside world. As one British historian has written: 'In their declared opinion the slightest criticism of SCAP amounted to something approaching sacrilege.'[24]

Yet this is not to decry either the personal achievement of General MacArthur or the nature of the Administration which he fathered on Japan. He gave the Japanese people good government at a time when they desperately needed it, when the very roots of their centuries-old political beliefs had withered in the ground, leaving them hopeless and helpless, a potential prey to Communism. For a people, reared and nurtured in the belief of the divinity of their Emperor, to see him degraded in status to that of a ceremonial monarch,[25] 'deriving his position from the sovereign will of the people',[26] it was necessary to have some strong and durable foundation on which to build anew. This MacArthur gave them and they were appreciative. Had the Allied occupation been distinguished by overbearance, corruption and inefficiency, much would certainly have been heard of this during the anti-American reaction which followed its termination. In fact the reverse was the case and on all sides, except the Communist, it was hailed as having been benevolent in intention.

Moreover, the Supreme Commander's very foibles, his magnificence of bearing, even though it approached pomposity; the military grandees of his court; his refusal to expose himself more than was absolutely necessary to the public eye, except on ceremonial occasions; his rejection of all popular contact: these were characteristics which an Oriental people accustomed to tradition could understand and appreciate. 'As conscious as the Japanese themselves of the tremendous drama of history,' one of his American successors claims, 'General MacArthur wrote his name on its pages in even larger letters in peace than he did in war. It will stand as one of the great names in Japanese history, surpassed by few in Japan's long annals and unrivalled by any since the stirring days of the Meiji period.'[27]

This is high praise indeed and it carries with it its own sequel. For it was because General MacArthur had reached this degree of eminence and veneration that the Japanese people may have learned more about democracy from his dismissal by President Truman than from anything which he or his Administration had done or said during his years in Tokyo.

V

The first stage of the planning for the Japanese Peace Treaty was based on the general premise that its guiding principle was the prevention of the recrudescence of Japan's expansionist and militaristic policies. The primary precept of the Allied occupation, as defined in the Initial Post-Surrender Policy Directive, was 'to ensure that Japan will not again become a menace to the United States or to the peace and security of the world', and to this end it was decreed that 'Japan will be completely disarmed and demilitarized. The authority of the militarists and the influences of militarism will be totally eliminated from her political, economic and social life.'[28]

Though there was general agreement on this as a fundamental objective of the Administration established by the Allied Powers, there were various, and to some extent conflicting, ideas as to how it should be implemented. The State Department in Washington favoured in general the speedy conclusion of a peace treaty which should give legal form to the principles laid down in the Post-Surrender Policy Directive. On the other hand there were those in the Departments of the Army and the Navy who envisaged an indefinite occupation, following a preliminary treaty which should merely re-establish diplomatic relations between Japan and the world but should not make full restoration of Japanese sovereignty.[29]

As between these two schools of thought General MacArthur en-couraged the idea of the early termination of the occupation of Japan, which was alleged to be costing a million dollars a day, and the speedy conclusion of a treaty of peace under which the United States, or the United Nations, would assume the protection of the Japanese homeland. It was the Supreme Commander's proclaimed conviction that, having passed through the fiery ordeal of war and defeat, the Japanese people had undergone a change of heart unparalleled in world history. 'Japan today understands as thoroughly as any nation that war does not pay', he asserted. 'Her spiritual revolution has been probably the greatest the world has ever seen.'[30]

One is frequently reminded of the wisdom of Bismarck's dictum that 'What matters is not truth but what people believe to be true'. General MacArthur was convinced of the truth of his belief that Japan's deep-seated desire was for neutral status as 'the Switzerland of the Pacific'. To this end he incorporated into the new Constitution, which he gave to Japan in the name of the Allies, the famous Article 9, which stated:

> War, as a sovereign right of the nation and the threat or use of force, is forever renounced [by Japan] as a means of settling disputes with other nations. The maintenance of land, sea and air forces, as well as other war potential, will never be authorized. The right of belligerency of the State will not be recognized.[31]

Having framed their mental state for the Japanese people and in-terpreted it to them by means of their fundamental law, the Supreme Commander was consistent in his recommendation for defence pro-visions in a treaty of peace. Japan, he advised, should be allowed no armed services, beyond a police force sufficient to deal with internal disorders. Her defence should be undertaken by the United Nations.[32]

It was against this background of conflicting thought that the first tentative steps were taken by the United States Department of State towards a Four-Power agreement on Japan. In the early months of 1946 they prepared a draft treaty on the disarmament and demilitarization of Japan, which was submitted to the Governments of the United Kingdom, the U.S.S.R. and China on 21 June 1946.[33]*

The preamble to this document stated that 'It remains to ensure that the total disarmament and demilitarization of Japan will be enforced as long as the peace and security of the world may require. Only this assurance will permit the nations of Asia and the world to return single-

---

* The suggested treaty paralleled a similar draft agreement between the U.S.A., the U.K., the U.S.S.R. and France, put forward at approximately the same time, for the disarmament and demilitarization of Germany.

mindedly to the habits of peace.' It was thus implied, though not stated, that the disarmament and demilitarization of Japan would apparently continue at the will of the four Contracting Powers and that, at some unspecified moment of time, these might be terminated, despite the provision of Article 9 of the Japanese Constitution that 'The maintenance of land, sea and air forces . . . will never be authorized'.*

The draft treaty of 1946 for Japanese disarmament and demilitarization never achieved fruition because of Soviet intransigence, although both Britain and China accepted its provisions, and a similar fate awaited the attempts of the State Department to initiate negotiations for a peace treaty in 1947. In March of that year two important events occurred. On 17 March, General MacArthur announced to the Press that the military phase of the tasks of the Allied occupation of Japan had been completed and that in his opinion the time was ripe for the conclusion of a peace treaty. When asked when the negotiations should begin, he made the somewhat Delphic reply: 'I will say as soon as possible.'[35] During the same month a State Department working party, headed by Dr Hugh Borton, Special Assistant to the Director of the Office of Far Eastern Affairs, produced draft articles for a treaty of peace which were circulated to the British, Soviet and Chinese Governments.†

As a preliminary, the United States Government suggested in July 1947 that the countries represented on the Far Eastern Commission‡ should convene in a conference of deputies and experts, voting by a two-thirds majority, in the following month of August to work out a definitive treaty of peace with Japan.

The text of the Borton Draft has never been published, but there exist in various American publications a fairly clear summary, as it were from an inspired and informed source.[36] It would appear to have reflected the general view that all precautions must be taken against a military renaissance and that therefore, in accordance with Article 9 of the Constitution, Japan must have no military force, other than police, and no military potential. During a period of not less than twenty-five

---

* It should be noted that, despite the unequivocal provisions of Article 9 of the Constitution of 1946 and before the modifications contained in the Treaty of San Francisco in 1951 had been enacted, foreign observers were able to report in 1950 that 'the nucleus of an army is being formed [in Japan]: the 75,000 strong National Police Reserve will be a highly trained and adequately armed quasi-military body with the functions of maintaining internal order and of combating subversive activity. It will certainly be an efficient force.' Indeed it was, if for no other reason than that, it was alleged, its nucleus was composed of former Japanese soldiers.[34]

In fairness to the Japanese Government, however, it must be stated that this measure of rearmament was very much an American initiative. From 1950 onwards the United States Government, perhaps understandably, pressed strongly for Japanese rearmament.

† The Borton Draft was revised in August 1947 and in January 1948.

‡ See above, p. 491.

years Japan must accept the surveillance of an Allied Commission of Inspection as a surety of her good faith.

There was to be a Council of Ambassadors, composed of representatives of the Powers constituting the Far Eastern Commission, charged with the enforcement of these restrictive provisions and to whom the Commission of Inspection was to report. The Council was also empowered to enforce the continuance of both the economic reforms and the limitations on office-holding imposed under the occupation. No mention was made of the post-treaty security status of Japan, nor of grants of bases to the United States.

The Borton Draft derived more from the spirit of the Second World War than from that of the Cold War, and it was criticized accordingly. Those who shared the somewhat euphoric view of General MacArthur that Japan had undergone a change of heart unparalleled in the history of mankind, denounced the draft as being too draconian and retaliatory and thus rendered unworkable and self-defeating. As one of them commented: 'It was the Treaty of Versailles all over again' – forgetting perhaps that under the provisions of that treaty Japan had made a determined effort to annex the province of Shantung from China!

At the other end of the balance were the American Service Departments who, disgruntled and amazed, marked the lack of provision in the Borton Draft for any means of self-defence for Japan and a strict adherence to the principle of Article 9 of the Constitution. They were deeply distrustful of the capacity of the United Nations to undertake the defence of Japan – indeed the U.N. ability to fill a power vacuum had, in the blunt language of Secretary of the Navy Forrestal, been 'oversold'.[37] They envisaged the United States, already widely committed strategically in the Pacific, as being compelled to assume full responsibility for the defence of a militarily denuded Japan.

The Service Departments were perhaps thinking further ahead than the Borton group, of a clash of interests with the U.S.S.R. in the Pacific, a confrontation in which their hand would be materially strengthened if the United States were in more or less permanent control of the former Japanese island mandates and of the Ryukyu Islands as strategic bases and also if they could count on some degree of support from a potential Japanese Defence Force. The Army favoured an abrogation of Article 9 of the Constitution and a rebuilding of Japan's military forces; together with the Navy, they demanded bases and airfields on Japanese soil and freedom of movement over the whole of the islands. What they infinitely preferred was no peace treaty at all and the continuation of the occupation for an indefinite period.

The views of the British Commonwealth Powers in the Pacific

approximated more nearly to those of the Borton Draft. Neither Australia nor New Zealand was convinced by Japan's newly assumed guise as a peace-loving nation, despite General MacArthur's championship of her sincerity in this role. 'In spite of the complete and apparently willing submission of the Japanese people to the occupation and the display of enthusiasm for democratic concepts,' ran official New Zealand opinion, 'few competent observers are now prepared to be sure that this attitude indicates a change of any permanence. Positive democracy cannot be imposed from outside. . . . In cases of doubt the substance of physical disarmament should not be sacrificed for the shadow of democratic reform.'[38] So much for a Pacific view of Japan's readiness to become 'the Switzerland of the Pacific'.

In effect, however, this first phase of tentative discussions for a Japanese peace treaty petered out ineffectively for a variety of reasons. The original invitation to a conference had been issued from Washington on 11 July 1947 and the date proposed had been a month later, 19 August.[39] This in itself was short notice and rendered British acceptance impossible because of a conflict of dates. Arrangements had already been made, before the receipt of the American invitation, for a Commonwealth Conference at Canberra, at which the whole question of a Japanese peace settlement would be reviewed. The British Government, therefore, begged to be excused, though accepting the general principle of the American proposal that a Japanese treaty should be drafted at a conference of the Powers represented on the Far Eastern Commission, voting by a two-thirds majority.

All the other Powers which had received the United States invitation accepted, with the two vitally important exceptions of China and Russia. The Chinese Government (still at that time the Nationalist régime of Generalissimo Chiang Kai-shek), while accepting the drafting of the treaty within the framework of the F.E.C. Powers, objected to the mode of voting proposed. China first proposed that a negative vote by any two of the Pacific Big Four would constitute a veto,* but later made a sudden and unexpected switch in support of the Soviet proposal that a negative vote by a single one of these Powers would constitute a veto. When this was rejected China declined the invitation.†

---

* This is the account given by Professor Frederick Dunn, but Robert Fearey has a slightly different version to the effect that the first Chinese proposal was that voting be by a two-thirds majority including the affirmative vote of three of the Far Eastern Big Four.[40]

† Professor Dunn conjectures that 'the motivation for this switch was probably fear that Chinese participation in a peace conference from which the Soviet Union abstained would be construed by the latter as a violation of the Sino-Soviet agreement of 1945, which forbade a separate peace with Japan, and that the Soviet Union would then have a legal excuse for aiding the Chinese Communists'.[41]

But the chief source of obstruction was the intransigent objections of the Soviet Government to the whole matter of procedure. Moscow descried at once that a conference such as proposed by Washington, with a provision for a two-thirds majority, would place the Soviet Government at a disadvantage. It was therefore contended that the American proposal was not viable because, on the authority of the Potsdam Protocol of 2 August 1945, the task of drafting peace treaties with the ex-enemy states was delegated to the Council of Foreign Ministers, in which body the method of unanimity of voting obtained, and therefore the weapon of the veto.

It was a fact, however, that Japan was not named in this Protocol because it was framed before the Soviet Union's entry into the Pacific War.* The present Soviet proposal was that it would be in conformity with the spirit of the Protocol for the Council of Foreign Ministers, on which for this purpose China should replace France, to become the body responsible for the drafting of the Japanese treaty preparatory to its submission to the United Nations.

Bearing in mind the current record of obstruction and delay resulting from the adamant attitude of the Soviet Government in the Council of Foreign Ministers over the treaties with the European ex-enemy states, which had made it impossible to frame any peace treaty with Germany,† the State Department neatly side-stepped the Soviet contention with the counter-argument that, since Japan was not mentioned in the terms of reference of the Council of Foreign Ministers, any extension of the competence of that body could be accomplished only with the consent of all. If therefore one of the Council Powers refused its co-operation, the Council would remain constitutionally incapable of drafting a Japanese peace treaty, and it was left fairly obvious which Power that might be.

Thus a stalemate resulted and, in view of the manifestly unfruitful prospects of a conference in which Great Britain could not, and the Soviet Union and China would not, participate, the United States Government accepted the inevitable and resigned itself to a period of 'marking time'.

VI

When the second phase of consideration for a Japanese peace treaty opened in the spring of 1950 it did so against an altogether new back-cloth of world events and with an almost entirely new cast. In May 1947 the United States had taken over from Britain the responsibility for

---

* See above, p. 384.   † See above, Chs. 18 and 19.

aiding Greece and Turkey against Soviet-inspired Communist threats. *
By the end of 1948 the Cold War was a thing in being – in Europe with
the Soviet blockade of Berlin in full swing and in Asia with ample
evidence that the Soviet High Command was building up the armed
forces of North Korea with a view to striking at her southern neighbour.
A further Asiatic complication was the complete triumph of Communist
arms on the mainland of China and the withdrawal of the Nationalist
Government to the island of Taiwan (Formosa).

The United States had entered the lists as the champion of democratic government against Communist aggression and she rapidly discovered that she needed all the support, direct and indirect, that was
available. In the case of Japan this new situation produced divided
counsels at Washington, but more and more the thinking at the highest
level tended to shift away from a punitive and restrictive settlement.
What was now required of Japan was a status and bearing of friendly
co-operation, with the Americans banking on the durability of the
lesson in democratic government which they had administered during
the occupation.† Step by step Japan was treated less and less as a defeated enemy and more and more as being ready for readmission into
membership of the family of nations.

This trend reached a climacteric in November 1948 when President
Truman's National Security Council took the momentous decision
that, in order to foster the goodwill of the Japanese people after termination of the occupation, a considerable degree of responsibility in all
fields was to be shifted from General MacArthur to the Japanese
Government and that the Supreme Commander's personnel was to be
considerable reduced. Moreover, the national police force was to be
increased to 150,000 and Japan was to be allowed to assimilate the
reforms included in the new Constitution at her own pace and in her
own way.‡

This was indeed a long way from the Borton Draft and Article 9 of
the new Constitution and also from that hazy mirage of Japan as 'the
Switzerland of the Pacific' – and this was but a beginning.§

* See below, p. 563.

† But it was the recorded view of John Alison, Director of the Office of Northern
Asiatic Affairs in the State Department, 'that, under the best circumstances and
management, the chances were not better than even that after the occupation the
Japanese people would continue the liberal, democratic and peaceful society we [the
United States] had sought to establish'.[42]

‡ This decision, which greatly diminished the impact of the effects of the occupation,
derived much in origin from recommendations made by George Kennan to General
Marshall (the Secretary of State) after his return from a confidential mission to Japan
in February and March of 1948.[43]

§ It is a matter of interest that the notion of a punitive peace died hard. In a new
draft for a treaty with Japan prepared in the State Department as late as September

On 7 January 1949, President Truman announced the resignation of General Marshall as Secretary of State and the nomination of Dean Acheson as his successor. It was an epic decision, for it brought to be the President's highest adviser on foreign policy a man who had the most outstanding qualifications of statesmanship – wisdom, courage, humour, imagination and determination. This is not to say that Mr Acheson was not a controversial figure. He had never not been that. His elegant and aristocratic bearing, his waspish and irrepressible wit, and his frank refusal to suffer fools gladly – or, indeed, at all – had brought him both friends and enemies in Washington, and even his personal loyalty to a friend – as displayed in his refusal 'to turn his back' on Alger Hiss, a former law associate and State Department colleague, after his conviction for perjury – had been turned against him. He was more than suspected of Leftist propensities by die-hard elements in both political parties, and his fearless conduct of American foreign policy, along sometimes somewhat unconventional lines, evoked vituperative criticism of the most bitter nature.

Convinced that the issue of a Japanese treaty should be both revitalized and refurbished, Acheson began at once to take soundings within his own Department and that of Defence. The result was a monumental row which threatened the practical continuation of the bipartisan approach to foreign affairs which had rendered the foreign policy of the United States so forceful and effective.[45]

It took the better part of a year before, as a general result of Dean Acheson's cajolery and compulsion, the State Department, the Defence Department and the Supreme Commander were in accord, first as to whether a treaty with Japan were desirable or not, and secondly what kind of a treaty it should be. The search for a formula which was acceptable to all three parties was materially facilitated when, in September 1950, President Truman recalled General George Marshall from retirement and appointed him Secretary of Defence in the room of Colonel Louis A. Johnson.

In the midst of all this welter of personalities and clash of departmental interests, the Secretary of State pressed forward with his own studies and preparations for a treaty. He was increasingly anxious to reach a state of stability in Japanese affairs, a climate of ideas which

---

1949, there was very little change from the Borton Draft of January 1948. Although there was no provision for reparation payments in the draft of September 1949, it did contain restrictions on Japanese sovereignty and on the nation's war-making ability. The Japanese were not to be permitted to engage in certain manufactures which had a war-potential, and troops, of which 85 per cent were to be United States forces, were to be stationed in Japan for an unspecified period after the peace settlement had come into force.[44]

would render the restored relations between Japan and her former enemies amicable rather than *revanchiste*, and pave the way for a new era of understanding in the Pacific.

While the increasing tempo of the Cold War was an ever-galling goad to reduce the situation in the Pacific to one of normality and readiness to meet any crisis which might arise in that area, Dean Acheson was also under pressure from America's principal ally, Britain, to hasten the process of treaty-making. Mr Attlee's Government were themselves being pressed to this end by Parliament and by the Governments of the Commonwealth countries, and it was inevitable that this issue would figure prominently in the discussions at the forthcoming Commonwealth Conferences at Canberra in November 1949 and at Colombo in January 1950.

As a result of this long-distance needling and of a series of very important conversations in Washington during the visit in mid-September of Ernest Bevin and his chief adviser on Far Eastern affairs, Sir Esler Dening, a joint Anglo-American communiqué was issued on 14 September 1949 to the effect that both countries had agreed on the urgency of a peace treaty with Japan.[46] Two weeks later, on 29 September, an instruction was issued to the divisions of the State Department concerned to prepare with speed a new draft treaty for communication to the British and Commonwealth Governments.

This draft, which was completed by 13 October 1949, marks the first step towards a non-punitive peace with Japan, the first instrument which took into consideration the existence of the Cold War, President Truman's 'containment' policy and the vital decisions of the National Security Council in November 1948. It was as important and significant in its way as the decision of the Conference of Foreign Ministers taken in New York a year later to rearm Germany.

The new draft, because of the speed which attended its inception, was an incomplete document. It dealt mainly with the political and social aspects of the treaty, leaving the security provisions to be inserted after further consultation with the Defence Department – and agreement here was a very long time a-borning. But it served as a basis for a step forward in joint United States–British–Commonwealth thinking, and this in itself was worth while.

The October 1949 draft had for its basic concept the restoration of Japanese sovereignty, if not totally at least with as few restrictions as possible. The F.E.C., the Allied Council and the office of the Supreme Commander were to be terminated, and no machinery for control or inspection (as had been envisaged in the Borton Drafts) was to replace them. Japan was to be required to observe and maintain the democratic principles contained in the New Constitution, but the agrarian, labour and other reforms imposed by the occupation were left for their execution to the discretion and sense of timing of the Japanese Government. Japan was to make reparation to those states which had been victims of her aggressive policies.[47]

Though Dean Acheson was himself in approval of the terms of the draft of 13 October, he foresaw that there were rocks and shoals ahead which must be negotiated before any craft built on these lines could be brought safely to port. The British might conceivably, and in the long run, accept the principle of a non-punitive treaty, but the Commonwealth Governments, notably Australia and New Zealand, were in no such forgiving mood and it would require all the moral courage, political guile, sincere faith and sheer physical guts at the Secretary of State's disposal before a United States Senate, mindful of the collective memories of its constituents and of the Bataan March and many subsequent Japanese atrocities which had been suffered by American prisoners of war, could be persuaded to accept a treaty which was not only in the main non-punitive but provided for the continuation of American economic aid to Japan.

Moreover, the very personality and record of the Secretary of State militated against him, and he knew it. 'Can you imagine my asking Congress for this kind of treaty?' he once said. 'They would say, "Here comes this communist Acheson. Now he wants to help the Japs!"'[48] Dean Acheson knew that if the treaty were to have the remotest chance of success it must draw forcefully upon the support of the bipartisan foreign policy in the Senate, and he also knew that there was growing Republican dissatisfaction on that score.[49]* What was necessary was not just a bipartisan block of votes but the introduction of certain eminent Republicans into the highest level of the State Department hierarchy who should bear a part in the planning of Far Eastern policy and shoulder a share in the burden of responsibility for bringing that policy to fruition.

Acheson took soundings on Capitol Hill, notably from Senator Arthur Vandenberg (then a very sick man), and made certain recommendations to the President with the result that on 19 April 1950 President Truman announced the appointment of John Foster Dulles, up to that moment a potential Republican contestant for the Governorship of the State of New York, as principal consultant to the Secretary of State on bipartisan foreign policy. It was tacitly understood, though

* George Kennan wrote, somewhat lugubriously and not perhaps quite accurately, in his diary on 30 August 1949: 'It is ironic that our principal reason for wanting a treaty of peace [with Japan] at this time is that it appears to be the only way of solving internal administrative difficulties within our own Government.'[50]

it was not explicitly stated, that his duties would be exclusively concerned with the preparation of the final draft of the Japanese Peace Treaty.[51]*

With the wisdom of hindsight it may be said that in his handling of this episode of the Japanese Peace Treaty, that remarkable and volatile statesman, John Foster Dulles, achieved his 'finest hour'. Certain it is, on the authority of his widow, that he later looked back to this diplomatic assignment as one of the most important achievements of his life.[52] Nor was he in error. The assignment called upon his most vital attributes, but not to excess. He was enabled to give free rein to his natural peripateticism without incurring the – perhaps justifiably – exasperated comment of Adlai Stevenson: 'Don't do something, Foster, just stand there.' He flew many hundreds of thousands of miles in fact-finding tours and in his searches for a treaty formula which might prove acceptable to all concerned. He was patient and single-minded and, on the whole, truthful – attributes of his which later in his career were to be called in question. Perhaps most important of all, he was not, as he subsequently became, in competition with anyone – neither with Adlai Stevenson at home nor Anthony Eden abroad. The result was a magnificent piece of bipartisan statesmanship, worthy of the grandson and nephew of American Secretaries of State.

It was in the middle of Foster Dulles's first visit to Japan, in June 1950, that the invasion of South Korea by North Korean armoured columns on 25 June wrought a complete change in the whole concept of Pacific relations. Now it became clear in the United States that pressure of events had swept away all idea of a punitive peace with Japan or that the conclusion of a treaty should be long delayed. In circumstances of open warfare against Communism in Korea, the evolution of a friendly and symbiotic Japan was highly desirable. Obstacles, hitherto seemingly insurmountable, were swept away; opposition crumbled. The potential danger now came from too great a swing of the pendulum, namely that concessions might go too fast and too far.

Foster Dulles now found himself in a triangular quandary. The United States had swung well away from a punitive peace and was willing to go a long way towards restoring to Japan both her complete sovereignty and her right of self-defence. Japan was anxious to profit to the hilt from this change of front, but at the same time to avoid giving the impression that she avidly desired to rearm. The Government of Prime Minister Shigeru Yoshida therefore pursued a course of policy which seemed to involve an endless series of permutations

* At the same time another prominent Republican, destined for future high office and performance, was appointed to the State Department in a consultative capacity – John Sherman Cooper.

and tergiversations, and which was at once evocative of exasperation and suspicion.[53]

There remained also those Pacific states which had felt in their own throats the iron-shod heel of Japan triumphant. Australia, New Zealand and the Philippine Republic deprecated the rearmament of Japan and called for a full indemnity in reparation. It was all very well for the United States, with its great wealth and power and its evident brevity of memory, to propound now the doctrine of a 'soft' peace with Japan, but, as a Filipino spokesman announced: 'The United States is rich but we are not . . . we have said repeatedly that the Pacific peace treaty must not be a unilateral or bilateral operation. If that is true technically, it is also true morally.'[54]

The only solution to this dilemma of conflicting views seemed to Mr Dulles to lie in the United States assuming greater security liabilities in the Pacific area. The very natural and understandable fears of the Pacific Powers aroused at the prospect of a rearmed Japan, uninhibited by the imposition of reparation payments and therefore on the way to an economic recovery which would place her in lively industrial and agricultural competition with her neighbours, would only be assuaged if the United States could undertake certain major specific security obligations vis-à-vis both Japan and the Pacific states.

This view Dulles expounded to Dean Acheson who, with the approval of the Defence Department, accepted his thesis and endorsed it in a lengthy memorandum to President Truman, dated 7 August 1950. A month later, on 8 September, the President gave a formal directive for the preparation of a final treaty of peace to be concluded with all possible speed, and gave to Dulles the authority to negotiate bilateral treaties with all states concerned.[55] It was the enunciation of this Presidential fiat which paved the way for the convening of the San Francisco Conference and the signing of the Treaty of Peace with Japan just one year later.

VII

The new and penultimate phase of the Japanese Peace Treaty began during the session of the General Assembly of the United Nations in New York on 22 September 1950. On this day, John Foster Dulles, as the special representative of President Truman, handed to the representatives of the fourteen other states represented on the F.E.C.* a 'tentative and suggestive' document outlining the views of the United

---

* The fourteen recipient states were Australia, Burma, Canada, Ceylon, China, France, India, Indonesia, the Netherlands, New Zealand, Pakistan, the Philippine Republic, the Soviet Union and the United Kingdom.

States on a desirable treaty with Japan, and suggesting that 'after there has been an opportunity to study this outline, there will be a series of informal discussions designed to elaborate on it and make clear any points which may be obscure at a glance'.[56]

The Americans' view was itself summarized in a Memorandum of Seven Points:

1. The treaty should be signed by all the states which had been at war with Japan, forty-nine in all, including China.
2. All signatories of the treaty should undertake to support Japan's admission to the United Nations.
3. The Bonin and Ryukyu Islands should be placed under United States trusteeship, while Korea was to become independent. The future of the Kurile Islands and of Formosa was to be settled by the Big Four, or, if they failed to produce an agreed settlement within one year, by the U.N. General Assembly.
4. Japan to make facilities available to the armed forces of the United States to assure Japan's security.
5. Japan to observe international agreements on fishing, drug-control, etc., and, pending the conclusion of new commercial agreements, to extend most-favoured-nation treatment, subject to the normal exceptions.
6. Signatories of the treaty were to retain Japanese assets within their territories, but to waive all claims against Japan for reparation.
7. All disputes concerning claims to be referred to a special tribunal of the International Court at The Hague or to be settled by the conventional machinery of diplomacy.[57]

It was clear from the United States Memorandum that Washington envisaged the forthcoming peace treaty as recalling Japan into the comity of nations without any economic limitations and enjoying the same rights of individual and collective self-defence as those of any other member-state of the United Nations. She was, in fact, to be allowed to rearm at her own discretion. This drew forth the liveliest symptoms of trepidation and protest from Canberra and from Wellington, which were expressed in the somewhat acrid debates of the Commonwealth Prime Ministers' Meeting in London in January 1951. All the countries of the West admitted the danger of Japan being overwhelmed and incorporated in the Communist empire and all were in accord that every kind of means must be taken to prevent such a catastrophe, but, as Lord Casey* has written, there were some states, such

* The Rt Hon. Richard, Baron Casey, K.G., former Australian Minister of External Affairs and Governor-General of Australia.

as Australia and New Zealand, 'which believed that this danger could still be guarded against if there were some limitations on the size and range of Japan's armed forces'.[58]

These apprehensive views did not prevail because John Foster Dulles was determined that they should not. He not only rejected them in principle, he went to Australia and New Zealand and castigated those who held them. His practical argument was that, if the treaty contained the limitations desired by Canberra and Wellington and Manila, who was to play policeman and enforce them? But his main belief was that any continuing limitation on Japanese sovereignty would render it less easy for Japan to be associated with the West and thus defeat the object of the operation. Completely and absolutely was he opposed to anything remotely smacking of a 'punitive peace', and he denounced the attitude of the Pacific Powers as being 'outdated' and resembling the mentality of the Versailles *Diktat*.[59]*

With characteristic dynamic energy, Mr Dulles pressed forward and carried his colleagues along with him on the wings of his own indefatigable ardour. In March 1951 a provisional United States draft treaty was circulated to the fourteen Powers, and also to the Republic of Korea, and early in April the United Kingdom handed to the United States Government an independently prepared draft, which was also circulated to all Commonwealth Governments.

The main grounds of disagreement between Britain and the United States was that of the representation of China. After the Commonwealth Prime Ministers' Conference of January 1951, Mr Bevin urged on the State Department the necessity of inviting the People's Republic of China to the conference talks, and, for good measure, proposed that Formosa be returned to that Government. This was a sternly practical view based on the pragmatic premise that Generalissimo Chiang Kai-shek was no longer a Head of State and that the Communist régime in China, however much it might be regretted, was indeed a *fait accompli*. But Dulles would have none of it, and Dean Acheson firmly refused even to approach the Peking Government for its views on this or any other subject – whereupon the British Government vetoed the inclusion of the Nationalist Government in Taipeh. The ensuing deadlock was resolved, in June 1951, at the suggestion of Mr Dulles, by a secret agreement between himself and Herbert Morrison, who had succeeded Bevin as Foreign Secretary, that neither Chinese régime should be invited to the Peace Conference provided that Japan concluded a

---

* Mr Dulles was equally trenchant in disposing of the claims of the Philippine Republic which, as Dean Acheson subsequently wrote, was left 'simmering in their dream of eight billion dollars in reparations'.[60]

bilateral treaty of peace, within three years of the coming into force of the general treaty, 'with any state that had been at war with Japan and had adhered to the Declaration of the United Nations of 1 January 1942'. Dulles and Morrison also agreed that Japan's future attitude towards China 'must necessarily be for determination by Japan itself in the sovereign and independent status contemplated by the treaty'.[61]*

Meanwhile the Soviet Union was obstinately adhering to its claim that the Conference of Foreign Ministers was alone the body empowered to draw up a peace treaty with Japan. In a note to the United States Government of 7 May, the Soviet view was reiterated, but with the mild concession that other countries which were at war with Japan might be brought into the preliminary drafting work. It was, however, clearly stated that no foreign troops or bases should be permitted in Japan following the coming into force of the peace treaty, and that Japan should not lose sovereignty over the Ryukyu and Bonin Islands. The People's Republic of China associated itself with the Soviet view. The reply of the United States, delivered on 19 May, and of which the Secretary of State was the chief architect, was couched in such terms as to earn from President Truman the *imprimatur* of approval: 'Dean; this document is a jewel. H.S.T.'[62] – but it did not quench the vehemence of Soviet expression. Moscow continued to insist upon the legal rectitude of the Russian thesis until the last possible moment when, much to the surprise of all – and the apprehension of many – she declared her intention of attending the San Francisco Conference.

By June 1951 the United States and United Kingdom Governments had reached a sufficient degree of accord for the completion of a joint draft treaty[63]† which, after discussion with the Powers chiefly concerned, was circulated on 20 July to all states at war with Japan. Early comments were invited and it was suggested that a conference for the formal conclusion of the treaty should meet at San Francisco in September.

---

* The Taipeh Government of Marshal Chiang Kai-shek was kept informed by the United States Government of the subsequent developments towards the conclusion of a treaty. A similar office was performed for the Peking Government by the Soviet Union.

For a discussion of the 'Yoshido Letter' incident, see below, App. B.

† The Anglo-American draft treaty was sent in the first instance on 3 July to the Powers chiefly concerned and received its wider circulation on 20 July. Certain amendments to the original text, which was made public on 12 July, were included in that circulated on 20 July, and as a result of subsequent comments further amendments were to be found in the text presented to the delegates to the San Francisco Conference on 4 September. This semi-final draft was published on 13 August.

VIII

The unusual, not to say unique, character of the preliminaries to the Japanese Peace Treaty was continued in the final phase of the saga. Under the courageous leadership and sagacious control of Dean Acheson, Foster Dulles's skill and determination had bulldozed America's war-time allies into accepting the kind of peace which America wanted and which America believed was best for the world. Apart from consultation within the British Commonwealth, there had been little or no attempt, or indeed opportunity, to exchange views among the Powers concerned on the American proposals, except bilaterally with Mr Dulles. The British Government had eventually sufficiently identified itself with the views of the United States to become a co-sponsor of the draft treaty of 20 July, but, in effect, there was no suggestion of equality between the two sponsors.

One by one those Powers which had raised objections to the Anglo-American draft had either been mollified or compensated by promises of American aid and protection. This had been achieved not by multilateral negotiations but by the indefatigable personal efforts of Mr Dulles. Never before in modern times had a great treaty, concerning the interests of some fifty-two sovereign states, been negotiated, and generally agreed, on the basis of bilateral discussions. Only the U.S.S.R. and the People's Republic of China had remained unmollified and unappeased, to the extent that, as a result, China, the earliest victim of Japanese aggression, was not a party to the treaty.*

As with the preliminaries, so with the 'end-product'. When the invitations to San Francisco were issued, the terms of reference of the conference were clearly laid down. The purpose of the conference was, not to negotiate, but 'for Conclusion and Signature of a Treaty of Peace with Japan' on the terms of the Anglo-American draft already generally agreed.[64]†

Though the proceedings of the conference partook somewhat of the cut-and-dried, only the brilliant and forceful presiding genius of Dean Acheson, who had been voted unanimously to the chair, preserved decorum and navigated the course of the sessions between the Scylla of ineptitude and the Charybdis of obstruction.[66] As might have been expected, the Soviet Union and its *cortège habituel* – in this case Poland

---

* Despite the fact that the Royal Italian Government of Marshal Badoglio had declared war on Japan in 1944, Italy, in company with the other ex-Axis Powers, was not invited to San Francisco.

† Mr Dulles, in his speech to the conference on behalf of the sponsors, made an extremely plausible and credible explanation as to how and why the United States had assumed so forthright an initiative in the preparation of the treaty.[65]

and Czechoslovakia – seized every opportunity to obstruct and occlude the proceedings of the conference, beginning from the first day.

For example, when the draft rules of procedure, based on the terms of the invitation, were moved for adoption, M. Gromyko, on behalf of the Soviet Union, took occasion to raise the question of the absence of the Chinese Communist Government. Mr Acheson ruled him out of order. M. Gromyko challenged the ruling, and his Polish colleague, Stefan Wierblowski, was allowed five minutes to support him. At the end of this period M. Wierblowski was still speaking; he went on and on, though the President had recognized the British delegate, the Hon. Kenneth Younger. He continued to talk despite repeated interruptions and admonitions from the chair. Finally, when Mr Younger had begun his own speech, the Pole reluctantly relinquished the podium and returned to his seat, still muttering, having, in the words of James Reston, 'out-shouted, outcharged, out-challenged and outraged' every other delegation.[67]

This incident was, in fact, the real 'crunch' of the conference. Dean Acheson's ruling was sustained by thirty-five votes to three. His chairmanship had prevailed and thereafter his authority was never seriously challenged.

The Treaty of Peace with Japan which was ultimately 'concluded and signed' on 8 September 1951 at San Francisco did not vary very greatly from the Anglo-American draft text. Its main provisions dealt with cession of territory, the question of security, economics, claims and property, and the settlement of disputes.[68]

The state of war between Japan and each of the Allied Powers was terminated and Japan's full sovereignty over her territories and territorial waters was recognized by these same Powers (Article 1).

The terms laid down in the Potsdam Declaration of 26 July 1945 had confined Japanese sovereignty to the four main islands of Honshu, Shikoku, Kyushu and Hokkaido, together with other minor adjacent islands, including Tsushima, and this was confirmed in the treaty; under Article 2, Japan renounced 'all rights, titles and claims' to Korea, Formosa and the Pescadores, to the Kurile Islands, southern Sakhalin, the former Pacific mandates, the Spratly and Paracel Islands and all connection with any part of the Antarctic area. The treaty did not determine the ultimate disposition of these territories. Indeed the conference side-stepped this important point with a mixture of agility and pusillanimity. In view of the absence of Allied unity as to the future of Formosa and the Pescadores, it was agreed that, in the interest of a speedy settlement, no attempt should be made in the treaty to resolve this complex question and that the conference should content itself with removing them from Japanese sovereignty.

The Ryukyu and Bonin Islands were not ceded by Japan, but Article 3 provided for the continued administration of these islands by the United States.

The treaty placed no restrictions on the Japanese economy, nor did it limit Japan's right to take part in the trade of the world. Agreements establishing permanent relations between Japan and the Allied Powers in trading, maritime and other commerical activities (Article 12), as well as high-seas fishing (Article 9) and international air transport (Article 13), were to be negotiated between Japan and such Allied Powers so desiring.

Article 14 of the treaty, which dealt with the general principle of reparations, was essentially a compromise between the views of those countries, such as Indonesia and the Philippines, which had suffered heavy damage as a result of Japanese aggression and wished to see their claims made good, and, on the other hand, the reasoning of the United States which had already expended over $2,000 million on providing Japan with essential imports of food and raw material. The Washington Government was understandably unwilling to continue America's economic assistance to Japan in order to make possible reparations to other countries, the payment of which would jeopardize the attainment of a self-sufficient Japanese economy. In order, therefore, to meet both points of view to some degree, Japan was called upon, under Article 14, to recognize her ability to make reparation payments for war damage inflicted by her on certain of the Allies, but the Allies as a whole for their part acknowledged her actual inability to make such payments because of her presently insufficient resources. In order to give some more practical measure of satisfaction and consolation to Japan's erstwhile victims, she was declared willing to compensate them by making available to them certain technical services in production, salvaging, etc. In addition, each of the Allied Powers was granted the right to dispose of Japan's assets within their jurisdiction.

There remained the problem of security which, for the Pacific Powers, constituted the whole crux of the matter of peace with Japan. Whether the threat to their security came from a potential revival of Japanese expansionist policies or from the current menace of Communist aggression,* it was keenly felt by Australia, New Zealand and the Philippine

* Not unnaturally it was the menace of Communist aggression which Mr Yoshida, on behalf of Japan, stressed in his statement to the San Francisco Conference, where he represented Japan as 'beaten and battered, dispossessed of her overseas possessions and resources . . . absolutely incapable of equipping herself for modern warfare to such an extent as to make her a military menace to her neighbours'.[69]

Republic that such a threat most certainly existed, and there was little within the peace treaty itself to allay their apprehensions.[70]

It was true that, by virtue of Article 5 of the treaty, Japan accepted the obligations set forth in Article 2 of the Charter of the United Nations and in particular those which required her to settle her international disputes by peaceful means 'in such a manner that international peace and security and justice are not endangered'; to refrain in her international relations from the threat or use of force against the territorial integrity or political independence of any state, 'or in any other manner inconsistent with the Purposes of the United Nations'; and to give to the United Nations every assistance in its efforts for the making and preservation of peace and to withhold such assistance from any law-breaking state against whom the United Nations was proceeding. But these were regarded as but pious affirmations of good intention, and the treaty imposed upon Japan nothing as sweeping as Article 9 of the new Constitution.* Indeed it was rather to the contrary. Under the last paragraph (c) (i) of Article 5, full recognition was made of the fact that Japan as a sovereign state possessed 'the inherent right of individual or collective self-defence referred to in Article 51 of the Charter of the United Nations and, further, that she might voluntarily enter into collective security arrangements'.†

In order to fulfil her obligations assumed under Article 3, paragraph (a) (iii), it would be a logical conclusion that Japan should revive and rearm her military forces, and it was in view of this that Australia and New Zealand had produced stringent criticisms of the early American proposals. Nor were they reassured by the attitude of the British Government. Although Britain's policy had not reached the degree of wholesale scuttle 'East of Suez' achieved by Harold Wilson's Labour Administration in the later sixties, there were already indications that His Majesty's Government in London could no longer assume massive measures of defence in the Pacific. It was as a result of this that the Australian and New Zealand Governments reluctantly capitulated to Mr Dulles's beguiling blandishments.

At this time the United States was not itself desirous of large-scale Japanese rearmament (this was to come later), but the only alternative to such rearmament was that others should assume the defence of Japan. This Mr Dulles was not prepared to advocate and there was some tentative consideration of the idea of a Pacific Pact.[71] Gradually, however, it became clear that if such a guarantee of Japanese security and

* See above, pp. 502–3.

† This wording is similar to that contained in Article 17 of the Austrian State Treaty of 1955 (see above, p. 484). Japan was admitted to membership of the United Nations in 1956.

continued disarmament was to be assumed it must be among those heavy burdens and responsibilities which America had undertaken in her new role of arbiter of the Pacific.

As a result, therefore, of this great realization of a sense of mission by America, three documents were signed, additional to the Treaty of San Francisco. The first, coincidentally on 8 September, was a Security Treaty between the United States and Japan. It contained only a preamble and four Articles. The preamble stated that, though under Article 5 of the Treaty of Peace Japan had assumed certain obligations vis-à-vis the United Nations, in pursuance of Articles 2 and 51 of the Charter, she was, in effect, not in possession of effective means of exercising her inherent right of self-defence because she had been disarmed. 'There is a danger to Japan in this situation because irresponsible militarism has not yet been driven from the world.' By reason of this danger 'Japan desires, as a provisional arrangement for its defence' that the United States should maintain troops and military installations on her territory. The temporary nature of the arrangement was underlined by the explicit expectation that 'Japan will itself increasingly assume responsibility for its own defence against direct or indirect aggression, always avoiding any armament which could be an offensive threat or serve other than to promote peace and security . . .'. In other words, Japan was granted the right, and indeed the duty, to make a progressive process of rearmament along conventional lines.

The treaty was of indefinite duration and was to expire whenever in the opinion of the two Governments 'there shall have come into force such United Nations arrangements for such alternative individual or collective security dispositions as will satisfactorily provide for the maintenance by the United Nations or otherwise of international peace and security in the Japan area'.†

Four days before the opening of the San Francisco Conference, and a week preceding the signature of the Security Treaty with Japan, the United States had concluded (on 1 September) a tripartite agreement with Australia and New Zealand, to be known as the ANZUS Treaty. This was the price of acceptance by the two senior Pacific members of

---

† Indeed a pious aspiration! When the terms of the U.S.–Japanese Security Treaty came to be reviewed in 1960, the agreement was recast on a basis of equality as a pact of mutual obligation. Ten years later, early in 1970, during conversations between President Nixon and Eisaku Sato, the Japanese Prime Minister, the latter stated that it was now accepted by his Government that, though Japan's 'self-defence forces' would only be used against 'active aggression', a retaliatory attack provoked by American combat operations mounted against a third country from bases in Japan would come under this heading.[72]

the British Commonwealth of the American line in the Japanese Peace Treaty. It also represented for the United States a further assumption of obligation for the defence of the West against Communism to those which she had already assumed in Europe under the North Atlantic Alliance and was about to assume in South-east Asia with less notable success.

Though the treaty comprised eleven articles, the essential provisions were contained in Articles II–IV, and there is a marked resemblance between them and those of the NATO Treaty of 1949, which had its genesis in the historic Vandenberg Resolution of the previous year.* The basic undertaking among the signatories was that they should consult together whenever any one of them should consider themselves the object of a threat to their territorial integrity, political independence or national security in the Pacific area (Article III) and that, by means of continuous and effective self-help and mutual aid, they would maintain and develop their individual and collective capacity to resist armed attack (Article II). It was agreed that since such an armed attack in the Pacific area on any of the three states would be dangerous to the peace and safety of all of them, all three would act to meet the common danger, each 'in accordance with its constitutional processes'.[73]

The third of the supplementary defence treaties was that between the United States and the Philippine Republic, signed at San Francisco on 30 August 1951. Like the ANZUS agreement, it was for mutual defence and its essence was contained in Article IV, wherein each party stated that an armed attack in the Pacific area upon either of them would be 'dangerous to its own peace and safety',‡ and added that 'it would act to meet the common dangers in accordance with its constitutional processes'. The remainder of the treaty provisions were, *mutatis mutandis*, virtually identical with the ANZUS Treaty.

By the conclusion of these three treaties for defence, the United States sought to forge a shield of security around the Pacific system established by the Treaty of San Francisco. It attempted to combat the threat of Communism and also to diminish the danger of a renewal of Japanese militarism and expansionist aggression. A further step towards the realization of both these objectives was taken with the signature at Manila, on 8 September 1954 (just three years after the Treaty of San Francisco), of the South-east Asia Collective Defence Treaty (SEATO), which extended the provisions of the ANZUS Treaty to a multilateral agreement in which Britain, France, Pakistan and Thailand joined the

---

* See below, pp. 582–3.
‡ These words are taken from President James Monroe's Message to Congress of 2 December 1823, which became historic as the Monroe Doctrine.

522   *The Semblance of Peace*

four parties of the ANZUS and Manila treaties. The eight Powers established a permanent South-East Asia Treaty Organization and enunciated a Pacific Charter.[74] It was to play a most insignificant future role.

IX

The Treaty of Peace with Japan was signed at San Francisco Opera House on the morning of Saturday, 8 September 1951* – just six years after the signature of Japan's Unconditional Surrender on the quarter-deck of U.S.S. *Missouri*. All those invited to the conference accepted the treaty with the exception of the Soviet bloc, comprising the U.S.S.R., Poland and Czechoslovakia. In addition, in view of the fact that neither of the Chinese régimes was represented, peace was not concluded between Japan and either Peking or Taipeh. †

The conference had been a particular triumph for John Foster Dulles, whose negotiating skill and pertinacity had made it possible. It was also a triumph for Dean Acheson who, first as temporary and then as permanent President, had borne the brunt of the task of controlling and directing the work of the conference, refusing to allow its proceedings to be side-tracked and diverted by the manœuvres of the Soviet Union and her allies. Both men were justly proud of their achievement, which had been accomplished in the remarkable short time of one year. In Dean Acheson's own words:

> There was nothing mean, nothing sordid, left in any corner of this treaty. There was nothing hidden, nothing that could not bear the broad light of day; and we were able to join in that sort of an effort, and we were able to settle our differences, because we were going forward in a great effort, making a new step in history, and hoping from this day forward that a new chapter is opening in the history of the world.[75]

Such, it is perhaps unnecessary to state, was not the view of the Soviet Government. From the first its representatives had rejected the

* In addition to the treaty, an Optional Protocol was signed by a number of countries relating to the question of contracts, periods of prescription and negotiable instruments, and the question of contracts of insurance. Japan signed this Protocol and also two declarations, one concerning her adherence to various agreements and the other relating to war graves.

The treaty was signed on behalf of the United Kingdom by Herbert Morrison, Secretary of State for Foreign Affairs, the Hon. Kenneth Younger, Minister of State, and Sir Oliver (later Lord) Franks, British Ambassador in Washington. The United States signatories were Dean Acheson, John Foster Dulles and Senators Alexander Wiley (Democrat) and John Sparkman (Republican). Shigeru Yoshida (Prime Minister), Hayato Ikeda (Foreign Minister) and four others signed on behalf of Japan.

† It should be remembered that under the Anglo-American draft treaty 'China', *per se*, was accorded the benefit of certain articles, though not a signatory.

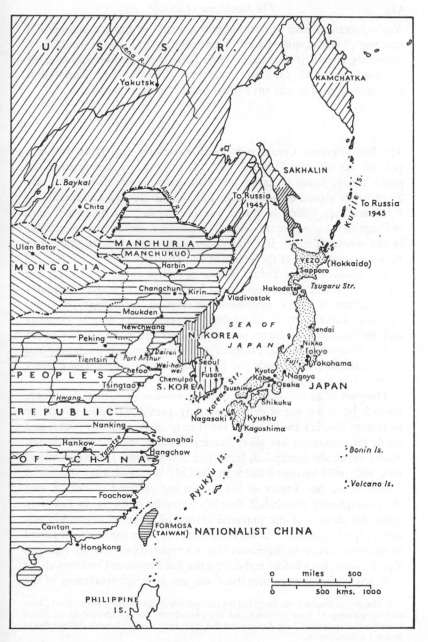

Japan after 1945

Anglo-American·draft as nothing but 'a treaty for the preparation of a new war',[76] and proposed a set of amendments to it which would have materially altered its nature.* When these were refused approval by the conference, M. Gromyko, together with his Czech and Polish colleagues, ceased to take any further interest in the proceedings.

X

The San Francisco Conference closed, therefore, with Japan still in a state of war with the U.S.S.R. and 'China', but, by Article 26 of the peace treaty, Japan declared her willingness to conclude 'with any State which signed or adhered to the United Nations Declaration of 1 January 1942,† and which is at war with Japan . . . a bilateral Treaty of Peace on the same, or substantially the same terms as are provided for in the present Treaty'. But this undertaking expired three years after the coming into force of the Treaty of San Francisco.‡

The Japanese Peace Treaty became operative on 28 April 1952, and on this same date Japan regularized her relations with the Nationalist Government of China, established in Taiwan, by a treaty of peace signed at Taipeh. By its provisions, the cession to China of Formosa and the Pescadores by Japan, sovereignty over which she had renounced under Article 2(*a*) of the Treaty of San Francisco, was confirmed and the remaining articles made the provisions of the general peace treaty applicable to Sino-Japanese relations.

The path of Soviet-Japanese relations was less easy. Stalin's attitude towards Japan was one of definite hostility, partly on account of a desire to recoup Russia's losses under the Treaty of Portsmouth (1905) and partly on account of her all-embracing hostility to the United States, whose vassal, she contended, Japan had now become. Japan had, therefore, willy-nilly become a factor in the Cold War, and when the Soviet Union signed her Treaty of Friendship and Alliance in Peking with the triumphantly established People's Republic of China, in February 1950, the menace of the potential revival of Japanese aggression was explicitly emphasized.[78] As has been seen, the same theme was apparent in the whole course of the Soviet Union's negotiations over the Japanese Peace Treaty, both before and during the San Francisco Conference.

It was not until 1953 that there was any apparent weakening of the

---

* The Soviet amendments included the recognition of the People's Republic of China and its sovereignty over Formosa and the Pescadores; the withdrawal of all Allied troops and installations from Japan; and the strict limitation of Japan's defence forces and her neutralization.[77]

† See below, p. 537.   ‡ See below, App. B, 'The Yoshida Letter'.

deadlock between the two countries. Then, with the death of Stalin and the somewhat more flexible attitudes of his successors, the international tension in the Orient was temporarily eased by the South-East Asian agreement reached at Geneva in July 1954. As a result of the general *détente*, the decision was taken in Moscow to make a new approach in the field of Soviet-Japanese relations, at least to the extent of considering separating them from Sino-Soviet and Sino-Japanese relations.

The first tentative indication of this new departure was on 12 September 1954, when M. Molotov announced that, if a mutual willingness for the normalization of Soviet-Japanese relations existed in both Moscow and Tokyo, something might come of it.[79] The Japanese response being deemed favourable, and after a further period of 'shadow negotiation' the Soviet Government made a definite *démarche* on 25 January 1955 for the opening of discussions towards a resumption of diplomatic relations.[80]

These discussions opened in London on 1 June, but not before certain major political changes had taken place in Japan, where the six-year rule of Shigeru Yoshida was descending into its twilight. Mr Yoshida had identified himself with the policy of the American alliance, but his successors, notably Ichiro Hatoyama, though they stood for the *status quo* created by the San Francisco Treaty and the Security Pact with the United States, advocated a wider degree of independence in Japanese foreign policy, as illustrated by their advocacy of the repeal of Article 9 of the new Constitution and the consequent rearmament of Japan.[81] Moreover, changes in Russian policy were also apparent, following upon the removal of the Soviet Premier, Georgi Malenkov, and his succession by Khrushchev and Bulganin in February 1955.

Finally, after a Japanese general election, from which Hatoyama and the Democrats emerged as the largest but not the over-all majority party, the London negotiations got off to a poor start on 1 June, with the Soviet Ambassador, Jacob Malik, and Shunichi Matsumoto, a career diplomat, as the plenipotentiaries. The course of this truly Oriental period of diplomatic exchanges, which lasted for eighteen months, fell into four separate phases (June–August 1955, January–March 1956, July–August 1956 and October–December 1956), two of which were held in London and two in Moscow.

This sequence of conversations was in no way a stately pavane of Old World diplomacy, nor even did it follow the artificial intricacies of a ritual dance; it was an exercise in catch-as-catch-can all-in wrestling, with no holds barred, in the course of which the Soviet Union for the

second time blackballed Japan from admission to the United Nations.*
At another moment, in late August 1956, John Foster Dulles, now
Secretary of State, added a further complication by threatening to
occupy Okinawa permanently if Japan ceded the islands of Etorofu
and Kunashiri to the U.S.S.R. Furthermore, the whole issue became
deeply enmeshed in the web of Japanese domestic politics.[82] Finally,
a Joint Declaration was signed on 19 October 1956 by Bulganin,
Khrushchev, Mikoyan and Gromyko, on behalf of the U.S.S.R., and
by Ichiro Hatoyama and Ichiro Kono on the part of Japan.

This document terminated the state of war which had been hastily
declared on Japan by the Soviet Union on 8 August 1945, between the
dropping of the first and second nuclear bombs.† It re-established
diplomatic relations between them and, with the exception of the
territorial settlement, which was postponed until the negotiation and
signature of a formal treaty of peace, agreement was reached on all
issues outstanding from the Second World War. Both states agreed that
their future relations would be regulated by the principles enunciated
in the Charter of the United Nations and that any disputes arising
between them would be settled by peaceful means, in accordance with
Article 2 of the Charter, 'in such a manner that international peace and
security and justice are not endangered'.

It was significant that, whereas the Soviet Union had strenuously
opposed at the San Francisco Conference the adoption of Article 5 of
the peace treaty which accorded to Japan the right of self-defence,‡
she now, in Article 3 of the Joint Declaration, specifically reaffirmed
with Japan her 'inalienable right of individual and collective self-defence'
stipulated in Article 51 of the Charter.

By Article 9 of the Joint Declaration both states agreed to continue
their negotiations for the conclusion of a formal treaty of peace, and
Russia undertook to return to Japan the islands of Habomai and
Shikotan after such a treaty had come into force. It is a matter of
record that all subsequent Soviet-Japanese negotiations to such an end
have so far (1971) proved fruitless.

The treaty signed by Japan with Nationalist China in 1952 and the
declaration with the Soviet Union in 1956 brought to a formal conclusion the state of war in the Far East which had been begun bilaterally
with the Japanese aggression against China in 1937 and had become

* In vetoing Japan's application for admission in December 1955, the U.S.S.R.
specifically stated that she would reverse her policy after the conclusion of a Soviet–
Japanese agreement. This she did a year later, when Japan was finally admitted to the
United Nations on 18 December 1956.

† See above, pp. 380–4.   ‡ See above, pp. 519 and 524.

general with the attacks on British and American Pacific possessions in December 1941. The Unconditional Surrender made by Japan on 14 August 1945 and formally signed in Tokyo Bay on 2 September, signified the opening of a period of non-belligerency which was to end, for the majority of states concerned, with the Treaty of San Francisco six years later.

The admission of Japan to the United Nations in December 1956 marked the reinclusion, with one exception, of all the ex-enemy states of the Second World War into the international community. The exception is, of course, Germany, which by reason of her dichotomized condition has been consistently denied membership.

21 | The Origins of the United Nations Organization

I

To understand fully the background and genesis of the United Nations Organization in 1945 it is necessary to give consideration to the nascent circumstances of the League of Nations some quarter of a century earlier, and to compare the two.

Separated as we are by fifty years of steady decline in international relations and the cataclysmic horror of the Second World War, it is increasingly difficult to recapture the atmosphere of idealism, hope and fervour which was strongly prevalent, at any rate in the Anglo-Saxon countries, during the latter years of what to the older of our generations is still the Great War. 'It must never happen again' was the keynote and the basic belief of much whole-souled thought in Britain and America from 1916 onwards, when the bloody bootlessness of the Somme convinced many of the horrid futility of war.

To young and old it became vitally apparent that the war, once it had been won, must indeed be a 'war to end war', and that, in its wake, the world must be 'made safe for democracy'. Subsequent disillusionment has resulted in the labelling of these aphorisms as mere cynical slogans; this is both untruthful and unjust. At the time of their origin they were articles of faith and were accepted as such both by many of those who had fought in battle and by those who were too old or too young to have done so. On this foundation was built the edifice of hope which was not destined to survive.

In Britain in the years 1916–18 certain men of high intellect put pen to paper: Leonard Woolf, G. Lowes Dickinson, H. N. Brailsford, C. R. Buxton and J. A. Hobson all produced thoughtful studies in international government, which provided varying methods for the pacific settlement of international disputes, for common action by member states against an aggressor and for the surrender of some modicum of the prerogatives of national sovereignty,[1] and to these names must be added that of a brilliant young athlete and intellectual, Philip Noel-Baker, a Quaker dedicated to the cause of peace.

Other plans for an international organization for the maintenance of peace were formulated by group action,* but in governmental circles there was little activity until 1918, when official committees were set up in Britain and in France, under the chairmanship respectively of Lord Phillimore, a judge of the High Court, and Léon Bourgeois, a veteran of the European peace movement, who had attended the two Hague Conferences of 1899 and 1907 and had been Prime Minister of France nearly a quarter of a century before. These committees were charged with collating and examining the various plans for peace which had been produced in their respective countries and with preparing official draft conventions for the establishment of what was by now becoming generally known as a League of Nations. †

In this same year two other plans of great importance were produced in England. The first, by Lord Robert Cecil, the second son of that great Marquess of Salisbury who had been both Prime Minister and Foreign Secretary, was presented to the Foreign Office in July,‡ the second was by the South African Minister of Defence, General Jan Christiaan Smuts, then serving as a member of the Imperial War Cabinet. His memorandum, submitted to his War Cabinet colleagues on 16 December,§ was later described by Mr Lloyd George as 'pellucid in style, eloquent in diction, penetrating in thought and broad in outlook'.[6]

When President Woodrow Wilson landed in Europe on 13 December 1918, with 'glory in his wings', and was accorded a reception worthy of a second Saviour of mankind, he found that little practical progress had been made towards the preliminary organization of the Peace Conference. Europe as a whole was still in a state of 'battle-fatigue', and in Britain and France the chief governmental interest and activity had been centered on the consultation of the public mind in general elections. Such thought as had been given to the work of the Peace Conference had tended to focus on the solution of the territorial problems arising from the defeat of the Central Powers rather than on the work of drafting a Covenant and putting the League of Nations into operation.

---

* Lord Bryce and some of his friends, the British League of Nations Society, the Fabian Society and the Union of Democratic Control, the American League to Enforce Peace, and the Central Organization for a Durable Peace at The Hague, all produced such plans.

† The Phillimore Committee presented its interim report together with a draft convention, to the Foreign Secretary, Arthur Balfour, on 20 March 1918. Their final report and commentary were submitted on 3 July.[2] The Bourgeois Committee reported in November 1918.[3]

‡ Lord Robert Cecil had already sent a brief draft of 'Proposals for the Maintenance of Future Peace' to the Foreign Office in October 1916.[4]

§ The original title of Smuts' paper, as sent to the Imperial War Cabinet, was 'A League of Nations: A Programme for the Peace Conference'. Later, when it was published, the title was changed to *The League of Nations: A Practical Suggestion.*[5]

This was diametrically opposed to the intentions of the President, who was unalterably determined to make the League a constituent part of the peace treaties and, more specifically, to insist upon the drafting of the Covenant being given first priority over all other business of the conference. President Wilson feared, and not without reason, that if consideration of the Covenant were left till the final stages of the conference it might never be considered at all, since the weary and exhausted delegates would seek to find some good reason for postponing so complicated a decision till a later date. The President's second reason for incorporating the Covenant in the treaties was that he counted on the machinery of the League to correct the mistakes which the peace-makers would inevitably make and to provide means of solution for the deadlocks arising in the deliberations of the conference, which would otherwise prove insurmountable obstacles to agreement.

The President's third reason stemmed from his own domestic political situation in America. There the measure of support on which he could count in the Senate was, to say the least of it, uncertain and there was no question but that he would incur the bitter and obstinate antagonism of the anti-League lobby of Republicans led by Senator Henry Cabot Lodge of Massachusetts. President Wilson anticipated this opposition, but neither he, nor anyone in Europe, expected that the United States Senate would go to the length of rejecting the terms of peace with Germany in the form of a treaty which had been signed by the President of the United States in person. He was determined therefore so to interweave the Covenant with the Treaty that refusal to ratify the former could not be effected without rejecting the latter as a whole.[7]

As is now a matter of tragic history, the President's confidence in his political strategy was misplaced and his power of estimating the length to which the Senate would not go was utterly lacking in reality. The inextricable intertwining of the Covenant with the Treaty merely succeeded in damning the one with the other and in dealing a pre-natal injury to the League of Nations from which it never really recovered.

At the time, however, President Wilson, perhaps to his surprise, met with no opposition from the Allied statesmen with whom he conferred in London and Paris and Rome when he visited these capitals, and later when the conference opened.

It was on the proposal of the British delegation that a draft of the Covenant presented by President Wilson was adopted as the basis for discussion, and when the President himself proposed that the terms of reference for the Commission on the League should include the provision that 'this League should be treated as an integral part of the general Treaty of Peace', it received unanimous approval.

The draft Covenant presented to the Commission by the President was of varied parentage. He had written his first draft on his own typewriter, making only one copy. He had then received the Phillimore Report and draft, which had been revised by Colonel House, and also the draft of Léon Bourgeois. He had read them all. As a result of his perusal he prepared a second draft of his own, and yet a third after he had studied and compared the proposals of General Smuts and Lord Robert Cecil. To this third draft he made further amendments after talks with Smuts and Cecil in Paris. The result was handed over to the British and American legal experts, Sir Cecil Hurst and David Hunter Miller, who prepared a provisional text of a convention, and it was this text that President Wilson presented to the plenary session of the Peace Conference on 25 January 1919.[8]

It was at this same plenary session that the committee to work out in detail the constitution of the League was appointed. It was composed of two delegates from each of the Great Powers and five selected by the smaller states.* But at the very first meeting of the committee, on 3 February, this latter group protested that the Great Powers would exercise too great a predominance and demanded that four more of their own number should be added. In spite of opposition from the British and Americans the small Powers carried their point and the composition of the committee was increased to nineteen.†

The committee, working under the chairmanship of President Wilson, had before it, in addition to the agreed Anglo-American text, two draft conventions presented by the French and Italians respectively,[9] but the two sponsoring Governments readily agreed to accept the Hurst–Miller draft as a foundation on which to build. After eleven days of intensive discussion, carried on with exemplary speed and efficiency, the committee, having sat each evening until after midnight, unanimously adopted that first draft Covenant which Wilson so proudly presented to the plenary session of the conference on 14 February with the words 'a living thing is born' – a remark which proved to be both premature and over-optimistic.

This draft, now made public, was the first indication that the con-

* The original members of the committee were: United States, President Wilson and Colonel Edward House; British Empire, Lord Robert Cecil and General Smuts; France, Léon Bourgeois and Ferdinand Lanaude; Italy, Vittorio Orlando and Vittorio Scialoja; Japan, Baron Makino and Viscount Chinda; Belgium, Paul Hymans; Brazil, Epitano Pessôa; China, Dr Wellington Koo; Portugal, Jayme Batalho Reis; Serbia, Milenko Vesnić.

† Those appointed later were: Greece, Eleftherios Venizelos; Poland, Paul Domowski; Rumania, Constantine Diamandy; Czechoslovakia, Karel Krámǎr.

ference as a whole, or the world at large, had of the proposals for this purpose. President Wilson's drafts and those of the British, French and Italian Governments, as well as those of General Smuts and Lord Robert Cecil, had all been kept secret. This was the first declaration to the world of the means under contemplation for the implementing of the last of the President's Fourteen Points which had stated that 'a general association of nations must be formed under specific covenants for the purpose of affording mutual guarantees of political independence and territorial integrity to great and small states alike'.

Having presented the draft Covenant to the conference, President Wilson returned to the United States, where his own political fences were in dire need of mending, leaving the field free for discussion. Much constructive criticism was provoked, more especially from some of the British Commonwealth countries, such as Canada and Australia. Certain new voices were also heard. A number of those countries which had remained neutral during the war were by no means pleased that they had been granted no say in the initial planning of the League, claiming that, because of their neutrality, they were able to take a more dispassionate view than could those States which had been belligerents. They were dissatisfied with many aspects of the draft Covenant, but specifically they complained that the inclusion of Germany was not envisaged, that the Great Powers exercised too great a degree of influence and that there was lacking any provision for compulsory arbitration for the settlement of international justifiable disputes.

After considerable discussion it was agreed that, though the former belligerent Powers were not prepared to admit participation by ex-neutral states in the preparation of the peace terms as a whole, in this specific case informal discussion might be sanctioned, and accordingly a delegation from the League of Nations Committee of the Conference, which included Colonel House, Lord Robert Cecil and Léon Bourgeois, met with the representatives of twelve neutral states on 20 and 21 March 1919. The basis of their discussion was, in addition to the draft Covenant, an *avant-projet* prepared and submitted by the three Scandinavian Governments of Sweden, Norway and Denmark.[10]*

Returning to Paris after a month's absence – this time with a somewhat diminished glory – President Wilson brought with him certain draft amendments to the draft Covenant which had been demanded of him by such Republican supporters of the League as ex-President

---

* The proceedings of the conference with the neutrals remained secret until a full report was made public as an annex to the explanatory memorandum which accompanied the Bill laid before the Dutch Parliament on 13 January 1920 to authorize the adherence of the Netherlands to the League of Nations.[11]

William H. Taft as the price which must be paid to secure sufficient votes for ratification in the United States Senate. He still believed, however, that, fierce though the conflict might be, the Senate would not repudiate his signature and it was in this confidence that he joined with Mr Lloyd George in giving to M. Clemenceau the Anglo-American treaties of guarantee against a future threat of aggression by Germany against France.*

The American amendments and those arising out of the discussions with the neutral states were considered by the committee at five meetings held on 22, 24 and 26 March and 10 and 11 April. The final draft was presented to the plenary session of the conference on 28 April 1919 and was unanimously adopted. It became Part I of the Treaties of Versailles, St Germain, Trianon, Neuilly and Sèvres.

Thus, though there had been certain consideration of the general problem of an international organization in the early months of 1918, the Covenant was conceived, framed and adopted between the first meeting of the League of Nations Committee on 3 February 1919 and the acceptance of the final text by the Peace Conference on 28 April. A three-month period of intense negotiation and discussion had therefore yielded up an international instrument which, if admittedly imperfect, was unique and original and represented a measure of progress towards international government which had been unforeseen at the outset. It constituted a major tribute to the efforts of statesmen who zealously and sincerely essayed to give practical shape and form to the prevailing spirit of the time that 'It must never happen again'.

The fate of the League of Nations in the United States is now ancient, if still tragic, history. Determined opposition to ratification by Senator Lodge and his allies was matched by adamant intransigence on the part of President Wilson to the acceptance of any form of concession, and this resulted, on 19 March 1920, in the wholesale jettisoning by the Senate of the Treaty, the Covenant and the American guarantee to France. The League was therefore deprived at the outset of one of its chief pillars of support, a loss from which it never fully recovered and which materially changed the whole course of history.†

* The British and American treaties of guarantee were made interdependent, the one with the other, and their ratification was dependent in each case upon ratification of the Treaty of Versailles.

† It is worth recalling that at no time were all the Great Powers simultaneously members of the League of Nations. The United States, of course, never joined. Germany was elected in 1926 and withdrew in 1933. Japan resigned in 1933 and Italy in 1937. The U.S.S.R. was admitted in 1934 and was expelled in 1939. Britain and France alone remained members from 1920, when the Covenant came into force, until 1946, when the last Assembly of the League pronounced its own demise and its succession by the United Nations.

II

If, as has been alleged, the League of Nations was too hastily conceived and lacked sufficient preliminary consideration before being incorporated in the treaties of peace, this criticism could not be made of the United Nations. Whereas the League was not given serious excogitation before mid-1918 and was proclaimed a working organism a year later, the United Nations, though it achieved a semi-official existence as early as 1941, was not formally initiated for another four years.

This was perhaps a part of the profound and fundamental difference between the two world wars. The progressive failure and ultimate collapse of the 'Geneva Institution' had saddened many and soured some. As a result, there were those who were in no hurry to repeat what they regarded as the futilities of an international organization. There were also those who still believed in the possible success, or at least the inevitability, of some further adventure in the field of international government and who were anxious that the planning and preparation for such another experiment should be of the most detailed and complete nature, full cognizance being taken of the weaknesses and failures of the Covenant and means found to obviate their repetition. The combination of the two forces made for procrastination.

The first official announcement of the intention to create a post-war international organization was made on the occasion of the signing of the London Declaration at St James's Palace on 12 June 1941, when representatives of fourteen states announced their determination to pursue their common struggle against Nazi and Fascist tyranny to a victorious conclusion and that none of them would enter into a separate peace with the enemy. They then declared their intention of creating a world in which, 'relieved of the menace of aggression, all may enjoy economic and social security'.[12]*

Two months later, under dramatic circumstances, a further declaration of intent for post-war international co-operation for peace was made to the world in three clauses of the Atlantic Charter.

The historic meeting in Placentia Bay in August 1941 has been considered earlier in this book,† and it will be recalled that both Winston Churchill and the American Under-Secretary of State, Sumner Welles, had tried in vain to find inclusion within the terms of the Atlantic Charter of some specific, if general, provision for 'effective international organization' after the end of hostilities, as a means to future world security.[13] To this President Roosevelt was originally strongly opposed, for reasons which he clearly and firmly stated.

* See above, p. 32.   † See above, pp. 36–43.

President Roosevelt had himself been, in a sense, a political casualty in the cause of the League of Nations some twenty years before when, as Vice-Presidential candidate on the Democratic ticket with Governor James Cox of Ohio, he had gone down to defeat in the electoral débâcle of 1920. A shrewd and astute political operator, he had learned much from this experience and he now applied the full measure of this awareness. Genuinely in favour of some form of international peace-keeping machinery after the war, the President had not yet made up his mind as to what form he wished it to take or what was practicable. He knew that to many the term 'League of Nations' had an unacceptable connotation, by reason of the taint of 'Wilsonism' which attached to it and of its record of progressive failure. He himself had not progressed further in his thinking than the enunciation of the great basic truths of the Four Freedoms: Freedom of Speech and Expression, Freedom of Worship, Freedom from Want and Freedom from Fear.* He was still toying in his own mind with the somewhat fanciful idea of 'international policemen' – namely the Great Powers, the United States, Britain, Russia and China – who should exercise supervisory peace-keeping powers. Above all his amazingly sensitive political instinct told him that this was no time to make pledges in favour of a revamped League of Nations or even of a newly constituted international organization, and also – equally important – that any organization which did, or might, eventually emerge must be kept scrupulously apart and separate from the peace treaties which should conclude the war.

It was with these thoughts in mind that President Roosevelt withstood the desires of the British Prime Minister and of his own Under-Secretary of State for the inclusion of some reference to 'effective international organization'.

> The President replied [Mr Welles has recorded] that he did not feel that he could agree to this because of the suspicions and opposition that such a statement on his part would create in the United States. He said that he himself would not be in favour of the creation of a new Assembly of the League of Nations, at least until after a period of time had passed and during which an international police force composed of the United States and Great Britain had had an opportunity of functioning.[15]

In order to meet the President's point and yet give some encouragement to those in Europe who placed hope in the future of an international peace structure, Mr Churchill, after consultation with his War

---

* The 'Four Freedoms' were announced by President Roosevelt in his State of the Union message of 6 January 1941 in which he requested Congress for legislation which subsequently became the Lend-Lease Act.[14]

Cabinet colleagues, produced a different formula designed to satisfy both points of view. In this he proposed the disarmament of the aggressor Axis nations as 'essential', 'pending the establishment of a wider and more permanent system of general security', and with this form of words the President readily concurred.[16]

Thus, in the final text, the last paragraph, Point VIII, of the Atlantic Charter read as follows:

> They believe that all the nations of the world, for realistic as well as spiritual reasons, must come to the abandonment of the use of force. Since no future peace can be maintained if land, sea or air armaments continue to be employed by nations which threaten, or may threaten, aggression outside of their frontiers, they believe, pending the establishment of a wider and permanent system of general security, that the disarmament of such nations is essential. They will likewise aid and encourage all other practicable measures which will lighten for peace-loving peoples the crushing burden of armaments.*

In order that it might not appear that the Atlantic Charter constituted an Anglo-American prescriptive preserve in the consideration of post-war peace-keeping agreements, the British Government was anxious to align its belligerent Allies in support of the Charter's enunciation of principles. This was particularly desirable in the case of the Soviet Union, which was already giving indications of its belief that the Charter, with its affirmations against 'territorial aggrandizement' and 'territorial changes that do not accord with the freely expressed wishes of the peoples concerned', and its provision for 'the right of all peoples to choose the form of government under which they will live', was covertly directed against the U.S.S.R.† It was therefore arranged at a further meeting at St James's Palace on 24 September 1941 for the Governments of the British Dominions, the European Governments-in-exile, the representatives of General de Gaulle, and the Soviet Union to adhere formally to the principles of the Atlantic Charter.

It was at this meeting of the Allied nations that M. Maisky, the Soviet Ambassador, made certain pertinent statements on behalf of his Government which have a curious ring in the light of subsequent events. Soviet foreign policy, he said, was guided by 'the principle of

---

* It will be remembered that the fourth of President Wilson's Fourteen Points of 8 January 1918 read as follows: 'Adequate guarantees given and taken that national armaments will be reduced to the lowest point consistent with domestic safety'; and that the Preamble to Part v of the Treaty of Versailles stated: 'In order to render possible the initiation of a general limitation of the armaments of all nations, Germany undertakes strictly to observe the military, naval and air clauses which follow.'

† These arguments were indeed pursued by Marshal Stalin in his discussion with Anthony Eden in December 1941 during the negotiations preliminary to the signing of the Anglo-Soviet Treaty of Alliance of 26 May 1942 (see above, pp. 44–50).

self-determination of nations ... one of the pillars on which the political structure of the U.S.S.R. is built', * and that his Government defended the right of every nation to its independence, its territorial integrity and to such social order and form of government 'as it deems opportune and necessary'. He added, however:

> Considering that the practical application of these principles [of the Atlantic Charter] will necessarily adapt itself to the circumstances, needs and historic peculiarities of particular countries, the Soviet Government can state that a consistent application of these principles will secure the most energetic support on the part of the Government and peoples of the Soviet Union.[18]

Less than four months after the momentous meeting in Placentia Bay, Japanese aggression had transformed the United States from a benevolent neutral into an active belligerent, and immediately President Roosevelt took the initiative in defining more clearly the ideals and objectives which had been nascent or inherent in the Atlantic Charter.

On New Year's Day 1942 at a ceremony at the White House in Washington there was signed the 'Declaration by the United Nations'. The term 'United Nations' had been coined by President Roosevelt, an inspired choice since it avoided all connotation of 'alliance' or 'League' which had stuck so firmly in the craw of American Senators on an earlier occasion.

It was also significant that the text of the Declaration had been agreed as a result of joint drafting by the United States Secretary of State and the British, Soviet and Chinese Ambassadors in Washington, and that the four Great Powers, led by President Roosevelt and Mr Churchill, signed it first before it was thrown open to general signature and adherence.[19]

In the United Nations Declaration the signatories subscribed to the 'common programme of purpose and principles' embodied in the Atlantic Charter, pledged themselves to the defence and preservation of life, liberty, independence and religious freedom and 'to preserve human rights and justice in their own lands as well as in other lands', and further undertook (i) to employ their full resources, military or eco-

---

* The principle of self-determination was clearly affirmed in the Decree of Peace promulgated and adopted by the Congress of Soviets on 8 November 1917, in the following terms: 'If any nation whatsoever is detained by force within the boundaries of a certain state and if [that nation], contrary to its expressed desire – whether such desire is made manifest in the Press, national assemblies, party relations or in protests and uprisings against national oppression – is not given the right to determine the form of its State life by free voting and completely free from the presence of the troops of the annexing or stronger State and without the least pressure, then the adjoining of that nation by the stronger State is annexation, i.e. seizure by force and violence.'[17]

nomic, against the Axis Powers, and (ii) not to make a separate armistice or peace with the enemy.[20]*

In Britain Anthony Eden was also looking towards the future. He had not been present at the Placentia Bay meeting, for that had been very much Mr Churchill's own show, and it must be confessed that, like many others, he was not too clear what and how much importance should be attached to the terms of the Atlantic Charter,† but no one had a greater knowledge and a wider experience than the Foreign Secretary of international organizations and their problems. His reputation had been, to a great extent, built up on the efforts which he had made, first as Under-Secretary of State for Foreign Affairs, then as Lord Privy Seal, then as Minister for League of Nations Affairs and finally as Foreign Secretary, to make the machinery of the League of Nations work. The fact that he had failed was not held against him, nor had it daunted his confidence in the necessity for setting up some sort of international peace-keeping machinery after the defeat of the Axis Powers. He had accepted as the basis of policy the agreement reached between President Roosevelt and Mr Churchill that the establishment of such an international organization must be secondary, and not primary, in order of post-war priority planning, and that a certain provisional 'overlordship' must be exercised by the Great Powers before a permanent body could be installed. It was on this basis that Mr Eden submitted his first paper on the United Nations to his Cabinet colleagues in January 1943.[22]

The proposal was for political and economic world councils, which depended on the victorious Great Powers agreeing on a common world policy and being prepared to act together to enforce it. 'Failing this,' the Foreign Secretary wrote in a flash of hideously accurate prophecy, 'we shall be confronted by the prospect of a world in precarious balance, with the great powers, each with its circle of client States, facing

---

* The Declaration was signed by all those who had been signatory to the two Declarations of St James's of 1941 and also by Costa Rica, Cuba, the Dominican Republic, El Salvador, Guatemala, Haiti, Honduras, Nicaragua and Panama. It was subsequently adhered to by Mexico, the Philippines, Ethiopia, Iraq, Brazil, Bolivia, Iran, Colombia, Liberia, Ecuador, Peru, Chile, Paraguay, Venezuela, Uruguay, Turkey, Egypt, Saudi Arabia, Syria and the Lebanon.

France and Denmark were deemed to have been identified with the United Nations by reason of the fact that in the case of France a representative of General de Gaulle had signed the two Declarations of London on 12 June and 24 September 1941 and, in the case of Denmark, that the Danish Minister in Washington had repudiated all actions of his Government as being taken under duress and had signified the adherence of all free Danes to the Allied cause.

† For instance King George VI, the Canadian Prime Minister Mackenzie King and the Conservative Chief Whip, Sir David Margesson, were all somewhat sceptical of the implementation of the Charter and believed that the main responsibility for and burden of this would fall upon the United States and Britain.[21]

each other in a rivalry which will merge imperceptibly into hostility.'

The Eden proposals, while encouraging the formation of regional groupings, laid emphasis on the fact that there must not be any measure of 'limited liability' system whereby one Power was solely responsible for keeping the peace in a given area. On the contrary, it was desirable and, indeed, essential that the Great Powers should in principle be equally interested in maintaining the peace everywhere in the world and that they should act together whenever and wherever it might be threatened. In other words, the success or failure of any international organization would depend on the degree to which the principle of the indivisibility of peace and the system of collective security were accepted by the Great Powers.

Six months later, and having undergone some little metamorphosis, the British proposals were presented to the State Department in Washington on 14 July 1943.[23] They included provision for a United Nations Commission for Europe, composed of high-ranking political representatives of Great Britain, the United States, the Soviet Union, France, the other European Allies and any British Dominion which might be prepared to contribute to the policing of Europe. The Commission would be directed by a Steering Committee, operating under the unanimity rule and composed of British, American, Soviet and French members. The British proposals further envisaged machinery not only for problems of occupation and the transitional period after the termination of hostilities but also for a wide range of long-term activities.

The British memorandum forced the State Department to take certain decisions and to determine certain lines of thought which it had hitherto shrunk from doing. The recommendation of the establishment of a Commission for Europe, for example, brought to a head the whole regional issue on which official opinion in Washington was still divided. In view of this new development, therefore, and also mindful that a further meeting between the President and the Prime Minister was scheduled for 17 August at Quebec, the State Department recast its thinking, and Mr Hull presented to the President on 10 August a new set of proposals.

These differed radically from the British project. They took a firm position against the British plans for regional organization and came down strongly for an international organization of global rather than regional foundation. Accordingly they made provision for a single transitional United Nations Agency, charged with the preparation of plans for dealing with enemy countries and liberated areas and for the handling of the various long-range problems, and which would also be required 'to create and set into motion various pieces of necessary machinery, each step to be subject to ratification by the constitutional governments'. In the view of the State Department, machinery initiated on this basis could evolve into a 'fully operating permanent international organization' by continual adaptation along functional and 'in some cases' regional lines, but always 'within the framework of unified policy'.[24]

The President, canny as always, would only approve in principle this basic programme for establishing a provisional United Nations organization. In so far as a public statement was concerned he would not go beyond a declaration of intentions by the Great Powers. For this restraint he had good reason, prompted by past personal and historical experience. Woodrow Wilson's failure to enlist Republican support for the League of Nations had been one of the fundamental causes for the defeat of the Treaty of Versailles and the Covenant. Franklin Roosevelt had no intention of repeating this egregious error of judgement and strategy.

The President knew that leaders of the Republican Party were about to meet at Mackinac Island, in Michigan, in order to consider their future policy on foreign affairs. He knew also that the followers of his erstwhile Presidential opponent, Wendell Wilkie (still the party's nominal standard-bearer), favoured some form of post-war international organization and America's participation in it. He was determined to take no irrevocable step without having previously secured Congressional approval on a bipartisan basis, and Republican support was a *conditio sine qua non* of such approval.

As was true in most instances of domestic politics, the President's judgement was faultless. The Republican meeting of leaders at Mackinac adopted on 7 September, largely owing to the leadership of Senator Vandenberg, a cautious but unanimous resolution in favour of 'responsible participation by the United States in post-war co-operative organization among sovereign nations to prevent military aggression and to attain permanent peace with organized justice in a free world'.[25] When Congress reconvened in the autumn, the House of Representatives adopted on 21 September, on the recommendation of its Committee on Foreign Affairs, a resolution, sponsored by Congressman William Fulbright of Arkansas, favouring the creation of 'appropriate international machinery, with power adequate to establish and maintain a joint and lasting peace . . . and as favouring participation therein of the United States through its constitutional processes'. The resolution was passed by 360 votes to 29.[26]

In the Senate, the constitutional body charged with the ratification of treaties, matters were tardier and less smooth of passage. However, after a long debate, distinguished for the high quality of its argument, Senator Tom Connally of Texas, chairman of the Committee on Foreign Relations, succeeded in securing the adoption on 5 November, by 85 votes to 5, of a resolution of which the two most vital paragraphs were as follows:

> That the United States, acting through its constitutional processes, join with free and sovereign nations in the establishment and mainte- nance of international authority with power to prevent aggression and to preserve the peace of the world.
>
> That the Senate recognizes the necessity of there being established at the earliest practicable date a general international organization, based on the principle of the sovereign equality of all peace-loving states, and open to membership by all such states, large and small, for the maintenance of international peace and security.[27]

Thus buttressed and protected, his flanks secured against snipers and enfilading fire, President Roosevelt was enabled to go forward with assurance towards the ultimate goal of his ambition. Indeed he could register substantial progress on the higher diplomatic level even before the Connally Resolution was finally passed.

The President and Mr Churchill had sought unsuccessfully to persuade Marshal Stalin to join them at Quebec in August and had offered to meet him more than half-way by going to Alaska if he would come this far. But the most that the Marshal would concede was a meeting of Foreign Ministers in Moscow in October. This was agreed, and to the shadow of the Kremlin came Mr Eden and Mr Hull, the latter bolstered by the passing of the Fulbright Resolution in the House of Representatives on 21 September and confident that, however long the Senate took to talk itself out, the votes were there for the success of the Connally Resolution.

Considering the personalities involved, for few men could have less in common than Anthony Eden, Vyacheslav Molotov and Cordell Hull, the Moscow Conference was remarkably successful. Although the agenda had been agreed beforehand, it was evident that each major protagonist had one subject to which he attached particular importance:

> The Russians were concerned for a second front in Europe in the spring of 1944 [Lord Avon has written]. The subject nearest Hull's heart was a Four-Power Declaration on war aims and international organization to keep the peace. My purpose was to get agreement to set up machinery for consultation between the Allies on European questions connected with the war.[28]

Remarkably enough all their major objectives were realized, and the main achievements of the conference have been already recounted

elsewhere in this book.* The Four-Power Declaration, for the discussion of which the Chinese Ambassador in Moscow, Foo Ping-shen,
had been co-opted, contained a provision (paragraph 4) endorsing, in
language almost identical with that of the subsequent Connally Resolution in the Senate, the necessity of establishing as soon as possible a
permanent general international organization for the maintenance of
peace.[29]

When the three great architects of Allied victory did eventually meet
for the first time in Tehran at the end of November 1943,† in so far as the
matter of an international organization was concerned they did no more
than reaffirm the Moscow Declaration. Their language was somewhat
more flowery and loosely rhetorical but the sentiments were the same.
There was indeed present some vestigal dreaming and hankering after
the earlier idea of the 'four policemen', but events had far outstripped
this fanciful idea. Already, as the statesmen met at Tehran, the experts
in Washington and London – and presumably in Moscow – were busily
preparing their respective drafts for a basic instrument for the United
Nations, comparable to the Covenant of the League. Planning liaison
was maintained, at any rate between the British and the Americans, and
by February 1944 Secretary Hull, who was rightly regarded as the
patriarchal elder statesman of the project, felt that sufficient progress
had been made to warrant an exchange of drafts between the three
Governments.‡

Arrangements were accordingly made for a meeting of high-level
officials and experts of the four Great Powers to be held in Washington,
and this was duly opened on 21 August 1944. Though nominally
quadripartite in character, the representatives of the Four Powers
never met together at any one time. For the first period (21 August to
28 September) the British, American and Soviet delegations, led
respectively by Sir Alexander Cadogan, Edward Stettinius and Andrei
Gromyko, exchanged drafts and views, and for the second part of the
discussions (29 September to 7 October) M. Gromyko withdrew and was
replaced by Dr Wellington Koo, the Chinese Ambassador in Washington. This somewhat farcical arrangement was necessitated by reason of
the fact that the Soviet Union was not yet a belligerent participant in the
Pacific War and was still scrupulous in her observance of her existing

---

* See above, pp. 103–21.   † See above, pp. 143–67.

‡ As Herbert Nicholas has pointed out in his admirable book on the United Nations,
'About the evolution of British official thinking curiously little has been disclosed;
there is no counterpart to the wealth of material documenting the British role in the
shaping of the League'.[30] The names of Gladwyn Jebb (later Lord Gladwyn) and of Sir
Charles Webster will rightfully find an important place in the history of British
planning, but the record is exiguous. By contrast the story of American planning has
been fairly fully told.

treaty of neutrality and non-aggression with Japan.* It also reflected the ambiguous position of China as not enjoying absolutely full membership of the Great Power club.

The subtropical climate of Washington in August may well have been regarded as offering an atmosphere both unsalubrious and unsuitable for diplomatic conversation and also unconducive to the finding of felicitous conclusions. But the fact that the conference met at Dumbarton Oaks, a residence and estate presented for public use by the munificence of former Ambassador Robert Bliss and his wife Mildred, rendered negligible most of the inherent inconveniences of climate. There, in surroundings of comfort and luxury, of spaciousness and greenery reminiscent of an English country house of the Edwardian era, the members of the conference met at ease and in secret. Their discussions were marked by cordiality and co-operation and they made an amazing amount of progress. The document which finally emerged from the Dumbarton Oaks Conference presented in outline all the main features of the United Nations as we know it today.[31]

As in the framework of the League of Nations, the new organization was to have four principal organs: a Security Council, a General Assembly, an International Court of Justice and an international Secretariat. On the creation of these bodies and on their method of functioning, which differed in a number of instances from those of the League, there was general and comparatively speedy agreement, but there were certain important aspects on which there was major disagreement, and in the final analysis there was a fairly amicable 'agreement to disagree'.

The main gap was on that side of the work of the United Nations which touched upon the trusteeship and administration of former colonial territories. As the chief colonial Power involved, the British representatives were sensitive on this issue and they received unexpected support for the postponement of a decision from the Americans who, for quite different reasons connected with their interest as the prospective legatee of Japanese colonization, were also desirous of avoiding a discussion of this topic at this time.

The major ground of disagreement, however, was the crucial one of the use of the veto by members of the Security Council. The agreed draft provided that for one of the five Great Powers to vote against a resolution in the Council was tantamount to a veto and would thus prevent action being taken. The point on which disagreement arose was the extent to which any Great Power could fall back on the use of the veto when it was a party to the dispute in question. In short, should a Great

* See above, p. 346.

Power which was a party to a dispute before the Council continue to enjoy the privilege of veto?

The Soviet Union delegates, with acute political foresight, wanted a comprehensive Great Power veto. The British advanced the view that a party to a dispute should not vote on its own case. The United States representatives, though at first undecided on the issue, later announced that they were ready to agree with the British view. An attempt to find a compromise formula failed of success and it was eventually decided to refer this decision to the forthcoming meeting of the Big Three, together with the wholly fanciful claim by the Russians that the sixteen component republics of the U.S.S.R. should be eligible for separate membership in the United Nations Organization. Thus a place for their decision was found in the already overcrowded agenda of the unhappy and ill-fated Yalta Conference.[32]*

There did not lack those who criticized the Dumbarton Oaks proposals – and with reason – for their lack of humanity and warmth, and they were indeed drafted by men with official background and training whose anxiety it was to avoid the use of language which might, by emotional appeal, effectually obscure the actual facts of the case. But in all fairness it must be admitted, as a member of the British delegation has noted, that 'It is, no doubt, advisable to include in such a document aspirations, which the authors know cannot be immediately realized, to make, as it were, an appeal to posterity. But that is a process better left to politicians, and they eventually did all that was necessary at San Francisco.'[33]

Like so many of the decisions taken at Yalta, the agreements relative to the United Nations bore the marks of haste, fatigue, impatience and wishful thinking. As Herbert Nicholas has so accurately written, 'they papered over the deep differences between the national interests and policies of the Big Three with formulas which would not stand the strain of the world's inspection and the wear and tear of the Organization's own functioning'.[34]

Moreover, there were the various personal aspects to be considered. Stalin had come to Yalta with a determination to exploit to the full both the success of Russian arms on the Eastern Front and the fact that at that moment the United States was desperately anxious for Soviet participation in the Far Eastern theatre of operations as soon as the war against Germany should be concluded.† He was thus in a position to ask a high price for his acquiescence on various issues, and he did so.

President Roosevelt, apart from indifferent health and in addition to an urgent wishfulness to gain Russia's co-operation in the Pacific War,

* See above, pp. 233–4.   † See above, pp. 350–1.

was also determined to gain Three-Power agreement on outstanding United Nations issues so that the Charter might be drawn up and made operative as soon as possible and certainly before the conclusion of hostilities in Europe. He was prepared therefore to make concessions in order to achieve this.

Mr Churchill's overriding desire was to bring the war in Europe to a victorious finish and then to concentrate on the defeat of Japan. He deprecated the idea of bringing the world organization into official being during war-time, and was reluctant to see any energies directed to peace-time tasks. This attitude was resented by the Americans, more expecially as the principle of an early nativity for the United Nations had already been agreed some time before.[35]

When therefore the Big Three, with their Foreign Ministers and military and civilian advisers, met at Yalta in February 1945, their accords in regard to the United Nations were reached, not *in vacuo*, but as a part of greater decisions and wider issues, and must be judged accordingly.

The two major difficulties involved dealt with Council voting and membership. On the first of these there was considerable disagreement and long discussions on the expert level.[36] Eventually agreement was reached on the basis of an Anglo-American compromise which provided that the veto by the Great Powers would not apply to 'decisions on procedural matters' and that a decision could be taken on a majority vote; a party to a dispute, it was further agreed, would not vote when peaceful adjustments of disputes were involved, but in all decisions involving enforcement measures there could be a veto since Great Power unanimity was required, even if a Great Power was a party to the dispute in question.

This agreed formula was far from ideal but it represented a basis of realistic compromise. Some means must necessarily be found to ensure that the Great Powers, which, 'when the chips were down', were ultimately responsible for the major share of any enforcement measures, were not stampeded by lesser colleagues on the Council into involvement in some collective action of which they did not necessarily approve. If the provisions of the Charter did not provide protection against such a contingency, it is doubtful whether it would ever have received ratification at the hands of the United States Senate and it might even have suffered the same fate as the Covenant of the League of Nations. On the other hand, if, under the Charter, a Great Power might find itself confronted with a combination of lesser Powers by reason of the fact that it could not exercise its right of veto, it is of the greatest improbability that the U.S.S.R. would have accepted membership of the United Nations and, as Field-Marshal Smuts wrote to Mr Churchill of such an occurrence: 'Should a World Organization be formed which does not include Russia, she will become the power-centre of another group. We shall then be heading for a Third World War.'*

The issue of membership also presented some interesting aspects – and indeed grounds for compromise. The Russian bid for membership for the sixteen constituent republics of the U.S.S.R., which had been advanced at Dumbarton Oaks, had been reaffirmed by Stalin between the Washington conversations and the Yalta Conference. It will never be known whether this was ever a 100 per cent serious proposal on the part of the Marshal, or whether he had proposed it in a moment of puckish humour, or whether – which is considerably more likely – he used it as an instance of the 'asking price and taking price' technique, intending to gain for himself a reputation for sweet reasonableness by scaling down claims which he had placed outrageously high in the first place but never expected to get; it certainly had the latter effect. President Roosevelt had been inclined to 'pooh-pooh' the matter when it was first proposed by Gromyko, but when it was repeated by Stalin he took it seriously, recognizing the threat inherent in such a matter to the chances of approval of the Charter by the Senate when it came up for ratification. When he met with members of the Foreign Relations Committee before leaving for Yalta, he had assured them that he would demand membership in the United Nations for all the forty-eight of the United States of America if Stalin insisted on his sixteen republics.†

As a matter of fact a complete solution for this conundrum was not found at Yalta. It was agreed that all Governments which had declared war on the Axis Powers by 1 March 1945 should be eligible for U.N. membership, but though Stalin contented himself with only demanding recognition of Byelorussia and the Ukraine for eligibility, and though this claim was supported by Mr Churchill, who was anxious to obtain the admission of India as a special case before her complete independence within the framework of the British Commonwealth,‡ President

* It should be noted that this was the prevailing *Zeitgeist* of 1945; judged in the light of the experience of a quarter of a century later the conclusion might well be different.

† Both Secretary of State Byrnes in his memoirs and Robert Sherwood in his biography of Harry Hopkins have reported this episode incorrectly by saying that the President had told the Senate that he would demand forty-eight for the United States if Stalin insisted on *two* additional memberships (which was what was eventually agreed). Neither the British nor the Americans had any knowledge before the opening of the Yalta Conference that Stalin would abate his claims.[37]

‡ It will be recalled that India had become a charter member of the League of Nations in 1919 by virtue of her being an original signatory of the Treaty of Versailles (of which the Covenant was an integral part), and despite the fact that her constitutional status did not at that time comply with the conditions for membership laid down in the Preamble to the Covenant. A similar position had now arisen in that the Government of India had declared war on the Axis and had been a signatory of both the St James's Palace Declarations of 1941.

Roosevelt was adamant. He would not agree to additional Soviet representation and insisted that this decision should be referred for settlement to the founding conference of the United Nations. However, he secretly promised Stalin to vote for the Russian proposal, and Mr Churchill followed suit.[38]*

While the principals found – or failed to find – compromise solutions on the major issues, progress was made at the Foreign Ministers' level towards practical decisions. Once it had been agreed that the founding Conference of the United Nations should be convened for the summer of 1945, discussion turned on where it should be held. All favoured the United States, partly because it was separated geographically from the continents on which war was being waged and partly because it was felt, certainly by the British, that if the United States Government were hosts to the conference this would be an added commitment in their support of the United Nations and an additional reinsurance against the risks of a subsequent withdrawal. Credit for the choice of San Francisco as a venue for the conference must go to Anthony Eden. There were some among the Americans who, anxious to avoid the selection of a populous centre in the eastern states, canvassed a site in the Middle West. 'For this,' writes Mr Eden, 'I felt little enthusiasm and later suggested California to Stettinius. San Francisco was in my mind, because I thought it geographically well placed. I had also been disappointed not to be able to see the city on my last visit to the United States. Stettinius worked the oracle.'[39]

After certain sinister vicissitudes the United Nations Conference opened at San Francisco on 25 April 1945.

III

'This time', President Roosevelt assured Congress on 1 March 1945, reporting on the Yalta Conference, 'we are not making the mistake of waiting until the end of the war to set up the machinery of peace. This time, as we fight together to win the war finally, we work together to keep it from happening again'.[40]

The conference which assembled in the San Francisco Opera House on 25 April 1945 to give life to the United Nations was perhaps as different as it was possible to be from that which, a quarter of a century earlier, had met together in Paris to make delivery of the Covenant of the League.† At San Francisco, for one thing, the delegates gathered under

* See above, pp. 246–7.
† There is still lacking an adequate account of the proceedings of the San Francisco United Nations Conference. Whereas the Paris Conference had its Keynes, its Mantoux, its David Hunter Miller, its Harold Nicolson and its Florence Wilson, to narrate

the shadow of the death – rather than in the presence – of a great President of the United States, and the outstanding qualities of his successor were as yet unapparent and unrecognized; for another, the atmosphere of the conference was already polluted by the acts of perfidy committed by the Soviet Union since the Yalta Conference.*

But perhaps the most important aspect of the conference was that its assigned task, in the words of the Four-Power official invitation, was 'to prepare a charter for a general international organization for the maintenance of international peace and security'. Its duty, therefore, was clear and specific; its terms of reference had nothing to do with the treaties of peace or the settlement of territorial problems; it had but one purpose. And when one considers what happened when the Peace Conference of the Second World War did indeed meet in Paris a year later, one cannot but be thankful for this fact.†

There were nostalgic moments, linking the present with the past, as when the conference was addressed by Field-Marshal Smuts and Dr Wellington Koo, both of whom had been members of the committee of the Peace Conference of 1919 which drew up the Covenant of the League of Nations; and there were moments of poignancy, recalling old shame, as when Jan Masaryk concluded his speech with the words – additionally tragic for their bearing on the future – 'Fellow delegates, my country has been one concentration camp since 1939'.

Generally speaking, however, the birth of the Charter was less spectacular and less dramatic than that of the Covenant. This was partly due to the fact that there was little novelty about it. Whereas the details of the League framework were kept secret until they had been agreed and accepted by the Conference of Paris, the draft proposals of the Dumbarton Oaks Conference had been fully publicized before the delegates even reached San Francisco and a number of amendments had already been tabled.

There was, moreover, a feeling of *déjà vu* – of 'This is where I came in' – which overhung San Francisco. 'The peculiar thrill and promise

---

its story, San Francisco had no such chroniclers and, indeed, there is only a chapter in Sir Charles Webster's book. Lord Avon's memoirs give us no picture of the conference nor a scent of its atmosphere, and even Field-Marshal Smuts' substantial contribution is accorded scant space by his biographer. We are, however, indebted, as usual, to the United States in the matter of documents.[41]

* The *coup d'état* in Rumania of 2 March 1945, whereby King Michael was compelled by Vyshinsky to install a Communist Government in a Bucharest ringed by Soviet tanks, must have been planned at the moment that Stalin was signing the Declaration on Liberated Europe at Yalta (see below, Document 3, pp. 631–2); the arrest and disappearance of the leaders of the Polish Home Army in Warsaw by Soviet military authorities took place at the end of March 1945 (see above, pp. 288–9).

† See above, Ch. 18.

that comes of doing something for the first time was inevitably absent', one British commentator has written. 'At San Francisco history was not so much made as re-made. The world was having a second try',[42] and he might have added: 'Humanity was getting its second chance.'

Never was the Wilsonian doctrine of 'open covenants openly arrived at' more fully honoured than at San Francisco. For two months, in a blaze of publicity, the delegates hammered out the details of the Charter clause by clause. Decisions were taken by vote, a two-thirds majority being necessary, under the eyes of 2,636 newspaper correspondents.

When it opened, the conference had before it the Dumbarton Oaks proposals, submitted by the four sponsoring Powers, and the accumulated amendments which had been put forward subsequently, but it was soon apparent that there existed a considerable degree of dissatisfaction among the small Powers. Under the able and waspish leadership of the late Dr Herbert Evatt, then Australian Minister of External Affairs, these states launched a series of attacks against the proposals of the Great Powers, centring mainly on the veto provisions by which, they maintained, the Great Powers had arrogated to themselves collectively a position of almost absolute authority in the Security Council over the other members, and had, individually, carefully protected themselves from any possibility of having the measures of enforcement action applied to them by the United Nations.

Dr Evatt and his colleagues did not hope to compel the Great Powers to retreat from the impregnable position which they had taken up. By persistent guerrilla warfare, however, and, alternatively, by intensive application of the technique of the Importunate Widow, they did achieve a series of tactical victories which materially strengthened their own position.

On 22 May a 'Questionnaire on Exercise of Veto in Security Council' was submitted to the four sponsoring powers on behalf of the smaller nations. It comprised twenty-three questions designed to clarify the voting formula arrived at at Yalta and, if possible, to secure certain concessions in the use of the veto power.[43]

This action precipitated the one serious crisis of the conference, and for a week its proceedings were at a standstill while intensive negotiations took place behind the scenes among the Great Powers. Though Britain and the United States were disposed to make concessions, the Soviet Union stood out for a 100 per cent use of the veto power, demanding its application even to the decision of whether a question were 'procedural' or not, and, moreover – which occasioned an even greater degree of discomposure – to apply it also to the decision as to whether or not an item should be placed on the agenda. It was felt by the

American, British, Chinese and French Governments that such an insistence would make freedom of decision impossible on the Security Council, but the Russians stood pat.

Molotov had left the conference on 8 May for Moscow, and Stettinius returned to Washington on the twenty-third. After consultation with President Truman on 2 June, it was agreed that, as Harry Hopkins was at that very moment in Moscow on his famous if fanciful goodwill mission to Stalin,* he should be asked to make a direct approach to the Marshal on the issue under dispute. A week later Hopkins reported that Stalin had overruled Molotov – on the grounds that he [Stalin] 'had not understood the issues' – and that instructions had been sent to the Soviet delegation in San Francisco, now led by Gromyko, to place Russia's view on the use of the veto in consonance with those of her fellow Great Powers.[44]

As a result of the concession by Stalin it was possible for the five Great Powers on the Security Council to take a consolidated stand in their reply to the smaller states. On 7 June, therefore, they made reply to the Questionnaire. It was not calculated to give complete satisfaction to Dr Evatt and his friends. Not a word of the Yalta formula was changed, and it became Article 27 of the Charter; nor were explicit answers given to the twenty-three questions submitted on 22 May. But an interpretation of the formula was offered, of which the nub was contained in the following passages:

> No individual member of the Council can alone prevent considera-
> tion and discussion by the Council of a dispute or situation brought
> to its attention. . . . Nor can parties to such dispute be prevented by
> these means from being heard by the Council. . . .
> Beyond this point, decisions and actions by the Security Council
> may well have major political consequences and may even initiate a
> chain of events which might, in the end, require the Council under its
> responsibilities to invoke measures of enforcement. . . . This chain of
> events begins when the Council decides to make an investigation, or
> determines that the time has come to call upon states to settle their
> differences, or make recommendations to the parties. It is to such
> decisions and actions that unanimity of the permanent members
> applies, with the important proviso referred to above, for abstention
> from voting by parties to a dispute.[45]

It cannot be pretended that this interpretation on the part of the Great Powers gave great comfort or satisfaction to the smaller nations. Before the voting procedure, as defined at Yalta, was finally accepted, there was a display of great disgruntlement on the part of the small states and also a formal and deliberate refusal on their part to endorse the joint

* See above, pp. 305–7.

interpretation of the sponsoring Powers. The hopes of those states which had sought to gain some mitigation of the Yalta formula, though doomed to immediate disappointment, received some glimmering of encouragement by the adoption of Article 109 of the Charter which provided that if, after ten years, the Charter had not been amended by the ordinary machinery (provided by Article 108), the Assembly by a majority of one, plus the Security Council by a vote, *to which the veto would not apply*, could together summon a Charter revision conference.[46]*

With the veto crisis thus, at least temporarily, disposed of – if not solved – the San Francisco Conference had no further major obstacles. It was brought to a formal conclusion on 26 June by President Truman after a ceremony of mass adherence in which more than five hundred delegates from fifty-one nations affixed their several signatures to five official texts – one for each official language – and took eight hours to do it. With his usual proclivity for not allowing grass to grow under his feet, the President presented the Charter to the United States Senate within a week of signature and that august body signified its ratification on 28 July, by 89 votes.

Under Article 110 the ratification by all five Great Powers, plus a majority of the other signatory states, was required to bring the Charter into effect and the United Nations Organization into being. This was formally attained on 24 October 1945. UNO's subsequent chequered record of success and failure is now a matter of history.

It is no part of the purpose of this book to make a comparison between the Covenant and the Charter, more especially since this has been done so admirably by Herbert Nicholas,[47] but it is legitimate to compare the means by which the League of Nations and UNO were brought into active being.

IV

By Articles 6 and 7 of the Covenant of the League of Nations, the Secretary-General, who was named in the Annex as being Sir Eric Drummond (later the Earl of Perth), was established at the seat of the League, which was declared to be Geneva. He was charged with convening the first meetings of the Council and the Assembly; these took place respectively on 16 January and 15 November 1920.

In 1945 the United Nations had no Secretary-General because the machinery for his appointment existed only on paper. The responsibility for the preliminary arrangements was vested by the San Francisco

---

* For the record, it should be noted that neither in 1955 nor in 1965 did the Powers take advantage of this provision to call a revision conference. Certain amendments to Charter have however, been adopted.

Conference in a Preparatory Commission, composed of delegations from all Governments signatory to the Charter. This Commission was assisted by an Executive Committee of fourteen, whose Secretary was Gladwyn Jebb, with Charles Webster as a kind of unofficial 'floor-manager'. The Preparatory Commission met in London from August to November 1945, and among its duties was the convening of the General Assembly which held its first session, also in London, on 10 January 1946. The Security Council met for the first time on 19 January to receive a complaint from Iran against the U.S.S.R.*

By virtue of Article 97 of the Charter, the Secretary-General of UNO is appointed by the General Assembly. Accordingly at its first session there was some jockeying for candidates. The West advanced the suggestion of Lester Pearson of Canada or Dr Elko van Kleffens of the Netherlands; the Soviet Union expressed a preference for M. Simić of Yugoslavia. Without much difficulty, however, agreement was reached on Trygve Lie of Norway, who was duly appointed on 1 February 1946.

And at Geneva on 18 April the last session of the Assembly brought the League of Nations to a close, after twenty-six years of life.

Much thought was naturally given to the location of the seat of UNO. Those with nostalgic leanings hankered after Geneva, where the Palais des Nations now housed the ghosts of earlier hopes. But there was little support for this inclination, it being rightly believed that the new organization would have a better chance of success if it were completely divorced from association with the old.

Sites were offered in London, Paris and The Hague, but these were distasteful to those nations which did not regard the United Nations – as the League had been – as a basically European institution. More conservative elements, on the other hand, were opposed to such esoteric suggestions as Tangier and Jerusalem.

More and more opinion turned towards the New World, partly because it was felt to offer more of a world approach than any European city and partly because the cynics believed that, once housed in the United States, it would be virtually impossible for the United Nations Organization to be abandoned by America. Once this trend of thought became known, offers of locations and invitations for establishment poured in from a variety of cities. Chicago and San Francisco were in the van and the State of Wyoming even offered to set aside an area of several square miles, on which a City of Peace should be erected. Some cities

* It is a coincidence of some interest that the first dispute to be submitted to the Council of the League of Nations in 1920 was a protest from Iran (then Persia) against the bombardment and subsequent occupation of the Iranian port of Enzeli on the Caspian Sea by the Soviet Union.[48]

made it clear that under no circumstances did they wish to become even involuntary hosts to a horde of foreigners. The United Kingdom plumped for Philadelphia. The United States made it known that they would accept any alternative to Washington.

Finally the brothers Rockefeller solved the problem by offering to the United Nations some twenty-six acres of slum and abattoir property in New York on the East Side of Manhattan, overlooking Turtle Bay, an act of generosity which was gladly seized upon by the General Assembly as a reason for deciding to house UNO in New York.

On this site, so handsomely provided, there arose what Harold Macmillan has not unfairly described as 'a vast glass edifice filled with people throwing stones at each other'.[49]

22 | The Coming of the Cold War

I

WHEN may the Cold War be said to have actually begun? Manifestly the challenge was present from the moment that the Soviet Union became an active belligerent and Stalin disclosed to Anthony Eden in Moscow in December 1941 the territorial claims which Russia was determined to make upon a post-war Europe.* Mr Eden's astute handling of the situation prevented an immediate endorsement of Stalin's demands. However, in the course of the period of Western appeasement of the Soviet Government, which began at Tehran, reached its apogee at Yalta and its reaffirmation at Potsdam, the fact remains that Stalin obtained by one means or another all that he had gained from his nefarious pact with Hitler in 1939, and a good deal more. Moreover, by the time the victorious Allies met at Potsdam, it was apparent that Stalin's ambitions in Europe and in Asia even surpassed the paranoiac schemings of the most extreme fanatics of the Tsarist school of expansionism. For what was alarming about this new menace from the East was that it germinated from an unholy mating of Marxist ideology with Tsarist imperialism and Pan-Slavism, a truly fearsome amalgam, with an inexorable drive for domination.†

But at what moment in history was this challenge accepted and taken up? and why? and how?

Was the final point of conflict reached at that agonising moment of revelation on 24 March 1945 when President Roosevelt cried out in anger that 'We can't do business with Stalin. He has broken every one of the promises he made at Yalta'?‡ Or was it to be found in that historic letter from President Truman to Secretary of State Byrnes in January 1946, after the latter's return from Moscow, which concluded with the words 'I'm sick of babying the Soviets'?§ For America the die had certainly been cast by 12 March 1947 when the President, before the

---

* See above, pp. 44–50.
† By far the best analysis of the origins of the Cold War is to be found in Professor Arthur Schlesinger Jr's article in *Foreign Affairs*, Oct 1967.[1]
‡ See above, p. 298.   § See above, p. 429.

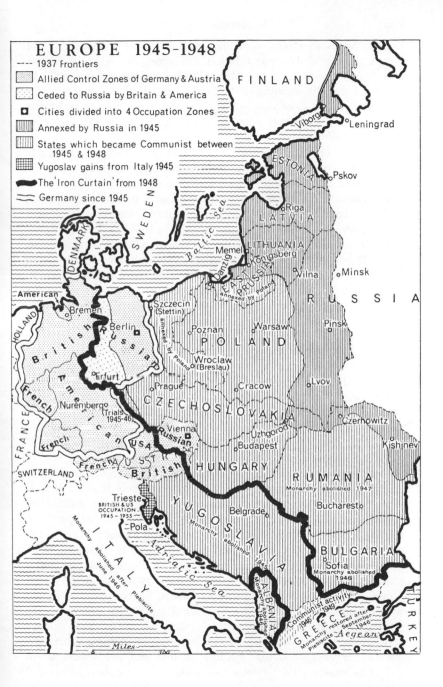

EUROPE 1945-1948

- - - - 1937 Frontiers

Allied Control Zones of Germany & Austria

Ceded to Russia by Britain & America

Cities divided into 4 Occupation Zones

Annexed by Russia in 1945

States which became Communist between 1945 & 1948

Yugoslav gains from Italy 1945

The 'Iron Curtain' from 1948

Germany since 1945

FINLAND

Viborg

Leningrad

ESTONIA

Pskov

SWEDEN

Baltic Sea

Riga

LATVIA

Memel

LITHUANIA

DENMARK

Königsberg

EAST PRUSSIA

Vilna

Minsk

annexed by Poland

American

Bremen

Szczecin (Stettin)

Berlin

annexed by Poland

RUSSIA

Poznan

Warsaw

Pinsk

HOLLAND

British

Russian

POLAND

Wroclaw (Breslau)

FRANCE

American

Erfurt

Prague

Cracow

Lvov

French

Nuremberg (Trials 1945-46)

CZECHOSLOVAKIA

French

Vienna

Russian

USA

Uzhgorod

Czernowitz

SWITZERLAND

French

AUSTRIA

British

HUNGARY

Budapest

Kishinev

RUMANIA

Monarchy abolished 1947

Trieste

BRITISH & US OCCUPATION 1945-1955

Pola

YUGOSLAVIA

Belgrade

Bucharest

ITALY

Monarchy abolished after June 1946 Plebiscite

Adriatic Sea

Monarchy abolished 1945

BULGARIA

Sofia

Monarchy abolished 1946

ALBANIA

Monarchy abolished 1946

Communist activity 1946 1949

GREECE

Monarchy restored after September 1946 Plebiscite

Aegean

TURKEY

Miles

100

United States Congress, promulgated the Truman Doctrine.* For Russia the crucial date was 1 July of the same year, when her representatives walked out of the Marshall Plan conference in Paris.† In Britain, Ernest Bevin clung to the hope of peace a little longer, but by December, at the Conference of Foreign Ministers in London, he was compelled, by Molotov's outrageous strategy, to exclaim: 'Now 'e's gone too bloody far.'‡

Whichever of these dates was crucial, the fact remains unavoidable that by the close of 1947 the Cold War was a thing in being.

Readers of this book will have realized that it is the view of its authors, based upon careful research and analysis, that Russia's foreign policy, as disclosed during the war and practised thereafter, was a re-embodiment of those imperial ambitions which in the glory of the Tsarist expansionist period had led to the Crimean War, the Russo-Turkish War, the colonization of the Transcaucasian territories and of Manchuria, the penetration of the Balkans and the Middle East, and the threat to Britain's 'lifeline' to India. To this old-fashioned imperialist policy was added the further threat of the proliferation of Communism in Europe to the detriment of what the Communists themselves term 'bourgeois democracy'.

It was in recognition of the threat inherent in this policy that, with supreme reluctance, the Western Powers were constrained to accept the Soviet challenge and to make a brave and essential response of free men against aggression. It was completely irrelevant to the issue that both sides had very shortly before been engaged in a life-and-death struggle against a common aggressor from another quarter.

These are the facts as we believe them and this is our interpretation of them. But it would be foolish to maintain that there does not exist, in both Britain and America, a Revisionist School of thought whose views are totally at variance with ours. The thesis of these scholars is that, after the death of Franklin Roosevelt and the conclusion of the Second World War, the United States deliberately abandoned the policy of collaboration and friendship with Russia and, exhilarated by the possession of the atomic bomb, undertook a course of aggression of its own designed to expel all Soviet influence from Eastern Europe and to establish democratic–capitalist states on the very border of the Soviet Union. It is the contention of this Revisionist School that, confronted with the adoption by President Truman of a policy of insensate anti-Communism, Stalin had no alternative but to take measures in defence of Russia's own borders and its own spiritual revolutionary heritage, with the result that Europe became divided into two armed camps

* See below, p. 565.   † See below, p. 574.   ‡ See above, p. 473.

represented by the North Atlantic Treaty and the Warsaw Pact.*

Between our views and those of the Revisionists there is clearly a stark contrast which is irreconcilable. Some of the facts as we know them have already been stated; others follow.

II

On 5 May 1944 the Soviet Ambassador in London, Fedor Gusev, called, by invitation, at the Foreign Office to discuss with Anthony Eden a general suggestion which the latter had put forward that, for the time being, the U.S.S.R. should temporarily regard Rumanian affairs as mainly their concern until the end of hostilities while leaving Greece as the province of Great Britain. The object of this proposal was to prevent a Soviet take-over in Greece, while recognizing the inevitability of such a measure in Rumania, and also to safeguard British interests against a Soviet penetration to the Aegean and the Mediterranean. It was still Mr Eden's hope that the whole rearrangement of the map of Europe would await the final peace settlement at the conclusion of the war. In the meantime, in order to prevent a major conflict of policy in the Balkans, he sought to gain time. His proposal was not to create spheres of influence but to establish a means of securing the interests of the Greeks, who were, in Mr Churchill's words, 'in our assigned theatre, who are our old allies, and for whom we sacrificed 40,000 men in 1941'.[3]

Gusev's reaction to the Eden proposals was not unfavourable. He was, however, guarded in his acceptance. He was immensely correct. Had the British Government consulted President Roosevelt? Were the Americans in agreement? It was most important that Allied solidarity be maintained. If Washington accepted, Moscow would agree.

The American response to Mr Eden's proposal when first communicated to the State Department by Lord Halifax was distinctly chilly. The proposal ran counter to all Cordell Hull's prejudices and convictions. It savoured of all the abominations of pre-war European diplomacy, of 'balance of power' and 'spheres of influence' and the bartering away of small nations in the avaricious interests of Great Powers. The Secretary of State was, in the main, supported by his

---

* The chief protagonists of this thesis are Professor D. F. Fleming, Dr David Horowitz and Gar Alperowitz, the last being the more subtle. As Professor Arthur Schlesinger so wisely reminds us, the fact that, in some aspects, the Revisionist thesis parallels the official Soviet argument must not, of course, prevent consideration of the case on its merits, nor raise questions about the motives of the writers.[2] Having said this, it is also incumbent to state that, whereas Professor Fleming's vast work pertains to scholarship, many of his statements are based on newspaper articles and even on the reflections of columnists, whereas Mr Alperowitz puts an interpretation on the sources he quotes which we find it impossible to accept.

departmental associates and advisers, and the counsel tendered to President Roosevelt was to have nothing to do with such a deal. To this view the President assented and expressed his dissent from the proposed Anglo-Russian agreement in a message to Mr Churchill on 10 June.

Relieved and reassured, Mr Hull went off for a short vacation, confident that he had prevented a piece of devious 'un-American' diplomacy. But he reckoned without the persuasiveness of Mr Churchill and the instability of President Roosevelt.

The Prime Minister, in a long and forceful telegram to the President, reiterated and reinforced his arguments in favour of Mr Eden's Anglo-Russian proposals and suggested that they be given a three months' trial, following which they would be reviewed by the three Great Powers. Without consulting his Secretary of State or informing the State Department, the President accepted the three months' proposal. When Mr Hull returned to his office on 12 June the matter was already '*accompli*', yet it was not until 30 June – and then only indirectly – that he was informed of the President's decision, which amounted to a complete reversal of policy.[4]

Mr Hull was, however, to win in the end, and in alliance with none other than Stalin. When Mr Churchill put his plans to Stalin on 11 July by telegram, the Marshal proved evasive. He had already consulted the United States Government direct through his Ambassador in Washington, Andrei Gromyko, on 1 July and had received an unenthusiastic confirmation of the President's acceptance of the Eden proposals for a period of three months.[5] Thus, in replying to Mr Churchill on 15 July, Stalin was able to state that 'One thing is clear to me, that the U.S. Government has certain doubts about this matter'. He therefore postponed for the moment all consideration of Mr Eden's suggestion,[6] which temporarily disappeared from the board.

Whether Stalin's motives in thus torpedoing the Eden proposals were dictated by a desire to please the Americans at the expense of the British is not entirely clear. What would seem to be certain is that he expected at this moment to include both Rumania *and* Greece within the Soviet orbit, thus aligning the whole of the Balkan Peninsula. It was clearly with this end in view that early in August 1944 he secretly dispatched a Soviet mission from Italy into northern Greece to co-operate with ELAS, the Greek Communist militants. It was in consideration of this further instance of Soviet malfeasance that the British Government abandoned all efforts to reach a major understanding with the Russians until Mr Churchill's next meeting with Stalin some two months later.

When this encounter occurred in October 1944 Mr Churchill, notwithstanding earlier evidence of Soviet bad faith, again reopened with Stalin the issue of a temporary Balkan settlement on the basis of the Eden proposals. There resulted the famous 'Percentage Agreement'. 'As far as Britain and Russia are concerned,' the Prime Minister suggested, 'how would it do for you to have ninety per cent predominance in Rumania, for us to have ninety per cent say in Greece and go fifty-fifty about Yugoslavia?' And he wrote on half a sheet of paper:

Rumania	
Russia	90 per cent
The others	10 per cent
Greece	
Great Britain	90 per cent
(in accord with U.S.A.)	
Russia	10 per cent
Yugoslavia	50–50 per cent
Hungary	50–50 per cent
Bulgaria	
Russia	75 per cent
The others	25 per cent[7]

Stalin at once accepted and, though next day (10 October) Molotov, in conversation with Eden, made a certain display of 'dragging his feet',[8] the 'Percentage Agreement' became policy.*

The results of the 'Percentage Agreement' were far-reaching beyond the anticipation of the Prime Minister. Mr Churchill was understandably satisfied with the outcome of his somewhat rough-and-ready diplomacy, and it must be admitted that, in so far as the primary purpose of circumventing Soviet interference in Greek affairs was concerned, the 'Percentage Agreement' was an unqualified success. Stalin proved himself to be a man of his word, and his word was soon to be put to the test.

During the winter of 1944 Greece, in the throes of liberation from German occupation – a campaign in which British troops actively participated – found herself in the grip of a civil war, in which the Communist-controlled ELAS and E.A.M. organizations made a determined attempt to seize the government of the country. This resulted in Mr Churchill's dramatic personal intervention during Christmas 1944 and the consequent establishment of an interim Govern-

---

* Even Mr Churchill, when he had brought off his successful negotiation, was somewhat alarmed at the almost light-hearted way in which the agreement had been reached. 'Might it not', he asked Stalin, 'be thought rather cynical if it seemed we had disposed of these issues, so fateful to millions of people, in such an offhand manner?' And he suggested that the paper be destroyed. 'No, you keep it', said Stalin.

ment, with Archbishop Damaskinos acting as Regent, pending the holding of elections and a referendum on the return of the King.

Throughout this difficult and delicate period Mr Churchill and his Government were subjected to vehement attacks in the House of Commons and the the British Press for having imposed a reactionary régime upon the Greek people in defiance of their desire for a Government of the Left led by George Papandreou. The American Press also violently condemned British policy and vilified the Prime Minister and Anthony Eden, while the new Secretary of State, Edward Stettinius, issued a distinctly critical statement.

Yet, throughout the same period, Stalin remained faithful to his compact. He gave no support to ELAS and, while *The Times* and the *Manchester Guardian* and the *New York Times* fulminated against Mr Churchill, his Government and his policy, no word of reproach came from Stalin or was to be found in the columns of *Pravda* or *Izvestia*.

It is not without irony that this display of integrity on the part of the Soviet Government was to redound very greatly to their advantage in the future. It created in Mr Churchill's mind a belief in the fundamental trustworthiness of Stalin's promises, and this in its turn was to have disastrous results all too soon. On 11 December 1944 the Prime Minister minuted to Anthony Eden:

> I am increasingly impressed up to date with the loyalty with which, under much temptation and very likely pressure, Stalin has kept off Greece in accordance with our agreement, and I believe that we shall gain in influence with him and strengthen a moderate policy for the Soviets by showing them how our mind works.[9]

It was under the influence of this illusion that Mr Churchill attended the Yalta Conference two months later, where, predisposed by the success of his Greek policy, he entered into further agreements with Stalin for the future government of those Balkan states in which, under the 'Percentage Agreement', Russia exercised a major degree of control.* It may have been due to his overpowering desire to maintain Anglo-American unity of thought and purpose and therefore his willingness to follow President Roosevelt's lead in his policy of appeasement towards Russia, or it may have been a genuine belief in Soviet integrity induced by Marshal Stalin's guile and charm, but, whatever the cause, Mr Churchill certainly told the House of Commons on his return from the Yalta Conference:

> The impression I brought back from the Crimea, and from all my other contacts, is that Marshal Stalin and the Soviet leaders wish to live in honourable friendship and equality with the Western demo-

* See above, p. 240.

cracies. I feel also that their word is their bond. I know of no Government which stands to its obligations, even in its own despite, more solidly than the Russian Soviet Government.[10]

This was pure delusion, as Mr Churchill was himself swift to recognise and admit. Even as he addressed the House of Commons the Soviet Government was violating in Rumania the pledge which Stalin had given in the Yalta Declaration on Liberated Europe.* And now the results of misplaced trust became apparent. Stalin, probably quite genuinely, had believed that under the 'Percentage Agreement' and at Yalta, the British and the Americans had acquiesced in the establishment of a Soviet sphere of influence in the Balkan countries other than Greece, and he had behaved accordingly. In his view, if the British installed a 'reactionary' Government in Greece, was he not free to install a Communist Government in Rumania? The Western Allies were now hampered by their previous agreements with Russia, which Russia had loyally observed. It was true that Stalin had broken the agreements entered into at Yalta but, as Mr Churchill honestly admitted, 'if I pressed him too much he might say, "I did not interfere with your action in Greece: why do you not give me the same latitude in Rumania?"'[11]

Thus the hands of the British and American Governments were tied in respect of their reproaches to Stalin, and their protests regarding Rumania were weakened accordingly. But they clung to Greece as an outpost of democracy in the Balkan Peninsula and, under British leadership, maintained their position there with courage and tenacity; but not for long.

No sooner had the curtain fallen at Potsdam upon the last act of the farce of quadripartite solidarity than the naked ambition of Soviet foreign policy was made apparent. Only seven months separated V.J. Day from that moment of revelation at Fulton, Missouri, when, on 5 March 1946, Mr Churchill, in a historic address, gave public recognition to the imminent danger of the power and behaviour of Stalin's Russia. A year later the crisis was in full spate.

By a curious irony of history this new situation made demands upon Britain which, with the best will in the world, she was unable to meet. A disastrous concatenation of circumstances deprived her of the power to make good her pledges to Greece – among other countries – and thereby changed the course of history.

The first event in this threnody of woe had been the precipitate termination without previous warning of Lend-Lease, authorization for which was signed by President Truman on 11 May 1945, without his

* See above, p. 331 n.

having previously read the document.[12]* The result of this capricious action was to throw the British economy violently and harmfully out of gear, and, to save it from immediate disaster, it was necessary for the United States to grant a credit of some $3,750 million. Delay in America's ratifying this financial agreement – which was not accomplished until July 1946 – and the rapid decline in exchange value deprived the credit of much of its benefit.

On top of these staggering blows to her economic stability, Britain was now to suffer the calamitous winter of 1946–7, bringing with it a congeries of disaster. Beginning on 25 January, a succession of driving blizzards, almost unparalleled in British meteorological annals, blanketed the country. Even before these snowstorms arrived the British Isles were afflicted by a severe coal shortage which had already forced an extensive temporary industrial 'shut-down'. Early in January Mr Attlee's Government had been compelled to cut the allocation of coal to industry by 50 per cent, for the simple reason that there was no more than this to allocate; there were no more reserves. The supply of electricity to industry was also drastically curtailed. Food too was severely rationed, bread being placed on coupons for the first time in British history.

All this was before the blizzards and the storms which accompanied them. When they struck they simply froze transport by rail and road into immobility and rendered even portage by sea impossible. The winter wheat withered on the ground. Such industry as had previously managed to continue in production now began to close, and when, on 7 February, the Government announced in the House of Commons that all electricity would be cut off from factories for several days and that domestic consumption would be cut off for five hours of the day, five million workers were confronted with loss of employment and with heatless homes.

All Europe was held in the pitiless grip of this savage winter which was to have so memorable an effect on the history of the Continent. In country after country recently installed democratic Governments, already grappling with the wellnigh insurmountable problems of post-war reconstruction, were now confronted with appalling additional burdens of feeding and maintaining their ravaged populations in the wake of these horrible conditions. One Power alone stood to benefit by this calamitous situation. As in state after state democratic régimes staggered in the throes of their predicament, the Soviet Union girt itself to take full advantage of the embarrassment in which European

* This lapse from good sense taught President Truman a salutary lesson. 'After that first sad experience with the Lend-Lease termination', he subsequently wrote, 'I never put my initials of approval on a piece of paper without reading it with care.'[13] (See above, pp. 318–21.)

'bourgeois-democracy' found itself. Indeed, at the beginning of 1947 it seemed as if nothing could withstand the advance of Stalin's rapidly expanding empire.

Nowhere was this more true than in Greece and Turkey, where since 1944 successive British Governments had been according the economic and military aid necessary to stave off the disaster of a surrender by these states to Communist pressure and to a penetration which would result in the emergence of Soviet influence in force upon the shores of the Mediterranean.

Manifestly Britain, in her own parlous state, could not continue to sustain her two pensionaries – Greek requirements alone for 1947 amounted to between $250 and $280 million; manifestly, also, the annexation of Greece and Turkey to the Soviet-dominated sphere of influence must not be allowed to occur. For the third time in less than half a century there came to the United States the appeal to save Europe.

At this moment in Washington there was a moment of mutation. President Truman had just appointed the third of his Secretaries of State (the first two had been Edward Stettinius and James Byrnes) in the person of General George Marshall, whom he had summoned back from a not altogether happy ambassadorial mission to China. Though he had been but a month in office, General Marshall had already reached one vitally important conclusion, which was soon to be confirmed as a result of his experience at the Moscow meeting of the Conference of Foreign Ministers,* namely that European recovery could not await 'compromise through exhaustion' and must proceed, if necessary, without Four-Power agreement. The United States must take the initiative.

In pursuance of this conviction he had with some care, and with the perhaps infelicitous assistance of the State Department speech-writers, prepared, as his first major public utterance since assuming office, an address which he would give at Princeton University on 22 February.† In it he drew the attention of his student audience to the potential of the United States, to the responsibility which this potential implied and to the basic orientation of United States policy in the discharge of this responsibility:

> You should fully understand the special position that the United States now occupies in the world geographically, financially, militarily and scientifically, and the implications involved. The development of a

* See above, p. 471.
† As Professor Louis Hallé in his admirable book on the Cold War justifiably points out, 'the language of this statement is so awkward as to cry out for comment. . . . What the Secretary of State said in this, his first major utterance since taking office, was denied any possibility of moral or intellectual authority by the crippled English in which he said it.'[14]

sense of responsibility for world order and security, the development of a sense of overwhelming importance of this country's acts and failures to act, in relation to world order and security – these, in my opinion, are great 'musts' for your generation.[15]

Even as General Marshall thus addressed the young men of Princeton on the new facts of life, with which they and their country were confronted willy-nilly, events were taking place in Washington which added an immediate effect to his words.

The General had left his office in the State Department for Princeton early in the afternoon of Friday, 21 February, and scarcely had he gone than the British Ambassador, Lord Inverchapel, telephoned a request for an immediate appointment with him. At the earliest the Secretary of State could not return to Washington until Saturday evening and would not be back at his desk before Monday morning, the twenty-fourth. To his brilliant and understanding deputy, Dean Acheson, now Acting Secretary of State, it seemed undesirable to summon the Secretary back precipitately; he deserved, Acheson thought, at least some part of a weekend free if it could be arranged. Inquiry at the British Embassy elucidated the fact that Lord Inverchapel's request for an appointment was for the purpose of delivering two Notes announcing the decision of the British Government to withdraw their troops from Greece and terminate their economic and financial assistance to that hard-pressed and distressed country and also to Turkey. Acheson, with practical common sense, suggested that copies of the Notes should be delivered informally; that consideration of their contents could begin immediately by the competent officials of the State Department and, if necessary, continue throughout the weekend; that General Marshall would be briefed accordingly on his return on Monday morning to his office and, having had time to study the matter, could receive the Ambassador that same evening when the formal handing over of the Notes could take place. Meanwhile, he assured the Embassy, both the President and the Secretary of State would be informed.

It thus happened that later in the afternoon of Friday, 21 February, Herbert Sichell, a member of the great family firm of wine importers and currently a First Secretary in the British Foreign Service, sat down with Loy Henderson, Director of the Office of Near Eastern and African Affairs in the State Department, who had been one of that scintillating group of Kremlinologists which William C. Bullitt had taken with him to Moscow in 1934. Sichell now told Henderson, both verbally and in writing, of Britain's intention to withdraw from her role as protector of Greece and Turkey within thirty-eight days.[16]

This news, which was tantamount to an official announcement of the liquidation of the *Pax Britannica*, by which Britain had for a century and a half discharged her responsibilities throughout the world, did not come as a complete surprise to the State Department. For some days their Embassies in Athens and London had been reporting rumours of such a decision and the disastrous effect which it would have, particularly in Greece, where the economic structure was already crumbling, resulting inevitably in hardship and political unrest and the imminent intention of the Communists to seize the country. It seemed inevitable that the Soviet Empire would replace Britain as the dominant force in the Eastern Mediterranean unless the United States, breaking with its ancient prejudices against 'entangling alliances', were to move with courage and celerity to fill the vacuum first.

The issue was never for a moment in doubt in the percipient mind of Dean Acheson. As he was to tell the House of Representatives later: 'A Communist-dominated Government in Greece would be considered dangerous to United States security.'[17] It was as simple as that. Soviet Russia predominant in the Eastern Mediterranean was recognized as a threat to the vital interests of America, and not only of America but of the whole Western world. And America alone was capable of meeting and dealing with this threat.

The Under-Secretary of State communicated his views to the President and to General Marshall, in both of whom he found warm supporters. After consultation with Congressional leaders and with the members of his Cabinet, whose approval he obtained, President Truman went before a joint session of Congress on 12 March and asked them to vote legislation which would provide the sum of $250 million for Greece and $150 million for Turkey, and he warned them that this would be only a beginning.

There followed a debate of greater length and acerbity than had been anticipated, but the House of Representatives approved the measure on 22 April and the Senate passed it on 9 May. On 22 May, just three months after Britain had given notice of her compulsory withdrawals, the President signed the bill and thus gave legal form to the Truman Doctrine that

> we [the United States] shall not realize our objectives unless we are willing to help free people to maintain their institutions and their national integrity against aggressive movements that seek to impose upon them totalitarian régimes. This is no more than a frank recognition that totalitarian régimes imposed on free peoples, by direct or indirect aggression, undermine the foundation of international peace and hence the security of the United States.

By endorsing this Doctrine Congress had placed itself squarely behind the President. As Truman himself was to write later, 'America had served notice that the march of Communism would not be allowed to succeed by default'.[18] It was this Doctrine which, through the instrument of the Marshall Plan, was to save Western Europe and was also to save West Berlin from Soviet annexation; it was also to lead the United States into full-scale conventional wars in Korea and Vietnam. It was the beginning of the third great American adventure into active world politics.

III

When the President of the United States and his advisers took the decision to recommend to Congress the necessary means for the protection of Greece and Turkey from Soviet aggression, they were very well aware of what they did. When Congress enacted the legislation for this purpose, and the President signed it, there was no doubt in the minds of those who directed the foreign relations of the United States that America had not engaged in an isolated and individual act of policy but had assumed the leadership of the Western world in accepting a challenge from Moscow which had been proximate since Yalta and imminent since Potsdam.

If this leadership were to amount to anything more than a grandiloquent gesture, instant preparation must be made to give aid and succour to those European countries where, as Under-Secretary of State William Clayton wrote in a memorandum of prescient warning, systematic campaigns were in process to destroy national integrity and independence. 'Feeding on hunger, economic slavery and frustration, these attacks have already been successful in some of the liberated countries', Mr Clayton continued, and went on to advise that prompt and effective aid for gravely threatened countries was essential to America's own security and that the President and the Secretary of State must shock the country into a realization of its peril by telling it the facts which daily poured into Washington in cables from American missions abroad.

Time was of the essence in this matter, but it was essential that no major step should be taken before the President and his Administration had secured both Congressional and popular support. Planning towards both these ends could, however, be set in hand.

Because both his chief, General Marshall, and his principal colleague, Will Clayton, were in Europe, the main responsibility for this early planning devolved upon Dean Acheson. It could scarcely have been in more efficient hands. He at once returned to a suggestion originally made by General Dwight Eisenhower, then Chief of the General Staff, that the appeal to Congress for support for Greece and Turkey should also request funds for other countries resisting Communist penetration. For reasons of time, and in order not to complicate the immediate issue unduly, it had been decided not to adopt the General's suggestion at that time, but it was soon evident that the general situation in Europe would shortly demand a much larger programme of American assistance and that the first thing to be done was to collect the facts and estimate accordingly. This Dean Acheson did, setting up, as early as 5 March, inter-departmental planning machinery to prepare a comprehensive brief for General Marshall's consideration on his return from Moscow.

While this activity was in progress an opportunity presented itself for a preliminary move for the enlightenment of the nation. President Truman asked Dean Acheson to substitute for him as principal speaker at a meeting of the Delta Council to be held at the town of Cleveland, Mississippi. The occasion would be one for a major statement on foreign policy. Acheson agreed, and in due course delivered a speech which President Truman subsequently termed 'the prologue to the Marshall Plan'.[19]

Before his departure for Mississippi, Acheson was able to get the first-hand views of General Marshall, who came back from Moscow in the last days of April.* Here there was but cold comfort. The Secretary of State returned with the absolute conviction that the Soviet Union had no intention of co-operating with the United States in the interests of world peace or of humanity, being merely concerned with the cold and pitiless exploitation of the helpless condition of Europe for the further expansion of Communist power and Russian imperialism.

Thus, when Dean Acheson spoke at Cleveland, Mississippi, on 8 May, he did so with the authority and backing of both the President and the Secretary of State. Indeed General Marshall had himself given the keynote in his radio report to the nation on 28 April on the course of the Moscow Conference. He gave his hearers a harrowing picture, by no means exaggerated, of 'the impoverished and suffering people of Europe who are crying for help, for coal, for food, and for most of the necessities of life. . . . The recovery of Europe has been slower than had been expected. Disintegrating forces are becoming evident. The patient is sinking while the doctors deliberate . . . action cannot await compromise through exhaustion.'[20]

It was in pursuance of this sombre warning that Dean Acheson addressed the members of the Delta Council in the auditorium of the

* The authorities are at variance as to the exact date of General Marshall's return to Washington. President Truman (II 112) gives it as 26 April, Mr Acheson (pp. 227-8) as 28 April.

Teachers' College of Cleveland, Mississippi. Clearly and forcefully he
described the situation in Europe and explained how and why it had
come about. Then he defined for them the remedy, which lay in increased exports to Europe from the United States. But since Europe
needed exports to the tune of $16 billion and could find imports to the
United States to pay for them of only half that sum, the deficit would
have to be made up by loans and grants and credits from the United
States, and by new methods of financing which would avoid exhausting
the already gravely depleted reserves of the stricken countries, leaving
them bankrupt and hopeless. The new methods would include the
increase of imports from Europe to close the gap and also selective
exports to European areas of special concern to the United States and
her purposes, that is to say the countries of the Western world.

America's objective in this matter, Acheson emphasized, was neither
relief nor charity, but a revival of the agriculture, the industry and the
trade of these stricken countries so that they might again become self-
supporting. To do this it was necessary to obtain from Congress new
powers to allocate commodities and shipping, and also new finance
grants. And beyond all other considerations, time was running out. He
concluded:

> Not only do human beings and nations exist in narrow economic
> margins, but also human dignity, human freedom, and democratic
> constitutions. It is one of the principal aims of our foreign policy
> today to use our economic and financial resources to widen these
> margins. It is necessary if we are to preserve our own freedoms and
> our own democratic institutions. It is necessary for our national
> security. And it is our duty and our privilege as human beings.[21]

This eloquent appeal of Dean Acheson's deserved a wider response
than it received. It did not cause much of a stir at home or abroad on a
broad public scale, though on both sides of the Atlantic it stimulated
a good deal of discussion among those who appreciated the grave impact
of the message it contained. Nevertheless it achieved a certain degree
of reaction which in itself was important in the grand strategy of the
campaign. Above all, its indomitable author was not cast down. 'I did
not think at the time', Mr Acheson wrote later, 'that my trumpet note
from Cleveland was the call to arms which would start the American
people on one of the greatest and most honourable adventures in
history. . . . Perhaps it is not too much to say that it was reveille, which
awoke them to the duties of that day of decision. At least the trumpet
did not give an uncertain sound.'[22]

In the days that followed, the need for American action in Europe
became more pressing. How was the State Department to keep up and

increase the momentum generated by Dean Acheson's Cleveland speech? As he explained to General Marshall: 'I've kicked a fairly important ball pretty high in the air, but it's falling rapidly. It's time you caught it and ran with it.' It was indeed. Hungary had just fallen to a *coup d'état* which had placed the Communist Party in control of the machinery of government.

The difficulty seemed to be just how to 'get the show on the road'. Should the approach be through diplomatic channels or through the public media or both? And, if both, which first? And to whom should it be addressed? To all European countries or to Western Europe only? Meanwhile two fundamental principles crystallized. First, America must run this show, though Europe must produce her own plan for her own salvation; secondly, Russia must not be permitted to obstruct the production of the show.

The answers to at least some of these questions were forthcoming when the Secretary of State decided that he himself would make a major statement of policy. General Marshall bethought himself of an earlier invitation to accept an honorary degree from Harvard University, which he had temporarily refused. He learned that the next Commencement exercises were to be held on 5 June. He telephoned to Harvard and was informed by a somewhat flummoxed official that the University would be delighted to confer the degree upon him and that a short speech would be in order.

A brilliant galaxy of experts were now charged to contribute their thoughts for the Secretary's forthcoming speech, Dean Acheson, Will Clayton, George Kennan and 'Chip' Bohlen among them. Finally, having read all their offerings, the General went home and wrote his own text. He showed it to nobody. It is not actually known that he discussed it with the President, though it is supposed that he did. He left for Cambridge, Massachusetts, on 4 June with an uncompleted text, and the State Department was never told in advance of its final form, which was telephoned from Harvard at the last moment.[23]*

Meanwhile Dean Acheson had lost no opportunity of making use of the technique of the 'calculated leak'. On 22 May John Balfour, then Minister at the British Embassy, had invited Acheson to lunch to meet Gerald Barry, then editor of the London *News Chronicle*, at the Metropolitan Club, Washington. The repercussions and implications of the Cleveland, Mississippi, speech were still fresh in mind and over a preprandial dry martini Jock Balfour raised the subject directly.

---

* A text of sorts was made available by the State Department on the afternoon of 4 June. It was a hastily composed mixture of drafts reflecting its varied parentage. Some of their ideas were dissimilar and even contradictory.

In answer to a question of mine over a cocktail before luncheon [Sir John wrote later*] Dean Acheson said that in the not too far distant future General Marshall might also be expected to speak on the subject of world recovery. Drawing a deep breath he then gave Gerald Barry and myself what appeared to be almost identical with the text of the Harvard speech. While unwilling to say whether his chief would make any concrete recommendations, Acheson left us in no doubt that the time was past when America would respond to piecemeal approaches for assistance. It would, he said, be of great help to the Administration in making an extensive programme of further financial aid palatable to Congress and public opinion if the Governments of individual European countries were to give as much proof as possible of their willingness to co-operate together in promoting co-ordinated recovery over a wide Continental area. Britain and France should give a lead to others. The time factor was all important.

When leaving the Club Gerald Barry and I exchanged the glances of happy explorers who had just sighted a promised land. On my return to the Chancery I reported what Acheson had said to my then chief, Archie Inverchapel, who promptly called a meeting of Embassy experts to examine the implications of this novel and most encouraging development in American policy. Their combined views were set out in a letter from myself to the Head of the American Department [then Sir Nevile Butler] which reached the Foreign Office the very day that the Harvard speech was delivered.

Some two weeks later Dean Acheson grasped a further opportunity gratuitously and fortuitously presented to him by three British correspondents. Leonard Miall of the B.B.C., René MacColl of the *Daily Express* and Malcolm Muggeridge of the *Daily Telegraph*, on 2 June, also invited him to luncheon at the United Nations Club on 19th Street. He came with Lincoln White, Press Officer of the State Department, and was in due course questioned about his Cleveland speech and the Continental Plan which it had envisaged. How official was it, they asked, and what was the next step to be? Acheson told them just how important and how serious he considered it to be but explained that unless there was some dramatic initiative to formulate an agreed plan on the European side of the Atlantic nothing would happen. He made no mention, however, of the fact that General Marshall's speech was imminent.[24]

The speech which General Marshall delivered on 5 June at Harvard partook strongly of the General's own characteristics. It was forceful and straightforward, wise and courageous, far-seeing and compassionate, making up in integrity and directness of approach what it lacked in

---

* The authors of this book are deeply grateful to Sir John Balfour for his permission to quote this extract from his as yet unpublished memoirs.

polished eloquence. Placed in juxtaposition with the elegance of Mr Acheson's appeal at Cleveland, Mississippi, it epitomizes the supremely complementary relationship which existed between the two men, the Under-Secretary providing the perfect foil for the Secretary of State.

General Marshall spoke in language which Dean Acheson has described as 'simple, short and altogether brilliant'. It was clearly his own and not that of professional speech-writers. He set forth the condition of Europe and the causes of it, and then defined the governmental policy of the United States towards Europe as a desire to relieve not only want but fear.

> Our policy [he said] is directed not against any country or doctrine but against hunger, poverty, desperation and chaos. Its purpose should be the revival of a working economy in the world so as to permit the emergence of political and social conditions in which free institutions can exist.
>
> Such assistance, I am convinced, must not be on a piecemeal basis as various crises develop. Any assistance that this government may render in the future should provide a cure rather than a palliative.
>
> Any government that is willing to assist in the task of recovery will find full co-operation, I am sure, on the part of the United States Government. Any government which manœuvres to block the recovery of other countries cannot expect help from us. Furthermore, governments, political parties, or groups which seek to perpetuate human misery in order to profit therefrom politically or otherwise will encounter the opposition of the United States.[25]

In this last paragraph notice was served unequivocally as to the intended policy of the United States. Without mentioning her name, Russia was invited to participate in the restoration of Europe. If she preferred not to help she was asked not to hinder. If she elected to hamper the work of rehabilitation she was warned that she would incur 'the opposition of the United States'. No declaration of intention could have been clearer.

Lest it should be thought by some that Europe was to be reduced to the status of a Grand Pensionary, or by others that the United States was to assume the passive attitude of a milch-cow whose udders lay in transatlantic hands, General Marshall proceeded to outline the role of Europe in its own economic restoration. The European countries must, as far as possible, work out their plans for their own salvation in co-operation with the United States.

> It would be neither fitting nor efficacious for this [the American] government to undertake to draw up unilaterally a programme designed to place Europe on its feet economically.
> This is the business of Europeans.

The initiative, I think, must come from Europe.

The programme should be a joint one, agreed to by a number of, if not all, European nations.

The role of this country should consist of friendly aid in the drafting of a European programme and of later support of such a programme so far as it may be practical for us to do so.[26]

The responsibility for taking the initiative was therefore laid at the door of Europe. If European nations, all or some, would get together and agree upon what their various needs were, then the United States would respond. But would they do so? Were they so sunk in their Slough of Despond that further effort was impossible? Was there in Europe 'peradventure one just man' who might give a lead?*

From his corner room on the first floor of the Foreign Office Ernest Bevin had watched with growing gloom and apprehension the course of events in Europe. As Russian obstruction developed into Russian aggression and there was still no clear indication of policy from Washington his anxiety deepened, for behind the silence there lurked the underlying fear that the United States would once again retreat behind the banner of isolation. Bevin had been agreeably impressed by the response which the Truman Administration had made to his appeal on behalf of Greece and Turkey, but there had been no indication that this was any more than an isolated instance of emergency action. The British Embassy in Washington had given no encouragement as to the intention of the Administration, and without the backing of America, Bevin was convinced, there was no possibility of halting the economic depression in Western Europe and the consequent drift towards Communism. There was imminent danger that Russia might succeed in extending her power and doctrine by reason of the very inability of Western Europe to pull itself up by its own bootstraps.

By the evening of 5 June, however, there were indications that the answers to at least some of Mr Bevin's problems were on the way. He turned on the little portable radio in his bedroom to catch the nine o'clock news. This contained a brief version of the Marshall speech, but at 10.30 p.m. the Foreign Secretary heard, in the B.B.C. 'American Commentry', the voice of Leonard Miall proclaiming 'glad tidings of great joy'.†

* General Marshall had originally toyed with the idea of warning Mr Bevin privately beforehand of the significance of his overture, but had decided against it for fear of offending Georges Bidault, the French Foreign Minister.

† The unwitting inaccuracy of historical writing – indeed the whole impossibility of achieving historical truth *in toto* – is something with which the modern historian has to contend. Dependent upon the frailty of human memory, he is at the mercy of either deliberate rationalization or the sheer inability of man to recall and record any event with absolute precision of detail. In after years, when speaking of the Marshall Plan,

Armed with the interpretation which Acheson had given at the journalists' luncheon, Miall, when he read the text of the Marshall speech in the State Department release, at once grasped its vital importance and put all that he had into his 'American Commentary' that evening.* The importance of what Miall said was that he emphasized what Dean Acheson had told him (but which was not in the Marshall speech), namely, that the success or failure of the Marshall proposal depended on whether there was an immediate European response. As Mr Bevin listened to his words a new hope was born.

> The first thought that came into his mind [Lord Franks has written] was not that this gave a prospect of American economic help for Europe. He saw that, and grasped the chance with both hands; but first came the realization that his chief fear had been banished for good. The Americans were not going to do as they had done after the First World War and retreat into their hemisphere. They had enlarged their horizon and their understanding of the intention of the United States to take in the Atlantic and the several hundred million of Europeans who lived beyond it. The keystone of Bevin's foreign policy had swung into place.[27]

The Foreign Secretary was first with the news at the Foreign Office next morning, and here he met with the wet blanket of professional diplomacy. The Washington correspondent of *The Times* (Sir Willmot Lewis) had failed to mention the Marshall speech at all.† It was only featured in the *Daily Express* and the *Telegraph*. There was no telegram from the Embassy in Washington, but there was Jock Balfour's long letter to Nevile Butler, which had just arrived. Sir William Strang, the Permanent Under-Secretary, was of the opinion that they should not be precipitate but should telegraph to the Embassy in Washington instructing them to inquire at the State Department as to exactly what General Marshall had in mind. This piece of cautious counsel was rejected by Mr Bevin. He would not, he said, pry into what General Marshall was thinking about; what General Marshall had said was good enough for him and it demanded immediate action.[28]

Having read Balfour's letter, the Foreign Secretary forthwith tele-

---

Mr Bevin would state that, early in the morning of 6 June, he heard the voice of General Marshall on his little bedside radio. In point of fact, according to contemporary B.B.C. records, the voice that he heard was that of Leonard Miall, whose message from Washington, the 'American Commentary', was broadcast at 10.30 on the evening of 5 June.

  * Similarly prompted by Dean Acheson's remarks, MacColl and Muggeridge also reported vehemently on the Marshall speech, but the other British correspondents, and indeed the national Press of America also, failed to appreciate the fact that it contained a great statement of policy which was to change the course of history.

  † *The Times* of 6 June carried only a very brief dispatch from Reuter's.

phoned Georges Bidault in Paris and arranged to meet him there on 17 June. As a result of their joint invitation, M. Molotov joined them on 27 June and there followed four days of abrasive discussion. This concluded on 1 July when Molotov withdrew, formally refusing to have any part in any combined programme of European recovery, and rejecting the fundamental basis of the American offer on the grounds that such a programme would constitute a 'violation of national sovereignty'.

The rapidity with which Mr Bevin moved after 5 June ('I grasped the opportunity with both hands and went to Paris') came as a surprise – an agreeable surprise – to the American Secretary of State and his Department, who had expected dalliance abroad and opposition at home. That the latter did not make itself apparent for some weeks was due in all probability to the dramatic rapidity with which the Western Powers responded, under Mr Bevin's leadership, to a formal consideration of ways and means.* 'History will give credit', said General Marshall some two years later, 'to those European statesmen who responded with such energy and vision to the needs of the moment.'[29]†

Their task made in a sense much easier by the departure of Molotov, Mr Bevin and M. Bidault jointly issued on 4 July an invitation to twenty-two countries to a conference to be held in Paris on 12 July. Of those invited seventeen accepted, Moscow having vetoed the participation of Poland, Rumania, Hungary and Bulgaria, and Spain

* 'I like to think', Sir John Balfour wrote later, 'that Mr Bevin's magnificent initiative was greatly facilitated by the detached background information made available by Dean Acheson's calculated disclosure to myself.' Like most great historical events, the Marshall Plan is not without its mythology, and perhaps the most unfounded and unjustified of the myths is that associated with Sir John Balfour, to the effect that he dismissed it as 'one more university speech' and refused to telegraph the text to London. The picture has grown up, and is even recorded in print by Joseph Marion Jones (on p. 256 of the paperback edition of his book *Fifteen Weeks*), of a somewhat bumbling diplomatic figure of fun sending the text of the Harvard speech by sea-bag because he did not appreciate its importance. In the light of what has been recorded above, it will be seen how unfair this image is. It was in effect Dean Acheson's 'calculated leak' and Jock Balfour's quick appraisal of its value that materially contributed to the ability of the Foreign Secretary to make up his mind so quickly and to grasp the initiative with such vigour. It is perfectly true that Sir John sent the text of the Harvard speech by bag, but he knew that his Press Officer, Philip Jordan, was aware of Acheson's conversation with the three journalists and he anticipated that the text would be immediately available in London through the Press. In view of the strong requests from London for economy in cables, he therefore determined to save money on sending a telegram, but for very different reasons from those which have been attributed to him.

† In view of this encomium from the author of the Marshall Plan, it is difficult to understand, or take seriously, the criticisms of such scholars as Professor P. Kindleberger of the Massachusetts Institute of Technology who, as lately as 1968, attacked Mr Bevin for tardiness in his response to the Marshall speech and, incidentally, repeated, without full knowledge of the facts, the allegation of Sir John Balfour's sending the text of the speech by bag.[30]

standing apart. But when the conference formally convened on 12 July 1947 only sixteen states were present.* For the last time Czechoslovakia had exercised her liberty of action as a free nation in accepting the invitation. There followed grim retribution. Jan Masaryk, the Foreign Minister, was summoned to Moscow and ordered to rescind her acceptance. He did so with reluctance and humiliation. Seven months later Czechoslovakia had passed behind the Iron Curtain in the *coup d'état* of 25 February 1948, and shortly thereafter Jan Masaryk himself was dead.

The Paris Conference set up a Committee on European Economic Co-operation which, on 22 September, presented an over-all plan – really a sublimated 'shopping-list' – to the United States Government, retailing their immediate and less immediate needs. In due course, after the usual preliminary consultations with Congressional leaders, President Truman summoned a special session of Congress and re-quested them, on 19 December 1947, to authorize the appropriation of the gigantic sum of $17 billion dollars, representing the estimated cost over a four-year period of European recovery. He also asked that $6 billion of this amount be provided by 1 April 1948 to cover the initial – and most critical – period of fifteen months, to 30 June 1949.

Congress acted with becoming celerity, but they did not vote the whole sum asked for by the President. They enacted the first European Recovery Act as quickly as it was possible to do so, and President Truman signed it on 3 April 1948. Its appropriation was for thirteen instead of seventeen billion dollars.[31]†

The Marshall Plan will surely be recorded as one of America's greatest contributions to the peace of the world. Without it it would have been difficult for Western Europe to have remained free from the tyranny of Communism. It was, as Winston Churchill has written, 'the most unsordid act in history', and the men who achieved it, in McGeorge Bundy's splendid words, 'still walk with the pride of heroes who know they put their mark on history'.[32]

IV

When Soviet Russia in the summer of 1947 rejected the Marshall Plan as 'a violation of national sovereignty' and deliberately prevented her

---

* Austria, Belgium, Denmark, France, Greece, Iceland, Ireland, Italy, Luxembourg, the Netherlands, Norway, Portugal, Sweden, Switzerland, Turkey and the United Kingdom.

† On 16 April, immediately after the passage of the European Recovery Act, the Organization for European Economic Co-operation (O.E.E.C.) was established in Paris for the implementation of the Marshall Plan.

satellite states – including in this category for the first time Czechoslovakia – from participating in the Paris Conference, she made a
clear-cut decision. The alternative presented to Russia by General
Marshall's speech and Mr Bevin's subsequent initiative was either to
join the West or fight – an adaptation of Theodore Roosevelt's advice
to 'put up or shut up'. Russia, clearly and wittingly, chose the latter
course. Thenceforth the term 'Iron Curtain' took on a grimmer and
more definite character. The lines of battle were drawn in Europe
which would be increasingly now divided into two armed camps. The
Cold War was on.

Moscow moved first. In October, at an international Communist
gathering in Poland, there was set up (5 October) the Cominform
(Communist Information Bureau), a lineal descendant of the Comintern
(Communist International) which had been disbanded during the war.
The Cominform, which was located in Belgrade, was dedicated to the
undoing of 'bourgeois democracy'. It was the Soviet riposte to the
Truman Doctrine and the Marshall Plan, which were represented as
'imitating the Hitlerites, the new aggressors are using blackmail and
distortion'. The first fruits were seen in France and Italy. There, by
means of strikes and industrial disturbances promoted by the Communist parties, attempts were made in the winter of 1947 to disrupt the
economic life of both countries. They failed, and in December 1947
the last session of the Conference of Foreign Ministers, meeting in
London, adjourned *sine die*.* Moscow then ordered the Prague *coup* of
25 February 1948, whereby the deeply afflicted Czechoslovak democracy was again sacrificed to a totalitarian régime.

It was now time for the West to take up the running. On 22 January
1948 Mr Bevin, in a speech in the House of Commons, called upon the
states of Western Europe to unite for their own protection and advantage. 'The free nations of Western Europe must now draw closely
together. . . . I believe the time is ripe for a consolidation of Western
Europe.'[33] The response was immediate. On 17 March the Pact of
Brussels was signed by representatives of Britain, France, Belgium, the
Netherlands and Luxembourg for the purpose of closer collaboration in
economic, social and cultural matters and for collective self-defence.
Western Europe, sure now of American support, was beginning to take
heed of Mr Churchill's warning at Fulton, uttered a full two years before,
that there was nothing that Russia admired so much as strength.

In the United States also there were signs of girding for the battle.
On 17 March 1948, the same day that the Western European Pact was
signed in Brussels, President Truman addressed Congress, called in

---

* See above, p. 473.

special session, and gave them grave warning of the past Soviet record and future Soviet intentions:

> Since the close of the hostilities, the Soviet Union and its agents have destroyed the independence and democratic character of a whole series of nations in Eastern and Central Europe. It is this ruthless course of action, and the design to extend it to the remaining free nations of Europe, that have brought about the critical situation in Europe today. . . .
>
> Faced with this growing menace, there have been encouraging signs that the free nations of Europe are drawing closer together for their economic well-being and common defence against aggression. . . .
>
> This action [the Pact of Brussels] has great significance, for this agreement was not imposed by a decree of a powerful neighbour. It was the free choice of independent governments representing the will of their people. . . .
>
> I am sure that the determination of the free countries of Europe to protect themselves will be matched by an equal determination on our part to help them to protect themselves.[34]

Thereupon the President urged Congress to complete legislative action on the European Recovery Programme and, which was even more significant, to provide for the strengthening of national defence through the reintroduction of universal military training and the restoration of Selective Service which had been terminated three years before at the close of the war. This resort to compulsory service by the United States, for the fourth time in her national history and the second in what were somewhat ironically termed 'times of peace', served notice upon the world, to friend and foe alike, that America meant business.

The Government of the Soviet Union was not intimidated. The aggressive nature of Russian foreign policy was intensified as the year progressed. In February 1948 Czechoslovakia was made prisoner, and the following month Norway was menaced with demands for a mutual defence agreement with the Soviet Government, which she sturdily rejected.

Meanwhile in Germany tension was also growing acute. The British and American authorities there found their difficulties with the Russians outweighing all others – even the obstructiveness of the French. On 3 May 1946 General Clay halted reparations deliveries to the Soviet authorities from the American Zone. By the end of the same year the Americans and the British had become so concerned about their mutual problems in Germany – which until then they had been handling independently of one another – that on 2 December 1946 they carried out the economic fusion of their occupation areas into what became known as Bizonia.[35] In making this arrangement, which greatly improved prospects for German trade and economic development, they stressed that the other two occupying Powers would be welcome to join them. Nevertheless, Bizonia bore witness to the progressive collapse of quadri-partite rule in Germany. It was not until 1948 that the French brought their zone into the Western economic unit. The Russians, of course, never allowed the Eastern Zone to be co-ordinated with the others.

Lack of Soviet co-operation in the economic field went side by side with disturbing political developments in the Soviet Zone itself. Aided by their German collaborators, the Soviet authorities pushed through measures of land reform and economic control which obviously had implications for the political future of Germany, even if in themselves they were not without merit.[36]* More important was the enforced merger of the Social Democratic Party (S.P.D.) with the Communists in a new organization called the Socialist Unity Party (S.E.D.). The S.P.D. was the most important working-class party in Germany, and before Hitler's accession to power it had always exceeded the Com-munists in popularity. When, by the spring of 1946, its fusion into the S.E.D. had been accepted by the S.P.D. Chairman in Berlin, Otto Grotewohl, it seemed that German Social Democracy was about to be swallowed up in a Communist-directed front organization of the kind which was becoming familiar in Eastern Europe.

That this did not happen was partly due to the will-power of rank-and-file Social Democrats and partly to the Western presence in Berlin. The Social Democrats in the German capital refused to be intimidated by the Soviet authorities and were supported in their resistance by the Western representatives on the *Kommandatura*. A poll conducted among S.P.D. members in the Western sectors of the city on 31 March 1946 rejected fusion with the S.E.D., and at elections for the Berlin city council held in October the S.P.D. gained nearly 50 per cent of the vote as against only 20 per cent for the S.E.D.[38] This was a startling demon-stration of the importance for German politics of a Western presence in Berlin.†

Meanwhile in the British and American Zones of Germany political life among the Germans was being allowed to revive, at first on a local

---

* There had been a discussion in London during the war about the use of social reform as a means of undermining German militarism and enabling Germany to build on healthier political foundations in the future. Mr Attlee was eager that the Prussian landowners and the controllers of German heavy industry should not be restored to positions of influence, and perceptively remarked in July 1944 that military authorities always tended to work with what they considered to be forces of 'law and order'.[37]

† It should not be supposed that the S.P.D. in the Western zones would have accepted fusion with the Communists. But the failure of the S.E.D. in Berlin was a serious blow to Communist prestige throughout Germany. The Communist Party (K.P.D.) kept its independent identity in Western Germany until it was finally declared to be unconstitutional in 1956. A new Communist Party, the D.K.P., was set up in West Germany in 1968.

and then on a provincial, or *Land*, level. By the end of 1946 a number of German regional areas, or *Länder*, had been created with democratic constitutions and elected parliaments. Although historic German *Land* boundaries were taken into account when delineating these regions, in only one case – that of Bavaria – was it possible to revive a German *Land* which had existed before the war. In many ways the new *Länder* were more viable as administrative units than the old, and one standing anomaly from the time of Imperial and Republican Germany – the overwhelming preponderance of Prussia – finally ceased to exist. On 25 February 1947 the State of Prussia was formally abolished by order of the A.C.C.[39]

The three major parties which were to dominate post-war German politics in the Western zones – the S.P.D., the Christian Democratic Union (C.D.U.) and the liberal Free Democratic Party (F.D.P.) – had also established themselves and were independent of centralized control in Berlin. After Bizonia had been created in December 1946, an Economic Parliament was established whose members were chosen by the *Länder* Diets. The institutions established to run Bizonia were obviously models for a future German administration. Parallel action was taken in the Soviet Zone, where a German Economic Council was set up in June 1947. The two halves of Germany were steadily growing apart.

At the same time the four occupying Powers had come no nearer to agreeing on a peace settlement for Germany. Meetings of the Council of Foreign Ministers in London, Moscow and Paris proved fruitless. M. Molotov confirmed his reputation as a stonewall negotiator, harping on the need for recognition of the Soviet claim for $10 billion reparations and Four-Power control of the Ruhr.* When taken in conjunction with Russian pressure for a centralized Government, these claims could only result in economic disaster and the political radicalization of Germany.

The leaders of the Western countries were not prepared to pay Molotov's price and their resistance hardened to the point that, in December 1947, they refused to continue sterile parleying with the Russians any longer. A month later they met by themselves to discuss Germany, inviting the Benelux countries to join them. By this time the Truman Doctrine and the Marshall Plan had already made it plain that the United States was committed to support European recovery and resistance to Soviet penetration. Changes in the political complexion of the French Government, which the Communists had left in 1947, were also making Western co-operation easier. Robert Schuman was French Foreign Minister in 1948 and under his guidance France sought her security in closer political and economic integration with her neighbours.[40]

* See above, p. 472.

One result of these developments was an agreement in June 1948 between the Western occupying Powers and the Benelux countries, according to which the Ruhr should be placed under their joint economic control but not separated from Germany. At the same time it was agreed that the Governments of the German *Länder* should convene a Constituent Assembly to draw up a Constitution covering the three Western zones.[41]

Naturally these activities provoked lively protests from the Russians. They denounced the Western Powers for wrecking the inter-Allied control machinery in Germany and for trying to divide the country. On 20 March 1948 General Sokolovsky accused the Western Allies of 'tearing up the agreement on control machinery' and 'destroying the Control Council and burying it'.[42] He and the other Soviet representatives then flounced out of the Allied Control Council in Berlin, claiming that their Western colleagues were negotiating behind their backs and were discussing German problems with other Powers. This was indeed true, but it was a natural consequence of the deadlock over Germany which had developed since 1945.

One of the most urgent issues facing Bizonia in 1948 was the inflation of the German currency. It had been a chronic cause of difficulty since the beginning of the occupation, and as early as the spring of 1946 General Clay's financial advisers told him that revaluation was an urgent necessity.[43] No agreement over this could be reached on the A.C.C. because the Russians would not allow any effective controls over the fiduciary issue in their zone. By 1948 the Anglo-Americans were ready to act independently to provide their zones with a stable currency.

On 18 June the three Western Powers – the French having agreed to participate – began to introduce a reformed *Deutschmark* into Western Germany. Stalin's response was rapid and seemed decisive. Apart from announcing their own reformed currency – which was to be introduced into the whole of Berlin as well as into the Soviet zone – the Russians imposed a blockade on the Western sectors of the capital. On 24 June all land and water traffic to Berlin was halted indefinitely for 'technical' reasons. Soviet obstruction of Western supply routes to the capital had been building up in the months before the blockade; the Western Powers were now faced with a serious crisis there.

Suggestions that an armed incursion along one of the *Autobahn* routes to Berlin might call the Soviet bluff – if it were bluff – were discarded as too dangerous. It hardly seemed possible to keep the city going by air since it required a minimum of 4,500 tons of supplies a day. Increased air traffic was at first seen by the Allied Governments as a means of playing for time in the hope that the Russians would be willing to negotiate.[44]

General Lucius D. Clay had other ideas. He was convinced of the need to hold Berlin and had expressed himself forcibly on this subject the previous April, when proposals had been made to evacuate American families from the city:

> We have [he said] lost Czechoslovakia. Norway is threatened. We retreat from Berlin. When Berlin falls, Western Germany will be next. If we mean . . . to hold Europe against communism, we must not budge. We can take humiliation and pressure short of war on Berlin without losing face. If we withdraw, our position is threatened. . . .[45]

The General threw himself vigorously into the task of supplying Berlin exclusively from the air. Under his inspired leadership the airlift became one of the most remarkable technical achievements of modern aviation. American and British aircraft landed in Berlin at five-minute intervals and persistently raised their level of cargoes even in bad weather. The tonnage of imported supplies climbed steadily until by the spring of 1949 the average figure was 8,000 tons per day. By that time the Soviet blockade had clearly failed. At midnight on 11–12 May 1949, after 323 days, the barriers to land traffic were lifted.

The Berlin airlift was perhaps the most dramatic confrontation in the Cold War and its success was hailed as a major triumph over Communism. The Mayor of Berlin, Ernst Reuter, summed up the general feeling when he declared:

> Without the bold initiative and admirable devotion of all those who created the airlift and co-operated in its development Berlin could not have withstood the pressure; it would have disappeared into the Soviet Zone. The consequences for the whole world would have been incalculable. . . .[46]

Such sentiments were understandable, though exaggerated. Nevertheless it was a major victory for the West and it had far-reaching repercussions, not the least of which were the establishment of the North Atlantic Treaty Organization, the creation in 1949 of a Federal German Republic from the occupation zones of the Western Allies, and the decision to integrate a rearmed Western Germany with Western Europe.

For, against this background of tension, vitally important decisions had been reached by the United States Government, which had been for some time in receipt of warnings from Britain and France of the necessity for a wider system of defence. The attitude of Washington, however, had been that, until some evidence had been shown that

Western Europe was prepared to do something for its own protection, further American assistance would not be forthcoming. The signature of the Pact of Brussels had provided that evidence and, as has been seen, the response of President Truman had been immediate and material. Now the display of Soviet aggression and defiance was an added proof that America must still further justify the role of world leadership which had become her reluctant but inescapable heritage from the Second World War.

The genesis of NATO was certainly transatlantic, but Canadian rather than American. On 28 April 1948 the idea of a single material defence system, including and superseding the Brussels Treaty system, was publicly advocated in the Canadian House of Commons by the Prime Minister, Louis Saint-Laurent.[47] It was welcomed by Ernest Bevin in the British Parliament a week later,[48] but the major result occurred on 12 May, when Senator Arthur H. Vandenberg, the ranking Republican on the Senate Foreign Relations Committee, offered a resolution recommending 'the association of the United States by constitutional process, with such regional and other collective arrangements as are based on continuous and effective self-help and mutual aid, and as affect its national security'.[49] The resolution – United States Resolution 239 – was adopted on 11 June 1948 by 64 votes to 4.

This truly remarkable evolution in American foreign and defence policies in time of peace made it possible for the United States to enter a North Atlantic Alliance, and President Truman made all possible speed. On 2 July, he directed that the Vandenberg Resolution should be implemented 'to the fullest extent possible' and at once. Negotiations began between the United States, Canada and the parties to the Brussels Pact on 6 July.

Two problems were at once apparent: first, that the combined forces of the negotiating parties were insufficient for their defence and, secondly, the degree of security to be afforded by the new alliance.

In the first case it was seen that an enemy occupation of the territories of Norway, Denmark, Iceland, Ireland and Portugal, none of which were parties to the Brussels Pact, would represent a threat to the security of Western Europe and of the United States. It was agreed to invite these states to join the alliance and all did so with the exception of the Republic of Ireland.[50]

The second point was more difficult of solution. The Brussels Powers wanted the terms of the new alliance to state definitely that if one of the contracting parties was attacked the others would come to its aid immediately with all the military and other aid and assistance in their power. In other words, they wanted automatic action, which implied going to war. The American representatives could not and would not, in view of their Constitution, accept such an obligation.

Between these conflicting theses the negotiations hung on a dead centre. Finally, a Canadian compromise was forthcoming. This provided that any attack on a member state should be considered by the other contracting parties as an attack upon themselves. Instead, however, of becoming immediately in a state of war, each nation would be expected to give aid and assistance to the victim of aggression in accordance with its own constitutional processes. This compromise was found to be acceptable to all and was incorporated in the final draft, as Article V.[51]

The North Atlantic Treaty was signed at Washington by the Foreign Ministers of its twelve member states on 4 April 1949.* Its intentions, which, it was emphasized, were not directed against any nation or group of nations, but only against the forces of aggression, were defined as the outcome of the decision of its signatories 'to safeguard the freedom, common heritage and civilization of these peoples, founded on the principle of democracy, individual liberty and the rule of law; to promote stability and well-being in the North Atlantic area; and to unite their efforts for collective defence and for the preservation of peace and security'. On 17 October of the same year both Greece and Turkey were invited to join the alliance, it being considered that 'the security of the North Atlantic will be enhanced' by their accession They were admitted as from February 1952.

The treaty was to remain in force for ten years (i.e. until 1959) after which time it might be reviewed at the request of any of the parties. After it had been in force for twenty years (i.e. in 1969) any party might cease to be bound by its provisions after giving one year's notice of such termination.

The North Atlantic Treaty was the answer of the West to the renewed threat of Soviet aggression. It has become fashionable in certain quarters to denigrate it as an example of capitalist–imperialist diplomacy directed against a well-intentioned Soviet Union, or, at best, an act prompted by unnecessary and unwarranted panic. This is simply not true. The threat was assuredly present. As that veteran adviser of American Presidents, the Hon. John J. McCloy, has written: 'Revisionist historians who question the original need for NATO forget or ignore conditions in Europe both at the end of the war and twenty-five years later'.

The North Atlantic Alliance was a logical, and almost inevitable, progression from the Truman Doctrine, the Marshall Plan and the

* The twelve signatories were Belgium, Canada, Denmark, France, Iceland, Italy, Luxembourg, the Netherlands, Norway, Portugal, the United Kingdom and the United States of America.

Brussels Pact; just as it was the logical and, perhaps, inevitable precursor of the European Defence Community and the Western European Union.* It was the tangible proof of the new orientation of American foreign policy, and as such it ranks as a great and historic state paper. For practical value it ranks very high in that it was based on the two most binding elements in statecraft: common fear in the face of common danger,† and mutual self-interest. It is sternly practical, having in its language few vague generalities. In many ways it is a watershed in the post-war history of the modern world.

V

There remained the problem of Germany. The Four-Power policy agreed upon at the Potsdam Conference in August 1945 had been founded upon two basic principles: first, that though, for occupational purposes, Germany was to be divided into four zones, this segmentation was in no way to prejudice the fundamental unity of the German state nor the subsequent formation of a central German Government;‡ and, secondly, that in order to achieve the underlying purpose for which two world wars had been fought and won Germany should remain disarmed and no effort should be spared to eradicate the militaristic spirit from the German mind.

Accordingly the Germans were, in consonance with the Four-Power Agreement of 20 September 1945[52] and by subsequent rulings of the Allied Control Council,[53] prohibited from military organization in any form and, when the West German Federal Republic was established in 1949, particular care was taken to safeguard the permanency of these provisions.§ If ever provision was made for the permanent suppression and exorcism of German militarism it was during the years 1945–52.

However, between 1950 and 1955 there occurred a complete transmogrification of the German scene.

Quadripartite solidarity remained in being until the conclusion of the trial of the Nazi war criminals at Nuremberg in October 1946‖ and thenceforth markedly and rapidly deteriorated. By 1948 it was fully

* See below, pp. 599–600.
† It was Rudyard Kipling who asserted that the British Empire was held together by 'ties of common funk' ('The Puzzler', in *Actions and Reactions*).
‡ For the setting-up of the zones, see above, Ch. 13. The agreements concerning the occupation zones (6 February 1945) and the control of Germany (2 August 1945) were repudiated by the U.S.S.R. on 27 November 1958.
§ Article 139 of the Bonn Constitution reads: 'The legal provisions enacted for the liberation of the German people from National Socialism and militarism shall not be affected by the provisions of this Basic Law.'
‖ See above, pp. 391–416.

apparent that the Potsdam propositions had reached a condition of *reductio ad absurdum* by reason of the fact that the Iron Curtain separated East Germany impenetrably from the West, and from behind it were perceptible all the premonitory symptoms of the revival of militarism under direct Russian supervision.

In face of this progressive change on the part of the Soviet Union from the status of respected ally, which she had enjoyed at the end of the war, to that of suspect aggressor and saboteur of peace, the Western Powers were compelled to take their own measures of defence. It was certainly not to the interests of Britain, the United States and France – or indeed of Germany herself – to allow all of the former Reich to drift into the Communist camp through inertia on the part of the three Western occupying Powers inspired by an over-nice respect for the principle of German unity. Under the impulse of a joint Anglo-American initiative, therefore, agreement was reached to restore a limited degree of sovereignty to a West German Federal Republic, composed of the three Western zones of occupation, with its capital at Bonn, it being still emphasized that, despite this temporary dichotomy, the ultimate desire of the three Powers was for a united Germany.

The Federal Republic of Germany came into formal existence on 23 May 1949,* and on 21 September the People's Council of the Soviet-controlled zone of occupation was converted into a provisional People's Chamber. This body, on 7 October 1949, proclaimed and enacted the constitution of the 'German Democratic Republic'.

The subsidiary organization of NATO proceeded apace, once the alliance had been called into being. A North Atlantic Council was formed on 17 September 1949, composed of the Foreign Ministers of the twelve participant states, while the Defence Ministers constituted a Defence Committee, having under it a Military Committee comprising high-ranking naval, military and air force commanders of the twelve nations. By January 1950 these bodies had worked out and approved a plan of defence for the NATO area and this was formally approved by President Truman on 27 January.

Good though this progress was, it was inevitably incomplete. There lacked one essential factor – the inevitable, but in some cases dreaded, presence of Germany as a military participant.

To plan for the defence of Germany without her participation was manifestly, from a military point of view, impossible and ludicrous. Yet to include her evoked the age-old dread and memories in France

---

* On the same day an Occupation Statute, signed by the three Western Powers, reduced considerably the responsibilities of the occupying authorities, while this Statute itself was materially modified by the Petersburg Agreement of 22 November 1949.

and the Low Countries of German invasion and dominance. The fear of Germany had preoccupied French political thinking ever since 1945, and had found expression in the Treaty of Dunkirk signed with Britain on 4 March 1947, whereby both Powers agreed to come to each other's support in the event of renewed German aggression. The Pact of Brussels had been concluded 'against aggression' *per se*, though it was generally believed that this was primarily Muscovite in character, but there were those among the signatories who still looked upon it as a bulwark and a guarantee against a further outbreak of the *furor Teutonicus*.

On the obverse side of the medal was the consideration that Russia was indeed the primary source of menace, that a vacuum in Central Europe offered by an unarmed Germany could only be for Soviet advantage and that it was still just possible that, if left out in the cold, Germany might again resort to the Rapallo strategy of 1922 and throw in her lot with Soviet Russia, even as Hitler and Stalin had concluded their 'Pact of Infamy' in 1939.

Thus by her very absence Germany dominated the NATO scene. France frankly feared the inclusion of Germany; the Benelux countries called for an understanding from Britain that she, as well as France, would take part in the actual defence arrangements in North-western Europe. Above all, all the other eleven NATO Powers looked towards the United States to find out what – and how much – she was prepared to do.

Thus matters stood when Dean Acheson, who had succeeded General Marshall as Secretary of State on 7 January 1949, met with Ernest Bevin and Robert Schuman at a session of the North Atlantic Council in New York in September 1950.† Here the question of German participation dragged out of the closet – jangling and naked – the horrifying skeleton of German rearmament. At once the reaction was one of terror. If Germany were allowed to rearm, how could she be controlled and contained within limits? If a rearmed Germany entered NATO would she not dominate the whole concern and reduce the other military contingents to the status of mere helots? What guarantee would the United States and Canada and Britain offer against the exercise of such a domination?

Acheson was convinced that only a unified defence force with German participation could effectively meet the needs of the North Atlantic Powers. He won over Bevin, after some difficulty, but he failed to win the French. Schuman and Moch, who had now been joined by their Prime Minister, René Pleven, remained adamant, hypnotised by the

---

† The three Defence Ministers, General Marshall, Emanuel Shinwell and Jules Moch, were also present.

fear of Germany – a most understandable fear[54] – yet terrified of Acheson's threat that the United States would withdraw her troops from Europe altogether if agreement were not reached on some formula for a circumscribed German rearmament.

At the close of the meeting the question of Germany was left unresolved, though Pleven had given ground to the extent of accepting in principle the participation of German units in existing regimental combat teams.

The whole European strategic development had undergone a massive acceleration as a result of the Korean War, which came suddenly out of the blue on 25 June 1950, when North Korean forces, armed and equipped by Soviet Russia, crossed the 38th parallel.* This new example of Communist aggression in another quarter of the globe further stressed the essential importance of NATO defence and – inevitably – the inclusion, in some form or other, of German manpower. President Truman and his Secretary of State were emphatic that this should and must be done. The former victims of Nazi aggression were radically reluctant to see any kind of resuscitation of the German military machine, which had so recently crushed their liberties and destroyed their countries. The problem therefore – seemingly insoluble – was to devise some means whereby German manpower might be made available to the NATO alliance without any concomitant of a German war mentality or a national rearmament of Germany. Above all it was highly undesirable that any re-creation of a German General Staff, whether clandestine or overt, be permitted.

* The ancient Empire of Korea, which, since Japan's victories over China and Russia in 1894 and 1905, had become virtually a Japanese protectorate, was formally annexed by Japan in 1910. The restoration of Korean independence had been promised at the Cairo Conference of 1943 (see above, p. 137) and at the close of the Japanese War the country was occupied by Russian and American troops to enforce the surrender of Japanese forces. The country had been divided for mutual military convenience into two portions, separated by the 38th parallel, and abortive negotiations between Washington and Moscow as to the future of Korea continued until 1946. Thereafter the Soviet military authorities proclaimed the Korean People's Republic in their zone in 1948 and in the same year Dr Syngman Rhee was inaugurated President of the Republic of Korea in Seoul. Bitter fighting followed the North Korean invasion in the summer of 1950, the brunt of which was borne by United States forces, though troops of fourteen United Nations member states, including British and Commonwealth contingents, were also in the field. General MacArthur was appointed Supreme Allied Commander-in-Chief. He first stabilized his line north of Toegu and along the Nakling river and then, on 14 September, in a brilliant amphibious operation at Inchon, began a victorious advance which thrust the invaders back beyond the 38th parallel. At this point General MacArthur, under the ambiguous authority of a United Nations General Assembly resolution and with the vociferous support of President Rhee, pressed forward and by the last week of October was well beyond the North Korean capital of Pyongyang. There, on 26 November, he was first checked and then repulsed by a powerful and well-equipped force of Chinese 'volunteers' who compelled his retreat to the 38th parallel.

Within West Germany itself there was divided feeling and also a growing sense of insecurity. That singularly articulate and clear-sighted statesman, Dr Konrad Adenauer, the ablest Chancellor to be produced by Germany since Bismarck, was keenly aware that, in any attack by Soviet Russia against Western Europe, Germany could not fail to be the cockpit of the initial assault. Moreover the Soviet authorities in Eastern Germany had encouraged the Government of the German Democratic Republic to raise a so-called 'People's Police', 50,000 strong, heavily armed and equipped by the Soviet military command. Chancellor Adenauer now urged that his Government should be allowed to equip a West German force of similar size and strength and repeatedly suggested that the United States should dispatch reinforcements to Europe, especially armoured divisions.

Not unaware of the added prestige and advantage accruing to Western Germany from participation in any associated military formation, Chancellor Adenauer, on 23 August 1950, announced that he favoured the creation of a Western European Army, adding that 'if Germany is called upon to provide a contingent for this army, she is ready, under certain conditions, to make sacrifices for her own and Western Europe's sake'.[55]

The unhappy René Pleven was unwilling to alienate American support yet fearful of the reactions of France to the idea of German rearmament. In his dilemma he essayed to appease Washington and reassure his own countrymen by producing a proposal so fantastic and impracticable that it is a cause of wonderment that it achieved as much approval and backing as it did from European and American statesmen.

What became known as the Pleven Plan was introduced by the French Prime Minister into the National Assembly on 24 October 1950. It called for 'the creation of a European army linked to the political institutions of a united Europe'. Under this project there would be 'a complete fusion of all the human and material elements' of the proposed force. A European Minister of Defence, responsible to a European Assembly, would be appointed by the participating Governments. This European Army would be integrated with the NATO defence forces, to which Germany would contribute, both financially and militarily, despite the fact that she was not a member of the alliance; nor indeed was she, at that moment in full possession of her own sovereignty.

The debate which followed was one of some acerbity. It became evident that neither chauvinism nor fear was dead in France. The National Assembly, however, with a marked lack of enthusiasm, approved the Pleven proposals as a basis of negotiation among the NATO states for the solution of both the problem of constituting a militarily viable defence force for Western Europe and also of German participation in such a formation.

Some further advance was achieved in mid-December. With the Chinese intervention in the Korean War and the consequent reverses suffered by General MacArthur's United Nations forces, President Truman announced a state of national emergency on 16 December, declaring that 'Our homes, our nation, all the things we believe in, are in great danger', and he placed the United States on a war footing. Two days later, at their session in Brussels, the North Atlantic Council agreed to the constitution of an integrated military force under the supreme command of an American General. They requested President Truman to designate such a commander and unofficially expressed the unanimous hope that his choice would be General Eisenhower. He was duly appointed and in January 1951 set up his headquarters (SHAPE) at Versailles. His command extended over the military forces of the Brussels Pact Powers, now absorbed into NATO, and also the American, British and French occupation forces in Germany and Austria.[56]

Meanwhile the adoption of the Pleven Plan by the French National Assembly had resulted in a series of laborious, circuitous and protracted negotiations, distinguished chiefly for their lack of reality and enthusiasm. The conference for the establishment of a European Defence Community (E.D.C.), which the French Government called in Paris in February 1951 and which sat intermittently for some fifteen months, called forth the usual crop of difficulties. The French were anxious to bind Britain and the United States to E.D.C. by definite treaties of association, and to this both London and Washington were inimical. The German Government made the plea that the E.D.C. agreement should include provision for immediate mutual action by all member and associated Powers in the event of an act of aggression being committed against any of them, but this was opposed by the Netherlands Government as going beyond the terms of the NATO Treaty, of which Article V was based on the Canadian compromise formula.* At the same time parallel talks between the three occupying Powers and Germany on the subject of German participation were completely abortive.

By the time the Labour Party gave place to the Conservatives in Britain, in October 1951, the situation was virtually one of deadlock. Herbert Morrison, whose health and eyesight were declining when he succeeded Ernest Bevin as Foreign Secretary in March and whose interests in foreign affairs was certainly not primary, was correspondingly unconstructive.

* See above, p. 583.

The new Foreign Secretary, Mr Eden, had inherited a difficult situation in which national prejudices and phobias predominated. He was
fortunate in having the friendship and support of Dean Acheson, with
whom he had considerable community of interest. The United States
was not urging Britain to join E.D.C., but recommended a 'close
association' with it, a course which they themselves were prepared to
follow. When Mr Churchill and Mr Eden visited Paris in mid-December
1951, they made Britain's position clear. The British Government,
they said, would 'associate themselves as closely as possible' with E.D.C.
and the United Kingdom land, sea and air forces under General
Eisenhower's command would be linked with those of E.D.C.[57]

This, however, was not enough to satisfy the French, whose motive
in demanding a formal treaty between Britain and E.D.C., rather than
a declaration of association, was twofold: first, against the contingency
of outside aggression (i.e. the U.S.S.R.), and, secondly, against the event
of the secession or misbehaviour of a member of E.D.C. itself (i.e.
Germany). The difficulties involved in meeting these French requirements were taxing even to one of Mr Eden's diplomatic abilities and
experience, since other national sensibilities were involved besides those
of the French. By the beginning of 1952 the Paris Conference was again
at a deadlock from which the only release was found in the adoption of a
resolution on 14 March requesting the United Kingdom to enter into
a treaty relationship with E.D.C.

'I realized', Lord Avon wrote later of this juncture, 'that if the entire
E.D.C. project was to be saved from a breakdown, for which we [the
British] would be blamed, Her Majesty's Government would have to
make a positive response to these approaches.'[58] This indeed he did to
the extent of reversing the heretofore adamant refusal of the British
Government to consider a treaty. Conversations in Paris with the
European leaders convinced him of the necessity for this and, after some
discussion, he overcame the objections of some of his Cabinet colleagues
and carried them with him. He did more. After further consultation
with Dean Acheson, the United States Government were persuaded to
pursue a similar course of action and also to enter with Britain in making
a joint declaration which amounted to a kind of Anglo-American
Monroe Doctrine.

This reversal of policy on the part of Britain and America, which
must be accepted as justified on the supposition that E.D.C. was worth
saving, removed most of the French objections. It paved the way for a
series of events which was supposed to set the seal upon European
security, to close the period of war and to usher in the new age of
European co-operation in the face of a common enemy.

On 27 May 1952 there was signed at Paris, in the Salle de l'Horloge of the Quai d'Orsay – where the Covenant of the League of Nations had been adopted and the Kellogg–Briand Pact signed – an agreement constituting the European Defence Community, the primary purpose of which was to merge the armed forces of its six signatory Powers – France, West Germany, Italy, Belgium, the Netherlands and Luxembourg – into one defence force. It was, however, bolstered by a number of additional undertakings: first, a treaty of mutual assistance between the six Powers and the United Kingdom against aggression from without; second, a protocol extending to West Germany the guarantees of the North Atlantic Treaty; third, a declaration by the United States and the United Kingdom that any threat to the integrity of E.D.C. would be considered a threat to them; fourth, an agreement on the part of the United States and the United Kingdom to station in Europe 'such forces as they deem necessary and appropriate to contribute to a joint defence of the North Atlantic area'.[59]

As a necessary preliminary to the signing of the E.D.C. agreements, the three occupying Powers and West Germany had signed on the previous day at Bonn a convention which both terminated the Allied occupation of Germany and returned to the Bonn Government the essential sovereignty of Germany which had been thrown into commission as a result of Unconditional Surrender.* The Bonn Convention would become effective only after the E.D.C. agreement had been ratified by all the signatories. Thus E.D.C. was made the condition for the restoration of German sovereignty and for the termination of a state of war. †

VI

After the First World War it took seven years from the date of the Armistice of 11 November 1918 before Germany was readmitted to the European polity of nations by her signature of the Locarno agreements on 1 December 1925 and her entry into the League of Nations in the following September. After the Second World War it took precisely the same period from the Unconditional Surrender of 7 May 1945 to the signature of the European Defence Community agreement on 27 May 1952.

Yet there was a difference. The diplomacy of Gustav Stresemann achieved German rehabilitation in the teeth of considerable opposition and not without devious means. It did not include the rearmament of

---

* See above, pp. 250–65.

† By proclamation dated 24 October 1951, President Truman had already ended the state of war with Germany in so far as the United States was concerned.

Germany, yet the foundations for that rearmament were being clandestinely laid, nevertheless. It admitted Germany to a free platform in the League of Nations from which to demonstrate for treaty revision, more especially for the abolition of reparation payments' and for general disarmament.

By contrast, the diplomacy of Konrad Adenauer was confronted with both greater and lesser problems. In that the German defeat of 1945 was more consummate and more abject than in 1918 and that Germany had for the time being surrendered her sovereignty to the victorious Allies, Adenauer started further behind the line than did Stresemann. But once the start had been made his task was considerably easier. To begin with, Germany was not saddled with a staggering burden of reparation payments, and though her disarmament had been more complete than in 1918 her rearmament had no reason to partake of the secret and nefarious. She was virtually begged to rearm by the Western Powers and at their expense, though the actual form of her rearmament was the cause of dissent. Ironically also, whereas her rearmament had been effected during the twenties with the furtive co-operation of the Soviet Union, who was then her only ally, her rearmament in the fifties was necessitated by the aggressive policies of that same Russia, who threatened not only Germany but the whole of the West.

To achieve her new status, Western Germany's sovereignty was returned to her by the Bonn Contractual Agreement and the Allied occupation status was terminated.* Unlike Germany in 1926, however, she was not admitted to the United Nations, since her election was blocked by the hostile vote of the Soviet Union and its satellites. And furthermore, perhaps most important of all, Germany was divided into two parts.

VII

It was confidently believed that the new order initiated by the E.D.C. agreement would begin forthwith, or at least by the beginning of 1953. Such confidence soon proved baseless.

Slowly the ratifications of the E.D.C. agreement were deposited, the outstanding absentees being France and Italy. The situation in Indo-China and the unresolved wrangle over Trieste were partly responsible for their respective delays, but at heart, in the case of France, the cause of her hesitancy to ratify was her basic fear of Germany and her lack of

---

* It will be remembered that it was not until four years after the Locarno agreements that Stresemann succeeded in persuading the British, French and Belgian Governments to terminate their occupation of German territory. This was achieved at the Hague Conference on 30 August 1929, as part of a 'package deal' on the acceptance of the Young Plan for the 'final settlement' on German reparation payments.[60]

faith in the real efficacy of the status of 'association' which Britain and the United States had assumed towards E.D.C. What successive French Governments still hankered after were the specific undertakings contained in the Anglo-American treaties of guarantee signed with France as a part of the Peace Settlement of Paris in 1919 but which failed of effect when the United States Senate rejected the Treaty of Versailles and its concomitant agreements. The Treaty of Dunkirk had gone far in this direction but, from the French point of view, not far enough, and this, of course, did not commit the United States.*

The death of Stalin on 5 March 1953 gave rise to hopes in certain countries, and especially France, that there would be a change of heart and a change of policy in Soviet Russia which would make possible a *détente* and a *rapprochement* with the West, thereby rendering the creation of a European Army, and the resultant rearmament of Germany, unnecessary. This too was seized upon in Paris as an excuse for further delay, and when on 11 May Sir Winston Churchill publicly proposed a 'conference at the summit', this also gave encouragement to those in France who lacked enthusiasm for the E.D.C. agreement to hold out a little longer before committing themselves to its provisions and obligations.

Governments rose and fell in Paris and no Prime Minister could summon up the inclination or the intestinal fortitude to present the E.D.C. agreement to the National Assembly for ratification. It seemed an age since René Pleven had gained the original consent of that body to accept his plan for a European Army as a basis for negotiation with other NATO Powers. Truly 'hope deferred maketh the heart sick'.

The final crisis developed in the summer of 1954. The Geneva Conference, called to consider the ever-worsening situation in Indo-China, appeared to be deadlocked – so much so that the United States Government decided to terminate its participation. The Government of Joseph Laniel failed to obtain a vote of confidence in the French Assembly on 12 June and consequently resigned. After a week of negotiations, that remarkable apparition upon the French political stage, Pierre Mendès-France, succeeded in forming a Government. In his declaration of policy on 17 June the new Prime Minister promised a settlement in Indo-China by 20 July and added, incidentally, that he would propose amendments to the E.D.C. agreement before submitting it to the National Assembly for ratification.

Three days later, on 20 June, Mendès-France told a somewhat different story to General Walter Bedell Smith, the United States

---

* As Raymond Aron has written: '*Entre janvier et août 1954, se déchaîna la plus grande querelle idéologico-politique que la France ait connue probablement depuis l'affaire Dreyfus, querelle dont l'enjeu le plus visible était le réarmament de l'Allemagne mais dont le sens dernier intéressait le principe même de l'existence française de l'État national.*'[61]

Under-Secretary of State, during the latter's visit to Paris on his way home from the Geneva Conference. He was deferring action on the E.D.C. agreement, he said, until after the termination of the Indo-China war had enhanced his prestige and would enable him to obtain ratification by a large majority. He might propose certain amendments to the text in due course, but ratification must come first.[62]

What followed was extraordinary. By the end of July Mendès-France was convinced that there was no majority in the Assembly for the E.D.C. agreement. He therefore informed Anthony Eden that he proposed to call a conference of E.D.C. Powers at Brussels on 19 August and present them with a schedule of amendments. If the other Powers agreed to these textual changes, he would then present the agreement to the Assembly on the understanding that the amendments would be incorporated after ratification.

The proposed amendments – and President Eisenhower* did not hesitate to designate them as 'shocking' – included indefinite postponement of plans for the standardization of the European armed forces, a veto power for any signatory over any and all E.D.C. actions and decisions, and deferment for a period of eight years of the setting-up of the supra-national court. These proposed alterations changed the whole concept of E.D.C. and were unhesitatingly rejected by the other signatory Powers.

There followed a brief period of confusion. Mendès-France conferred at Chartwell with Churchill and Eden, but to little purpose. The French Prime Minister was unwilling to submit the agreement for ratification without the amendments and argued strongly against the idea of a meeting of the United States, the United Kingdom, Germany and the Benelux countries in the event of France rejecting the agreement. The British Ministers urged the French Premier to make a brave effort to wring ratification from the National Assembly, and this Mendès-France grudgingly agreed to do. In the interests of his success, Mr Eden dissuaded an enraged President Eisenhower from calling an Eight-Power conference excluding France, in order to demonstrate French isolation.†
On 30 August 1954, by a vote of 319 to 264, with 43 abstentions, the National Assembly rejected the E.D.C. agreement. In the two days of bitter and emotional debate which preceded this decision, Mendès-France, in the opinion of Lord Avon, 'was more referee than advocate'.[63]

---

* General Eisenhower had been elected President on 4 November 1952.

† At the meeting of President Eisenhower, Sir Winston Churchill and M. Laniel, together with their Foreign Ministers, at Bermuda in December 1953, John Foster Dulles had warned the French that if, as a result of the rejection of E.D.C., France and Germany were once again to become enemies, continental Europe would never be safe and that 'would compel an agonizing reappraisal of basic United States policy'.

VIII

The brave, if perhaps impracticable efforts to achieve some kind of European defence unity, coupled with a controlled degree of German rearmament – efforts which had dragged out for the better part of four mortal years – had at last collapsed in a welter of frustration, distrust, disappointment and recrimination. The spirit of European unity had touched its post-war nadir; the defence edifice, so carefully conceived and created, had crumbled, leaving it all too clear to the Soviet Union that it was opposed by anything but a staunch alliance. Germany, which for the last two years had existed in a kind of suspended animation – neither independent nor occupied – relapsed legally into that state of 'sovereignty in commission' which had followed Unconditional Surrender, since the Bonn Contractual Agreement of 26 May 1952 had been made dependent upon E.D.C. coming into operation.

It was a moment of decision which might have been a moment of tragedy for Europe. A gesture of despair, even of undue irritation, might have undone the work of years and destroyed the hard-won fruits of post-war statesmanship. It required little at this moment to precipitate once again the old animosity between France and Germany, bringing in its wake a disinclination on the part of Britain to participate in European affairs and in the United States an 'agonizing reappraisal' of policy. That this tragedy did not occur, but rather that a better solution eventually emerged from the embers of E.D.C., is due very largely to the leadership of Anthony Eden and the wisdom of Konrad Adenauer.

Eden had not been taken entirely unawares. His experienced eye had detected all the potential rocks and shoals endemic in French politics. Some preparation for dealing with the problem of German sovereignty in the event of the possible collapse of E.D.C. had therefore already been made when Sir Winston Churchill and Mr Eden visited Washington in June 1954. It had then been agreed with President Eisenhower and Mr Dulles that, in view of the manifest uncertainty of the situation, it was necessary to free the Bonn Conventions from their dependence on E.D.C. coming into force and to make some more dependably viable provision for the restoration of German sovereignty, which should leave her free to make her own alliances on a basis of equality.

Fully aware of the necessity for speedy action yet unwilling to settle for a patched-up, 'warmed-over', diluted version of E.D.C., the Foreign Secretary took his problems away for a period of quiet seclusion and reflection at his Wiltshire cottage at Broad Chalke during the weekend of 4–5 September, and there, like Archimedes and the theory of displacement, while in his bath, he lit upon the solution of the enigma of Western European defence.*

There lay to his hand the Brussels Treaty of 1948, which had originally been directed in large measure against a recrudescence of German aggression. With knowledge and experience of a lifetime spent in diplomacy and statecraft, Mr Eden reverted to the magic formula of Locarno which had brought about a drastic change in Germany's relations with the West under somewhat similar circumstances some thirty years before. If Germany and Italy could be brought into the Brussels Pact as full members and the whole instrument transformed into a mutual defence pact against aggression from whatever quarter, the result would be a new political framework for Europe in which, because it would lack the supranational features of E.D.C., Britain would be enabled to assume full membership, even to the extent of increasing her military commitments on the Continent.

This colourful and imaginative idea appealed to Sir Winston Churchill whose attitude towards the collapse of E.D.C. had been one not of blame for the French rejection of the project but only for their having invented it,[65] and he gave his blessing to the idea that Mr Eden should make a rapid tour of the Brussels Pact capitals preliminary, if the results of this journey should prove fruitful, to the calling of a Nine-Power Conference in London at the end of the month. The Foreign Secretary, during the ensuing period of 11–17 September, achieved a very considerable measure of success, though the problems raised in various of the capitals which he visited gave warning that hard and intricate negotiation lay ahead before full achievement would be forthcoming.[66]†

Nor were all Eden's difficulties European; some were transatlantic. Never was the disappearance from public office of a great American statesman felt more acutely than now. 'History, I am sure, will list Dean Acheson among the truly great Secretaries of State our nation has had', President Truman has written. 'There are few men who come to the secretaryship as fully prepared for the job and as eminently qualified as Acheson was. His keen mind, cool temper and broad vision served him well for handling the day-to-day business of the great issues of policy as well as the Department of State.'[68] These words,

---

* There is here a conflict of record between two ex-Prime Ministers and Foreign Secretaries. Mr Macmillan recalls that he had raised with Mr Eden the idea of using the machinery of the Brussels Pact as an alternative to E.D.C. at the end of August 1954 and that Eden accepted this idea 'in the course of a talk on 8 September 1954'.[64]

† Mr Macmillan writes warmly of Eden's 'high degree of diplomatic skill . . . with his charm and powers of persuasion, his journey proved a turning-point, although Dulles did his best to throw a spanner in the works'.[67]

glowing though not exaggerated, could never be applied, even in a most diluted form by his most devoted and purblind admirer, to Dean Acheson's successor. Impulsive to the point of irresponsibility, devious to the point of deceit, and of a mental attitude of superiority amounting to arrogance, John Foster Dulles, though he dreamed for years of being Secretary of State and had briefed himself as zealously as any man may for the job, lacked the great qualities of Dean Acheson, lacked his wisdom and perspective and composure and, in some ways most important of all, lacked the ability to make *rapport* with Anthony Eden.*

Foster Dulles now made a negative contribution to the situation by conducting a European tour of his own, paralleling if not in actual competition with Mr Eden's. He produced a series of spanners and threw them into the works with a meticulously accurate aim, thereby undermining the pattern of unanimity which Anthony Eden had been at such pains to create. Still smarting under the rebuff which France had administered to United States policy in rejecting E.D.C., Dulles pointedly visited Bonn and then London, deliberately missing out Paris from his itinerary. Moreover, where he did light, with what Harold Macmillan has called his 'elephantine obstinacy', he displayed a curious lack of appreciation of the realities of the situation, urging that any solution which did not provide for the creation of a supranational institution must be regarded as makeshift.

Indeed, he went further and told Mr Eden in London that since Congress had been 'sold' on the E.D.C. solution as a means of uniting Europe, American support for any non-supranational plan would be most unlikely and that some reduction of the American military presence in Europe might be regarded as inevitable. Much to his credit and to his patience, Anthony Eden, having listened to this diatribe, eventually persuaded Mr Dulles not only to agree to attend the Nine-Power Conference but to make a declaration of support if the new plan was approved.

The conference opened in London on 28 September.[70]† At first things did not go well, M. Mendès-France was determined to be difficult. He was resentful of Mr Dulles's omission of a call in Paris and chose to interpret it as an indication that the United States was preparing to support Germany all the way in opposition to France. For his part, Mr Dulles did not show himself warmly disposed towards the whole affair.

* 'Mr Dulles makes a speech every day', Mr Churchill once said of him 'has a Press conference every other day; and preaches on Sundays. All this tends to rob his utterances of real significance.'[69]

† Britain, the United States, Canada, France, Western Germany, Italy, Belgium, the Netherlands and Luxembourg participated.

From the chair Anthony Eden felt the conflicting currents of opinion and kept a firm though pliant hand upon the tiller. He had reached the conclusion that to achieve success a new emollient was necessary. This success might stand or fall upon the issue of British participation and, on the day before the conference opened, he had warned Sir Winston Churchill that it might be necessary to make an announcement, at the appropriate moment and if necessary, of a new and unprecedented British commitment on the Continent. Britain would undertake to maintain her forces in Europe at their existing strength (i.e. four divisions and the Tactical Air Force), and not to withdraw them against the wishes of the majority of the enlarged Brussels Treaty Powers, except in specified emergency circumstances, such as an acute balance of payments deficit or a sudden overseas crisis. The Prime Minister had agreed in principle and the Cabinet had been informed of this possible contingency, but it yet remained to obtain their formal consent.

By the end of the first day of the conference it was clear that either stalemate or outright conflict of thought lay ahead unless drastic action were taken. Anthony Eden took it. He first sought and obtained the approval of the British Cabinet for the action he had proposed and, on the strength of this, persuaded a still somewhat reluctant Mr Dulles to stand by with a similar promise.

On the second day, 29 September, Mr Eden threw in all his reserves. By agreement, Mr Dulles batted first and renewed on behalf of the United States the pledge which had been given to E.D.C. – 'In reason, you can count on us'. The Foreign Secretary followed with Britain's own assurances made 'in the same spirit as Mr Dulles spoke just now'. From then on it was pretty plain sailing. In view of British and American promises – promises which France had sought for thirty-five years – the fears of the 'Continentals' were largely assuaged and they gave proof of this. The Benelux countries renounced the right to manufacture chemical, bacteriological or atomic weapons. Germany went further and, in addition, surrendered her claim to guided missiles, bombers and large naval vessels. Only M. Mendès-France remained dissatisfied.[71]

It took five days of hard bargaining and technical discussion to reach a final agreement and further time thereafter to translate this agreement from draft into a final text. However, on 23 October 1954, there was signed in Paris, again in the Salle de l'Horloge, a series of documents, known as the Paris Agreements. By virtue of these it was enacted:

(1) that the occupation of Germany should cease as soon as possible;

(2) that Germany and Italy should adhere to the Pact of Brussels,

which should become the Western European Union,* with headquarters in London;

(3) that an agency for European arms control should be created; and

(4) that the immediate entry of Germany into NATO would be
recommended to the next meeting of the ministerial committee of
the North Atlantic Council.

But still the vessel of European defence and security was not safely
home in port, and again the chief obstacle was France. When, at 5 a.m.
on the morning of Christmas Eve, a vote was taken in the French
National Assembly – despite the fact that M. Mendès-France had
proved a doughtier champion of W.E.U. than he had of E.D.C. –
Article 1 of the main agreement was rejected. It dealt with the establishment of W.E.U. and the admission of Germany into NATO and was
therefore crucial.

The debate in the Assembly was due to continue on Wednesday,
29 December, when a final vote on ratification would be taken. Sir
Anthony Eden now, for the first time in the seemingly endless series of
negotiations, applied pressure rather than persuasiveness to the French.
Abandoning the carrot, he made use of the stick. On the evening of
24 December a Foreign Office statement made it clear to the French,
and to the world, that rejection of W.E.U. by France would not halt
the progress of German rearmament. It was no longer a question of
whether Western Germany should rearm but of *how* she should rearm.
The statement concluded: 'The United Kingdom commitment, offered
at the London Conference, to maintain British forces on the continent
of Europe, depends on the ratification of the Paris Agreement by all
parties.'

There were indications also that this notification by Britain that the
end of her patience had been reached would find an echo in Washington.
The French Assembly, in a modern phrase, 'got the message' and the
Paris Agreements were ratified on 29 December 1954.

If Dean Acheson may be regarded as the 'hero' and chief architect of
the Marshall Plan, to Sir Anthony Eden must go the major credit for
salvaging the essentials from the wreck of E.D.C. and creating a new
European framework of defence and security. In bringing W.E.U.,
almost single-handed, into being he concluded negotiations which that
great Continental statesman Paul-Henri Spaak has described as
'*certainement parmi les plus heureuses de sa carrière. Il l'a conduite du*

* The original suggestion had been to call the new organization simply 'Western
Union', but it was then objected that this might cause confusion with the great American telegraphic agency!

début jusqu'à la fin avec maîtrise, tour à tour conciliant et ferme, enfin, pour enlever la décision finale, imaginatif et audacieux.[72]

With speed as his watchword, Sir Anthony, within a month of the rejection by France of E.D.C. on 30 August, had achieved, by the preliminary accords reached at the London Nine-Power Conference, a new hope for European defence and security and for the future of the North Atlantic Alliance. Navigating with patience, skill and understanding between the varied personalities of Konrad Adenauer, Pierre Mendès-France and John Foster Dulles, he had attained success at last. *'Il est vraiment le père des Accords de Londres et du Traité de Paris'*, M. Spaak has written. *'Sans lui, je le confirme, il est peu probable qu'un accord ait été trouvé. Il a, en 1954 et en 1955, sauvé l'Alliance atlantique.'*[73]*

IX

When, in his famous Zürich speech of September 1946, Mr Churchill spoke of his hope that Soviet Russia might be numbered among 'the friends and sponsors of a new Europe', he was guilty of an almost euphoric optimism. The Soviet Union was already committed to a certain line of policy which precluded any such role and, as the West drew together to meet the Russian challenge, so did Moscow seek to disrupt this unifying process.

Yet for a brief period in 1953 hopes did blaze up irrepressibly. The death of Stalin on 5 March, followed by President Eisenhower's appeal, on 16 April, to the new rulers of the Soviet Union to give tangible evidence of their genuine desire for peace,[74] followed in its turn by the East Berlin rising of 17 June, gave rise to a certain sanguine expectancy that, for one reason or another, a 'breakthrough' might be possible, or even imminent, and a *détente* conceivable between Moscow and the West.

However, like many another hope in this connection, these were doomed to disappointment. The anti-Communist demonstrations in East Berlin were put down, with some savagery, by Soviet troops, and the reply of Moscow to President Eisenhower's advances, though it lacked the hectoring abuse which had characterized Stalin's communications, still gave indication that, whatever outward changes might be apparent, while Molotov remained in charge of Soviet external affairs it would be a case of 'new presbyter is but old priest writ large'. The Russians demanded as the price of German reunification the conclusion of a formal peace treaty, the withdrawal of occupation troops and the signing of a European security pact.

---

* For the controversy in Britain over the British Government's attitude towards Europe at this time, see below, App. C.

None the less there existed, both in London and in Washington, a desire to explore once more the possibility of a meeting of Foreign Ministers which should at least exchange views on current problems. This was agreed in principle between Sir Winston Churchill, President Eisenhower and Joseph Laniel at the Three-Power Conference at Bermuda in December 1953.

By this time E.D.C. had been signed and was awaiting ratification and it became evident that if Soviet diplomacy could delay this consummation of a European defence framework it would be to her material advantage. When therefore tentative proposals were made by the West for the purpose of convening a Four-Power Conference of Foreign Ministers which should discuss 'the first steps which should lead to a satisfactory solution of the German problem, namely, the organization of free elections and the establishment of a free all-German Government', they were met by a Soviet *non possumus*, on 4 August 1953. The Western proposals were summarily rejected as involving 'leaving Germany divided into western and eastern parts' and rendering the conclusion of a peace treaty as distant as ever.

Having thus disposed of the West's proposals, the Soviet Government made its own strategic bid, reversing the basis of the Allied offer. On 23 August Georgi Malenkov made a public pronouncement that a peace conference, for the purpose of drawing up a peace treaty with Germany, should be summoned as soon as possible and that, at the conference and in all stages of preparation of the treaty, the participation of German representatives must be guaranteed. He also proposed that, in contradistinction to the Allied plan, the formation of an all-German Government should precede the holding of all-German elections without the interference or supervision of foreign states.*

The Western Governments rejected these Soviet proposals as frankly specious but countered with an invitation to a Four-Power Conference which the Soviet Government accepted on condition that it became a Five-Power Conference, including Red China. As a result of this *détente*

---

* On the same day a protocol was signed between the Soviet Union and the German Democratic Republic providing for (1) the cancellation of all reparation payments by East Germany to the Soviet Union as from 1 January 1954 (it was stated that the balance still due amounted to $2,537 million at 1938 world prices); (2) the return by Russia of the industrial enterprises taken over from East Germany after the war; (3) Soviet occupation costs to be limited to 5 per cent of the East German national income; (4) the cancellation of all foreign debts which had arisen in connection with reparation payments. It was also announced in a separate communiqué that the Soviet Government had promised a pardon to all German prisoners of war who had been sentenced for offences committed during hostilities, except those guilty of 'particularly grave crimes against peace and humanity'. The Soviet Government also undertook to grant a credit to the German Democratic Republic of 485 million roubles at 2 per cent payable over two years from 1955.

and of the Bermuda Conference in December, a conference did indeed
meet in Berlin on 25 January 1954. In so far as the problem of Germany
was concerned it achieved nothing. The three Western Powers put forward a plan for German reunification through free elections leading to an
all-German Government with which a peace treaty could be concluded.
The plan was rejected by the Soviet Government, which was not ready to
permit free elections or to abandon its control over East Germany.*

The Soviet Government had reluctantly to recognize that they had
lost this particular round of the game but still pinned their faith to some
degree on the failure of E.D.C. When therefore the French rejection of
the E.D.C. agreements on 30 August 1954 seemed to betoken the collapse
of all hopes for the creation of a European defence system, Soviet hopes
rose again only to be dashed by the amazingly quick recovery effected
by Anthony Eden's extension and development of the Brussels Treaty
organization into W.E.U., into which Western Germany was admitted.

The Khrushchev–Bulganin leadership in Moscow now took a new
course of action. The time had come, in their opinion, to concentrate
their hold upon Stalin's legacy in Eastern Europe and transform it into
some kind of political and military organization. While Stalin lived he
exercised an authoritative control over the Eastern European satellites
by the sheer awe of his personality. When this dominating factor disappeared with the Marshal's death in 1953, it was realized that, as they
stood, these satellites were no more than wasting assets – 'little more',
as one writer has aptly observed, 'than a secret policeman's paradise'.†
What was clearly needed in order to face the new political situation in
international affairs occasioned by Stalin's death was to get the various
Eastern and Central European states concerned to develop some degree
of individual life of their own, under appropriate Soviet direction, control and co-ordination, in the fields of foreign policy and political and
economic affairs.

The conclusion of the W.E.U. agreements in Paris on 23 October 1954
provided an opportunity for a new initiative in Soviet policy towards
their satellites. On the very same day the Soviet Foreign Ministry, in a
note to the Governments of twenty-three European countries,‡ denounced W.E.U. as a 'violation of international agreements' in that it

* The conference, which dispersed on 18 February, was more successful in other
fields. It reached agreement on calling a Seven-Power Conference at Geneva to
consider the problem of Indo-China, and the subsequent holding of an exchange of
views on disarmament. It also made some progress towards the conclusion of an
Austrian State Treaty (see above, p. 479).

† An excellent study of the Warsaw Pact and its origins has been written by Malcolm
Mackintosh of the Institute for Strategic Studies.[75]

‡ Copies of the Note were also sent to the Governments of the United States and the
People's Republic of China.

provided for the remilitarization of Western Germany and her inclusion in a military grouping against other states. The Note repeated the Soviet proposals for the immediate withdrawal of occupation troops and proposed that a conference should be held 'without delay' to establish a system of collective security for Europe. The Western Powers replied collectively that they were not averse to a further meeting of the four Foreign Ministers or to a possible European security conference but that both these must await the ratification of the Paris Agreements by the countries concerned and the consequent entry into force of W.E.U. Whereupon the Soviet Government convened a satellite security conference on 29 November* and announced that, if the Paris Agreements were ratified, a joint military organization for Eastern and Central Europe would be set up.

Ratification of the Paris Agreements was duly completed on 5 May 1955 and four days later West Germany joined NATO, as well as W.E.U. The Soviet Government thereupon, on 7 May, denounced the Anglo-Soviet Treaty of 1942 and the Franco-Soviet Treaty of 1944, both of which had a validity of twenty years, and on 14 May there was signed at Warsaw a pact between the U.S.S.R. and her seven satellites.

This agreement, which was also to have a twenty years' duration, was not dissimilar to the NATO Treaty, to which, it was claimed, it owed its being. The Warsaw Pact would cease to be valid as soon as NATO was abandoned by the Western Powers and a European security system came into being as a substitute for both groupings. Meanwhile the Pact provided for the abstention by its members from violence and for the pacific settlement of disputes arising between them; for readiness to co-operate in all international actions with the purpose of achieving peace and security; for mutual consultation on all important international problems and immediate consultation and assistance in the event of aggression against any member state; for the setting-up of a joint command of armed forces‡ and of a political consultative committee; for an undertaking not to interfere in one another's internal affairs;§ and for the adhesion of other states to the protocol of the Pact.‖

* Those states attending were the Soviet Union, Albania, Bulgaria, Czechoslovakia, East Germany, Hungary, Poland and Rumania.

‡ The first Commander-in-Chief of the Warsaw Pact forces was Marshal Ivan Koniev of the Red Army.

§ The acts of the Soviet Government in Czechoslovakia in August 1968 afford an interesting commentary on the manner in which this provision of the Warsaw Pact came to be interpreted in Moscow.

‖ In a speech immediately after the signing of the Pact, Marshal Bulganin emphasized that it was purely defensive and inspired by the principle of peaceful coexistence. He further elaborated this theme in a speech before the Indian Parliament on 21 November 1955.

Thus ten years after the Unconditional Surrender of Germany and the solemn undertaking on the part of the occupying Powers who assumed the sovereignty of the German state that this occupation did not prejudice the principle of German unity, there existed two German republics, each of which is an integral and sovereign equal partner in a rival political defence grouping. Europe stood sharply divided in 1955 – and so remains fifteen years later: the Western European Union and the North Atlantic Treaty Organization representing the forces of the freedom-loving peoples and the nations of the Warsaw Pact the organized might of Communist power.

As a result of this confrontation we are presented with the Semblance of Peace.

Epilogue:
'By Manifold Illusion'

'PEACE, you must know, is perhaps a hundred times more difficult to make than war', the great Boer soldier and statesman, Louis Botha, told cheering crowds on 24 July 1919 on his return to Cape Town from attending the Peace Conference of Paris, and he added: 'Sometimes the action of a fool can start a war, but it takes the wisdom of the world to make peace again.'[1] In the profundity of these words, taken in conjunction with those of Thucydides with which this book began, namely that men rarely adhere to the same views during the course of war which they held upon entering it,* lies the kernel of the book's purpose.

Britain and France began the war in 1939 in a mist of illusion and concluded it in 1945, having changed their views considerably and radically, in a fog of further illusion which had become manifold. This was also true of the United States.

To be sure we were less naïve in 1945 than we had been in 1919. There was no talk of our having fought a 'war to end war', and though there was still the lurking chimera that we were out to 'make the world safe for democracy', it died a speedy death under the impact of Soviet diplomacy. We began to drop our reference to democracy as the be-all and end-all of our aims and to substitute a more significant formula of 'the defence of the free world', which at least had some foundation in reality. That we were deeply perturbed in the face of the Russian menace we did not attempt to deny, but equally we adopted a frank and honourable policy of pledging, in the defence of that in which we believed, 'our lives, our fortunes and our sacred honour'. This, remarkably enough, was the basic principle of the North Atlantic Treaty.

Contemplating the state of our world society a quarter of a century after the end of the Second World War, one can descry little of which to be proud, little indeed to evoke a major degree of satisfaction or confidence. Our world is divided into two armed camps, within which

* See above, p. 4.

there are symptoms of considerable disagreement, though each camp maintains an appearance of united opposition to the other. It is not impossible that the existing menace of Communist China to both the U.S.S.R. and the United States may have a relatively beneficial effect in the form of some unwritten, unagreed state of affairs whereby the Soviet Union will not bring matters to a confrontation with the United States while China is in her present mood.

The United Nations, destroyed as an effective peace-keeping force by its universality and egalitarianism, has reached a nadir of uselessness in this its major purpose more completely and more rapidly than was ever achieved by the League of Nations. Its status, except as an international welfare organization, is derisory, and its place as a factor of security has been taken by such regional organizations as NATO – even, in a sense, the Warsaw Pact – composed of states bound together by what Rudyard Kipling called 'ties of common funk'.*

The two great warrior states among the former Axis Powers, Germany and Japan, have both been disarmed and demilitarized. But, in the course of the years and in answer to the exigencies of world affairs, Germany – now, perhaps happily, but 'half a Reich' – has been rearmed, largely at the expense of the United States. Both Germany and Japan stand now among the richest and most prosperous of the nations, linked in honourable alliance in defence of the Western world.

Theoretically we live, though some may doubt it, in a world in which aggression has been outlawed, for the Kellogg–Briand Pact of 1928, by which the contracting parties renounced war as an instrument of national policy, still remains a technically viable undertaking because it contained no time limit and was indeed concluded *in perpetuam*. As will be remembered, it played its not inconsiderable role in the Indictment of the major war criminals at Nuremburg and at Tokyo. Though its present obligation may be regarded, perhaps, as somewhat nebulous,

---

* Constructive proposals for improving and rendering more efficient the peace-keeping powers of the Security Council were advanced by the British Foreign Secretary, Sir Alec Douglas-Home, in New York on 21 October 1970. Sir Alec forthrightly stated that the Council had been diverted from its intended role as a peace-making body and had become a virtual extension of the General Assembly. To remedy this he proposed that:

1. Except in emergencies, states calling the Security Council into session should have positive and workable proposals ready for the start of the meeting.
2. The United Nations should equip itself with the physical means of keeping the peace (but there was no specific suggestion for a standing U.N. force).
3. The Council should utilize its existing, but usually neglected, powers to investigate disputes.
4. Support should be given to a Brazilian plan for setting up small working groups of member states to investigate and report on situations threatening world peace.

In essence the Foreign Secretary declared that the Security Council must have the will to settle disputes peacefully and the machinery to do it effectively.[2]

it has made one curious, if largely negative, contribution to our post-war world.

Since we do not recognize a state of war, and certainly we do not perceptibly enjoy the blessings of peace, we have a new set of circumstances, a sort of mutation of the somewhat lunatic formula which Trotsky propounded at Brest–Litovsk of 'no war–no peace'. What has developed in various parts of the world as an intermediary stage in international affairs is 'non-belligerency' – a state of affairs in which a full condition of war no longer obtains but the international status of the nations concerned has still not been regulated in a completely normal fashion.

This, for example, was the condition which obtained in Japan from the Unconditional Surrender of September 1945 to the conclusion of the Treaty of San Francisco six years later. It exists in a different degree in Germany where, by reason of partition, no treaty of peace has brought the state of war declared in 1939 to an end. Hostilities were terminated by the Unconditional Surrender of May 1945 but, at least in so far as the Federal Republic of Germany is concerned, sovereignty had to be somewhat hastily and arbitrarily restored by the three Western Allies so that the Bonn Government might be a participating party in the Western European Union.

A further, and strangely successful, example of 'non-belligerency' is the situation created by the armistice agreement of Panmunjom, which brought to an end the Korean War in 1953. Though no treaty of peace has been signed between the North and South Korean republics, the line defined by the armistice agreement has been generally respected and remains intact.

There remain two less recognizable instances of 'non-belligerency'. One is to be found in the Middle East, where, though there have been three wars between Israel and the Arab states since 1948, none of these has been 'declared' and there has been no peace treaty after any of them. The situation, moreover, is infinitely complicated in that one group of belligerents refuses to recognize the legal existence of the other.

The other 'illusory' instance of 'non-belligerency' is in Vietnam, where there exists a full-scale conventional state of hostilities in which, at one moment, some 600,000 United States armed forces were committed and which has defied the efforts of President Johnson to win and of President Nixon to liquidate. This supremely tragic situation, which has humiliated, divided and weakened the United States beyond belief, is not a 'declared' war, nor is it a United Nations operation, as was the case in Korea. Like Topsy, 'it just growed', varying in intensity, accelerating and decelerating, from the initial act by President Kennedy to the present day. It remains an extreme example of 'non-belligerency' and adds poignancy to the inevitable reflection: 'A mad world, my masters.'

There remains, however, another thought. In the midst of the gloomy prospect which confronts the world at this moment there emerges one point, at least, of pale, almost anaemic, hope. It is ineluctably true that our civilization has been spared the horror of a major armed conflict for a longer period since the conclusion of the Second World War than was the case between the wars. Admittedly we have not experienced those euphoric years which followed the Treaty of Locarno and preceded the Great Depression and the rise of Nazi Germany in Europe; admittedly, too, we have never been since 1945 in anything but a state of uncertainty, suspicion and apprehension. The first shots of the Cold War may well have been fired before the Unconditional Surrender of Germany and Japan. But the fact remains that no major crisis – and there have been many in this period which might in an earlier age have provoked a world conflagration – has been permitted to go beyond the state of what is somewhat ironically termed 'conventional' warfare.

It is not that we are better or kinder or more compassionate in our attitude to one another. It is not that we have abandoned or outgrown that combative instinct which is thought to be inherently natural to the human and to the animal species. It is that we are desperately afraid. If, 'ties of common funk' are the most potent bonds of alliance, so is mutual fear of destruction the surest shield against a major conflict. A United States estimate has it that in an all-out nuclear exchange between Russia and America the United States might have to face casualties in the nature of 150 million. One believes that the Russian losses could not be less.

Faced with so horrifying a holocaust – which, of course, would not be confined to the two major antagonists – the world has been petrified in a stalemate of terror. The threat of nuclear war has for nearly a quarter of a century proved a powerful and, so far, effective deterrent, which has resulted in a curious degree of added caution in the handling of international crises lest they produce a clash which, in its turn, might lead to dangerous escalation.

As that eminent diplomat, Lord Caccia, once told an audience at Ditchley:

> The more Governments know from their own experience what nuc-
> lear weapons are like, the less glibly they speak of their use and the
> more reluctant they are to be a party to their dissemination. . . . We
> cannot, of course, be sure that our views will always be acceptable to

others on nuclear matters. Nor can they. But they, like we, are interested in survival and this is an argument about the means of survival rather than threats of annihilation.[3]

It is, of course, a sad comment on the standard of our contemporary morals and ethics that we accept with relief and gratitude a state of affairs which permits 'conventional' warfare almost as a humanitarian activity, even when it assumes the bitter ferocity and recurrence of the Middle East struggle or the major proportion of the hostilities in Vietnam. It is as if an affrighted world had heard, and fearfully heeded, the warning of Euripides to Athens on the eve of the departure of the first ill-fated expedition to Sicily: 'A fool among men is he who sacks cities, brings desolation on the temples, the groves, the hallowed places of the dead, and thus has brought destruction too upon himself. . . .'[4] There is, indeed, a strange impression of our having struck a bargain with Fate, but the nightmare which rides our dreams, as we teeter on the razor-edge of uncertainty, is – how long will this bargain hold?

You cannot prove a negative, that is to say that you cannot 'go nap' on the premise that the Bomb will not be used. But, at the moment, the threat of the consequence of the use of the Bomb has ensured the peace of our planet for the last five-and-twenty years.

Here again, in our sombre relief, we cannot escape a tragic sense of failure. Whether inevitably or not, for the second time in half a century a great international organization, born in each case on the crest of the wave of the hope of the world, has failed to ensure peace and to promote security. The United Nations, like its predecessor the League, has realized neither the hopes nor the desires of its founders, and today our protection against a general war is not the assurance of collective action by the international community, but the deterrent effect of nuclear potential in the hands of two major Powers.

That great Canadian statesman, Lester Pearson, admitted in Westminster Hall, on the occasion of the twenty-fifth birthday of the United Nations Charter: 'The knowledge that even the victor is vanquished in a nuclear war has become our main guarantee of peace; and is likely to remain so until we find something better and more permanent; yet peace rests uneasily on a hydrogen bomb; and an inter-continental missile is a weak foundation for lasting security.'[5]*

---

* A similar American view was expressed by MacGeorge Bundy in his Ditchley Foundation Lecture of 1969: 'This is a painful conclusion because what it continues to mean, twenty-five years after D-Day and twenty-four after Hiroshima, is that the peace of Europe depends on the stable will of Washington and that Washington in turn must depend upon a form of strength whose actual use – as President Kennedy once said – would be a confession of terrible failure.'[6]

That this is really the sum total of our united achievement after two world wars may well be a cause for tears, something for weeping, but it at least justifies the verse with which this book begins:

> Civilization is hooped together, brought
> Under a rule, under the semblance of peace,
> By manifold illusion.

APPENDIX A

Note on the Present Position of the Munich Agreement of 29 September 1938

THE Munich Agreement, concluded between Germany, the United Kingdom, France and Italy for the cession of the Sudeten German territory by Czechoslovakia, although officially dated 29 September 1938, was in reality signed in the small hours of the morning of 30 September.[1] To it was annexed a declaration by the British and French Governments guaranteeing the new boundaries of the Czechoslovak state against unprovoked aggression. Germany and Italy also agreed to give a similar guarantee to Czechoslovakia 'when the question of the Polish and Hungarian minorities in Czechoslovakia had been settled'. It was further declared that the problems of these minorities in Czechoslovakia, if not settled within three months by agreement between the respective Governments, 'shall form the subject of another meeting of the Heads of the Governments of the four Powers here present'.

Because of its nature, the Munich Agreement was not subject to the usual forms of ratification, and no provision for such procedure was included in its text. Parliamentary approval was accorded to Mr Chamberlain and to M. Daladier, on 6 and 5 October respectively, by means of votes of confidence but by the time these had been given in the House of Commons and the Chamber of Deputies the terms of the Munich Agreement were already a *fait accompli.*

On 2 November 1938 the German and Italian Foreign Ministers, Ribbentrop and Ciano, handed down the First Vienna Award, which, without consultation with, or reference to, the British and French Governments, adjudicated the fate of the Polish and Hungarian minorities in Czechoslovakia, in violation of the annexe to the Munich Agreement.[2]

The structure set up by the Munich Agreement was destroyed on 15 March 1939 when Hitler proclaimed that 'Czechoslovakia has ceased to exist'. Slovakia and Ruthenia proclaimed their independence on 14 March and the provinces of Bohemia and Moravia were annexed to the German Reich as a Protectorate.[3]

On the second anniversary of the signing of the Munich Agreement (30 September 1940), Winston Churchill in a broadcast to the Czechoslovak people announced that the Agreement had been destroyed by the Germans,[4] and on 18 July of the following year the Czechoslovak Provisional Government was officially recognized by the British Government and by General de Gaulle's National Committee.[5] It was not, however, until 5 August 1942 that this statement was given official form. On that day the British Foreign Secretary,

Anthony Eden, announced in the House of Commons that he had sent a Note to the Czechoslovak Ambassador, Jan Masaryk, declaring that 'as Germany has deliberately destroyed the arrangements concerning Czechoslovakia reached in 1938, in which His Majesty's Government in the United Kingdom participated, His Majesty's Government regard themselves as free from any engagements in this respect. At the final settlement of the Czechoslovak frontiers to be reached at the end of the war, they will not be influenced by any changes effected in and since 1938.'[6]

Of the other two signatories, France and Italy, General de Gaulle declared on 29 September 1942 that France considered the Munich Agreement to be null and void,[7] and a similar statement was made by the Government of Ivanoe Bonomi, on behalf of Italy, on 26 September 1944.[8]

At the conclusion of hostilities in Europe in May 1945 and the consequent resumption by Czechoslovakia of her full sovereignty and independence, the Czechoslovak state reconstituted itself within its pre-Munich frontiers. This act received tacit approval from the British, American, Soviet and French Governments, but the question of the Munich frontiers was not raised at the Potsdam Conference and therefore finds no mention in the Protocol of 2 August 1945. The reason for this was that three of the four signatory Munich Powers had repudiated the Agreement and that no German Government existed at that moment. The matter was therefore left over until a final peace treaty with Germany was formally concluded.

When it became apparent, however, that the conclusion of such a peace treaty would be long postponed, successive German Federal Chancellors announced their repudiation of the Munich Agreement. Thus, on 15 October 1964, Dr Ludwig Erhard declared that in no circumstances would Western Germany present territorial claims against Czechoslovakia,[9] and his successor, Dr Kurt Kiesinger, on 5 July 1968, was even more definite, announcing explicitly that in so far as Germany was concerned 'the Munich Agreement no longer exists'.[10]

Thus all the four participants in the Pact of Munich have repudiated their signatures and, as far as Her Majesty's Government is concerned, there has been no basic change in policy since Mr Eden's statement of August 1942. Indeed it has been re-emphasized. Michael Stewart, during his first tenure of office as Foreign Secretary, took the opportunity, during an official visit to Prague in April 1965, to assure Czechoslovak Ministers that 'the Munich Agreement was detestable, unjust and dangerous as events have shown to the peace of Europe'. He added that it was 'completely dead and had been dead for many years . . .'. The mere historical fact that it was once made could not justify any future claims against Czechoslovakia. When the time came for a final determination of Germany's frontiers by a peace treaty, the treaty discussions would start from the basis that Czechoslovak frontiers were not in question.[11]

Explicit though this statement may appear to be, it was not sufficiently definite to satisfy the Czechoslovak Government, who took advantage of the thirtieth anniversary of the signing of the Munich Agreement to make a further *démarche*. On 27 September 1968 the Czechoslovak Ambassador called at the Foreign Office and made a formal request to the Minister of State,

Goronway Roberts, that Britain should make a formal declaration to the effect that the Pact of Munich was null and void. He was informed that his request would be 'examined'.[12]

Though the matter is of purely academic interest – except perhaps to the Czechoslovaks – there might possibly be a good reason to make a formal Four-Power Declaration which should bury the ghost of the Munich Agreement once and for all. In view of the powerful initiative taken by the British Government to bring the Agreement into being in 1938, it might well be considered a gracious act on their part to take the initial steps towards its formal repudiation.

APPENDIX B

The Yoshida Letter

IN the secret agreement reached between John Foster Dulles and Herbert Morrison, then Foreign Secretary, in June 1951, it was agreed that neither the Nationalist Chinese Government in Taipeh nor the Communist régime in Peking should be invited to the Conference of San Francisco and, moreover, that Japan's future attitude towards 'China' 'must necessarily be for determination by Japan itself in the sovereign and independent status contemplated by the treaty'.[1]* The agreement was to have some interesting repercussions.

It was on Mr Dulles's personal plea that the British Foreign Secretary agreed to the terms of secrecy, this being alien to both his own personal inclination and to the avowed policy of the Labour Party, who were traditionally averse to 'secret diplomacy'. However, Mr Dulles had specifically asked that no public statement disclosing the nature of their agreement should be made, as 'it would embarrass me', and Mr Morrison therefore reluctantly assented.[2]

For a while all went well. Shigeru Yoshida, the Japanese Prime Minister, who knew of the Anglo-American agreement, behaved throughout the San Francisco Conference with impeccable dignity and in conformity with all that Mr Dulles could have desired, and there is good evidence that American influence was even exerted on him to restrain his obvious anti-Communist sympathies.

Up to the moment of the signing of the treaty on 8 September 1951, therefore, both sides had remained loyal to the terms of the Morrison–Dulles accord and to the preservation of its secrecy, but almost immediately thereafter the situation became complicated and murky. The kindest explanation of what followed is that it was the result of bungling misunderstanding on the part of the State Department, but there do not lack those who interpret the result as one of deliberate sharp practice on the part of John Foster Dulles.

The interpretation placed upon the Morrison–Dulles accord by the British Foreign Office was that 'the sovereignty and independent status' of Japan, to which reference was made in the accord, could only exist when the treaty which created it had become effective upon the ratification, and this interpretation was known – and presumably understood – by both the United States and Japanese Governments.[3] However, an unforeseen difficulty now arose.

The rejection of the Treaty of Versailles by the United States Senate in

* See above, p. 524.

1920 and the consequent mortification of President Woodrow Wilson has had a traumatic and lasting effect upon successive Presidents, Secretaries of State and majority party leaders in the Senate. 'Never again' has become their watchword, and they are determined that no President and Administration shall again be subjected to so humiliating a defeat. Inevitably, therefore, it has become axiomatic that when a major treaty is about to come before the Senate and its powerful Committee on Foreign Relations, every possible precaution is taken so to prepare the ground in advance that the danger of rejection is avoided.

It was in accordance with this policy that by mid-September, shortly before the Treaty of San Francisco was to be submitted to the Senate, some fifty-six Senators sympathetic to its ratification wrote warningly to President Truman that 'Prior to the submission of the Japanese Treaty to the Senate, we desire to make it clear that we would consider the recognition of Communist China by Japan or the negotiating of a bilateral treaty with the Communist China régime to be adverse to the best interests of the people of both Japan and the United States'.[4]

President Truman was no weakling in politics, but he was a very shrewd politician well attuned to the grass roots. The fear of Communism was rife in the land and the United States was heavily committed to the Cold War. In this minatory and ominous senatorial warning he sensed the premonitory symptoms of trouble, and he urged Mr Dulles to clear up this matter once and for all.

It must also be realized that Mr Yoshida had himself been guilty of confusing the issue.* Doubtless for purposes of his own internal and domestic political policies, he had made statements in the Diet, in the course of the debates on the Japanese ratification of the treaty, of a perplexing and ambiguous nature, leaving the matter of Japan's future attitude towards China rather less than clear. It was these ambivalent utterances which had aroused the senatorial doubts as to where indeed he really did stand, and especially in the breasts of two Senators, Alexander Smith and John Sparkman, who were members of the Far Eastern Committee of the Senate's Committee on Foreign Relations which would give first consideration to the examination of the treaty.

Finally it was decided that Mr Dulles, together with Senators Smith and Sparkman, should go to Tokyo to clear up the matter with Mr Yoshida personally. This they did in mid-December 1951. As a result of their discussions and immediately after their return to Washington, the Japanese Prime Minister handed to the American Ambassador in Tokyo on 24 December the famous 'Yoshida Letter', addressed to Dulles, which was to have such far-reaching repercussions. It read as follows:[5]

Dear Ambassador Dulles:
    While the Japanese Peace Treaty and the U.S.–Japan Security Treaty were being debated in the House of Representatives and the House of Councillors of the Diet, a number of questions were put and statements made relative to Japan's future policy towards China. Some of the

---

* It should be noted that no mention of this whole incident of the letter is made in the Yoshida memoirs.

statements, separated from their context and background, gave rise to misapprehensions which I should like to clear up.

The Japanese Government desires ultimately to have a full measure of political peace and commercial intercourse with China which is Japan's close neighbor.

At the present time it is, we hope, possible to develop that kind of relationship with the National Government of the Republic of China, which has the seat, voice and vote of China in the United Nations, which exercises actual governmental authority over certain territory, and which maintains diplomatic relations with most of the members of the United Nations. To that end my Government on November 17, 1951, established a Japanese Government Overseas Agency in Formosa, with the consent of the National Government of China. This is the highest form of relationship with other countries which is now permitted to Japan, pending the coming into force of the multilateral Treaty of Peace. The Japanese Government Overseas Agency in Formosa is important in its personnel, reflecting the importance which my government attaches to relations with the National Government of the Republic of China. My government is prepared as soon as legally possible to conclude with the National Government of China, if that government so desires, a Treaty which will reestablish normal relations between the two Governments in conformity with the principles set out in the multilateral Treaty of Peace. The terms of such bilateral treaty shall, in respect of the Republic of China, be applicable to all territories which are now, or which may hereafter be, under the control of the National Government of the Republic of China. We will promptly explore this subject with the National Government of China.

As regards the Chinese Communist regime, that regime stands actually condemned by the United Nations of being an aggressor and in consequence, the United Nations has recommended certain measures against that regime, in which Japan is now concurring and expects to continue to concur when the multilateral Treaty of Peace comes into force pursuant to the provisions of Article 5(a)(iii), whereby Japan has undertaken 'to give the United Nations every assistance in any action it takes in accordance with the Charter and to refrain from giving assistance to any State against which the United Nations may take preventive or enforcement action'. Furthermore, the Sino-Soviet Treaty of Friendship, Alliance and Mutual Assistance concluded in Moscow in 1950 is virtually a military alliance aimed against Japan. In fact there are many reasons to believe that the Communist regime in China is backing the Japan Communist Party in its program of seeking violently to overthrow the constitutional system and the present Government of Japan. In view of these considerations, I can assure you that the Japanese Government has no intention to conclude a bilateral Treaty with the Communist regime of China.

Yours sincere
Shigeru Yoshida.

It is abundantly clear that the content and tenor of this letter were not in accordance with the British interpretation of the terms of the Morrison–Dulles accord of June 1951, with which both Dulles and Yoshida were familiar. The American interpretation, however, as now developed by Foster Dulles, was that Japan's 'sovereign and independent status contemplated in the treaty' would, as a practical matter, exist when the Allied occupation and the Supreme

Commander's authority over Japanese relations with foreign countries had been terminated. This, Dulles claimed, had already occurred and been recognized by many signatories of the treaty, as shown by their acceptance of negotiations with Japan. It was an argument which Dean Acheson regards as 'not answerable but respectable'.[6] But however conflicting views may be in this judgement, it was obvious that a situation had arisen among allies which demanded clarification and frank discussion.

A fortuitous opportunity for such consultation was immediately forthcoming. In the General Election of October 1951 the British electorate had rejected Mr Attlee and the Labour Party and, as a result, Mr Churchill had formed his third Administration, with Mr Eden back at the Foreign Office. The new Prime Minister and Foreign Secretary paid their 'duty call' on the American President and Secretary of State in January 1952. By this time, according to Dean Acheson, the Yoshida Letter had been shown to the British Ambassador, Sir Oliver Franks,* and it had been assumed by the State Department that he had communicated its contents to Mr Eden. On 10 January, Acheson, Eden, Dulles and Franks met to talk about the need for a public statement by Japan on her China policy. According to Dean Acheson the Yoshida Letter was not mentioned,[7] but Mr Eden in his memoirs records that the Americans explained their domestic political difficulties arising out of the machinations of the 'China lobby' which, they said, might be able to defeat the ratification of the peace treaty in the Senate if Japan did not give some indication of her intention to recognize and treat with Chiang Kai-shek's régime. Mr Eden was sympathetic to their problems but repeated that the views of the British Government had not changed and were still based on the Morrison–Dulles accord. At this point Mr Eden recalls, 'Mr Dulles had mentioned a communication he had received from Mr Yoshida, the Japanese Prime Minister, and hinted that it might be necessary to use this during the Senate's debate on ratification. I was not shown the text, or informed that there was any immediate intention to make it public. I made it clear, however, that I must not be regarded as having acquiesced in the development which had taken place.'[8]

Thus, by an absurd chance of fate, Mr Eden had been made aware of the existence and purport of the Yoshida Letter, though not of the background to it nor the intention to make it public. He had not been consulted as to its procurement nor shown the text of it. In view of the fact that he could not prevent its use by the State Department, he had made it clear that neither he personally nor the British Government were a party to the whole business.

Still in ignorance of what was afoot, Mr Eden left New York on the late afternoon of 15 January, after an exchange of compliments and felicitations. He arrived next morning in London to be greeted with the news of simultaneous publications in Washington and Tokyo of a letter from the Japanese

---

* Mr Dulles's semi-official biographer, Louis L. Gerson, states (on p. 93) that Herbert Morrison had also been informed of the tenor of the Yoshida Letter, but this statement must surely belong to the 'Department of Utter Confusion'. Morrison had ceased to be Foreign Secretary some two months before the letter was ever written, and if Mr Eden, as his successor, had not been informed of it, why should a member, even a leading member, of the Opposition?

Prime Minister to Mr Dulles dated 24 December, of the existence of which Mr Eden was totally unaware.*

There ensued a period of abrasive bewilderment. Much was at stake, including the amicable continuation of Anglo-American relations. Mr Eden wisely permitted a 'cooling-off' period of two weeks before making a statement in the House of Commons. However, on 30 January, in answer to questions, he said without equivocation that the British Government had frequently made its position clear to the United States Government, namely that, pursuant to the Morrison–Dulles accord, the matter of their attitude towards China should be left to the Japanese to decide after the treaty of peace had come into operation. As for the Yoshida Letter, there had been no previous consultation with the British Embassy and no British participation in the drafting or publishing of the document; the British diplomatic mission in Tokyo had only been made aware of its existence on the morning of its publication.[9]

Mr Eden had studiously refrained from making any specific charges of chicanery against John Foster Dulles (a fact to which Dean Acheson pays grateful tribute in his memoirs[10]), but Herbert Morrison had taken great umbrage. A month later, at the end of February, he emphatically accused Dulles of acting against both the spirit and the letter of their accord of June 1951 in bringing pressure to bear on the Japanese Government to state, before the treaty came up for ratification by the Senate, its intention to recognize the Taipeh Government of Chiang Kai-shek.[11] In view of this breach of contract, he later wrote in his memoirs, 'I may be forgiven if I resolved there and then not fully to trust Dulles again'.[12]

The repercussions of the Yoshida Letter incident – which, to put it at its best, was a matter of stupidity on the part of the State Department and, at its worst, a piece of bad faith on the part of John Foster Dulles† – were widely dispersed and unfortunate. The letter certainly served its turn in alleviating the apprehensions of certain Senators, and the Japanese Peace Treaty was ratified by the United States on 28 April 1952. The primary objective of Dulles's manœuvre had therefore been successfully achieved. But it had left a trail of suspicion behind it.

In Japan the victim was Yoshida himself. The fact that his Government had signed a treaty of peace and recognition with Taiwan on the same day as the Treaty of San Francisco‡ generally came into force was seized upon by his parliamentary opponents, and especially the Japanese Communist Party, for a series of damaging attacks on the Yoshida Government on the ground that its obsequious pursuit of a foreign policy in consonance with that of the United States was evidence that, despite whatever was stated in the peace

---

* In his memoirs (*Full Circle*, pp. 19–20) and in conversations with Louis Gerson and with Sir John Wheeler-Bennett, Lord Avon stated that he had not seen the text of the Yoshida Letter before its publication, and spoke of his surprise at its simultaneous release in Washington and Tokyo.

† Mr Acheson, as Secretary of State, had been at pains to declare that in his opinion Mr Dulles had not violated either the letter or the spirit of his agreement with Mr Morrison, and gave Dulles the full support and covering of his high office, though whether from conviction or policy is not entirely clear.[13]

‡ See above, p. 524.

treaty and the withdrawal of the Allied occupation, Japan's full and unfettered sovereignty and international status had not in actual fact been restored to her. She was, it was alleged, still the vassal of Washington, and the name of Dulles became as obnoxious in Japan as in certain European countries where he was felt to qualify for the label with which C. P. Scott had once tagged Mr Asquith – 'a champion in the arts of chicane'.[14] The issue proved severely hurtful to Yoshida's position, hitherto virtually impregnable.

Anglo-American relations also suffered from the impact of the Yoshida Letter. By the summer of 1952 it had become highly probable that General Eisenhower, the Supreme Allied Commander at SHAPE, would be the next President of the United States. With the conclusion of President Truman's term of office there came an end to the domination of the American scene by the Democratic Party which had begun twenty years before with the election of Franklin D. Roosevelt. All the auguries pointed to a Republican victory at the polls in November 1952, and their natural candidate – the very personification of the father-image dear to the hearts of the American people – was Dwight D. Eisenhower.

It was made clear to the General that the Republican nomination was his if he desired it (despite some opposition from the Old Guard supporters of Senator Robert Taft), and he consented to his name being put forward. In June 1952 he laid down his command, forsaking a military career, in which he had distinguished himself pre-eminently, for the field of politics in which he was to prove less than qualified.

On his way home to America General Eisenhower took the opportunity of informal discussions with Mr Churchill and Mr Eden, both of whom evinced great interest, in the event of his being elected, as to his appointment of a Secretary of State. According to the General's recollection, Anthony Eden went further than 'great interest': he 'expressed the hope', wrote Eisenhower, 'that I might appoint someone other than Dulles'.

If indeed Mr Eden had put the point thus bluntly the General might well have been as amazed as he says he was. 'From anyone else', he wrote, 'I would have resented such a suggestion as an unwarranted intrusion in American affairs. But my long association and friendship with him [Eden] during war and peace, involving the frankest kind of exchanges between us, made such a remark understandable. So, at that moment, I made no reply except to say that I knew of no other American so well qualified as Foster to take over the duties of that particular office.'[15]

John Foster Dulles's biographer, with perhaps precipitate judgement, states categorically that 'the immediate cause of Eden's extraordinary attempt to influence Eisenhower's decision resulted from Dulles's negotiations for the Japanese Treaty'[16] and the violation of the Morrison–Dulles accord. This is an easy and plausible assumption but very difficult to substantiate.

Though he had not shared in the public manifestation of outraged breast-beating in which Herbert Morrison had indulged, Eden would have been more than justified in developing some elements of mistrust towards Dulles as a result of that statesman's devious behaviour in the matter of the Yoshida Letter; indeed he would have been less than human had he not done so. But that he, a veteran statesman and diplomatist, would have employed so clumsy,

620 The Semblance of Peace

tactless and generally 'ham-fisted' a method of approach as a head-on frontal attack on Dulles in conversation is past all belief. Whatever his private views on Dulles may have been, Eden was not the man to disclose them; nor, in fact, did he.

'The foolish tale is now abroad that I had volunteered an opinion against Dulles to Ike. That is not true', Lord Avon later recorded. 'When we were breakfasting together in the British Embassy in Paris, alone and for a confidential talk at his suggestion, he asked me what I knew of various possible candidates for Secretary of State. I praised Dewey, and said that I felt sure he would be good. In reply to a question I said that I had not worked with Dulles,* indicating that I therefore had no view myself, but admitting the difficulties which Morrison had reported to me that he had had with Dulles.'[17]

Later, during the 'lame-duck' period in American politics (between the Presidential election in November 1952 and the inauguration in January 1953) Eden and Eisenhower met again at luncheon in New York, during one of the former's visits to the United Nations. Eisenhower had already announced the members of his Cabinet, with Dulles as Secretary of State. Now he drew Eden apart after lunch and explained (or justified) this appointment on the grounds of Dulles's long training and experience in foreign affairs and the fact that the Republican Party had regarded him as the foregone nominee for this position. However, the President-elect added that this was not at all important in view of his long-standing personal friendship with Eden. Eden must always feel free to get into touch with him and he looked forward to their two Governments working closely together.[18]

Alas, so auspicious a beginning was to have the unhappiest of endings.

* Mr Eden had, in point of fact, only met Dulles on two previous occasions, first at the Foreign Office towards the end of the war (see *The Reckoning*, p. 341) and secondly during his visit to Washington in January 1952 retailed above.

APPENDIX C

Britain and Europe in 1951

IT has been stated, with some severity, by leading members of the Conservative Party* that had it not been for the mutation and tergiversation, the lack of enthusiasm and the lukewarm support on the part of the British Government – and notably Winston Churchill and Anthony Eden – E.D.C. would have been saved and the creation of a European Army assured. More specifically, it is said that Mr Eden, at a Press conference in Rome on the evening of 28 November 1951, 'torpedoed' a more optimistic statement which Sir David Maxwell Fyfe (later the Earl of Kilmuir) had made that morning at the Consultative Assembly of the Council of Europe† at Strasbourg. As a result of this conduct, it is alleged, Paul-Henri Spaak resigned the Presidency of the Consultative Assembly to lead a campaign for a 'Little Federation of the Six', excluding Britain, and the British Conservative delegates to the Assembly sent a formal telegraphic protest to the Prime Minister, to which they received no reply. Finally, there is the ungracious sneer of Sir David Maxwell Fyfe that 'Eden, who bears such a heavy responsibility for this diplomatic catastrophe [the collapse of E.D.C.], was forced to hasten round the capitals of Europe within a few years to guarantee that British forces would remain in Europe, and to accept almost all the implications of the policy he had so brusquely dismissed in 1951'.[2]

Looking back a decade it seems ludicrous that E.D.C. with its fantastic and impracticable supranational features – with what Harold Macmillan has described as 'its elaborate and almost unworkable machinery' – should have stirred such passions, more especially when it is compared with the workman-like and proficient aspects of W.E.U., but the spirit of 'Europeanism' was in vogue in the fifties – partly for ideological reasons and partly for reasons of political expediency – and one has to accept the prevailing *Zeitgeist*.

When, however, the acid test of factual accuracy and historical judgement

* Notably Lord Kilmuir and Lord Boothby.[1]

† Established by the European Convention of 1949, the Council of Europe consists of eighteen European countries who 'accept the principles of the rule of law and the enjoyment by all persons within [their] jurisdiction of human rights and fundamental freedoms'. The Council has two organs, the Committee of Foreign Ministers and the Consultative Assembly, consisting of 147 persons elected or appointed by their national parliaments. The original members were Belgium, Denmark, France, the Irish Republic, Italy, Luxembourg, the Netherlands, Norway, Sweden and the United Kingdom. Greece and Turkey joined in 1949, Iceland in 1950, the Federal Republic of Germany in 1951, Austria in 1956, Cyprus in 1961, Switzerland in 1963 and Malta in 1965. Its headquarters are at Strasbourg.

in perspective is applied to the accusations against Churchill and Eden, they wither and decay. It may certainly be true that, in producing his original plan for a European Army, René Pleven drew his inspiration from the great speeches which Mr Churchill – then in opposition in the House of Commons – had made at Zürich in September 1946 and at The Hague in May 1948, in which he had called strongly for European unity. But Mr Churchill had made it abundantly clear on both occasions that, while Britain was anxious – nay, eager – to work closely with Europe, and any European structure, she had neither the desire nor the intention of being 'integrated' with it. Rather did he see Britain and the Commonwealth equated with the United States – and possibly the Soviet Union – as 'friends and sponsors of the new Europe'.*

Even before the proposals for E.D.C. Mr Churchill had, in August 1950, declared in favour of 'the immediate creation of a European army under a unified command in which we should bear a worthy and honourable part',[3] but when the Pleven Plan was made public, with its federal implications and supranational overtones, Mr Churchill found it quite unacceptable. The French proposals for a European Defence Community were totally different from those of which he had conceived; he had always thought in terms of a Western defence force founded on the principle of a Grand Alliance. 'He was particularly distressed by the plans for a European army', writes Lord Normanbrook, then Secretary to the Cabinet, 'an integrated organization of the kind then envisaged would not in his view provide an effective fighting force'.[4] He did not hesitate to dub the projected military formation as 'a sludgy amalgam' and, as we have seen, his final verdict, as expressed to President Eisenhower, was that he did not blame the French for having rejected E.D.C. but for having invented it.†

The reception accorded to the Pleven Plan by the British Government of the day had been less than cordial. 'The French Government have now produced a proposal for a European Army . . .', Mr Bevin had told the House of Commons on 29 November 1950. 'His Majesty's Government do not favour this proposal.'[5] All the innate British repugnance to unnecessary surrender of sovereignty was made manifest in their attide towards E.D.C. and only the pressure of the United States and the absence of an adequate alternative mitigated this natural hostility to the extent of permitting Mr Bevin's successor, Herbert Morrison, to join with Dean Acheson and Robert Schuman on 14 September 1951 in a Three-Power declaration of support to

---

* At Zürich on 19 September 1946 Mr Churchill had said: 'We must create the European family in a regional structure called – it may be – the United States of Europe, and the first practical steps will be to form a Council of Europe. . . . In all this urgent work France and Germany must take the lead together. Great Britain, the British Commonwealth of Nations, mighty America, and, I trust, Soviet Russia – for then, indeed, all would be well – must be the friends and sponsors of the new Europe and must champion its right to live.' Two years later, at The Hague on 7 May 1948, he said: 'Mutual aid in the economic field and joint military defence must inevitably be accompanied step by step with a parallel policy of closer political unity. It is said with truth that this involves some sacrifice or merger of national sovereignty. But it is also possible to regard it as the gradual assumption by all nations concerned of that larger sovereignty which can alone protect their diverse and distinctive customs and characters and national traditions. . . .'

† See above, p. 596.

the effect that 'The Government of the United Kingdom desire to establish the closest possible association with the European Continental Community at all stages of its development'.

The implication of this statement is clear. There was, and would be, no pledge of British participation in E.D.C. As *The Times* made comment: 'The choice of words makes it plain, even if it were not explicitly stated, that Britain will remain outside this European community and will make no direct contribution to the European Army.'[6]

Such was the policy of the Labour Government and such was the policy which the Conservative Party, the following month, inherited, endorsed and pursued with complete consistency. At no time – either before or after the General Election – did Winston Churchill or Anthony Eden contemplate full British participation in E.D.C., though they did consider the possibility of a limited contribution. From the first, Anthony Eden had his doubts as to the possibility of success for E.D.C. Like Winston Churchill, he supported the concept of a European community of some kind, but the federal, supranational features of M. Pleven's lucubration did not appeal. Both men in their attitude to Europe at this time reflected the opinion of the Conservative Government and, as that keen and candid observer, Sir Winston's Principal Private Secretary, John Colville, has pointed out, 'the strongly held convictions of the House of Commons, the electorate and the Commonwealth'.[7]

It seemed correct for the new British Government to make its position clear, and two occasions for doing this were imminent. The Home Secretary, Sir David Maxwell Fyfe, was about to attend a meeting of the Consultative Assembly of the Council of Europe at Strasbourg and Mr Eden was due in Rome for a meeting of the North Atlantic Council. Before leaving London the general tone of the statements which both would make was agreed between them and with their colleagues.

Sir David spoke on 28 November. He was legally elusive but it was difficult to misunderstand his meaning:

> If a new organization emerges, we shall consider how best to associate ourselves with it in a practical way. . . . I cannot promise you that our eventual association with the European Defence Community will amount to full and unconditional participation, because this, as I have said, is a matter which must, in our view, be left to inter-governmental discussion elsewhere. But I can assure you of our determination that no genuine method shall fail for lack of the thorough examination which one gives to the needs of trusted comrades.[8]

This statement, though eloquent, promised nothing, save that the British Government would be happy to give a 'thorough examination' to the Pleven Plan. It could under no circumstances be construed as a constructive commitment.

A few hours later in Rome, Anthony Eden made the position clearer, but he did not change the premise. In a Press conference he said that British units and British formations would not participate in a European Army, but that there might be some other form of association. 'I thought it better', he wrote later, 'to make plain at once what we could not do, so that we might agree on what we could do.'[9]

The wisdom of this policy bore fruit, as has been seen, within a month when, as a result of conversations with Dean Acheson concerning the common attitude of Britain and America towards E.D.C., Mr Churchill and Mr Eden, in the course of a visit to Paris, issued a joint communiqué with the French Government to the effect that, in addition to Britain being associated with E.D.C. 'in all stages of its military and political development', 'The United Kingdom forces under the direction of the Supreme Allied Commander in Europe will be linked with those of the European Defence Community for training, supply and operations by land, sea and air'.*

In view of these facts, the stand taken later by Lord Kilmuir and Lord Boothby becomes the more inexplicable. There was little but additional clarity on Mr Eden's part to distinguish his statement from that of the Home Secretary at Strasbourg and this was as it should be, since both statements were based on the same agreed governmental policy. Nor is Lord Kilmuir's graceless jibe at Lord Avon remotely deserved. Rather is it true that the wisdom of Anthony Eden's instinctive distrust of E.D.C. preserved Britain from being enmeshed in the federalist fatuity of its framework. Britain's whole-hearted participation was thus reserved for the practical provisions of W.E.U., of which organization he can claim paternity.

As for the alleged anger and frustration of Paul-Henri Spaak, whatever that splendid statesman may have felt in 1950, by the time he wrote his memoirs some twenty years later, he viewed events in the light of historical perspective. His tribute to Anthony Eden's great achievement in fashioning W.E.U. from the ruins of E.D.C. has already been noted,† but it is worth while to quote him on the subject of British Conservative consistency of opinion in the matter of the European Defence Community:

> *Soyons juste* [he has written], *c'est cette thèse que Churchill avait exposé à Zurich. Sa présence au Congrès de la Haye, ses interventions à l'Assemblée Consultative, sa proposition de créer une armée européenne avaient entretenu les illusions. Retrouvant les responsabilités du pouvoir, il faisait précise sa position: la Grande-Bretagne ne s'associerait pas à une Europe intégrée. Elle ne participerait même aux tentatives d'intégration partielle.*[10]

Thus, in M. Spaak's view, the Conservative leaders, when their party returned to power in October 1951, merely made their position the more clear and more precise; they did not change or modify it in any way.[11]

---

* See above, p. 590.   † See above, p. 600.

CHRONOLOGY

1939   23 August: German–Soviet Non-aggression Pact.
       25 August: Anglo-Polish Alliance.
       1 September: German invasion of Poland.
       3 September: Great Britain and France declare war on Germany.
       4 September: Mr Chamberlain's broadcast to the German people.
       17 September: Russian invasion of Poland.

1940   9 April: German invasion of Denmark and Norway.
       10 May: German invasion of Belgium, Holland and Luxembourg.
       10 June: Italy declares war on Britain and France.
       22 June: Franco-German Armistice.
       24 June: Franco-Italian Armistice.

1941   12 June: United Nations Declaration of St James's Palace against a separate peace.
       22 June: German invasion of Russia.
                 Russian adherence to Declaration of St James's Palace.
       30 July: Russo-Polish agreement signed.
       12 August: Atlantic Charter agreed between Roosevelt and Churchill.
       24 September: United Nations Declaration of St James's Palace adhering to Atlantic Charter.
       7/8 December: Japanese attack on Pearl Harbor and Philippines.
                 United States enters the war.
       11 December: Germany declares war on the United States.
       12–20 December: Mr Eden in Moscow.

1942   26 May: Anglo-Russian Treaty of Alliance signed.
       12–16 August: First Moscow Conference: Stalin–Churchill.

1943   14–24 January: Casablanca Conference: Churchill–Roosevelt (Unconditional Surrender).
       1 February: Unconditional surrender of Field-Marshal Paulus's Sixth Army at Stalingrad.
       12–25 May: Washington Conference: Churchill–Roosevelt.
       12/13 May: Unconditional surrender of Axis forces in North Africa.
       17–24 August: First Quebec Conference: Churchill–Roosevelt.
       8 September: Unconditional surrender of Italy.
       13 October: Italy declares war on Germany.
       18–30 October: Second Moscow Conference: Hull–Eden–Molotov (War Criminals, Austria, E.A.C.).

22–6 November: First Cairo Conference: Churchill–Roosevelt–Chiang Kai-shek.

28 November–1 December: Tehran Conference: Churchill–Roosevelt–Stalin (post-war treatment of Germany).

4–7 December: Second Cairo Conference: Churchill–Roosevelt–Inönü.

1944 6 June: Allied invasion of France.

21–9 August: Dumbarton Oaks Conference (post-war security and United Nations Organization).

11–16 September: Second Quebec Conference (Morgenthau Plan).

9–18 October: Third Moscow Conference: Churchill–Eden–Stalin–Molotov–Mikolajczyk.

10 December: Franco-Soviet Treaty of Alliance signed.

1945 20 January: Hungarian Armistice signed.

30 January–2 February: Malta Conference.

4–11 February: Yalta Conference: Churchill–Roosevelt–Stalin.

5 April: Denunciation by Russia of her treaty of neutrality and non-aggression with Japan.

12 April: Death of President Roosevelt.

25 April: Russian and American forces meet at Torgau on the Elbe.

25 April–26 June: San Francisco Conference on United Nations.

28 April: Mussolini and twelve members of his Cabinet executed by Italian partisans.

29 April–1 May: Unconditional surrender of German armies in northern Italy to Field-Marshal Alexander.

30 April: Suicide of Adolf Hitler in Berlin.

2 May: Unconditional surrender of Berlin to Russians.

4 May: Unconditional surrender of German armies in Holland, north-western Germany and Denmark to Field-Marshal Montgomery.

7 May: Unconditional surrender of Germany to Western Allies and Russia at Rheims.

8 May: V–E Day.

9 May: Final Act of Unconditional Surrender in Berlin.

31 May–4 June: United Nations War Crimes Commission. Conference in London.

26 June: United Nations Charter signed at San Francisco.

26 June–8 August: Four Power Conference in London on Trial of War Criminals.

16 July–2 August: Potsdam Conference: Churchill–Attlee–Truman–Stalin.

6 August: First atomic bomb dropped on Hiroshima.

8 August: Russia declares war on Japan.

9 August: Second atomic bomb dropped on Nagasaki.

14 August: Japan signifies willingness to make unconditional surrender. Sino-Soviet Agreement signed in Moscow.

15 August: V–J Day.

2 September: Unconditional surrender of Japan signed in Tokyo Bay.

11 September–2 October: First session of Council of Foreign Ministers (Bevin–Byrnes–Molotov–Bidault–Wang Shih-chieh) in London.

18 October: Conference of the International Military Tribunal in Berlin.

20 November: Trial of major war criminals opened before the International Military Tribunal in Nuremberg.

16–26 December: Conference of Foreign Ministers in Moscow.

1946 10 January: First session of United Nations General Assembly opened in London.

19 January: Trial of Japanese war criminals opened in Tokyo.

26 April–17 May: Second session of Council of Foreign Ministers in Paris.

29 July–15 October: Peace Conference in Paris. Treaties signed with Italy, Rumania, Bulgaria, Finland and Hungary.

1 October: Close of trial of major war criminals in Nuremberg.

1947 4 March: Treaty of Dunkirk between Britain and France.

12 July: Paris Conference called by Bevin and Bidault to respond to Marshall Plan.

5 October: Establishment of Cominform.

1948 25 February: Pro-Soviet coup in Czechoslovakia.

17 March: Brussels Pact signed (Britain, France and Benelux).

3 April: President Truman signs Marshall Plan legislation.

28 June: Berlin Blockade begins.

12 November: Close of trial of Japanese war criminals in Tokyo.

1949 4 April: Establishment of NATO.

12 May: Berlin Blockade ends.

23 May: Establishment of German Federal Republic.

7 October: Establishment of German Democratic Republic.

1950 25 June: Korean War begins.

1951 1 September: ANZUS Treaty signed.

8 September: Treaty of Peace with Japan signed (effective 28 February 1952).

American–Japanese Security Treaty signed.

1952 26 May: German Contractual Agreement signed in Bonn.

1953 5 March: Death of Stalin.

1954 8 September: SEATO Pact signed in Manila.

1955 14 May: Warsaw Pact signed.

15 May: Austrian State Treaty signed.

1956 19 October: Russo-Japanese Declaration resuming diplomatic relations.

BIBLIOGRAPHY

I. BOOKS

ACHESON, Hon. DEAN, *Present at the Creation: My Years in the State Department* (London, 1970).

ADUARD, Baron E. J. LEWE VAN, *Japan from Surrender to Peace* (New York, 1954).

ALDERMAN, SYDNEY, *Negotiating with the Russians* (New York, 1951).

ALEXANDER, CHARLES W., and KEESHAN, ANNE, *Justice at Nuremberg* (New York, 1946).

ALEXANDER OF TUNIS, Field-Marshal Earl, *Memoirs 1940–1945* (London, 1962).

ALPEROWITZ, GAR, *Atomic Diplomacy: Hiroshima and Potsdam* (New York, 1965).

ALSOP, JOSEPH, and KINTNER, ROBERT, *American White Paper* (London, 1940).

AMBROSE, STEPHEN, *Eisenhower and Berlin: The Decision to Halt at the Elbe* (New York, 1967).

AMERY, Rt Hon. LEOPOLD, *My Political Life*, vol. III: *The Unforgiving Years, 1929–1940* (London, 1955).

ARMSTRONG, ANNE, *Unconditional Surrender. The Impact of the Casablanca Policy upon World War II* (New Brunswick, 1961).

ARON, RAYMOND, and LERNER, DANIEL (eds), *Essais d'analyse sociologiques* (Paris, 1956).

ATTLEE, Rt Hon. Earl, *As It Happened* (London, 1954).

——, (with FRANCIS WILLIAMS), *A Prime Minister Remembers* (London, 1961).

AVON, Rt Hon. Earl of (ANTHONY EDEN), *Full Circle* (London, 1960).

——, *The Reckoning* (London, 1965).

BALFOUR, MICHAEL, and MAIR, JOHN, *Four Power Control in Germany and Austria 1945–1946* (London, 1956).

BEAL, JOHN ROBINSON, *John Foster Dulles: A Biography* (New York, 1957).

BELL, CORAL, *Negotiations from Strength* (London, 1965).

BELL, W. MACMAHON, *Japan: Enemy or Ally?* (New York, 1949).

BELOFF, Professor MAX, *Soviet Policy in the Far East, 1944–1951* (Oxford, 1953).

BENEŠ, President EDUARD, *Memoirs*, trans. Godfrey Lias (London, 1954).

BERNADOTTE, Count FOLKE, *The Curtain Falls* (New York, 1945).

BIDDLE, Hon. FRANCIS, *In Brief Authority* (New York, 1962).

BLOOM, Hon. SOLOMON, *Autobiography* (New York, 1948).

BLUM, JOHN MORTON, *From the Morgenthau Diaries: Years of War, 1941–1945* (Boston, 1967).

BOHLEN, Hon. CHARLES E., *The Transformation of American Foreign Policy* (New York, 1969).

BOOTHBY, Lord, *My Yesterday, Your Tomorrow* (London, 1962).

BROWN, COURTNEY, *Tojo*, paperback ed. (London, 1969).

BRYANS, J. LONSDALE, *Blind Victory* (London, 1951).

BRYANT, Sir ARTHUR, *The Turn of the Tide* (London, 1957).

——, *Triumph in the West* (London, 1959).

BULLOCK, ALAN, *Hitler: A Study in Tyranny*, paperback ed. (New York, 1964).

BÜLOW, Prince BERNHARD VON, *Memoirs, 1849–1919* (London, 1931–2).

BUTCHER, Commander HARRY C., *Three Years with Eisenhower* (London, 1946).

BUTOW, Professor ROBERT J. C., *Japan's Decision to Surrender* (Stanford, Calif., 1954).

BYRNES, Hon. J. F., *Speaking Frankly* (London, 1948).

——, *All in one Lifetime* (London, 1960).

CADOGAN, Sir ALEXANDER. *The Diaries of Sir Alexander Cadogan 1938–1945*, ed. David Dilkes (London, 1971).

CASEY, Rt Hon. RICHARD G., *Friends and Neighbours: Australia, the U.S. and the World* (East Lansing, Mich., 1955).

CASTELLANO, General GIUSEPPE, *La Guerra Continua: la Vera Storia dell' 8 Settembre con documenti inediti* (Milan, 1963).

CHIANG KAI-SHEK, Generalissimo, *Collected War-time Messages, 1937–1945* (New York, 1945).

CHURCHILL, Rt Hon. Sir WINSTON, *The Second World War*, vol. III: *The Grand Alliance* (London, 1950); vol. IV: *The Hinge of Fate* (London, 1951); vol. V: *Closing the Ring* (London, 1952); vol. VI: *Triumph and Tragedy* (London, 1954).

——, *The Tide of Victory* (London, 1954).

——, *War Speeches, 1939–1945*, 3 vols, ed. Charles Eade (London, 1952).

CIECHANOWSKY, JAN, *Defeat in Victory* (New York, 1947).

CLARK, General MARK, *Calculated Risk*, paperback ed. (London, 1956).

——, *From the Danube to the Yalu* (New York, 1954).

CLAY, General LUCIUS, *Decision in Germany* (New York, 1950).

CLAYTON, WILL. *Selected Papers of Will Clayton*, ed. Fred J. Dobney (Baltimore, Md, 1971).

CLEMENS, D. S., *Yalta* (New York, 1970).

COFFEY, THOMAS M., *Imperial Tragedy. Japan in World War II* (New York, 1970).

COHEN, BERNARD C., *The Political Process and Foreign Policy: The Making of the Japanese Peace Settlement* (Princeton, 1957).

COLVILLE, J. R., in *Action this Day: Working with Churchill*, ed. Sir John Wheeler-Bennett (London, 1968).

CONNALLY, Senator THOMAS, *My Name is Tom Connally* (New York, 1954).

COUNSELL, JOHN, *Counsell's Opinion* (London, 1963).

COWLES, VIRGINIA, *The Russian Dagger* (London, 1969).

CROCKER, GEORGE N., *Roosevelt's Road to Russia* (Chicago, 1959).

CROZIER, BRIAN, *Franco* (London, 1967).

DAVIDSON, W. P., *The Berlin Blockade* (Princeton, 1958).

DEAKIN, F. W., *The Brutal Friendship* (London, 1962).

DEANE, Major-General JOHN R., *The Strange Alliance* (London, 1947).

DEDIJER, VLADIMIR, *Josip Broz Tito* (Belgrade, 1953).

DEUTSCH, HAROLD C., *The Conspiracy against Hitler in the Twilight War* (Minneapolis, 1968).

DICKINSON, G. LOWES, BRAILSFORD, H. N., and BUXTON, C. R., *Toward a Lasting Settlement* (London, 1917).

DIVINE, ROBERT A., *Roosevelt and World War II* (Baltimore, Md, 1969).

DIXON, PIERS (ed.), *Double Diploma: The Life of Sir Pierson Dixon* (London, 1968).

DJILAS, MILOVAN, *Conversations with Stalin* (London, 1963).

DOENITZ, Grand-Admiral KARL, *Memoirs* (London, 1959).

DONOVAN, FRANK, *Mr Roosevelt's Four Freedoms* (New York, 1966).

DRAPER, GERALD I. A. D., *The Red Cross Conventions* (London, 1958).

DRUKS, HERBERT, *Harry S. Truman and the Russians, 1945–1953* (New York, 1966).

DULLES, ELEANOR LANSING, *John Foster Dulles: The Last Year* (New York, 1963).

DUNN, FREDERICK S., *Peacemaking and the Settlement with Japan* (Princeton, 1963).

EHRMAN, JOHN, *Grand Strategy*, vols V and VI (London, 1956).

EISENHOWER, General DWIGHT D., *Crusade in Europe* (London, 1948).

——, *Mandate for Change, 1952–1956* (London, 1963).

EUBANK, KEITH, *The Summit Conferences, 1919–1960* (Norman, Okla., 1966).

FARNSWORTH, BEATRICE, *William C. Bullitt and the Soviet Union* (Bloomington, Ind., 1967).

FEAREY, ROBERT A., *The Occupation of Japan: Second Phase, 1948–1950* (New York, 1950).

FEIS, HERBERT, *Churchill, Roosevelt, Stalin* (Princeton, 1957).

——, *Between War and Peace* (Princeton, 1960).

——, *The Atomic Bomb and the End of World War II* (Princeton, 1966).

——, *From Trust to Terror: The Onset of the Cold War* (New York, 1970).

FINLETTER, Hon. THOMAS K., *Interim Report on the American Search for a Substitute for Isolation* (New York, 1968).

FLEMING, D. F., *The Cold War and its Origins* (New York, 1961).

FORRESTAL, Hon. JAMES, *Diaries*, ed. Walter Millis (London, 1952).

GAULLE, General CHARLES DE, *Mémoires de Guerre: Le Salut 1944–1946* (Paris, 1959).

GERSON, LOUIS L., *John Foster Dulles* (New York, 1967).

GILDERSLEEVE, VIRGINIA C., *Many a Good Crusade* (New York, 1954).

GRAYSON, Rear-Admiral CARY T., *Woodrow Wilson: An Intimate Memoir* (New York, 1959).

GREW, Hon. JOSEPH, *Turbulent Era*, 2 vols (London, 1953).

GRINROD, MURIEL, *The Rebuilding of Italy* (London, 1955).

GROVES, Lieutenant-General LESLIE R., *Now It Can Be Told* (New York, 1962).

GUINGAND, Major-General Sir FRANCIS DE, *Operation Victory* (London, 1947).

HALIFAX, Rt Hon. Earl of, *Fulness of Days* (London, 1957).

HALLÉ, LOUIS J., *The Cold War as History* (London, 1966).

HANCOCK, Sir KEITH, *Smuts: The Sanguine Years, 1870–1919* (Cambridge, 1962).

——, *Smuts: The Fields of Force, 1919–1950* (Cambridge, 1968).

HARRIMAN, Hon. AVERELL, *America and Russia in a Changing World: A Half-Century of Personal Observation* (New York, 1971).

HARPER, N., and SISSONS, D. C., *Australia and the United Nations* (New York, 1959).

HASSELL, ULRICH VON, *Vom andern Deutschland* (Zürich, 1946).

HELLMANN, Professor DONALD C., *Japanese Domestic Politics and Foreign Policies: The Peace Agreement with the Soviet Union* (Berkeley and Los Angeles, 1969).

HIGGINS, Professor TRUMBULL, *Winston Churchill and the Second Front* (New York, 1957).

HILLMAN, WILLIAM (ed.), *Mr President: Personal Diaries, Private Letters, Papers, and Revealing Interviews of Harry S. Truman* (London, 1952).

HITLER, ADOLF, *Collected Speeches 1922–1939*, 2 vols, ed. Norman H. Baynes (London, 1942).

HOBSON, J. A., *Towards International Government* (London, 1918).

HOCHHUTH, ROLF, *The Soldiers* (London, 1967).

HOLBORN, Professor HAJO, *American Military Government* (New Haven, 1947).

HOROWITZ, DAVID, *The Free World Colossus* (New York, 1965).

HOWARD, MICHAEL, *The Mediterranean Strategy in the Second World War* (London, 1968).

HULL, Hon. CORDELL, *Memoirs*, 2 vols (New York, 1948).

HUNTER, ROBERT, *Security in Europe* (London, 1969).

HYDE, H. MONTGOMERY, *Norman Birkett* (London, 1962).

ICKES, Hon. HAROLD L., *Secret Diary*, vol. III: *The Lowering Clouds, 1939–1941* (London, 1955).

ISMAY, General Lord, *Memoirs* (London, 1960).

——, *NATO: The First Five Years, 1949–1954* (Paris, 1954).

JACKSON, Hon. ROBERT H., *The Nuremberg Case* (New York, 1947).

——, *Report on the International Conference on Military Trials* (Washington, 1948).

JONES, JOSEPH MARION, *The Fifteen Weeks*, paperback ed. (New York, 1964).

KANAI, KAZUO, *Japan's American Interlude* (Chicago, 1960).

KASE, TOSHIKAZU, *Eclipse of the Rising Sun* (London, 1951).

KAUFMAN, THEODORE N., *Germany Must Perish* (Newark, N.J., 1941).

KENNAN, Hon. GEORGE, *Memoirs, 1925–1950* (New York, 1968).

KENNEY, ELINOR M., *The Origin of the Marshall Plan* (privately printed at the Bookman Press, Los Angeles, n.d.).

KEYNES, JOHN MAYNARD, *The Economic Consequences of the Peace* (London, 1920).

KILMUIR, Rt Hon. the Earl of (Sir DAVID MAXWELL FYFE), *Political Adventure* (London, 1962).

KING, Fleet Admiral E. J., and WHITEHILL, W. M., *Fleet Admiral King: A Naval Record* (London, 1953).

KLEFFENS, Jonkheer EELKO VAN, *The Rape of the Netherlands* (London, 1940).

KLEIST, PETER, *Zwischen Hitler und Stalin* (Bonn, 1950).

KLUYVERS, C. A., *Documents on the League of Nations* (The Hague, 1920).

KNAPP, WILFRID, *A History of War and Peace, 1939–1965* (Oxford, 1967).

KOLKO, G., *The Politics of War: Allied Diplomacy and the World Crisis of 1943–45* (London, 1968).

KORDT, ERICH, *Nicht aus den Akten* (Stuttgart, 1950).

LANGER, WILLIAM L., and GLEASON, S. EVERETT, *The Undeclared War* (New York, 1953).

LEAHY, Admiral WILLIAM D., *I Was There* (London, 1950).

LEONHARD, WOLFGANG, *Child of the Revolution* (London, 1957).

LLOYD GEORGE, Rt Hon. DAVID, *The Truth about the Treaties*, 2 vols (London, 1938).

LOHBECK, DON, *Patrick J. Hurley* (Chicago, 1956).

LÜDDE-NEURATH, WALTER, *Regierung Doenitz* (Göttingen, 1964).

MACARTHUR, General DOUGLAS, *Reminiscences*, paperback ed. (New York, 1965).

MACARTNEY, C. A., *October Fifteenth*, 2 vols (Edinburgh, 1957).

McCLOY, Hon. JOHN J., *The Atlantic Alliance: Its Origin and Future* (New York, 1969).

MACCOLL, RENÉ, *Deadline and Dateline* (London, 1956).

McINTIRE, Vice-Admiral ROSS T., *Twelve Years with Roosevelt* (London, 1964).

MACMILLAN, Rt Hon. HAROLD, *Winds of Change, 1914–1939* (London, 1966).

——, *The Blast of War, 1939–1945* (London, 1967).

——, *Tides of Fortune, 1945–1955* (London, 1968).

McNEILL, WILLIAM HARDY, *America, Britain and Russia* (Oxford, 1953).

MASAO, MARUYAMA, *Thought and Behaviour in Modern Japanese Politics* (Oxford, 1963).

MEINTJES JOHANNES, *General Louis Botha* (London, 1970).

MENZIES, Rt Hon. Sir ROBERT, *Afternoon Light* (London, 1967).

MIKOLAJCZYK, STANISLAS, *The Rape of Poland* (New York, 1948).

MILLER, DAVID HUNTER, *The Drafting of the Covenant*, 2 vols (New York, 1928).

MINEAR, RICHARD H., *Victors' Justice. The Tokyo War Crimes Trials* (Princeton, N.J., 1971).

MOEBLHAUSEN, EITEL FRIEDRICH, *Die gebrochene Axis* (Leine, 1949).

MOFFAT, Hon. JAY PIERPOINT, *The Moffat Papers, 1919–1941* (Cambridge, Mass., 1956).

MONTGOMERY OF ALAMEIN, Field-Marshal the Viscount, *Memoirs* (London, 1958).

MORAN, Lord, *Churchill: Taken from the Diaries of Lord Moran* (London, 1966).

MORGENTHAU, Hon. HENRY, *Germany is our Problem* (New York, 1945).

MORISON, ELTING E., *Turmoil and Tradition: A Study of the Life and Times of Henry L. Stimson* (Boston, 1960).

MORRISON OF LAMBETH, Rt Hon. Lord, *Herbert Morrison: An Autobiography* (London, 1960).

MORTON, H. V., *Atlantic Meeting, 1941* (London, 1943).

MOSELEY, Hon. PHILIP, *The Kremlin and World Politics* (New York, 1960).

MOSLEY, LEONARD, *Hirohito, Emperor of Japan* (London, 1966).

MULLINS, CLAUD, *The Leipzig Trials* (London, 1921).

MURPHY, Hon. ROBERT, *Diplomat among Warriors* (London, 1964).

NEUMANN, WILLIAM L., *After Victory* (New York, 1967).

NICHOLAS, HERBERT G., *The United Nations as a Political Institution*, 3rd ed. (Oxford, 1967).

NICOLSON, Hon. Sir HAROLD, *Peacemaking, 1919*, rev. (London, 1943).

——, *Diaries and Letters 1937–1962*, 3 vols, ed. Nigel Nicolson (London, 1966–8).

NORMANBROOK, Rt Hon. Lord, in *Action this Day: Working with Churchill*, ed. Sir John Wheeler-Bennett (London, 1968).

NORTH, ROBERT C., *Moscow and the Chinese Communists* (Stanford, Calif., 1953).

OPIE, REDVERS, *et al.*, *The Search for Peace Settlements* (Washington, 1951).

OPPEN, B. RUHM VON, *Documents on Germany under Occupation 1945–1954* (Oxford, 1955).

PACIFIC WAR RESEARCH SOCIETY OF TOKYO, *Japan's Longest Day* (London, 1968).

PARKER, R. A. C., *Europe 1919–1945* (London, 1969).

PAWLE, GERALD, *The War and Colonel Warden* (London, 1963).

PICK, F. W., *Peacemaking in Perspective* (Oxford, 1950).

POGUE, FORREST C., *George C. Marshall: Ordeal and Hope, 1939–1942* (New York, 1966).

——, *The Meaning of Yalta* (Baton Rouge, La, 1958).

PRATT, JULIUS W., *Cordell Hull* (New York, 1964).

RACZYŃSKI, Count EDWARD, *In Allied London*, introduction by Sir John Wheeler-Bennett (London, 1962).

READ, JAMES MORGAN, *Atrocity Propaganda* (New York, 1941).

REESE, TREVOR R., *Australia, New Zealand and the United States* (Oxford, 1969).

REISCHAUER, Hon. EDWIN O., *The United States and Japan*, paperback ed. (New York, 1966).

ROOSEVELT, ELLIOTT, *As He Saw It* (New York, 1946).

—— (ed.), *The Roosevelt Letters*, vol. III: *1928–1945* (London, 1952).

ROOSEVELT, Hon. FRANKLIN DELANO, *Public Papers and Addresses: War – and Aid to the Democracies* (New York, 1941).

ROSENMAN, Judge SAMUEL L., *Working with Roosevelt* (London, 1952).

ROZEK, E. J., *Allied Wartime Diplomacy: A Pattern in Poland* (New York, 1958).

RUSSELL, RUTH B., *A History of the United Nations Charter* (Washington, 1958).

RUSSELL OF LIVERPOOL, Lord, *The Knights of Bushido* (London, 1958).

SAPIN, BURTON, 'The Role of the Military in Formulating the Japanese Peace Treaty', in *A History of Military Affairs in Western Society since the Eighteenth Century*, ed. George B. Turner (New York, 1953).

SCHUMANN, FRANZ, and SCHELL, ORVILLE (ed.), *Communist China* (New York, 1967).

SCHWARTZ, H. P., *Vom Reich zur Bundesrepublik: Deutschland im Widerstreit der aussenpolitischen Konzeptionen in den Jahren der Besatzungsherrschaft 1944–1949* (Neuwied and Berlin, 1966).

SCHWERIN VON KROSIGK, Count LUTZ, *Es Geschah in Deutschland* (Tübingen, 1951).

SEBALD, Hon. WILLIAM J., *With MacArthur in Japan* (London, 1967).

SHAWCROSS, Rt Hon. Lord, *et al.*, *Mr Justice Jackson: Four Lectures in his Honour* (New York, 1969).

SHERWOOD, ROBERT, *Roosevelt and Hopkins: An Intimate History* (New York, 1948). Published in Britain as:

——, *The White House Papers of Harry L. Hopkins*, vols. I and II (London, 1948–9).

SHIGEMITSU, MAMORU, *Japan and her Destiny* (London, 1958).

SIEGLER, HEINRICH, *et al.*, *Austria: Problems and Achievements since 1945* (Bonn, 1965).

SLESSOR, Marshal of the Royal Air Force Sir JOHN, *The Central Blue* (London, 1956).

SMITH, DENNYS, *America and the Axis War* (London, 1942).

SMITH, GENE, *When the Cheering Stopped* (New York, 1964).

SNELL, JOHN L., *Wartime Origins of the East-West Dilemma over Germany* (New Orleans, 1959).

SORLEY, C. H., *Marlborough and Other Poems* (Cambridge, 1914).

SPAAK, PAUL-HENRI, *Combat machevés*, vol. I: *De l'indépendance a l'alliance* (Paris, 1969); vol. II: *De l'espoir aux déceptions* (Paris, 1969).

Stalin's Correspondence with Churchill, Attlee, Roosevelt and Truman, 1941–1945, 2 vols in one (London, 1958).

STEINERT, MARLIS G., *Capitulation, 1945: The Story of the Doenitz Régime* (London, 1969).

STETTINIUS, Hon. EDWARD R., *Roosevelt and the Russians at Yalta* (New York, 1949).

STILLWELL, Lieutenant-General JOSEPH V., *Papers*, ed. Theodore H. White (New York, 1948).

STIMSON, Hon. HENRY L., and BUNDY, MCGEORGE, *On Active Service in Peace and War* (New York, 1948).

STORRY, RICHARD, *A History of Modern Japan*, Penguin ed. (Harmondsworth, 1968).

STRANG, Lord, *Home and Abroad* (London, 1956).

——, *Britain in World Affairs* (London, 1961).

STRONG, Major-General Sir KENNETH, *Intelligence at the Top: Recollections of an Intelligence Officer* (London, 1968).

SYKES, CHRISTOPHER, *Troubled Loyalty: A Biography of Adam von Trott* (London, 1968).

TÁBORSKÝ, EDUARD, *The Czechoslovak Cause in International Law* (London, 1944).

TAYLOR, A. J. P., *The Origins of the Second World War*, with introductory chapter to Penguin ed. (Harmondsworth, 1965).

TEMPLEWOOD, Rt Hon. the Viscount (Sir SAMUEL HOARE), *Ambassador on Special Mission* (London, 1946).

TENNANT, KYLIE, *Evatt, Politics and Justice* (London, 1970).

TETLOW, EDWIN, *The United Nations* (London, 1970).

THOMPSON, CARLOS, *The Assassination of Winston Churchill* (Gerrards Cross, 1969).

THUCYDIDES, *Peloponnesian War*, trans. Rex Warner.

TOGO, SHIGENORI, *The Cause of Japan* (New York, 1956).

TOWNLEY, RALPH, *The United Nations* (New York, 1968).

TREVOR-ROPER, Professor HUGH, *The Last Days of Hitler*, 2nd ed. (London, 1950).

TRUMAN, Hon. HARRY S., *Year of Decisions* (New York, 1955).

——, *Years of Trial and Hope* (New York, 1956).

TUGWELL, Hon. REXFORD, *The Democratic Roosevelt* (Garden City, N.Y., 1957).

VANDENBERG, Senator ARTHUR, *Private Papers* (London, 1953).

WALKER, RICHARD L., 'E. R. Stettinius, Jr', in *The American Secretaries of State and their Diplomacy*, ed. Robert H. Ferrell, vol. XIV (New York, 1965).

WALTERS, FRANCIS P., *A History of the League of Nations* (Oxford, 1967).

WARNE, Wing-Commander J. D., *NATO and its Prospects* (London, 1954).

WEBSTER, Sir CHARLES, 'The Making of the Charter of the United Nations', in *Art and Practice of Diplomacy* (London, 1961).

WEINSTEIN, MARTIN E., *Japan's Post-war Defence Policy 1947–1968* (New York, 1971).

WELLES, Hon. SUMNER, *The Time for Decision* (New York, 1944).

——, *Where are we heading?* (London, 1947).

——, *Seven Major Decisions* (London, 1951).

WHEELER-BENNETT, Sir JOHN, *The Problem of Security* (London, 1927).

——, (with HUGH LATIMER), *The Reparation Settlement, 1929–1930* (London, 1930).

——, *Disarmament and Security since Locarno, 1925–1931* (London, 1932).

——, *Disarmament Deadlock* (London, 1934).

——, *Munich: Prologue to Tragedy* (London, 1948).

——, *The Nemesis of Power* (London, 1953).

——, *King George VI: His Life and Reign* (London, 1958).

——, *John Anderson, Viscount Waverley* (London, 1962).

——, *Brest-Litovsk: The Forgotten Peace, March 1918*, rev. ed. (London, 1966).

WILHELMINA, Princess of the Netherlands, *Lonely but not Alone* (London, 1960).

WILMOT, CHESTER, *The Struggle for Europe* (London, 1952).

WILSON, EDITH BOLLING, *My Memoir* (New York, 1939).

WILSON, FLORENCE, *The Origins of the League Covenant* (London, 1928).

WILSON, THEODORE A., *The First Summit* (Boston, 1969).

WINDSOR, PHILIP, *City on leave: a History of Berlin* (London, 1963).

WOODWARD, Sir LLEWELLYN, *British Foreign Policy in the Second World War* (London, 1962).

WOOLF, LEONARD, *International Government* (London, 1916).

——, *The Framework of a Lasting Peace* (1917).

YOSHIDA, SHIGERU, *Memoirs* (London, 1961).

YOST, Hon. CHARLES, *The Insecurity of Nations* (New York, 1968).

ZACHARIAS, Captain ELLIS M., U.S.N., *Secret Missions* (New York, 1946).

2. ARTICLES, LECTURES, PAMPHLETS, ETC.

ASQUITH OF YARNBURY, Baroness, B.B.C. interview with Kenneth Harris, *The Listener*, 13 Apr 1967.

BALFOUR, MICHAEL, 'Another Look at Unconditional Surrender', *International Affairs*, Oct 1970.

BERNAYS, MURRAY C., 'Legal Basis of the Nuremberg Trial', *Survey Graphic* (New York), Jan 1946.

BRAND, Lord, interview with Kenneth Harris, *Observer*, 8 Jan 1961.

BRUENN, Dr HOWARD G., 'Clinical Notes on the Illness and Death of President Franklin D. Roosevelt', *Annals of Internal Medicine* (Philadelphia), Apr 1970.

BULLITT, Hon. WILLIAM C., 'How we Won the War and Lost the Peace', *Life Magazine*, 30 Aug 1948.

BUNDY, HARVEY, 'Remembered Words', *Atlantic Monthly*, Mar 1957.

BUNDY, Hon. MCGEORGE, *The Americans and Europe: Rhetoric and Reality* (Ditchley Foundation Lecture No. VIII) July 1969.

CACCIA, Lord, *The Roots of British Foreign Policy, 1929–1965* (Ditchley Foundation Lecture No. IV), Nov 1965.

CRANKSHAW, EDWARD, 'When we Wanted war', *Observer*, 23 Aug 1964.

FEIS, HERBERT, 'When Roosevelt Died', *Virginia Quarterly Review*, autumn 1970.

FISHEL, WESLEY R., 'A Japanese Peace Manœuvre in 1944', *Far Eastern Quarterly* (now the *Journal for Asian Studies*) (New York), Aug 1949.

FRANKLIN, WILLIAM M., 'Zonal Boundaries and Access Routes to Berlin', *World Politics*, Oct 1963.

FRANKS, Lord, article in *The Listener*, 14 June 1956.

GREEN, L. C., 'Making Peace with Japan', *Year Book of World Affairs* (1952).

HASLUCK, PAWL, 'Australia and the Formation of the United Nations', XL(3), *Journal of the Royal Australian Historical Society*.

JOLL, JAMES, 'The Decline of Europe', *International Affairs*, Nov 1970.

KANAI, KAZUO, '*Mokusatsu:* Japan's Response to the Potsdam Declaration', *Pacific Historical Review*, Nov 1950.

KINDLEBERGER, CHARLES P., 'The Marshall Plan and the Cold War', *International Journal* (Canadian Institute of International Affairs), summer 1968.

KREISKY, BRUNO, in *Österrich in Geschichte und Literatur*, no. 3 (1957).

MACKINTOSH, MALCOLM, *The Evolution of the Warsaw Pact*, Institute for Strategic Studies, Adelphi Papers No. 58 (London, 1969).

MENZIES, Rt Hon. Sir ROBERT, 'The Pacific Settlement as seen from Australia', *Foreign Affairs*, Jan 1952.

MOLTMANN, GÜNTER, 'Unconditional Surrender and War Propaganda', *Wiener Library Bulletin*, Oct 1964.

NICHOLAS, HERBERT G., 'From League to United Nations', *International Affairs*, Nov 1970.

NICOLSON, Hon. Sir HAROLD, B.B.C. Home Service broadcast 'News Talk', 11 Aug 1946.

PICK, Commander CHARLES F., U.S.N.R., 'Torpedo on the Starboard Beam', *United States Naval Institute Proceedings*, Aug 1970.

RENNER, KARL, interview in *Wiener Zeitung*, 20 Dec 1945.

SEABURY, PAUL, 'Cold War Origins I', *Journal of Contemporary History*, vol. 3, no. 1 (1968).

SCHLESINGER, ARTHUR, Jr, 'The Origins of the Cold War', *Foreign Affairs*, Oct 1967.

STIMSON, Hon. HENRY L., 'The Nuremberg Trial: Landmark in Law', *Foreign Affairs*, Jan 1947.

——, 'The Decision to Use the Atom Bomb', *Harper's Magazine*, Feb 1947.

STRANG, Lord, *et al.*, 'Potsdam after Twenty-five Years', *International Affairs*, July 1970.

THOMAS, BRIAN, 'Cold War Origins II', *Journal of Contemporary History*, vol. 3, no. 1 (1968).

THOMAS, General GEORG, 'Gedanken und Ereignisse', *Schweizerische Monatshefte*, Dece 1945.

THOMPSON, Hon. LLEWELLYNN, interview in *Corriere della Sera*, 15 Oct 1954

WARNER, GEOFFREY, 'The United States and the Origins of the Cold War', *International Affairs*, July 1970.

3. NEWSPAPERS, PERIODICALS, ETC.

Annals of Internal Medicine (Philadelphia, Pa.)
Atlantic Monthly
Corriere della Sera
Daily Telegraph
Das Reich
Evening Standard
Far Eastern Quarterly
Foreign Affairs
Harper's Magazine

International Affairs (Royal Institute of International Affairs)
International Journal (Canadian Institute of International Affairs)
Journal of the Royal Australian Historical Society
Life Magazine
New York Herald-Tribune
New York Times
Observer
Österreich in Geschichte und Literatur
Pacific Historical Review
Pravda
Soviet News
Sunday Telegraph
Sunday Times
Survey Graphic
The Times
U.S. State Department Bulletin
Völkischer Beobachter
Wall Street Journal
Washington Post
Wiener Library Bulletin
Wiener Zeitung

4. DOCUMENTS, ETC.
I. *Governmental*

Australian Government
United Nations Conference on International Organization held at San Francisco from 23 April–25 June 1945: Report by the Australian Delegation, Cmd 24 F4311 (Canberra, 1945).

Belgian Government
Belgium: The Official Account of What Happened (New York, 1941).

British Government
Blue Book, *Miscellaneous No. 9*, Cmd 6106 (1939).
Blue Book, *Miscellaneous No. 4*, Cmd 6560 (1944).
Blue Book, Cmd 6693 (1945).
Blue Book, Cmd 7022 (1947).
White Paper, Cmd 6285 (1941).
White Paper, Cmd 6315 (1941).
White Paper, Cmd 6321 (1941).

Commentary on the United Nations Charter (London, 1948).

The Italian Campaign, 12 December 1944–2 May 1945: A Report to the Combined Chiefs of Staff by the Supreme Allied Commander, Mediterranean, Field-Marshal Viscount Alexander of Tunis (London, 1951).

House of Commons Debates.

House of Lords Debates.

Canadian Government
Report of the Royal Commission appointed under Order in Council P.C. 411 of February 5, 1946 (Ottawa, 1946).
Report on the United Nations Conference on International Organization held at San Francisco, April 25–June 26, 1945, Cmd No. 2 (Ottawa, 1945).

Czechoslovak Government
Documents diplomatiques rélatifs aux Conventions d'Alliance conclués par la République Tchéchoslovaque avec le Royaume des Serbes, Croats et Slovènes et le Royaume de Roumanie, décembre 1919–août 1921 (Prague, 1923).

Japanese Government
Explanatory Study of the Draft Japanese Peace Treaty (Tokyo, 1951).

Netherlands Government
Orange Book, June 1919–April 1920 (The Hague, 1920).

New Zealand Government
Report on the Conference held at San Francisco, April 25–June 26, 1945 (Wellington, 1945).
The Conference of Paris: Report of the New Zealand Delegation (Wellington, 1947).
Japanese Peace Settlement: British Commonwealth Conference, July 26–September 3, 1947 (Wellington,, 1947).
Japanese Peace Settlement: Report of the New Zealand Delegation (Wellington, 1951).

Rumanian Government
Rapport du Ministre des Finances au Conseil des Ministres sur la situation créée à la Roumanie par la politique des Réparations et des Dettes Inter-Alliés, 4 vols (Bucharest, 1925).

United States Government
Department of State
Conference on the Limitation of Armament: Verbatim Report, December 1921–February 1922 (Washington, 1922).
Foreign Relations of the United States: Diplomatic Papers, 1945, 9 vols.
The Conferences at Washington 1941–1942, and Casablanca 1943 (Washington, 1968).
The Conference at Cairo and Tehran, 1943 (Washington, 1961).
The Conferences at Malta and Yalta, 1945 (Washington, 1956).
The Conference of Berlin (Potsdam), 1945, 2 vols (Washington, 1960).
Co-operative War Effort (Washington, 1942).
Paris Peace Conference, 1946: Selected Documents (Washington, 1946).
United States and Italy, 1936–1946 (Washington, 1946).
Comments and Proposed Amendments concerning the Dumbarton Oaks Proposals (San Francisco, 1945).
The United Nations Conference on International Organization, San Francisco, April 25–June 26, 1945 (Washington, 1946).
The Occupation of Japan: Policy and Progress (Washington, 1946).
The Axis in Defeat (Washington, 1946).

Making the Peace Treaties 1941–1947 (Washington, 1947).

Nazi–Soviet Relations (Washington, 1948).

Postwar Foreign Policy Preparation 1939–1945 (Washington, 1949).

A Decade of American Foreign Policy 1941–1949 (Washington, 1950).

Laying Foundations for Peace in the Pacific (Washington, 1951).

Record of Proceedings of the Conference for the Conclusion and Signature of the Peace Treaty with Japan, San Francisco, California, September 4–8, 1951 (Washington, 1951).

United States Treaties and Other International Agreements, vol. 3, pt 3, 1952 (Washington, 1955).

The Far Eastern Commission: A Study in International Co-operation, 1945–1952, by George H. Blakeslee (Washington, 1953).

Report by the Supreme Commander for the Allied Powers (Governmental Section): Political Orientation of Japan, September 1945–September 1948 (Washington, 1959).

Department of the Army

Official History, *European Operations: Cross-Channel Attack* (Washington, 1951).

Command Decisions (Washington, 1967).

Department of Defence

The Entry of the Soviet Union into the War against Japan (Washington, 1955).

United States Senate

Committee on Foreign Relations:

Hearings on the Nomination of the Hon. Joseph Grew as Under-Secretary of State (Washington, 1944).

Hearings on the Military Situation in the Far East: United States Relations with China (Washington, 1949).

Hearings on the Japanese Peace Treaty and other Treaties relating to Security in the Pacific, January 21–23, 1952 (Washington, 1952).

Hearings on the Nomination of the Hon. Charles Bohlen as Ambassador to Moscow (Washington, 1953).

Committee on the Judiciary (Subcommittee on Internal Security):

Interlocking Subversion in Government Departments (Washington, 1955).

Scope of Soviet Activity in the United States (Washington, 1956).

Report on the Administration of the Internal Security Act and other Internal Security laws (The Morgenthau Diaries), 2 vols (Washington, 1967).

The Warsaw Insurrection: The Communist Version versus the Facts (Washington, 1969).

U.S.S.R. Government

'Documents: The Crimea and Potsdam Conferences of the Leaders of the Three Great Powers', *International Affairs*, nos 6–10 (Moscow, June-Oct 1965).

II. *International*

Record of the International Military Tribunal, 42 vols (Nuremberg, 1947).

Transcript of the International Tribunal of the Far East, 75 vols (Tokyo, 1948).

Report on the International Conference on Military Trials by Mr Justice, Jackson (Washington, 1948).

United Nations

Verbatim Report of the Sessions of the General Assembly (New York).

Documents of the United Nations Conference on International Organization, 22 vols (New York, 1945–55).

The Charter and the Judgement: Memorandum by the Secretary-General (Lake Success, N.Y., 1949).

International Court of Justice

Advisory Opinion of March 30, 1950: Interpretation of the Peace Treaties with Bulgaria, Hungary and Rumania (Leyden, 1950).

Order of May 5, 1950 (Leyden, 1950).

Advisory Opinion of July 18, 1950 (Leyden, 1950).

III. *Miscellaneous*

Gooderich, L. M., and Carrol, M. J. (eds), *Documents on American Foreign Relations*, vol. v (Boston, 1944); vol. vi (Boston, 1945); vol. viii (Boston, 1948).

Documents on German Foreign Policy, 1918–1945, series c, vol. v: *The Third Reich: First Phase, March 5–October 31, 1936* (London and Washington 1966); series D, vol. xii: *The War Years: February 1–June 22, 1941* (London and Washington, 1962).

Documents on International Affairs, 1938, 3 vols, Royal Institute on International Affairs (Oxford, 1941–53).

Documents on International Affairs, 1955 (Oxford, 1958).

Cherwell Papers, Nuffield College, Oxford.

Wheeler-Bennett Papers, St Antony's College, Oxford.

NOTES

Chapter 1: Introduction: Some Thoughts on Peace-making

1. Thucydides, *Peloponnesian War*, Bk I, chap. cxl.
2. Prince Bernhard von Bülow, *Memoirs, 1849–1919* (London, 1931–2) vol. III, pp. 156–65.
3. *The Times*, 31 July 1946.
4. *H.C.Deb.*, 3 Oct 1938, col. 32.
5. Broadcast to the German People, *British Blue Book*, no. 144, Cmd 6106 (1939).
6. Sir John Wheeler-Bennett, *King George VI: His Life and Reign* (London, 1958) pp. 719–31.
7. Rear-Admiral Cary T. Grayson, *Woodrow Wilson: An Intimate Memoir* (New York, 1959), p. 05, Edith Bolling Wilson, *My Memoir* (New York, 1939) p. 248.
8. For the *ex post facto* diagnosis of thrombosis, together with medical arguments, see Gene Smith, *When the Cheering Stopped* (New York, 1964) pp. 105–6.
9. Vice-Admiral Ross T. McIntire, *Twelve Years with Roosevelt* (London, 1964) pp. 216–17. See also Dr Howard G. Bruenn's article, 'Clinical Notes on the Illness and Death of President Franklin D. Roosevelt', *Annals of Internal Medicine* (American College of Physicians, Philadelphia) Apr 1970.
10. e.g. Sir Winston Churchill, *The Second World War*, vol. VI: *Triumph and Tragedy* (London, 1954) p. 416; General Lord Ismay, *Memoirs* (London, 1960) p. 393.
11. Grayson, *Woodrow Wilson*, p. 85.
12. Sir John Wheeler-Bennett, *The Nemesis of Power* (London, 1953) pp. 119–148.

Chapter 2: From the Phoney War to the Atlantic Charter

1. Wheeler-Bennett, *Nemesis of Power*, pp. 404–24; Erich Kordt, *Nicht aus den Akten* (Stuttgart, 1950) pp. 279–80.
2. Wheeler-Bennett, *Nemesis of Power*, pp. 444–5, 453 n.; Kordt, *Nicht aus den Akten*, pp. 311–19, 377–8.
3. Sir John Wheeler-Bennett, *Munich: Prologue to Tragedy* (London, 1948) pp. 429–33.
4. C. H. Sorley, *Marlborough and Other Poems* (Cambridge, 1914).
5. Sir John Wheeler-Bennett, *John Anderson, Viscount Waverley* (London, 1962) pp. 238–47.
6. Leopold Amery, *My Political Life*, vol. III: *The Unforgiving Years, 1929–1940* (London, 1955) p. 330.
7. *H.C.Deb.*, 12 Oct 1939, cols 563–6.
8. Jonkheer Eelco van Kleffens (Netherlands Foreign Minister, 1939–1945), *The Rape of the Netherlands* (London, 1940) pp. 85–8; *Belgium, the Official Account of What Happened*, published for the Belgian Ministry of Foreign Affairs (New York, 1941) pp. 12–14.
9. *The Times*, 13 Nov 1939.
10. *Belgium*, p. 15; for text of documents, see International Military Tribunal Document T.C. 058a.
11. Kordt, *Nicht aus den Akten*, p. 369.
12. Ulrich von Hassell, *Vom andern Deutschland* (Zürich, 1946) pp. 127–33, 147–9; J. Lonsdale Bryans, *Blind Victory* (London, 1951).
13. An account of Dr Josef Müller's conversations in Rome is to be found in the papers of Lt-Col. Groscurth (vol. II, section iv) in the Federal Archives at Coblenz. See also General Georg Thomas's 'Gedanken und Ereignisse', *Schweizerische Monatshefte*, 1945; Hassell,

Vom andern Deutschland, p. 140; and the evidence of Dr Müller himself at the second Huppenkotten Trial at Munich on 14 Oct 1952.

14. Wheeler-Bennett, *King George VI*, p. 463.

15. Elliott Roosevelt (ed.), *The Roosevelt Letters*, vol. III: *1928–1945* (London, 1952) p. 280.

16. Dennys Smith, *America and the Axis War* (London, 1942) p. 224.

17. Wheeler-Bennett, *Nemesis of Power*, pp. 487–8; also Christopher Sykes, *Troubled Loyalty: A Biography of Adam von Trott* (London, 1968).

18. Joseph Alsop and Robert Kintner, *American White Paper* (London, 1940) p. 127.

19. Cordell Hull, *Memoirs* (New York, 1948) vol. I, p. 711; Julius W. Pratt, *Cordell Hull* (New York, 1964) vol. I, p. 336.

20. Alsop and Kintner, *American White Paper*, p. 126.

21. *Harold L. Ickes Diary*, vol. III: *The Lowering Clouds, 1939–1941* (London, 1955) p. 138; Hull, *Memoirs*, vol. I, p. 737.

22. Hull, *Memoirs*, vol. I, p. 202.

23. Alsop and Kintner, *American White Paper*, p. 128.

24. Ickes, *Secret Diary*, vol. III, p. 138.

25. Sumner Welles, *The Time for Decision* (New York, 1944) p. 77.

26. Rexford Tugwell, *The Democratic Roosevelt* (Garden City, N.Y., 1957) pp. 516–17; Pratt, *Cordell Hull*, pp. 339–340.

27. Hull, *Memoirs*, vol. I, pp. 738–9.

28. Welles, *Time for Decision*, p. 74.

29. For text of letters, see *Roosevelt Letters*, vol. III, pp. 306–7.

30. For accounts of the Welles Mission, see Welles, *Time for Decision*, pp. 73–147; also Jay Pierpoint Moffat, *The Moffat Papers, 1919–1941* (Cambridge, Mass., 1956) pp. 291–304. Pierpoint Moffat also wrote a second account of the mission of a highly confidential nature; unfortunately, however, no trace of this report has been found either in his papers or in the archives of the State Department. The text of the Welles Report is printed in *Foreign Relations of the United States,*

1940 (Washington, 1945) vol. I, pp. 21–117.

31. Hull, *Memoirs*, vol. I, p. 740.

32. *The Times*, 30 Mar 1940.

33. Edward Crankshaw, 'When we Wanted War', *Observer*, 23 Aug 1964.

34. For documents of the Soviet–Germany negotiations and agreements, see *Nazi–Soviet Relations* (Washington, 1948).

35. *The Times*, 14 Mar 1940.

36. Ibid. 28 May 1941.

37. Ibid., 12 June 1941.

38. British White Paper, Cmd 6285 (1941).

39. Sir Winston Churchill, *The Second World War*, vol. III: *The Grand Alliance* (London, 1950) pp. 331–3, 351–2.

40. Ibid., p. 349.

41. Count Edward Raczyński, *In Allied London* (London, 1962) pp. 96–8.

42. *H.C.Deb.*, 30 July 1941, col. 1504.

43. Wheeler-Bennett, *King George VI*, pp. 526–7.

44. Robert Sherwood, *The White House Papers of Harry L. Hopkins*, vol. I. (London 1948) p. 351.

45. Accounts of the Atlantic Meeting are to be found in Churchill *The Grand Alliance*, pp. 385–400; Sumner Welles, *Where are we Heading?* (London, 1947) pp. 1–16; Sherwood, *White House Papers*, vol. I, pp. 350–66. See also H. V. Morton, *Atlantic Meeting, 1941* (London, 1943) and Theodore A. Wilson, *The First Summit* (Boston, 1969).

46. Churchill, *The Grand Alliance*, p. 385.

47. Welles, *Where are we Heading?*, pp. 5–6.

48. Sherwood, *White House Papers*, vol. I, p. 312.

49. Churchill, *The Grand Alliance*, p. 386.

50. Sherwood, *White House Papers*, vol. I, p. 368.

51. Welles, *Where are we Heading?*, p. 12.

52. Ismay, *Memoirs*, p. 221.

53. British White Paper, Cmd 6321 (1941).

54. British White Paper, Cmd 6315 (1941).

Chapter 3: The Anglo-Russian Treaty

1. Hull, *Memoirs*, vol. II, p. 1163.

2. Churchill, *The Grand Alliance*, pp. 470–3.

3. Hull, *Memoirs*, vol. II, pp. 1165–6; Sumner Welles, *Seven Major Decisions* (London, 1951) p. 129.

4. For Lord Avon's own account of his Moscow mission, see *The Reckoning* (London, 1965) pp. 285-303; also his dispatch to Mr Churchill quoted in *The Grand Alliance*, pp. 558-9.

5. Avon, *The Reckoning*, pp. 302-3.

6. *The Times*, 9 Feb 1942.

7. Avon, *The Reckoning*, pp. 318-20. In his official history Sir Llewellyn Woodward writes that 'the Foreign Office drew up a memorandum'. *British Foreign Policy in the Second World War* (London, 1962) p. 192. Lord Avon leaves no doubt that he was the author of this paper.

8. Sir Winston Churchill, *The Second World War*, vol. IV: *The Hinge of Fate* (London, 1951) p. 293.

9. Hull, *Memoirs*, vol. II, pp. 1168-72; *Moffat Papers*, p. 380.

10. Avon, *The Reckoning*, pp. 325-9.

Chapter 4: Casablanca and Unconditional Surrender

1. Ismay, *Memoirs*, p. 283.

2. In his diary for 4 Nov 1942. Wheeler-Bennett, *King George VI*, p. 553.

3. Sir John Slessor, *The Central Blue* (London, 1956) p. 433.

4. Churchill, *The Hinge of Fate*, p. 583.

5. Ibid., p. 584.

6. Ibid., p. 586.

7. Sir Arthur Bryant, *The Turn of the Tide* (London, 1957) pp. 530-5.

8. Churchill, *The Hinge of Fate*, p. 583. See also William Hardy McNeill, *Survey of International Affairs, 1939-1946: America, Britain and Russia* (Oxford, 1953) pp. 263 ff.

9. Harold Macmillan, *The Blast of War, 1939-1945* (London, 1967) p. 221; *Stalin's Correspondence with Churchill, Attlee, Roosevelt and Truman, 1941-1945* (London, 1958) p. 80.

10. Churchill, *The Hinge of Fate*, p. 594.

11. Cf. views expressed on American strategy by Lord Attlee in *A Prime Minister Remembers* (London, 1961) pp. 51-3. It was perhaps unfortunate from the British point of view that General Marshall had only experienced the last year of the First World War on the Western Front, when German resistance to the policy of the 'big push' was weakening.

12. Dwight D. Eisenhower, *Crusade in Europe* (London, 1948) p. 213.

13. Harry C. Butcher, *Three Years with Eisenhower* (London, 1946) p. 208.

14. Robert E. Sherwood, *The White House Papers of Henry L. Hopkins*, vol. II (London, 1949) p. 667.

15. Churchill, *The Hinge of Fate*, p. 177.

16. Herbert Feis, *Churchill, Roosevelt, Stalin* (Princeton, 1957) pp. 108-13.

17. Ismay, *Memoirs*, p. 285.

18. Butcher, *Three Years with Eisenhower*, p. 205. Cf. Bryant, *The Turn of the Tide*, pp. 537 ff.

19. Bryant, *The Turn of the Tide*, p. 552.

20. Cf. ibid., pp. 525-36, 548-9, 560.

21. Ibid., p. 544.

22. Ibid., p. 545.

23. Ibid., p. 540, citing the unpublished diary of Sir Ian Jacob, 14 Jan 1943.

24. Admiral W. D. Leahy, *I Was There* (London, 1950), p. 145.

25. *Foreign Relations of the United States, Conferences at Washington 1941-1942, and Casablanca, 1943*. (Washington, 1968) pp. 627-37. Hereafter cited as *Casablanca*. See also Bryant, *The Turn of the Tide*, pp. 549-50.

26. Leahy, *I Was There*, p. 145. For an entertaining and informative picture of these negotiations, see Macmillan, *The Blast of War*, pp. 248-56.

27. Feis, *Churchill, Roosevelt, Stalin*, p. 117.

28. For a harsher view of Elliott's testimony, see Feis, *Churchill, Roosevelt, Stalin*, p. 110.

29. Churchill, *The Hinge of Fate*, p. 613.

30. Ibid., p. 614. Also Woodward, *British Foreign Policy in the Second World War*, pp. 436-7.

31. *Casablanca*, pp. 836-7; Sherwood, *White House Papers*, vol. II, p. 693.

32. *Casablanca*, p. 635 n, and pp. 833-6; Churchill, *The Hinge of Fate*, p. 615. See also Feis, *Churchill, Roosevelt, Stalin*, pp. 111-13.

33. Feis, *Churchill, Roosevelt, Stalin*, p. 111.

34. Ibid., p. 113. The statement was made to the White House Press Correspondents' Association.

35. *H.C.Deb.*, 21 July 1949, col. 1585.

36. Ibid.

37. Churchill, *The Hinge of Fate*, p. 617.

38. Senator Arthur Vandenberg, *Private Papers* (London, 1953), p. 56 ff.

39. See Günter Moltmann, 'Unconditional Surrender and War Propaganda', *Wiener Library Bulletin*, Oct 1964.

40. Feis, *Churchill, Roosevelt, Stalin*, p. 113.

41. *H.C.Deb.*, 18 Jan 1945, cols 423–4.

42. For an interesting discussion of this topic, see Michael Balfour, 'Another Look at Unconditional Surrender', *International Affairs*, Oct 1970.

Chapter 5: The Unconditional Surrender of Italy

1. Churchill, *The Hinge of Fate*, p. 614.

2. Winston S. Churchill, *War Speeches, 1939–1945*, ed. Charles Eade (London, 1952) vol. II, p. 368.

3. *Documents on American Foreign Relations*, ed. L. M. Goodrich and M. J. Carroll (Boston, 1944) vol. V, p. 170.

4. Churchill, *War Speeches*, vol. II, p. 368.

5. Wheeler-Bennett, *King George VI*, p. 561.

6. Cf. Sir Winston Churchill, *The Second World War*, vol. V: *Closing the Ring* (London, 1952), p. 48.

7. Sherwood, *White House Papers*, vol. II, p. 740.

8. Churchill, *Closing the Ring*, pp. 42–3.

9. Ibid., p. 45.

10. Ibid., p. 51. Also Sherwood, *White House Papers*, pp. 737–8.

11. Churchill, *Closing the Ring*, p. 51.

12. Ibid., p. 52.

13. F. W. Deakin, *The Brutal Friendship* (London, 1962), pp. 501–2.

14. *H.C.Deb.*, 27 July 1943, cols 1397–1402.

15. Ibid.

16. Robert Murphy, *Diplomat among Warriors* (London, 1964) p. 232. Macmillan, *Blast of War*, pp. 373–4, records simply that Washington and London were consulted and disliked the idea of a broadcast.

17. Murphy, *Diplomat among Warriors*, pp. 206–7. For Macmillan's account of the Italian surrender, see *Blast of War*, pp. 371–408.

18. Murphy, *Diplomat among Warriors*, p. 235.

19. Macmillan, *Blast of War*, p. 385.

20. Friedrich-Karl von Plehwe, *The End of an Alliance; Rome's Defection From the Axis in 1943* (London 1971) pp. 81 ff.

21. Murphy, *Diplomat among Warriors*, p. 234.

22. Ibid., p. 234. See also General Giuseppe Castellano, *La Guerra Continua: La Vera Storia dell' 8 Settembre con documenii inedite* (Milan, 1963) p. 57, and Viscount Templewood (Sir Samuel

Hoare), *Ambassador on Special Mission* (London, 1946) pp. 213–16.

23. Churchill, *Closing the Ring*, pp. 92–94.

24. For the minutes of this meeting, see Castellano, *La Guerra Continua*, pp. 64–6. Also Major-General Sir Kenneth Strong, *Intelligence at the Top: Recollections of an Intelligence Officer* (London, 1968) pp. 100–26.

25. Castellano, *La Guerra Continua*, pp. 201–2.

26. Ibid., pp. 203–4. Cf. Churchill, *Closing the Ring*, pp. 93–4.

27. Castellano, *La Guerra Continua*, p. 67. The time mentioned by Smith was five or six hours.

28. Ibid., p. 206.

29. Murphy, *Diplomat among Warriors*, p. 236.

30. Churchill, *Closing the Ring*, p. 86.

31. Murphy, *Diplomat among Warriors*, p. 237; Macmillan, *Blast of War*, p. 388. Mr Churchill felt that the estimate of German divisions he had received was exaggerated, since it included leading elements and H.Q.s in several cases, rather than whole divisions. Churchill, *Closing the Ring*, p. 86.

32. Castellano, *La Guerra Continua*, pp. 78–81.

33. Murphy, *Diplomat among Warriors*, p. 238.

34. Ibid., p. 239.

35. Ibid. The attack does not seem to have taken place.

36. Ibid., pp. 240–4; Macmillan, *Blast of War*, p. 391.

37. Murphy, *Diplomat among Warriors*, p. 237; Macmillan, *Blast of War*, p. 385.

38. Woodward, *British Foreign Policy in the Second World War*, pp. 227 n., 230. Also Macmillan, *Blast of War*, p. 384.

39. Churchill, *Closing the Ring*, p. 57.

40. Woodward, *British Foreign Policy in the Second World War*, p. 232.

41. Murphy, *Diplomat among Warriors*, p. 242.

42. General Mark Clark, *Calculated Risk* (paperback ed., London, 1956) p. 169.

43. Murphy, *Diplomat among Warriors*, p. 242.

44. Castellano, *La Guerra Continua*, pp. 128–9.

45. Ibid., p. 119.

46. Ibid., p. 123.

47. Murphy, *Diplomat among Warriors*, p. 250.

48. Castellano, *La Guerra Continua*, p. 207.

Chapter 6: 'Trident', 'Quadrant' and the Moscow Conference of Foreign Ministers

1. Bryant, *The Turn of the Tide*, p. 673.

2. Ismay, *Memoirs*, p. 298.

3. Leahy, *I Was There*, p. 162. Roosevelt was only willing to consider an assault through Rumania, Bulgaria and Turkey. Ibid., p. 159.

4. Ibid., p. 160: 'Field-Marshal Wavell explained all the many objections to a Burma campaign and failed to offer any helpful advice.'

5. Ibid., pp. 162–3.

6. *Foreign Relations of the United States: The Conferences at Cairo and Tehran, 1943* (hereafter called *Cairo and Tehran*) (Washington, 1961). Message from Harriman to Roosevelt, 5 July 1943, p. 15.

7. In December 1941, April 1942, November–December 1942. *Cairo and Tehran*, p. 3.

8. Sherwood, *White House Papers*, vol. II. p. 729. Standley, however presented Davies to Stalin on his arrival. *Cairo and Tehran*, p. 5.

9. *Cairo and Tehran*, p. 5. The President did not want the meeting to be held in Iceland because 'It . . . would make it, quite frankly, difficult not to invite Prime Minister Churchill at the same time'.

10. Sherwood, *White House Papers*, vol. II, pp. 733–4.

11. *Cairo and Tehran*, p. 11. Roosevelt to Churchill, 28 June 1943.

12. Ismay, *Memoirs*, p. 300.

13. Churchill, *The Hinge of Fate*, p. 726.

14. *Stalin's Correspondence*, vol. I, p. 132.

15. Ibid., p. 135.

16. *Cairo and Tehran*, p. 9. Roosevelt was in Virginia when the message from Stalin arrived in Washington. By the time he returned Churchill had sent him a copy of his proposed reply and asked the President to return the compliment.

17. *Stalin's Correspondence*, vol. I, pp. 137–8.

18. Peter Kleist, *Zwischen Hitler und Stalin* (Bonn, 1950) pp. 239–55, 265–80. See also McNeill, *America, Britain and Russia*, p. 324 n.

19. *Cairo and Tehran*, p. 13. Harriman to Roosevelt, 5 July 1943.

20. Ibid., p. 10. Churchill to Roosevelt, 25 June 1943.

21. Sherwood, *White House Papers*, vol. II, p. 730: 'he [Churchill] sent off a scorching cable to which Roosevelt would never have agreed had he been given a chance to read it in advance'.

22. *Cairo and Tehran*, p. 11. Roosevelt to Churchill, 28 June, 1943.

23. Ibid., pp. 12–13. Churchill to Roosevelt, 28 and 29 June 1943.

24. *Foreign Relations of the United States, 1943* (hereafter cited as *Foreign Relations*), vol. I (Washington, 1963) p. 484. Hull to U.S. Ambassador in Turkey, 13 Mar 1943.

25. Ibid., pp. 486 ff. Aide-mémoire from the British Embassy, Washington, 6 Apr 1943.

26. C. A. Macartney, *October Fifteenth* (Edinburgh, 1957) vol. II, p. 169 and n.

27. On Rumania, see *Foreign Relations*, 1943, vol. I, p. 493. Report from U.S. Minister in Stockholm, 14 Aug 1943. On Hungary, see McGeorge Macartney, *October Fifteenth*, vol. II, p. 176.

28. Henry Stimson and McGeorge Bundy, *On Active Service in Peace and War* (New York, 1948), pp. 223–6.

29. Bryant, *The Turn of the Tide*.

30. Stimson and Bundy, *On Active Service*, p. 228.

31. Sherwood, *White House Papers*, vol. II, p. 733. Specific mention of these two areas was made in a memorandum on the urgent need for a Second Front given to the President by Lord Beaverbrook. Roosevelt returned to the idea of an attack on Rumania at the Tehran Conference. Ibid. p. 775.

32. Stimson and Bundy, *On Active Service*, p. 229.

33. Harold Nicolson, *Peacemaking 1919* (rev. ed., London, 1943), p. ix.

34. Hull, *Memoirs*, vol. II, p. 1168.

35. Woodward, *British Foreign Policy in the Second World War*, p. 434. Memorandum by Mr Jebb (early October 1942).

36. Ibid., p. 443.

37. Churchill, *The Hinge of Fate*, p. 837. Minute to Sir Alexander Cadogan.

38. Sherwood, *White House Papers*, vol. II, pp. 715–16.

39. Leahy, *I Was There*, p. 145. Hull, *Memoirs*, vol. II, p. 961.

40. Sherwood, *White House Papers*, vol. II, p. 710.

41. Churchill, *The Hinge of Fate*, p. 716.

42. Lord Avon, *The Reckoning*, p. 399.

43. Ibid., p. 398.

44. Churchill, *The Hinge of Fate*, p. 717.

45. The British had repudiated the Munich Agreement in August 1942. See Woodward, *British Foreign Policy in the Second World War*, pp. 296 f. The French did the same in September 1942. See *Memoirs of Dr Eduard Beneš*, trans. Godfrey Lias (London, 1954) p. 232. On his visit to Washington in the spring of 1943 Beneš claimed that the U.S. authorities confirmed to him that the United States had never recognized the frontiers set out under the Munich Agreement. Ibid., p. 182.

46. The Polish Government's exploitation of the Munich crisis was embarrassing to at least one of its more sensitive and perceptive representatives abroad. See Raczyński, *In Allied London*, pp. 8–10.

47. Ibid., p. 119. On 5 Aug 1942 Mr Eden told a questioner in the House of Commons that Britain's repudiation of Munich did not apply to the Polish acquisition of Teschen.

48. Ibid., p. 104. On 28 July 1943 President Roosevelt told the Polish Ambassador in Washington, M. Ciechanowsky, that East Prussia would belong to Poland after the war and that the Germans there would be forced to leave. 'No more Polish Corridor, Mr Ambassador, no more corridor this time', the President is supposed to have remarked. Jan Ciechanowsky, *Defeat in Victory* (New York, 1947) pp. 185–6. In Moscow on 16 Dec 1941 Stalin suggested to Mr Eden that East Prussia should go to Poland, Woodward, *British Foreign Policy in the Second World War*, p. 191.

49. Woodward, *British Foreign Policy in the Second World War*, p. 191.

50. Ibid.

51. Ibid.

52. Ciechanowsky, *Defeat in Victory*, p. 78.

53. Sherwood, *White House Papers*, vol. II, p. 710.

54. Raczyński, *In Allied London*, pp. 130–40.

55. See *inter alia* E. J. Rozek, *Allied Wartime Diplomacy: A Pattern in Poland* (New York, 1958) pp. 123–33.

56. Rolf Hochhuth, *The Soldiers* (London, 1967); Carlos Thompson, *The Assassination of Winston Churchill* (Gerrards Cross, 1969).

57. Beneš, *Memoirs*, pp. 185, 193.

58. Woodward, *British Foreign Policy in the Second World War*, p. 296 n; *Foreign Relations*, 1943, vol. I, p 626.

59. Raczyński, *In Allied London*, pp. 45–6.

60. Ibid., pp. 86–7.

61. Sherwood, *White House Papers*, vol. II, p. 712.

62. Ibid., p. 708.

63. Earl of Halifax, *Fulness of Days* (London, 1957) pp. 249–50.

64. Gerald Pawle, *The War and Colonel Warden* (London, 1963) pp. 249–250.

65. Sherwood, *White House Papers*, vol. II, p. 714.

66. Ibid., p. 717.

67. Woodward, *British Foreign Policy in the Second World War*, p. 441.

68. Ibid., p. 440 n.

69. Ibid.

70. Hull, *Memoirs*, vol. II, p. 1234.

71. Churchill, *Closing the Ring*, pp. 62 ff.

72. Bryant, *The Turn of the Tide*, p. 699. See also U.S. Army Department History, European Operations, *Cross-Channel Attack* (Washington, 1951), p. 903.

73. Bryant, *The Turn of the Tide*, p. 693.

74. Churchill, *The Hinge of Fate*, p. 702.

75. Bryant, *The Turn of the Tide*, p. 703.

76. E. J. King and W. M. Whitehill, *Fleet Admiral King: A Naval Record* (London, 1953) p. 485.

77. Bryant, *The Turn of the Tide*, p. 706.

78. Ibid., p. 718.

79. Churchill, *Closing the Ring*, p. 83. The report went on to say that 'unanimous agreement has been expressed in a masterly report by the Combined Chiefs of Staff, which the President and I both approved'.

80. Lord Avon, *The Reckoning*, pp. 402–3.

81. Hull, *Memoirs*, vol. II, p. 1232.

82. Avon, *The Reckoning*, p. 403.

83. Hull, *Memoirs*, vol. II, p. 1232.

84. Avon, *The Reckoning*, p. 403.

85. Hull, *Memoirs*, vol. II, p. 1237.

86. Ibid., p. 1238.

87. Avon, *The Reckoning*, pp. 402–3.

88. Ibid.

89. Churchill, *Closing the Ring*, pp. 248–50.

90. *Foreign Relations*, 1943, vol. I, p. 543.

91. Woodward, *British Foreign Policy in the Second World War*, p. 251 and n.

92. Cf. *Foreign Relations*, 1943, vol. I, pp. 630–2.

93. Churchill, *Closing the Ring*, pp. 254–5.

94. Ibid., pp. 251–2.

95. Ibid., pp. 606–7, 705–8.

96. Ibid., pp. 645–9, 730–6.

97. Avon, *The Reckoning*, pp. 402–3.

98. Hull, *Memoirs*, vol. II, p. 1255.

99. Ibid., p. 1249.

100. Sherwood, *White House Papers*, vol. II, pp. 713–15.

101. Hull, *Memoirs*, vol. II, p. 1257.

102. *Foreign Relations*, 1943, vol. I, pp. 541–3; also Hull, *Memoirs*, vol. II, p. 1265.

103. *Foreign Relations*, 1943, vol. I, p. 542.

104. Ibid.

105. Ibid.

106. Ibid.

107. Milovan Djilas, *Conversations with Stalin* (London, 1962) p. 163.

108. *Foreign Relations*, 1943, vol. I, p. 542.

109. Ibid., p. 539. Cable from Hull to Winant.

110. Hull, *Memoirs*, vol. II, p. 1277; Avon, *The Reckoning*, p. 410.

111. *Foreign Relations*, 1943, vol. I, p. 570.

112. See, for example, Ismay, *Memoirs*, p. 324.

113. Avon, *The Reckoning*, pp. 412–13.

114. Ibid., p. 411.

115. Hull, *Memoirs*, vol. II, p. 1292.

116. Avon, *The Reckoning*, pp. 412–13.

117. *Foreign Relations*, 1943, vol. I, p. 580.

118. Ibid., pp. 778–81.

119. Ibid., p. 584.

120. Avon, *The Reckoning*, p. 413.

121. Churchill, *The Hinge of Fate*, pp. 623–42.

122. *Foreign Relations*, 1943, vol. I, p. 585.

123. Avon, *The Reckoning*, p. 416.

124. *Foreign Relations*, 1943, vol. I, p. 621.

125. Ibid., pp. 618–19; Avon, *The Reckoning*, p. 414.

126. *Foreign Relations*, 1943, vol. I, p. 607.

127. Ibid., pp. 629, 651, 653.

128. Ibid., p. 664.

129. Ibid., pp. 609–13, 714.

130. Ibid., p. 761.

131. Ibid., p. 638.

132. Ibid., pp. 639, 762.

133. Ibid., p. 639.

134. Ibid., p. 652.

135. Ibid., p. 651.

136. Avon, *The Reckoning*, pp. 415–16; *Foreign Relations*, 1943, vol. I, p. 623.

137. Hull, *Memoirs*, vol. II, p. 1272.

138. *Foreign Relations*, 1943, vol. I, pp. 597, 668.

139. Ibid., pp. 602–3.

140. Ibid., p. 596.

141. Hull, *Memoirs*, vol. II, p. 1297.

142. *Cairo and Tehran*, p. 45.

143. Avon, *The Reckoning*, p. 414.

144. *Foreign Relations*, 1943, vol. I, p. 642.

145. Ibid., p. 654.

146. Ibid., p. 698.

147. Ibid., p. 667.

148. Ibid., p. 769.

149. Ibid.

150. Ibid., pp. 402–5 ff.

151. Ibid., p. 762.

152. Ibid., pp. 760–1.

153. Cf. ibid., p. 685.

154. Avon, *The Reckoning*, p. 418.

155. *Foreign Relations*, 1943, vol. I, p. 685; Hull, *Memoirs*, vol. II, p. 1293.

156. *Foreign Relations*, 1943, vol. I, pp. 764–8.

157. *Cairo and Tehran*, p. 152.

Chapter 7: First Cairo and the Road to Tehran

1. Roosevelt to Churchill, 22 Oct 1943. *Cairo and Tehran*, pp. 37–8. Part of this message is quoted in Churchill, *Closing the Ring*, p. 276.

2. Churchill to Roosevelt, 23 Oct 1943. Churchill, *Closing the Ring*, p. 277.

3. Lord Avon, *The Reckoning*, p. 415. Cf. also Sherwood, *White House Papers*, vol. II, p. 790.

4. Roosevelt to Stalin, 21 Oct 1943. *Cairo and Tehran*, p. 36. Harriman to Roosevelt, 26 Oct 1943. Ibid., p. 43.

5. For the President's views on Soviet participation in staff talks, see Roosevelt to Churchill, 26 Oct 1943. *Cairo and Tehran*, p. 42. Also Churchill, *Closing the Ring*, p. 279. On the possibility of even a flying visit by Stalin to Basra, see President Roosevelt to Cordell Hull, 28 Oct 1943. *Cairo and Tehran*, p. 49.

6. Cordell Hull to Roosevelt, 31 Oct 1943. *Cairo and Tehran*, pp. 57–8.

7. Marshall to Leahy, 25 Oct 1943. *Cairo and Tehran*, p. 41.

8. Churchill to Roosevelt, 27 Oct 1943. *Cairo and Tehran*, pp. 47–8. Churchill, *Closing the Ring*, pp. 279–80.

9. Churchill to Roosevelt, 26 Oct 1943. *Cairo and Tehran*, p. 41.

10. Churchill to Roosevelt, 26 Oct 1943. *Cairo and Tehran*, pp. 41–2. Churchill to Roosevelt, 30 Oct 1943. Ibid., pp. 54–5. Churchill to Roosevelt, 2 Nov 1942. Ibid., 60–1.

11. Hull to Roosevelt, 30 Oct 1943. *Cairo and Tehran*, p. 53.

12. Churchill to Roosevelt, 2 Nov 1943. *Cairo and Tehran*, p. 60.

13. Roosevelt to Churchill, 30 Oct 1943. Ibid., p. 55.

14. Roosevelt to Churchill, 5 Nov 1943. Ibid., pp. 66–7.

15. Churchill, *Closing the Ring*, p. 281. Also Churchill to Roosevelt, 6 Nov 1943, and Harriman to Roosevelt, 7 Nov 1943. *Cairo and Tehran*, pp. 69–70.

16. Harriman to Roosevelt, 4 Nov 1943. *Cairo and Tehran*, p. 65.

17. Ibid., p. 71 n.

18. Memorandum by the First Secretary of the Embassy in the Soviet Union, 9 Nov 1943. Ibid., pp. 74–5.

19. Stalin to Roosevelt, 10 Nov 1943. Ibid., p. 78. Roosevelt to Churchill, 11 Nov 1943. Ibid., p. 79.

20. Ibid., p. 79. Also Churchill, *Closing the Ring*, p. 282.

21. *Cairo and Tehran*, p. 79. Also Churchill, *Closing the Ring*, p. 283.

22. Harriman to Roosevelt, 12 Nov 1943. *Cairo and Tehran*, p. 80.

23. 'The President's Log en route to Cairo, November 11–21, 1943', *Cairo and Tehran*, pp. 273–7. See also Leahy, *I Was There*, pp. 195 ff.; Sherwood, *White House Papers*, vol. II, pp. 762–5.

24. This incident is described in the President's Log, *Cairo and Tehran*, p. 280, in Sherwood, *White House Papers*, vol. II, pp. 763–4, and in more detail in Commander C. F. Pick, 'Torpedo on the Starboard Beam', in *Proceedings of the United States Naval Institute* (Aug 1970) pp. 90–3.

25. Leahy, *I Was There*, pp. 201, 209: 'The British bulldog tenacity did not let go of a desire to retain a controlling hold on the Mediterranean in the Near East', and 'The Prime Minister, devoted to the preservation of the power of the British Empire, apparently gave in, perhaps with reluctance [i.e. to the fixing of the date for "Overlord" in May 1944 – author], to the arguments of his top advisers'. For a similar view on the Far East, see Sherwood, *White House Papers*, vol. II, p. 767.

26. Letter from Stimson to Hopkins, 10 Nov 1943: 'The task for our Commander-in-Chief to hold the situation firmly to the straight road which has been agreed to and which it is now on. He should tolerate no departures from the programme. Once we approach within two or three months of the attack, I anticipate no further efforts to depart and a steady acceleration of British support.' *Cairo and Tehran*, pp. 175–6. See also Sherwood, *White House Papers*, vol. II, p. 762.

27. Sherwood, *White House Papers*, vol. II, p. 809.

28. *Cairo and Tehran*, pp. 259–60.

29. Sherwood, *White House Papers*, vol. II, p. 775. See also Feis, *Churchill, Roosevelt, Stalin*, p. 260 n.

30. Churchill, *Closing the Ring*, pp. 269–70.

31. Sherwood, *White House Papers*, vol. II, p. 782.

32. Ibid., pp. 756–7.

33. Memoranda of the Joint Chiefs of Staff drawn up for the President by the Joint Chiefs of Staff, 17 Nov 1943. *Cairo and Tehran*, pp. 203–9.

34. Minutes of the President's meeting with the Joint Chiefs of Staff, 19 Nov 1943. *Cairo and Tehran*, pp. 248–9.

35. Memorandum by the Department of State, sent to Roosevelt on 11 Nov 1943. *Cairo and Tehran*, p. 187.

36. Minutes of the President's meeting

with the Joint Chiefs of Staff, 19 Nov 1943. *Cairo and Tehran*, p. 253.

37. William M. Franklin, 'Zonal Boundaries and Access Routes to Berlin', *World Politics*, Oct 1963.

38. Ibid.

39. Minutes of the President's meeting with the Joint Chiefs of Staff, 15 Nov 1943. *Cairo and Tehran*, pp. 194–5.

40. Minutes of the President's meeting with Joint Chiefs of Staff, 19 Nov 1943. *Cairo and Tehran*, pp. 254–6.

41. Ibid., p. 256.

42. Ibid., p. 256.

43. Ibid., p. 260.

44. President's Log, 22 Nov 1943. *Cairo and Tehran*, p. 293. See also Leahy, *I Was There*, p. 199.

45. Churchill, *Closing the Ring*, pp. 287–8.

46. Ibid., pp. 289–90.

47. President's Log, *Cairo and Tehran*, p. 294. Also account of plenary meeting, 23 Nov 1943. Ibid., p. 311.

48. Meeting of Combined Chiefs of Staff, 24 Nov 1943. *Cairo and Tehran*, pp. 342–4. The amount demanded was 10,000 tons per month.

49. Churchill, *Closing the Ring*, p. 290. See also *Cairo and Tehran*, p. 350.

50. Feis, *Churchill, Roosevelt, Stalin*, p. 250 n. Also John Ehrman, *Grand Strategy*, vol. v (London, 1956) p. 167, and *Cairo and Tehran*, pp. 358–65.

51. Churchill, *Closing the Ring*, pp. 291–4.

52. Ibid., p. 289.

53. Avon, *The Reckoning*, p. 426.

54. President's Log, *Cairo and Tehran*, p. 296. For discussion of sources for this meeting, see ibid., p. 322. We have accepted Elliott Roosevelt's claim to have been at the dinner (see Elliott Roosevelt, *As he saw it*, pp. 164–5) since this agrees with the list given in the Log.

55. Chinese Summary Record of Roosevelt–Chiang meeting, 23 Nov 1943. *Cairo and Tehran*, p. 324.

56. Memorandum by the Co-Chairman of the Anglo-American Caribbean Commission, Washington, 16 January 1945. *Cairo and Tehran*, p. 887. See also Leahy to Stettinius, 29 May 1945. Ibid., p. 888.

57. Ibid., p. 425.

58. Avon, *The Reckoning*, p. 425.

59. Ibid., p. 426.

60. Cf. Byrnes to Truman, 3 Sept 1945, and the U.S. Ambassador to China to Byrnes, 11 Aug 1945. *Cairo and Tehran*, p. 889.

61. Roosevelt to Hull, 24 Jan 1944. *Cairo and Tehran*, p. 872.

62. Communiqué issued by Roosevelt, Chiang and Churchill, 1 Dec 1943. *Cairo and Tehran*, p. 448.

63. Avon, *The Reckoning*, p. 424.

64. Ibid., p. 425.

65. See memorandum by the Assistant Secretary of War (McCloy) sent to Hopkins, 25 Nov 1943. *Cairo and Tehran*, pp. 416–17.

66. Ibid., pp. 416–20.

67. Ibid., p. 418.

68. American–British Conversations on Civil Affairs, 26 Nov 1943. *Cairo and Tehran*, pp. 351–4. Also Lord Avon, *The Reckoning*, p. 425. Major D. J. F. Morton was also present at these talks on the British side.

69. *Cairo and Tehran*, p. 352.

70. McCloy to Hopkins, 30 Nov 1943. *Cairo and Tehran*, p. 445. Also draft agreement on E.A.C. prepared by the American delegation. Ibid., p. 446.

71. *Cairo and Tehran*, pp. 189–90.

72. Minutes of the meeting of the Combined Chiefs of Staff, 24 Nov 1943. *Cairo and Tehran*, p. 333. Also meeting of Combined Chiefs of Staff, 26 Nov 1943. Ibid., pp. 358–65.

73. Churchill, *Closing the Ring*, p. 302; Avon, *The Reckoning*, p. 426.

74. Roosevelt to Stalin, 22 Nov 1943. *Cairo and Tehran*, pp. 373–4.

75. Reilly to Spaman in Cairo, 24 Nov 1943. *Cairo and Tehran*, p. 397.

76. Hurley to the President, 26 Nov 1943. *Cairo and Tehran*, p. 440.

77. The President's Log at Tehran, *Cairo and Tehran*, p. 463 and n.

78. Mr Churchill, though recording his own support for the move, tells how Molotov 'produced a story that the Soviet Secret Intelligence had unearthed a plot to kill one or more of the "Big Three"'. Churchill, *Closing the Ring*, p. 303. The decision to accept Stalin's invitation was certainly criticized in the U.S.A. See Ciechanowsky, *Defeat in Victory*, p. 244. The President's Log at Tehran, *Cairo and Tehran*, p. 463 n.

79. Ibid.

80. Ibid.

Chapter 8: Tehran and Second Cairo

1. Roosevelt said 'I am glad to see you, I have tried for a long time to bring this about'. Roosevelt–Stalin meeting 28 Nov 1943, 3 p.m. *Cairo and Tehran*, pp. 482 ff. For other general accounts of the Tehran meetings, see Feis, *Churchill, Roosevelt, Stalin*. pp. 254 ff, and McNeill, *America, Britain and Russia*, pp. 348–75.

2. *Cairo and Tehran*, p. 485.

3. Churchill, *Closing the Ring*, p. 307.

4. Leahy. *I Was There*, p. 207.

5. Lord Moran, *Churchill, taken from the Diaries of Lord Moran* (London, 1966) pp. 146–7.

6. Bryant, *Triumph in the West* (London, 1959) pp. 90–1; 98–100.

7. Leahy, *I Was There*, p. 204.

8. *Cairo and Tehran*, 'Bohlen Minutes', pp. 487–97, and 'Combined Chiefs of Staff Minutes', pp. 497–508. There are differences in these texts – especially in Marshal Stalin's views. Cf. Churchill, *Closing the Ring*, p. 307.

9. Butcher, *Three Years with Eisenhower*, p. 384; Ehrman, *Grand Strategy*, vol. v, pp. 156.

10. *Cairo and Tehran*, pp. 492, 502.

11. Ibid., p. 496.

12. Bryant, *Triumph in the West*, p. 91.

13. *Cairo and Tehran*, pp. 509–12. Tripartite Dinner Meeting, 28 Nov 1943. See also Churchill, *Closing the Ring*, pp. 317–20.

14. *Cairo and Tehran*, pp. 513–14, Bohlen Supplementary Memorandum of Stalin's views as expressed during the evening of 28 Nov 1943.

15. Ibid., p. 510.

16. Ibid., p. 511.

17. Ibid., p. 511.

18. Churchill, *Closing the Ring*, p. 319.

19. *Cairo and Tehran*, p. 512. The Bohlen minutes of this conversation make it clear that Stalin was rather less willing to accept Mr Churchill's enthusiasm for a discussion on Poland than the latter's memoirs suggest. Stalin seems to have been very reticent and ironical when replying to both Eden and Churchill.

20. Ibid.

21. Lord Avon, *The Reckoning*, p. 427.

22. Moran, *Churchill*, p. 145.

23. *Cairo and Tehran*, p. 514. Combined Chiefs of Staff Minutes of Tripartite Military Meeting, 29 Nov 1943.

24. Bryant, *Triumph in the West*, pp. 90, 92.

25. Ibid., p. 91.

26. Churchill, *Closing the Ring*, p. 320. Cf. McNeill, *America, Britain and Russia*, p. 355.

27. *Cairo and Tehran*, p. 529. Bohlen Minutes of Roosevelt–Stalin meeting, 29 Nov 1943, n. 1.

28. Ibid., pp. 531–2. Bohlen Minutes of Roosevelt–Stalin meeting, 29 Nov 1943.

29. Cf McNeill, *America, Britain and Russia*, pp. 356–7. McNeill points to the possibility that Stalin did not want all of Germany to go Communist because this might threaten Stalin's own position. It seems more likely that he wanted to exploit the Germans to repair Russia's shattered economy, and hoped that his allies would take responsibility for the harsh measures which this would involve.

30. *Cairo and Tehran*, pp. 533–40. Bohlen Minutes of the Second Plenary Meeting, 29 Nov 1943.

31. Ibid. Cf. also Bryant, *Triumph in the West*, p. 92.

32. *Cairo and Tehran*, pp. 552–5. Bohlen Minutes of Tripartite Dinner Meeting, 29 Nov 1943.

33. *Cairo and Tehran*, p. 602.

34. Ibid. Also Churchill, *Closing the Ring*, pp. 329–30.

35. Ibid., p. 333.

36. Ibid.

37. *Cairo and Tehran*, p. 564. Minutes of Combined Chiefs of Staff Meeting, 30 Nov 1943.

38. Ibid., pp. 565–8. Roosevelt–Stalin–Churchill luncheon meeting, 30 Nov 1943.

39. *Cairo and Tehran*, pp. 324, 891.

40. Ibid., pp. 568–76. Ware Minutes on Hopkins–Eden–Molotov luncheon. See also Sherwood, *White House Papers*, vol. II, p. 786.

41. *Cairo and Tehran*, p. 571.

42. Sherwood, *White House Papers*, vol. II, p. 786; *Cairo and Tehran*, pp. 572–4.

43. *Cairo and Tehran*, pp. 576–8. Bohlen Minutes of Third Plenary Meeting, 20 Nov 1943.

44. Cf. Feis, *Churchill, Roosevelt, Stalin*, p. 264.

45. Bryant, *Triumph in the West*, p. 100.

46. *Cairo and Tehran*, Boettiger

Minutes of Tripartite Dinner Meeting, 30 Nov 1943, pp. 582–5.
47. Churchill, *Closing the Ring*, p. 342; Bryant, *Triumph in the West*, p. 100.
48. Bryant, *Triumph in the West*, p. 101.
49. *Cairo and Tehran*, p. 585.
50. *Cairo and Tehran*, pp. 585–93. Bohlen Minutes of Tripartite Luncheon Meeting, 1 Dec 1943. Churchill, *Closing the Ring*, pp. 334–7. The Bohlen minutes and the account given in Sherwood, *White House Papers*, vol. II, pp. 787–8, stress American opposition to the Turkish project rather more than Mr Churchill's version. In particular, Hopkins inserted his views on the impossibility of offering the Turks an assault on Rhodes into the minutes of the meeting so as to make the American position absolutely clear on this point.
51. *Cairo and Tehran*, p. 591.
52. Ibid., p. 594. Bohlen Minutes of Roosevelt–Stalin Meeting, 1 Dec 1943, 3.20 p.m. The sense of this conversation was glossed over in Sherwood's account in the Hopkins Papers as follows: 'Roosevelt felt it necessary to explain to Stalin that there were six or seven million Americans of Polish extraction, and others of Lithuanian, Latvian, and Estonian origin who had the same rights and the same votes as anyone else and whose opinions must be respected. Stalin said that he understood this, but subsequently suggested that some "propaganda work" should be done among these people.' Sherwood, *White House Papers*, vol. II, pp. 788–9. From this it might be implied that Roosevelt's purpose had been to restrain Stalin in Poland. The Bohlen minutes make it clear that such was not the case.

53. *Cairo and Tehran*, p. 596, n. 6, citing Thomas Connally, *My Name is Tom Connally* (New York, 1954) p. 265.
54. *Cairo and Tehran*, pp. 596–604. Bohlen Minutes of Tripartite Political Meeting, 1 Dec 1943, 6 p.m.
55. Avon, *The Reckoning*, pp. 427–8.
56. Moran, *Churchill*, p. 150.
57. *Cairo and Tehran*, p. 883, Memorandum by H. D. White, Assistant to the Secretary of the United States Treasury, 15 Aug 1944.
58. Ibid., p. 884. Memorandum by H. D. White of a conversation at dinner in the Citadel, Quebec, on 13 Sep 1944.
59. Ibid., pp. 879, 881, 883.
60. Bryant, *Triumph in the West*, pp. 102–9; McNeill, *America, Britain and Russia*, pp. 368–75.
61. *Cairo and Tehran*, p. 803.
62. Ibid., p. 722.
63. See Byrnes's memorandum to President Truman, 3 Sep 1945. *Cairo and Tehran*, p. 889. On the question of a Chinese loan, see State Department memorandum of 27 Dec 1943. Ibid., p. 861.
64. Ibid., p. 680.
65. See Churchill's minute to Ismay of 29 Sep 1943. Churchill, *Closing the Ring*, p. 475.
66. Avon, *The Reckoning*, p. 430; *Cairo and Tehran*, p. 850.
67. *Cairo and Tehran*, p. 844.
68. Ibid., pp. 833 ff.; see also Churchill's message to Roosevelt of 9 Mar 1944 claiming that the question had been discussed on 8 Dec 1943. This was impossible as Roosevelt left on the 7th. Ibid., pp. 878–9; Churchill, *Closing the Ring*, p. 697.
69. *Cairo and Tehran*, pp. 846–8.

Chapter 9: The Morgenthau Plan and JCS 1067

1. This decision was the subject of a conversation between Anthony Eden and Harry Dexter White, Assistant to the U.S. Secretary of the Treasury Henry Morgenthau, Jr, in London on Sunday 13 Aug 1944. Mr White reported accordingly. See *Cairo and Tehran*, pp. 881–2.
2. Letter to Queen Wilhelmina of the Netherlands, 26 Aug 1944. *The Roosevelt Letters*, vol. III, p. 509.
3. Hull, *Memoirs*, vol. I, p. 207.
4. John Morton Blum, *From the Morgenthau Diaries: Years of War, 1941–1945* (Boston, 1967) p. 338.

5. Reports of the U.S. Senate Internal Security Subcommittee, *Interlocking Subversion in Government Departments* (Washington, 1955) and *Scope of Soviet Activity in the United States* (Washington, 1956).
6. *Report on the Morgenthau Diaries prepared by the Subcommittee of the Senate Committee of the Judiciary appointed to investigate the Administration of the Internal Security Act and other Internal Security Laws* (Washington, 1967), vol. I, p. 81.
7. Hull, *Memoirs*, vol. II, pp. 1602–

1603; Blum, *Morgenthau Diaries*, pp. 348 ff.

8. Blum, *Morgenthau Diaries*, p. 342.

9. Stimson and Bundy, *On Active Service*, pp. 570–5; Hull, *Memoirs*, vol. II, pp. 1604–10.

10. A photographic copy of this 'Top Secret' document, entitled 'Program to Prevent Germany from starting a World War III', is printed as a frontispiece to Mr Morgenthau's book *Germany is our Problem* (New York, 1945).

11. Stimson and Bundy, *On Active Service*, p. 575.

12. Ibid., p. 575; Moran, *Churchill*, p. 179.

13. Memorandum by Harry Dexter White for the Secretary of the Treasury, dated 25 Sep 1944, *Cairo and Tehran*, p. 884; Memorandum by the Deputy Director of the Office of European Affairs (H. Freeman Matthews) for the Secretary of State, dated 20 Sep 1944, in *Foreign Relations of the United States: The Conferences at Malta and Yalta, 1945* (Washington, 1956) p. 134; Moran, *Churchill*, pp. 177–8.

14. Lord Brand interviewed by Kenneth Harris, 'How a Banker Watched History Happen', *Observer*, 8 Jan 1961; letter from the Earl of Birkenhead to Sir John Wheeler-Bennett, 2 June 1966; Cherwell Papers. Nuffield College, Oxford.

15. Blum, *Morgenthau Diaries*, p. 373.

16. Winston S. Churchill, *The Tide of Victory* (London, 1954) pp. 138–9; Matthews Memorandum, *Malta and Yalta*, p. 134.

17. Stimson and Bundy, *On Active Service*, pp. 576–7; *Senate Judiciary Subcommittee Report*, pp. 620–1.

18. Feis, *Churchill, Roosevelt, Stalin*, p. 380 n.

19. Unsigned memorandum dated 14 Sep, OFF 23.2. *Cherwell Papers*, Nuffield College, Oxford.

20. Feis, *Churchill, Roosevelt, Stalin*, p. 371.

21. John L. Snell, *Wartime Origins of the East–West Dilemma over Germany* (New Orleans, 1959) pp. 87–8.

22. Hull, *Memoirs*, vol. II, pp. 1613–1614.

23. Memorandum for the Secretary of the Treasury by Harry Dexter White of a meeting at the Senate Department on 20 September, at which were present Secretaries Hull, Stimson and Morgenthau, together with their advisers. *Malta and Yalta*, pp. 136–41.

24. Moran, *Churchill*, p. 179.

25. Avon, *The Reckoning*, pp. 475–6.

26. Dexter White Memorandum of meeting on 20 Sep 1944. *Malta and Yalta*, p. 137.

27. Hull, *Memoirs*, vol. II, p. 1614.

28. Ibid., pp. 1616–19.

29. Stimson's diary for 3 Oct 1944, quoted by Elting E. Morison in *Turmoil and Tradition: A Study of the Life and Times of Henry L. Stimson* (Boston, 1960) p. 609; Stimson and Bundy, *On Active Service*, pp. 577–83.

30. Sherwood, *White House Papers*, vol. II, p. 824.

31. *Washington Post*, 21 Sep 1944.

32. *New York Times*, 22 Sep 1944, 2 Nov 1944; *Wall Street Journal*, 23 Sep 1944.

33. Hull, *Memoirs*, vol. II, p. 162a.

34. *Das Reich*, 30 June 1944.

35. Theodore N. Kaufman, *Germany Must Perish* (Newark, N.J., 1941).

36. *Das Reich*, 21 Oct 1944.

37. *Völkischer Beobachter*, quoted by Chester Wilmot in *The Struggle for Europe* (London, 1952) p. 550.

38. *Senate Judiciary Subcommittee Report*, p. 41 and nn.

39. Woodward, *British Foreign Policy in the Second World War*, p. 11.

40. Hull, *Memoirs*, vol. II, p. 162; Philip E. Moseley, *The Kremlin and World Politics* (New York, 1960) p. 177.

41. Blum, *Morgenthau Diaries*, pp. 383–90; *Senate Judiciary Subcommittee Report*, pp. 43–5.

42. Murphy, *Diplomat among Warriors*, p. 251.

43. General Lucius C. Clay, *Decision in Germany* (New York, 1950) p. 18.

44. Memorandum from Douglas to General Clay dated 1 May 1945 (made available to Sir John Wheeler-Bennett by Hon. Lewis W. Douglas, Feb 1968).

Chapter 10: The Road to Yalta

1. Churchill, *Triumph and Tragedy*, p. 208.

2. Some idea of the atmosphere in which Soviet policy discussions took place can be obtained from Djilas's account in his *Conversations with Stalin*. It is known

from Soviet military memoirs that strategic differences on the Russian side were as lively as those in London and Washington.

3. On 23 Aug 1944 he visited the Pope, with whom he discussed the danger of Communist expansion. Churchill, *Triumph and Tragedy*, pp. 102–3. Cf. Moran, *Churchill*, p. 185 (U.S. edition), where Moran remarks on 21 Aug 1944 that 'Winston never talks of Hitler these days: he is always harping on the dangers of Communism'. It is worth pointing out that Mr Churchill's fears seem to have been most acute with regard to Greece and Turkey (cf. ibid., p. 174) and that he became more satisfied with the Russians in the autumn of 1944, when Stalin seemed ready to set limits to Soviet ambitions in the Balkans.

4. For Churchill's dismay over the progress of the war in December 1944, see his letter to Field-Marshal Smuts of 3 Dec 1944 and his letter to Roosevelt, 6 Dec 1944. Churchill, *Triumph and Tragedy*, pp. 233–6. For the dissatisfaction with Eisenhower, see Bryant, *Triumph in the West*, pp. 322, 334 ff. For the fears at SHAEF that Eisenhower might be forced to accept a Land Commander, see Strong, *Intelligence at the Top*, pp. 168–70.

5. Churchill, *Triumph and Tragedy*, p. 120.

6. Slessor, *The Central Blue*, p. 612, cited in Michael Howard, *The Mediterranean Strategy in the Second World War* (London, 1968) p. 65. See also a study entitled *The Warsaw Insurrection: The Communist Version versus the Facts*, prepared for the Subcommittee on Internal Security of the United States Senate Committee on the Judiciary (Washington, 1969).

7. See his message to the British Prime Minister on this subject dated 26 Aug 1944. Churchill, *Triumph and Tragedy*, p. 123.

8. Woodward, *British Foreign Policy in the Second World War*, p. 299 and n.

9. Ibid., p. 284.
10. Ibid., p. 287.
11. Ibid.
12. A promise which did not please Mr Eden, who was aware how little it was worth. Avon, *The Reckoning*, p. 464. See also *Malta and Yalta*, pp. 202 ff., Ambassador Harriman in Moscow to

President Roosevelt, 14 Oct 1944. This volume of documents will henceforth be cited as *Yalta*.

13. Woodward, *British Foreign Policy in the Second World War*, p. 300.
14. Ibid., p. 291. Also Avon, *The Reckoning*, p. 439.
15. *Yalta*, p. 6. 4 Oct 1944.
16. Avon, *The Reckoning*, p. 483; Woodward, *British Foreign Policy in the Second World War*, pp. 307–8.
17. Churchill, *Triumph and Tragedy*, p. 198. As mentioned above, Molotov persistently argued about the size of the percentages in negotiations with Mr Eden. Nevertheless, the main feature of the agreement – that Russian leadership in Bulgaria and Rumania should be accepted in exchange for British pre-eminence in Greece – remained unaffected.
18. Feis, *Churchill, Roosevelt, Stalin*, p. 453.
19. *Yalta*, pp. 202 ff. Harriman to Roosevelt, 14 Oct 1944, and Mikolajczyk to Harriman, 16 Oct 1944.
20. Avon, *The Reckoning*, p. 487.
21. *Yalta*, p. 207.
22. Ibid., p. 209.
23. Churchill, *Triumph and Tragedy*, p. 208.
24. Bryant, *Triumph in the West*, p. 311.
25. George F. Kennan, *Memoirs, 1925–1950* (London, 1968) pp. 218–19.
26. Feis, *Churchill, Roosevelt, Stalin*, p. 296.
27. Ibid., p. 436.
28. Stimson and Bundy, *On Active Service*, pp. 327–8.
29. *Yalta*, p. 165.
30. Ibid., p. 315. Memorandum from Morgenthau to Roosevelt, 10 Jan 1945.
31. Stimson and Bundy, *On Active Service*, p. 341; Woodward, *British Foreign Policy in the Second World War*, pp. 573–4.
32. *Yalta*, pp. 107–8.
33. Avon, *The Reckoning*, p. 496.
34. Leahy, *I Was There*, p. 285.
35. Ibid., pp. 276–8.
36. Sherwood, *White House Papers*, vol. II. 824.
37. See, for example, Richard L. Walker, 'E. R. Stettinius, Jr', in *The American Secretaries of State and their Diplomacy*, ed. Robert H. Ferrell, vol. XIV (New York, 1965) pp. 21–4.
38. *Yalta*, pp. 64–6.

39. *Yalta*, p. 95. Hickerson to Stettinius, 8 Jan 1945.
40. Ibid.
41. Ibid.
42. Ibid., pp. 97–100.
43. Ibid., p. 106. Attachment to Briefing Book Paper 'American Policy toward Spheres of Influence'. Leahy's letter was dated 16 May 1944. Leahy was writing to Hull.
44. Ibid., p. 102.
45. Stimson and Bundy, *On Active Service*, p. 359. Stimson's diary, 23 Apr 1945. Mr Bundy was evidently uneasy about this passage and a footnote is appended which claims that 'Stimson had no intention of excluding the democracies of Western Europe, for example, from his list of nations that understand the free ballot'.
46. *Yalta*, pp. 242–3. The document read: 'While Hungary must of course renounce the territorial gains made at the expense of Czechoslovakia and Yugoslavia with German help, the United States would favour for example, an eventual negotiated settlement which would transfer to Hungary some of the predominantly Hungarian-populated districts of Southern Slovakia.' It then went on to refer to the promising prospects facing Maort, a subsidiary of Standard Oil of New Jersey. Maort had concessions for oil-fields in Hungary.
47. Sherwood, *White House Papers*, vol. II, pp. 836–7.
48. Ibid.

49. *Yalta*, p. 29. Hopkins to Roosevelt, 24 Jan 1945.
50. Churchill, *Triumph and Tragedy*, p. 295.
51. *Yalta*, p. 31. Churchill to Roosevelt, 8 Jan 1945.
52. Ibid., p. 33. Churchill to Roosevelt, 10 Jan 1945.
53. There is little published material about Hopkins's visit to London, but it seems to have satisfied him and to have pleased the British. Sherwood, *White House Papers*, vol. II, p. 839; Avon, *The Reckoning*, p. 507; *Yalta*, p. 39; Churchill, *Triumph and Tragedy*, p. 298. The latter simply repeats Sherwood's account without comment.
54. See, for example, *Yalta*, p. 291. Roosevelt to Churchill, 6 Dec 1944.
55. General de Gaulle, *Mémoires de Guerre: Le Salut, 1944–1946* (Paris, 1959) p. 80.
56. Ibid., p. 81
57. *Yalta*, p. 296. French Note to the British, U.S. and Soviet Governments, 16 Jan 1945.
58. De Gaulle, *Le Salut*, p. 88. For a record of Hopkins's conversation with de Gaulle, see ibid., pp. 389–92.
59. Leahy, for example, retained his low opinion of de Gaulle. He records that Roosevelt shrugged off the French refusal to come to Algiers with the remark: 'Well I just wanted to discuss some of our problems with him. If he doesn't want to, it doesn't make any difference to me'. Leahy, *I Was There*, p. 327.

Chapter 11: The Yalta Conference

1. Bryant, *Triumph in the West*, p. 398. This did not mean, of course, that many German troops did not go on fighting deperately right until the final surrender.
2. Ibid., p. 395.
3. *Yalta*, p. 543. Record of Chiefs of Staff Meeting with Roosevelt and Churchill, 2 Feb 1945.
4. Ibid. The quotation is given in reported speech. Also Churchill, *Triumph and Tragedy*, p. 300.
5. *Yalta*, p. 478. Memorandum by the British Chiefs of Staff, 30 Jan 1945.
6. Avon, *The Reckoning*, p. 510.
7. Ibid.
8. Leahy, *I Was There*, pp. 297–9; Sherwood, *White House Papers*, vol. II, p. 842.
9. *Yalta*, p. 499 n.

10. Ibid. p. 500.
11. Avon, *The Reckoning*, pp. 510–11.
12. *Yalta*, pp. 502–3. The plan had already been communicated to the Foreign Office in London. The term 'Emergency High Commission' was preferred to that of 'Provisional Security Council'.
13. Ibid., pp. 504 n., 661.
14. Ibid., p. 501.
15. Ibid., p. 378.
16. Ibid., p. 379. Memorandum of the Division of Territorial Studies on the Kuriles.
17. Leahy, *I Was There*, p. 288.
18. Ibid.
19. *Yalta*, p. 330. Cordell Hull to Ambassador Morris in Tehran, 16 Oct 1944.
20. Ibid., p. 501.

21. Ibid., pp. 505–6.

22. No attempt has been made to deal exhaustively with the talks at Malta. Further reference will be made to them later in the chapter. Otherwise the reader is referred to *Yalta*, pp. 598–607.

23. Cf. J. F. Byrnes, *Speaking Frankly* (London, 1948) p. 23.

24. Avon, *The Reckoning*, p. 512.

25. Ibid.

26. Sherwood, *White House Papers*, vol. II, p. 841.

27. Moran, *Churchill*, p. 242.

28. Ibid., p. 234.

29. Leahy, *I Was There*, pp. 290, 313.

30. Byrnes, *Speaking Frankly*, p. 22.

31. Ibid., p. 23.

32. At one point on the flight ice formed on the wings of the President's aeroplane and his Secret Service agents wanted him to don a Mae West. Leahy, *I Was There*, p. 296.

33. Avon, *The Reckoning*, p. 513.

34. Moran, *Churchill*, p. 237.

35. *Yalta*, p. 559. The President's Log.

36. Avon, *The Reckoning*, p. 519.

37. *Yalta*, p. 567.

38. Ibid., p. 570. This is taken from the Hiss notes of informal discussions among the American delegation. 'Mr B' is presumably Bohlen.

39. Ibid., p. 566.

40. Ibid., pp. 570–3. Roosevelt–Stalin meeting, 4 Feb 1945, Bohlen Minutes.

41. Ibid., p. 400. Churchill to Roosevelt, 22 Oct 1944. See also Foreign Secretaries' discussions at Malta, p. 506.

42. Churchill, *Triumph and Tragedy*, p. 305.

43. *Yalta*, p. 575; Bryant, *Triumph in the West*, p. 402; Churchill, *Triumph and Tragedy*, p. 304.

44. *Yalta*, p. 590.

45. Ibid.

46. Ibid., p. 590.

47. Ibid., pp. 611–23. Bohlen Minutes of Second Plenary Meeting, 5 Feb 1945; pp. 624–33, Matthews Minutes.

48. Ibid., pp. 611–12, 624.

49. Ibid., pp. 179, 187. Briefing Book Paper: 'The Treatment of Germany'.

50. Avon, *The Reckoning*, p. 516; Woodward, *British Foreign Policy in the Second World War*, p. 475.

51. Woodward, *British Foreign Policy in the Second World War*, pp. 469–70.

52. Churchill, *Triumph and Tragedy*, p. 306. Memorandum to Eden, 4 Jan 1945.

53. *Yalta*, pp. 655 ff. Meeting of the Foreign Ministers, 6 Feb 1945; also Avon, *The Reckoning*, p. 516.

54. *Yalta*, p. 809.

55. *Yalta*, p. 920; Sherwood, *White House Papers*, vol. II, p. 851.

56. *Yalta*, pp. 978–9.

57. Sherwood, *White House Papers*, vol. II, p. 851.

58. *Yalta*, pp. 620–9. Second Plenary Session of the Conference, Bohlen Minutes.

59. Ibid., p. 634.

60. Ibid., p. 704. Foreign Ministers' meeting, 7 Feb 1945.

61. Ibid., p. 979.

62. See Byrnes, *Speaking Frankly*, p. 29.

63. *Yalta*, pp. 660–3. Third Plenary Meeting, 6 Feb 1945.

64. Ibid., p. 664.

65. Byrnes, *Speaking Frankly*, p. 37.

66. *Yalta*, p. 667.

67. Ibid., p. 77. Third Plenary Meeting 6 Feb 1945, Matthews Minutes.

68. Ibid., p. 669. Third Plenary Meeting, Bohlen Minutes.

69. Ibid.

70. Ibid., p. 726 and n. Draft letter, Roosevelt to Stalin.

71. Ibid., p. 727. Letter, Roosevelt to Stalin, 6 Feb 1945. Also Avon, *The Reckoning*, pp. 516–17.

72. *Yalta*, p. 716. Plenary session, 7 Feb 1945, Bohlen Minutes.

73. For British proposals on the settlement of the Polish problem at the conference, see *Yalta*, pp. 869–70, 870–1, 8 Feb 1945. The British refused to recognize anything other than a representative Polish Government and refused to accept mention of the Western Neisse in any communiqué.

74. Leahy, *I Was There*, p. 284.

75. Woodward, *British Foreign Policy in the Second World War*, p. 349.

76. *Yalta*, p. 781. Fifth Plenary Meeting, 8 Feb 1945, Bohlen Minutes.

77. Ibid., p. 782.

78. Ibid., p. 849. Sixth Plenary Meeting, 9 Feb 1945, 4 p.m.

79. Ibid., p. 820. Memorandum from the British Delegation to the Soviet Delegation regarding the Yugoslav Government, 6 Feb 1945.

80. Ibid., pp. 900–1.
81. Ibid., pp. 712–13. Fourth Plenary Session, 7 Feb 1945. Bohlen Minutes.
82. Ibid.; also Sherwood, *White House Papers*, vol. II, p. 847.
83. Dean Acheson, *Present at the Creation: My Years in the State Department* (London, 1970), p. 103.
84. Avon, *The Reckoning*, p. 517.
85. *Yalta*, p. 714; Sherwood, *White House Papers*, vol. II, p. 852.
86. *Yalta*, p. 746.
87. Ibid., p. 735.
88. Ibid., p. 794.
89. Ibid., pp. 738–40.
90. Avon, *The Reckoning*, p. 515.
91. *Yalta*, p. 767. Roosevelt–Stalin meeting, 8 Feb 1945.
92. Ibid., p. 768. The text is in reported speech.
93. Ibid., p. 984.
94. Avon, *The Reckoning*, p. 513.
95. *Yalta*, pp. 358–61. Briefing Book Paper, 'Postwar Status of Korea'.

96. Ibid., p. 775. Fifth Plenary Session, 8 Feb 1945, Bohlen Minutes.
97. Ibid., p. 84. Memorandum on International Trusteeship submitted to Stettinius, 23 Jan 1945.
98. Ibid.
99. Stimson and Bundy, *On Active Service*, pp. 350–1.
100. Woodward, *British Foreign Policy in the Second World War*, p. 531.
101. Ibid. and n.
102. *Yalta*, p. 844.
103. Avon, *The Reckoning*, p. 514.
104. *Yalta*, p. 844.
105. Ibid., p. 977. Protocol of the proceedings of the conference.
106. Avon, *The Reckoning*, p. 514.
107. *Yalta*, pp. 966–7. Exchange of letters, 10–11 Feb 1945.
108. Ibid., p. 976.
109. Ibid., p. 992.
110. Ibid., pp. 898–900. Seventh Plenary Session, 10 Feb 1945, Bohlen Minutes.
111. Ibid., pp. 849–50.
112. Avon, *The Reckoning*, p. 522.

Chapter 12: Unconditional Surrender of the German Armed Forces

1. *Yalta*, p. 978.
2. Leahy, *I Was There*, p. 387.
3. Ibid.; Major-General John R. Deane, *The Strange Alliance* (London, 1947) pp. 63–4.
4. Churchill, *Triumph and Tragedy*, p. 388; Leahy, *I Was There*, p. 389.
5. Churchill, *Triumph and Tragedy*, p. 392.
6. Leahy, *I Was There*, pp. 390–2; Churchill, *Triumph and Tragedy*, p. 394.
7. Churchill, *Triumph and Tragedy*, p. 398.
8. Leahy, *I Was There*, p. 388.
9. Diary entry for 17 Mar 1945; see Stimson and Bundy, *On Active Service*, p. 607.
10. Leahy, *I Was There*, p. 392.
11. Churchill, *Triumph and Tragedy*, p. 495.
12. Field-Marshal Earl Alexander of Tunis, *Memoirs 1940–1945* (London, 1962) p. 149; *The Italian Campaign, 12 December 1944–2 May 1945: A Report to the Combined Chiefs of Staff by the Supreme Allied Commander, Mediterranean, Field-Marshal Viscount Alexander of Tunis* (London, 1951) Appendix E, 'Negotiations for the German Capitulation'. For an entertaining account of these events, see Eitel Friedrich Moebl-

housen, *Die gebrochene Achse* (Leine, 1949).
13. Wheeler-Bennett, *The Nemesis of Power*, pp. 577–8.
14. Churchill, *Triumph and Tragedy*, pp. 465–6; a somewhat different account, though substantially the same, appears in Count Bernadotte's book *The Curtain Falls* (New York, 1945) pp. 105–29, 136–55. See also Professor Hugh Trevor-Roper's *The Last Days of Hitler*, 2nd ed. (London, 1950) pp. 117, 128–9, 139, and Walter Schellenberg's affidavit sworn at Nuremberg on January 23, 1946.
15. Churchill, *Triumph and Tragedy*, pp. 466–7; Harry S. Truman, *Year of Decisions* (New York, 1955) pp. 88–94; Leahy, *I Was There*, pp. 415–16.
16. Churchill, *Triumph and Tragedy*, pp. 467–8; *Stalin's Correspondence*, vol. I, pp. 332–5; vol. II, pp. 222–3.
17. Field-Marshal the Viscount Montgomery of Alamein, K.G., *Memoirs* (London, 1958) pp. 334–40; Major-General Sir Francis de Guingand, *Operation Victory* (London, 1947) pp. 453–4; Eisenhower, *Crusade in Europe*, p. 463; Grand-Admiral Karl Doenitz, *Memoirs* (London, 1959) pp. 45–46; Walter Lüdde-Neurath, *Regierung Doenitz* (Göttingen, 1964) pp. 61–7; Count Lutz Schwerin von Krosigk, *Es*

Geschan in Deutschland (Tübingen, 1951) pp. 367–70; also 'The Beginning and the End', Diary of Count Lutz Schwerin von Krosigk, 5 Nov 1932–5 February 1933 and 15 Apr–1 May 1945 (Wheeler-Bennett Papers, St Antony's College, Oxford); Marlis G. Steinert, *Capitulation 1945* (London, 1969); Strong, *Intelligence at the Top*, chap. 9.

18. Lord Strang, *Home and Abroad*.

(London, 1956) pp. 199–225; Moseley, *The Kremlin and World Politics*, pp. 142–154; John Counsell, *Counsel's Opinion* (London, 1963) pp. 148–53; Deane, *Strange Alliance*, pp. 166–71.

19. Eisenhower, *Crusade in Europe*, pp. 464–5; Butcher, *Three Years with Eisenhower*, pp. 682–93.

20. Bryant, *Triumph in the West*, p. 456.

Chapter 13: Germany Divided: the Zones of Occupation

1. Woodward, *British Foreign Policy*, pp. 524–6.

2. Ibid. When the Cabinet discussed the Treasury memorandum on 22 Mar, Mr Churchill reiterated his desire to see Prussia isolated from the rest of Germany.

3. *Yalta*, p. 187.

4. *Foreign Relations of the United States: The Conference of Berlin (Potsdam)* (Washington, 1960) vol. 1, p. 460. Hereafter cited as *Potsdam*.

5. Ibid., pp. 439–40, 447.

6. Woodward, *British Foreign Policy*, p. 465.

7. Ibid., p. 527; *Potsdam*, vol. 1, p. 445.

8. *Potsdam*, vol. 1, p. 50.

9. Ibid.

10. Ibid., p. 455.

11. H.-P. Schwarz, *Vom Reich zur Bundesrepublik. Deutschland im Widerstreit der aussenpolitischen Konzeptionen in den Jahren der Besatzungsherrschaft 1945–1949* (Neuwied and Berlin, 1966) p. 236. Also Wolfgang Leonhard, *Child of the Revolution* (London, 1957) pp. 289–3; Wheeler-Bennett, *Nemesis of Power*, pp. 614–21, 716–23.

12. Woodward, *British Foreign Policy*, pp. 469–70.

13. See William M. Franklin, 'Zonal Boundaries and Access Routes to Berlin', *World Politics* (Oct 1963) pp. 1–31.

14. Lord Strang, 'Prelude to Potsdam', in 'Potsdam after twenty-five years', *International Affairs* (July 1970) p. 450.

15. *Cairo and Tehran*, pp. 255–6; Franklin, 'Zonal Boundaries', p. 11.

16. Franklin, 'Zonal Boundaries', p. 12.

17. Franklin, 'Zonal Boundaries'. pp. 18–20.

18. George F. Kennan, *Memoirs 1925–1950* (Boston, 1967) p. 168; Franklin, 'Zonal Boundaries', p. 17; Strang, *Home and Abroad*, pp. 208, 212–15.

19. Kennan, *Memoirs*, pp. 168–71; also Feis, *Churchill, Roosevelt, Stalin*, p. 362.

20. Franklin, 'Zonal Boundaries', p. 23.

21. Churchill, *Triumph and Tragedy*, p. 489.

22. Churchill, *Triumph and Tragedy*, p. 469. This was a phrase used to Mr Eden but it summed up the Prime Minister's view.

23. Mr Churchill sent a message to Roosevelt on 5 Apr expressing concern about Austria, and urging the furthest possible eastward expansion of Anglo-American forces into Germany. See *Triumph and Tragedy*, p. 446. For his messages to Truman on this subject, see ibid., pp. 448, 450, 496–7, 524, 525–6.

24. Ibid., p. 448.

25. Ibid., p. 443.

26. Ibid., p. 525; Eisenhower, *Crusade in Europe*, pp. 517–18.

27. Cf. Ehrman, *Grand Strategy*, vol. VI, p. 152.

28. *Potsdam*, vol. 1, pp. 598–9. Winant to Secretary of State, 7 July 1945.

29. Ibid., pp. 603 4; vol. II, pp. 1001–2.

30. *Cairo and Tehran*, p. 254.

31. Clay, *Decision in Germany*, p. 26. See also Murphy, *Diplomat among Warriors*, pp. 322–3.

32. Murphy, *Diplomat among Warriors*, p. 281.

33. *Potsdam*, vol. II, pp. 1483–4.

34. Eisenhower, *Crusade in Europe*, p. 478; Clay, *Decision in Germany*, p. 107.

35. Moran, *Churchill*, p. 298.

36. Murphy, *Diplomat among Warriors*, p. 348.

37. Strang, *Home and Abroad*, p. 234. Cf. Lord Strang's conversation with the Mayor of Hamburg, Dr Petersen.

38. Soviet Military Administration Order No. 2. See B. Ruhm von Oppen, *Documents on Germany under Occupation, 1945–1954* (Oxford, 1955) pp. 37–8. Also

Philip Windsor, *City on Leave: A History of Berlin* (London, 1963) pp. 34-5.

39. Leonhard, *Child of the Revolution*, p. 303; Schwarz, *Vom Reich zur Bundes-*

republik. pp. 236-7 and n. 50, p. 748. Also Oppen, *Documents on Germany*, pp. 64-6.

40. Windsor, *City on Leave*, p. 14 n.

41. *Potsdam*, vol. II, pp. 1561-2.

Chapter 14: The Road to Potsdam

1. Quoted by Virginia Cowles in *The Russian Dagger* (London, 1969) p. 21.

2. *Stalin's Correspondence*, vol. I, pp. 306-8; vol. II, pp. 194-7.

3. Kennan, *Memoirs*, p. 252.

4. *Stalin's Correspondence*, vol. I, pp. 309-10, 313-16, 324-6, 330-1, 338-44, 346-8; vol. II, pp. 201-4, 211-13, 215-17, 218-20, 225-7, 228-9, 231-2; Woodward, *British Foreign Policy*, pp. 502-6, 507-14; Raczyński, *In Allied London*, pp. 284-99.

5. Told to Sir John Wheeler-Bennett by Harold Macmillan on 9 June 1964. Cf. *Winds of Change, 1914-1939* (London, 1966) p. 14.

6. Lord Strang, *Britain in World Affairs* (London, 1961) p. 55.

7. Television interview with Baroness Asquith of Yarnbury by Kenneth Harris on 13 Apr 1967. See *The Listener*, 17 Aug 1967.

8. John Colville in *Action This Day*, ed. Sir John Wheeler-Bennett (London, 1968) pp. 93, 97.

9. Churchill. *Triumph and Tragedy*, p. 496.

10. *Das Reich*, 25 Feb 1945; *The Times*, 3 May 1945 and 11 Oct 1966 (letter from Lord Conesford).

11. *Potsdam*, vol. I, p. 92.

12. Byrnes, *Speaking Frankly*, p. 74; *Potsdam*, vol. II, p. 362.

13. *The Novels of Thomas Love Peacock*, ed. David Garnett (London, 1948) p. 839.

14. Churchill, *Triumph and Tragedy*, pp. 498-9; *Potsdam*, vol. I, p. 9.

15. Duke of Alba's Report No. 502 (30 Oct 1943) on a conversation at luncheon with Mr Churchill on 22 Oct 1943. Quoted by Brian Croziei, *Franco* (London, 1967) pp. 378-9.

16. Viscount Templewood, *Ambassador on Special Mission* (London, 1946), p. 189.

17. Colville, in *Action this Day*, pp. 132-7.

18. Churchill, *The Hinge of Fate*, p. 177.

19. Hon. William Bullitt, 'How we Won the War and Lost the Peace', *Life Magazine*, 30 Aug 1948, p. 94.

20. Elliott Roosevelt, *As He Saw It*, p. 185.

21. Moran, *Churchill*, p. 132.

22. Djilas, *Conversations with Stalin*, p. 73.

23. Hon. James Forrestal *Diaries* (London, 1952) p. 53.

24. Leahy, *I Was There*, p. 340.

25. Letter from Mrs Paul Hoffman to the Hon. Averell Harriman dated 3 June 1963 (a copy of which has been given to Sir John Wheeler-Bennett). Mrs Hoffman adds: 'These were his exact words. I remembered them and verified them with Mrs Roosevelt shortly before her death' (on 7 Nov 1962). The fact that Mrs Hoffman lunched with the President and Mrs Roosevelt on 24 Mar is recorded by William D. Hassett, one of the President's assistant private secretaries, in *Off the Record with F.D.R. 1942-1945* (New Brunswick, N.J., 1958) p. 326.

26. *Stalin's Correspondence*, vol. II, pp. 207-8.

27. Ibid., p. 214.

28. Truman, *Year of Decisions*, p. 14.

29. *Mr President: Personal Diaries, Private Letters, Papers and Revealing Interviews of Harry S. Truman*, ed. William Hillman (London, 1952) p. 99.

30. Avon, *The Reckoning*, p. 529.

31. *Congressional Record – House*, 6 June 1967, p. H.6736.

32. See Minutes of the sixteenth meeting of the United States Delegation to the San Francisco Conference, 25 Apr 1945. *Foreign Relations of the United States: Diplomatic Papers, 1945* (Washington, 1967) vol. I, General: *The United Nations*, pp. 389-90.

33. *Congressional Record – House*, 6 June 1967, p. H.6736; Truman, *Year of Decisions*, pp. 70-2.

34. *Congressional Record*, ibid.

35. Churchill, *Triumph and Tragedy*, pp. 437-9, 496-7; Woodward, *British Foreign Policy*, pp. 518-20; Truman, *Year of Decisions*, pp. 255-6.

36. Truman, *Year of Decisions*, p. 265.

37. Hillman (ed.), *Mr President*, p. 99.

38. Sherwood, *White House Papers*, vol. II, pp. 874-5.

39. Hillman (ed.), *Mr President*, p. 99.
40. *Potsdam*, vol. I, pp. 21–2; *Stalin's Correspondence*, vol. II, p. 234.
41. *Potsdam*, vol. I, pp. 22–3.
42. Forrestal, *Diaries*, p. 73; Hillman (ed.), *Mr President*, p. 99.
43. Hillman (ed.), *Mr President*, pp. 98–9; *Potsdam*, vol. I, p. 63.
44. Avon, *The Reckoning*, p. 539. Diary entry for 29 May 1945.
45. Truman, *Year of Decisions*, p. 260.
46. Ibid., pp. 260–2; Leahy, *I Was There*, pp. 441–5; *Potsdam*, vol. I, pp. 64–81; Churchill, *Triumph and Tragedy*, pp. 502–5.
47. Hillman (ed.), *Mr President*, p. 99.
48. *Potsdam*, vol. I, pp. 24–60; Sherwood, *White House Papers*, vol. II, pp. 875–905.
49. Herbert Feis, *Between War and Peace* (Princeton, 1960) pp. 97–116.
50. *Potsdam*, vol. I, p. 61. Telegram to President Truman, 8 June 1945.
51. Kennan, *Memoirs*, pp. 212–13.

Chapter 15: San Francisco and Potsdam

1. Avon, *The Reckoning*, p. 525.
2. Ibid., p. 529.
3. For Anglo-American views and consultations on this point, see Woodward, *British Foreign Policy*, pp. 506–9; Leahy, *I Was There*, p. 353; Truman, *Year of Decisions*, p. 78.
4. Truman, *Year of Decisions*, p. 79.
5. Churchill, *Triumph and Tragedy*. p. 428.
6. Forrestal, *Diaries*, p. 80.
7. Truman, *Year of Decisions*, p. 80.
8. Forrestal, *Diaries*, p. 66; Truman, *Year of Decisions*, pp. 80–2.
9. Stimson and Bundy, *On Active Service*, p. 358.
10. Truman, *Year of Decisions*, pp. 83–5. The quotations have been transposed from reported to direct speech.
11. For Mr Harriman's strong warnings to the American delegation on the situation in Eastern Europe, see *Foreign Relations of the United States, 1945*, vol. I, pp. 389–90.
12. *Potsdam*, vol. I, p. 28.
13. Ibid., p. 39.
14. Woodward, *British Foreign Policy*, p. 507; Churchill, *Triumph and Tragedy*, pp. 384–5.
15. *Potsdam*, vol. I, p. 55.
16. *Foreign Relations, 1945*, vol. IV, p. 431. Report of conversation between Harriman and Beneš, 31 Mar 1945.
17. Kennan, *Memoirs*, p. 254.
18. *Foreign Relations, 1945*, vol. IV, p. 432.
19. Ibid., p. 445. Repeated in Churchill, *Triumph and Tragedy*, p. 442; see also Avon, *The Reckoning*, pp. 532–3.
20. *Foreign Relations, 1945*, vol. IV, p. 451.
21. John Ehrman, *Grand Strategy*, vol. VI, p. 161.
22. For American views on what happened in Czechoslovakia during May–July 1945, see ibid., pp. 456–78.
23. Ibid., vol. V, p. 990.
24. *Yalta*, p. 313.
25. See, for example, *Foreign Relations, 1945*, vol. V, p. 990.
26. Ibid., p. 999.
27. Truman, *Year of Decisions*, p. 145. Also *Foreign Relations, 1945*, vol. V, p. 1000.
28. Truman, *Year of Decisions*, p. 146.
29. *Potsdam*, vol. I, p. 35.
30. For statements of the Soviet and American points of view on Lend-Lease, see the discussion between Harriman and Mikoyan in Moscow on 11 June 1945, *Foreign Relations, 1945*, vol. V, pp. 1018–1021.
31. For Forrestal's fears, see Forrestal, *Diaries*, pp. 72–3. For Harriman's views, see *Foreign Relations, 1945*, vol. I, pp. 389–90.
32. *Potsdam*, vol. I, pp. 155, 242, 295, 320, 417, 505, 552, 596, 700, 781, 958, 971, 1009, 1052.
33. Churchill, *Triumph and Tragedy*, p. 529.
34. Ibid., pp. 530–1.
35. Moran, *Churchill*, p. 296.
36. Truman, *Year of Decisions*, p. 290.
37. Avon, *The Reckoning*, pp. 543–4.
38. Kennan, *Memoirs*, p. 364; also *Potsdam*, vol. II, p. 305.
39. Ehrman, *Grand Strategy*, vol. VI, p. 303.
40. This point is well made in G. Kolko, *The Politics of War: Allied Diplomacy and the World Crisis of 1943–45* (London, 1968) p. 539.
41. Churchill, *Triumph and Tragedy*, p. 553.
42. *Potsdam*, vol. II, pp. 47, 81–2, 378–9; Truman, *Year of Decisions*, p. 346.
43. Robert Cecil, 'Potsdam and its

Legends', in 'Potsdam after Twenty-five Years, *International Affairs*, XLVI, 3 (July 1970) 464–6.

44. Woodward, *British Foreign Policy*, pp. 538–9; *Potsdam*, vol. I, p. 320.

45. Avon, *The Reckoning*, p. 546.

46. Ibid.

47. Woodward, *British Foreign Policy*, p. 538.

48. Avon, *The Reckoning*, p. 546.

49. Truman, *Year of Decisions*. p. 265.

50. *Potsdam*, vol. II, p. 1584. Bohlen's reconstruction of the Truman–Stalin meeting on 17 July 1945.

51. Woodward, *British Foreign Policy*, p. 537.

52. For the draft of this U.S. proposal, see *Potsdam*, vol. II, p. 610.

53. *Potsdam*, vol. II, p. 67.

54. Ibid., pp. 1478–80.

55. Woodward, *British Foreign Policy*, p. 550.

56. Ibid., pp. 408–9, 538.

57. *Potsdam*, vol. II, p. 180.

58. Ibid., p. 207.

59. Ibid., pp. 228–32.

60. Ibid., p. 230.

61. Ibid., p. 380.

62. Ibid., p. 1494.

63. Ibid., pp. 1492–3.

64. Ibid., p. 729.

65. Ibid., pp. 274, 297.

66. Ibid., pp. 296–7, 863.

67. Ibid., p. 98.

68. Ibid., p. 1508.

69. Truman, *Year of Decisions*, p. 296.

70. *Potsdam*, vol. II, pp. 249–52.

71. Ibid., pp. 250, 386.

72. Ibid., pp. 1522–4.

73. Ibid., p. 356; and Rozek, *Allied Wartime Diplomacy*, pp. 408–9.

74. *Potsdam*, vol. II, pp. 381 ff.

75. Ibid., p. 384.

76. Ibid., p. 385.

77. Churchill, *Triumph and Tragedy*, p. 581.

78. Cecil, 'Potsdam and its Legends', p. 456.

79. Churchill, *Triumph and Tragedy*, p. 566.

80. Ibid., pp. 548–9.

81. Ibid. Also Moran, *Churchill*, p. 295.

82. Avon, *The Reckoning*, p. 545.

83. Leahy, *I Was There*, p. 412.

84. Ibid., Truman, *Year of Decisions*, p. 287.

85. *Potsdam*, vol. II, p. 461.

86. Clement Attlee, *As It Happened* (London, 1954) p. 149.

87. *Potsdam*, vol. II, p. 55.

88. Ibid., p. 459; Byrnes, *Speaking Frankly*, p. 79.

89. Leahy, *I Was There*, p. 420.

90. See *Potsdam*, vol. II, p. 1150; for U.S. proposal to this effect.

91. Ibid., pp. 471–7.

92. Ibid., p. 1538.

93. Ibid., p. 480.

94. Ibid., p. 485.

95. Woodward, *British Foreign Policy*, pp. 562–3; Churchill, *Triumph and Tragedy*, pp. 573–7.

96. *Potsdam*, vol. II, p. 519.

97. Woodward, *British Foreign Policy*, pp. 564–5.

98. *Potsdam*, vol. II, pp. 528–33.

99. Ibid., p. 1500.

100. For Bevin's difficulties with Byrnes in Moscow in December 1945, see Kennan, *Memoirs*, pp. 286–8.

101. Truman, *Year of Decisions*, p. 331.

Chapter 16: The Unconditional Surrender of Japan

1. *Documents on German Foreign Policy, 1918–1945*, series D (1937–45), vol. XII, pp. 376–83. Record of conversation between the Reich Foreign Minister [von Ribbentrop] and the Japanese Foreign Minister, at Berlin, on 27 Mar 1941.

2. Churchill, *The Grand Alliance*, pp. 528, 538–9.

3. Lieut.-General Joseph V. Stillwell, *Stillwell Papers*, ed. Theodore H. White (New York, 1948) p. 106.

4. Mamoru Shigemitsu, *Japan and her Destiny* (London, 1958) p. 214.

5. Forrest C. Pogue, *George C.

Marshall: Ordeal and Hope, 1939–1942* (New York, 1966) p. 239.

6. Sherwood, *White House Papers*, vol. II, p. 745.

7. Hull, *Memoirs*, vol. II, 1309–10.

8. Avon, *The Reckoning*, p. 418.

9. Ibid., p. 488.

10. Deane, *The Strange Alliance*, pp. 247–8. Lord Avon in his account of the Moscow Conference of 1944 makes no mention of this scene.

11. Churchill, *Triumph and Tragedy*, pp. 388–9.

12. *Yalta*, pp. 383–4.

13. Edward R. Stettinius, *Roosevelt and the Russians at Yalta* (New York, 1949) pp. 33–4; *Military Situation in the Far East*, Hearing before the Committee on Armed Services and the Committee on Foreign Relations, U.S. Senate, 82nd Congress, 1st Session, pt 4, p. 3120.

14. Sherwood, *White House Papers*, vol. II, p. 856; Truman, *Year of Decisions*, p. 265.

15. Stettinius, *Roosevelt and the Russians*, p. 90; *Yalta*, p. 396.

16. Avon, *The Reckoning*, pp. 507–8.

17. *Yalta*, pp. 894–7; Churchill, *Triumph and Tragedy*, pp. 341–2.

18. *Yalta*, p. 984.

19. Keith Eubank, *The Summit Conferences, 1919–1960* (Norman, Okla., 1966) p. 104.

20. Avon, *The Reckoning*, p. 513.

21. Stettinius, *Roosevelt and the Russians*, p. 94.

22. Shigeru Yoshida, *Memoirs* (London, 1961) p. 24.

23. Robert J. C. Butow, *Japan's Decision to Surrender* (Stanford, Calif., 1954) p. 14 and n. 15. Mr Butow's book, based upon meticulous research on documentary sources hitherto untapped, is of the greatest value.

24. Yoshida, *Memoirs*, pp. 22–3; Butow, *Japan's Decision to Surrender*, pp. 14–15. There is some discrepancy here. Butow asserts that the only result of this suggestion by Yoshida was 'a mutual pledge between himself and the Lord Privy Seal [Kido] to work for peace'. Yoshida, on the other hand, complains that, when sounded about the matter, Kido 'refrained from giving me a straight answer', and makes no mention of any mutual pledge.

25. Captain Ellis M. Zacharias, U.S.N., *Secret Missions* (New York, 1946) p. 321; Shigemitsu, *Japan and her Destiny*, p. 302.

26. Shigemitsu, *Japan and her Destiny*, p. 302.

27. Butow, *Japan's Decision to Surrender*, pp. 16–19.

28. Ibid., pp. 19–20, n. 37; Shigemitsu, *Japan and her Destiny*, pp. 326–7.

29. Wesley R. Fishel, 'A Japanese Peace Manœuvre in 1944', *Far Eastern Quarterly* (now the *Journal for Asian Studies*) (New York), Aug 1949.

30. Shigemitsu, *Japan and her Destiny*, pp. 338–9.

31. Butow, *Japan's Decision to Surrender*, pp. 54–5 ff.

32. Churchill, *Triumph and Tragedy*, pp. 478–9.

33. Truman, *Year of Decisions*, p. 207.

34. Ibid., p. 76.

35. *Potsdam*, vol. I, pp. 45–7.

36. Sherwood, *White House Papers*, vol. II, pp. 891–3.

37. *Potsdam*, vol. I, pp. 61–2.

38. Feis, *Between War and Peace*, pp. 112–13.

39. Truman, *Year of Decisions*, p. 265.

40. Ibid., pp. 268–70; *Stalin's Correspondence* vol. II, p. 246.

41. *United States Relations with China* (Washington, 1949) pp. 94–8; Ambassador Hurley's testimony in *Hearings on the Military Situation in the Far East*, before the U.S. Senate Committee on Armed Services and Foreign Relations (Washington, 1951) pp. 2827–62; Ambassador Bohlen's testimony in *Hearings of the Nomination of Charles E. Bohlen*, before the U.S. Senate Committee on Foreign Relations (Washington, 1953) pp. 2–113; *Communist China*, ed. Franz Schumann and Orville Schell (New York, 1967) pp. 237–42; A. Doak Barnett, *Communist China and Asia* (New York, 1961) pp. 337–51; Djilas, *Conversations with Stalin*, p. 182; Robert C. North, *Moscow and the Chinese Communists* (Stanford, Calif., 1953) pp. 208–28; Max Beloff, *Soviet Policy in the Far East, 1944–1951* (Oxford, 1953) pp. 20–53.

42. Truman, *Year of Decisions*, p. 265.

43. Ibid., p. 417.

44. Stimson and Bundy, *On Active Service*, p. 619; Morison, *Turmoil and Tradition*, p. 622.

45. U.S. Dept of Defence, *The Entry of the Soviet Union into the War against Japan: Military Plans, 1941–1945* (Washington, 1955) pp. 51–2.

46. Leahy, *I Was There*, p. 450.

47. *Potsdam*, vol. I, p. 910.

48. Deane, *The Strange Alliance*, pp. 262–5; *Entry of the Soviet Union into the War against Japan*, pp. 60–1.

49. Truman, *Year of Decisions*, pp. 314–15, 322–3, 411; *Potsdam*, vol. I, p. 909.

50. Conversations between John McCloy and James Forrestal, 8 Mar 1947. See Forrestal, *Diaries*, p. 83.

51. Sherwood, *White House Papers* vol. II, p. 892.

52. Shigenori Togo, *The Cause of Japan* (New York, 1956) pp. 289–90; Butow, *Japan's Decision to Surrender*, pp. 90–2.

53. Togo, *The Cause of Japan*, pp. 298–303; Shigemitsu, *Japan and her Destiny*, pp. 356–7.

54. *Potsdam*, vol. I, pp. 874–83.

55. Butow, *Japan's Decision to Surrender*, pp. 103–11.

56. Leahy, *I Was There*, p. 449.

57. Correspondence and personal conversations between Sir John Wheeler-Bennett and the Hon. Allen Dulles, Oct–Nov 1967.

58. Forrestal, *Diaries*, pp. 86–7.

59. *Potsdam*, vol. I, p. 893.

60. See a memorandum to Secretary of State Hull for the consideration of the State Department Postwar Planning Committee, dated Apr 1944; Joseph C. Grew, *Turbulent Era* (London, 1953) vol. II, pp. 1408–15; and also Mr Grew's evidence on the occasion of his appointment as Under-Secretary of State, 12 Dec 1944, *Hearings before the Committee on Foreign Relations*, 78th Congress, 2nd Session (Washington, 1944) pp. 17–19.

61. Hull, *Memoirs*, vol. II, pp. 1591–3.

62. Woodward, *British Foreign Policy*, pp. 570–1.

63. Forrestal, *Diaries*, p. 92; *Potsdam*, vol. II, p. 477.

64. The Marshal reported this conversation with the President in his address to the Chinese people on 1 Jan 1944. *The Collected War-time Messages of Generalissimo Chiang Kai-shek, 1937–1945* (New York, 1946) vol. II, p. 779.

65. *Potsdam*, vol. I, p. 44.

66. See Grew, *Turbulent Era*, vol. II, pp. 1421–5; Stimson and Bundy, *On Active Service*, pp. 619–27; *Potsdam*, vol. I, pp. 885–7; Forrestal, *Diaries*, pp. 79, 81–3.

67. *Potsdam*, vol. I, pp. 900–1.

68. Hull, *Memoirs*, vol. II, pp. 1593–4.

69. Truman, *Year of Decisions*, p. 417.

70. Ibid., p. 341.

71. Ibid., p. 341; Hillman (ed.), *Mr President*, p. 123.

72. Byrnes, *Speaking Frankly*, p. 205; and *All in One Lifetime* (London, 1960) p. 291.

73. *Potsdam*, vol. II, p. 1586.

74. For the account of the Churchill-Stalin conversation of 17 July, see Ehrman, *Grand Strategy*, vol, VI, p. 302.

75. For the account of the Churchill-Truman conversation of 18 July, see ibid., pp. 302–3.

76. *Potsdam*, vol. II, p. 1360.

77. Truman, *Year of Decisions*, p. 415.

78. *Potsdam*, vol. II, p. 1266.

79. Churchill, *Triumph and Tragedy*, pp. 551–2.

80. Avon, *The Reckoning*, p. 547.

81. Churchill, *Triumph and Tragedy*, p. 554. There is no known American record of this conversation.

82. *Potsdam*, vol. II, Document 1305, p. 1361.

83. Mr Stimson's diary entry for 21 and 22 July 1945; see *Potsdam*, vol. II, pp. 203, 225.

84. Murphy, *Diplomat among Warriors*, p. 338.

85. Harvey and Bundy, 'Remembered Words', *Atlantic Monthly* (Boston, Mass.) (Mar 1957) p. 57.

86. Churchill, *Triumph and Tragedy*, pp. 552–3; Truman, *Year of Decisions*, p. 419.

87. Leahy, *I Was There*, pp. 475–7.

88. Avon, *The Reckoning*, p. 547.

89. *Potsdam*, vol. II, p. 243.

90. Byrnes, *All in One Lifetime*, p. 285.

91. For a detailed account of the sequence of events leading to the British consent to use of the atomic weapon, see Ehrman, *Grand Strategy*, vol. VI, pp. 296–8; also *Potsdam*, vol. I, pp. 941–2, Minutes of a meeting of the Combined Policy Committee in Washington, 4 July 1945.

92. Churchill, *Triumph and Tragedy*, p. 553.

93. Truman, *Year of Decisions*, p. 416.

94. Byrnes, *All in One Lifetime*, pp. 300–1.

95. Churchill, *Triumph and Tragedy*, pp. 579–80.

96. *New York Herald Tribune*, 11 Feb 1950.

97. *Report of the Royal Commission appointed under Order in Council P.C. 411 of February 5, 1946* (Ottawa, 1946) pp. 447 ff.

98. Lieutenant-General Leslie R. Groves, *Now It Can Be Told* (New York, 1962) p. 184.

99. Mr Stimson's diary entry for 22 July 1945. *Potsdam*, vol. II, p. 225.

100. Herbert Feis, *The Atomic Bomb and the End of World War II* (Princeton, 1966) p. 102, n. 67; confirmed to Sir John

Wheeler-Bennett by the Hon. Averell Harriman, Jan 1968.

101. Churchill, *Triumph and Tragedy*, p. 553; Ehrman, *Grand Strategy*, vol. VI, p. 292.

102. Forrestal's diary entry for 28 July 1945 with record of conversation with Byrnes. Forrestal, *Diaries*, p. 90.

103. *Potsdam*, vol. II, Document 1213, pp. 1224-5.

104. Ibid., Document 1216, p. 1241; Byrnes, *All in One Lifetime*, p. 291.

105. Minutes of Tripartite Meeting of the Joint Chiefs of Staff, 24 July 1945. *Potsdam*, vol. II, p. 345.

106. U.S. Department of the Army, Office of the Chief of Military History, *Command Decisions* (Washington, 1967) p. 499; Truman, *Year of Decisions*, p. 11.

107. Wheeler-Bennett, *King George VI*, p. 645; Leahy, *I Was There*, pp. 502-3; Byrnes, *Speaking Frankly*, pp. 263-4.

108. Forrestal, *Diaries*, p. 90.

109. Leahy, *I Was There*, p. 431. Harriman later expressed similar views before a United States Congressional Committee: *MacArthur Hearings*, 82nd Congress, 1st Session (Washington, 1951) pt 5, p. 3341.

110. General Douglas MacArthur, *Reminiscences* (New York, 1965, paperback ed.) pp. 301-2.

111. Ehrman, *Grand Strategy*, vol. VI, pp. 301-3.

112. *Potsdam*, vol. I, pp. 897-9.

113. Truman, *Year of Decisions*, p. 387.

114. For an account of the Anglo-American exchanges and a comparison of the two drafts, see *Potsdam*, vol. II, pp. 1275-7.

115. Ehrman, *Grand Strategy*, vol. VI, p. 306; *Potsdam*, vol. II, pp. 1267-78.

116. *Potsdam*, vol. II, p. 1279.

117. Ibid., p. 1282; Truman, *Year of Decisions*, p. 390.

118. *Potsdam*, vol. II, p. 1275, n. 1; Truman, *Year of Decisions*, p. 387; Byrnes, *All in One Lifetime*, pp. 296-7.

119. *Potsdam*, vol. II, pp. 1474-6.

120. For a comparison of the Proclamation of 26 July 1945 with the policy of the Department of State see text of a memorandum prepared in the Office of Far Eastern Affairs for the consideration of the meeting of the Secretary of State's Staff Committee held on 30 July. *Potsdam*, vol. II, pp. 1284-9.

121. Zacharias, *Secret Missions*, pp. 370-1.

122. For text of broadcast, see Zacharias, *Secret Missions*, pp. 420-1.

123. Telegram from Acting Secretary of State Grew to Secretary Byrnes, 22 July 1945. See *Potsdam*, vol. II, pp. 1273-1274.

124. Ibid., pp. 1260-2.

125. Zacharias, *Secret Missions*, pp. 373-4.

126. Shigemitsu, *Japan and her Destiny*, p. 358.

127. Togo, *The Cause of Japan*, pp. 311-13.

128. *Potsdam*, vol. II, p. 1293.

129. Toshikazu Kase, *Eclipse of the Rising Sun* (London, 1951) p. 211.

130. Kazuo Kanai, 'Mokusatsu: Japan's Response to the Potsdam Declaration', *Pacific Historical Review* (Nov 1950) p. 413.

131. Togo, *The Cause of Japan*, p. 314.

132. Kanai, 'Mokusatsu', p. 412. For a considered discussion of this point, see Butow, *Japan's Decision to Surrender*, pp. 143-9.

133. Togo, *The Cause of Japan*, p. 314.

134. Stimson, 'The Decision to Use the Atom Bomb', *Harper's Magazine*, Feb 1947; Stimson and Bundy, *On Active Service*, p. 625.

135. *Potsdam*, vol. II, p. 1375.

136. Lord Attlee, 'The Hiroshima Choice', *Observer*, 6 Sep 1959.

137. Truman, *Year of Decisions*, pp. 420-1.

138. Ibid., pp. 412-13; Wheeler-Bennett, *King George VI*, pp. 643-4.

139. Truman, *Year of Decisions*, p. 421; Byrnes, *All in One Lifetime*, p. 304.

140. *Potsdam*, vol. II, p. 476.

141. Truman, *Year of Decisions*, pp. 401-2.

142. Byrnes, *All in One Lifetime*, pp. 297-8.

143. *Potsdam*, vol. II, pp. 1333-4. See also Byrnes, *Speaking Frankly*, pp. 208-9; *All in One Lifetime*, p. 298; Truman, *Year of Decisions*, pp. 403-4.

144. Leahy, *I Was There*, pp. 494-5.

145. *Stalin's Correspondence*, vol. II, p. 258.

146. Feis, *The Atomic Bomb and the End of World War II*, p. 111.

147. *Potsdam*, vol. II, pp. 1297-8; Ehrman, *Grand Strategy*, vol. VI, p. 308.

148. Togo, *The Cause of Japan*, p. 316.

149. Truman, *Year of Decisions*, p. 425.

150. *New York Times*, 9 Aug 1945.

151. Shigemitsu, *Japan and her Destiny*, p. 359.

152. Butow, *Japan's Decision to Surrender*, p. 151.

153. Shigemitsu, *Japan and her Destiny*, pp. 359–60.

154. Truman, *Year of Decisions*, p. 426.

155. Togo, *The Cause of Japan*, p. 315.

156. Byrnes, *Speaking Frankly*, p. 264.

157. Togo, *The Cause of Japan*, pp. 316–21; Shigemitsu, *Japan and her Destiny*, p. 361; Butow, *Japan's Decision to Surrender*, pp. 159–76.

158. Truman, *Year of Decisions*, p. 423.

159. Ibid., p. 425.

160. Stimson and Bundy, *On Active Service*, pp. 628–33; Forrestal, *Diaries*, pp. 94–5; Leahy, *I Was There*, p. 506; Grew, *Turbulent Era*, vol. II, pp. 1438–40.

161. Truman, *Year of Decisions*, pp. 428–9; Byrnes, *All in One Lifetime*, p. 305.

162. Truman, *Year of Decisions*, p. 430.

163. Pierson Dixon, *Double Diploma: The Life of Sir Pierson Dixon* (London, 1968) p. 180.

164. Ibid., pp. 180–1.

165. Ehrman, *Grand Strategy*, vol. VI, p. 312; Togo, *The Cause of Japan*, p. 324.

166. Truman, *Year of Decisions*, pp. 430–1; Byrnes, *All in One Lifetime*, p. 306.

167. Togo, *The Cause of Japan*, p. 335; Shigemitsu, *Japan and her Destiny*, pp. 364–6.

168. Togo, *The Cause of Japan*, pp. 324–34; Shigemitsu, *Japan and her Destiny*, pp. 362–3; Butow, *Japan's Decision to Surrender*, pp. 192–209; and also *Japan's Longest Day* (London, 1968), a publication of the Pacific War Research Society of Tokyo, on the events of 14–15 August 1945.

169. MacArthur, *Reminiscences*, p. 311.

170. For a moving Japanese account of the surrender in Tokyo Bay, see Kase, *Eclipse of the Rising Sun*, pp. 2–10.

Chapter 17: The Trial and Punishment of the Nazi War Criminals

1. *New York Times*, 22 Aug 1942.

2. Hull, *Memoirs*, vol. II, pp. 1289–90.

3. Henry L. Stimson, 'The Nuremberg Trial: Landmark in Law', *Foreign Affairs* (New York), Jan 1947.

4. Moran, *Churchill*, p. 141; Bohlen Minutes, *Cairo and Tehran*, pp. 553–4; Elliott Roosevelt, *As He Saw It*, pp. 188–189; Churchill, *Closing the Ring*, p. 330 and p. 621.

5. As quoted by Lord Curzon in a report on his negotiations in Paris to the Imperial War Cabinet on 20 Nov 1918; see David Lloyd George, *The Truth about the Treaties* (London, 1938) vol. I, p. 98.

6. Statement at the Inter-Allied Conference in London on 1 Dec 1918. Ibid., p. 142.

7. Ibid., p. 140.

8. Mr Lansing's Papers and Diaries have been deposited in the Library of Congress at Washington; a careful study of them in regard to this subject has been made by James Morgan Read in *Atrocity Propaganda 1914–1919* (New York, 1941).

9. Lloyd George, *The Truth about the Treaties*, vol. I, pp. 178, 463.

10. *The Times*, 1 Dec and 10 Dec 1918. See also John Maynard Keynes, *The Economic Consequences of the Peace* (London, 1920) pp. 129–31.

11. Princess Wilhelmina of the Netherlands, *Lonely but not alone* (London, 1960) p. 107; *Dutch Orange Book, June 1919–April 1920* (The Hague, 1920).

12. Claud Mullins, *The Leipzig Trials* (London, 1921).

13. *The Times*, 18 Sep 1927.

14. *The Times*, 12 July 1932.

15. *Collected Speeches of Adolf Hitler, 1922–1939*, ed. Norman H. Baynes (Oxford, 1942) vol. II, pp. 1335–6.

16. *Conference on the Limitation of Armament, November 12, 1921–February 6, 1922: Verbatim Report* (Washington, 1922) pp. 1608–9.

17. Judge Samuel L. Rosenman, *Working with Roosevelt* (London, 1952) p. 472.

18. For text of the American Memorandum, see Mr Justice Robert H. Jackson's *Report on the International Conference on Military Trials* (Washington, 1948) pp. 3–9; also *Yalta*, pp. 403–8. For the early planning which the memorandum embodies, see Stimson and Bundy, *On Active Service*, p. 584; Murray C. Bernays, 'Legal Basis of the Nuremberg Trials', *Survey Graphic* (New York), (Jan 1946) p. 4, and Robert H. Jackson, *The Nuremberg Case* (New York, 1947) p. v.

19. Truman, *Year of Decisions*, pp. 109–10.

20. Philip Howard, 'How the headlong rush of History ended in a cabinet quibble', *The Times*, 1 Jan 1972.

21. Rosenman, *Working with Roosevelt*, p. 493.

22. Ibid., p. 495; Woodward, *British Foreign Policy*, pp. 573–4.

23. *Jackson Report*, p. 21; Truman, *Year of Decisions*, pp. 282–4.

24. For text of Judge Rosenman's draft, see *Jackson Report*, pp. 23–7; for British amendments, see ibid., pp. 39–40.

25. For documents of the London Conference, see *Jackson Report*. See also, for accounts of the working and achievements of the Conference, the Earl of Kilmuir, *Political Adventure* (London, 1962) chap. 8, and Sydney Alderman, *Negotiating with the Russians* (New York, 1951) chap. iii.

26. *Potsdam*, vol. I, pp. 157–9.

27. Ibid., p. 198.

28. Ibid., p. 578.

29. For text of the Soviet proposals, see ibid., vol. II, pp. 984–5.

30. Ibid., p. 987.

31. Ibid., p. 573.

32. Ibid., p. 572.

33. For text of the British proposal, see ibid., p. 986, and for agreement on Stalin's proposal, ibid., p. 573; Truman, *Year of Decisions*, pp. 407–8.

34. *Potsdam*, vol. II, pp. 1489–90.

35. Ibid., p. 1507.

36. For text, see *Jackson Report*, pp. 420–9, and *Record of the Trial of the Major War Criminals before the International Military Tribunal at Nuremberg, November 14, 1945–October 1, 1946* (Nuremberg, 1947) vol. I, pp. 8–19; hereafter cited as *I.M.T. Record*.

37. Francis Biddle, *In Brief Authority* (New York, 1962) pp. 371–3.

38. H. Montgomery Hyde, *Norman Birkett* (London, 1962) pp. 494–5.

39. *I.M.T. Record*, vol. I, pp. 24–6.

40. Charles W. Alexander and Anne Keeshan, *Justice at Nuremberg* (New York, 1946) pp. 31, 43.

41. Papers placed at the disposal of Sir John Wheeler-Bennett by the late Hon. Francis Biddle.

42. For text of the Tribunal Judgement and sentences, see *I.M.T. Record*, vol. I, pp. 171–341.

43. Biddle, *In Brief Authority*, p. 464; *I.M.T. Record*, vol. XX, p. 490.

44. For text of Soviet dissenting opinions, see *I.M.T. Record*, vol. I, pp. 341–64.

45. Kilmuir, *Political Adventure*, pp. 329–39; Biddle, *In Brief Authority*, pp. 479–81; Stimson and Bundy, *On Active Service*, pp. 588–91; *Jackson Report*, pp. 46–51.

46. Byrnes, *Speaking Frankly*, pp. 85–6.

47. A. J. P. Taylor, *The Origins of the Second World War*, introductory chapter to Penguin ed. (Harmondsworth, 1965) pp. 22, 36.

48. *Documents on German Foreign Policy, 1918–1945* (London and Washington, 1966) series C, vol. V, pp. 853–62. This document first appeared at Nuremberg as Defence Exhibit Schacht, 48, but for some reason was not included in the document volumes of Record of the International Military Tribunal. It was used subsequently in Case XI of the *Trials of War Criminals before the Military Tribunals under Control Council Law No. 10.* (Washington, Oct 1948–Apr 1949) vol. XII, pp. 430–9.

49. 34th Plenary Meeting, *Verbatim Report of the General Assembly*, p. 684.

50. *U.S. State Department Bulletin*, XV (1946) 954–7; Biddle, *In Brief Authority*, p. 478.

51. *The Charter and Judgement of the Nürnberg Tribunal: Memorandum by the Secretary-General of the United Nations* (Lake Success, N.Y., 1949) p. 12.

52. Ibid., pp. 14–15.

53. *U.N. General Assembly Records* 5th session (1950), supp. 12 (A/1316); *General Assembly Records IX* (1953), supp. 12. (A/2645).

54. H. G. Nicholas, *The United Nations as a Political Institution*, 3rd ed. (Oxford, 1967) p. 133.

55. See *The United Nations and Human Rights* (New York, 1968); *Human Rights 1945–70* (New York, 1970); *International Covenants on Human Rights* (New York, 1967). All these documents are published under the auspices of the United Nations. See also Evan Luard (ed.), *The International Protection of Human Rights* (New York, 1967).

56. G. I. A. D. Draper, *The Red Cross Conventions* (London, 1958) p. 1.

57. For texts of the Conventions, see ibid., pp. 125–216.

Chapter 18: The Paris Peace Conference and the Five Peace Treaties

1. *Yalta*, pp. 974–5.
2. *Potsdam*, vol. II, pp. 1478–80.
3. Ibid., pp. 1492–3.
4. Ibid., p. 1479.
5. Ibid., p. 1480.
6. Ibid., p. 1479.
7. Accounts of the London meeting of the Council of Foreign Ministers are to be found in Dixon, *Double Diploma*, pp. 183–94; Byrnes, *Speaking Frankly*, pp. 93–106, and *All in One Lifetime*, pp. 313–317; Truman, *Year of Decisions*, pp. 516–8.
8. *H.C.Deb.*, 8 Jan 1942, cols 77–8.
9. U.S. Department of State, *Making the Peace Treaties, 1941–1947* (Washington, Feb 1947) pp. 16–18; F. W. Pick, *Peacemaking in Perspective* (Oxford, 1950) pp. 28–30.
10. *Making the Peace Treaties*, p. 71.
11. Dixon, *Double Diploma*, p. 195.
12. Kennan, *Memoirs*, pp. 290–5, 546–59.
13. Truman, *Year of Decisions*, pp. 546–7.
14. Byrnes, *Speaking Frankly*, pp. 107–108.
15. Ibid., p. 109.
16. Dixon, *Double Diploma*, p. 199.
17. Kennan, *Memoirs*, pp. 286–7.
18. Truman, *Year of Decisions*, pp. 539–44; Lord Attlee (with Francis Williams), *A Prime Minister Remembers* (London, 1961) pp. 97–101; Wheeler-Bennett, *John Anderson, Viscount Waverley*, pp. 333–6.
19. Truman, *Year of Decisions*, pp. 547–8; Vandenberg, *Private Papers*, pp. 227–9.
20. Kennan, *Memoirs*, p. 287.
21. *Making the Peace Treaties*, pp. 19–20.
22. Truman, *Year of Decisions*, p. 549.
23. Ibid., p. 552; Hillman (ed.) *Mr President*, pp. 25–9; Byrnes, *All in One Lifetime*, pp. 343–5.
24. Byrnes, *All in One Lifetime*, p. 343; Herbert Druks, *Harry S. Truman and the Russians, 1945–1953* (New York, 1966) p. 90.
25. For accounts of the Paris meetings, see Byrnes, *Speaking Frankly*, pp. 125–37, *All in One Lifetime*, pp. 357–60; Vandenberg, *Private Papers*, pp. 262–97; Dixon, *Double Diploma*, pp. 207–25; Pick, *Peacemaking in Perspective*, pp. 37–76; *Making the Peace Treaties*, pp. 22–9.

26. Vandenberg, *Private Papers*, p. 286.
27. Dixon, *Double Diploma*, pp. 213–214.
28. The five draft treaties were published in London as Cmds 6892, 6894, 6895, 6896 and 6897 (1946). See also U.S. Department of State, *Paris Peace Conference, 1946: Selected Documents* (Washington, 1946).
29. Harold Nicolson, *Diaries and Letters, 1945–1962* (London, 1968) p. 70.
30. Ibid., p. 69.
31. Redvers Opie *et al.*, *The Search for Peace Settlements* (Washington, 1951) p. 91.
32. *The Conference of Paris: Report of the New Zealand Delegation* (Wellington, 1947) pp. 14–18.
33. For verbatim reports of these operations, see *Paris Peace Conference*.
34. *Potsdam*, vol. II, p. 1492.
35. Harold Nicolson's 'News Talk', B.B.C. Home Service, 11 Aug 1946.
36. Byrnes, *All in One Lifetime*, pp. 362–3.
37. New Zealand, *Conference of Paris*, pp. 4–6.
38. Dixon, *Double Diploma*, pp. 229–230.
39. Byrnes, *All in One Lifetime*, pp. 370–6; Vandenberg, *Private Papers*, pp. 300–2; Truman, *Year of Decisions*, pp. 555–60.
40. Sir Pierson Dixon in his diary – doubtless inadvertently – refers to the meeting taking place on the *twenty-seventh* floor of the Waldorf. This is a misstatement. It was on the thirty-seventh floor, as confirmed by the management of the hotel. See *Double Diploma*, p. 235.
41. For details of the New York meeting of the Council of Foreign Ministers, see Byrnes, *Speaking Frankly*, pp. 152–5, *All in One Lifetime*, pp. 381–6; Dixon, *Double Diploma*, pp. 235–44; *Making the Peace Treaties*, pp. 52–62; Pick, *Peacemaking in Perspective*, pp. 102–4.
42. Byrnes, *Speaking Frankly*, p. 154.
43. McNeill, *America, Britain and Russia*, pp. 722–3.
44. Cf. Wheeler-Bennett, *Nemesis of Power*, p. 298, n. 1.
45. The texts of these documents are to be found in the British Blue Book, *Documents relating to the Completion of an Armistice with Italy, September-*

November 1943, Cmd 6693 (1945); U.S. Department of State, *A Decade of American Foreign Policy, 1941–1949* (Washington, 1950) pp. 455–6, and *The United States and Italy 1936–1946* (Washington, 1946) pp. 55–6. Excellent accounts of the surrender negotiations are to be found in Macmillan, *The Blast of War*, pp. 362–409, and Strong, *Intelligence at the Top*, pp. 100–23.

46. British Blue Book, *Treaties of Peace with Italy, Bulgaria, Rumania, Hungary and Finland*, Cmd 7022 (1947) pp. 7–78, hereinafter cited as *Peace Treaties*.

47. A good account of these colonial dispositions is given in Muriel Grinrod, *The Rebuilding of Italy* (London, 1955) pp. 36–7.

48. Ibid., pp. 32–3.

49. Lord Avon, *Full Circle* (London, 1960) pp. 177–8; Grinrod, *The Rebuilding of Italy*, pp. 33–6.

50. *Yalta*, pp. 888–9.

51. Some account of these negotiations was given by Ambassador Thompson in an interview with the *Corriere della Sera*, 15 Oct 1954.

52. *Text of Memorandum of Understanding*, Cmd 9288 (1954). For accounts of the events leading up to the conclusion of the final agreement, see Avon, *Full Circle*, pp. 177–87; Grinrod, *The Rebuilding of Italy*, pp. 136–53.

53. Avon, *Full Circle*, p. 188.

54. British White Paper, Treaty Series No. 15, Cmd 1747 (1922). See also *History of the Peace Conference* (London, 1920–4) vol. IV, pp. 139, 129; vol. V, p. 169; J. W. Wheeler-Bennett, *The Problem of Security* (London, 1927) pp. 74–5.

55. Wheeler-Bennett, *The Problem of Security*, pp. 74–6, 86–7; idem, *Disarmament and Security since Locarno, 1925–1931* (London, 1932) pp. 252–4; idem, *Disarmament Deadlock* (London, 1934) p. 152; *Rapport du Ministre des Finances au Conseil des Ministres sur la situation créée à la Roumanie par la politique des Réparations et des Dettes Inter-Alliés*, 2 vols (Bucharest, 1925).

56. See *Statesman's Year Books* for 1915, 1922 and 1965–66.

57. Czechoslovak White Book, *Documents diplomatiques rélatifs aux Conventions d'Alliance conclues par la République Tchéchoslovaque avec le Royaume des Serbes, Croates et Slovènes et le Royaume de Roumanie décembre 1919–août 1921* (Prague, 1923).

58. *Peace Treaties*, pp. 79–98.

59. British White Paper, *Text of Munich Agreement*, Cmd 5848 (1938) No. 4.

60. Wheeler-Bennett, *Munich*, pp. 306–315.

61. *Peace Treaties*, pp. 117–37.

62. Wheeler-Bennett, *Munich*, p. 349, n. 2.

63. *Peace Treaties*, pp. 98–116.

64. Ibid., pp. 138–51.

65. *Advisory Opinion of March 30, 1950: Interpretation of the Peace Treaties with Bulgaria, Hungary and Rumania*. Reports of Judgements. Advisory Opinions and Orders of the International Court of Justice 1950 (Leyden, 1950) pp. 65–78.

66. *Order of May 5, 1950*, ibid., pp. 121–3.

67. *Advisory Opinion of July 18, 1950*, ibid., pp. 221–230.

Chapter 19: The Austrian State Treaty

1. Alan Bullock, *Hitler: A Study in Tyranny*, paperback ed. (New York, 1964) p. 316.

2. Wheeler-Bennett, *Nemesis of Power*, p. 489; von Hassell, *Vom andern Deutschland*, pp. 127–33.

3. Harold C. Deutsch, *The Conspiracy against Hitler in the Twilight War* (Minneapolis, 1968) p. 297.

4. For text of the Moscow Declaration, see *Documents on American Foreign Relations, July 1943 to June 1944*, vol. VI (Boston, 1945) pp. 229–30.

5. Heinrich Siegler et al., *Austria: Problems and Achievements since 1945* (Bonn, 1965) p. 7.

6. Hajo Holbon, *American Military Government* (New Haven, 1947) pp. 78–81.

7. *Potsdam*, vol. II, p. 1490.

8. *Making the Peace Treaties*, pp. 24, 28–9.

9. Ibid., p. 62.

10. Murphy, *Diplomat among Warriors*, p. 305; General Mark W. Clark, *From the Danube to the Yalu* (New York, 1954) pp. 12–14. See also Opie, *The Search for Peace Settlements*, pp. 181–3.

11. Opie, *The Search for Peace Settlements*, p. 180.

12. Pick, *Peacemaking in Perspective*, p. 112.

13. Murphy, *Diplomat among Warriors*, p. 306.

14. Siegler, *Austria*, pp. 11–12.

15. For details of the Cherrière Plan, see ibid., p. 13; Pick, *Peacemaking in Perspective*, pp. 149–50; Opie, *The Search for Peace Settlements*, p. 189.

16. Communiqué of the Council of Foreign Ministers, 20 June 1949, in *U.S. Department of State Bulletin*, 4 July 1949, p. 858; British White Paper, *Miscellaneous No. 11*, Cmd 7729 (1949) pp. 19–22.

17. Cf. Pick, *Peacemaking in Perspective*, p. 230.

18. Karl Renner in the *Wiener Zeitung*, 20 Dec 1945.

19. Bruno Kreisky in *Österreich in Geschichte und Literatur* No. 3 (1957).

20. See British White Papers, *Miscellaneous No. 16*, Cmd 8979 (1953); *Miscellaneous No. 21*, Cmd 9008 (1953); *Miscellaneous No. 22* Cmd 9022 (1953);

Germany No. 4, Cmd 8945 (1953); and *Miscellaneous No. 1*, Cmd 9037 (1954).

21. For text of the five articles, see British White Paper, *Miscellaneous No. 1*, Cmd 9037 (1954) Annex D, pp. 167–70.

22. Avon, *Full Circle*, p. 65.

23. Cmd 9037 (1954) pp. 138–9.

24. Ibid., p. 143.

25. Avon, *Full Circle*, p. 74.

26. Cmd 9037 (1954) p. 165.

27. Avon, *Full Circle*, p. 289.

28. For text of the Moscow Memorandum, see Siegler, *Austria*, pp. 169–71.

29. Harold Macmillan, *Tides of Fortune, 1945–1955* (London, 1969) p. 594.

30. For texts of the Vienna Memorandum and the Franco-Austrian Memorandum, see Siegler, *Austria*, pp. 171–5.

31. Macmillan, *Tides of Fortune*, p. 601.

32. Ibid., pp. 599–600.

33. Ibid., p. 602.

Chapter 20: The Japanese Peace Treaty

1. Acheson, *Present at the Creation*, p. 427.

2. For text of 'The United States Initial Post-Surrender Policy', see *The Occupation of Japan: Policy and Progress*, Department of State Publication 2671, Far Eastern Series No. 17 (Washington, 1946) pp. 73–81.

3. MacArthur, *Reminiscences*, pp. 326–327.

4. *Occupation of Japan*, p. 75.

5. For background of the establishment of the Far Eastern Advisory Commission, see George H. Blakeslee, *The Far Eastern Commission: A Study in International Co-operation, 1945–1952*, Department of State Publication No. 5138. Far Eastern Series No. 60 (Washington, 1953) pp. 2–4; for text of the U.S. invitation, see *Occupation of Japan*, pp. 67–8.

6. Acheson, *Present at the Creation*, p. 427; Byrnes, *Speaking Frankly*, pp. 214–15.

7. Blakeslee, *The Far Eastern Commission*, p. 5.

8. For text, see *Occupation of Japan*, pp. 69–73.

9. Truman, *Year of Decisions*, pp. 519–521.

10. Ibid., pp. 549–50.

11. MacArthur, *Reminiscences*, pp. 334–335.

12. Ibid., p. 335.

13. Edwin O. Reischauer, *The United States and Japan*, paperback ed. (New York, 1966) p. 48. See also Ambassador William J. Sebald, *With MacArthur in Japan* (London, 1967) pp. 126–50, and W. Macmahon Bell, *Japan: Enemy or Ally?* (New York, 1949) p. 33.

14. Kazuo Kanai, *Japan's American Interlude* (Chicago, 1960) p. 22.

15. Courtney Brown, *Tojo*, paperback ed. (London, 1969) pp. 239–40.

16. For texts of the Supreme Commander's Proclamation and of the Charter of the International Military Tribunal for the Far East, see *Occupation of Japan*, pp. 146–53.

17. MacArthur, *Reminiscences*, p. 364.

18. Sebald, *With MacArthur in Japan*, pp. 151–76; Kanai, *Japan's American Interlude*, pp. 22–4; Robert A. Fearey, *The Occupation of Japan: Second Phase, 1948–1950* (New York, 1950) pp. 17–21.

19. Yoshida, *Memoirs*, p. 50.

20. Sebald, *With MacArthur in Japan*, pp. 161–5; Fearey, *The Occupation of Japan*, pp. 18–19.

21. Sebald, *With MacArthur in Japan*, pp. 168–9.

22. Fearey, *The Occupation of Japan*, pp. 19–20; Kanai, *Japan's American Interlude*, pp. 22–4.

23. Richard Storry, *A History of Modern Japan*, Penguin ed. (Harmondsworth, 1968) p. 240.

24. Ibid.

25. *Occupation of Japan*, pp. 133–5

'Imperial Rescript Denying the Divinity of the Emperor', 1 Jan 1946.

26. Ibid., p. 118, 'Constitution of Japan', 22 Apr 1946), Chapter I, Article 1.

27. Reischauer, *The United States and Japan*, p. 224.

28. *Occupation of Japan*, p. 74.

29. Yoshida, *Memoirs*, p. 244; Frederick S. Dunn, *Peacemaking and the Settlement with Japan* (Princeton, 1963) pp. 56–7.

30. Supreme Commander for the Allied Powers, Report of the Government Section, *Political Orientation of Japan: September 1945 to September 1948*, 2 vols (Washington, 1959) p. 785.

31. *Occupation of Japan*, p. 119.

32. Dunn, *Peacemaking and the Settlement with Japan*, p. 55.

33. For text, see *Occupation of Japan*, pp. 85–8.

34. *Observer*, 13 Aug 1950; *The Times*, 10 Aug 1950.

35. Sebald, *With MacArthur in Japan*, p. 244.

36. e.g. Dunn, *Peacemaking and the Settlement with Japan*, pp. 58–9; Sebald, *With MacArthur in Japan*, pp. 243–4; Fearey, *The Occupation of Japan*, pp. 185–8.

37. Forrestal, *Diaries*, p. 266.

38. New Zealand Department of External Affairs, *Japanese Peace Settlement: British Commonwealth Conference* [at Canberra], *July 26 to September 3, 1947* (Wellington, 1947) p. 8.

39. *Department of State Bulletin*, 27 July 1947, p. 182.

40. Dunn, *Peacemaking and the Settlement with Japan*, p. 65; Fearey, *The Occupation of Japan*, p. 183.

41. Dunn, *Peacemaking and the Settlement with Japan*, p. 65.

42. Acheson, *Present at the Creation*, p. 429.

43. Kennan, *Memoirs*, p. 391.

44. Dunn, *Peacemaking and the Settlement with Japan*, p. 78, n. 31.

45. Acheson, *Present at the Creation*, p. 430; Burton Sapin, 'The Role of the Military in Formulating the Japanese Peace Treaty', in Gordon B. Turner (ed.), *A History of Military Affairs in Western Society since the Eighteenth Century* (New York, 1953) pp. 751–62; Bernard C. Cohen, *The Political Process and Foreign Policy: The Making of the Japanese Peace Settlement* (Princeton, 1957) p. 12.

46. *New York Times*, 15 Sep 1949.

47. Dunn, *Peacemaking and the Settlement with Japan*, p. 84.

48. Louis L. Gerson, *John Foster Dulles* (New York, 1967) p. 55.

49. Vandenberg, *Private Papers*, pp. 546 ff.

50. Kennan, *Memoirs*, p. 394.

51. Acheson, *Present at the Creation*, p. 432; Gerson, *John Foster Dulles*, pp. 57–9; John Robinson Beal, *John Foster Dulles: A Biography* (New York, 1957) pp. 116–17.

52. Eleanor Lansing Dulles, *John Foster Dulles: The Last Year* (New York, 1963) p. 33.

53. For Yoshida's account of these preliminary negotiations, see his *Memoirs*, pp. 249–53.

54. *New York Times*, 20 Nov 1949.

55. Gerson, *John Foster Dulles*, pp. 63–4.

56. United States Information Service, *Summary of Events Leading to the Japanese Peace Treaty Conference*, p. 4.

57. For text of the Seven Points Memorandum, see *New York Times*, 25 Nov 1950 and, for an admirable comment, an article by L. C. Green entitled 'Making Peace with Japan' in the *Year Book of World Affairs* (1952).

58. Rt Hon. Richard G. Casey, *Friends and Neighbours: Australia, the U.S. and the World* (East Lansing, Mich., 1955) p. 58. See also Trevor R. Reese, *Australia, New Zealand and the United States* (Oxford, 1969) pp. 101–3; Dunn, *Peacemaking and the Settlement with Japan*, pp. 128–30.

59. State Department Publication 4148, *Laying Foundations for Peace in the Pacific*, an address by John Foster Dulles (Washington, Mar 1951).

60. Acheson, *Present at the Creation*, p. 540.

61. Ibid., pp. 540–1; Lord Morrison of Lambeth, *Herbert Morrison: An Autobiography* (London, 1960) p. 280.

62. Acheson, *Present at the Creation*, p. 540; *Department of State Bulletin*, 28 May 1951.

63. British White Paper, Cmd 8300 (1951).

64. Department of State Publication 4392, *Record of Proceedings of Conference for the Conclusion and Signature of the Peace Treaty with Japan, San Francisco, California, September 4–8, 1951* (Wash-

ington, Dec 1951) p. 19, hereafter cited as
Proceedings.

65. Ibid., p. 75.

66. Dean Acheson has left a most
entertaining account of the conference in
Present at the Creation, pp. 542–50.
Yoshida has also given his version in his
Memoirs, pp. 254–62.

67. James Reston, *New York Times*,
6 Sep 1951; also *Proceedings*, pp. 40–5.

68. Excellent commentaries on the
treaty and summaries of its contents are
to be found in Cohen, *The Political
Process*, pp. 17–21; New Zealand Department of External Affairs, Publication 106,
Japanese Peace Settlement (Wellington,
1951) pp. 14–16; Japanese Ministry of
Foreign Affairs, Public Information
Division Publication, *Explanatory Study
of Draft Japanese Peace Treaty* (Tokyo,
4 Aug 1951. See also Hearings before the
Committee on Foreign Relations, United
States Senate (82nd Congress, 2nd
session) on *The Japanese Peace Treaty
and other Treaties relating to Security in
the Pacific, January 21–23 and 24, 1952*
(Washington, 1952).

69. *Proceedings*, pp. 279–80.

70. Sir Robert Menzies, 'The Pacific
Settlement as Seen from Australia',
Foreign Affairs (Jan 1952) p. 191.

71. Reese, *Australia, New Zealand and
the United States*, pp. 107–25.

72. *The Times*, 26 Feb 1970. For text

of the joint Nixon–Sato communiqué
issued in Washington, see *New York
Times*, 22 Nov 1969.

73. Casey, *Friends and Neighbours*,
pp. 60–73; Reese, *Australia, New Zealand
and the United States*, pp. 126–49;
Dunn, *Peacemaking and the Settlement
with Japan*, pp. 187–204; Yoshida,
Memoirs, pp. 263–8; Rt Hon. Sir Robert
Menzies, *Afternoon Light* (London, 1967)
pp. 262–70.

74. Reese, *Australia, New Zealand and
the United States*, pp. 175–83; for texts
of the SEATO Treaty and the Pacific
Charter, see British White Papers, Cmd
9282 and 9299 (1954).

75. *Proceedings*, p. 308.

76. Ibid., p. 116.

77. Ibid., pp. 119–22.

78. For text, see *New York Times*, 15
Feb 1950.

79. *Pravda*, 13 Sep 1954.

80. Japanese Ministry of Foreign
Affairs, *Press Releases, December 1954–
December 1955* [212] p. 65.

81. Storry, *A History of Modern Japan*,
pp. 260–3.

82. An admirable summary of these
Soviet–Japanese discussions is given by
Professor Donald C. Hellmann in his
*Japanese Domestic Politics and Foreign
Policies: The Peace Agreement with the
Soviet Union* (Berkeley and Los Angeles,
1969) pp. 34–9.

Chapter 21: The Origins of the United Nations Organization

1. Leonard Woolf, *International
Government* (London, 1916) and *The
Framework of a Lasting Peace* (London,
1917); G. Lowes Dickinson, H. N.
Brailsford, C. R. Buxton, *Toward a
Lasting Settlement* (London, 1917); J. A.
Hobson, *Towards International Govern-
ment* (London, 1918).

2. For texts of the Reports of the
Phillimore Committee, see David Hunter
Miller, *The Drafting of the Covenant*
(New York, 1928) vol II, pp. 3–6; Florence
Wilson, *The Origins of the League Cove-
nant* (London, 1928) pp. 114–72.

3. For text, see Wilson, *The Origins of
the League Covenant*, pp. 189–98.

4. For texts of Cecil drafts of 1916 and
1918, see Miller, *The Drafting of the
Covenant*, vol. II, pp. 61–4; Wilson, *The
Origins of the League Covenant*, pp. 112–
113, 181–3.

5. Sir Keith Hancock, *Smuts: The

Sanguine Years, 1870–1919* (Cambridge,
1962) pp. 500–3; Miller, *The Drafting of
the Covenant*, vol. II, pp. 23–60; Wilson,
The Origins of the League Covenant,
pp. 184–8.

6. David Lloyd George, *The Truth about
the Treaties* (London, 1938) vol. II, p. 34.

7. Francis P. Walters, *A History of the
League of Nations* (Oxford, 1967) p. 31.

8. Wilson, *The Origins of the League
Covenant*, p. xi; Walters, *A History of the
League of Nations*, p. 32.

9. For text of the Italian plan, see
Miller, *The Drafting of the Covenant*, vol.
II, pp. 539–47; Wilson, *The Origins of the
League Covenant*, pp. 199–210.

10. For text of the Scandinavian draft
Convention, see Wilson, *The Origins of
the League Covenant*, pp. 211–56.

11. C. A. Kluyvers, *Documents on the
League of Nations* (The Hague, 1920)
pp. 174–82.

12. *The Times,* 13 June, 1941.

13. Churchill, *The Grand Alliance,* pp. 434–40; Welles, *Where are we Heading?,* pp. 11–14.

14. *Public Papers and Addresses of Franklin D. Roosevelt: War and Aid to the Democracies* (New York, 1941) p. 672.

15. Welles, *Where are we Heading?,* p. 11; William L. Langer and S. Everett Gleason, *The Undeclared War, 1940–1941* (New York, 1953) p. 685.

16. Churchill, *The Grand Alliance,* p. 441.

17. Sir John Wheeler-Bennett, *Brest-Litovsk: The Forgotten Peace, March 1918,* rev. ed. (London, 1966) pp. 68, 376.

18. British White Paper, *Miscellaneous No. 3* Cmd 6315 (1941) pp. 4–6.

19. Hull, *Memoirs,* vol. II, pp. 1114–24; Sherwood, *White House Papers,* vol. I, pp. 446–55. Churchill, *The Grand Alliance* pp. 664–6, 682–5.

20. U.S. Department of State, *Co-operative War Effort* (Washington, 1942) p. 1.

21. Wheeler-Bennett, *King George VI,* pp. 529–30.

22. Avon, *The Reckoning,* pp. 366–7.

23. Ruth B. Russell, *A History of the United Nations Charter* (Washington, 1958) pp. 114–15.

24. Ibid., pp. 118–19.

25. Vandenberg, *Private Papers,* pp. 56–8.

26. *Congressional Record,* vol. 89, Part 6 (78th Congress, 1st Session) pp. 7728–9.

27. U.S. Senate, Resolution 192 (78th Congress, 1st Session) 5 Nov 1943; Connally, *My Name is Tom Connally,* pp. 263–4; Vandenberg, *Private Papers,* pp. 38–9, 44–6.

28. Avon, *The Reckoning,* pp. 410–11.

29. Hull, *Memoirs,* vol. II, pp. 1292–1307; U.S. Department of State, *Toward the Peace Documents* (Washington, 1945) p. 6.

30. The best English accounts are to be found in Mr Nicholas's *The United Nations as a Political Institution* and in Sir Charles Webster's chapter entitled 'The Making of the Charter of the United Nations' in his *Art and Practice of Diplomacy* (London, 1961). The scholarly work of Ruth Russell, *A History of the United Nations Charter,* is a very full history of the subject. More popular books are *The United Nations* by Ralph

Townley (New York, 1968) and *Mr Roosevelt's Four Freedoms* by Frank Donovan (New York, 1966).

31. British White Paper, *Miscellaneous No. 4: Dumbarton Oaks Conversations on World Organization, 21 August–7 October. Statement of Tentative Proposals,* Cmd 6560 (1944).

32. Russell, *A History of the United Nations Charter,* pp. 445–54.

33. Webster, *Art and Practice of Diplomacy,* p. 26.

34. Nicholas, *The United Nations as a Political Institution,* p. 5.

35. Avon, *The Reckoning,* p. 517.

36. Russell, *A History of the United Nations Charter,* pp. 531–7; *Yalta,* pp. 710–40; Churchill, *Triumph and Tragedy,* pp. 356–60.

37. Russell, *A History of the United Nations Charter,* p. 507; Byrnes, *Speaking Frankly,* p. 40; Sherwood, *White House Papers,* vol. II, p. 848.

38. Russell, *A History of the United Nations Charter,* pp. 536–7; Stettinius, *Roosevelt and the Russians at Yalta,* pp. 196–7; *Yalta,* pp. 772, 991–2.

39. Avon, *The Reckoning,* p. 517.

40. *Congressional Record,* 79th Congress, vol. 91. pt. 5, p. 1654.

41. For American sources, see *Comments and Proposed Amendments concerning the Dumbarton Oaks Proposals* (San Francisco, 7 May 1945); *The United Nations Conference on International Organization, San Francisco, California, April 25–June 26, 1945: Selected Documents* (Washington, 1946); *Foreign Relations of the United States, Diplomatic Papers, 1945,* vol. I, General: *The United Nations* (Washington, 1967). This volume includes minutes of the discussions of the U.S. delegation. For British and Commonwealth sources, see New Zealand Department of External Affairs, *Report on the Conference held at San Francisco, April 25–June, 26 1945,* Publication No. 11 (Wellington, 1945); Canadian Department of External Affairs, *Report on the United Nations Conference on International Organization held at San Francisco, April 25–June 26, 1945,* Cmd No. 2 (Ottawa, 1945); Parliament of the Commonwealth of Australia, *United Nations Conference on International Organization, held at San Francisco from 25 April to 25 June, 1945: Report by the Australian Delegation,* Cmd 24.F4311 (Canberra, 1945).

See also *Documents of the United Nations Conference on International Organization*, 15 vols (United Nations Information Office, New York, 1946). For personal accounts see Vandenberg, *Private Papers*, pp. 172–98; Connally, *My Name is Tom Connally*, pp. 277–86; Sol Bloom, *Autobiography* (New York, 1948) pp. 275–84; Virginia C. Gilderleeve, *Many a Good Crusade* (New York, 1954) pp. 315–57.

42. Nicholas, *The United Nations as a Political Institution*, pp. 7–8.

43. Text in *Documents of the United Nations Conference on International Organization*, vol. II, pp. 699–709.

44. Truman, *Year of Decisions*, pp. 284–87; Sherwood, *White House Papers*, vol. II, pp. 900–2.

45. For text of statement, see *United Nations Conference Documents*, vol. XI, pp. 710–14.

46. For an admirable study of the problem of the Great Power veto, see Russell, *A History of the United Nations Charter*, pp. 713–49.

47. Nicholas, *The United Nations as a Political Institution*, pp. 14–40.

48. Francis P. Walters, *A History of the League of Nations* (Oxford, 1967) pp. 102–3.

49. Macmillan, *Tides of Fortune*, p. 606.

Chapter 22: The Coming of the Cold War

1. Arthur Schlesinger, Jr, 'The Origins of the Cold War', *Foreign Affairs*, Oct 1967.

2. D. F. Fleming, *The Cold War and its Origins* (New York, 1961); David Horowitz, *The Free World Colossus* (New York, 1965); Coral Bell, *Negotiations from Strength* (London, 1965); Gar Alperowitz, *Atomic Diplomacy: Hiroshima and Potsdam* (New York, 1965).

3. Churchill, *The Tide of Victory*, pp. 64–5.

4. Ibid., pp. 65–8; Hull, *Memoirs*, vol. II, pp. 1451–6.

5. Hull, *Memoirs*, vol. II, pp. 1457–8.

6. Churchill, *The Tide of Victory*, pp. 69–70; *Stalin's Correspondence*, pp. 235–6, 238.

7. Churchill, *The Tide of Victory*, p. 198.

8. Avon, *The Reckoning*, p. 483.

9. Churchill, *The Tide of Victory*, p. 617.

10. *H.C.Deb.*, 27 Feb 1945, cols. 1283–4.

11. Churchill, *The Tide of Victory*, p. 369.

12. Truman, *Year of Decisions*, pp. 227–8.

13. Harry S. Truman, *Years of Trial and Hope* (New York, 1956) p. 103.

14. Louis J. Hallé, *The Cold War as History* (London, 1966) p. 110, n. 1.

15. Ibid. pp. 109–10.

16. For the account of the origins of the Truman Doctrine, see Truman, *Years of Trial and Hope*, pp. 99–109; Acheson, *Present at the Creation*, pp. 217–25; Joseph Manon Jones, *The Fifteen Weeks*, paperback ed. (New York, 1964) pp. 1–23; Hallé, *The Cold War as History*, pp. 110–22.

17. *Congressional Record*, House of Representatives, 21 Mar 1947.

18. Truman, *Years of Trial and Hope*, p. 108.

19. For the history of the Delta Council speech, see Acheson, *Present at the Creation*, pp. 227–30; Truman, *Years of Trial and Hope*, pp. 113–14; Jones (one of the co-drafters of the speech), *The Fifteen Weeks*, pp. 24–30.

20. *Department of State Bulletin*, vol. XVI, 11 May 1947, pp. 919, 920, 924.

21. Acheson, *Present at the Creation*, pp. 229; *Department of State Bulletin*, vol. XVI, 18 May 1947, pp. 991–4.

22. Acheson, *Present at the Creation*, p. 230.

23. Ibid., pp. 232–3. For the origins of this historic episode, the best account is unfortunately in privately printed form, namely Elinor M. Kenney's *The Origin of the Marshall Plan* (the Bookman Press, Los Angeles, n.d.); see also Jones, *The Fifteen Weeks*, which is excellent; also George Kennan's *Memoirs*, pp. 325–53, and Acheson, *Present at the Creation*, pp. 230–3. It will doubtless be treated at length in a later volume of Dr Forrest Pogue's life of General Marshall.

24. The authors of this book are greatly obligated to Leonard Miall for making his records of these events available to them. He himself has written on this subject in *The Listener* for 4 May 1961, and also treated of it in a speech before the British–American Associates on 30 March 1954. Mr MacColl's account is given in pp. 171–5 of his book *Deadline*

and Dateline (London, 1956), and both he and Mr Muggeridge have confirmed the incident in letters to Sir John Wheeler-Bennett, dated 11 July and 22 July 1970 respectively.

25. *Department of State Bulletin*, 15 June 1947, vol. xvi, pp. 1159–60.

26. Ibid.

27. Sir Oliver Franks, in *The Listener*, 14 June 1956.

28. Acheson, *Present at the Creation*, p. 234.

29. *New York Herald Tribune*, 6 June 1949.

30. Charles P. Kindleberger, 'The Marshall Plan and the Cold War', *International Journal* (Ottawa) summer 1968, pp. 376–7.

31. Truman, *Years of Trial and Hope*, pp. 116–19.

32. Hon. McGeorge Bundy, *The Americans and Europe: Rhetoric and Reason*, Ditchley Foundation Lecture No. VIII (July 1969) p. 4.

33. *H.C.Deb.*, 22 Jan 1948, cols 395–6.

34. Truman, *Years of Trial and Hope*, p. 242.

35. For the decision to establish Bizonia, see Oppen, *Documents on Germany*, pp. 195–9.

36. For the text of the decree of 10 Sep 1945 on land reform in Saxony, see ibid., pp. 59–64.

37. Woodward, *British Foreign Policy*, p. 467.

38. Windsor, *City on Leave*, pp. 74–5.

39. Oppen, *Documents on Germany*, pp. 210–11.

40. See Wilfrid Knapp, *A History of War and Peace, 1939–1965* (Oxford, 1967) p. 118.

41. Oppen, *Documents on Germany*, pp. 286–90.

42. Ibid., p. 284.

43. Murphy, *Diplomat among Warriors*, p. 380.

44. W. P. Davidson, *The Berlin Blockade* (Princeton, 1958) p. 109. See also Windsor, *City on Leave*, pp. 98 ff.; Clay, *Decision in Germany*, p. 386.

45. Clay, *Decision in Germany*, p. 361.

46. Quoted in Windsor, *City on Leave*, p. 126.

47. *Canadian H.C.Deb.*, 28 Apr 1948.

48. *H.C.Deb.*, 5 May 1948, cols 1110–1.

49. *Congressional Record, United States Senate*, 11 June 1948, p. 8026. Truman, *Years of Trial and Hope*, p. 244; Vanden-berg, *Private Papers*, pp. 474–501; Kennan, *Memoirs*, pp. 397–414.

50. Truman, *Years of Trial and Hope*, p. 248.

51. Ibid., p. 249.

52. Text in *The Axis in Defeat*, U.S. Department of State Publication 2423 (Washington, 1946) pp. 7–81.

53. e.g. OMGUS Law No. 154, *Elimination and Prohibition of Military Training*, 14 July 1945; Control Council Order No. 4, *Confiscation of Literature and Material of a Nazi and Militant Nature*, 13 May 1946; Control Council Law No. 8, *Elimination and Prohibition of Military Training*, 30 Nov 1946; Control Council Law No. 23, *Prohibition of Military Construction in Germany*, 10 Apr 1946; Control Council Directive No. 18, *Disbandment and Dissolution of the German Armed Forces*, 12 Nov 1945.

54. Truman, *Years of Trial and Hope*, pp. 254–7; Acheson, *Present at the Creation*, pp. 435–40.

55. Lord Ismay, *NATO: The First Five Years, 1949–1954* (Paris, 1954) p. 32.

56. Truman, *Years of Trial and Hope*, pp. 257–8; Ismay, *NATO: The First Five Years*, pp. 33–8; Dwight D. Eisenhower, *Mandate for Change, 1952–1956* (London, 1963) pp. 12–18.

57. Avon, *Full Circle*, pp. 32–8.

58. Ibid., p. 42.

59. Eisenhower, *Mandate for Change*, pp. 398–9; Acheson, *Present at the Creation*, pp. 643–50.

60. John Wheeler-Bennett and Hugh Latimer, *The Reparation Settlement, 1929–1930* (London, 1930) pp. 137–49.

61. Raymond Aron and Daniel Lerner (eds), *Essais d'analyse sociologiques* (Paris, 1956) p. 9.

62. Eisenhower, *Mandate for Change*, pp. 401–2.

63. Avon, *Full Circle*, pp. 147–9; Eisenhower, *Mandate for Change*, p. 402.

64. Macmillan, *Tides of Fortune*, p. 481.

65. Eisenhower, *Mandate for Change*, p. 405.

66. Avon, *Full Circle*, pp. 151–62.

67. Macmillan, *Tides of Fortune*, p. 480–1.

68. Truman, *Years of Trial and Hope*, p. 429.

69. Macmillan, *Tides of Fortune*, p. 489.

70. Avon, *Full Circle*, pp. 162–74; Eisenhower, *Mandate for Change*, pp. 403–9.

71. Avon, *Full Circle*, p. 171.

72. Paul-Henri Spaak, *Combat machevés*, vol. 1: *De l'indépendance à l'alliance* (Paris, 1969) pp. 306–7.

73. Ibid., pp. 307–15.

74. Eisenhower, *Mandate for Change*, pp. 145–7.

75. Malcolm Mackintosh, *The Evolution of the Warsaw Pact*, Institute for Strategic Studies, Adelphi Papers No. 58 (London, June 1969).

Epilogue: 'By Manifold Illusion'

1. Johannes Meintjes, *General Louis Botha* (London, 1970) p. 295.

2. *The Times*, 22 Oct 1970.

3. Lord Caccia, *The Roots of British Foreign Policy, 1929–1965*, Ditchley Foundation Lecture No. IV (Nov 1965) p. 12.

4. Euripides, *The Trojan Women*, trans. Anon.

5. The Rt Hon. Lester Pearson in Westminster Hall on the occasion of the twenty-fifth anniversary of the signing of the United Nations Charter, Friday, 26 June 1970.

6. Bundy, *The Americans and Europe*, p. 6.

Appendix A: The Munich Agreement

1. British White Paper, Cmd 5848 (1938).

2. For text of Vienna Award, see R.I.I.A., *Documents on International Affairs* (1938) p. 351.

3. Norman H. Baynes (ed.), *Hitler's Speeches, 1922–1939* (Oxford, 1942) vol. II, p. 1585.

4. *The Times*, 1 Oct 1940.

5. Eduard Táborský, *The Czechoslovak Cause in International Law* (London, 1944) pp. 26–7.

6. *H.C.Deb.*, 5 Aug 1942, cols 1004–5; British White Paper, Cmd 6379 (1942).

7. Táborský, *The Czechoslovak Cause*, p. 89.

8. *Manchester Guardian*, 27 Sep 1944.

9. *The Times*, 16 Oct 1964.

10. Ibid., 5 July 1968.

11. Ibid., 24 Apr 1965.

12. *New York Times*, 28 Sep 1968.

Appendix B: The Yoshida Letter

1. Acheson, *Present at the Creation*, pp. 540–1.

2. Lord Morrison, *Herbert Morrison: An Autobiography*, p. 280.

3. Acheson, *Present at the Creation*, p. 603.

4. *Congressional Record*, 82nd Congress, 2nd Session, p. 2331.

5. *Department of State Bulletin*, vol. XXVI, 28 Jan 1952, p. 120.

6. Acheson, *Present at the Creation*, p. 604.

7. Ibid., pp. 603–4.

8. Avon, *Full Circle*, p. 19.

9. *H.C.Deb.*, 30 Jan 1952, cols 165–8; Avon, *Full Circle*, p. 20.

10. Acheson, *Present at the Creation*, p. 603.

11. *H.C.Deb.*, 26 Feb 1952, cols 948–60

12. Morrison, *Autobiography*, p. 280.

13. Acheson, *Present at the Creation*, p. 605.

14. *The Political Diaries of C. P. Scott, 1911–1928*, ed. Trevor Wilson (London, 1970) p. 166.

15. Eisenhower, *Mandate for Change*, p. 142.

16. Gerson, *John Foster Dulles*, p. 93.

17. Letter from Lord Avon to Sir John Wheeler-Bennett, dated 22 July 1970, giving extract quoted which was dictated in 1968; also conversations of 29–30 June 1970. Permission given to use this material was generously granted by Lord Avon in a letter dated 28 July 1970.

18. Ibid.

Appendix C: Britain and Europe in 1951

1. Kilmuir, *Political Adventure*, pp. 186–9; Lord Boothby, *My Yesterday, Your To-morrow* (London, 1962) pp. 81–85.

2. Kilmuir, *Political Adventures*, p. 188.

3. Avon, *Full Circle*, p. 30.

4. Lord Normanbrook, in *Action this Day*, p. 41.

5. *H.C.Deb.*, 29 Nov 1950, col. 1173.

6. *The Times*, 15 Sep 1951.

7. John Colville, in *Action this Day*, p. 127.

8. Council of Europe Consultative Assembly, 3rd Ordinary Session (General Part), *Official Report of Debates*, vol. IV, 28 Nov 1951, 21st sitting.

9. Avon, *Full Circle*, p. 33.

10. Paul-Henri Spaak, *Combat mach-evés*, vol. II: *De l'espoir aux déceptions* (Paris, 1969) p. 47.

11. An admirable paper, as yet unpublished, has been written on this subject by Mr B. J. Pimlott, of Worcester College, Oxford, entitled 'E.D.C., W.E.U. and Mr Eden'. The authors of this book have been permitted to consult this memorandum by favour of its writer and of Lord Avon.

INDEX

Index

689

EUROPEAN HISTORY TITLES IN
NORTON PAPERBOUND EDITIONS

Aron, Raymond. *On War.* N107

Aron, Raymond. *The Opium of the Intellectuals.* N106

Balfour, Michael. *The Kaiser and His Times.* N661

Benda, Julien. *The Treason of the Intellectuals.* N470

Bloch, Marc. *Strange Defeat: A Statement of Evidence Written in 1940.* N371

Brandt, Conrad. *Stalin's Failure in China.* N352

Brinton, Crane. *The Lives of Talleyrand.* N188

Butterfield, Herbert. *The Whig Interpretation of History.* N318

Calleo, David P. *Europe's Future: The Grand Alternatives.* N406

Cobban, Alfred. *Aspects of the French Revolution.* N512

Dehio, Ludwig. *Germany and World Politics in the Twentieth Century.* N391

East, W. Gordon. *The Geography Behind History.* N419

Eyck, Erich. *Bismarck and the German Empire.* N235

Feis, Herbert. *Contest Over Japan.* N466

Feis, Herbert. *The Spanish Story.* N339

Feis, Herbert. *Three International Episodes: Seen from E. A.* N351

Fischer, Fritz. *Germany's Aims in the First World War.*

Fox, Edward Whiting. *History in Geographic Perspective: The Other France.* N650

Ganshof, Francois Louis. *Frankish Institutions Under Charlemagne.* N500

Gatzke, Hans W. *Stresemann and the Rearmament of Germany.* N486

Gay, Peter. *The Party of Humanity: Essays in the French Enlightenment.* N607

Gulick, Edward Vose. *Europe's Classical Balance of Power.* N413

Hale, J. R. *Renaissance Exploration.* N635

Halperin, S. William. *Germany Tried Democracy.* N280

Haskins, Charles Homer. *The Normans in European History.* N342

Hobsbawm, E. J. *Primitive Rebels.* N328

Langer, William L. *Our Vichy Gamble.* N379

May, Arthur J. *The Hapsburg Monarchy: 1867-1914.* N460

Menéndez, Pidal, Ramón. *The Spaniards in Their History.* N353

Newhouse, John. *Collision in Brussels: The Common Market Crisis of 30 June 1965.*

Nichols, J. Alden. *Germany After Bismarck: The Caprivi Era, 1890-1894.* N463

Pirenne, Henri. *Early Democracies in the Low Countries.* N565

Roth, Cecil. *The Spanish Inquisition.* N255

Rowse, A. L. *Appeasement.* N139

Russell, Bertrand. *Freedom versus Organization: 1814-1914.* N136

Salvemini, Gaetano. *The French Revolution, 1788-1792.* N179

Sontag, Raymond J. *Germany and England: Background of Conflict, 1848-1894.* N180

Stansky, Peter and William Abrahams. *Journey to the Frontier: Two Roads to the Spanish Civil War.* N509

Talmon, J. L. *The Origins of Totalitarian Democracy.* N510

Taylor, A. J. P. *Germany's First Bid for Colonies, 1884-1885.* N530

Thompson, J. M. *Louis Napoleon and the Second Empire.* N403

Tucker, Robert C. *The Marxian Revolutionary Idea.* N539

Waite, Robert G. L. *Vanguard of Nazism: The Free Corps Movement in Postwar Germany, 1918-1923.* N181

Wedgwood, C. V. *William the Silent.* N185

Wheeler-Bennett, John W. *Brest-Litovsk: The Forgotten Peace, March 1918.* N576

Wheeler-Bennett, John W. and Anthony Nicholls. *The Semblance of Peace: The Political Settlement After the Second World War.* N709

Whyte, A. J. *The Evolution of Modern Italy.* N298

Wolfers, Arnold. *Britain and France between Two Wars.* N343

Wolf, John B. *Louis XIV.*

Wolff, Robert Lee. *The Balkans in Our Time.* N305

Zeldin, Theodore. *The Political System of Napoleon III.* N580

THE NORTON HISTORY OF
MODERN EUROPE

Rice, Eugene F., Jr. *The Foundations of Early Modern Europe, 1460-1559*

Dunn, Richard S. *The Age of Religious Wars, 1559-1689*

Krieger, Leonard. *Kings and Philosophers, 1689-1789*

Breunig, Charles. *The Age of Revolution and Reaction, 1789-1850*

Rich, Norman. *The Age of Nationalism and Reform, 1850-1890*

Gilbert, Felix. *The End of the European Era, 1890 to the Present*